International Law

Selected Documents

Editorial Advisory Board

Little, Brown and Company
Law Book Division

Richard A. Epstein
James Parker Hall Distinguished Service Professor of Law
University of Chicago

E. Allan Farnsworth
Alfred McCormack Professor of Law
Columbia University

Ronald J. Gilson
Professor of Law
Stanford University

Geoffrey C. Hazard, Jr.
Sterling Professor of Law
Yale University

James E. Krier
Earl Warren DeLano Professor of Law
University of Michigan

Elizabeth Warren
William A. Schnader Professor of Commercial Law
University of Pennsylvania

Bernard Wolfman
Fessenden Professor of Law
Harvard University

International Law

Selected Documents

Barry E. Carter
Professor of Law
Georgetown University Law Center

Phillip R. Trimble
Professor of Law
University of California, Los Angeles

LITTLE, BROWN AND COMPANY
Boston Toronto London

Copyright © 1991 by Barry E. Carter and Phillip R. Trimble

All rights reserved. No part of this book may be reproduced in any form or by any electronic or mechanical means including information storage and retrieval systems without permission in writing from the publishers, except by a reviewer who may quote brief passages in a review.

Library of Congress Catalog No. 90-64118

ISBN 0-316-13043-5

Second Printing

EB

Published simultaneously in Canada
by Little, Brown & Company (Canada) Limited

Printed in the United States of America

Contents

Alphabetical List of Documents ... ix
List of Abbreviations ... xiii
Preface ... xv

Chapter 1. What Is International Law? ... 1

United Nations Charter ... 1
International Court of Justice Statute ... 27
Cases Before the International Court of Justice:
   1946-September 1990 ... 41
U.S. International Emergency Economic Powers Act
   [See Chapter 3.]
Algiers Accord [See Chapter 3.]
N.Y. Convention on the Recognition and Enforcement
   of Foreign Arbitral Awards [See Chapter 4.]

Chapter 2. Treaties and Customary International Law ... 51

Vienna Convention on the Law of Treaties ... 51

Chapter 3. International Law in the United States ... 77

U.S. Constitution ... 77
U.S.-Japan Friendship, Commerce, and Navigation
   (FCN) Treaty ... 93

v

Trading with the Enemy Act	104
National Emergencies Act	106
International Emergency Economic Powers Act (IEEPA)	111
Algiers Accords (1981) (Algiers Declarations)	116

Chapter 4. International Dispute Resolution — 125

International Court of Justice Statute [See Chapter 1.]	
ICC Rules of Arbitration	125
N.Y. Convention on the Recognition and Enforcement of Foreign Arbitral Awards	135
Convention on the Settlement of Investment Disputes Between States and Nationals of Other States (ICSID Convention)	140
Canada-U.S. Free Trade Agreement	154

Chapter 5. States and Other Major International Entities — 177

U.N. Charter [See Chapter 1.]	
Treaty of Rome, as amended by the Single European Act (SEA)	177
SEA Title III	228
Rio Treaty (Inter-American Treaty of Reciprocal Assistance)	231
Organization of American States (OAS) Charter	237

Chapter 6. Foreign Sovereign Immunity and the Act of State Doctrine — 263

Foreign Sovereign Immunities Act (FSIA)	263
Vienna Convention on Diplomatic Relations	273

Chapter 7. Allocation of Legal Authority Among States — 287

U.S.-U.K. Extradition Treaty (1972)	287
U.S.-U.K. Supplementary Extradition Treaty (1985)	294
U.S.-U.K. Treaty on Mutual Legal Assistance	299
Hague Evidence Convention	307

Contents vii

Chapter 8. State Responsibility—Injuries to Aliens and International Human Rights — 317

U.S.-Egypt Bilateral Investment Treaty	317
ICSID Convention [See Chapter 4.]	
OECD Declaration on Multinationals	329
U.N. Proposed Code of Conduct on Transnational Corporations	338
Universal Declaration of Human Rights	352
Covenant on Civil and Political Rights	357
Optional Protocol to the Covenant	373
Covenant on Economic, Social and Cultural Rights	376
Convention on Racial Discrimination	385
Genocide Convention	395
U.S. Reservations to the Genocide Convention	398
Convention on Discrimination Against Women	399
Convention Against Torture	410
Convention on the Rights of the Child	420
European Human Rights Convention	429
Protocols to the Human Rights Convention (Nos. 1, 2, 4, 6, 7)	445
American Convention on Human Rights	451
African Charter on Human Rights	471
Helsinki Final Act	483
Charter of Paris for a New Europe (1990)	489

Chapter 9. Law of the Sea — 501

Territorial Sea and Contiguous Zone Convention	501
Continental Shelf Convention	509
High Seas Convention	512
Optional Protocol on Dispute Settlements	520
UNCLOS Resolution on Preparatory Commission	522
Law of the Sea Convention (1982)	525
Antarctic Treaty	682

Chapter 10. The Law Governing Airspace, Aviation, and Outer Space — 687

Convention on International Civil Aviation (Chicago Convention)	687
Outer Space Treaty	704

Chapter 11. International Environmental Law — 709

Stockholm Declaration — 709
Vienna Ozone Convention — 714
Montreal Ozone Protocol (1987) — 723
Helsinki Declaration — 730
Montreal Ozone Protocol (as amended and adjusted, 1990) — 731

Chapter 12. Use of Force and Arms Control — 749

U.N. Charter [See Chapter 1.]
"Uniting for Peace" Resolution — 749
Inter-American Treaty of Reciprocal Assistance (Rio Treaty) [See Chapter 5.]
OAS Charter [See Chapter 5.]
U.N. Participation Act — 755
Proposed Intelligence Authorization Act for Fiscal Year 1991 — 758
War Powers Resolution — 763
U.N. Security Council Resolutions re: Iraq (1990) — 770
Congressional Authorization for Use of Military Force Against Iraq (1991) — 782
President Bush's Letter to Congress re: Attack on Iraq (1991) — 784

Alphabetical List of Documents

African Charter on Human Rights	471
Algiers Accords (1981) (Algiers Declarations)	116
American Convention on Human Rights	451
Antarctic Treaty	682
Canada-U.S. Free Trade Agreement	154
Cases Before the International Court of Justice: 1946-September 1990	41
Charter of Paris for a New Europe (1990)	489
Congressional Authorization for Use of Military Force Against Iraq (1991)	782
Covenant on Civil and Political Rights	357
Covenant on Economic, Social and Cultural Rights	376
Continental Shelf Convention	509
Convention Against Torture	410
Convention on Discrimination Against Women	399
Convention on International Civil Aviation (Chicago Convention)	687
Convention on Racial Discrimination	385
Convention on the Rights of the Child	420
Convention on the Settlement of Investment Disputes Between States and Nationals of Other States (ICSID Convention)	140
European Human Rights Convention	429
Foreign Sovereign Immunities Act (FSIA)	263
Genocide Convention	395
Hague Evidence Convention	307
Helsinki Declaration	730
Helsinki Final Act	483
High Seas Convention	512

ICC Rules of Arbitration	125
Inter-American Treaty of Reciprocal Assistance (Rio Treaty)	231
International Court of Justice Statute	27
International Emergency Economic Powers Act (IEEPA)	111
Law of the Sea Convention (1982)	525
Montreal Ozone Protocol (as amended and adjusted, 1990	731
Montreal Ozone Protocol (1987)	723
National Emergencies Act	106
N.Y. Convention on the Recognition and Enforcement of Foreign Arbitral Awards	135
OECD Declaration on Multinationals	329
Optional Protocol to the Covenant on Civil and Political Rights	373
Optional Protocol on Dispute Settlements	520
Organization of American States (OAS) Charter	237
Outer Space Treaty	704
President Bush's Letter to Congress Re: Attack on Iraq (1991)	784
Proposed Intelligence Authorization Act for Fiscal Year 1991	758
Protocols to the European Human Rights Convention (Nos. 1, 2, 4, 6, 7)	445
Rio Treaty (Inter-American Treaty of Reciprocal Assistance)	231
Single European Act, Title III	228
Stockholm Declaration	709
Territorial Sea and Contiguous Zone Convention	501
Trading with the Enemy Act	104
Treaty of Rome, as amended by the Single European Act (SEA)	177
UNCLOS Resolution on Preparatory Commission	522
U.N. Charter	1
U.N. Proposed Code of Conduct on Transnational Corporations	338
U.N. Participation Act	755
U.N. Security Council Resolutions re: Iraq	770
U.S. Constitution	77
U.S.-Egypt Bilateral Investment Treaty	317
U.S.-Japan Friendship, Commerce, and Navigation (FCN) Treaty	93
U.S. Reservations to the Genocide Convention	398
U.S.-U.K. Extradition Treaty (1972)	287
U.S.-U.K. Supplementary Extradition Treaty (1985)	294

Alphabetical List of Documents

U.S.-U.K. Treaty on Mutual Legal Assistance	299
"Uniting for Peace" Resolution	749
Universal Declaration of Human Rights	352
Vienna Convention on Diplomatic Relations	273
Vienna Convention on the Law of Treaties	51
Vienna Ozone Convention	714
War Powers Resolution	763

Abbreviations List

A.J.I.L.	American Journal of International Law
Bevans	Bevans, Treaties and Other International Agreements of the United States of America, 1776-1949 (1968-76)
E.T.S.	European Treaty Series
G.A.Res.	United Nations General Assembly Resolution
I.L.M.	International Legal Materials
L.N.T.S.	League of Nations Treaty Series
O.A.S.	Organization of American States
Stat.	Statutes at Large, United States
T.I.A.S.	Treaties and Other International Acts Series
T.S.	Treaty Series
U.N.Doc.	United Nations Document
U.N.T.S.	United Nations Treaty Series
U.S.C.	United States Code
U.S.T.	United States Treaties and Other International Agreements

Preface

These documents should be useful for anyone working in the international law field who needs a compilation of the basic documents. They have been collected for use as a supplement to our International Law casebook published by Little, Brown and Company in 1991.

The documents, including ones from as late as January 1991, are organized according to the chapters in the casebook. Background information about a document's date of signing and entry into force, as well as the countries that have ratified it, are provided in a footnote to each document. Information about treaties is from: International Legal Materials (through October 1990); U.S. Department of State, Treaties in Force: A List of Treaties and Other International Agreements of the United States in Force on January 1, 1990; United Nations, Multilateral Treaties Deposited with the Secretary-General (status as at December 31, 1989); and from other published sources.

Because this collection is a reference book, the substantive provisions of each document are usually printed in full. When deemed peripheral, however, some of the materials have been omitted—for example, some of the preambles and the final paragraphs containing mere formalities. There has been substantial editing of some of the longer documents, whose complex provisions go well beyond what is needed here. These long documents include the Treaty of Rome, the 1982 Law of the Sea Convention, and the Canada-U.S. Free Trade Agreement. All omissions are indicated.

The editors acknowledge the invaluable assistance of many of the same student research assistants listed in the Acknowledgements section of the casebook.

We encourage any suggestions about possible additions or deletions in future editions.

Barry E. Carter
Phillip R. Trimble

January 23, 1991

International Law

Selected Documents

1

What Is International Law?

CHARTER OF THE UNITED NATIONS
(as amended)
June 26, 1945, 59 Stat. 1031, T.S. No. 993, 3 Bevans 1153*

We the peoples of the United Nations determined to save succeeding generations from the scourge of war, which twice in our lifetime has brought untold sorrow to mankind, and to reaffirm faith in fundamental human rights, in the dignity and worth of the human person, in the equal rights of men and women and of nations large and small, and to establish conditions under which justice and respect for the obligations arising from treaties and

---

*Signed at San Francisco on June 26, 1945. Entered into force on October 24, 1945. The latest amendments are at 24 U.S.T. 2225, T.I.A.S. 7739.
   The following are the 159 parties to the Charter and Member States of the United Nations: Afghanistan, Albania, Algeria, Angola, Antigua and Barbuda, Argentina, Australia, Austria, Bahamas, Bahrain, Bangladesh, Barbados, Belgium, Belize, Benin, Bhutan, Bolivia, Botswana, Brazil, Brunei Darussalam, Bulgaria, Burkina Faso, Burundi, Byelorussian Soviet Socialist Republic, Cameroon, Canada, Cape Verde, Central African Republic, Chad, Chile, China, Colombia, Comoros, Congo, Costa Rica, Cote d'Ivoire, Cuba, Cyprus, Czechoslovakia, Democratic Kampuchea, Denmark, Djibouti, Dominica, Dominican Republic, Ecuador, Egypt, El Salvador, Equatorial Guinea, Ethiopia, Fiji, Finland, France, Gabon, Gambia, Germany (Federal Republic), Ghana, Greece, Grenada, Guatemala, Guinea, Guinea-Bissau, Guyana, Haiti, Honduras, Hungary, Iceland, India, Indonesia, Iran (Islamic Republic of), Iraq, Ireland, Israel, Italy, Jamaica, Japan, Jordan, Kenya, Kuwait, Lao People's Democratic Republic, Lebanon, Lesotho, Liberia, Libyan Arab Jamahiriya, Liechtenstein, Luxembourg, Madagascar, Malawi, Malaysia, Maldives, Mali, Malta, Mauritania, Mauritius, Mexico, Mongolia, Morocco, Mozambique, Myanmar, Namibia, Nepal, Netherlands, New Zealand, Nicaragua, Niger, Nigeria, Norway, Oman, Pakistan, Panama, Papua New Guinea, Paraguay, Peru, Philippines, Poland, Portugal, Qatar, Romania, Rwanda, Saint Kitts and Nevis, Saint Lucia, Saint Vincent and the Grenadines, Samoa, Sao Tome and Principe, Saudi Arabia, Senegal, Seychelles, Sierra Leone, Singapore, Solomon Islands, Somalia, South Africa, Spain, Sri Lanka, Sudan, Suriname, Swaziland, Syrian Arab Republic, Thailand, Togo, Trinidad and Tobago, Tunisia, Turkey, Uganda, Ukranian Soviet Socialist Republic, Union of Soviet Socialist Republics, United Arab Emirates, United Kingdom of Great Britain and Northern Ireland, United Republic of Tanzania, United States of America, Uruguay, Vanuatu, Venezuela, Viet Nam, Yemen, Yugoslavia, Zaire, Zambia, and Zimbabwe.

other sources of international law can be maintained, and to promote social progress and better standards of life in larger freedom, and for these ends to practice tolerance and live together in peace with one another as good neighbors, and to unite our strength to maintain international peace and security, and to ensure, by the acceptance of principles and the institution of methods, that armed force shall not be used, save in the common interest, and to employ international machinery for the promotion of the economic and social advancement of all peoples, have resolved to combine our efforts to accomplish these aims.

Accordingly, our respective Governments, through representatives assembled in the city of San Francisco, who have exhibited their full powers found to be in good and due form, have agreed to the present Charter of the United Nations and do hereby establish an international organization to be known as the United Nations.

Chapter I. Purposes and Principles

Article 1

The Purposes of the United Nations are:

1. To maintain international peace and security, and to that end: to take effective collective measures for the prevention and removal of threats to the peace, and for the suppression of acts of aggression or other breaches of the peace, and to bring about by peaceful means, and in conformity with the principles of justice and international law, adjustment or settlement of international disputes or situations which might lead to a breach of the peace;

2. To develop friendly relations among nations based on respect for the principle of equal rights and self-determination of peoples, and to take other appropriate measures to strengthen universal peace;

3. To achieve international cooperation in solving international problems of an economic, social, cultural, or humanitarian character, and in promoting and encouraging respect for human rights and for fundamental freedoms for all without distinction as to race, sex, language, or religion; and

4. To be a center for harmonizing the actions of nations in the attainment of these common ends.

Article 2

The Organization and its Members, in pursuit of the Purposes stated in Article 1, shall act in accordance with the following Principles.

1. The Organization is based on the principle of the sovereign equality of all its Members.

2. All Members, in order to ensure to all of them the rights and benefits resulting from membership, shall fulfil in good faith the obligations assumed by them in accordance with the present Charter.

3. All Members shall settle their international disputes by peaceful means in such a manner that international peace and security, and justice, are not endangered.

4. All Members shall refrain in their international relations from the threat or use of force against the territorial integrity or political independence of any state, or in any other manner inconsistent with the Purposes of the United Nations.

5. All Members shall give the United Nations every assistance in any action it takes in accordance with the present Charter, and shall refrain from giving assistance to any state against which the United Nations is taking preventive or enforcement action.

6. The Organization shall ensure that states which are not Members of the United Nations act in accordance with these Principles so far as may be necessary for the maintenance of international peace and security.

7. Nothing contained in the present Charter shall authorize the United Nations to intervene in matters which are essentially within the domestic jurisdiction of any state or shall require the Members to submit such matters to settlement under the present Charter; but this principle shall not prejudice the application of enforcement measures under Chapter VII.

Chapter II. Membership

Article 3

The original Members of the United Nations shall be the states which, having participated in the United Nations Conference on International Organization at San Francisco, or having previously signed the Declaration by United Nations of January 1, 1942, sign the present Charter and ratify it in accordance with Article 110.

Article 4

1. Membership in the United Nations is open to all other peace-loving states which accept the obligations contained in the present Charter and, in the judgment of the Organization, are able and willing to carry out these obligations.

2. The admission of any such state to membership in the United Nations will be effected by a decision of the General Assembly upon the recommendation of the Security Council.

Article 5

A Member of the United Nations against which preventive or enforcement action has been taken by the Security Council may be suspended from the exercise of the rights and privileges of membership by the General Assembly upon the recommendation of the Security Council. The exercise of these rights and privileges may be restored by the Security Council.

Article 6

A Member of the United Nations which has persistently violated the Principles contained in the present Charter may be expelled from the Organization by the General Assembly upon the recommendation of the Security Council.

Chapter III. Organs

Article 7

1. There are established as the principal organs of the United Nations: a General Assembly, a Security Council, an Economic and Social Council, a Trusteeship Council, an International Court of Justice, and a Secretariat.

2. Such subsidiary organs as may be found necessary may be established in accordance with the present Charter.

Article 8

The United Nations shall place no restrictions on the eligibility of men and women to participate in any capacity and under conditions of equality in its principal and subsidiary organs.

Chapter IV. The General Assembly

Composition

Article 9

1. The General Assembly shall consist of all the Members of the United Nations.

2. Each Member shall have not more than five representatives in the General Assembly.

Functions and Powers

Article 10

The General Assembly may discuss any questions or any matters within the scope of the present Charter or relating to the powers and functions of any organs provided for in the present Charter, and, except as provided in Article 12, may make recommendations to the Members of the United Nations or to the Security Council or to both on any such questions or matters.

Article 11

1. The General Assembly may consider the general principles of cooperation in the maintenance of international peace and security, including the principles governing disarmament and the regulation of armaments, and may make recommendations with regard to such principles to the Members or to the Security Council or to both.

2. The General Assembly may discuss any questions relating to the maintenance of international peace and security brought before it by any Member of the United Nations, or by the Security Council, or by a state which is not a Member of the United Nations in accordance with Article 35,

paragraph 2, and, except as provided in Article 12, may make recommendations with regard to any such questions to the state or states concerned or to the Security Council or to both. Any such question on which action is necessary shall be referred to the Security Council by the General Assembly either before or after discussion.

3. The General Assembly may call the attention of the Security Council to situations which are likely to endanger international peace and security.

4. The powers of the General Assembly set forth in this Article shall not limit the general scope of Article 10.

Article 12

1. While the Security Council is exercising in respect of any dispute or situation the functions assigned to it in the present Charter, the General Assembly shall not make any recommendation with regard to that dispute or situation unless the Security Council so requests.

2. The Secretary-General, with the consent of the Security Council, shall notify the General Assembly at each session of any matters relative to the maintenance of international peace and security which are being dealt with by the Security Council and shall similarly notify the General Assembly, or the Members of the United Nations if the General Assembly is not in session, immediately the Security Council ceases to deal with such matters.

Article 13

1. The General Assembly shall initiate studies and make recommendations for the purpose of:

    a. promoting international cooperation in the political field and encouraging the progressive development of international law and its codification;

    b. promoting international cooperation in the economic, social, cultural, educational, and health fields, and assisting in the realization of human rights and fundamental freedoms for all without distinction as to race, sex, language, or religion.

2. The further responsibilities, functions, and powers of the General Assembly with respect to matters mentioned in paragraph 1(b) above are set forth in Chapters IX and X.

Article 14

Subject to the provisions of Article 12, the General Assembly may recommend measures for the peaceful adjustment of any situation, regardless of origin, which it deems likely to impair the general welfare or friendly relations among nations, including situations resulting from a violation of the provisions of the present Charter setting forth the Purposes and Principles of the United Nations.

Article 15

1. The General Assembly shall receive and consider annual and special reports from the Security Council; these reports shall include an account of

the measures that the Security Council has decided upon or taken to maintain international peace and security.

2. The General Assembly shall receive and consider reports from the other organs of the United Nations.

Article 16

The General Assembly shall perform such functions with respect to the international trusteeship system as are assigned to it under Chapters XII and XIII, including the approval of the trusteeship agreements for areas not designated as strategic.

Article 17

1. The General Assembly shall consider and approve the budget of the Organization.

2. The expenses of the Organization shall be borne by the Members as apportioned by the General Assembly.

3. The General Assembly shall consider and approve any financial and budgetary arrangements with specialized agencies referred to in Article 57 and shall examine the administrative budgets of such specialized agencies with a view to making recommendations to the agencies concerned.

Voting

Article 18

1. Each member of the General Assembly shall have one vote.

2. Decisions of the General Assembly on important questions shall be made by a two-thirds majority of the members present and voting. These questions shall include: recommendations with respect to the maintenance of international peace and security, the election of the non-permanent members of the Security Council, the election of the members of the Economic and Social Council, the election of members of the Trusteeship Council in accordance with paragraph 1(c) of Article 86, the admission of new Members to the United Nations, the suspension of the rights and privileges of membership, the expulsion of Members, questions relating to the operation of the trusteeship system, and budgetary questions.

3. Decisions on other questions, including the determination of additional categories of questions to be decided by a two-thirds majority, shall be made by a majority of the members present and voting.

Article 19

A Member of the United Nations which is in arrears in the payment of its financial contributions to the Organization shall have no vote in the General Assembly if the amount of its arrears equals or exceeds the amount of the contributions due from it for the preceding two full years. The General Assembly may, nevertheless, permit such a Member to vote if it is satisfied that the failure to pay is due to conditions beyond the control of the Member.

Procedure

Article 20

The General Assembly shall meet in regular annual sessions and in such special sessions as occasion may require. Special sessions shall be convoked by the Secretary-General at the request of the Security Council or of a majority of the Members of the United Nations.

Article 21

The General Assembly shall adopt its own rules of procedure. It shall elect its President for each session.

Article 22

The General Assembly may establish such subsidiary organs as it deems necessary for the performance of its functions.

Chapter V. The Security Council

Composition

Article 23

1. The Security Council shall consist of fifteen Members of the United Nations. The Republic of China, France, the Union of Soviet Socialist Republics, the United Kingdom of Great Britain and Northern Ireland, and the United States of America shall be permanent members of the Security Council. The General Assembly shall elect ten other Members of the United Nations to be non-permanent members of the Security Council, due regard being specially paid, in the first instance to the contribution of Members of the United Nations to the maintenance of international peace and security and to the other purposes of the Organization, and also to equitable geographical distribution.
2. The non-permanent members of the Security Council shall be elected for a term of two years. In the first election of the non-permanent members after the increase of the membership of the Security Council from eleven to fifteen, two of the four additional members shall be chosen for a term of one year. A retiring member shall not be eligible for immediate re-election.
3. Each member of the Security Council shall have one representative.

Functions and Powers

Article 24

1. In order to ensure prompt and effective action by the United Nations, its Members confer on the Security Council primary responsibility for the maintenance of international peace and security, and agree that in carrying

out its duties under this responsibility the Security Council acts on their behalf.

2. In discharging these duties the Security Council shall act in accordance with the Purposes and Principles of the United Nations. The specific powers granted to the Security Council for the discharge of these duties are laid down in Chapters VI, VII, VIII, and XII.

3. The Security Council shall submit annual and, when necessary, special reports to the General Assembly for its consideration.

Article 25

The Members of the United Nations agree to accept and carry out the decisions of the Security Council in accordance with the present Charter.

Article 26

In order to promote the establishment and maintenance of international peace and security with the least diversion for armaments of the world's human and economic resources, the Security Council shall be responsible for formulating, with the assistance of the Military Staff Committee referred to in Article 47, plans to be submitted to the Members of the United Nations for the establishment of a system for the regulation of armaments.

Voting

Article 27

1. Each member of the Security Council shall have one vote.
2. Decisions of the Security Council on procedural matters shall be made by an affirmative vote of nine members.
3. Decisions of the Security Council on all other matters shall be made by an affirmative vote of nine members including the concurring votes of the permanent members; provided that, in decisions under Chapter VI, and under paragraph 3 of Article 52, a party to a dispute shall abstain from voting.

Procedure

Article 28

1. The Security Council shall be so organized as to be able to function continuously. Each member of the Security Council shall for this purpose be represented at all times at the seat of the Organization.
2. The Security Council shall hold periodic meetings at which each of its members may, if it so desires, be represented by a member of the government or by some other specially designated representative.
3. The Security Council may hold meetings at such places other than the seat of the Organization as in its judgment will best facilitate its work.

Article 29

The Security Council may establish such subsidiary organs as it deems necessary for the performance of its functions.

Article 30

The Security Council shall adopt its own rules of procedure, including the method of selecting its President.

Article 31

Any Member of the United Nations which is not a member of the Security Council may participate, without vote, in the discussion of any question brought before the Security Council whenever the latter considers that the interests of that Member are specially affected.

Article 32

Any Member of the United Nations which is not a member of the Security Council or any state which is not a Member of the United Nations, if it is a party to a dispute under consideration by the Security Council, shall be invited to participate, without vote, in the discussion relating to the dispute. The Security Council shall lay down such conditions as it deems just for the participation of a state which is not a Member of the United Nations.

Chapter VI.   Pacific Settlement of Disputes

Article 33

1. The parties to any dispute, the continuance of which is likely to endanger the maintenance of international peace and security, shall, first of all, seek a solution by negotiation, enquiry, mediation, conciliation, arbitration, judicial settlement, resort to regional agencies or arrangements, or other peaceful means of their own choice.
2. The Security Council shall, when it deems necessary, call upon the parties to settle their dispute by such means.

Article 34

The Security Council may investigate any dispute, or any situation which might lead to international friction or give rise to a dispute, in order to determine whether the continuance of the dispute or situation is likely to endanger the maintenance of international peace and security.

Article 35

1. Any Member of the United Nations may bring any dispute, or any situation of the nature referred to in Article 34, to the attention of the Security Council or of the General Assembly.
2. A state which is not a Member of the United Nations may bring to

the attention of the Security Council or of the General Assembly any dispute to which it is a party if it accepts in advance, for the purposes of the dispute, the obligations of pacific settlement provided in the present Charter.

3. The proceedings of the General Assembly in respect of matters brought to its attention under this Article will be subject to the provisions of Articles 11 and 12.

Article 36

1. The Security Council may, at any stage of a dispute of the nature referred to in Article 33 or of a situation of like nature, recommend appropriate procedures or methods of adjustment.

2. The Security Council should take into consideration any procedures for the settlement of the dispute which have already been adopted by the parties.

3. In making recommendations under this Article the Security Council should also take into consideration that legal disputes should as a general rule be referred by the parties to the International Court of Justice in accordance with the provisions of the Statute of the Court.

Article 37

1. Should the parties to a dispute of the nature referred to in Article 33 fail to settle it by the means indicated in that Article, they shall refer it to the Security Council.

2. If the Security Council deems that the continuance of the dispute is in fact likely to endanger the maintenance of international peace and security, it shall decide whether to take action under Article 36 or to recommend such terms of settlement as it may consider appropriate.

Article 38

Without prejudice to the provisions of Articles 33 to 37, the Security Council may, if all the parties to any dispute so request, make recommendations to the parties with a view to a pacific settlement of the dispute.

Chapter VII. Action with Respect to Threats to the Peace, Breaches of the Peace, and Acts of Aggression

Article 39

The Security Council shall determine the existence of any threat to the peace, breach of the peace, or act of aggression and shall make recommendations, or decide what measures shall be taken in accordance with Articles 41 and 42, to maintain or restore international peace and security.

Article 40

In order to prevent an aggravation of the situation, the Security Council may, before making the recommendations or deciding upon the measures provided for in Article 39, call upon the parties concerned to comply with such provisional measures as it deems necessary or desirable. Such provisional measures shall be without prejudice to the rights, claims, or position of the parties concerned. The Security Council shall duly take account of failure to comply with such provisional measures.

Article 41

The Security Council may decide what measures not involving the use of armed force are to be employed to give effect to its decisions, and it may call upon the Members of the United Nations to apply such measures. These may include complete or partial interruption of economic relations and of rail, sea, air, postal, telegraphic, radio, and other means of communication, and the severance of diplomatic relations.

Article 42

Should the Security Council consider that measures provided for in Article 41 would be inadequate or have proved to be inadequate, it may take such action by air, sea, or land forces as may be necessary to maintain or restore international peace and security. Such action may include demonstrations, blockade, and other operations by air, sea, or land forces of Members of the United Nations.

Article 43

1. All Members of the United Nations, in order to contribute to the maintenance of international peace and security, undertake to make available to the Security Council, on its call and in accordance with a special agreement or agreements, armed forces, assistance, and facilities, including rights of passage, necessary for the purpose of maintaining international peace and security.
2. Such agreement or agreements shall govern the numbers and types of forces, their degree of readiness and general location, and the nature of the facilities and assistance to be provided.
3. The agreement or agreements shall be negotiated as soon as possible on the initiative of the Security Council. They shall be concluded between the Security Council and Members or between the Security Council and groups of Members and shall be subject to ratification by the signatory states in accordance with their respective constitutional processes.

Article 44

When the Security Council has decided to use force it shall, before calling upon a Member not represented on it to provide armed forces in fulfillment of the obligations assumed under Article 43, invite that Member, if the Member so desires, to participate in the decisions of the Security Council concerning the employment of contingents of that Member's armed forces.

Article 45

In order to enable the United Nations to take urgent military measures, Members shall hold immediately available national air-force contingents for combined international enforcement action. The strength and degree of readiness of these contingents and plans for their combined action shall be determined, within the limits laid down in the special agreement or agreements referred to in Article 43, by the Security Council with the assistance of the Military Staff Committee.

Article 46

Plans for the application of armed force shall be made by the Security Council with the assistance of the Military Staff Committee.

Article 47

1. There shall be established a Military Staff Committee to advise and assist the Security Council on all questions relating to the Security Council's military requirements for the maintenance of international peace and security, the employment and command of forces placed at its disposal, the regulation of armaments, and possible disarmament.

2. The Military Staff Committee shall consist of the Chiefs of Staff of the permanent members of the Security Council or their representatives. Any Member of the United Nations not permanently represented on the Committee shall be invited by the Committee to be associated with it when the efficient discharge of the Committee's responsibilities requires the participation of that Member in its work.

3. The Military Staff Committee shall be responsible under the Security Council for the strategic direction of any armed forces placed at the disposal of the Security Council. Questions relating to the command of such forces shall be worked out subsequently.

4. The Military Staff Committee, with the authorization of the Security Council and after consultation with appropriate regional agencies, may establish regional subcommittees.

Article 48

1. The action required to carry out the decisions of the Security Council for the maintenance of international peace and security shall be taken by all the Members of the United Nations or by some of them, as the Security Council may determine.

2. Such decisions shall be carried out by the Members of the United Nations directly and through their action in the appropriate international agencies of which they are members.

Article 49

The Members of the United Nations shall join in affording mutual assistance in carrying out the measures decided upon by the Security Council.

Article 50

If preventive or enforcement measures against any state are taken by the Security Council, any other state, whether a Member of the United

Nations or not, which finds itself confronted with special economic problems arising from the carrying out of those measures shall have the right to consult the Security Council with regard to a solution of those problems.

Article 51

Nothing in the present Charter shall impair the inherent right of individual or collective self-defense if an armed attack occurs against a Member of the United Nations, until the Security Council has taken the measures necessary to maintain international peace and security. Measures taken by Members in the exercise of this right of self-defense shall be immediately reported to the Security Council and shall not in any way affect the authority and responsibility of the Security Council under the present Charter to take at any time such action as it deems necessary in order to maintain or restore international peace and security.

Chapter VIII. Regional Arrangements

Article 52

1. Nothing in the present Charter precludes the existence of regional arrangements or agencies for dealing with such matters relating to the maintenance of international peace and security as are appropriate for regional action, provided that such arrangements or agencies and their activities are consistent with the Purposes and Principles of the United Nations.

2. The Members of the United Nations entering into such arrangements or constituting such agencies shall make every effort to achieve pacific settlement of local disputes through such regional arrangements or by such regional agencies before referring them to the Security Council.

3. The Security Council shall encourage the development of pacific settlement of local disputes through such regional arrangements or by such regional agencies either on the initiative of the states concerned or by reference from the Security Council.

4. This Article in no way impairs the application of Articles 34 and 35.

Article 53

1. The Security Council shall, where appropriate, utilize such regional arrangements or agencies for enforcement action under its authority. But no enforcement action shall be taken under regional arrangements or by regional agencies without the authorization of the Security Council, with the exception of measures against any enemy state, as defined in paragraph 2 of this Article, provided for pursuant to Article 107 or in regional arrangements directed against renewal of aggressive policy on the part of any such state, until such time as the Organization may, on request of the Governments concerned, be charged with the responsibility for preventing further aggression by such a state.

2. The term enemy state as used in paragraph 1 of this Article applies to any state which during the Second World War has been an enemy of any signatory of the present Charter.

Article 54

The Security Council shall at all times be kept fully informed of activities undertaken or in contemplation under regional arrangements or by regional agencies for the maintenance of international peace and security.

Chapter IX. International Economic and Social Cooperation

Article 55

With a view to the creation of conditions of stability and well-being which are necessary for peaceful and friendly relations among nations based on respect for the principle of equal rights and self-determination of peoples, the United Nations shall promote:

    a. higher standards of living, full employment, and conditions of economic and social progress and development;

    b. solutions of international economic, social, health, and related problems; and international cultural and educational cooperation; and

    c. universal respect for, and observance of, human rights and fundamental freedoms for all without distinction as to race, sex, language, or religion.

Article 56

All Members pledge themselves to take joint and separate action in cooperation with the Organization for the achievement of the purposes set forth in Article 55.

Article 57

1. The various specialized agencies, established by intergovernmental agreement and having wide international responsibilities, as defined in their basic instruments, in economic, social, cultural, educational, health, and related fields, shall be brought into relationship with the United Nations in accordance with the provisions of Article 63.

2. Such agencies thus brought into relationship with the United Nations are hereinafter referred to as specialized agencies.

Article 58

The Organization shall make recommendations for the coordination of the policies and activities of the specialized agencies.

Article 59

The Organization shall, where appropriate, initiate negotiations among the states concerned for the creation of any new specialized agencies required for the accomplishment of the purposes set forth in Article 55.

Article 60

Responsibility for the discharge of the functions of the Organization set forth in this Chapter shall be vested in the General Assembly and, under the authority of the General Assembly, in the Economic and Social Council, which shall have for this purpose the powers set forth in Chapter X.

Chapter X. The Economic and Social Council

Composition

Article 61

1. The Economic and Social Council shall consist of fifty-four Members of the United Nations elected by the General Assembly.

2. Subject to the provisions of paragraph 3, eighteen members of the Economic and Social Council shall be elected each year for a term of three years. A retiring member shall be eligible for immediate re-election.

3. At the first election after the increase in the membership of the Economic and Social Council from twenty-seven to fifty-four members, in addition to the members elected in place of the nine members whose term of office expires at the end of that year, twenty-seven additional members shall be elected. Of these twenty-seven additional members, the term of office of nine members so elected shall expire at the end of one year, and of nine other members at the end of two years, in accordance with arrangements made by the General Assembly.

4. Each member of the Economic and Social Council shall have one representative.

Functions and Powers

Article 62

1. The Economic and Social Council may make or initiate studies and reports with respect to international economic, social, cultural, educational, health, and related matters and may make recommendations with respect to any such matters to the General Assembly, to the Members of the United Nations, and to the specialized agencies concerned.

2. It may make recommendations for the purpose of promoting respect for, and observance of, human rights and fundamental freedoms for all.

3. It may prepare draft conventions for submission to the General Assembly, with respect to matters falling within its competence.

4. It may call, in accordance with the rules prescribed by the United Nations, international conferences on matters falling within its competence.

Article 63

1. The Economic and Social Council may enter into agreements with any of the agencies referred to in Article 57, defining the terms on which

the agency concerned shall be brought into relationship with the United Nations. Such agreements shall be subject to approval by the General Assembly.

2. It may coordinate the activities of the specialized agencies through consultation with and recommendations to such agencies and through recommendations to the General Assembly and to the Members of the United Nations.

Article 64

1. The Economic and Social Council may take appropriate steps to obtain regular reports from the specialized agencies. It may make arrangements with the Members of the United Nations and with the specialized agencies to obtain reports on the steps taken to give effect to its own recommendations and to recommendations on matters falling within its competence made by the General Assembly.

2. It may communicate its observations on these reports to the General Assembly.

Article 65

The Economic and Social Council may furnish information to the Security Council and shall assist the Security Council upon its request.

Article 66

1. The Economic and Social Council shall perform such functions as fall within its competence in connection with the carrying out of the recommendations of the General Assembly.

2. It may, with the approval of the General Assembly, perform services at the request of Members of the United Nations and at the request of specialized agencies.

3. It shall perform such other functions as are specified elsewhere in the present Charter or as may be assigned to it by the General Assembly.

Voting

Article 67

1. Each member of the Economic and Social Council shall have one vote.

2. Decisions of the Economic and Social Council shall be made by a majority of the members present and voting.

Procedure

Article 68

The Economic and Social Council shall set up commissions in economic and social fields and for the promotion of human rights, and such other commissions as may be required for the performance of its functions.

Article 69

The Economic and Social Council shall invite any Member of the United Nations to participate, without vote, in its deliberations on any matter of particular concern to that Member.

Article 70

The Economic and Social Council may make arrangements for representatives of the specialized agencies to participate, without vote, in its deliberations and in those of the commissions established by it, and for its representatives to participate in the deliberations of the specialized agencies.

Article 71

The Economic and Social Council may make suitable arrangements for consultation with nongovernmental organizations which are concerned with matters within its competence. Such arrangements may be made with international organizations and, where appropriate, with national organizations after consultation with the Member of the United Nations concerned.

Article 72

1. The Economic and Social Council shall adopt its own rules of procedure, including the method of selecting its President.
2. The Economic and Social Council shall meet as required in accordance with its rules, which shall include provision for the convening of meetings on the request of a majority of its members.

Chapter XI. Declaration Regarding Non-Self-Governing Territories

Article 73

Members of the United Nations which have or assume responsibilities for the administration of territories whose peoples have not yet attained a full measure of self-government recognize the principle that the interests of the inhabitants of these territories are paramount, and accept as a sacred trust the obligation to promote to the utmost, within the system of international peace and security established by the present Charter, the well-being of the inhabitants of these territories, and, to this end:

    a. to ensure, with due respect for the culture of the peoples concerned, their political, economic, social, and educational advancement, their just treatment, and their protection against abuses;

    b. to develop self-government, to take due account of the political aspirations of the peoples, and to assist them in the progressive development of their free political institutions, according to the particular circumstances of each territory and its peoples and their varying stages of advancement;

    c. to further international peace and security;

    d. to promote constructive measures of development, to encourage research, and to cooperate with one another and, when and where appropriate, with specialized international bodies with a view to the practical achievement of the social, economic, and scientific purposes set forth in this Article; and

    e. to transmit regularly to the Secretary-General for information purposes, subject to such limitation as security and constitutional considerations may require, statistical and other information of a technical nature relating to economic, social, and educational conditions in the territories for which they are respectively responsible other than those territories to which Chapters XII and XIII apply.

Article 74

Members of the United Nations also agree that their policy in respect of the territories to which this Chapter applies, no less than in respect of their metropolitan areas, must be based on the general principle of good-neighborliness, due account being taken of the interests and well-being of the rest of the world, in social, economic, and commercial matters.

Chapter XII.   International Trusteeship System

Article 75

The United Nations shall establish under its authority an international trusteeship system for the administration and supervision of such territories as may be placed thereunder by subsequent individual agreements. These territories are hereinafter referred to as trust territories.

Article 76

The basic objectives of the trusteeship system, in accordance with the Purposes of the United Nations laid down in Article 1 of the present Charter, shall be:

    a. to further international peace and security;

    b. to promote the political, economic, social, and educational advancement of the inhabitants of the trust territories, and their progressive development towards self-government or independence as may be appropriate to the particular circumstances of each territory and its peoples and the freely expressed wishes of the peoples concerned, and as may be provided by the terms of each trusteeship agreement;

    c. to encourage respect for human rights and for fundamental freedoms for all without distinction as to race, sex, language, or religion, and to encourage recognition of the interdependence of the peoples of the world; and

    d. to ensure equal treatment in social, economic, and commercial matters for all Members of the United Nations and their nationals, and also equal treatment for the latter in the administration of justice, without prejudice to the attainment of the foregoing objectives and subject to the provisions of Article 80.

Article 77

1. The trusteeship system shall apply to such territories in the following categories as may be placed thereunder by means of trusteeship agreements:
   a. territories now held under mandate;
   b. territories which may be detached from enemy states as a result of the Second World War; and
   c. territories voluntarily placed under the system by states responsible for their administration.

2. It will be a matter for subsequent agreement as to which territories in the foregoing categories will be brought under the trusteeship system and upon what terms.

Article 78

The trusteeship system shall not apply to territories which have become Members of the United Nations, relationship among which shall be based on respect for the principle of sovereign equality.

Article 79

The terms of trusteeship for each territory to be placed under the trusteeship system, including any alteration or amendment, shall be agreed upon by the states directly concerned, including the mandatory power in the case of territories held under mandate by a Member of the United Nations, and shall be approved as provided for in Articles 83 and 85.

Article 80

1. Except as may be agreed upon in individual trusteeship agreements, made under Articles 77, 79, and 81, placing each territory under the trusteeship system, and until such agreements have been concluded, nothing in this Chapter shall be construed in or of itself to alter in any manner the rights whatsoever of any states or any peoples or the terms of existing international instruments to which Members of the United Nations may respectively be parties.

2. Paragraph 1 of this Article shall not be interpreted as giving grounds for delay or postponement of the negotiation and conclusion of agreements for placing mandated and other territories under the trusteeship system as provided for in Article 77.

Article 81

The trusteeship agreement shall in each case include the terms under which the trust territory will be administered and designate the authority which will exercise the administration of the trust territory. Such authority, hereinafter called the administering authority, may be one or more states or the Organization itself.

Article 82

There may be designated, in any trusteeship agreement, a strategic area or areas which may include part or all of the trust territory to which the agreement applies, without prejudice to any special agreement or agreements made under Article 43.

Article 83

1. All functions of the United Nations relating to strategic areas, including the approval of the terms of the trusteeship agreements and of their alteration or amendment, shall be exercised by the Security Council.
2. The basic objectives set forth in Article 76 shall be applicable to the people of each strategic area.
3. The Security Council shall, subject to the provisions of the trusteeship agreements and without prejudice to security considerations, avail itself of the assistance of the Trusteeship Council to perform those functions of the United Nations under the trusteeship system relating to political, economic, social, and educational matters in the strategic areas.

Article 84

It shall be the duty of the administering authority to ensure that the trust territory shall play its part in the maintenance of international peace and security. To this end the administering authority may make use of volunteer forces, facilities, and assistance from the trust territory in carrying out the obligations towards the Security Council undertaken in this regard by the administering authority, as well as for local defense and the maintenance of law and order within the trust territory.

Article 85

1. The functions of the United Nations with regard to trusteeship agreements for all areas not designated as strategic, including the approval of the terms of the trusteeship agreements and of their alteration or amendment, shall be exercised by the General Assembly.
2. The Trusteeship Council, operating under the authority of the General Assembly, shall assist the General Assembly in carrying out these functions.

Chapter XIII.   The Trusteeship Council

Composition

Article 86

1. The Trusteeship Council shall consist of the following Members of the United Nations:
   a. those Members administering trust territories;
   b. such of those Members mentioned by name in Article 23 as are not administering trust territories; and
   c. as many other Members elected for three-year terms by the General Assembly as may be necessary to ensure that the total number of members of the Trusteeship Council is equally divided between those

Members of the United Nations which administer trust territories and those which do not.

2. Each member of the Trusteeship Council shall designate one specially qualified person to represent it therein.

Functions and Powers

Article 87

The General Assembly and, under its authority, the Trusteeship Council, in carrying out their functions, may:

    a. consider reports submitted by the administering authority;

    b. accept petitions and examine them in consultation with the administering authority;

    c. provide for periodic visits to the respective trust territories at times agreed upon with the administering authority; and

    d. take these and other actions in conformity with the terms of the trusteeship agreements.

Article 88

The Trusteeship Council shall formulate a questionnaire on the political, economic, social, and educational advancement of the inhabitants of each trust territory, and the administering authority for each trust territory within the competence of the General Assembly shall make an annual report to the General Assembly upon the basis of such questionnaire.

Voting

Article 89

1. Each member of the Trusteeship Council shall have one vote.
2. Decisions of the Trusteeship Council shall be made by a majority of the members present and voting.

Procedure

Article 90

1. The Trusteeship Council shall adopt its own rules of procedure, including the method of selecting its President.
2. The Trusteeship Council shall meet as required in accordance with its rules, which shall include provision for the convening of meetings on the request of a majority of its members.

Article 91

The Trusteeship Council shall, when appropriate, avail itself of the assistance of the Economic and Social Council and of the specialized agencies in regard to matters with which they are respectively concerned.

Chapter XIV. The International Court of Justice

Article 92

The International Court of Justice shall be the principal judicial organ of the United Nations. It shall function in accordance with the annexed Statute, which is based upon the Statute of the Permanent Court of International Justice and forms an integral part of the present Charter.

Article 93

1. All Members of the United Nations are *ipso facto* parties to the Statute of the International Court of Justice.

2. A state which is not a Member of the United Nations may become a party to the Statute of the International Court of Justice on conditions to be determined in each case by the General Assembly upon the recommendation of the Security Council.

Article 94

1. Each Member of the United Nations undertakes to comply with the decision of the International Court of Justice in any case to which it is a party.

2. If any party to a case fails to perform the obligations incumbent upon it under a judgment rendered by the Court, the other party may have recourse to the Security Council, which may, if it deems necessary, make recommendations or decide upon measures to be taken to give effect to the judgment.

Article 95

Nothing in the present Charter shall prevent Members of the United Nations from entrusting the solution of their differences to other tribunals by virtue of agreements already in existence or which may be concluded in the future.

Article 96

1. The General Assembly or the Security Council may request the International Court of Justice to give an advisory opinion on any legal question.

2. Other organs of the United Nations and specialized agencies, which may at any time be so authorized by the General Assembly, may also request advisory opinions of the Court on legal questions arising within the scope of their activities.

Chapter XV. The Secretariat

Article 97

The Secretariat shall comprise a Secretary-General and such staff as the Organization may require. The Secretary-General shall be appointed by the General Assembly upon the recommendation of the Security Council. He shall be the chief administrative officer of the Organization.

Article 98

The Secretary-General shall act in that capacity in all meetings of the General Assembly, of the Security Council, of the Economic and Social Council, and of the Trusteeship Council, and shall perform such other functions as are entrusted to him by these organs. The Secretary-General shall make an annual report to the General Assembly on the work of the Organization.

Article 99

The Secretary-General may bring to the attention of the Security Council any matter which in his opinion may threaten the maintenance of international peace and security.

Article 100

1. In the performance of their duties the Secretary-General and the staff shall not seek or receive instructions from any government or from any other authority external to the Organization. They shall refrain from any action which might reflect on their position as international officials responsible only to the Organization.

2. Each Member of the United Nations undertakes to respect the exclusively international character of the responsibilities of the Secretary-General and the staff and not to seek to influence them in the discharge of their responsibilities.

Article 101

1. The staff shall be appointed by the Secretary-General under regulations established by the General Assembly.

2. Appropriate staffs shall be permanently assigned to the Economic and Social Council, the Trusteeship Council, and, as required, to other organs of the United Nations. These staffs shall form a part of the Secretariat.

3. The paramount consideration in the employment of the staff and in the determination of the conditions of service shall be the necessity of securing the highest standards of efficiency, competence, and integrity. Due regard shall be paid to the importance of recruiting the staff on as wide a geographical basis as possible.

Chapter XVI. Miscellaneous Provisions

Article 102

1. Every treaty and every international agreement entered into by any Member of the United Nations after the present Charter comes into force shall as soon as possible be registered with the Secretariat and published by it.

2. No party to any such treaty or international agreement which has not been registered in accordance with the provisions of paragraph 1 of this Article may invoke that treaty or agreement before any organ of the United Nations.

Article 103

In the event of a conflict between the obligations of the Members of the United Nations under the present Charter and their obligations under any other international agreement, their obligations under the present Charter shall prevail.

Article 104

The Organization shall enjoy in the territory of each of its Members such legal capacity as may be necessary for the exercise of its functions and the fulfillment of its purposes.

Article 105

1. The Organization shall enjoy in the territory of each of its Members such privileges and immunities as are necessary for the fulfillment of its purposes.

2. Representatives of the Members of the United Nations and officials of the Organization shall similarly enjoy such privileges and immunities as are necessary for the independent exercise of their functions in connection with the Organization.

3. The General Assembly may make recommendations with a view to determining the details of the application of paragraphs 1 and 2 of this Article or may propose conventions to the Members of the United Nations for this purpose.

Chapter XVII. Transitional Security Arrangements

Article 106

Pending the coming into force of such special agreements referred to in Article 43 as in the opinion of the Security Council enable it to begin the exercise of its responsibilities under Article 42, the parties to the Four-Nation Declaration, signed at Moscow, October 30, 1943, and France, shall, in accordance with the provisions of paragraph 5 of that Declaration, consult with one another and as occasion requires with other Members of the United

Nations with a view to such joint action on behalf of the Organization as may be necessary for the purpose of maintaining international peace and security.

Article 107

Nothing in the present Charter shall invalidate or preclude action, in relation to any state which during the Second World War has been an enemy of any signatory to the present Charter, taken or authorized as a result of that war by the Governments having responsibility for such action.

Chapter XVIII. Amendments

Article 108

Amendments to the present Charter shall come into force for all Members of the United Nations when they have been adopted by a vote of two thirds of the members of the General Assembly and ratified in accordance with their respective constitutional processes by two thirds of the Members of the United Nations, including all the permanent members of the Security Council.

Article 109

1. A General Conference of the Members of the United Nations for the purpose of reviewing the present Charter may be held at a date and place to be fixed by a two-thirds vote of the members of the General Assembly and by a vote of any nine members of the Security Council. Each Member of the United Nations shall have one vote in the conference.

2. Any alteration of the present Charter recommended by a two-thirds vote of the conference shall take effect when ratified in accordance with their respective constitutional processes by two thirds of the Members of the United Nations including all the permanent members of the Security Council.

3. If such a conference has not been held before the tenth annual session of the General Assembly following the coming into force of the present Charter, the proposal to call such a conference shall be placed on the agenda of that session of the General Assembly, and the conference shall be held if so decided by a majority vote of the members of the General Assembly and by a vote of any seven members of the Security Council.

Chapter XIX. Ratification and Signature

Article 110

1. The present Charter shall be ratified by the signatory states in accordance with their respective constitutional processes.

2. The ratifications shall be deposited with the Government of the

United States of America, which shall notify all the signatory states of each deposit as well as the Secretary-General of the Organization when he has been appointed.

3. The present Charter shall come into force upon the deposit of ratifications by the Republic of China, France, the Union of Soviet Socialist Republics, the United Kingdom of Great Britain and Northern Ireland, and the United States of America, and by a majority of the other signatory states. A protocol of the ratifications deposited shall thereupon be drawn up by the Government of the United States of America which shall communicate copies thereof to all the signatory states.

4. The states signatory to the present Charter which ratify it after it has come into force will become original Members of the United Nations on the date of the deposit of their respective ratifications.

Article 111

The present Charter, of which the Chinese, French, Russian, English, and Spanish texts are equally authentic, shall remain deposited in the archives of the Government of the United States of America. Duly certified copies thereof shall be transmitted by that Government to the Governments of the other signatory states.

In faith whereof the representatives of the Governments of the United Nations have signed the present Charter.

Done at the city of San Francisco the twenty-sixth day of June, one thousand nine hundred and forty-five.

STATUTE OF THE INTERNATIONAL COURT OF JUSTICE

June 26, 1945, 59 Stat. 1055, T.S. No. 993, 3 Bevans 1179*

Article 1

The International Court of Justice established by the Charter of the United Nations as the principal judicial organ of the United Nations shall be constituted and shall function in accordance with the provisions of the present Statute.

Chapter I. Organization of the Court

Article 2

The Court shall be composed of a body of independent judges, elected regardless of their nationality from among persons of high moral character, who possess the qualifications required in their respective countries for appointment to the highest judicial offices, or are jurisconsults of recognized competence in international law.

Article 3

1. The Court shall consist of fifteen members, no two of whom may be nationals of the same state.
2. A person who for the purposes of membership in the Court could be regarded as a national of more than one state shall be deemed to be a national of the one in which he ordinarily exercises civil and political rights.

Article 4

1. The members of the Court shall be elected by the General Assembly and by the Security Council from a list of persons nominated by the national groups in the Permanent Court of Arbitration, in accordance with the following provisions.
2. In the case of Members of the United Nations not represented in the

---

*All Member States of the United Nations are automatically parties to the Statute (U.N. Charter, Art. 93). San Marino and Switzerland are also parties.

Permanent Court of Arbitration, candidates shall be nominated by national groups appointed for this purpose by their governments under the same conditions as those prescribed for members of the Permanent Court of Arbitration by Article 44 of the Convention of The Hague of 1907 for the pacific settlement of international disputes.

3. The conditions under which a state which is a party to the present Statute but is not a Member of the United Nations may participate in electing the members of the Court shall, in the absence of a special agreement, be laid down by the General Assembly upon recommendation of the Security Council.

Article 5

1. At least three months before the date of the election, the Secretary-General of the United Nations shall address a written request to the members of the Permanent Court of Arbitration belonging to the states which are parties to the present Statute, and to the members of the national groups appointed under Article 4, paragraph 2, inviting them to undertake, within a given time, by national groups, the nomination of persons in a position to accept the duties of a member of the Court.

2. No group may nominate more than four persons, not more than two of whom shall be of their own nationality. In no case may the number of candidates nominated by a group be more than double the number of seats to be filled.

Article 6

Before making these nominations, each national group is recommended to consult its highest court of justice, its legal faculties and schools of law, and its national academies and national sections of international academies devoted to the study of law.

Article 7

1. The Secretary-General shall prepare a list in alphabetical order of all the persons thus nominated. Save as provided in Article 12, paragraph 2, these shall be the only persons eligible.

2. The Secretary-General shall submit this list to the General Assembly and to the Security Council.

Article 8

The General Assembly and the Security Council shall proceed independently of one another to elect the members of the Court.

Article 9

At every election, the electors shall bear in mind not only that the persons to be elected should individually possess the qualifications required, but also that in the body as a whole the representation of the main forms of civilization and of the principal legal systems of the world should be assured.

Article 10

1. Those candidates who obtain an absolute majority of votes in the General Assembly and in the Security Council shall be considered as elected.

2. Any vote of the Security Council, whether for the election of judges or for the appointment of members of the conference envisaged in Article 12, shall be taken without any distinction between permanent and non-permanent members of the Security Council.

3. In the event of more than one national of the same state obtaining an absolute majority of the votes both of the General Assembly and of the Security Council, the eldest of these only shall be considered as elected.

Article 11

If, after the first meeting held for the purpose of the election, one or more seats remain to be filled, a second and, if necessary, a third meeting shall take place.

Article 12

1. If, after the third meeting, one or more seats still remain unfilled, a joint conference consisting of six members, three appointed by the General Assembly and three by the Security Council, may be formed at any time at the request of either the General Assembly or the Security Council, for the purpose of choosing by the vote of an absolute majority one name for each seat still vacant, to submit to the General Assembly and the Security Council for their respective acceptance.

2. If the joint conference is unanimously agreed upon any person who fulfils the required conditions, he may be included in its list, even though he was not included in the list of nominations referred to in Article 7.

3. If the joint conference is satisfied that it will not be successful in procuring an election, those members of the Court who have already been elected shall, within a period to be fixed by the Security Council, proceed to fill the vacant seats by selection from among those candidates who have obtained votes either in the General Assembly or in the Security Council.

4. In the event of an equality of votes among the judges, the eldest judge shall have a casting vote.

Article 13

1. The members of the Court shall be elected for nine years and may be re-elected; provided, however, that of the judges elected at the first

election, the terms of five judges shall expire at the end of three years and the terms of five more judges shall expire at the end of six years.

2. The judges whose terms are to expire at the end of the abovementioned initial periods of three and six years shall be chosen by lot to be drawn by the Secretary-General immediately after the first election has been completed.

3. The members of the Court shall continue to discharge their duties until their places have been filled. Though replaced, they shall finish any cases which they may have begun.

4. In the case of the resignation of a member of the Court, the resignation shall be addressed to the President of the Court for transmission to the Secretary-General. This last notification makes the place vacant.

Article 14

Vacancies shall be filled by the same method as that laid down for the first election, subject to the following provision: the Secretary-General shall, within one month of the occurrence of the vacancy, proceed to issue the invitations provided for in Article 5, and the date of the election shall be fixed by the Security Council.

Article 15

A member of the Court elected to replace a member whose term of office has not expired shall hold office for the remainder of his predecessor's term.

Article 16

1. No member of the Court may exercise any political or administrative function, or engage in any other occupation of a professional nature.

2. Any doubt on this point shall be settled by the decision of the Court.

Article 17

1. No member of the Court may act as agent, counsel, or advocate in any case.

2. No member may participate in the decision of any case in which he has previously taken part as agent, counsel, or advocate for one of the parties, or as a member of a national or international court, or of a commission of enquiry, or in any other capacity.

3. Any doubt on this point shall be settled by the decision of the Court.

Article 18

1. No member of the Court can be dismissed unless, in the unanimous opinion of the other members, he has ceased to fulfil the required conditions.

2. Formal notification thereof shall be made to the Secretary-General by the Registrar.

3. This notification makes the place vacant.

Article 19

The members of the Court, when engaged on the business of the Court, shall enjoy diplomatic privileges and immunities.

Article 20

Every member of the Court shall, before taking up his duties, make a solemn declaration in open court that he will exercise his powers impartially and conscientiously.

Article 21

1. The Court shall elect its President and Vice-President for three years; they may be re-elected.
2. The Court shall appoint its Registrar and may provide for the appointment of such other officers as may be necessary.

Article 22

1. The seat of the Court shall be established at The Hague. This, however, shall not prevent the Court from sitting and exercising its functions elsewhere whenever the Court considers it desirable.
2. The President and the Registrar shall reside at the seat of the Court.

Article 23

1. The Court shall remain permanently in session, except during the judicial vacations, the dates and duration of which shall be fixed by the Court.
2. Members of the Court are entitled to periodic leave, the dates and duration of which shall be fixed by the Court, having in mind the distance between The Hague and the home of each judge.
3. Members of the Court shall be bound, unless they are on leave or prevented from attending by illness or other serious reasons duly explained to the President, to hold themselves permanently at the disposal of the Court.

Article 24

1. If, for some special reason, a member of the Court considers that he should not take part in the decision of a particular case, he shall so inform the President.
2. If the President considers that for some special reason one of the members of the Court should not sit in a particular case, he shall give him notice accordingly.
3. If in any such case the member of the Court and the President disagree, the matter shall be settled by the decision of the Court.

Article 25

1. The full Court shall sit except when it is expressly provided otherwise in the present Statute.

2. Subject to the condition that the number of judges available to constitute the Court is not thereby reduced below eleven, the Rules of the Court may provide for allowing one or more judges, according to circumstances and in rotation, to be dispensed from sitting.

3. A quorum of nine judges shall suffice to constitute the Court.

Article 26

1. The Court may from time to time form one or more chambers, composed of three or more judges as the Court may determine, for dealing with particular categories of cases; for example, labor cases and cases relating to transit and communications.

2. The Court may at any time form a chamber for dealing with a particular case. The number of judges to constitute such a chamber shall be determined by the Court with the approval of the parties.

3. Cases shall be heard and determined by the chambers provided for in this Article if the parties so request.

Article 27

A judgment given by any of the chambers provided for in Articles 26 and 29 shall be considered as rendered by the Court.

Article 28

The chambers provided for in Articles 26 and 29 may, with the consent of the parties, sit and exercise their functions elsewhere than at The Hague.

Article 29

With a view to the speedy despatch of business, the Court shall form annually a chamber composed of five judges which, at the request of the parties, may hear and determine cases by summary procedure. In addition, two judges shall be selected for the purpose of replacing judges who find it impossible to sit.

Article 30

1. The Court shall frame rules for carrying out its functions. In particular, it shall lay down rules of procedure.

2. The Rules of the Court may provide for assessors to sit with the Court or with any of its chambers, without the right to vote.

Article 31

1. Judges of the nationality of each of the parties shall retain their right to sit in the case before the Court.

2. If the Court includes upon the Bench a judge of the nationality of one of the parties, any other party may choose a person to sit as judge. Such person shall be chosen preferably from among those persons who have been nominated as candidates as provided in Articles 4 and 5.

3. If the Court includes upon the Bench no judge of the nationality of

the parties, each of these parties may proceed to choose a judge as provided in paragraph 2 of this Article.

4. The provisions of this Article shall apply to the case of Articles 26 and 29. In such cases, the President shall request one or, if necessary, two of the members of the Court forming the chamber to give place to the members of the Court of the nationality of the parties concerned, and, failing such, or if they are unable to be present, to the judges specially chosen by the parties.

5. Should there be several parties in the same interest, they shall, for the purpose of the preceding provisions, be reckoned as one party only. Any doubt upon this point shall be settled by the decision of the Court.

6. Judges chosen as laid down in paragraphs 2, 3, and 4 of this Article shall fulfil the conditions required by Articles 2, 17 (paragraph 2), 20, and 24 of the present Statute. They shall take part in the decision on terms of complete equality with their colleagues.

Article 32

1. Each member of the Court shall receive an annual salary.

2. The President shall receive a special annual allowance.

3. The Vice-President shall receive a special allowance for every day on which he acts as President.

4. The judges chosen under Article 31, other than members of the Court, shall receive compensation for each day on which they exercise their functions.

5. These salaries, allowances, and compensation shall be fixed by the General Assembly. They may not be decreased during the term of office.

6. The salary of the Registrar shall be fixed by the General Assembly on the proposal of the Court.

7. Regulations made by the General Assembly shall fix the conditions under which retirement pensions may be given to members of the Court and to the Registrar, and the conditions under which members of the Court and the Registrar shall have their traveling expenses refunded.

8. The above salaries, allowances, and compensation shall be free of all taxation.

Article 33

The expenses of the Court shall be borne by the United Nations in such a manner as shall be decided by the General Assembly.

Chapter II. Competence of the Court

Article 34

1. Only states may be parties in cases before the Court.

2. The Court, subject to and in conformity with its Rules, may request of public international organizations information relevant to cases before it, and shall receive such information presented by such organizations on their own initiative.

3. Whenever the construction of the constituent instrument of a public international organization or of an international convention adopted thereunder is in question in a case before the Court, the Registrar shall so notify the public international organization concerned and shall communicate to it copies of all the written proceedings.

Article 35

1. The Court shall be open to the states parties to the present Statute.
2. The conditions under which the Court shall be open to other states shall, subject to the special provisions contained in treaties in force, be laid down by the Security Council, but in no case shall such conditions place the parties in a position of inequality before the Court.
3. When a state which is not a Member of the United Nations is a party to a case, the Court shall fix the amount which that party is to contribute towards the expenses of the Court. This provision shall not apply if such state is bearing a share of the expenses of the Court.

Article 36

1. The jurisdiction of the Court comprises all cases which the parties refer to it and all matters specially provided for in the Charter of the United Nations or in treaties and conventions in force.
2. The states parties to the present Statute may at any time declare that they recognize as compulsory *ipso facto* and without special agreement, in relation to any other state accepting the same obligation, the jurisdiction of the Court in all legal disputes concerning:
    a. the interpretation of a treaty;
    b. any question of international law;
    c. the existence of any fact which, if established, would constitute a breach of an international obligation;
    d. the nature or extent of the reparation to be made for the breach of an international obligation.
3. The declarations referred to above may be made unconditionally or on condition of reciprocity on the part of several or certain states, or for a certain time.
4. Such declarations shall be deposited with the Secretary-General of the United Nations, who shall transmit copies thereof to the parties to the Statute and to the Registrar of the Court.
5. Declarations made under Article 36 of the Statute of the Permanent Court of International Justice and which are still in force shall be deemed, as between the parties to the present Statute, to be acceptances of the compulsory jurisdiction of the International Court of Justice for the period which they still have to run and in accordance with their terms.
6. In the event of a dispute as to whether the Court has jurisdiction, the matter shall be settled by the decision of the Court.

Article 37

Whenever a treaty or convention in force provides for reference of a matter to a tribunal to have been instituted by the League of Nations, or to

Article 38

1. The Court, whose function is to decide in accordance with international law such disputes as are submitted to it, shall apply:

   a. international conventions, whether general or particular, establishing rules expressly recognized by the contesting states;

   b. international custom, as evidence of a general practice accepted as law;

   c. the general principles of law recognized by civilized nations;

   d. subject to the provisions of Article 59, judicial decisions and the teachings of the most highly qualified publicists of the various nations, as subsidiary means for the determination of rules of law.

2. This provision shall not prejudice the power of the Court to decide a case *ex aequo et bono,* if the parties agree thereto.

Chapter III. Procedure

Article 39

1. The official languages of the Court shall be French and English. If the parties agree that the case shall be conducted in French, the judgment shall be delivered in French. If the parties agree that the case shall be conducted in English, the judgment shall be delivered in English.

2. In the absence of an agreement as to which language shall be employed, each party may, in the pleadings, use the language which it prefers; the decision of the Court shall be given in French and English. In this case the Court shall at the same time determine which of the two texts shall be considered as authoritative.

3. The Court shall, at the request of any party, authorize a language other than French or English to be used by that party.

Article 40

1. Cases are brought before the Court, as the case may be, either by the notification of the special agreement or by a written application addressed to the Registrar. In either case the subject of the dispute and the parties shall be indicated.

2. The Registrar shall forthwith communicate the application to all concerned.

3. He shall also notify the Members of the United Nations through the Secretary-General, and also any other states entitled to appear before the Court.

Article 41

1. The Court shall have the power to indicate, if it considers that circumstances so require, any provisional measures which ought to be taken to preserve the respective rights of either party.

2. Pending the final decision, notice of the measures suggested shall forthwith be given to the parties and to the Security Council.

Article 42

1. The parties shall be represented by agents.
2. They may have the assistance of counsel or advocates before the Court.
3. The agents, counsel, and advocates of parties before the Court shall enjoy the privileges and immunities necessary to the independent exercise of their duties.

Article 43

1. The procedure shall consist of two parts: written and oral.
2. The written proceedings shall consist of the communication to the Court and to the parties of memorials, counter-memorials and, if necessary, replies; also all papers and documents in support.
3. These communications shall be made through the Registrar, in the order and within the time fixed by the Court.
4. A certified copy of every document produced by one party shall be communicated to the other party.
5. The oral proceedings shall consist of the hearing by the Court of witnesses, experts, agents, counsel, and advocates.

Article 44

1. For the service of all notices upon persons other than the agents, counsel, and advocates, the Court shall apply direct to the government of the state upon whose territory the notice has to be served.
2. The same provision shall apply whenever steps are to be taken to procure evidence on the spot.

Article 45

The hearing shall be under the control of the President or, if he is unable to preside, of the Vice-President; if neither is able to preside, the senior judge present shall preside.

Article 46

The hearing in Court shall be public, unless the Court shall decide otherwise, or unless the parties demand that the public be not admitted.

Article 47

1. Minutes shall be made at each hearing and signed by the Registrar and the President.
2. These minutes alone shall be authentic.

Article 48

The Court shall make orders for the conduct of the case, shall decide the form and time in which each party must conclude its arguments, and make all arrangements connected with the taking of evidence.

Article 49

The Court may, even before the hearing begins, call upon the agents to produce any document or to supply any explanations. Formal note shall be taken of any refusal.

Article 50

The Court may, at any time, entrust any individual, body, bureau, commission, or other organization that it may select, with the task of carrying out an enquiry or giving an expert opinion.

Article 51

During the hearing any relevant questions are to be put to the witnesses and experts under the conditions laid down by the Court in the rules of procedure referred to in Article 30.

Article 52

After the Court has received the proofs and evidence within the time specified for the purpose, it may refuse to accept any further oral or written evidence that one party may desire to present unless the other side consents.

Article 53

1. Whenever one of the parties does not appear before the Court, or fails to defend its case, the other party may call upon the Court to decide in favor of its claim.
2. The Court must, before doing so, satisfy itself, not only that it has jurisdiction in accordance with Articles 36 and 37, but also that the claim is well founded in fact and law.

Article 54

1. When, subject to the control of the Court, the agents, counsel, and advocates have completed their presentation of the case, the President shall declare the hearing closed.
2. The Court shall withdraw to consider the judgment.
3. The deliberations of the Court shall take place in private and remain secret.

Article 55

1. All questions shall be decided by a majority of the judges present.
2. In the event of an equality of votes, the President or the judge who acts in his place shall have a casting vote.

Article 56

1. The judgment shall state the reasons on which it is based.
2. It shall contain the names of the judges who have taken part in the decision.

Article 57

If the judgment does not represent in whole or in part the unanimous opinion of the judges, any judge shall be entitled to deliver a separate opinion.

Article 58

The judgment shall be signed by the President and by the Registrar. It shall be read in open court, due notice having been given to the agents.

Article 59

The decision of the Court has no binding force except between the parties and in respect of that particular case.

Article 60

The judgment is final and without appeal. In the event of dispute as to the meaning or scope of the judgment, the Court shall construe it upon the request of any party.

Article 61

1. An application for revision of a judgment may be made only when it is based upon the discovery of some fact of such a nature as to be a decisive factor, which fact was, when the judgment was given, unknown to the Court and also to the party claiming revision, always provided that such ignorance was not due to negligence.
2. The proceedings for revision shall be opened by a judgment of the Court expressly recording the existence of the new fact, recognizing that it has such a character as to lay the case open to revision, and declaring the application admissible on this ground.
3. The Court may require previous compliance with the terms of the judgment before it admits proceedings in revision.
4. The application for revision must be made at latest within six months of the discovery of the new fact.
5. No application for revision may be made after the lapse of ten years from the date of the judgment.

Article 62

1. Should a state consider that it has an interest of a legal nature which may be affected by the decision in the case, it may submit a request to the Court to be permitted to intervene.
2. It shall be for the Court to decide upon this request.

Article 63

1. Whenever the construction of a convention to which states other than those concerned in the case are parties is in question, the Registrar shall notify all such states forthwith.

2. Every state so notified has the right to intervene in the proceedings; but if it uses this right, the construction given by the judgment will be equally binding upon it.

Article 64

Unless otherwise decided by the Court, each party shall bear its own costs.

Chapter IV. Advisory Opinions

Article 65

1. The Court may give an advisory opinion on any legal question at the request of whatever body may be authorized by or in accordance with the Charter of the United Nations to make such a request.

2. Questions upon which the advisory opinion of the Court is asked shall be laid before the Court by means of a written request containing an exact statement of the question upon which an opinion is required, and accompanied by all documents likely to throw light upon the question.

Article 66

1. The Registrar shall forthwith give notice of the request for an advisory opinion to all states entitled to appear before the Court.

2. The Registrar shall also, by means of a special and direct communication, notify any state entitled to appear before the Court or international organization considered by the Court, or, should it not be sitting, by the President, as likely to be able to furnish information on the question, that the Court will be prepared to receive, within a time limit to be fixed by the President, written statements, or to hear, at a public sitting to be held for the purpose, oral statements relating to the question.

3. Should any such state entitled to appear before the Court have failed to receive the special communication referred to in paragraph 2 of this Article, such state may express a desire to submit a written statement or to be heard; and the Court will decide.

4. States and organizations having presented written or oral statements or both shall be permitted to comment on the statements made by other states or organizations in the form, to the extent, and within the time limits which the Court, or, should it not be sitting, the President, shall decide in each particular case. Accordingly, the Registrar shall in due time communicate any such written statements to states and organizations having submitted similar statements.

Article 67

The Court shall deliver its advisory opinions in open court, notice having been given to the Secretary-General and to the representatives of Members of the United Nations, of other states and of international organizations immediately concerned.

Article 68

In the exercise of its advisory functions the Court shall further be guided by the provisions of the present Statute which apply in contentious cases to the extent to which it recognizes them to be applicable.

Chapter V. Amendment

Article 69

Amendments to the present Statute shall be effected by the same procedure as is provided by the Charter of the United Nations for amendments to that Charter, subject however to any provisions which the General Assembly upon recommendation of the Security Council may adopt concerning the participation of states which are parties to the present Statute but are not Members of the United Nations.

Article 70

The Court shall have power to propose such amendments to the present Statute as it may deem necessary, through written communications to the Secretary-General, for consideration in conformity with the provisions of Article 69.

CASES BEFORE THE INTERNATIONAL COURT OF JUSTICE
1946-September 1990*

A. LIST OF CASES

1. *Contentious Cases*

Title	Date
Territorial Dispute (Libyan Arab Jamahiriya/Chad)	1990–
Arbitral Award of 31 July 1989 (Guinea-Bissau v. Senegal)	1989–
Certain Phosphate Lands in Nauru (Nauru v. Australia)	1989–
Aerial Incident of 3 July 1988 (Islamic Republic of Iran v. United States of America)	1989–
Maritime Delimitation in the Area between Greenland and Jan Mayen (Denmark v. Norway)	1988–
Elettronica Sicula S.p.A. (ELSI) (United States of America v. Italy) [case referred to a Chamber)	1987–1989
Land, Island and Maritime Frontier Dispute (El Salvador/Honduras) [case referred to a Chamber)	1986–
Border and Transborder Armed Actions (Nicaragua v. Honduras)	1986–
Border and Transborder Armed Actions (Nicaragua v. Costa Rica)	1986–1987
Application for Revision and Interpretation of the Judgment of 24 February 1982 in the Case concerning the Continental Shelf (Tunisia/Libyan Arab Jamahiriya) (Tunisia v. Libyan Arab Jamahiriya)	1984–1985
Military and Paramilitary Activities in and against Nicaragua (Nicaragua v. United States of America)	1984–
Frontier Dispute (Burkina Faso/Republic of Mali) [case referred to a Chamber]	1983–1986

*The list of cases is from the I.C.J. Yearbook 1989-1990 and from the actual I.C.J. Reports. The synopsis of all the cases, except for *Elettronica Sicula* (which is from the I.C.J. Reports), is quoted from Weiss, Judicial Independence and Impartiality: A Preliminary Inquiry, in The International Court of Justice at a Crossroads 135-139 (L. Damrosch ed. 1987).

41

Continental Shelf (Libyan Araba Jamahiriya/Malta)	1982–1985
Delimitation of the Maritime Boundary in the Gulf of Maine Area (Canada/United States of America) [case referred to a Chamber)	1981–1984
United States Diplomatic and Consular Staff in Tehran (United States of America v. Iran)	1979–1981
Continental Shelf (Tunisia/Libyan Arab Jamahiriya	1978–1982
Aegean Sea Continental Shelf (Greece v. Turkey)	1976–1978
Trial of Pakistani Prisoners of War (Pakistan v. India)	1973
Nuclear Tests (New Zealand v. France)	1973–1974
Nuclear Tests (Australia v. France)	1973–1974
Fisheries Jurisdiction (Federal Republic of Germany v. Iceland)	1972–1974
Fisheries Jurisdiction (United Kingdom v. Iceland)	1972–1974
Appeal Relating to the Jurisdiction of the ICAO Council (India v. Pakistan)	1971–1972
North Sea Continental Shelf (Federal Republic of Germany/Denmark; Federal Republic of Germany/Netherlands)	1967–1969
Barcelona Traction, Light and Power Company, Limited (New Application: 1962) (Belgium v. Spain)	1962–1970
Northern Cameroons (Cameroon v. United Kingdom)	1961–1963
South West Africa (Ethiopia v. South Africa; Liberia v. South Africa)	1960–1966
Temple of Preah Vihear (Cambodia v. Thailand)	1959–1962
Aerial Incident of 7 November 1954 (United States v. USSR)	1959
Compagnie du Port, des Quais et des Entrepôts de Beyrouth and Société Radio-Orient (France v. Lebanon)	1959–1960
Barcelona Traction, Light and Power Company, Limited (Belgium v. Spain)	1958–1961
Aerial Incident of 4 September 1954 (United States v. USSR)	1958
Arbitral Award Made by the King of Spain on 23 December 1906 (Honduras v. Nicaragua)	1958–1960
Sovereignty over Certain Frontier Land (Belgium/Netherlands)	1957–1959
Aerial Incident of 27 July 1955 (United Kingdom v. Bulgaria)	1957–1959
Aerial Incident of 27 July 1955 (United States v. Bulgaria)	1957–1960
Aerial Incident of 27 July 1955 (Israel v. Bulgaria)	1957–1959
Interhandel (Switzerland v. United States)	1957–1959
Application of the Convention of 1902 Governing the Guardianship of Infants (Netherlands v. Sweden)	1957–1958
Right of Passage over Indian Territory (Portugal v. India)	1955–1960
Certain Norwegian Loans (France v. Norway)	1955–1957
Aerial Incident of 7 October 1952 (United States. v. USSR)	1955–1956
Antarctica (United Kingdom v. Chile)	1955–1956
Antarctica (United Kingdom v. Argentina)	1955–1956
Aerial Incident of 10 March 1953 (United States v. Czechoslovakia)	1955–1956
Treatment in Hungary of Aircraft and Crew of United States of America (United States v. USSR)	1954
Treatment in Hungary of Aircraft and Crew of United States of America (United States v. Hungary)	1954

Electricité de Beyrouth Company (France v. Lebanon)	1953–1954
Monetary Gold Removed from Rome in 1943 (Italy v. France, United Kingdom and United States)	1953–1954
Nottebohm (Liechtenstein v. Guatemala)	1951–1955
Minquiers and Ecrehos (France/United Kingdom)	1951–1953
Anglo-Iranian Oil Co. (United Kingdom v. Iran)	1951–1952
Ambatielos (Greece v. United Kingdom)	1951–1953
Haya de la Torre (Colombia v. Peru)	1950–1951
Request for Interpretation of the Judgment of 20 November 1950 in the Asylum case (Colombia v. Peru)	1950
Rights of Nationals of the United States of America in Morocco (France v. United States)	1950–1952
Asylum (Colombia/Peru)	1949–1950
Protection of French Nationals and Protected Persons in Egypt (France v. Egypt)	1949–1950
Fisheries (United Kingdom v. Norway)	1949–1951
Corfu Channel (United Kingdom v. Albania)	1947–1949

2. Advisory Cases

Title	Dates
Applicability of Article VI, Section 22, of the Convention on the Privileges and Immunities of the United Nations	1989–
Applicability of the Obligation to Arbitrate under Section 21 of the United Nations Headquarters Agreement of 26 June 1947	1988
Application for Review of Judgment No. 333 of the United Nations Administrative Tribunal	1984–1987
Application for Review of Judgment No. 273 of the United Nations Administrative Tribunal	1981–1982
Interpretation of the Agreement of 25 March 1951 between the WHO and Egypt	1980
Western Sahara	1974–1975
Application for Review of Judgment No. 158 of the United Nations Administrative Tribunal	1972–1973
Legal Consequences for States of the Continued Presence of South Africa in Namibia (South West Africa) notwithstanding Security Council Resolution 276 (1970)	1970–1971
Certain Expenses of the United Nations (Article 17, paragraph 2, of the Charter)	1961–1962
Constitution of the Maritime Safety Committee of the Inter-Governmental Maritime Consultative Organization	1959–1960
Admissibility of Hearings of Petitioners by the Committee on South West Africa	1955–1956
Judgments of the Administrative Tribunal of the ILO upon Complaints Made against Unesco	1955–1956

Voting Procedure on Questions relating to Reports and Petitions concerning the Territory of South West Africa	1954–1955
Effect of Awards of Compensation Made by the United Nations Administrative Tribunal	1953–1954
Reservations to the Convention on the Prevention and Punishment of the Crime of Genocide	1950–1951
International Status of South West Africa	1949–1950
Competence of the General Assembly for the Admission of a State to the United Nations	1949–1950
Interpretation of Peace Treaties with Bulgaria, Hungary and Romania	1949–1950
Reparation for Injuries Suffered in the Service of the United Nations	1948–1949
Conditions of Admission of a State to a Membership in the United Nations (Article 4 of Charter)	1947–1948

B. SYNOPSES OF IMPORTANT DECISIONS IN MAJOR CONTENTIOUS CASES

CASE CONCERNING ELETTRONICA SICULA S.p.A. (Elsi) (U.S.A. v. Italy)
— 1989 I.C.J. — (Judgment of July 20). Decision by a chamber (4-1) in favor of Italy on a claim by the United States that the seizure of an Italian subsidiary of two U.S. companies was not an expropriation under a treaty between Italy and the United States.

MILITARY AND PARAMILITARY ACTIVITIES IN AND AGAINST NICARAGUA (Nicar. v. U.S.)
— 1986 I.C.J. 14 (Merits: Judgment of 27 June).
— 1984 I.C.J. 392 (Preliminary Objections: Judgment of 26 Nov.). Decision that Court had jurisdiction in the case under Articles 36(2) and 36(1) (the latter through the Friendship, Commerce and Navigation Treaty). The Court joined adjudication of the Vandenberg Reservation to the merits.
— 1984 I.C.J. 215 (Order of 4 Oct.: Intervention of the Republic of El Sal.). Ruling against intervention at this stage of the proceedings. Joint separate opinion: Argentina, FRG, Italy, U.K., France.
— 1984 I.C.J. 170 (Order of 10 May: Interim Measures). Order to the U.S. to cease from acts of aggression and to both parties to refrain from aggravating the situation until the Court ruled on the merits. Joint separate opinion: FRG and U.K.

FRONTIER DISPUTE (Burkina Faso/Mali)
— 1986 I.C.J. 3 (Interim Measures: Order of 10 Jan.) (Communique No. 86/2). The Court unanimously indicated provisional measures, requiring both governments to withdraw their armed forces to such positions as to be agreed upon, and to continue to observe the cease-fire.

— 1985 I.C.J. 10 (Formation of a Chamber: Order of 5 Apr.). Unanimous votes forming and electing a Chamber, as requested by the Parties.

APPLICATION FOR REVISION AND INTERPRETATION OF THE JUDGMENT OF 24 FEBRUARY 1982 IN THE CASE CONCERNING THE CONTINENTAL SHELF (Tunisia/Libyan Arab Jamahiriya), 1985 I.C.J. 192 (Judgment of 10 Dec.) (Communique No. 85/21). Decision providing interpretation of the prior judgment and rejecting Tunisia's request for revision as inadmissible.

DELIMITATION OF THE MARITIME BOUNDARY OF THE GULF OF MAINE AREA (Can./U.S.)
— 1984 I.C.J. 246 (Judgment of 12 Oct: Chamber Proceeding). Decision delineating a new boundary for the Gulf of Maine.
— 1982 I.C.J. 3 (Order of 20 January: Constitution of Chamber). Order establishing a Chamber as requested.

CONTINENTAL SHELF (Libyan Arab Jamahiriya/Malta)
— 1985 I.C.J. 13 (Judgment of 3 June). Decision upon request delineating the boundaries between the parties. Joint separate opinion: Argentina, Algeria, and Libya (*ad hoc*).
— 1984 I.C.J. 3 (Judgment of 21 Mar: Application by Italy for Permission to Intervene). Decision refusing to grant intervention. Court noted the sanctity of a special agreement between two parties conferring jurisdiction on the Court.

CONTINENTAL SHELF (Tunisia/Libyan Arab Jamahiriya)
— 1982 I.C.J. 18 (Judgment of 24 Feb.). Decision upon request delineating the boundary between the parties.
— 1981 I.C.J. 3 (Judgment of 14 Apr.: Application by Malta for Permission to Intervene). Decision against intervention.

UNITED STATES DIPLOMATIC AND CONSULAR STAFF IN TEHRAN (U.S. v. Iran)
— 1980 I.C.J. 3 (Judgment of 24 May). Decision that Iran violated her legal obligations by holding U.S. citizens hostage in Iran, and ordering her to take immediate steps to redress and repatriate.
— 1979 I.C.J. 7 (Order of 15 Dec.: Interim Measures). Award of interim measures to the U.S., ordering Iran to release the hostages and to redress the situation.

AEGEAN SEA CONTINENTAL SHELF (Greece v. Turkey).
— 1978 I.C.J. 3 (Judgment of 19 Dec.). Decision declining jurisdiction to hear the case.
— 1976 I.C.J. 3 (Order of 11 Dec.: Interim Measures). Order against interim measures.

NUCLEAR TESTS (Australia v. France; New Zealand v. France)
— 1974 I.C.J. 253, 457 (Judgments of 20 Dec.). Decision dismissing case.

Since France had ceased atmospheric nuclear testing, the Court indicated there was no longer any purpose to the claim. Joint dissenting opinion: Nigeria, U.S., Uruguay, and U.K. This is one of the Court's weakest votes; only five judges voted with the opinion, four judges concurred with the dismissal but not with the reasons, and six judges dissented.
— 1973 I.C.J. 99, 135 (Orders of 22 June: Interim Measures). Order granting the applicants interim measures.
— 1973 I.C.J. 320, 324 (Orders of 12 July: Application by Fiji to Intervene). Decision to defer consideration of intervention by Fiji.

FISHERIES JURISDICTION (U.K. v. Iceland; F.R.G. v. Iceland)
— 1974 I.C.J. 3, 175 (Judgments of 25 July). Decision in favor of the fishing rights of U.K. and F.R.G. on the three issues presented to the Court. Joint separate opinion: Senegal, Philippines, Uruguay, India, and Argentina.
— 1973 I.C.J. 3, 49 (Orders of 2 Feb: Jurisdiction of the Court). Decision that Court had jurisdiction of dispute.
— 1972 I.C.J. 12, 30 (Orders of 17 Aug: Interim Measures). Decision of Court to award interim measures against Iceland.

APPEAL RELATING TO THE JURISDICTION OF THE ICAO COUNCIL (India v. Pak.), 1972 I.C.J. 46 (Judgment of 18 Aug.). Decision that Court had jurisdiction to determine whether or not the case should go before the ICAO, and determination that it should.

BARCELONA TRACTION, LIGHT, AND POWER COMPANY, LIMITED (Belg. v. Spain)
— 1970 I.C.J. 4 (New Application: 1962, Judgment of 5 Feb.). Decision that Belgium did not have standing to bring the case before the Court.
— 1964 I.C.J. 6 (Judgment of 24 July: New Application: 1962). Decision rejecting two of Spain's preliminary objections and joining two to the merits.

NORTH SEA CONTINENTAL SHELF (F.R.G. v. Den; F.R.G. v. Neth.), 1969 I.C.J. 3 (Judgment of 20 Feb.). Decision that using the equidistant method for delimiting the continental shelf was optional, and that principles of equity should prevail.

SOUTH WEST AFRICA (Ethiopia v. S. Afr.; Liberia v. S. Afr.)
— 1966 I.C.J. 6 (Judgment of 18 July: Second Phase). Decision that the Applicants did not have a legal interest sufficient to bring the claim.
— 1962 I.C.J. 319 (Judgment of 21 Dec.). Decision rejecting South Africa's preliminary objections and finding that the Mandate conferred by the League of Nations to South Africa had survived the demise of the League. Joint dissenting opinion: U.K. and Australia.

NORTHERN CAMEROONS (Cameroon v. U.K.), 1963 I.C.J. 15 (Judgment of 2 Dec.: Preliminary Objections). Decision that adjudication of the claim would have no purpose.

TEMPLE OF PREAH VIHEAR (Cambodia v. Thailand)
— 1962 I.C.J. 6 (Judgment of 15 June: Merits). Decision that the temple

was part of Cambodian territory and that Thailand was to withdraw from the temple and return any artifacts.
— 1961 I.C.J. 17 (Judgment of 26 May: Preliminary Objections). Unanimous rejection of Thailand's objection that her acceptance of jurisdiction under Article 36(2) was invalid in view of the Israel v. Bulgaria decision.

RIGHTS OF PASSAGE OVER INDIAN TERRITORY (Port. v. India)
— 1960 I.C.J. 6 (Judgment of 12 Apr.). Decision rejecting India's remaining preliminary objections and finding that although Portugal did have a right to passage for private citizens, under the circumstances, it could not be said that India had violated its obligations. Joint dissenting opinions: Egypt and Poland.
— 1957 I.C.J. 125 (Judgment of 26 Nov.: Preliminary Objections). Decision overruling several of India's preliminary objections and joining the remaining ones to adjudication of the merits. Joint dissenting opinion: Norway and Portugal, *ad hoc.*

ARBITRAL AWARD MADE BY THE KING OF SPAIN ON 23 DECEMBER 1906 (Hond. v. Nicar.), 1960 I.C.J. 192 (Judgment of 18 Nov.). Decision requiring Nicaragua to abide by the original arbitral award.

INTERHANDEL (Switz. v. U.S.)
— 1959 I.C.J. 6 (Judgment of 21 Mar.). Judgment in favor of the preliminary objection of the U.S. that Switzerland had not exhausted her remedies before bringing the case to the I.C.J. Pakistan judge concurred with the U.S. judge's separate opinion.
— 1957 I.C.J. 105 (Judgment of 24 Oct.: Interim Measures). Refusal to order interim measures. Court found that the assets in dispute were tied up in the U.S. court system and were not in danger of being dissipated. Joint separate opinion: Norway, U.S., and Canada.

AERIAL INCIDENT OF 27 JULY 1955 (Israel v. Bulgaria), 1959 I.C.J. 127 (Judgment of 26 May). Decision that Article 36(5) did not convert Bulgaria's acceptance of the compulsory jurisdiction of the P.C.I.J. to acceptance of I.C.J. jurisdiction because its declaration had lapsed before Bulgaria was admitted to the U.N. Joint dissenting opinion: U.K., China, and Australia.

SOVEREIGNTY OVER CERTAIN FRONTIER LAND (Belg. v. Neth.), 1959 I.C.J. 209 (Judgment of 20 June). Decision that the sovereignty of the disputed land belonged to Belgium.

APPLICATION OF THE CONVENTION OF 1902 GOVERNING THE GUARDIANSHIP OF INFANTS (Neth. v. Swed.), 1958 I.C.J. 55 (Judgment of 28 Nov.). Decision rejecting the claim of the Netherlands on the grounds that the matter before the Court fell outside the Convention of 1902. Pakistan concurred with China's separate opinion.

CERTAIN NORWEGIAN LOANS (Fr. v. Nor.), 1957 I.C.J. 9 (Judgment of 6 July). Judgment that Norway, by virtue of reciprocity, could invoke France's self-judging domestic jurisdiction reservation and bar jurisdiction.

NOTTEBOHM (Liechtenstein v. Guat.)
— 1955 I.C.J. 4 (Second Phase: Judgment of 6 Apr.). Decision that the claim by Liechtenstein in behalf of Nottebohm was inadmissible in that Nottebohm could not be considered a Liechtenstein citizen in relation to Guatemala.
— 1953 I.C.J. 111 (Preliminary Objection: Judgment of 18 Nov.). Ruling that once the Court is seised of a case, a party cannot withdraw jurisdiction over the case. The expiration of Guatemala's acceptance of compulsory jurisdiction after seisin did not affect the jurisdiction of the Court.

MONETARY GOLD REMOVED FROM ROME IN 1943 (Italy v. Fr., U.K., and U.S.), 1954 I.C.J. 19 (Preliminary Question: Judgment of 15 June). Decision that the Court could not rule on Italy's claim because to do so would require the adjudication of the rights of a state, Albania, that was not before the Court.

MINQUIERS AND ECREHOS (U.K./FR.), 1953 I.C.J. 47 (Judgment of 17 Nov.). Decision that the separate groups of islands known as the Minquiers and the Ecrehos were both under the sovereignty of the U.K.

AMBATIELOS (Greece v. U.K.)
— 1953 I.C.J. 10 (Merits: Obligation to Arbitrate: Judgment of 19 May). Decision that U.K. must enter into arbitration with Greece over its claim, as required by the Declaration of 1926. Joint dissenting opinion: U.K., France, Norway, and Canada.
— 1952 I.C.J. 28 (Preliminary Objection: Judgment of 1 July). Ruling that while the Court could not adjudicate the merits of the claim by Greece, it did have jurisdiction to decide whether the U.K. was under an obligation to submit the claim to arbitration.

ANGLO-IRANIAN OIL CO. (U.K. v. Iran)
— 1952 I.C.J. 93 (Judgment of 22 July: Preliminary Objections). Decision that the claim by the U.K. did not present disputes arising "in regard to situations or facts relating directly or indirectly to the application of treaties or conventions accepted by Persia and subsequent to the ratification of this Declaration," as required by the Persian acceptance of the Court's compulsory jurisdiction, and that therefore, the Court did not have jurisdiction.
— 1951 I.C.J. 89 (Interim Measures: Judgment of 5 July). Award of interim measures to U.K. which were designed to preserve the status quo, pending final adjudication of the dispute by the parties. Joint dissenting opinion: Poland and Egypt.

RIGHTS OF NATIONALS OF THE UNITED STATES OF AMERICA IN MOROCCO (Fr. v. U.S.), 1952 I.C.J. 176, Judgment of 27 August). Decision against France on its claims and against the U.S. on most of its cross claims. The results were generally more favorable for the U.S. Joint dissenting opinion: U.S., Egypt, Brazil, and India.

HAYA DE LA TORRE (Colom. v. Peru), 1951 I.C.J. 71 (Judgment of 13 June). Decision that Colombia was under no obligation to surrender Victor Raul Haya de la Torre to the Peruvian authorities.

REQUEST FOR THE INTERPRETATION OF THE JUDGMENT OF NOVEMBER 20TH, 1950 IN THE ASYLUM CASE (Colom. v. Peru), 1959 I.C.J. 395 (Judgment of 27 Nov.). Court refused to clarify the issues raised by Colombia, finding that they were new issues, necessitating a new case.

ASYLUM (Colom. v. Peru) 1950 I.C.J. 266 (Judgment of 20 Nov.). Decision that the grant of asylum by Colombia to Victor Raul Haya de la Torre was not in compliance with the Convention of Asylum, signed in Havana in 1928.

FISHERIES (U.K. v. Nor.), 1951 I.C.J. 116 (Judgment of 18 Dec.). Rejection of the U.K.'s claim, because it could not be said that Norway had violated international law in the drawing of fishery boundaries.

CORFU CHANNEL (U.K. v. Alb.)
— 1949 I.C.J. 244 (Assessment of the Amount of Compensation Due From the People's Republic of Albania: Judgment of 15 Dec.). Decision fixing the amount of damages owed by Albania to the U.K.
— 1949 I.C.J. 4 (Merits: Judgment of 9 Apr.). Court determination that Albania was financially responsible for the damage caused by the mines in her waters.
— 1948 I.C.J. 124 (Preliminary Objections: Judgment of 25 Mar.). Decision rejecting Albania's objection to jurisdiction in the case. Joint Separate Opinion: France, Poland, USSR, Egypt, Yugoslavia, Chile and Belgium.

2

Treaties and Customary International Law

VIENNA CONVENTION ON THE LAW OF TREATIES
May 23, 1969, U.N. Doc. A/CONF. 39/27*

The States Parties to the present Convention,
Considering the fundamental role of treaties in the history of international relations,

Recognizing the ever-increasing importance of treaties as a source of international law and as a means of developing peaceful co-operation among nations, whatever their constitutional and social systems,

Noting that the principles of free consent and of good faith and the *pacta sunt servanda* rule are universally recognized,

Affirming that disputes concerning treaties, like other international disputes, should be settled by peaceful means and in conformity with the principles of justice and international law,

Recalling the determination of the peoples of the United Nations to establish conditions under which justice and respect for the obligations arising from treaties can be maintained,

Having in mind the principles of international law embodied in the Charter of the United Nations, such as the principles of the equal rights and self-determination of peoples, of the sovereign equality and independence

---

*Concluded at Vienna on May 23, 1969. Entered into force on January 27, 1980. The United States has not ratified the convention.

The 59 parties to the convention are: Algeria, Argentina, Australia, Austria, Barbados, Bulgaria, Byelorussian SSR, Canada, Central African Republic, Chile, Columbia, Congo, Cyprus, Czechoslovakia, Denmark, Egypt, Finland, German Democratic Republic, Germany (Federal Republic), Greece, Haiti, Holy See, Honduras, Hungary, Italy, Jamaica, Japan, Kuwait, Lesotho, Liberia, Malawi, Mauritius, Mexico, Mongolia, Morocco, Nauru, Netherlands, New Zealand, Niger, Nigeria, Panama, Paraguay, Philippines, Republic of Korea, Rwanda, Senegal, Solomon Islands, Spain, Sweden, Syrian Arab Republic, Togo, Tunisia, Ukrainian SSR, Union of Soviet Socialist Republics, United Kingdom, United Republic of Tanzania, Uruguay, Yugoslavia, and Zaire.

of all States, of non-interference in the domestic affairs of States, of the prohibition of the threat or use of force and of universal respect for, and observance of, human rights and fundamental freedoms for all,

Believing that the codification and progressive development of the law of treaties achieved in the present Convention will promote the purposes of the United Nations set forth in the Charter, namely, the maintenance of international peace and security, the development of friendly relations and the achievement of co-operation among nations,

Affirming that the rules of customary international law will continue to govern questions not regulated by the provisions of the present Convention,

Have agreed as follows:

Part I. Introduction

Article 1. Scope of the Present Convention

The present Convention applies to treaties between States.

Article 2. Use of Terms

1. For the purposes of the present Convention:

(a) "treaty" means an international agreement concluded between States in written form and governed by international law, whether embodied in a single instrument or in two or more related instruments and whatever its particular designation;

(b) "ratification", "acceptance", "approval" and "accession" mean in each case the international act so named whereby a State establishes on the international plane its consent to be bound by a treaty;

(c) "full powers" means a document emanating from the competent authority of a State designating a person or persons to represent the State for negotiating, adopting or authenticating the text of a treaty, for expressing the consent of the State to be bound by a treaty, or for accomplishing any other act with respect to a treaty;

(d) "reservation" means a unilateral statement, however phrased or named, made by a State, when signing, ratifying, accepting, approving or acceding to a treaty, whereby it purports to exclude or to modify the legal effect of certain provisions of the treaty in their application to that State;

(e) "negotiating State" means a State which took part in the drawing up and adoption of the text of the treaty;

(f) "contracting State" means a State which has consented to be bound by the treaty, whether or not the treaty has entered into force;

(g) "party" means a State which has consented to be bound by the treaty and for which the treaty is in force;

(h) "third State" means a State not a party to the treaty;

(i) "international organization" means an intergovernmental organization.

2. The provisions of paragraph 1 regarding the use of terms in the

present Convention are without prejudice to the use of those terms or to the meanings which may be given to them in the internal law of any State.

Article 3. International Agreements not Within the Scope of the Present Convention

The fact that the present Convention does not apply to international agreements concluded between States and other subjects of international law or between such other subjects of international law, or to international agreements not in written form, shall not affect:

(a) the legal force of such agreements;

(b) the application to them of any of the rules set forth in the present Convention to which they would be subject under international law independently of the Convention;

(c) the application of the Convention to the relations of States as between themselves under international agreements to which other subjects of international law are also parties.

Article 4. Non-Retroactivity of the Present Convention

Without prejudice to the application of any rules set forth in the present Convention to which treaties would be subject under international law independently of the Convention, the Convention applies only to treaties which are concluded by States after the entry into force of the present Convention with regard to such States.

Article 5. Treaties Constituting International Organizations and Treaties Adopted Within an International Organization

The present Convention applies to any treaty which is the constituent instrument of an international organization and to any treaty adopted within an international organization without prejudice to any relevant rules of the organization.

Part II. Conclusion and Entry into Force of Treaties

Section 1. Conclusion of Treaties

Article 6. Capacity of States to Conclude Treaties

Every State possesses capacity to conclude treaties.

Article 7. Full Powers

1. A person is considered as representing a State for the purpose of adopting or authenticating the text of a treaty or for the purpose of expressing the consent of the State to be bound by a treaty if:

(a) he produces appropriate full powers; or

(b) it appears from the practice of the States concerned or from other circumstances that their intention was to consider that person as representing the State for such purposes and to dispense with full powers.

2. In virtue of their functions and without having to produce full powers, the following are considered as representing their State:

(a) Heads of State, Heads of Government and Ministers for Foreign Affairs, for the purpose of performing all acts relating to the conclusion of a treaty;

(b) heads of diplomatic missions, for the purpose of adopting the text of a treaty between the accrediting State and the State to which they are accredited;

(c) representatives accredited by States to an international conference or to an international organization or one of its organs, for the purpose of adopting the text of a treaty in that conference, organization or organ.

Article 8. Subsequent Confirmation of an Act Performed Without Authorization

An act relating to the conclusion of a treaty performed by a person who cannot be considered under article 7 as authorized to represent a State for that purpose is without legal effect unless afterwards confirmed by that State.

Article 9. Adoption of the Text

1. The adoption of the text of a treaty takes place by the consent of all the States participating in its drawing up except as provided in paragraph 2.

2. The adoption of the text of a treaty at an international conference takes place by the vote of two-thirds of the States present and voting, unless by the same majority they shall decide to apply a different rule.

Article 10. Authentication of the Text

The text of a treaty is established as authentic and definitive:

(a) by such procedure as may be provided for in the text or agreed upon by the States participating in its drawing up; or

(b) failing such procedure, by the signature, signature *ad referendum* or initialling by the representatives of those States of the text of the treaty or of the Final Act of a conference incorporating the text.

Article 11. Means of Expressing Consent to be Bound by a Treaty

The consent of a State to be bound by a treaty may be expressed by signature, exchange of instruments constituting a treaty, ratification, acceptance, approval or accession, or by any other means if so agreed.

Article 12. Consent to be Bound by a Treaty Expressed by Signature

1. The consent of a State to be bound by a treaty is expressed by the signature of its representative when:

(a) the treaty provides that signature shall have that effect;

(b) it is otherwise established that the negotiating States were agreed that signature should have that effect; or

(c) the intention of the State to give that effect to the signature appears from the full powers of its representative or was expressed during the negotiation.

2. For the purposes of paragraph 1:

(a) the initialling of a text constitutes a signature of the treaty when it is established that the negotiating States so agreed;

(b) the signature *ad referendum* of a treaty by a representative, if confirmed by his State, constitutes a full signature of the treaty.

Article 13. Consent to be Bound by a Treaty Expressed by an Exchange of Instruments Constituting a Treaty

The consent of States to be bound by a treaty constituted by instruments exchanged between them is expressed by that exchange when:

(a) the instruments provide that their exchange shall have that effect; or

(b) it is otherwise established that those States were agreed that the exchange of instruments should have that effect.

Article 14. Consent to be Bound by a Treaty Expressed by Ratification, Acceptance or Approval

1. The consent of a State to be bound by a treaty is expressed by ratification when:

(a) the treaty provides for such consent to be expressed by means of ratification;

(b) it is otherwise established that the negotiating States were agreed that ratification should be required;

(c) the representative of the State has signed the treaty subject to ratification; or

(d) the intention of the State to sign the treaty subject to ratification appears from the full powers of its representative or was expressed during the negotiation.

2. The consent of a State to be bound by a treaty is expressed by acceptance or approval under conditions similar to those which apply to ratification.

Article 15. Consent to be Bound by a Treaty Expressed by Accession

The consent of a State to be bound by a treaty is expressed by accession when:

(a) the treaty provides that such consent may be expressed by that State by means of accession;

(b) it is otherwise established that the negotiating States were agreed that such consent may be expressed by that State by means of accession; or

(c) all the parties have subsequently agreed that such consent may be expressed by that State by means of accession.

Article 16. Exchange or Deposit of Instruments of Ratification, Acceptance, Approval or Accession

Unless the treaty otherwise provides, instruments of ratification, acceptance, approval or accession establish the consent of a State to be bound by a treaty upon:

(a) their exchange between the contracting States;

(b) their deposit with the depositary; or

(c) their notification to the contracting States or to the depositary, if so agreed.

Article 17. Consent to be Bound by Part of a Treaty and Choice of Differing Provisions

1. Without prejudice to articles 19 to 23, the consent of a State to be bound by part of a treaty is effective only if the treaty so permits or the other contracting States so agree.

2. The consent of a State to be bound by a treaty which permits a choice between differing provisions is effective only if it is made clear to which of the provisions the consent relates.

Article 18. Obligation not to Defeat the Object and Purpose of a Treaty Prior to Its Entry Into Force

A State is obliged to refrain from acts which would defeat the object and purpose of a treaty when:

(a) it has signed the treaty or has exchanged instruments constituting the treaty subject to ratification, acceptance or approval, until it shall have made its intention clear not to become a party to the treaty; or

(b) it has expressed its consent to be bound by the treaty, pending the entry into force of the treaty and provided that such entry into force is not unduly delayed.

SECTION 2. RESERVATIONS

Article 19. Formulation of Reservations

A State may, when signing, ratifying, accepting, approving or acceding to a treaty, formulate a reservation unless:

(a) the reservation is prohibited by the treaty;

(b) the treaty provides that only specified reservations, which do not include the reservation in question, may be made; or

(c) in cases not falling under sub-paragraphs (a) and (b), the reservation is incompatible with the object and purpose of the treaty.

Article 20. Acceptance of and Objection to Reservations

1. A reservation expressly authorized by a treaty does not require any subsequent acceptance by the other contracting States unless the treaty so provides.

2. When it appears from the limited number of the negotiating States and the object and purpose of a treaty that the application of the treaty in its entirety between all the parties is an essential condition of the consent of each one to be bound by the treaty, a reservation requires acceptance by all the parties.

3. When a treaty is a constituent instrument of an international organization and unless it otherwise provides, a reservation requires the acceptance of the competent organ of that organization.

4. In cases not falling under the preceding paragraphs and unless the treaty otherwise provides:

(a) acceptance by another contracting State of a reservation constitutes the reserving State a party to the treaty in relation to that other State if or when the treaty is in force for those States;

(b) an objection by another contracting State to a reservation does not preclude the entry into force of the treaty as between the objecting and reserving States unless a contrary intention is definitely expressed by the objecting State;

(c) an act expressing a State's consent to be bound by the treaty and containing a reservation is effective as soon as at least one other contracting State has accepted the reservation.

5. For the purposes of paragraphs 2 and 4 and unless the treaty otherwise provides, a reservation is considered to have been accepted by a State if it shall have raised no objection to the reservation by the end of a period of twelve months after it was notified of the reservation or by the date on which it expressed its consent to be bound by the treaty, whichever is later.

Article 21. Legal Effects of Reservations and of Objections to Reservations

1. A reservation established with regard to another party in accordance with articles 19, 20 and 23:

(a) modifies for the reserving State in its relations with that other party the provisions of the treaty to which the reservation relates to the extent of the reservation; and

(b) modifies those provisions to the same extent for that other party in its relations with the reserving State.

2. The reservation does not modify the provisions of the treaty for the other parties to the treaty *inter se.*

3. When a State objecting to a reservation has not opposed the entry into force of the treaty between itself and the reserving State, the provisions to which the reservation relates do not apply as between the two States to the extent of the reservation.

Article 22. Withdrawal of Reservations and of Objections to Reservations

1. Unless the treaty otherwise provides, a reservation may be withdrawn at any time and the consent of a State which has accepted the reservation is not required for its withdrawal.

2. Unless the treaty otherwise provides, an objection to a reservation may be withdrawn at any time.

3. Unless the treaty otherwise provides, or it is otherwise agreed:

(a) the withdrawal of a reservation becomes operative in relation to another contracting State only when notice of it has been received by that State;

(b) the withdrawal of an objection to a reservation becomes operative only when notice of it has been received by the State which formulated the reservation.

Article 23. *Procedure Regarding Reservations*

1. A reservation, an express acceptance of a reservation and an objection to a reservation must be formulated in writing and communicated to the contracting States and other States entitled to become parties to the treaty.

2. If formulated when signing the treaty subject to ratification, acceptance or approval, a reservation must be formally confirmed by the reserving State when expressing its consent to be bound by the treaty. In such a case the reservation shall be considered as having been made on the date of its confirmation.

3. An express acceptance of, or an objection to, a reservation made previously to confirmation of the reservation does not itself require confirmation.

4. The withdrawal of a reservation or of an objection to a reservation must be formulated in writing.

SECTION 3. ENTRY INTO FORCE AND PROVISIONAL APPLICATION OF TREATIES

Article 24. *Entry into Force*

1. A treaty enters into force in such manner and upon such date as it may provide or as the negotiating States may agree.

2. Failing any such provision or agreement, a treaty enters into force as soon as consent to be bound by the treaty has been established for all the negotiating States.

3. When the consent of a State to be bound by a treaty is established on a date after the treaty has come into force, the treaty enters into force for that State on that date, unless the treaty otherwise provides.

4. The provisions of a treaty regulating the authentication of its text, the establishment of the consent of States to be bound by the treaty, the manner or date of its entry into force, reservations, the functions of the depositary and other matters arising necessarily before the entry into force of the treaty apply from the time of the adoption of its text.

Article 25. *Provisional Application*

1. A treaty or a part of a treaty is applied provisionally pending its entry into force if:
(a) the treaty itself so provides; or
(b) the negotiating States have in some other manner so agreed.

2. Unless the treaty otherwise provides or the negotiating States have otherwise agreed, the provisional application of a treaty or a part of a treaty with respect to a State shall be terminated if that State notifies the other States between which the treaty is being applied provisionally of its intention not to become a party to the treaty.

Part III. Observance, Application and Interpretation of Treaties

SECTION 1. OBSERVANCE OF TREATIES

Article 26. Pacta Sunt Servanda

Every treaty in force is binding upon the parties to it and must be performed by them in good faith.

Article 27. Internal Law and Observance of Treaties

A party may not invoke the provisions of its internal law as justification for its failure to perform a treaty. This rule is without prejudice to article 46.

SECTION 2. APPLICATION OF TREATIES

Article 28. Non-Retroactivity of Treaties

Unless a different intention appears from the treaty or is otherwise established, its provisions do not bind a party in relation to any act or fact which took place or any situation which ceased to exist before the date of the entry into force of the treaty with respect to that party.

Article 29. Territorial Scope of Treaties

Unless a different intention appears from the treaty or is otherwise established, a treaty is binding upon each party in respect of its entire territory.

Article 30. Application of Successive Treaties Relating to the Same Subject-Matter

1. Subject to Article 103 of the Charter of the United Nations, the rights and obligations of States parties to successive treaties relating to the same subject-matter shall be determined in accordance with the following paragraphs.
2. When a treaty specifies that it is subject to, or that it is not to be considered as incompatible with, an earlier or later treaty, the provisions of that other treaty prevail.
3. When all the parties to the earlier treaty are parties also to the later treaty but the earlier treaty is not terminated or suspended in operation

under article 59, the earlier treaty applies only to the extent that its provisions are compatible with those of the later treaty.

4. When the parties to the later treaty do not include all the parties to the earlier one:

(a) as between States parties to both treaties the same rule applies as in paragraph 3;

(b) as between a State party to both treaties and a State party to only one of the treaties, the treaty to which both States are parties governs their mutual rights and obligations.

5. Paragraph 4 is without prejudice to article 41, or to any question of the termination or suspension of the operation of a treaty under article 60 or to any question of responsibility which may arise for a State from the conclusion or application of a treaty the provisions of which are incompatible with its obligations towards another State under another treaty.

SECTION 3. INTERPRETATION OF TREATIES

Article 31. General Rule of Interpretation

1. A treaty shall be interpreted in good faith in accordance with the ordinary meaning to be given to the terms of the treaty in their context and in the light of its object and purpose.

2. The context for the purpose of the interpretation of a treaty shall comprise, in addition to the text, including its preamble and annexes:

(a) any agreement relating to the treaty which was made between all the parties in connexion with the conclusion of the treaty;

(b) any instrument which was made by one or more parties in connexion with the conclusion of the treaty and accepted by the other parties as an instrument related to the treaty.

3. There shall be taken into account, together with the context:

(a) any subsequent agreement between the parties regarding the interpretation of the treaty or the application of its provisions;

(b) any subsequent practice in the application of the treaty which establishes the agreement of the parties regarding its interpretation;

(c) any relevant rules of international law applicable in the relations between the parties.

4. A special meaning shall be given to a term if it is established that the parties so intended.

Article 32. Supplementary Means of Interpretation

Recourse may be had to supplementary means of interpretation, including the preparatory work of the treaty and the circumstances of its conclusion, in order to confirm the meaning resulting from the application of article 31, or to determine the meaning when the interpretation according to article 31:

(a) leaves the meaning ambiguous or obscure; or

(b) leads to a result which is manifestly absurd or unreasonable.

Article 33. Interpretation of Treaties Authenticated in Two or More Languages

1. When a treaty has been authenticated in two or more languages, the text is equally authoritative in each language, unless the treaty provides or the parties agree that, in case of divergence, a particular text shall prevail.
2. A version of the treaty in a language other than one of those in which the text was authenticated shall be considered an authentic text only if the treaty so provides or the parties so agree.
3. The terms of the treaty are presumed to have the same meaning in each authentic text.
4. Except where a particular text prevails in accordance with paragraph 1, when a comparison of the authentic texts discloses a difference of meaning which the application of articles 31 and 32 does not remove, the meaning which best reconciles the texts, having regard to the object and purpose of the treaty, shall be adopted.

Section 4. Treaties and Third States

Article 34. General Rule Regarding Third States

A treaty does not create either obligations or rights for a third State without its consent.

Article 35. Treaties Providing for Obligations for Third States

An obligation arises for a third State from a provision of a treaty if the parties to the treaty intend the provision to be the means of establishing the obligation and the third State expressly accepts that obligation in writing.

Article 36. Treaties Providing for Rights for Third States

1. A right arises for a third State from a provision of a treaty if the parties to the treaty intend the provision to accord that right either to the third State, or to a group of States to which it belongs, or to all States, and the third State assents thereto. Its assent shall be presumed so long as the contrary is not indicated, unless the treaty otherwise provides.
2. A State exercising a right in accordance with paragraph 1 shall comply with the conditions for its exercise provided for in the treaty or established in conformity with the treaty.

Article 37. Revocation or Modification of Obligations or Rights of Third States

1. When an obligation has arisen for a third State in conformity with article 35, the obligation may be revoked or modified only with the consent of the parties to the treaty and of the third State, unless it is established that they had otherwise agreed.
2. When a right has arisen for a third State in conformity with article 36, the right may not be revoked or modified by the parties if it is established

that the right was intended not to be revocable or subject to modification without the consent of the third State.

Article 38. Rules in a Treaty Becoming Binding on Third States Through International Custom

Nothing in articles 34 to 37 precludes a rule set forth in a treaty from becoming binding upon a third State as a customary rule of international law, recognized as such.

Part IV. Amendment and Modification of Treaties

Article 39. General Rule Regarding the Amendment of Treaties

A treaty may be amended by agreement between the parties. The rules laid down in Part II apply to such an agreement except in so far as the treaty may otherwise provide.

Article 40. Amendment of Multilateral Treaties

1. Unless the treaty otherwise provides, the amendment of multilateral treaties shall be governed by the following paragraphs.
2. Any proposal to amend a multilateral treaty as between all the parties must be notified to all the contracting States, each one of which shall have the right to take part in:
   (a) the decision as to the action to be taken in regard to such proposal;
   (b) the negotiation and conclusion of any agreement for the amendment of the treaty.
3. Every State entitled to become a party to the treaty shall also be entitled to become a party to the treaty as amended.
4. The amending agreement does not bind any State already a party to the treaty which does not become a party to the amending agreement; article 30, paragraph 4(b), applies in relation to such State.
5. Any State which becomes a party to the treaty after the entry into force of the amending agreement shall, failing an expression of a different intention by that State:
   (a) be considered as a party to the treaty as amended; and
   (b) be considered as a party to the unamended treaty in relation to any party to the treaty not bound by the amending agreement.

Article 41. Agreements to Modify Multilateral Treaties Between Certain of the Parties Only

1. Two or more of the parties to a multilateral treaty may conclude an agreement to modify the treaty as between themselves alone if:
   (a) the possibility of such a modification is provided for by the treaty; or
   (b) the modification in question is not prohibited by the treaty and:

(i) does not affect the enjoyment by the other parties of their rights under the treaty or the performance of their obligations;

(ii) does not relate to a provision, derogation from which is incompatible with the effective execution of the object and purpose of the treaty as a whole.

2. Unless in a case falling under paragraph 1(a) the treaty otherwise provides, the parties in question shall notify the other parties of their intention to conclude the agreement and of the modification to the treaty for which it provides.

Part V. Invalidity, Termination and Suspension of the Operation of Treaties

SECTION 1. GENERAL PROVISIONS

Article 42. Validity and Continuance in Force of Treaties

1. The validity of a treaty or of the consent of a State to be bound by a treaty may be impeached only through the application of the present Convention.

2. The termination of a treaty, its denunciation or the withdrawal of a party, may take place only as a result of the application of the provisions of the treaty or of the present Convention. The same rule applies to suspension of the operation of a treaty.

Article 43. Obligations Imposed by International Law Independently of a Treaty

The invalidity, termination or denunciation of a treaty, the withdrawal of a party from it, or the suspension of its operation, as a result of the application of the present Convention or of the provisions of the treaty, shall not in any way impair the duty of any State to fulfil any obligation embodied in the treaty to which it would be subject under international law independently of the treaty.

Article 44. Separability of Treaty Provisions

1. A right of a party, provided for in a treaty or arising under article 56, to denounce, withdraw from or suspend the operation of the treaty may be exercised only with respect to the whole treaty unless the treaty otherwise provides or the parties otherwise agree.

2. A ground for invalidating, terminating, withdrawing from or suspending the operation of a treaty recognized in the present Convention may be invoked only with respect to the whole treaty except as provided in the following paragraphs or in article 60.

3. If the ground relates solely to particular clauses, it may be invoked only with respect to those clauses where:

(a) the said clauses are separable from the remainder of the treaty with regard to their application;

(b) it appears from the treaty or is otherwise established that acceptance of those clauses was not an essential basis of the consent of the other party or parties to be bound by the treaty as a whole; and

(c) continued performance of the remainder of the treaty would not be unjust.

4. In cases falling under articles 49 and 50 the State entitled to invoke the fraud or corruption may do so with respect either to the whole treaty or, subject to paragraph 3, to the particular clauses alone.

5. In cases falling under articles 51, 52 and 53, no separation of the provisions of the treaty is permitted.

Article 45. Loss of a Right to Invoke a Ground for Invalidating, Terminating, Withdrawing from or Suspending the Operation of a Treaty

A State may no longer invoke a ground for invalidating, terminating, withdrawing from or suspending the operation of a treaty under articles 46 to 50 or articles 60 and 62 if, after becoming aware of the facts:

(a) it shall have expressly agreed that the treaty is valid or remains in force or continues in operation, as the case may be; or

(b) it must by reason of its conduct be considered as having acquiesced in the validity of the treaty or in its maintenance in force or in operation, as the case may be.

SECTION 2. INVALIDITY OF TREATIES

Article 46. Provisions of Internal Law Regarding Competence to Conclude Treaties

1. A State may not invoke the fact that its consent to be bound by a treaty has been expressed in violation of a provision of its internal law regarding competence to conclude treaties as invalidating its consent unless that violation was manifest and concerned a rule of its internal law of fundamental importance.

2. A violation is manifest if it would be objectively evident to any State conducting itself in the matter in accordance with normal practice and in good faith.

Article 47. Specific Restrictions on Authority to Express the Consent of a State

If the authority of a representative to express the consent of a State to be bound by a particular treaty has been made subject to a specific restriction, his omission to observe that restriction may not be invoked as invalidating the consent expressed by him unless the restriction was notified to the other negotiating States prior to his expressing such consent.

Article 48. Error

1. A State may invoke an error in a treaty as invalidating its consent to be bound by the treaty if the error relates to a fact or situation which was

assumed by that State to exist at the time when the treaty was concluded and formed an essential basis of its consent to be bound by the treaty.

2. Paragraph 1 shall not apply if the State in question contributed by its own conduct to the error or if the circumstances were such as to put that State on notice of a possible error.

3. An error relating only to the wording of the text of a treaty does not affect its validity; article 79 then applies.

Article 49. Fraud

If a State has been induced to conclude a treaty by the fraudulent conduct of another negotiating State, the State may invoke the fraud as invalidating its consent to be bound by the treaty.

Article 50. Corruption of a Representative of a State

If the expression of a State's consent to be bound by a treaty has been procured through the corruption of its representative directly or indirectly by another negotiating State, the State may invoke such corruption as invalidating its consent to be bound by the treaty.

Article 51. Coercion of a Representative of a State

The expression of a State's consent to be bound by a treaty which has been procured by the coercion of its representative through acts or threats directed against him shall be without any legal effect.

Article 52. Coercion of a State by the Threat or Use of Force

A treaty is void if its conclusion has been procured by the threat or use of force in violation of the principles of international law embodied in the Charter of the United Nations.

Article 53. Treaties Conflicting with a Preemptory Norm of General International Law (Jus Cogens)

A treaty is void if, at the time of its conclusion, it conflicts with a preemptory norm of general international law. For the purposes of the present Convention, a peremptory norm of general international law is a norm accepted and recognized by the international community of States as a whole as a norm from which no derogation is permitted and which can be modified only by a subsequent norm of general international law having the same character.

SECTION 3. TERMINATION AND SUSPENSION OF THE OPERATION OF TREATIES

Article 54. Termination of or Withdrawal from a Treaty Under Its Provisions or by Consent of the Parties

The termination of a treaty or the withdrawal of a party may take place:
  (a) in conformity with the provisions of the treaty; or

(b) at any time by consent of all the parties after consultation with the other contracting States.

Article 55. Reduction of the Parties to a Multilateral Treaty Below the Number Necessary for its Entry into Force

Unless the treaty otherwise provides, a multilateral treaty does not terminate by reason only of the fact that the number of the parties falls below the number necessary for its entry into force.

Article 56. Denunciation of or Withdrawal from a Treaty Containing No Provision Regarding Termination, Denunciation or Withdrawal

1. A treaty which contains no provision regarding its termination and which does not provide for denunciation or withdrawal is not subject to denunciation or withdrawal unless:
   (a) it is established that the parties intended to admit the possibility of denunciation or withdrawal; or
   (b) a right of denunciation or withdrawal may be implied by the nature of the treaty.
2. A party shall give not less than twelve months' notice of its intention to denounce or withdraw from a treaty under paragraph 1.

Article 57. Suspension of the Operation of a Treaty Under its Provisions or by Consent of the Parties

The operation of a treaty in regard to all the parties or to a particular party may be suspended:
   (a) in conformity with the provisions of the treaty; or
   (b) at any time by consent of all the parties after consultation with the other contracting States.

Article 58. Suspension of the Operation of a Multilateral Treaty by Agreement Between Certain of the Parties Only

1. Two or more parties to a multilateral treaty may conclude an agreement to suspend the operation of provisions of the treaty, temporarily and as between themselves alone, if:
   (a) the possibility of such a suspension is provided for by the treaty; or
   (b) the suspension in question is not prohibited by the treaty and:
      (i) does not affect the enjoyment by the other parties of their rights under the treaty or the performance of their obligations;
      (ii) is not incompatible with the object and purpose of the treaty.
2. Unless in a case falling under paragraph 1(a) the treaty otherwise provides, the parties in question shall notify the other parties of their intention to conclude the agreement and of those provisions of the treaty the operation of which they intend to suspend.

Article 59. Termination or Suspension of the Operation of a Treaty Implied by Conclusion of a Later Treaty

1. A treaty shall be considered as terminated if all the parties to it conclude a later treaty relating to the same subject-matter and:
    (a) it appears from the later treaty or is otherwise established that the parties intended that the matter should be governed by that treaty; or
    (b) the provisions of the later treaty are so far incompatible with those of the earlier one that the two treaties are not capable of being applied at the same time.
2. The earlier treaty shall be considered as only suspended in operation if it appears from the later treaty or is otherwise established that such was the intention of the parties.

Article 60. Termination or Suspension of the Operation of a Treaty as a Consequence of its Breach

1. A material breach of a bilateral treaty by one of the parties entitles the other to invoke the breach as a ground for terminating the treaty or suspending its operation in whole or in part.
2. A material breach of a multilateral treaty by one of the parties entitles:
    (a) the other parties by unanimous agreement to suspend the operation of the treaty in whole or in part or to terminate it either:
        (i) in the relations between themselves and the defaulting State, or
        (ii) as between all the parties;
    (b) a party specially affected by the breach to invoke it as a ground for suspending the operation of the treaty in whole or in part in the relations between itself and the defaulting State;
    (c) any party other than the defaulting State to invoke the breach as a ground for suspending the operation of the treaty in whole or in part with respect to itself if the treaty is of such a character that a material breach of its provisions by one party radically changes the position of every party with respect to the further performance of its obligations under the treaty.
3. A material breach of a treaty, for the purposes of this article, consists in:
    (a) a repudiation of the treaty not sanctioned by the present Convention; or
    (b) the violation of a provision essential to the accomplishment of the object or purpose of the treaty.
4. The foregoing paragraphs are without prejudice to any provision in the treaty applicable in the event of a breach.
5. Paragraphs 1 to 3 do not apply to provisions relating to the protection of the human person contained in treaties of a humanitarian character, in particular to provisions prohibiting any form of reprisals against persons protected by such treaties.

Article 61. *Supervening Impossibility of Performance*

1. A party may invoke the impossibility of performing a treaty as a ground for terminating or withdrawing from it if the impossibility results from the permanent disappearance or destruction of an object indispensable for the execution of the treaty. If the impossibility is temporary, it may be invoked only as a ground for suspending the operation of the treaty.

2. Impossibility of performance may not be invoked by a party as a ground for terminating, withdrawing from or suspending the operation of a treaty if the impossibility is the result of a breach by that party either of an obligation under the treaty or of any other international obligation owed to any other party to the treaty.

Article 62. *Fundamental Change of Circumstances*

1. A fundamental change of circumstances which has occurred with regard to those existing at the time of the conclusion of a treaty, and which was not foreseen by the parties, may not be invoked as a ground for terminating or withdrawing from the treaty unless:

   (a) the existence of those circumstances constituted an essential basis of the consent of the parties to be bound by the treaty; and

   (b) the effect of the change is radically to transform the extent of obligations still to be performed under the treaty.

2. A fundamental change of circumstances may not be invoked as a ground for terminating or withdrawing from a treaty:

   (a) if the treaty establishes a boundary; or

   (b) if the fundamental change is the result of a breach by the party invoking it either of an obligation under the treaty or of any other international obligation owed to any other party to the treaty.

3. If, under the foregoing paragraphs, a party may invoke a fundamental change of circumstances as a ground for terminating or withdrawing from a treaty it may also invoke the change as a ground for suspending the operation of the treaty.

Article 63. *Severance of Diplomatic or Consular Relations*

The severance of diplomatic or consular relations between parties to a treaty does not affect the legal relations established between them by the treaty except in so far as the existence of diplomatic or consular relations is indispensable for the application of the treaty.

Article 64. *Emergence of a New Peremptory Norm of General International Law* (**Jus Cogens**)

If a new peremptory norm of general international law emerges, any existing treaty which is in conflict with that norm becomes void and terminates.

Section 4. Procedure

Article 65. Procedure to be Followed with Respect to Invalidity, Termination, Withdrawal from or Suspension of the Operation of a Treaty

1. A party which, under the provisions of the present Convention, invokes either a defect in its consent to be bound by a treaty or a ground for impeaching the validity of a treaty, terminating it, withdrawing from it or suspending its operation, must notify the other parties of its claim. The notification shall indicate the measure proposed to be taken with respect to the treaty and the reasons therefor.

2. If, after the expiry of a period which, except in cases of special urgency, shall not be less than three months after the receipt of the notification, no party has raised any objection, the party making the notification may carry out in the manner provided in article 67 the measure which it has proposed.

3. If, however, objection has been raised by any other party, the parties shall seek a solution through the means indicated in Article 33 of the Charter of the United Nations.

4. Nothing in the foregoing paragraphs shall affect the rights or obligations of the parties under any provisions in force binding the parties with regard to the settlement of disputes.

5. Without prejudice to article 45, the fact that a State has not previously made the notification prescribed in paragraph 1 shall not prevent it from making such notification in answer to another party claiming performance of the treaty or alleging its violation.

Article 66. Procedures for Judicial Settlement, Arbitration and Conciliation

If, under paragraph 3 of article 65, no solution has been reached within a period of 12 months following the date on which the objection was raised, the following procedures shall be followed:

(a) any one of the parties to a dispute concerning the application or the interpretation of article 53 or 64 may, by a written application, submit it to the International Court of Justice for a decision unless the parties by common consent agree to submit the dispute to arbitration;

(b) any one of the parties to a dispute concerning the application or the interpretation of any of the other articles in Part V of the present Convention may set in motion the procedure specified in the Annex to the Convention by submitting a request to that effect to the Secretary-General of the United Nations.

Article 67. Instruments for Declaring Invalid, Terminating, Withdrawing from or Suspending the Operation of a Treaty

1. The notification provided for under article 65, paragraph 1 must be made in writing.

2. Any act declaring invalid, terminating, withdrawing from or suspending the operation of a treaty pursuant to the provisions of the treaty or of paragraphs 2 or 3 of article 65 shall be carried out through an instrument

communicated to the other parties. If the instrument is not signed by the Head of State, Head of Government or Minister for Foreign Affairs, the representative of the State communicating it may be called upon to produce full powers.

Article 68. Revocation of Notifications and Instruments Provided for in Articles 65 and 67

A notification or instrument provided for in articles 65 or 67 may be revoked at any time before it takes effect.

SECTION 5. CONSEQUENCES OF THE INVALIDITY, TERMINATION OR SUSPENSION OF THE OPERATION OF A TREATY

Article 69. Consequences of the Invalidity of a Treaty

1. A treaty the invalidity of which is established under the present Convention is void. The provisions of a void treaty have no legal force.
2. If acts have nevertheless been performed in reliance on such a treaty:
    (a) each party may require any other party to establish as far as possible in their mutual relations the position that would have existed if the acts had not been performed;
    (b) acts performed in good faith before the invalidity was invoked are not rendered unlawful by reason only of the invalidity of the treaty.
3. In cases falling under articles 49, 50, 51 or 52, paragraph 2 does not apply with respect to the party to which the fraud, the act of corruption or the coercion is imputable.
4. In the case of the invalidity of a particular State's consent to be bound by a multilateral treaty, the foregoing rules apply in the relations between that State and the parties to the treaty.

Article 70. Consequences of the Termination of a Treaty

1. Unless the treaty otherwise provides or the parties otherwise agree, the termination of a treaty under its provisions or in accordance with the present Convention:
    (a) releases the parties from any obligation further to perform the treaty;
    (b) does not affect any right, obligation or legal situation of the parties created through the execution of the treaty prior to its termination.
2. If a State denounces or withdraws from a multilateral treaty, paragraph 1 applies in the relations between that State and each of the other parties to the treaty from the date when such denunciation or withdrawal takes effect.

Article 71. Consequences of the Invalidity of a Treaty Which Conflicts with a Peremptory Norm of General International Law

1. In the case of a treaty which is void under article 53 the parties shall:
    (a) eliminate as far as possible the consequences of any act performed

in reliance on any provision which conflicts with the peremptory norm of general international law; and

(b) bring their mutual relations into conformity with the peremptory norm of general international law.

2. In the case of a treaty which becomes void and terminates under article 64, the termination of the treaty:

(a) releases the parties from any obligation further to perform the treaty;

(b) does not affect any right, obligation or legal situation of the parties created through the execution of the treaty prior to its termination; provided that those rights, obligations or situations may thereafter be maintained only to the extent that their maintenance is not in itself in conflict with the new peremptory norm of general international law.

Article 72. Consequences of the Suspension of the Operation of a Treaty

1. Unless the treaty otherwise provides or the parties otherwise agree, the suspension of the operation of a treaty under its provisions or in accordance with the present Convention:

(a) releases the parties between which the operation of the treaty is suspended from the obligation to perform the treaty in their mutual relations during the period of the suspension;

(b) does not otherwise affect the legal relations between the parties established by the treaty.

2. During the period of the suspension the parties shall refrain from acts tending to obstruct the resumption of the operation of the treaty.

Part VI. Miscellaneous Provisions

Article 73. Cases of State Succession, State Responsibility and Outbreak of Hostilities

The provisions of the present Convention shall not prejudge any question that may arise in regard to a treaty from a succession of States or from the international responsibility of a State or from the outbreak of hostilities between States.

Article 74. Diplomatic and Consular Relations and the Conclusion of Treaties

The severance or absence of diplomatic or consular relations between two or more States does not prevent the conclusion of treaties between those States. The conclusion of a treaty does not in itself affect the situation in regard to diplomatic or consular relations.

Article 75. Case of an Aggressor State

The provisions of the present Convention are without prejudice to any obligation in relation to a treaty which may arise for an aggressor State in consequence of measures taken in conformity with the Charter of the United Nations with reference to that State's aggression.

Part VII. Depositaries, Notifications, Corrections and Registration

Article 76. *Depositaries of Treaties*

1. The designation of the depositary of a treaty may be made by the negotiating States, either in the treaty itself or in some other manner. The depositary may be one or more States, an international organization or the chief administrative officer of the organization.

2. The functions of the depositary of a treaty are international in character and the depositary is under an obligation to act impartially in their performance. In particular, the fact that a treaty has not entered into force between certain of the parties or that a difference has appeared between a State and a depositary with regard to the performance of the latter's functions shall not affect that obligation.

Article 77. *Functions of Depositaries*

1. The functions of a depositary, unless otherwise provided in the treaty or agreed by the contracting States, comprise in particular:

(a) keeping custody of the original text of the treaty and of any full powers delivered to the depositary;

(b) preparing certified copies of the original text and preparing any further text of the treaty in such additional languages as may be required by the treaty and transmitting them to the parties and to the States entitled to become parties to the treaty;

(c) receiving any signatures to the treaty and receiving and keeping custody of any instruments, notifications and communications relating to it;

(d) examining whether the signature or any instrument, notification or communication relating to the treaty is in due and proper form and, if need be, bringing the matter to the attention of the State in question;

(e) informing the parties and the States entitled to become parties to the treaty of acts, notifications and communications relating to the treaty;

(f) informing the States entitled to become parties to the treaty when the number of signatures or of instruments of ratification, acceptance, approval or accession required for the entry into force of the treaty has been received or deposited;

(g) registering the treaty with the Secretariat of the United Nations.

(h) performing the functions specified in other provisions of the present Convention.

2. In the event of any difference appearing between a State and the depositary as to the performance of the latter's functions, the depositary shall bring the question to the attention of the signatory States and the contracting States or, where appropriate, of the competent organ of the international organization concerned.

Article 78. Notifications and Communications

Except as the treaty or the present Convention otherwise provide, any notification or communication to be made by any State under the present Convention shall:

(a) if there is no depositary, be transmitted direct to the States for which it is intended, or if there is a depositary, to the latter;

(b) be considered as having been made by the State in question only upon its receipt by the State to which it was transmitted or, as the case may be, upon its receipt by the depositary;

(c) if transmitted to a depositary, be considered as received by the State for which it was intended only when the latter State has been informed by the depositary in accordance with article 77, paragraph 1(e).

Article 79. Correction of Errors in Texts or in Certified Copies of Treaties

1. Where, after the authentication of the text of a treaty, the signatory States and the contracting States are agreed that it contains an error, the error shall, unless they decide upon some other means of correction, be corrected:

(a) by having the appropriate correction made in the text and causing the correction to be initialled by duly authorized representatives;

(b) by executing or exchanging an instrument or instruments setting out the correction which it has been agreed to make; or

(c) by executing a corrected text of the whole treaty by the same procedure as in the case of the original text.

2. Where the treaty is one for which there is a depositary, the latter shall notify the signatory States and the contracting States of the error and of the proposal to correct it and shall specify an appropriate time-limit within which objection to the proposed correction may be raised. If, on the expiry of the time-limit:

(a) no objection has been raised, the depositary shall make and initial the correction in the text and shall execute a *procès-verbal* of the rectification of the text and communicate a copy of it to the parties and to the States entitled to become parties to the treaty;

(b) an objection has been raised, the depositary shall communicate the objection to the signatory States and to the contracting States.

3. The rules in paragraphs 1 and 2 apply also where the text has been authenticated in two or more languages and it appears that there is a lack of concordance which the signatory States and the contracting States agree should be corrected.

4. The corrected text replaces the defective text *ab initio*, unless the signatory States and the contracting States otherwise decide.

5. The correction of the text of a treaty that has been registered shall be notified to the Secretariat of the United Nations.

6. Where an error is discovered in a certified copy of a treaty, the depositary shall execute a *procès-verbal* specifying the rectification and communicate a copy of it to the signatory States and to the contracting States.

Article 80. Registration and Publication of Treaties

1. Treaties shall, after their entry into force, be transmitted to the Secretariat of the United Nations for registration or filing and recording, as the case may be, and for publication.

2. The designation of a depositary shall constitute authorization for it to perform the acts specified in the preceding paragraph.

Part VIII. Final Provisions

Article 81. Signature

The present Convention shall be open for signature by all States Members of the United Nations or of any of the specialized agencies or of the International Atomic Energy Agency or parties to the Statute of the International Court of Justice, and by any other State invited by the General Assembly of the United Nations to become a party to the Convention, as follows: . . .

Article 82. Ratification

The present Convention is subject to ratification. The instruments of ratification shall be deposited with the Secretary-General of the United Nations.

Article 83. Accession

The present Convention shall remain open for accession by any State belonging to any of the categories mentioned in article 81. The instruments of accession shall be deposited with the Secretary-General of the United Nations.

Article 84. Entry into Force

1. The present Convention shall enter into force on the thirtieth day following the date of deposit of the thirty-fifth instrument of ratification or accession.

2. For each State ratifying or acceding to the Convention after the deposit of the thirty-fifth instrument of ratification or accession, the Convention shall enter into force on the thirtieth day after deposit by such State of its instrument of ratification or accession. . . .

ANNEX

1. A list of conciliators consisting of qualified jurists shall be drawn up and maintained by the Secretary-General of the United Nations. To this end, every State which is a Member of the United Nations or a party to the present Convention shall be invited to nominate two conciliators, and the names of the persons so nominated shall constitute the list. The term of a conciliator, including that of any conciliator nominated to fill a casual va-

cancy, shall be five years and may be renewed. A conciliator whose term expires shall continue to fulfil any function for which he shall have been chosen under the following paragraph.

2. When a request has been made to the Secretary-General under article 66 the Secretary-General shall bring the dispute before a conciliation commission constituted as follows:

The State or States constituting one of the parties to the dispute shall appoint:

   (a) one conciliator of the nationality of that State or of one of those States, who may or may not be chosen from the list referred to in paragraph 1; and

   (b) one conciliator not of the nationality of that State or of any of those States, who shall be chosen from the list.

The State or States constituting the other party to the dispute shall appoint two conciliators in the same way. The four conciliators chosen by the parties shall be appointed within sixty days following the date on which the Secretary-General receives the request.

The four conciliators shall, within sixty days following the date of the last of their own appointments, appoint a fifth conciliator chosen from the list, who shall be chairman.

If the appointment of the chairman or of any of the other conciliators has not been made within the period prescribed above for such appointment, it shall be made by the Secretary-General within sixty days following the expiry of that period. The appointment of the chairman may be made by the Secretary-General either from the list or from the membership of the International Law Commission. Any of the periods within which appointments must be made may be extended by agreement between the parties to the dispute.

Any vacancy shall be filled in the manner prescribed for the initial appointment.

3. The Conciliation Commission shall decide its own procedure. The Commission, with the consent of the parties to the dispute, may invite any party to the treaty to submit to it its views orally or in writing. Decisions and recommendations of the Commission shall be made by a majority vote of the five members.

4. The Commission may draw the attention of the parties to the dispute to any measures which might facilitate an amicable settlement.

5. The Commission shall hear the parties, examine the claims and objections, and make proposals to the parties with a view to reaching an amicable settlement of the dispute.

6. The Commission shall report within twelve months of its constitution. Its report shall be deposited with the Secretary-General and transmitted to the parties to the dispute. The report of the Commission, including any conclusions stated therein regarding the facts or questions of law, shall not be binding upon the parties and it shall have no other character than that of recommendations submitted for the consideration of the parties in order to facilitate an amicable settlement of the dispute.

7. The Secretary-General shall provide the Commission with such assistance and facilities as it may require. The expenses of the Commission shall be borne by the United Nations.

3

International Law in the United States

THE CONSTITUTION OF THE UNITED STATES

We the People of the United States, in Order to form a more perfect Union, establish Justice, insure domestic Tranquility, provide for the common defence, promote the general Welfare, and secure the Blessings of Liberty to ourselves and our Posterity, do ordain and establish this Constitution for the United States of America.

Article I

Section 1. All legislative Powers herein granted shall be vested in a Congress of the United States, which shall consist of a Senate and House of Representatives.

Section 2. [1] The House of Representatives shall be composed of Members chosen every second Year by the People of the several States, and the Electors in each State shall have the Qualifications requisite for Electors of the most numerous Branch of the State Legislature.

[2] No Person shall be a Representative who shall not have attained to the Age of twenty five Years, and been seven Years a Citizen of the United States, and who shall not, when elected, be an Inhabitant of that State in which he shall be chosen.

[3] Representatives and direct Taxes shall be apportioned among the several States which may be included within this Union, according to their respective Numbers, which shall be determined by adding to the whole Number of free Persons, including those bound to Service for a Term of Years, and excluding Indians not taxed, three fifths of all other Persons. The actual Enumeration shall be made within three Years after the first Meeting of the Congress of the United States, and within every subsequent Term of ten Years, in such Manner as they shall by Law direct. The Number of Representatives shall not exceed one for every thirty Thousand, but each

State shall have at Least one Representative; and until such enumeration shall be made, the State of New Hampshire shall be entitled to chuse three, Massachusetts eight, Rhode Island and Providence Plantations one, Connecticut five, New York six, New Jersey four, Pennsylvania eight, Delaware one, Maryland six, Virginia ten, North Carolina five, South Carolina five, and Georgia three.

[4] When vacancies happen in the Representation from any State, the Executive Authority thereof shall issue Writs of Election to fill such Vacancies.

[5] The House of Representatives shall chuse their Speaker and other Officers; and shall have the sole Power of Impeachment.

Section 3. [1] The Senate of the United States shall be composed of two Senators from each State, chosen by the Legislature thereof, for six Years; and each Senator shall have one Vote.

[2] Immediately after they shall be assembled in Consequence of the first Election, they shall be divided as equally as may be into three Classes. The Seats of the Senators of the first Class shall be vacated at the Expiration of the second Year, of the second Class at the Expiration of the fourth Year, and of the third Class at the Expiration of the sixth Year, so that one third may be chosen every second Year; and if Vacancies happen by Resignation, or otherwise, during the Recess of the Legislature of any State, the Executive thereof may make temporary Appointments until the next Meeting of the Legislature, which shall then fill such Vacancies.

[3] No Person shall be a Senator who shall not have attained to the Age of thirty Years, and been nine Years a Citizen of the United States, and who shall not, when elected, be an Inhabitant of that State for which he shall be chosen.

[4] The Vice President of the United States shall be President of the Senate, but shall have no Vote, unless they be equally divided.

[5] The Senate shall chuse their other Officers, and also a President pro tempore, in the absence of the Vice President, or when he shall exercise the Office of President of the United States.

[6] The Senate shall have the sole Power to try all Impeachments. When sitting for that Purpose, they shall be on Oath or Affirmation. When the President of the United States is tried, the Chief Justice shall preside: And no Person shall be convicted without the Concurrence of two thirds of the Members present.

[7] Judgment in Cases of Impeachment shall not extend further than to removal from Office, and disqualification to hold and enjoy any Office of honor, Trust or Profit under the United States: but the Party convicted shall nevertheless be liable and subject to Indictment, Trial, Judgment and Punishment, according to Law.

Section 4. [1] The Times, Places and Manner of holding Elections for Senators and Representatives, shall be prescribed in each State by the Legislature thereof; but the Congress may at any time by Law make or alter such Regulations, except as to the Places of chusing Senators.

[2] The Congress shall assemble at least once in every Year, and such Meeting shall be on the first Monday in December, unless they shall by Law appoint a different Day.

Section 5. [1] Each House shall be the Judge of the Elections, Returns and Qualifications of its own Members, and a Majority of each shall constitute a Quorum to do Business; but a smaller Number may adjourn from day to day, and may be authorized to compel the Attendance of absent Members, in such Manner, and under such Penalties as each House may provide.

[2] Each House may determine the Rules of its Proceedings, punish its Members for disorderly Behavior, and, with the Concurrence of two thirds, expel a Member.

[3] Each House shall keep a Journal of its Proceedings, and from time to time publish the same, excepting such Parts as may in their Judgment require Secrecy; and the Yeas and Nays of the Members of either House on any question shall, at the Desire of one fifth of those Present, be entered on the Journal.

[4] Neither House, during the Session of Congress, shall, without the Consent of the other, adjourn for more than three days, nor to any other Place than that in which the two Houses shall be sitting.

Section 6. [1] The Senators and Representatives shall receive a Compensation for their Services, to be ascertained by Law, and paid out of the Treasury of the United States. They shall in all Cases, except Treason, Felony and Breach of the Peace, be privileged from Arrest during their Attendance at the Session of their respective Houses, and in going to and returning from the same; and for any Speech or Debate in either House, they shall not be questioned in any other Place.

[2] No Senator or Representative shall, during the Time for which he was elected, be appointed to any civil Office under the Authority of the United States, which shall have been created, or the Emoluments whereof shall have been encreased during such time; and no Person holding any Office under the United States, shall be a Member of either House during his Continuance in Office.

Section 7. [1] All Bills for raising Revenue shall originate in the House of Representatives; but the Senate may propose or concur with Amendments as on other Bills.

[2] Every Bill which shall have passed the House of Representatives and the Senate, shall, before it become a Law, be presented to the President of the United States; If he approve he shall sign it, but if not he shall return it, with his Objections to the House in which it shall have originated, who shall enter the Objections at large on their Journal, and proceed to reconsider it. If after such Reconsideration two thirds of that House shall agree to pass the Bill, it shall be sent, together with the Objections, to the other House, by which it shall likewise be reconsidered, and if approved by two thirds of that House, it shall become a Law. But in all such Cases the Votes of both Houses shall be determined by yeas and Nays, and the Names of the Persons voting for and against the Bill shall be entered on the Journal of each House respectively. If any Bill shall not be returned by the President within ten Days (Sundays excepted) after it shall have been presented to him, the Same shall be a Law, in like Manner as if he had signed it, unless the Congress by their Adjournment prevents its Return, in which Case it shall not be a Law.

[3] Every Order, Resolution, or Vote to Which the Concurrence of the

Senate and House of Representatives may be necessary (except on a question of Adjournment) shall be presented to the President of the United States; and before the Same shall take Effect, shall be approved by him, or being disapproved by him, shall be repassed by two thirds of the Senate and House of Representatives, according to the Rules and Limitations prescribed in the Case of a Bill.

Section 8. [1] The Congress shall have Power To lay and collect Taxes, Duties, Imposts and Excises, to pay the Debts and provide for the common Defence and general Welfare of the United States; but all Duties, Imposts and Excises shall be uniform throughout the United States;

[2] To borrow money on the credit of the United States.

[3] To regulate Commerce with foreign Nations, and among the several States, and with the Indian Tribes;

[4] To establish an uniform Rule of Naturalization, and uniform Laws on the subject of Bankruptcies throughout the United States;

[5] To coin Money, regulate the Value thereof, and of foreign Coin, and fix the Standard of Weights and Measures;

[6] To provide the Punishment of counterfeiting the Securities and current Coin of the United States;

[7] To establish Post Offices and post Roads;

[8] To promote the Progress of Science and useful Arts, by securing for limited Times to Authors and Inventors the exclusive Right to their respective Writings and Discoveries;

[9] To constitute Tribunals inferior to the supreme Court;

[10] To define and punish Piracies and Felonies committed on the high Seas, and Offenses against the Law of Nations;

[11] To declare War, grant Letters of Marque and Reprisal, and make Rules concerning Captures on Land and Water;

[12] To raise and support Armies, but no Appropriation of Money to that Use shall be for a longer Term than two Years;

[13] To provide and maintain a Navy;

[14] To make Rules for the Government and Regulation of the land and naval Forces;

[15] To provide for calling forth the Militia to execute the Laws of the Union, suppress Insurrections and repeal Invasions;

[16] To provide for organizing, arming, and disciplining, the Militia, and for governing such Part of them as may be employed in the Service of the United States, reserving to the States respectively, the Appointment of the Officers, and the Authority of training the Militia according to the discipline prescribed by Congress;

[17] To exercise exclusive Legislation in all Cases whatsoever, over such District (not exceeding ten Miles square) as may, by Cession of particular States, and the Acceptance of Congress, become the Seat of the Government of the United States, and to exercise like Authority over all Places purchased by the Consent of the Legislature of the State in which the Same shall be, for the Erection of Forts, Magazines, Arsenals, dock-Yards, and other needful Buildings; — And

[18] To make all Laws which shall be necessary and proper for carrying into Execution the foregoing Powers, and all other Powers vested by this

Constitution in the Government of the United States, or in any Department or Officer thereof.

Section 9. [1] The Migration or Importation of such Persons as any of the States now existing shall think proper to admit, shall not be prohibited by the Congress prior to the Year one thousand eight hundred and eight, but a Tax or duty may be imposed on such Importation, not exceeding ten dollars for each Person.

[2] The privilege of the Writ of Habeas Corpus shall not be suspended, unless when in Cases of Rebellion or Invasion the public Safety may require it.

[3] No Bill of Attainder or ex post facto Law shall be passed.

[4] No Capitation, or other direct, Tax shall be laid, unless in Proportion to the Census or Enumeration herein before directed to be taken.

[5] No Tax or Duty shall be laid on Articles exported from any State.

[6] No Preference shall be given by any Regulation of Commerce or Revenue to the Ports of one State over those of another: nor shall Vessels bound to, or from, one State, be obliged to enter, clear, or pay Duties in another.

[7] No Money shall be drawn from the Treasury, but in Consequence of Appropriations made by Law; and a regular Statement and Account of the Receipts and Expenditures of all public Money shall be published from time to time.

[8] No Title of Nobility shall be granted by the United States: And no Person holding any Office of Profit or Trust under them, shall, without the Consent of the Congress, accept of any present, Emolument, Office, or Title, of any kind whatever, from any King, Prince, or foreign State.

Section 10. [1] No State shall enter into any Treaty, Alliance, or Confederation; grant Letters of Marque and Reprisal; coin Money; emit Bills of Credit; make any Thing but gold and silver Coin a Tender in Payment of Debts; pass any Bill of Attainder, ex post facto Law, or Law impairing the Obligation of Contracts, or grant any Title of Nobility.

[2] No State shall, without the Consent of the Congress, lay any Imposts or Duties on Imports or Exports, except what may be absolutely necessary for executing its inspection Laws: and the net Produce of all Duties and Imposts, laid by any State on Imports or Exports, shall be for the Use of the Treasury of the United States; and all such Laws shall be subject to the Revision and Controul of the Congress.

[3] No State shall, without the Consent of Congress, lay any Duty of Tonnage, keep Troops, or Ships of War in time of Peace, enter into any Agreement or Compact with another State, or with a foreign Power, or engage in War, unless actually invaded, or in such imminent Danger as will not admit of delay.

Article II

Section 1. [1] The executive Power shall be vested in a President of the United States of America. He shall hold his Office during the Term of four Years, and, together with the Vice President, chosen for the same Term, be elected, as follows:

[2] Each State shall appoint, in such Manner as the Legislature thereof may direct, a Number of Electors, equal to the whole Number of Senators and Representatives to which the State may be entitled in the Congress: but no Senator or Representative, or Person holding an Office of Trust or Profit under the United States, shall be appointed an Elector.

[3] The Electors shall meet in their respective States, and vote by Ballot for two Persons, of whom one at least shall not be an Inhabitant of the same State with themselves. And they shall make a List of all the Persons voted for, and of the Number of Votes for each; which List they shall sign and certify, and transmit sealed to the Seat of the Government of the United States, directed to the President of the Senate. The President of the Senate shall, in the Presence of the Senate and House of Representatives, open all the Certificates, and the Votes shall then be counted. The Person having the greatest Number of Votes shall be the President, if such Number be a Majority of the whole Number of Electors appointed; and if there be more than one who have such Majority, and have an equal Number of Votes, then the House of Representatives shall immediately chuse by Ballot one of them for President; and if no Person have a Majority, then from the five highest on the List the said House shall in like Manner chuse the President. But in chusing the President, the Votes shall be taken by States, the Representation from each State having one Vote; a quorum for this Purpose shall consist of a Member or Members from two thirds of the States, and a Majority of all the States shall be necessary to a Choice. In every Case, after the Choice of the President, the Person having the greatest Number of Votes of the Electors shall be the Vice President. But if there should remain two or more who have equal Votes, the Senate shall chuse from them by Ballot the Vice President.

[4] The Congress may determine the Time of chusing the Electors, and the Day on which they shall give their Votes; which Day shall be the same throughout the United States.

[5] No person except a natural born Citizen, or a Citizen of the United States, at the time of the Adoption of this Constitution, shall be eligible to the Office of President; neither shall any Person be eligible to that Office who shall not have attained to the Age of thirty five Years, and been fourteen Years a Resident within the United States.

[6] In case of the removal of the President from Office, or of his Death, Resignation or Inability to discharge the Powers and Duties of the said Office, the Same shall devolve on the Vice President, and the Congress may by Law provide for the Case of Removal, Death, Resignation or Inability, both of the President and Vice President, declaring what Officer shall then act as President, and such Officer shall act accordingly, until the Disability be removed, or a President shall be elected.

[7] The President shall, at stated Times, receive for his Services, a Compensation, which shall neither be increased nor diminished during the Period for which he shall have been elected, and he shall not receive within that Period any other Emolument from the United States, or any of them.

[8] Before he enter on the Execution of his Office, he shall take the following Oath or Affirmation: "I do solemnly swear (or affirm) that I will faithfully execute the Office of President of the United States, and will to the

best of my Ability, preserve, protect and defend the Constitution of the United States."

Section 2. [1] The President shall be Commander in Chief of the Army and Navy of the United States, and of the Militia of the several States, when called into the actual Service of the United States; he may require the Opinion, in writing, of the principal Officer in each of the executive Departments, upon any subject relating to the Duties of their respective Offices, and he shall have Power to grant Reprieves and Pardons for Offenses against the United States, except in Cases of Impeachment.

[2] He shall have Power, by and with the Advice and Consent of the Senate, to make Treaties, provided two thirds of the Senators present concur; and he shall nominate, and by and with the Advice and Consent of the Senate, shall appoint Ambassadors, other public Ministers and Consuls, Judges of the supreme Court, and all other Officers of the United States, whose Appointments are not herein otherwise provided for, and which shall be established by Law: but the Congress may by Law vest the Appointment of such inferior Officers, as they think proper, in the President alone, in the Courts of Law, or in the Heads of Departments.

[3] The President shall have Power to fill up all Vacancies that may happen during the Recess of the Senate, by granting Commissions which shall expire at the End of their next Session.

Section 3. He shall from time to time give to the Congress Information of the State of the Union, and recommend to their Consideration such Measures as he shall judge necessary and expedient; he may, on extraordinary Occasions, convene both Houses, or either of them, and in Case of Disagreement between them, with Respect to the Time of Adjournment, he may adjourn them to such Time as he shall think proper; he shall receive Ambassadors and other public Ministers; he shall take Care that the Laws be faithfully executed, and shall Commission all the Officers of the United States.

Section 4. The President and all civil Officers of the United States, shall be removed from Office on Impeachment for, and Conviction of, Treason, Bribery, or other high Crimes and Misdemeanors.

Article III

Section 1. The judicial Power of the United States, shall be vested in one supreme Court, and in such inferior Courts as the Congress may from time to time ordain and establish. The Judges, both of the supreme and inferior Courts, shall hold their Offices during good Behaviour, and shall, at stated Times, receive for their Services, a Compensation, which shall not be diminished during their Continuance in Office.

Section 2. [1] The Judicial Power shall extend to all Cases, in Law and Equity, arising under this Constitution, the Laws of the United States, and Treaties made, or which shall be made, under their Authority; — to all Cases affecting Ambassadors, other public Ministers and Consuls; — to all Cases of admiralty and maritime Jurisdiction; — to Controversies to which the United States shall be a Party; — to Controversies between two or more States; — between a State and Citizens of another State; — between Citizens of different States; — between Citizens of the same State claiming Lands under Grants of different States, and between a State, or the Citizens thereof, and foreign States, Citizens or Subjects.

[2] In all Cases affecting Ambassadors, other public Ministers and Consuls, and those in which a State shall be a Party, the supreme Court shall have original Jurisdiction. In all the other Cases before mentioned, the supreme Court shall have appellate Jurisdiction, both as to Law and Fact, with such Exceptions, and under such Regulations as the Congress shall make.

[3] The trial of all Crimes, except in Cases of Impeachment, shall be by Jury; and such Trial shall be held in the State where the said Crimes shall have been committed; but when not committed within any State, the Trial shall be at such Place or Places as the Congress may by Law have directed.

Section 3. [1] Treason against the United States, shall consist only in levying War against them, or in adhering to their Enemies, giving them Aid and Comfort. No person shall be convicted of Treason unless on the Testimony of two Witnesses to the same overt Act, or on Confession in open Court.

[2] The Congress shall have Power to declare the Punishment of Treason, but no Attainder of Treason shall work Corruption of Blood, or Forfeiture except during the Life of the Person attainted.

Article IV

Section 1. Full Faith and Credit shall be given in each State to the public Acts, Records, and judicial Proceedings of every other State. And the Congress may by general Laws prescribe the Manner in which such Acts, Records and Proceedings shall be proved, and the Effect thereof.

Section 2. [1] The Citizens of each State shall be entitled to all Privileges and Immunities of Citizens in the several States.

[2] A Person charged in any State with Treason, Felony, or other Crime, who shall flee from Justice, and be found in another State, shall on demand of the executive Authority of the State from which he fled, be delivered up, to be removed to the State having Jurisdiction of the Crime.

[3] No Person held to Service or Labour in one State, under the Laws thereof, escaping into another, shall, in Consequence of any Law or Regulation therein, be discharged from such Service or Labour, but shall be delivered up on Claim of the Party to whom such Service or Labour may be due.

Section 3. [1] New States may be admitted by the Congress into this Union; but no new State shall be formed or erected within the Jurisdiction of any other State; nor any State be formed by the Junction of two or more States, or Parts of States, without the Consent of the Legislatures of the States concerned as well as of the Congress.

[2] The Congress shall have Power to dispose of and make all needful Rules and Regulations respecting the Territory or other Property belonging to the United States; and nothing in this Constitution shall be so construed as to Prejudice any Claims of the United States, or of any particular State.

Section 4. The United States shall guarantee to every State in this Union a Republican Form of Government, and shall protect each of them against

Invasion; and on Application of the Legislature, or of the Executive (when the Legislature cannot be convened) against domestic Violence.

Article V

The Congress, whenever two thirds of both Houses shall deem it necessary, shall propose Amendments to this Constitution, or, on the Application of the Legislatures of two thirds of the several States, shall call a Convention for proposing Amendments, which, in either Case, shall be valid to all Intents and Purposes, as part of this Constitution, when ratified by the Legislatures of three fourths of the several States, or by Conventions in three fourths thereof, as the one or the other Mode of Ratification may be proposed by the Congress; Provided that no Amendment which may be made prior to the Year One thousand eight hundred and eight shall in any Manner affect the first and fourth Clauses in the Ninth Section of the first Article; and that no State, without its Consent, shall be deprived of its equal Suffrage in the Senate.

Article VI

[1] All Debts contracted and Engagements entered into, before the Adoption of this Constitution, shall be as valid against the United States under this Constitution, as under the Confederation.

[2] This Constitution, and the Laws of the United States which shall be made in Pursuance thereof; and all Treaties made, or which shall be made, under the Authority of the United States, shall be the supreme Law of the Land; and the Judges in every State shall be bound thereby, any Thing in the Constitution or Laws of any State to the Contrary notwithstanding.

[3] The Senators and Representatives before mentioned, and the Members of the several State Legislatures, and all executive and judicial Officers, both of the United States and of the several States, shall be bound by Oath or Affirmation, to support this Constitution; but no religious Test shall ever be required as a Qualification to any Office or public Trust under the United States.

Article VII

The Ratification of the Conventions of nine States shall be sufficient for the Establishment of this Constitution between the States so ratifying the Same.

Done in Convention by the Unanimous Consent of the States present the Seventeenth Day of September in the Year of our Lord one thousand seven hundred and Eighty seven and of the Independence of the United States of America the Twelfth.

ARTICLES IN ADDITION TO, AND AMENDMENT OF, THE CONSTITUTION OF THE UNITED STATES OF AMERICA, PROPOSED BY CONGRESS, AND RATIFIED BY THE LEGISLATURES OF THE SEVERAL STATES, PURSUANT TO THE FIFTH ARTICLE OF THE ORIGINAL CONSTITUTION

Amendment I [1791]

Congress shall make no law respecting an establishment of religion, or prohibiting the free exercise thereof; or abridging the freedom of speech, or of the press; or the right of the people peaceably to assemble, and to petition the Government for a redress of grievances.

Amendment II [1791]

A well regulated Militia, being necessary to the security of a free State, the right of the people to keep and bear Arms, shall not be infringed.

Amendment III [1791]

No Soldier shall, in time of peace be quartered in any house, without the consent of the Owner, nor in time of war, but in a manner to be prescribed by law.

Amendment IV [1791]

The right of the people to be secure in their persons, houses, papers, and effects, against unreasonable searches and seizures, shall not be violated, and no Warrants shall issue, but upon probable cause, supported by Oath or affirmation, and particularly describing the place to be searched, and the persons or things to be seized.

Amendment V [1791]

No person shall be held to answer for a capital, or otherwise infamous crime, unless on a presentment or indictment of a Grand Jury, except in cases arising in the land or naval forces, or in the Militia, when in actual service in time of War or public danger; nor shall any person be subject for the same offense to be twice put in jeopardy of life or limb; nor shall be compelled in any criminal case to be a witness against himself, nor be deprived of life, liberty, or property, without due process of law; nor shall private property be taken for public use, without just compensation.

Amendment VI [1791]

In all criminal prosecutions, the accused shall enjoy the right to a speedy and public trial, by an impartial jury of the State and district wherein the crime shall have been committed, which district shall have been previously ascertained by law, and to be informed of the nature and cause of the accusation; to be confronted with the witnesses against him; to have compulsory process for obtaining witnesses in his favor, and to have the Assistance of Counsel for his defence.

Amendment VII [1791]

In Suits at common law, where the value in controversy shall exceed twenty dollars, the right of trial by jury shall be preserved, and no fact tried by a jury, shall be otherwise re-examined in any Court of the United States, than according to the rules of the common law.

Amendment VIII [1791]

Excessive bail shall not be required, nor excessive fines imposed, nor cruel and unusual punishments inflicted.

Amendment IX [1791]

The enumeration in the Constitution, of certain rights, shall not be construed to deny or disparage others retained by the people.

Amendment X [1791]

The powers not delegated to the United States by the Constitution, nor prohibited by it to the States, are reserved to the States respectively, or to the people.

Amendment XI [1798]

The Judicial power of the United States shall not be construed to extend to any suit in law or equity, commenced or prosecuted against one of the United States by Citizens of another State, or by Citizens or Subjects of any Foreign State.

Amendment XII [1804]

The Electors shall meet in their respective states and vote by ballot for President and Vice-President, one of whom, at least, shall not be an inhabitant of the same state with themselves; they shall name in their ballots the person voted for as President, and in distinct ballots the person voted for as Vice-President, and they shall make distinct lists of all persons voted for as President, and of all persons voted for as Vice-President, and of the number of votes for each, which lists they shall sign and certify, and transmit sealed to the seat of the government of the United States, directed to the President of the Senate; — The President of the Senate shall, in the presence of the Senate and House of Representatives, open all the certificates and the votes shall then be counted; — The person having the greatest number of votes for President, shall be the President, if such number be a majority of the whole number of Electors appointed; and if no person have such majority, then from the persons having the highest numbers not exceeding three on the list of those voted for as President, the House of Representatives shall choose immediately, by ballot, the President. But in choosing the President, the votes shall be taken by states, the representation from each state having one vote; a quorum for this purpose shall consist of a member or members from two-thirds of the states, and a majority of all the states shall be necessary to a choice. And if the House of Representatives shall not choose a President whenever the right of choice shall devolve upon them, before the fourth day of March next following, then the Vice-President shall act as President, as in the case of the death or other constitutional disability of the President. — The person having the greatest number of votes as Vice-President, shall be the Vice-President, if such number be a majority of the whole number of Electors appointed, and if no person have a majority, then from the two highest numbers on the list, the Senate shall choose the Vice-President; a quorum for the purpose shall consist of two-thirds of the whole number of Senators, and a majority of the whole number shall be necessary to a choice. But no person constitutionally ineligible to the office of President shall be eligible to that of Vice-President of the United States.

Amendment XIII [1865]

Section 1. Neither slavery nor involuntary servitude, except as a punishment for crime whereof the party shall have been duly convicted, shall exist within the United States, or any place subject to their jurisdiction.

Section 2. Congress shall have power to enforce this article by appropriate legislation.

Amendment XIV [1868]

Section 1. All persons born or naturalized in the United States, and subject to the jurisdiction thereof, are citizens of the United States and of the State wherein they reside. No State shall make or enforce any law which shall abridge the privileges or immunities of citizens of the United States; nor shall any State deprive any person of life, liberty, or property, without due process of law; nor deny to any person within its jurisdiction the equal protection of the laws.

Section 2. Representatives shall be apportioned among the several States according to their respective numbers, counting the whole number of persons in each State, excluding Indians not taxed. But when the right to vote at any election for the choice of electors for President and Vice President of the United States, Representatives in Congress, the Executive and Judicial officers of a State, or the members of the Legislature thereof, is denied to any of the male inhabitants of such State, being twenty-one years of age, and citizens of the United States, or in any way abridged, except for participation in rebellion, or other crime, the basis of representation therein shall be reduced in the proportion which the number of such male citizens shall bear to the whole number of male citizens twenty-one years of age in such State.

Section 3. No person shall be a Senator or Representative in Congress, or elector of President and Vice President, or hold any office, civil or military, under the United States, or under any State, who, having previously taken an oath, as a member of Congress, or as an officer of the United States, or as a member of any State legislature, or as an executive or judicial officer of any State, to support the Constitution of the United States, shall have engaged in insurrection or rebellion against the same, or given aid or comfort to the enemies thereof. But Congress may by a vote of two-thirds of each House, remove such disability.

Section 4. The validity of the public debt of the United States, authorized by law, including debts incurred for payment of pensions and bounties for services in suppressing insurrection or rebellion, shall not be questioned. But neither the United States nor any State shall assume or pay any debt or obligation incurred in aid of insurrection or rebellion against the United

States, or any claim for the loss of emancipation of any slave; but all such debts, obligations and claims shall be held illegal and void.

Section 5. The Congress shall have power to enforce, by appropriate legislation, the provisions of this article.

Amendment XV [1870]

Section 1. The right of citizens of the United States to vote shall not be denied or abridged by the United States or by any State on account of race, color, or previous condition of servitude.

Section 2. The Congress shall have power to enforce this article by appropriate legislation.

Amendment XVI [1913]

The Congress shall have power to lay and collect taxes on incomes, from whatever source derived, without apportionment among the several States, and without regard to any census or enumeration.

Amendment XVII [1913]

[1] The Senate of the United States shall be composed of two Senators from each State, elected by the people thereof, for six years; and each Senator shall have one vote. The electors in each State shall have the qualifications requisite for electors of the most numerous branch of the State legislatures.

[2] When vacancies happen in the representation of any State in the Senate, the executive authority of such State shall issue writs of election to fill such vacancies: *Provided,* That the legislature of any State may empower the executive thereof to make temporary appointments until the people fill the vacancies by election as the legislature may direct.

[3] This amendment shall not be so construed as to affect the election or term of any Senator chosen before it becomes valid as part of the Constitution.

Amendment XVIII [1919]

Section 1. After one year from the ratification of this article the manufacture, sale, or transportation of intoxicating liquors within, the importation thereof into, or the exploration thereof from the United States and all territory subject to the jurisdiction thereof for beverage purposes is hereby prohibited.

Section 2. The Congress and the several States shall have concurrent power to enforce this article by appropriate legislation.

Section 3. This article shall be inoperative unless it shall have been ratified as an amendment to the Constitution by the legislatures of the several States, as provided in the Constitution, within seven years from the date of the submission hereof to the States by the Congress.

Amendment XIX [1920]

[1] The right of the citizens of the United States to vote shall not be denied or abridged by the United States or by any State on account of sex.

[2] Congress shall have power to enforce this article by appropriate legislation.

Amendment XX [1933]

Section 1. The terms of the President and Vice President shall end at noon on the 20th day of January, and the terms of Senators and Representatives at noon on the 3d day of January, of the years in which such terms would have ended if this article had not been ratified; and the terms of their successors shall then begin.

Section 2. The Congress shall assemble at least once in every year, and such meeting shall begin at noon on the 3d day of January, unless they shall by law appoint a different day.

Section 3. If, at the time fixed for the beginning of the term of the President, the President elect shall have died, the Vice President elect shall become President. If a President shall not have been chosen before the time fixed for the beginning of his term, or if the President elect shall have failed to qualify, then the Vice President elect shall act as President until a President shall have qualified; and the Congress may by law provide for the case wherein neither a President elect nor a Vice President elect shall have qualified, declaring who shall then act as President, or the manner in which one who is to act shall be selected, and such person shall act accordingly until a President or Vice President shall have qualified.

Section 4. The Congress may by law provide for the case of the death of any of the persons from whom the House of Representatives may choose a President whenever the right of choice shall have devolved upon them, and for the case of the death of any of the persons from whom the Senate may choose a Vice President whenever the right of choice shall have devolved upon them.

Section 5. Sections 1 and 2 shall take effect on the 15th day of October following the ratification of this article.

Section 6. This article shall be inoperative unless it shall have been ratified as an amendment to the Constitution by the legislatures of three-fourths of the several States within seven years from the date of its submission.

Amendment XXI [1933]

Section 1. The eighteenth article of amendment to the Constitution of the United States is hereby repealed.

Section 2. The transportation or importation into any State, Territory, or possession of the United States for delivery or use therein of intoxicating liquors, in violation of the laws thereof, is here by prohibited.

Section 3. This article shall be inoperative unless it shall have been ratified as an amendment to the Constitution by conventions in the several States, as provided in the Constitution, within seven years from the date of the submission hereof to the States by the Congress.

Amendment XXII [1951]

Section 1. No person shall be elected to the office of the President more than twice, and no person who has held the office of President, or acted as President, for more than two years of a term to which some other person was elected President shall be elected to the office of the President more than once. But this Article shall not apply to any person holding the office of President when this Article was proposed by the Congress, and shall not prevent any person who may be holding the office of President, or acting as President, during the term within which the Article becomes operative from holding the office of President or acting as President during the remainder of such term.

Section 2. This article shall be inoperative unless it shall have been ratified as an amendment to the Constitution by the legislatures of three-fourths of the several States within seven years from the date of its submission to the States by the Congress.

Amendment XXIII [1961]

Section 1. The District constituting the seat of Government of the United States shall appoint in such manner as the Congress may direct:

A number of electors of President and Vice President equal to the whole number of Senators and Representatives in Congress to which the District would be entitled if it were a State, but in no event more than the least populous State; they shall be in addition to those appointed by the States, but they shall be considered, for the purposes of the election of President and Vice President, to be electors appointed by a State; and they shall meet in the District and perform such duties as provided by the twelfth article of amendment.

Section 2. The Congress shall have power to enforce this article by appropriate legislation.

Amendment XXIV [1964]

Section 1. The right of citizens of the United States to vote in any primary or other election for President or Vice President, for electors for President or Vice President, or for Senator or Representative in Congress, shall not be denied or abridged by the United States or any State by reason of failure to pay any poll tax or other tax.

Section 2. The Congress shall have power to enforce this article by appropriate legislation.

Amendment XXV [1967]

Section 1. In case of the removal of the President from office or of his death or resignation, the Vice President shall become President.

Section 2. Whenever there is a vacancy in the office of the Vice President, the President shall nominate a Vice President who shall take office upon confirmation by a majority vote of both Houses of Congress.

Section 3. Whenever the President transmits to the President pro tempore of the Senate and the Speaker of the House of Representatives his written declaration that he is unable to discharge the powers and duties of his office, and until he transmits to them a written declaration to the contrary, such powers and duties shall be discharged by the Vice President as Acting President.

Section 4. Whenever the Vice President and a majority of either the principal officers of the executive departments or of such other body as Congress may by law provide, transmit to the President pro tempore of the Senate and the Speaker of the House of Representatives their written declaration that the President is unable to discharge the powers and duties of his office, the Vice President shall immediately assume the powers and duties of the office as Acting President.

Thereafter, when the President transmits to the President pro tempore of the Senate and the Speaker of the House of Representatives his written declaration that no inability exists, he shall resume the powers and duties of his office unless the Vice President and a majority of either the principal officers of the executive department or of such other body as Congress may by law provide, transmit within four days to the President pro tempore of the Senate and the Speaker of the House of Representatives their written declaration that the President is unable to discharge the powers and duties of his office. Thereupon Congress shall decide the issue, assembling within forty-eight hours for that purpose if not in session. If the Congress, within twenty-one days after receipt of the latter written declaration, or, if Congress is not in session, within twenty-one days after Congress is required to assemble, determines by two-thirds vote of both Houses that the President is unable to discharge the powers and duties of his office, the Vice President shall continue to discharge the same as Acting President; otherwise, the President shall resume the powers and duties of his office.

Amendment XXVI [1971]

Section 1. The right of citizens of the United States, who are eighteen years of age or older, to vote shall not be denied or abridged by the United States or by any State on account of age.

Section 2. The Congress shall have power to enforce this article by appropriate legislation.

UNITED STATES-JAPAN TREATY OF FRIENDSHIP, COMMERCE AND NAVIGATION

April 2, 1953, 4 U.S.T. 2063, T.I.A.S. No. 2863*

The United States of America and Japan, desirous of strengthening the bonds of peace and friendship traditionally existing between them and of encouraging closer economic and cultural relations between their peoples, and being cognizant of the contributions which may be made toward these ends by arrangements promoting mutually advantageous commercial intercourse, encouraging mutually beneficial investments, and establishing mutual rights and privileges, have resolved to conclude a Treaty of Friendship, Commerce and Navigation, based in general upon the principles of national and of most-favored-nation treatment unconditionally accorded, and for that purpose have appointed as their Plenipotentiaries, . . .

Who, having communicated to each other their full powers found to be in due form, have agreed upon the following Articles:

Article I

1. Nationals of either Party shall be permitted to enter the territories of the other Party and to remain therein: (a) for the purpose of carrying on trade between the territories of the two Parties and engaging in related commercial activities; (b) for the purpose of developing and directing the operations of an enterprise in which they have invested, or in which they are actively in the process of investing, a substantial amount of capital; and (c) for other purposes subject to the laws relating to the entry and sojourn of aliens.

2. Nationals of either Party, within the territories of the other Party, shall be permitted: (a) to travel therein freely, and to reside at places of their choice; (b) to enjoy liberty of conscience; (c) to hold both private and public religious services; (d) to gather and to transmit material for dissemination to the public abroad; and (e) to communicate with other persons inside and outside such territories by mail, telegraph and other means open to general public use.

---

*Signed in Tokyo on April 2, 1953. Entered into force on October 30, 1953.

3. The provisions of the present Article shall be subject to the right of either Party to apply measures that are necessary to maintain public order and protect the public health, morals and safety.

Article II

1. Nationals of either Party within the territories of the other Party shall be free from unlawful molestations of every kind, and shall receive the most constant protection and security, in no case less than that required by international law.

2. If, within the territories of either Party, a national of the other Party is taken into custody, the nearest consular representative of his country shall on the demand of such national be immediately notified. Such national shall: (a) receive reasonable and humane treatment; (b) be formally and immediately informed of the accusations against him; (c) be brought to trial as promptly as is consistent with the proper preparation of his defense; and (d) enjoy all means reasonably necessary to his defense, including the services of competent counsel of his choice.

Article III

1. Nationals of either Party shall be accorded national treatment in the application of laws and regulations within the territories of the other Party that establish a pecuniary compensation, or other benefit or service, on account of disease, injury or death arising out of and in the course of employment or due to the nature of employment.

2. In addition to the rights and privileges provided in paragraph 1 of the present Article, nationals of either Party shall, within the territories of the other Party, be accorded national treatment in the application of laws and regulations establishing compulsory systems of social security, under which benefits are paid without an individual test of financial need: (a) against loss of wages or earnings due to old age, unemployment, sickness or disability, or (b) against loss of financial support due to the death of father, husband or other person on whom such support had depended.

Article IV

1. Nationals and companies of either Party shall be accorded national treatment and most-favored-nation treatment with respect to access to the courts of justice and to administrative tribunals and agencies within the territories of the other Party, in all degrees of jurisdiction, both in pursuit and in defense of their rights. It is understood that companies of either Party not engaged in activities within the territories of the other Party shall enjoy such access therein without registration or similar requirements.

2. Contracts entered into between nationals and companies of either Party and nationals and companies of the other Party, that provide for the settlement by arbitration of controversies, shall not be deemed unenforce-

able within the territories of such other Party merely on the grounds that the place designated for the arbitration proceedings is outside such territories or that the nationality of one or more of the arbitrators is not that of such other Party. Awards duly rendered pursuant to any such contracts, which are final and enforceable under the laws of the place where rendered, shall be deemed conclusive in enforcement proceedings brought before the courts of competent jurisdiction of either Party, and shall be entitled to be declared enforceable by such courts, except where found contrary to public policy. When so declared, such awards shall be entitled to privileges and measures of enforcement appertaining to awards rendered locally. It is understood, however, that awards rendered outside the United States of America shall be entitled in any court in any State thereof only to the same measure of recognition as awards rendered in other States thereof.

Article V

1. Neither Party shall take unreasonable or discriminatory measures that would impair the legally acquired rights or interests within its territories of nationals and companies of the other Party in the enterprises which they have established, in their capital, or in the skills, arts or technology which they have supplied; nor shall either Party unreasonably impede nationals and companies of the other Party from obtaining on equitable terms the capital, skills, arts and technology it needs for its economic development.

2. The Parties undertake to cooperate in furthering the interchange and use of scientific and technical knowledge, particularly in the interests of increasing productivity and improving standards of living within their respective territories.

Article VI

1. Property of nationals and companies of either Party shall receive the most constant protection and security within the territories of the other Party.

2. The dwellings, offices, warehouses, factories and other premises of nationals and companies of either Party located within the territories of the other Party shall not be subject to unlawful entry or molestation. Official searches and examinations of such premises and their contents, when necessary, shall be made only according to law and with careful regard for the convenience of the occupants and the conduct of business.

3. Property of nationals and companies of either Party shall not be taken within the territories of the other Party except for a public purpose, nor shall it be taken without the prompt payment of just compensation. Such compensation shall be in an effectively realizable form and shall represent the full equivalent of the property taken; and adequate provision shall have been made at or prior to the time of taking for the determination and payment thereof.

4. Nationals and companies of either Party shall in no case be accorded,

within the territories of the other Party, less than national treatment and most-favored-nation treatment with respect to the matters set forth in paragraphs 2 and 3 of the present Article. Moreover, enterprises in which nationals and companies of either Party have a substantial interest shall be accorded, within the territories of the other Party, not less than national treatment and most-favored-nation treatment in all matters relating to the taking of privately owned enterprises into public ownership and to the placing of such enterprises under public control.

Article VII

1. Nationals and companies of either Party shall be accorded national treatment with respect to engaging in all types of commercial, industrial, financial and other business activities within the territories of the other Party, whether directly or by agent or through the medium of any form of lawful judicial entity. Accordingly, such nationals and companies shall be permitted within such territories: (a) to establish and maintain branches, agencies, offices, factories and other establishments appropriate to the conduct of their business; (b) to organize companies under the general company laws of such other Party, and to acquire majority interests in companies of such other Party; and (c) to control and manage enterprises which they have established or acquired. Moreover, enterprises which they control, whether in the form of individual proprietorships, companies or otherwise, shall, in all that relates to the conduct of the activities thereof, be accorded treatment no less favorable than that accorded like enterprises controlled by nationals and companies of such other Party.

2. Each Party reserves the right to limit the extent to which aliens may within its territories establish, acquire interests in, or carry on public utilities enterprises or enterprises engaged in shipbuilding, air or water transport, banking involving depository or fiduciary functions, or the exploitation of land or other natural resources. However, new limitations imposed by either Party upon the extent to which aliens are accorded national treatment, with respect to carrying on such activities within its territories, shall not be applied as against enterprises which are engaged in such activities therein at the time such new limitations are adopted and which are owned or controlled by nationals and companies of the other Party. Moreover, neither Party shall deny to transportation, communications and banking companies of the other Party the right to maintain branches and agencies to perform functions necessary for essentially international operations in which they are permitted to engage.

3. The provisions of paragraph 1 of the present Article shall not prevent either Party from prescribing special formalities in connection with the establishment of alien-controlled enterprises within its territories; but such formalities may not impair the substance of the rights set forth in said paragraph.

4. Nationals and companies of either Party, as well as enterprises controlled by such nationals and companies, shall in any event be accorded most-favored-nation treatment with reference to the matters treated in the present Article.

Article VIII

1. Nationals and companies of either Party shall be permitted to engage, within the territories of the other Party, accountants and other technical experts, executive personnel, attorneys, agents and other specialists of their choice. Moreover, such nationals and companies shall be permitted to engage accountants and other technical experts regardless of the extent to which they may have qualified for the practice of a profession within the territories of such other Party, for the particular purpose of making examinations, audits and technical investigations exclusively for, and rendering reports to, such nationals and companies in connection with the planning and operation of their enterprises, and enterprises in which they have a financial interest, within such territories.

2. Nationals of either Party shall not be barred from practicing the professions within the territories of the other Party merely by reason of their alienage; but they shall be permitted to engage in professional activities therein upon compliance with the requirements regarding qualifications, residence and competence that are applicable to nationals of such other Party.

3. Nationals and companies of either Party shall be accorded national treatment and most-favored-nation treatment with respect to engaging in scientific, educational, religious and philanthropic activities within the territories of the other Party, and shall be accorded the right to form associations for that purpose under the laws of such other Party.

Article IX

1. Nationals and companies of either Party shall be accorded within the territories of the other Party: (a) national treatment with respect to leasing land, buildings and other immovable property appropriate to the conduct of activities in which they are permitted to engage pursuant to Articles VII and VIII and for residential purposes, and with respect to occupying and using such property; and (b) other rights in immovable property permitted by the applicable laws of the other Party.

2. Nationals and companies of either Party shall be accorded within the territories of the other Party national treatment and most-favored-nation treatment with respect to acquiring, by purchase, lease, or otherwise, and with respect to owning and possessing, movable property of all kinds, both tangible and intangible. However, either Party may impose restrictions on alien ownership of materials dangerous from the standpoint of public safety and alien ownership of interests in enterprises carrying on the activities listed in the first sentence of paragraph 2 of Article VII, but only to the extent that this can be done without impairing the rights and privileges secured by Article VII or by other provisions of the present Treaty.

3. Nationals and companies of either Party shall be permitted freely to dispose of property within the territories of the other Party with respect to the acquisition of which through testate or intestate succession their alienage has prevented them from receiving national treatment, and they shall be permitted a term of at least five years in which to effect such disposition.

4. Nationals and companies of either Party shall be accorded within the

territories of the other Party national treatment and most-favored-nation treatment with respect to disposing of property of all kinds.

Article X

Nationals and companies of either Party shall be accorded, within the territories of the other Party, national treatment and most-favored-nation treatment with respect to obtaining and maintaining patents of invention, and with respect to rights in trade marks, trade names, trade labels and industrial property of every kind.

Article XI

1. Nationals of either Party residing within the territories of the other Party, and nationals and companies of either Party engaged in trade or other gainful pursuit or in scientific, educational, religious or philanthropic activities within the territories of the other Party, shall not be subject to the payment of taxes, fees or charges imposed upon or applied to income, capital, transactions, activities or any other object, or to requirements with respect to the levy and collection thereof, within the territories of such other Party, more burdensome than those borne by nationals and companies of such other Party.

2. With respect to nationals of either Party who are neither resident nor engaged in trade or other gainful pursuit within the territories of the other Party, and with respect to companies of either Party which are not engaged in trade or other gainful pursuit within the territories of the other Party, it shall be the aim of such other Party to apply in general the principle set forth in paragraph 1 of the present Article.

3. Nationals and companies of either Party shall in no case be subject, within the territories of the other Party, to the payment of taxes, fees or charges imposed upon or applied to income, capital, transactions, activities or any other object, or to requirements with respect to the levy and collection thereof, more burdensome than those borne by nationals, residents and companies of any third country.

4. In the case of companies of either Party engaged in trade or other gainful pursuit within the territories of the other Party, and in the case of nationals of either Party engaged in trade or other gainful pursuit within the territories of the other Party but not resident therein, such other Party shall not impose or apply any tax, fee or charge upon any income, capital or other basis in excess of that reasonably allocable or apportionable to its territories, nor grant deductions and exemptions less than those reasonably allocable or apportionable to its territories. A comparable rule shall apply also in the case of companies organized and operated exclusively for scientific, educational, religious or philanthropic purposes.

5. Each Party reserves the right to: (a) extend specific tax advantages on the basis of reciprocity; (b) accord special tax advantages by virtue of agreements for the avoidance of double taxation or the mutual protection of revenue; and (c) accord to its own nationals and to residents of contiguous countries more favorable exemptions of a personal nature with respect to income taxes and inheritance taxes than are accorded to other non-resident persons.

Article XII

1. Nationals and companies of either Party shall be accorded by the other Party national treatment and most-favored-nation treatment with respect to payments, remittances and transfers of funds or financial instruments between the territories of the two Parties as well as between the territories of such other Party and of any third country.

2. Neither Party shall impose exchange restrictions as defined in paragraph 5 of the present Article except to the extent necessary to prevent its monetary reserves from falling to a very low level or to effect a moderate increase in very low monetary reserves. It is understood that the provisions of the present Article do not alter the obligations either Party may have to the International Monetary Fund or preclude imposition of particular restrictions whenever the Fund specifically authorizes or requests a Party to impose such particular restrictions.

3. If either Party imposes exchange restrictions in accordance with paragraph 2 above, it shall, after making whatever provision may be necessary to assure the availability of foreign exchange for goods and services essential to the health and welfare of its people, make reasonable provision for the withdrawal, in foreign exchange in the currency of the other Party, of: (a) the compensation referred to in Article VI, paragraph 3, of the present Treaty, (b) earnings, whether in the form of salaries, interest, dividends, commissions, royalties, payments for technical services, or otherwise, and (c) amounts for amortization of loans, depreciation of direct investments, and capital transfers, giving consideration to special needs for other transactions. If more than one rate of exchange is in force, the rate applicable to such withdrawals shall be a rate which is specifically approved by the International Monetary Fund for such transactions or, in the absence of a rate so approved, an effective rate which, inclusive of any taxes or surcharges on exchange transfers, is just and reasonable.

4. Exchange restrictions shall not be imposed by either Party in a manner unnecessarily detrimental or arbitrarily discriminatory to the claims, investments, transport, trade, and other interests of the nationals and companies of the other Party, nor to the competitive position thereof.

5. The term "exchange restrictions" as used in the present Article includes all restrictions, regulations, charges, taxes, or other requirements imposed by either Party which burden or interfere with payments, remittances, or transfers of funds or of financial instruments between the territories of the two Parties.

Article XIII

Commercial travelers representing nationals and companies of either Party engaged in business within the territories thereof shall, upon their entry into and departure from the territories of the other Party and during their sojourn therein, be accorded most-favored-nation treatment in respect of the customs and other matters, including, subject to the exceptions in paragraph 5 of Article XI, taxes and charges applicable to them, their samples and the taking of orders, and regulations governing the exercise of their functions.

Article XIV

1. Each Party shall accord most-favored-nation treatment to products of the other Party, from whatever place and by whatever type of carrier arriving, and to products destined for exportation to the territories of such other Party, by whatever route and by whatever type of carrier, with respect to customs duties and charges of any kind imposed on or in connection with importation or exportation or imposed on the international transfer of payments for imports or exports, and with respect to the method of levying such duties and charges, and with respect to all rules and formalities in connection with importation and exportation. . . .

Article XVI

1. Products of either Party shall be accorded, within the territories of the other Party, national treatment and most-favored-nation treatment in all matters affecting internal taxation, sale, distribution, storage and use. . . .

Article XVII

1. Each Party undertakes (a) that enterprises owned or controlled by its Government, and that monopolies or agencies granted exclusive or special privileges within its territories, shall make their purchases and sales involving either imports or exports affecting the commerce of the other Party solely in accordance with commercial considerations, including price, quality, availability, marketability, transportation and other conditions of purchase or sale; and (b) that the nationals, companies and commerce of such other Party shall be afforded adequate opportunity, in accordance with customary business practice, to compete for participation in such purchases and sales.

2. Each Party shall accord to the nationals, companies and commerce of the other Party fair and equitable treatment, as compared with that accorded to the nationals, companies and commerce of any third country, with respect to: (a) the governmental purchase of supplies, (b) the awarding of concessions and other government contracts, and (c) the sale of any service sold by the Government or by any monopoly or agency granted exclusive or special privileges.

Article XVIII

1. The two Parties agree that business practices which restrain competition, limit access to markets or foster monopolistic control, and which are engaged in or made effective by one or more private or public commercial enterprises or by combination, agreement or other arrangement among such enterprises, may have harmful effects upon commerce between their respective territories. Accordingly, each Party agrees upon the request of the other Party to consult with respect to any such practices and to take such measures as it deems appropriate with a view to eliminating such harmful effects.

2. No enterprise of either Party, including corporations, associations, and government agencies and instrumentalities, which is publicly owned or

controlled shall, if it engages in commercial, industrial, shipping or other business activities within the territories of the other Party, claim or enjoy, either for itself or for its property, immunity therein from taxation, suit, execution of judgment or other liability to which privately owned and controlled enterprises are subject therein.

Article XIX

1. Between the territories of the two Parties there shall be freedom of commerce and navigation.

2. Vessels under the flag of either Party, and carrying the papers required by its law in proof of nationality, shall be deemed to be vessels of that Party both on the high seas and within the ports, places and waters of the other Party.

3. Vessels of either Party shall have liberty, on equal terms with vessels of the other Party and on equal terms with vessels of any third country, to come with their cargoes to all ports, places and waters of such other Party open to foreign commerce and navigation. Such vessels and cargoes shall in all respects be accorded national treatment and most-favored-nation treatment within the ports, places and waters of such other Party.

4. Vessels of either Party shall be accorded national treatment and most-favored-nation treatment by the other Party with respect to the right to carry all products that may be carried by vessel to or from the territories of such other Party; and such products shall be accorded treatment no less favorable than that accorded to like products carried in vessels of such other Party, with respect to: (a) duties and charges of all kinds, (b) the administration of the customs, and (c) bounties, drawbacks and other privileges of this nature. . . .

6. Notwithstanding any other provision of the present Treaty, each Party may reserve exclusive rights and privileges to its own vessels with respect to the coasting trade, national fisheries and inland navigation, or may admit foreign vessels thereto only on a reciprocity basis.

7. The term "vessels", as used herein, means all types of vessels, whether privately owned or operated, or publicly owned or operated; but this term does not, except with reference to paragraphs 2 and 5 of the present Article, include fishing vessels or vessels of war.

Article XX

There shall be freedom of transit through the territories of each Party by the routes most convenient for international transit:
 (a) for nationals of the other Party, together with their baggage;
 (b) for other persons, together with their baggage, en route to or from the territories of such other Party; and
 (c) for products of any origin en route to or from the territories of such other Party.

Such persons and things in transit shall be exempt from customs duties, from duties imposed by reason of transit, and from unreasonable charges and requirements; and shall be free from unnecessary delays and restrictions. They shall, however, be subject to measures referred to in paragraph

3 of Article I, and to nondiscriminatory regulations necessary to prevent abuse of the transit privilege.

Article XXI

1. The present Treaty shall not preclude the application of measures:
   (a) regulating the importation or exportation of gold or silver;
   (b) relating to fissionable materials, to radioactive by-products of the utilization or processing thereof, or to materials that are the source of fissionable materials;
   (c) regulating the production of or traffic in arms, ammunition and implements of war, or traffic in other materials carried on directly or indirectly for the purpose of supplying a military establishment;
   (d) necessary to fulfill the obligations of a Party for the maintenance or restoration of international peace and security, or necessary to protect its essential security interests; and
   (e) denying to any company in the ownership or direction of which nationals of any third country or countries have directly or indirectly the controlling interest, the advantages of the present Treaty, except with respect to recognition of juridical status and with respect to access to courts of justice and to administrative tribunals and agencies. . . .

3. The provisions of the present Treaty relating to the treatment of goods shall not preclude action by either Party which is required or specifically permitted by the General Agreement on Tariffs and Trade during such time as such Party is a contracting party to the General Agreement. Moreover, either Party may withhold advantages negotiated under the aforesaid Agreement from those countries which by their own choice are not contracting parties thereto.

4. Nationals of either Party admitted into the territories of the other Party for limited purposes shall not enjoy rights to engage in gainful occupations in contravention of limitations expressly imposed, according to law, as a condition of their admittance.

5. Nothing in the present Treaty shall be deemed to grant or imply any right to engage in political activities.

Article XXII

1. The term "national treatment" means treatment accorded within the territories of a Party upon terms no less favorable than the treatment accorded therein, in like situations, to nationals, companies, products, vessels or other objects, as the case may be, of such Party.

2. The term "most-favored-nation treatment" means treatment accorded within the territories of a Party upon terms no less favorable than the treatment accorded therein, in like situations, to nationals, companies, products, vessels or other objects, as the case may be, of any third country.

3. As used in the present Treaty, the term "companies" means corporations, partnerships, companies and other associations, whether or not with limited liability and whether or not for pecuniary profit. Companies constituted under the applicable laws and regulations within the territories of either Party shall be deemed companies thereof and shall have their juridical status recognized within the territories of the other Party.

4. National treatment accorded under the provisions of the present Treaty to companies of Japan shall, in any State, Territory or possession of the United States of America, be the treatment accorded therein to companies created or organized in other States, Territories, and possessions of the United States of America. . . .

Article XXIV

1. Each Party shall accord sympathetic consideration to, and shall afford adequate opportunity for consultation regarding, such representations as the other Party may make with respect to any matter affecting the operation of the present Treaty.

2. Any dispute between the Parties as to the interpretation or application of the present Treaty, not satisfactorily adjusted by diplomacy, shall be submitted to the International Court of Justice, unless the Parties agree to settlement by some other pacific means.

Article XXV

1. The present Treaty shall be ratified, and the ratifications thereof shall be exchanged at Washington as soon as possible.

2. The present Treaty shall enter into force one month after the day of exchange of ratifications. It shall remain in force for ten years and shall continue in force thereafter until terminated as provided herein.

3. Either Party may, by giving one year's written notice to the other Party, terminate the present Treaty at the end of the initial ten-year period or at any time thereafter. . . .

TRADING WITH THE ENEMY ACT
(1917, as amended)

Act Oct. 6, 1917, C. 106, 40 Stat. 411, 50 U.S.C. App. §§1-5 (1982)

§5. Suspension of Provisions Relating to Ally of Enemy; Regulation of Transactions in Foreign Exchange of Gold or Silver, Property Transfers, Vested Interests, Enforcement and Penalties

(b)(1) During the time of war, the President may, through any agency that he may designate, and under such rules and regulations as he may prescribe, by means of instructions, licenses, or otherwise —

(A) investigate, regulate, or prohibit, any transactions in foreign exchange, transfers of credit or payments between, by, through, or to any banking institution, and the importing, exporting, hoarding, melting, or earmarking of gold or silver coin or bullion, currency or securities, and

(B) investigate, regulate, direct and compel, nullify, void, prevent or prohibit, any acquistion holding, withholding, use, transfer, withdrawal, transportation, importation or exportation of, or dealing in, or exercising any right, power, or privilege with respect to, or transactions involving, any property in which any foreign country or a national thereof has any interest,

by any person, or with respect to any property, subject to the jurisdiction of the United States; and any property or interest of any foreign country or national thereof shall vest, when, as, and upon the terms, directed by the President, in such agency or person as may be designated from time to time by the President, and upon such terms and conditions as the President may prescribe such interest or property shall be held, used, administered, liquidated, sold, or otherwise dealt with in the interest of and for the benefit of the United States, and such designated agency or person may perform any and all acts incident to the accomplishment or furtherance of these purposes; and the President shall, in the manner hereinabove provided, require any person to keep a full record of, and to furnish under oath, in the form of reports or otherwise, complete information relative to any act or transaction referred to in this subdivision either before, during, or after the completion thereof, or relative to any interest in foreign property, or relative to any property in which any foreign country or any national thereof has or has had any interest, or as may be otherwise necessary to enforce the provisions of this subdivision, and in any case in which a report could be required, the

Trading with the Enemy Act

President may, in the manner hereinabove provided, require the production, or if necessary to the national security or defense, the seizure, of any books of account, records, contracts, letters, memoranda, or other papers, in the custody or control of such person. . . .

(3) As used in this subdivision the term "United States" means the United States and any place subject to the jurisdiction thereof: *Provided, however,* That the foregoing shall not be construed as a limitation upon the power of the President, which is hereby conferred to prescribe from time to time, definitions, not inconsistent with the purposes of this subdivision, for any or all of the terms used in this subdivision. As used in this subdivision the term "person" means an individual, partnership, association, or corporation.

(As amended Dec. 28, 1977, Pub. L. 95-223, Title I, §§101(a), 102, 103(b), 91 Stat. 1625, 1626.)

1977 Amendment. Subsec. (b)(1). Pub. L. 95-223, §§101(a), 102, substituted "During the time of war, the President may, through any agency that he may designate, and under such rules and regulations" for "During the time of war or during any other period of national emergency declared by the President, the President may, through any agency, that he may designate, or otherwise, and under such rules and regulations" in the provisions preceding subpar. (A), and, in the provisions following subpar. (B), struck out "; and the President may, in the manner hereinabove provided, take other and further measures not inconsistent herewith for the enforcement of this subdivision".

NATIONAL EMERGENCIES ACT
50 U.S.C. §§1601-1651

Subchapter I — Terminating Existing Declared Emergencies

§1601. Termination of Existing Declared Emergencies

(a) All powers and authorities possessed by the President, any other officer or employee of the Federal Government, or any executive agency, as defined in section 105 of Title 5, as a result of the existence of any declaration of national emergency in effect on September 14, 1976 are terminated two years from September 14, 1976. Such termination shall not affect —

   (1) any action taken or proceeding pending not finally concluded or determined on such date;
   (2) any action or proceeding based on any act committed prior to such date; or
   (3) any rights or duties that matured or penalties that were incurred prior to such date.

(b) For the purpose of this section, the words "any national emergency in effect" means a general declaration of emergency made by the President.

(Pub. L. 94-412, Title I, §101, Sept. 14, 1976, 90 Stat. 1255.)

Subchapter II — Declarations of Future National Emergencies

§1621. Declaration of National Emergency by President; Publication in Federal Register; Effect on Other Laws; Superseding Legislation

(a) With respect to Acts of Congress authorizing the exercise, during the period of a national emergency, of any special or extraordinary power, the President is authorized to declare such national emergency. Such proclamation shall immediately be transmitted to the Congress and published in the Federal Register.

(b) Any provisions of law conferring powers and authorities to be exercised during a national emergency shall be effective and remain in effect (1) only when the President (in accordance with subsection (a) of this section), specifically declares a national emergency, and (2) only in accordance with this chapter. No law enacted after September 14, 1976, shall supersede this subchapter unless it does so in specific terms, referring to this subchapter, and declaring that the new law supersedes the provisions of this subchapter.

(Pub. L. 94-412.)

§1622. National Emergencies

(a) Termination Methods

Any national emergency declared by the President in accordance with this subchapter shall terminate if —

(1) there is enacted into law a joint resolution terminating the emergency; or

(2) the President issues a proclamation terminating the emergency.

Any national emergency declared by the President shall be terminated on the date specified in any joint resolution referred to in clause (1) or on the date specified in a proclamation by the President terminating the emergency as provided in clause (2) of this subsection, whichever date is earlier, and any powers or authorities exercised by reason of said emergency shall cease to be exercised after such specified date, except that such termination shall not affect —

(A) any action taken or proceeding pending not finally concluded or determined on such date;

(B) any action or proceeding based on any act committed prior to such date; or

(C) any rights or duties that matured or penalties that were incurred prior to such date.

(b) Termination Review of National Emergencies by Congress

Not later than six months after a national emergency is declared, and not later than the end of each six-month period thereafter that such emergency continues, each House of Congress shall meet to consider a vote on a joint resolution to determine whether that emergency shall be terminated.

(c) Joint Resolution; Referral to Congressional Committees; Conference Committee in Event of Disagreement; Filing of Report; Termination Procedure Deemed Part of Rules of House and Senate

(1) A joint resolution to terminate a national emergency declared by the President shall be referred to the appropriate committee of the House of Representatives or the Senate, as the case may be. One such joint resolution shall be reported out by such committee together with its recommendations within fifteen calendar days after the day on which such

resolution is referred to such committee, unless such House shall otherwise determine by the yeas and nays.

(2) Any joint resolution so reported shall become the pending business of the House in question (in the case of the Senate the time for debate shall be equally divided between the proponents and the opponents) and shall be voted on within three calendar days after the day on which such resolution is reported, unless such House shall otherwise determine by yeas and nays.

(3) Such a joint resolution passed by one House shall be referred to the appropriate committee of the other House and shall be reported out by such committee together with its recommendations within fifteen calendar days after the day on which such resolution is referred to such committee and shall thereupon become the pending business of such House and shall be voted upon within three calendar days after the day on which such resolution is reported, unless such House shall otherwise determine by yeas and nays.

(4) In the case of any disagreement between the two Houses of Congress with respect to a joint resolution passed by both Houses, conferees shall be promptly appointed and the committee of conference shall make and file a report with respect to such joint resolution within six calendar days after the day on which managers on the part of the Senate and the House have been appointed. Notwithstanding any rule in either House concerning the printing of conference reports or concerning any delay in the consideration of such reports, such report shall be acted on by both Houses not later than six calendar days after the conference report is filed in the House in which such report is filed first. In the event the conferees are unable to agree within forty-eight hours, they shall report back to their respective Houses in disagreement.

(5) Paragraphs (1)-(4) of this subsection, subsection (b) of this section, and section 1651(b) of this title are enacted by Congress —

(A) as an exercise of the rulemaking power of the Senate and the House of Representatives, respectively, and as such they are deemed a part of the rules of each House, respectively, but applicable only with respect to the procedure to be followed in the House in the case of resolutions described by this subsection; and they supersede other rules only to the extent that they are inconsistent therewith; and

(B) with full recognition of the constitutional right of either House to change the rules (so far as relating to the procedure of that House) at any time, in the same manner, and to the same extent as in the case of any other rule of that House.

(d) *Automatic Termination of National Emergency; Continuation Notice from President to Congress; Publication in Federal Register*

Any national emergency declared by the President in accordance with this subchapter, and not otherwise previously terminated, shall terminate on the anniversary of the declaration of that emergency if, within the ninety-day period prior to each anniversary date, the President does not publish in the Federal Register and transmit to the Congress a notice stating that such emergency is to continue in effect after such anniversary.

(Pub. L. 94-412, Title II, §202, Sept. 14, 1976, 90 Stat. 1255; amended Pub. L. 99-93, Title VIII, §801, Aug. 16, 1985, 99 Stat. 448.)

1985 Amendment. Subsec. (a)(1). Pub. L. 99-93, §801(1)(A), substituted "there is enacted into law a joint resolution terminating the emergency" for "Congress terminates the emergency by concurrent resolution".
  Subsec. (a). Pub. L. 99-93, §801(1)(B), in the provisions following par. (2) substituted "joint resolution" for "concurrent resolution".
  Subsec. (b). Pub. L. 99-93, §801(2), substituted "joint resolution" for "concurrent resolution".
  Subsec. (c)(1) to (4). Pub. L. 99-93, §801(3), substituted "joint resolution" for "concurrent resolution" wherever appearing.

Subchapter III — Exercise of Emergency Powers and Authorities

§1631. Declaration of National Emergency by Executive Order; Authority; Publication in Federal Register, Transmittal to Congress

When the President declares a national emergency, no powers or authorities made available by statute for use in the event of an emergency shall be exercised unless and until the President specifies the provisions of law under which he proposes that he, or other officers will act. Such specification may be made either in the declaration of a national emergency, or by one or more contemporaneous or subsequent Executive orders published in the Federal Register and transmitted to the Congress.

(Pub. L. 94-412.)

Subchapter IV — Accountability and Reporting Requirements of the President

§1641. Accountability and Reporting Requirements of the President

(a) Maintenance of File and Index of Presidential Orders, Rules and Regulations During National Emergency

When the President declares a national emergency, or Congress declares war, the President shall be responsible for maintaining a file and index of all significant orders of the President, including Executive orders and proclamations, and each Executive agency shall maintain a file and index of all rules and regulations, issued during such emergency or war issued pursuant to such declarations.

(b) Presidential Orders, Rules and Regulations; Transmittal to Congress

All such significant orders of the President, including Executive orders, and such rules and regulations shall be transmitted to the Congress promptly under means to assure confidentiality where appropriate.

(c) Expenditures During National Emergency; Presidential Reports to Congress

When the President declares a national emergency or Congress declares war, the President shall transmit to Congress, within ninety days after the end of each six-month period after such declaration, a report on the total expenditures incurred by the United States Government during such six-month period which are directly attributable to the exercise of powers and authorities conferred by such declaration. Not later than ninety days after the termination of each such emergency or war, the President shall transmit a final report on all such expenditures.

(Pub. L. 94-412.)

INTERNATIONAL EMERGENCY ECONOMIC POWERS ACT
(1977, as amended)

50 U.S.C. §§1701-1706

§1701. Unusual and Extraordinary Threat; Declaration of National Emergency; Exercise of Presidential Authorities

(a) Any authority granted to the President by section 1702 of this title may be exercised to deal with any unusual and extraordinary threat, which has its source in whole or substantial part outside the United States, to the national security, foreign policy, or economy of the United States, if the President declares a national emergency with respect to such threat.

(b) The authorities granted to the President by section 1702 of this title may only be exercised to deal with an unusual and extraordinary threat with respect to which a national emergency has been declared for purposes of this chapter and may not be exercised for any other purpose. Any exercise of such authorities to deal with any new threat shall be based on a new declaration of national emergency which must be with respect to such threat.

§1702. Presidential Authorities

(a)(1) At the times and to the extent specified in section 1701 of this title, the President may, under such regulations as he may prescribe, by means of instructions, licenses, or otherwise —

(A) investigate, regulate, or prohibit —

(i) any transactions in foreign exchange,

(ii) transfers of credit or payments between, by, through, or to any banking institution, to the extent that such transfers or payments involve any interest of any foreign country or a national thereof,

(iii) the importing or exporting of currency or securities; and

(B) investigate, regulate, direct and compel, nullify, void, prevent or prohibit, any acquistion, holding, withholding, use, transfer, withdrawal, transportation, importation or exportation of, or dealing in, or exercising any right, power, or privilege with respect to, or transactions involving, any property in which any foreign country or a national thereof has any interest;

by any person, or with respect to any property, subject to the jurisdiction of the United States.

(2) In exercising the authorities granted by paragraph (1), the President may require any person to keep a full record of, and to furnish under oath, in the form of reports or otherwise, complete information relative to any act or transaction referred to in paragraph (1) either before, during, or after the completion thereof, or relative to any interest in foreign property, or relative to any property in which any foreign country or any national thereof has or has had any interest, or as may be otherwise necessary to enforce the provisions of such paragraph. In any case in which a report by a person could be required under this paragraph, the President may require the production of any books of account, records, contracts, letters, memoranda, or other papers, in the custody or control of such person.

(3) Compliance with any regulation, instruction, or direction issued under this chapter shall to the extent thereof be a full acquittance and discharge for all purposes of the obligation of the person making the same. No person shall be held liable in any court for or with respect to anything done or omitted in good faith in connection with the administration of, or pursuant to and in reliance on, this chapter, or any regulation, instruction, or direction issued under this chapter.

(b) The authority granted to the President by this section does not include the authority to regulate or prohibit, directly or indirectly —

(1) any postal, telegraphic, telephonic, or other personal communication, which does not involve a transfer of anything of value; or

(2) donations, by persons subject to the jurisdiction of the United States, of articles, such as food, clothing, and medicine, intended to be used to relieve human suffering, except to the extent that the President determines that such donations (A) would seriously impair his ability to deal with any national emergency declared under section 1701 of this title, (B) are in response to coercion against the proposed recipient or donor, or (C) would endanger Armed Forces of the United States which are engaged in hostilities or are in a situation where imminent involvement in hostilities is clearly indicated by the circumstances; or

(3) the importation from any country, or the exportation to any country whether commercial or otherwise, of publications, films, posters, phonograph records, photographs, microfilms, microfiche, tapes, or other information materials, which are not otherwise controlled for export under section 2404 of the Appendix to this title or with respect to which no acts are prohibited by chapter 37 of Title 18.

(Pub. L. 95-223, Title II, §203, Dec. 28, 1977, 91 Stat. 1626, amended Pub. L. 100-418, Title II, §2502(b)(1), Aug. 23, 1988, 102 Stat. 1371.)

International Emergency Economic Powers Act

§1703. Consultation and Reports

(a) Consultation with Congress

The President, in every possible instance, shall consult with the Congress before exercising any of the authorities granted by this chapter and shall consult regularly with the Congress so long as such authorities are exercised.

(b) Report to Congress Upon Exercise of Presidential Authorities

Whenever the President exercises any of the authorities granted by this chapter, he shall immediately transmit to the Congress a report specifying —
   (1) the circumstances which necessitate such exercise of authority;
   (2) why the President believes those circumstances constitute an unusual and extraordinary threat, which has its source in whole or substantial part outside the United States, to the national security, foreign policy, or economy of the United States;
   (3) the authorities to be exercised and the actions to be taken in the exercise of those authorities to deal with those circumstances;
   (4) why the President believes such actions are necessary to deal with those circumstances; and
   (5) any foreign countries with respect to which such actions are to be taken and why such actions are to be taken with respect to those countries.

(c) Periodic Follow-up Reports

At least once during each succeeding six-month period after transmitting a report pursuant to subsection (b) of this section with respect to an exercise of authorities under this chapter, the President shall report to the Congress with respect to the actions taken, since the last such report, in the exercise of such authorities, and with respect to any changes which have occurred concerning any information previously furnished pursuant to paragraphs (1) through (5) of subsection (b) of this section.

(d) Supplemental Requirements

The requirements of this section are supplemental to those contained in title IV of the National Emergencies Act [50 U.S.C. 1641].

§1704. Authority to Issue Regulations

The President may issue such regulations, including regulations prescribing definitions, as may be necessary for the exercise of the authorities granted by this chapter.

§1705. Penalties

(a) A civil penalty of not to exceed $10,000 may be imposed on any person who violates any license, order, or regulation issued under this chapter.

(b) Whoever willfully violates any license, order, or regulation issued under this chapter shall, upon conviction, be fined not more than $50,000, or, if a natural person, may be imprisoned for not more than ten years, or both; and any officer, director, or agent of any corporation who knowingly participates in such violation may be punished by a like fine, imprisonment, or both.

§1706. Savings Provisions

(a) *Termination of National Emergencies Pursuant to National Emergencies Act*

(1) Except as provided in subsection (b) of this section, notwithstanding the termination pursuant to the National Emergencies Act [50 U.S.C. 1601 et seq.] of a national emergency declared for purposes of this chapter, any authorities granted by this chapter, which are exercised on the date of such termination on the basis of such national emergency to prohibit transactions involving property in which a foreign country or national thereof has any interest, may continue to be so exercised to prohibit transactions involving that property if the President determines that the continuation of such prohibition with respect to that property is necessary on account of claims involving such country or its nationals.

(2) Notwithstanding the termination of the authorities described in section 101(b) of this Act, any such authorities, which are exercised with respect to a country on the date of such termination to prohibit transactions involving any property in which such country or any national thereof has any interest, may continue to be exercised to prohibit transactions involving that property if the President determines that the continuation of such prohibition with respect to that property is necessary on account of claims involving such country or its nationals.

(b) *Congressional Termination of National Emergencies by Concurrent Resolution*

The authorities described in subsection (a)(1) of this section may not continue to be exercised under this section if the national emergency is terminated by the Congress by concurrent resolution pursuant to section 202 of the National Emergencies Act [50 U.S.C. 1622] and if the Congress specifies in such concurrent resolution that such authorities may not continue to be exercised under this section.

(c) Supplemental Savings Provisions; Supersedure of Inconsistent Provisions . . .

(d) Periodic Reports to Congress

If the President uses the authority of this section to continue prohibitions on transactions involving foreign property interests, he shall report to the Congress every six months on the use of such authority.

(Pub. L. 95-223, title II, §207, Dec. 28, 1977, 91 Stat. 1628.)

ALGIERS ACCORDS
United States-Iran, Jan. 19, 1981, 20 I.L.M. 223 (1981)*

1. Declaration of the Government of the Democratic and Popular Republic of Algeria

The Government of the Democratic and Popular Republic of Algeria, having been requested by the Governments of the Islamic Republic of Iran and the United States of America to serve as an intermediary in seeking a mutually acceptable resolution of the crisis in their relations arising out of the detention of the 52 United States nationals in Iran, has consulted extensively with the two governments as to the commitments which each is willing to make in order to resolve the crisis within the framework of the four points stated in the resolution of November 2, 1980, of the Islamic Consultative Assembly of Iran. On the basis of formal adherences received from Iran and the United States, the Government of Algeria now declares that the following interdependent commitments have been made by the two governments:

GENERAL PRINCIPLES

The undertakings reflected in this Declaration are based on the following general principles:

A. Within the framework of and pursuant to the provisions of the two Declarations of the Government of the Democratic and Popular Republic of Algeria, the United States will restore the financial position of Iran, in so far as possible, to that which existed prior to November 14, 1979. In this context, the United States commits itself to ensure the mobility and free transfer of all Iranian assets within its jurisdiction, as set forth in Paragraphs 4-9.

B. It is the purpose of both parties . . . to terminate all litigation as between the Government of each party and the nationals of the other, and to bring about the settlement and termination of all such claims through

---

*The Algiers Accords were agreements between the Islamic Republic of Iran and the United States of America. The Accords took the form of Declarations by the government of the Democratic and Popular Republic of Algeria regarding the commitments made by the United States and Iran.

binding arbitration. Through the procedures provided in the Declaration, relating to the Claims Settlement Agreement, the United States agrees to terminate all legal proceedings in United States courts involving claims of United States persons and institutions against Iran and its state enterprises, to nullify all attachments and judgments obtained therein, to prohibit all further litigation based on such claims, and to bring about the termination of such claims through binding arbitration.

Point I: Non-Intervention in Iranian Affairs

1. The United States pledges that it is and from now on will be the policy of the United States not to intervene, directly or indirectly, politically or militarily, in Iran's internal affairs.

Points II and III: Return of Iranian Assets and Settlement of U.S. Claims

2. Iran and the United States (hereinafter "the parties") will immediately select a mutually agreeable central bank (hereinafter "the Central Bank") to act, under the instructions of the Government of Algeria and the Central Bank of Algeria (hereinafter "The Algerian Central Bank") as depositary of the escrow and security funds hereinafter prescribed and will promptly enter into depositary arrangements with the Central Bank in accordance with the terms of this declaration. . . .

3. The depositary arrangements shall provide that, in the event that the Government of Algeria certifies to the Algerian Central Bank that the 52 U.S. nationals have safely departed from Iran, the Algerian Central Bank will thereupon instruct the Central Bank to transfer immediately all monies or other assets in escrow with the Central Bank pursuant to this declaration. . . .

Assets in the Federal Reserve Bank

4. Commencing upon completion of the requisite escrow arrangements with the Central Bank, the United States will bring about the transfer to the Central Bank of all gold bullion which is owned by Iran and which is in the custody of the Federal Reserve Bank of New York, together with all other Iranian assets (or the cash equivalent thereof) in the custody of the Federal Reserve Bank of New York . . .

Assets in Foreign Branches of U.S. Banks

5. Commencing upon the completion of the requisite escrow arrangements with the Central Bank, the United States will bring about the transfer to the Central Bank, to the account of the Algerian Central Bank, of all

Iranian deposits and securities which on or after November 14, 1979, stood upon the books of overseas banking offices of U.S. banks, together with interest thereon through December 31, 1980 . . .

ASSETS IN U.S. BRANCHES OF U.S. BANKS

6. . . . [T]he United States will act to bring about the transfer to the Central Bank, within six months from such date, of all Iranian deposits and securities in U.S. banking institutions in the United States, together with interest thereon, to be held by the Central Bank in escrow . . .

7. As funds are received by the Central Bank pursuant to Paragraph 6 above, the Algerian Central Bank shall direct the Central Bank to (1) transfer one-half of each such receipt to Iran and (2) place the other half in a special interest-bearing security account in the Central Bank, until the balance in the security account has reached the level of $1 billion. After the $1 billion balance has been achieved, the Algerian Central Bank shall direct all funds received pursuant to Paragraph 6 to be transferred to Iran. All funds in the security account are to be used for the sole purpose of securing the payment of, and paying, claims against Iran in accordance with the claims settlement agreement. Whenever the Central Bank shall thereafter notify Iran that the balance in the security account has fallen below $500 million, Iran shall promptly make new deposits sufficient to maintain a minimum balance of $500 million in the account. The account shall be so maintained until the President of the Arbitral Tribunal established pursuant to the claims settlement agreement has certified to the Central Bank of Algeria that all arbitral awards against Iran have been satisfied in accordance with the claims settlement agreement, at which point any amount remaining in the security account shall be transferred to Iran.

OTHER ASSETS IN THE U.S. AND ABROAD

8. . . . [T]he United States will act to bring about the transfer to the Central Bank of all Iranian financial assets (meaning funds or securities) which are located in the United States and abroad, apart from those assets referred to in Paragraph 5 and 6 above, to be held by the Central Bank in escrow until their transfer or return is required by Paragraph 3 above.

9. . . . [T]he United States will arrange, subject to the provisions of U.S. law applicable prior to November 14, 1979, for the transfer to Iran of all Iranian properties which are located in the United States and abroad and which are not within the scope of the preceding paragraphs.

NULLIFICATION OF SANCTIONS AND CLAIMS

10. Upon the making by the Government of Algeria of the certification described in Paragraph 3 above, the United States will revoke all trade sanctions which were directed against Iran in the period November 4, 1979, to date.

11. . . . [T]he United States will promptly withdraw all claims now pending against Iran before the International Court of Justice and will thereafter bar and preclude the prosecution against Iran of any pending or future claim of the United States or a United States national arising out of events occurring before the date of this declaration related to (A) the seizure of the 52 United States nationals on November 4, 1979, (B) their subsequent detention, (C) injury to United States property or property of the United States nationals within the United States Embassy compound in Tehran after November 3, 1979, and (D) injury to the United States nationals or their property as a result of popular movements in the course of the Islamic Revolution in Iran which were not an act of the Government of Iran. The United States will also bar and preclude the prosecution against Iran in the courts of the United States of any pending or future claim asserted by persons other than the United States nationals arising out of the events specified in the preceding sentence.

POINT IV: RETURN OF THE ASSETS OF THE FAMILY OF THE FORMER SHAH

12. . . . [T]he United States will freeze, and prohibit any transfer of, property and assets in the United States within the control of the estate of the former Shah or of any close relative of the former Shah served as a defendant in U.S. litigation brought by Iran to recover such property and assets as belonging to Iran. As to any such defendant, including the estate of the former Shah, the freeze order will remain in effect until such litigation is finally terminated. Violation of the freeze order shall be subject to the civil and criminal penalties prescribed by U.S. law.

13. . . . [T]he United States will order all persons within U.S. jurisdiction to report to the U.S. Treasury within 30 days, for transmission to Iran, all information known to them, as of November 3, 1979, and of the date of the order, with respect to the property and assets referred to in Paragraph 12. . . .

14. [T]he United States will make known, to all appropriate U.S. courts, that in any litigation of the kind described in Paragraph 12 above the claims of Iran should not be considered legally barred either by sovereign immunity principles or by the act of state doctrine and that Iranian decrees and judgments relating to such assets should be enforced by such courts in accordance with United States law.

15. As to any judgment of a U.S. court which calls for the transfer of any property or assets to Iran, the United States hereby guarantees the enforcement of the final judgment to the extent that the property of assets exist within the United States.

16. If any dispute arises between the parties as to whether the United States has fulfilled any obligation imposed upon it by Paragraph 12-15, inclusive, Iran may submit the dispute to binding arbitration by the tribunal established by, and in accordance with the provisions of, the claims settlement agreement. If the tribunal determines that Iran has suffered a loss as a result of a failure by the United States to fulfill such obligation, it shall

make an appropriate award in favor of Iran which may be enforced by Iran in the courts of any nation in accordance with its laws.

SETTLEMENT OF DISPUTES

17. If any other dispute arises between the parties as to the interpretation or performance of any provision of this declaration, either party may submit the dispute to binding arbitration by the tribunal established by, and in accordance with the provisions of, the claims settlement agreement. Any decision of the tribunal with respect to such dispute, including any award of damages to compensate for a loss resulting from a breach of this declaration or the claims settlement agreement, may be enforced by the prevailing party in the courts of any nation in accordance with its laws.

Initialed on January 19, 1981. . . .

2. Declaration of the Government of the Democratic and Popular Republic of Algeria Concerning the Settlement of Claims by the Government of the United States of America and the Government of the Islamic Republic of Iran

The Government of the Democratic and Popular Republic of Algeria, on the basis of formal notice of adherence received from the Government of the Islamic Republic of Iran and the Government of the United States of America, now declares that Iran and the United States have agreed as follows:

Article I

Iran and the United States will promote the settlement of the claims described in Article II by the parties directly concerned. Any such claims not settled within six months from the date of entry into force of this agreement shall be submitted to binding third-party arbitration in accordance with the terms of this agreement. The aforementioned six months' period may be extended once by three months at the request of either party.

Article II

1. An International Arbitral Tribunal (the Iran United States Claims Tribunal) is hereby established for the purpose of deciding claims of nationals of the United States against Iran and claims of nationals of Iran against the United States, and any counterclaim which arises out of the same contract, transaction or occurrence that constitutes the subject matter of that national's claim, if such claims and counterclaims are outstanding on the date of this agreement, whether or not filed with any court, and arise out of debts, contracts (including transactions which are the subject of letters of credit or bank guarantees), expropriations or other measures affecting property rights, excluding claims described in Paragraph 11 of the Declara-

tion of the Government of Algeria of January 19, 1981, and claims arising out of the actions of the United States in response to the conduct described in such paragraph, and excluding claims arising under a binding contract between the parties specifically providing that any disputes thereunder shall be within the sole jurisdiction of the competent Iranian courts in response to the Majlis position.

2. The Tribunal shall also have jurisdiction over official claims of the United States and Iran against each other arising out of contractual arrangements between them for the purchase and sale of goods and services.

3. The Tribunal shall have jurisdiction, as specified in Paragraphs 16-17 of the Declaration of the Government of Algeria of January 19, 1981, over any dispute as to the interpretation or performance of any provision of that declaration.

Article III

1. The Tribunal shall consist of nine members or such larger multiple of three as Iran and the United States may agree are necessary to conduct its business expeditiously. Within ninety days after the entry into force of this agreement, each government shall appoint one-third of the members. Within thirty days after their appointment, the members so appointed shall by mutual agreement select their remaining third of the members and appoint one of the remaining third President of the Tribunal. Claims may be decided by the full Tribunal or by a panel of three members of the Tribunal as the President shall determine. Each such panel shall be composed by the President and shall consist of one member appointed by each of the three methods set forth above.

2. Members of the Tribunal shall be appointed and the Tribunal shall conduct its business in accordance with the arbitration rules of the United Nations Commission on International Trade Law (UNCITRAL) except to the extent modified by the parties or by the Tribunal to ensure that this agreement can be carried out. The UNCITRAL rules for appointing members of three-member Tribunals shall apply *mutatis mutandis* to the appointment of the Tribunal.

3. Claims of nationals of the United States and Iran that are within the scope of this agreement shall be presented to the Tribunal either by claimants themselves, or, in the case of claims of less than $250,000, by the Government of such national.

4. No claim may be filed with the Tribunal more than one year after the entry into force of this agreement or six months after the date the President is appointed, whichever is later. These deadlines do not apply to the procedures contemplated by Paragraphs 16 and 17 of the Declaration of the Government of Algeria of January 19, 1981.

Article IV

1. All decisions and awards of the Tribunal shall be final and binding.

2. The President of the Tribunal shall certify, as prescribed in Paragraph 7 of the Declaration of the Government of Algeria of January 19, 1981, when all arbitral awards under this agreement have been satisfied.

3. Any award which the Tribunal may render against either government shall be enforceable against such government in the courts of any nation in accordance with its laws.

Article V

The Tribunal shall decide all cases on the basis of respect for law, applying such choice of law rules and principles of commercial and international law as the Tribunal determines to be applicable, taking into account relevant usages of the trade, contract provisions and changed circumstances.

Article VI

1. The seat of the Tribunal shall be The Hague, The Netherlands, or any other place agreed by Iran and the United States.

2. Each government shall designate an agent at the seat of the Tribunal to represent it to the Tribunal and to receive notices or other communications directed to it or to its nationals, agencies, instrumentalities, or entitled in connection with proceedings before the Tribunal.

3. The expenses of the Tribunal shall be born equally by the two governments.

4. Any question concerning the interpretation or application of this agreement shall be decided by the Tribunal upon the request of either Iran or the United States.

Article VII

For the purpose of this agreement:

1. A "national" of Iran or of the United States, as the case may be, means (a) a natural person who is a citizen of Iran or the United States; and (b) a corporation or other legal entity which is organized under the laws of Iran or the United States or any of its states or territories, the District of Columbia or the Commonwealth of Puerto Rico, if, collectively, natural persons who are citizens of such country hold, directly or indirectly, an interest in such corporation or entity equivalent to fifty per cent or more of its capital stock.

2. "Claims of Nationals" of Iran or the United States, as the case may be, means claims owned continuously, from the date on which the claim arose to the date on which this agreement enters into force, by nationals of that state, including claims that are owned indirectly by such nationals through ownership of capital stock or other proprietary interests in juridical persons, provided that the ownership interests of such nationals, collectively, were sufficient at the time the claim arose to control the corporation or other entity, and provided, further, that the corporation or other entity is not itself entitled to bring a claim under the terms of this agreement. Claims referred to the Arbitral Tribunal shall, as of the date of filing of such claims with the Tribunal, be considered excluded from the jurisdiction of the courts of Iran, or of the United States, or of any other court.

3. "Iran" means the Government of Iran, any political subdivision of

Iran, and any agency, instrumentality, or entity controlled by the Government of Iran or any political subdivision thereof.

4. The "United States" means the Government of the United States, any political subdivision of the United States, any agency, instrumentality or entity controlled by the Government of the United States or any political subdivision thereof.

Article VIII

This agreement shall enter into force when the Government of Algeria has received from both Iran and the United States a notification of adherence to the agreement.

Initialed on January 19, 1981.

4

International Dispute Resolution

INTERNATIONAL CHAMBER OF COMMERCE (ICC) RULES OF ARBITRATION*

Article 1. Court of Arbitration.

1. The Court of Arbitration of the International Chamber of Commerce is the international arbitration body attached to the International Chamber of Commerce. Members of the Court are appointed by the Council of the International Chamber of Commerce. The function of the Court is to provide for the settlement by arbitration of business disputes of an international character in accordance with these Rules.

2. In principle, the Court meets once a month. It draws up its own internal regulations.

3. The Chairman of the Court of Arbitration or his deputy shall have power to take urgent decisions on behalf of the Court, provided that any such decision shall be reported to the Court at its next session.

4. The Court may, in the manner provided for in its internal regulations, delegate to one or more groups of its members the power to take certain decisions provided that any such decision shall be reported to the Court at its next session.

5. The Secretariat of the Court of Arbitration shall be at the Headquarters of the International Chamber of Commerce.

---

*These arbitration rules of the International Chamber of Commerce (ICC) were in force as of Jan. 1, 1988.

Article 2. The Arbitral Tribunal.

1. The Court of Arbitration does not itself settle disputes. Insofar as the parties shall not have provided otherwise, it appoints, or confirms the appointments of, arbitrators in accordance with the provisions of this Article. In making or confirming such appointment, the Court shall have regard to the proposed arbitrator's nationality, residence and other relationships with the countries of which the parties or the other arbitrators are nationals.

2. The disputes may be settled by a sole arbitrator or by three arbitrators. In the following Articles the word "arbitrator" denotes a single arbitrator or three arbitrators as the case may be.

3. Where the parties have agreed that the disputes shall be settled by a sole arbitrator, they may, by agreement, nominate him for confirmation by the Court. If the parties fail so to nominate a sole arbitrator within 30 days from the date when the Claimant's Request for Arbitration has been communicated to the other party, the sole arbitrator shall be appointed by the Court.

4. Where the dispute is to be referred to three arbitrators, each party shall nominate in the Request for Arbitration and the Answer thereto respectively one arbitrator for confirmation by the Court. Such person shall be independent of the party nominating him. If a party fails to nominate an arbitrator, the appointment shall be made by the Court.

The third arbitrator, who will act as chairman of the arbitral tribunal, shall be appointed by the Court, unless the parties have provided that the arbitrators nominated by them shall agree on the third arbitrator within a fixed time limit. In such a case the Court shall confirm the appointment of such third arbitrator. Should the two arbitrators fail, within the time limit fixed by the parties or the Court, to reach agreement on the third arbitrator, he shall be appointed by the Court.

5. Where the parties have not agreed upon the number of arbitrators, the Court shall appoint a sole arbitrator, save where it appears to the Court that the dispute is such as to warrant the appointment of three arbitrators. In such a case the parties shall each have a period of 30 days within which to nominate an arbitrator.

6. Where the Court is to appoint a sole arbitrator or the chairman of an arbitral tribunal, it shall make the appointment after having requested a proposal from a National Committee of the ICC that it considers to be appropriate. If the Court does not accept the proposal made, or if said National Committee fails to make the proposal requested within the time-limit fixed by the Court, the Court may repeat its request or may request a proposal from another appropriate National Committee.

Where the Court considers that the circumstances so demand, it may choose the sole arbitrator or the chairman of the arbitral tribunal from a country where there is no National Committee, provided that neither of the parties objects within the time-limit fixed by the Court.

The sole arbitrator or the chairman of the arbitral tribunal shall be chosen from a country other than those of which the parties are nationals. However, in suitable circumstances and provided that neither of the parties objects within the time-limit fixed by the Court, the sole arbitrator or the

ICC Rules of Arbitration

chairman of the arbitral tribunal may be chosen from a country of which any of the parties is a national.

Where the Court is to appoint an arbitrator on behalf of a party which has failed to nominate one, it shall make the appointment after having requested a proposal from the National Committee of the country of which the said party is a national. If the Court does not accept the proposal made, or if said National Committee fails to make the proposal requested within the time-limit fixed by the Court, or if the country of which the said party is a national has no National Committee, the Court shall be at liberty to choose any person whom it regards as suitable, after having informed the National Committee of the country of which such person is a national, if one exists.

7. Every arbitrator appointed or confirmed by the Court must be and remain independent of the parties involved in the arbitration.

Before appointment or confirmation by the Court, a prospective arbitrator shall disclose in writing to the Secretary General of the Court any facts or circumstances which might be of such a nature as to call into question the arbitrator's independence in the eyes of the parties. Upon receipt of such information, the Secretary General of the Court shall provide it to the parties in writing and fix a time-limit for any comments from them.

An arbitrator shall immediately disclose in writing to the Secretary General of the Court and the parties any facts or circumstances of a similar nature which may arise between the arbitrator's appointment or confirmation by the Court and the notification of the final award.

8. A challenge of an arbitrator, whether for an alleged lack of independence or otherwise, is made by the submission to the Secretary General of the Court of a written statement specifying the facts and circumstances on which the challenge is based.

For a challenge to be admissible, it must be sent by a party either within 30 days from receipt by that party of the notification of the appointment or confirmation of the arbitrator by the Court; or within 30 days from the date when the party making the challenge was informed of the facts and circumstances on which the challenge is based, if such date is subsequent to the receipt of the aforementioned notification.

9. The Court shall decide on the admissibility, and at the same time if need be on the merits, of a challenge after the Secretary General of the Court has accorded an opportunity for the arbitrator concerned, the parties and any other members of the arbitral tribunal to comment in writing within a suitable period of time.

10. An arbitrator shall be replaced upon his death, upon the acceptance by the Court of a challenge, or upon the acceptance by the Court of the arbitrator's resignation.

11. An arbitrator shall also be replaced when the Court decides that he is prevented *de jure* or *de facto* from fulfilling his functions, or that he is not fulfilling his functions in accordance with the Rules or within the prescribed time-limits.

When, on the basis of information that has come to its attention, the Court considers applying the preceding subparagraph, it shall decide on the matter after the Secretary General of the Court has provided such information in writing to the arbitrator concerned, the parties and any other members of the arbitral tribunal, and accorded an opportunity to them to comment in writing within a suitable period of time.

12. In each instance where an arbitrator is to be replaced, the procedure indicated in the preceding paragraphs 3, 4, 5 and 6 shall be followed. Once reconstituted, and after having invited the parties to comment, the arbitral tribunal shall determine if and to what extent prior proceedings shall again take place.

13. Decisions of the Court as to the appointment, confirmation, challenge or replacement of an arbitrator shall be final.

The reasons for decisions by the Court as to the appointment, confirmation, challenge, or replacement of an arbitrator on the grounds that he is not fulfilling his functions in accordance with the Rules or within the prescribed time-limits, shall not be communicated.

Article 3. Request for Arbitration.

1. A party wishing to have recourse to arbitration by the International Chamber of Commerce shall submit its Request for Arbitration to the Secretariat of the Court through its National Committee or directly. In this latter case the Secretariat shall bring the Request to the notice of the National Committee concerned.

The date when the Request is received by the Secretariat of the Court shall, for all purposes, be deemed to be the date of commencement of the arbitral proceedings.

2. The Request for Arbitration shall inter alia contain the following information:

a) names in full, description, and addresses of the parties,
b) a statement of the Claimant's case,
c) the relevant agreements, and in particular the agreement to arbitrate, and such documentation or information as will serve clearly to establish the circumstances of the case,
d) all relevant particulars concerning the number of arbitrators and their choice in accordance with the provisions of Article 2 above.

3. The Secretariat shall send a copy of the Request and the documents annexed thereto to the Defendant for his Answer.

Article 4. Answer to the Request.

1. The Defendant shall within 30 days from the receipt of the documents referred to in paragraph 3 of Article 3 comment on the proposals made concerning the number of arbitrators and their choice and, where appropriate, nominate an arbitrator. He shall at the same time set out his defence and supply relevant documents. In exceptional circumstances the Defendant may apply to the Secretariat for an extension of time for the filing of his defence and his documents. The application must, however, include the Defendant's comments on the proposals made with regard to the number of arbitrators and their choice and also, where appropriate, the nomina-

tion of an arbitrator. If the Defendant fails so to do, the Secretariat shall report to the Court, which shall proceed with the arbitration in accordance with these Rules.

2. A copy of the Answer and of the documents annexed thereto, if any, shall be communicated to the Claimant for his information.

Article 5. Counter-Claim.

1. If the Defendant wishes to make a counter-claim, he shall file the same with the Secretariat, at the same time as his Answer as provided for in Article 4.

2. It shall be open to the Claimant to file a Reply with the Secretariat within 30 days from the date when the counter-claim was communicated to him.

Article 6. Pleadings and Written Statements, Notifications or Communications.

1. All pleadings and written statements submitted by the parties, as well as all documents annexed thereto, shall be supplied in a number of copies sufficient to provide one copy for each party, plus one for each arbitrator, and one for the Secretariat.

2. All notifications or communications from the Secretariat and the arbitrator shall be validly made if they are delivered against receipt or forwarded by registered post to the address or last known address of the party for whom the same are intended as notified by the party in question or by the other party as appropriate.

3. Notification or communication shall be deemed to have been effected on the day when it was received, or should, if made in accordance with the preceding paragraph, have been received by the party itself or by its representative.

4. Periods of time specified in the present Rules or in the Internal Rules or set by the Court pursuant to its authority under any of these Rules shall start to run on the day following the date a notification or communication is deemed to have been effected in accordance with the preceding paragraph. When, in the country where the notification or communication is deemed to have been effected, the day next following such date is an official holiday or a nonbusiness day, the period of time shall commence on the first following working day. Official holidays and non-working days are included in the calculation of the period of time. If the last day of the relevant period of time granted is an official holiday or a non-business day in the country where the notification or communication is deemed to have been effected, the period of time shall expire at the end of the first following working day.

Article 7. Absence of Agreement to Arbitrate.

Where there is no prima facie agreement between the parties to arbitrate or where there is an agreement but it does not specify the International Chamber of Commerce, and if the Defendant does not file an Answer within the period of 30 days provided by paragraph 1 of Article 4 or refuses arbitration by the International Chamber of Commerce, the Claimant shall be informed that the arbitration cannot proceed.

Article 8. *Effect of the Agreement to Arbitrate.*

1. Where the parties have agreed to submit to arbitration by the International Chamber of Commerce, they shall be deemed thereby to have submitted ipso facto to the present Rules.

2. If one of the parties refuses or fails to take part in the arbitration, the arbitration shall proceed notwithstanding such refusal or failure.

3. Should one of the parties raise one or more pleas concerning the existence or validity of the agreement to arbitrate, and should the Court be satisfied of the *prima facie* existence of such an agreement, the Court may, without prejudice to the admissibility or merits of the plea or pleas, decide that the arbitration shall proceed. In such a case any decision as to the arbitrator's jurisdiction shall be taken by the arbitrator himself.

4. Unless otherwise provided, the arbitrator shall not cease to have jurisdiction by reason of any claim that the contract is null and void or allegation that it is inexistent provided that he upholds the validity of the agreement to arbitrate. He shall continue to have jurisdiction, even though the contract itself may be inexistent or null and void, to determine the respective rights of the parties and to adjudicate upon their claims and pleas.

5. Before the file is transmitted to the arbitrator, and in exceptional circumstances even thereafter, the parties shall be at liberty to apply to any competent judicial authority for interim or conservatory measures, and they shall not by so doing be held to infringe the agreement to arbitrate or to affect the relevant powers reserved to the arbitrator.

Any such application and any measures taken by the judicial authority must be notified without delay to the Secretariat of the Court of Arbitration. The Secretariat shall inform the arbitrator thereof.

Article 9. *Advance to Cover Costs of Arbitration.*

1. The Court shall fix the amount of the advance on costs in a sum likely to cover the costs of arbitration of the claims which have been referred to it.

Where, apart from the principal claim, one or more counter-claims are submitted, the Court may fix separate advances on costs for the principal claim and the counter-claim or counter-claims.

2. The advance on costs shall be payable in equal shares by the Claimant or Claimants and the Defendant or Defendants. However, any one party shall be free to pay the whole of the advance on costs in respect of the claim or the counterclaim should the other party fail to pay its share.

3. The Secretariat may make the transmission of the file to the arbitrator conditional upon the payment by the parties or one of them of the whole or part of the advance on costs to the International Chamber of Commerce.

4. When the Terms of Reference are communicated to the Court in accordance with the provisions of Article 13, the Court shall verify whether the requests for the advance on costs have been complied with. The Terms

of Reference shall only become operative and the arbitrator shall only proceed in respect of those claims for which the advance on costs has been duly paid to the International Chamber of Commerce.

Article 10. Transmission of the File to the Arbitrator.

Subject to the provisions of Article 9, the Secretariat shall transmit the file to the arbitrator as soon as it has received the Defendant's Answer to the Request for Arbitration, at the latest upon the expiry of the time limits fixed in Articles 4 and 5 above for the filing of these documents.

Article 11. Rules Governing the Proceedings.

The rules governing the proceedings before the arbitrator shall be those resulting from these Rules and, where these Rules are silent, any rules which the parties (or, failing them, the arbitrator) may settle, and whether or not reference is thereby made to a municipal procedural law to be applied to the arbitration.

Article 12. Place of Arbitration.

The place of arbitration shall be fixed by the Court, unless agreed upon by the parties.

Article 13. Terms of Reference.

1. Before proceeding with the preparation of the case, the arbitrator shall draw up, on the basis of the documents or in the presence of the parties and in the light of their most recent submissions, a document defining his Terms of Reference. This document shall include the following particulars:

a) the full names and description of the parties,
b) the addresses of the parties to which notifications or communications arising in the course of the arbitration may validly be made,
c) a summary of the parties' respective claims,
d) definition of the issues to be determined,
e) the arbitrator's full name, description and address,
f) the place of arbitration,
g) particulars of the applicable procedural rules and, if such is the case, reference to the power conferred upon the arbitrator to act as amiable compositeur,
h) such other particulars as may be required to make the arbitral award enforceable in law, or may be regarded as helpful by the Court of Arbitration or the arbitrator.

2. The document mentioned in paragraph 1 of this Article shall be signed by the parties and the arbitrator. Within two months of the date when the file has been transmitted to him, the arbitrator shall transmit to the Court the said document signed by himself and by the parties. The Court may, pursuant to a reasoned request from the arbitrator or if need be on its own initiative, extend this time-limit if it decides it is necessary to do so.

Should one of the parties refuse to take part in the drawing up of the said document or to sign the same, the Court, if it is satisfied that the case is one of those mentioned in paragraphs 2 and 3 of Article 8, shall take such action as is necessary for its approval. Thereafter the Court shall set a time-limit for the signature of the statement by the defaulting party and on expiry of that time-limit the arbitration shall proceed and the award shall be made.

3. The parties shall be free to determine the law to be applied by the arbitrator to the merits of the dispute. In the absence of any indication by the parties as to the applicable law, the arbitrator shall apply the law designated as the proper law by the rule of conflict which he deems appropriate.

4. The arbitrator shall assume the powers of an amiable compositeur if the parties are agreed to give him such powers.

5. In all cases the arbitrator shall take account of the provisions of the contract and the relevant trade usages.

Article 14. *The Arbitral Proceedings.*

1. The arbitrator shall proceed within as short a time as possible to establish the facts of the case by all appropriate means. After study of the written submissions of the parties and of all documents relied upon, the arbitrator shall hear the parties together in person if one of them so requests; and failing such a request he may of his own motion decide to hear them.

In addition, the arbitrator may decide to hear any other person in the presence of the parties or in their absence provided they have been duly summoned.

2. The arbitrator may appoint one or more experts, define their Terms of Reference, receive their reports and/or hear them in person.

3. The arbitrator may decide the case on the relevant documents alone if the parties so request or agree.

Article 15.

1. At the request of one of the parties or if necessary on his own initiative, the arbitrator, giving reasonable notice, shall summon the parties to appear before him on the day and at the place appointed by him and shall so inform the Secretariat of the Court.

2. If one of the parties, although duly summoned, fails to appear, the arbitrator, if he is satisfied that the summons was duly received and the party is absent without valid excuse, shall have power to proceed with the arbitration, and such proceedings shall be deemed to have been conducted in the presence of all parties.

3. The arbitrator shall determine the language or languages of the arbitration, due regard being paid to all the relevant circumstances and in particular to the language of the contract.

4. The arbitrator shall be in full charge of the hearings, at which all the parties shall be entitled to be present. Save with the approval of the arbitrator and of the parties, persons not involved in the proceedings shall not be admitted.

ICC Rules of Arbitration

5. The parties may appear in person or through duly accredited agents. In addition, they may be assisted by advisers.

Article 16.

The parties may make new claims or counter-claims before the arbitrator on condition that these remain within the limits fixed by the Terms of Reference provided for in Article 13 or that they are specified in a rider to that document, signed by the parties and communicated to the Court.

Article 17. Award by Consent.

If the parties reach a settlement after the file has been transmitted to the arbitrator in accordance with Article 10, the same shall be recorded in the form of an arbitral award made by consent of the parties.

Article 18. Time-Limit for Award.

1. The time-limit within which the arbitrator must render his award is fixed at six months. Once the terms of Article 9(4) have been satisfied, such time-limit shall start to run from the date of the last signature by the arbitrator or of the parties of the document mentioned in Article 13, or from the expiry of the time-limit granted to a party by virtue of Article 13(2), or from the date that the Secretary General of the Court notifies the arbitrator that the advance on costs is paid in full, if such notification occurs later.
2. The Court may, pursuant to a reasoned request from the arbitrator or if need be on its own initiative, extend this time-limit if it decides it is necessary to do so.
3. Where no such extension is granted and, if appropriate, after application of the provisions of Article 2 (11), the Court shall determine the manner in which the dispute is to be resolved.

Article 19. Award by Three Arbitrators.

When three arbitrators have been appointed, the award is given by a majority decision. If there be no majority, the award shall be made by the Chairman of the arbitral tribunal alone.

Article 20. Decision as to Costs of Arbitration.

1. The arbitrator's award shall, in addition to dealing with the merits of the case, fix the costs of the arbitration and decide which of the parties shall bear the costs or in what proportions the costs shall be borne by the parties.
2. The costs of the arbitration shall include the arbitrator's fees and the administrative costs fixed by the Court in accordance with the scale annexed to the present Rules, the expenses, if any, of the arbitrator, the fees and expenses of any experts, and the normal legal costs incurred by the parties.
3. The Court may fix the arbitrator's fees at a figure higher or lower than that which would result from the application of the annexed scale if in the exceptional circumstances of the case this appears to be necessary.

Article 21. Scrutiny of Award by the Court.

Before signing an award, whether partial or definitive, the arbitrator shall submit it in draft form to the Court. The Court may lay down modifications as to the form of the award and, without affecting the arbitrator's liberty of decision, may also draw his attention to points of substance. No award shall be signed until it has been approved by the Court as to its form.

Article 22. Making of Award.

The arbitral award shall be deemed to be made at the place of the arbitration proceedings and on the date when it is signed by the arbitrator.

Article 23. Notification of Award to Parties.

1. Once an award has been made, the Secretariat shall notify to the parties the text signed by the arbitrator; provided always that the costs of the arbitration have been fully paid to the International Chamber of Commerce by the parties or by one of them.

2. Additional copies certified true by the Secretary-General of the Court shall be made available, on request and at any time, to the parties but to no one else.

3. By virtue of the notification made in accordance with paragraph 1 of this article, the parties waive any other form of notification or deposit on the part of the arbitrator.

Article 24. Finality and Enforceability of Award.

1. The arbitral award shall be final.

2. By submitting the dispute to arbitration by the International Chamber of Commerce, the parties shall be deemed to have undertaken to carry out the resulting award without delay and to have waived their right to any form of appeal insofar as such waiver can validly be made.

Article 25. Deposit of Award.

An original of each award made in accordance with the present Rules shall be deposited with the Secretariat of the Court.

The arbitrator and the Secretariat of the Court shall assist the parties in complying with whatever further formalities may be necessary.

Article 26. General Rule.

In all matters not expressly provided for in these Rules, the Court of Arbitration and the arbitrator shall act in the spirit of these Rules and shall make every effort to make sure that the award is enforceable at law.

NEW YORK CONVENTION ON THE RECOGNITION AND ENFORCEMENT OF FOREIGN ARBITRAL AWARDS

June 10, 1958, 21 U.S.T. 2517, T.I.A.S. No. 6997, 330 U.N.T.S 38*

Article I

1. This Convention shall apply to the recognition and enforcement of arbitral awards made in the territory of a State other than the State where the recognition and enforcement of such awards are sought, and arising out of differences between persons, whether physical or legal. It shall also apply to arbitral awards not considered as domestic awards in the State where their recognition and enforcement are sought.

2. The term "arbitral awards" shall include not only awards made by arbitrators appointed for each case but also those made by permanent arbitral bodies to which the parties have submitted.

3. When signing, ratifying or acceding to this Convention, or notifying extension under article X hereof, any State may on the basis of reciprocity declare that it will apply the Convention to the recognition and enforcement of awards made only in the territory of another Contracting State. It may also declare that it will apply the Convention only to differences arising out of legal relationships, whether contractual or not, which are considered as commercial under the national law of the State making such declaration.

Article II

1. Each Contracting State shall recognize an agreement in writing under which the parties undertake to submit to arbitration all or any differ-

---

*Done at New York on June 10, 1958. Entered into force on June 7, 1959, and for the United States on December 29, 1970.

The 83 parties to the convention are: Algeria, Antigua and Barbuda, Argentina, Australia, Austria, Bahrain, Belgium, Benin, Botswana, Bulgaria, Burkina Faso, Byelorussian Soviet Socialist Republic, Cambodia, Cameroon, Canada, Central African Republic, Chile, China, Colombia, Costa Rica, Cuba, Cyprus, Czechoslovakia, Denmark, Djibouti, Dominica, Ecuador, Egypt, Finland, France, German Democratic Republic, Germany (Federal Republic), Ghana, Greece, Guatemala, Haiti, Holy See, Hungary, India, Indonesia, Ireland, Israel, Italy, Japan, Jordan, Kenya, Korea, Kuwait, Lesotho, Luxembourg, Madagascar, Malaysia, Mexico, Monaco, Morocco, Netherlands, New Zealand, Niger, Nigeria, Norway, Panama, Peru, Philippines, Poland, Romania, San Marino, Singapore, South Africa, Spain, Sri Lanka, Sweden, Switzerland, Syrian Arab Republic, Tanzania, Thailand, Trinidad and Tobago, Tunisia, Ukrainian Soviet Socialist Republic, Union of Soviet Socialist Republic, United Kingdom, United States, Uruguay, and Yugoslavia.

ences which have arisen or which may arise between them in respect of a defined legal relationship, whether contractual or not, concerning a subject matter capable of settlement by arbitration.

2. The term "agreement in writing" shall include an arbitral clause in a contract or an arbitration agreement, signed by the parties or contained in an exchange of letters or telegrams.

3. The court of a Contracting State, when seized of an action in a matter in respect of which the parties have made an agreement within the meaning of this article, shall, at the request of one of the parties, refer the parties to arbitration, unless it finds that the said agreement is null and void, inoperative or incapable of being performed.

Article III

Each Contracting State shall recognize arbitral awards as binding and enforce them in accordance with the rules of procedure of the territory where the award is relied upon, under the conditions laid down in the following articles. There shall not be imposed substantially more onerous conditions or higher fees or charges on the recognition or enforcement of arbitral awards to which this Convention applies than are imposed on the recognition or enforcement of domestic arbitral awards.

Article IV

1. To obtain the recognition and enforcement mentioned in the preceding article, the party applying for recognition and enforcement shall, at the time of the application, supply:

(a) The duly authenticated original award or a duly certified copy thereof;

(b) The original agreement referred to in article II or a duly certified copy thereof.

2. If the said award or agreement is not made in an official language of the country in which the award is relied upon, the party applying for recognition and enforcement of the award shall produce a translation of these documents into such language. The translation shall be certified by an official or sworn translator or by a diplomatic or consular agent.

Article V

1. Recognition and enforcement of the award may be refused, at the request of the party against whom it is invoked, only if that party furnishes to the competent authority where the recognition and enforcement is sought, proof that:

(a) The parties to the agreement referred to in article II were, under the law applicable to them, under some incapacity, or the said agreement is not valid under the law to which the parties have subjected it or, failing any indication thereon, under the law of the country where the award was made; or

(b) The party against whom the award is invoked was not given proper notice of the appointment of the arbitrator or of the arbitration proceedings or was otherwise unable to present his case; or

(c) The award deals with a difference not contemplated by or not falling within the terms of the submission to arbitration, or it contains decisions on matters beyond the scope of the submission to arbitration, provided that, if the decisions on matters submitted to arbitration can be separated from those not so submitted, that part of the award which contains decisions on matters submitted to arbitration may be recognized and enforced; or

(d) The composition of the arbitral authority or the arbitral procedure was not in accordance with the agreement of the parties, or, failing such agreement, was not in accordance with the law of the country where the arbitration took place; or

(e) The award has not yet become binding on the parties, or has been set aside or suspended by a competent authority of the country in which, or under the law of which, that award was made.

2. Recognition and enforcement of an arbitral award may also be refused if the competent authority in the country where recognition and enforcement is sought finds that:

(a) The subject matter of the difference is not capable of settlement by arbitration under the law of that country; or

(b) The recognition or enforcement of the award would be contrary to the public policy of that country.

Article VI

If an application for the setting aside or suspension of the award has been made to a competent authority referred to in article V (1) *(e)*, the authority before which the award is sought to be relied upon may, if it considers it proper, adjourn the decision on the enforcement of the award and may also, on the application of the party claiming enforcement of the award, order the other party to give suitable security.

Article VII

1. The provisions of the present Convention shall not affect the validity of multilateral or bilateral agreements concerning the recognition and enforcement of arbitral awards entered into by the Contracting States nor deprive any interested party of any right he may have to avail himself of an arbitral award in the manner and to the extent allowed by the law or the treaties of the country where such award is sought to be relied upon.

2. The Geneva Protocol on Arbitration Clauses of 1923 and the Geneva Convention on the Execution of Foreign Arbitral Awards of 1927 shall cease to have effect between Contracting States on their becoming bound and to the extent that they become bound, by this Convention.

Article VIII

1. This Convention shall be open until 31 December 1958 for signature on behalf of any Member of the United Nations and also on behalf of any

other State which is or hereafter becomes a member of any specialized agency of the United Nations, or which is or hereafter becomes a party to the Statute of the International Court of Justice, or any other State to which an invitation has been addressed by the General Assembly of the United Nations.

2. This Convention shall be ratified and the instrument of ratification shall be deposited with the Secretary-General of the United Nations.

Article IX

1. This Convention shall be open for accession to all States referred to in article VIII.

2. Accession shall be effected by the deposit of an instrument of accession with the Secretary-General of the United Nations.

Article X

1. Any State may, at the time of signature, ratification or accession, declare that this Convention shall extend to all or any of the territories for the international relations of which it is responsible. Such a declaration shall take effect when the Convention enters into force for the State concerned.

2. At any time thereafter any such extension shall be made by notification addressed to the Secretary-General of the United Nations and shall take effect as from the ninetieth day after the day of receipt by the Secretary-General of the United Nations of this notification, or as from the date of entry into force of the Convention for the State concerned, whichever is the later.

3. With respect to those territories to which this Convention is not extended at the time of signature, ratification or accession, each State concerned shall consider the possibility of taking the necessary steps in order to extend the application of this Convention to such territories, subject, where necessary for constitutional reasons, to the consent of the Governments of such territories.

Article XI

In the case of a federal or non-unitary State, the following provisions shall apply:

(a) With respect to those articles of this Convention that come within the legislative jurisdiction of the federal authority, the obligations of the federal Government shall to this extent be the same as those of Contracting States which are not federal States;

(b) With respect to those articles of this Convention that come within the legislative jurisdiction of constituent states or provinces which are not, under the constitutional system of the federation, bound to take legislative action, the federal Government shall bring such articles with a favourable recommendation to the notice of the appropriate authorities of constituent states or provinces at the earliest possible moment;

(c) A federal State Party to this Convention shall, at the request of any other Contracting State transmitted through the Secretary-General of the United Nations, supply a statement of the law and practice of the federation

and its constituent units in regard to any particular provision of this Convention, showing the extent to which effect has been given to that provision by legislative or other action.

Article XII

1. This Convention shall come into force on the ninetieth day following the date of deposit of the third instrument of ratification or accession.

2. For each State ratifying or acceeding to this Convention after the deposit of the third instrument of ratification or accession, this Convention shall enter into force on the ninetieth day after deposit by such State of its instrument of ratification or accession.

Article XIII

1. Any Contracting State may denounce this Convention by a written notification to the Secretary-General of the United Nations. Denunciation shall take effect one year after the date of receipt of the notification by the Secretary-General.

2. Any State which has made a declaration or notification under article X may, at any time thereafter, by notification to the Secretary-General of the United Nations, declare that this Convention shall cease to extend to the territory concerned one year after the date of the receipt of the notification by the Secretary-General.

3. This Convention shall continue to be applicable to arbitral awards in respect of which recognition or enforcement proceedings have been instituted before the denunciation takes effect.

Article XIV

A Contracting State shall not be entitled to avail itself of the present Convention against other Contracting States except to the extent that it is itself bound to apply the Convention. . . .

CONVENTION ON THE SETTLEMENT OF INVESTMENT DISPUTES BETWEEN STATES AND NATIONALS OF OTHER STATES

March 18, 1965, 17 U.S.T. 1270, T.I.A.S. No. 6090, 575 U.N.T.S. 159*

The Contracting States

Considering the need for international cooperation for economic development, and the role of private international investment therein;

Bearing in mind the possibility that from time to time disputes may arise in connection with such investment between Contracting States and nationals of other Contracting States;

Recognizing that while such disputes would usually be subject to national legal processes, international methods of settlement may be appropriate in certain cases;

Attaching particular importance to the availability of facilities for international conciliation or arbitration to which Contracting States and nationals of other Contracting States may submit such disputes if they so desire;

Desiring to establish such facilities under the auspices of the International Bank for Reconstruction and Development;

Recognizing that mutual consent by the parties to submit such disputes to conciliation or to arbitration through such facilities constitutes a binding agreement which requires in particular that due consideration be given to any recommendation of conciliators, and that any arbitral award be complied with; and

Declaring that no Contracting State shall by the mere fact of its ratifica-

---

*Done at Washington on March 18, 1965. Entered into force on October 14, 1966. The 92 parties to the convention are: Afghanistan, Austria, Bangladesh, Barbados, Belgium, Benin, Botswana, Burkina Faso, Burundi, Cameroon, Central African Republic, Chad, China, Comoros, Congo, Cote d'Ivoire, Cyprus, Denmark, Ecuador, Egypt, El Salvador, Fiji, Finland, France, Gabon, Gambia, Germany (Federal Republic), Ghana, Greece, Guinea, Guyana, Iceland, Indonesia, Ireland, Israel, Italy, Jamaica, Japan, Jordan, Kenya, Korea, Kuwait, Lesotho, Liberia, Luxembourg, Madagascar, Malawi, Malaysia, Mali, Mauritania, Mauritius, Morocco, Nepal, Netherlands, New Zealand, Niger, Nigeria, Norway, Pakistan, Papua New Guinea, Paraguay, Philippines, Portugal, Romania, Rwanda, Saint Lucia, Saudi Arabia, Senegal, Seychelles, Sierra Leone, Singapore, Solomon Islands, Somalia, Sri Lanka, Sudan, Swaziland, Sweden, Switzerland, Togo, Trinidad & Tobago, Tunisia, Uganda, United Arab Emirates, United Kingdom, United States, Western Samoa, Yugoslavia, Zaire, and Zambia.

tion, acceptance or approval of this Convention and without its consent be deemed to be under any obligation to submit any particular dispute to conciliation or arbitration,

Have agreed as follows:

Chapter I. International Centre for Settlement of Investment Disputes

SECTION 1. ESTABLISHMENT AND ORGANIZATION

Article 1

(1) There is hereby established the International Centre for Settlement of Investment Disputes (hereinafter called the Centre). [Also known as ICSID.]

(2) The purpose of the Centre shall be to provide facilities for conciliation and arbitration of investment disputes between Contracting States and nationals of other Contracting States in accordance with the provisions of this Convention.

Article 2

The seat of the Centre shall be at the principal office of the International Bank for Reconstruction and Development (hereinafter called the Bank). . . .

Article 5

The President of the Bank shall be *ex officio* Chairman of the Administrative Council (hereinafter called the Chairman) but shall have no vote. During his absence or inability to act and during any vacancy in the office of President of the Bank, the person for the time being acting as President shall act as Chairman of the Administrative Council. . . .

SECTION 4. THE PANELS

Article 12

The Panel of Conciliators and the Panel of Arbitrators shall each consist of qualified persons, designated as hereinafter provided, who are willing to serve thereon.

Article 13

(1) Each Contracting State may designate to each Panel four persons who may but need not be its nationals.

(2) The Chairman may designate ten persons to each Panel. The persons so designated to a Panel shall each have a different nationality.

Article 14

(1) Persons designated to serve on the Panels shall be persons of high moral character and recognized competence in the fields of law, commerce, industry or finance, who may be relied upon to exercise independent judgment. Competence in the field of law shall be of particular importance in the case of persons on the Panel of Arbitrators.

(2) The Chairman, in designating persons to serve on the Panels, shall in addition pay due regard to the importance of assuring representation on the Panels of the principal legal systems of the world and of the main forms of economic activity.

Article 15

(1) Panel members shall serve for renewable periods of six years.

(2) In case of death or resignation of a member of a Panel, the authority which designated the member shall have the right to designate another person to serve for the remainder of that member's term.

(3) Panel members shall continue in office until their successors have been designated.

Article 16

(1) A person may serve on both Panels.

(2) If a person shall have been designated to serve on the same Panel by more than one Contracting State, or by one or more Contracting States and the Chairman, he shall be deemed to have been designated by the authority which first designated him or, if one such authority is the State of which he is a national, by that State.

(3) All designations shall be notified to the Secretary-General and shall take effect from the date on which the notification is received.

SECTION 5. FINANCING THE CENTRE

Article 17

If the expenditure of the Centre cannot be met out of charges for the use of its facilities, or out of other receipts, the excess shall be borne by Contracting States which are members of the Bank in proportion to their respective subscriptions to the capital stock of the Bank, and by Contracting States which are not members of the Bank in accordance with rules adopted by the Administrative Council. . . .

Chapter II. Jurisdiction of the Centre

Article 25

(1) The jurisdiction of the Centre shall extend to any legal dispute arising directly out of an investment, between a Contracting State (or any constituent subdivision or agency of a Contracting State designated to the Centre by that State) and a national of another Contracting State, which the parties to the dispute consent in writing to submit to the Centre. When the parties have given their consent, no party may withdraw its consent unilaterally.

(2) "National of another Contracting State" means:

(a) any natural person who had the nationality of a Contracting State other than the State party to the dispute on the date on which the parties consented to submit such dispute to conciliation or arbitration as well as on the date on which the request was registered pursuant to paragraph (3) of Article 28 or paragraph (3) of Article 36, but does not include any person who on either date also had the nationality of the Contracting State party to the dispute; and

(b) any juridical person which had the nationality of a Contracting State other than the State party to the dispute on the date on which the parties consented to submit such dispute to conciliation or arbitration and any juridical person which had the nationality of the Contracting State party to the dispute on that date and which, because of foreign control, the parties have agreed should be treated as a national of another Contracting State for the purposes of this Convention.

(3) Consent by a constituent subdivision or agency of a Contracting State shall require the approval of that State unless that State notifies the Centre that no such approval is required.

(4) Any Contracting State may, at the time of ratification, acceptance or approval of this Convention or at any time thereafter, notify the Centre of the class or classes of disputes which it would or would not consider submitting to the jurisdiction of the Centre. The Secretary-General shall forthwith transmit such notification to all Contracting States. Such notification shall not constitute the consent required by paragraph (1).

Article 26

Consent of the parties to arbitration under this Convention shall, unless otherwise stated, be deemed consent to such arbitration to the exclusion of any other remedy. A Contracting State may require the exhaustion of local administrative or judicial remedies as a condition of its consent to arbitration under this Convention.

Article 27

(1) No Contracting State shall give diplomatic protection, or bring an international claim, in respect of a dispute which one of its nationals and another Contracting State shall have consented to submit or shall have submitted to arbitration under this Convention, unless such other Contract-

ing State shall have failed to abide by and comply with the award rendered in such dispute.

(2) Diplomatic protection, for the purposes of paragraph (1), shall not include informal diplomatic exchanges for the sole purpose of facilitating a settlement of the dispute.

Chapter III. Conciliation

Section 1. Request for Conciliation

Article 28

(1) Any Contracting State or any national of a Contracting State wishing to institute conciliation proceedings shall address a request to that effect in writing to the Secretary-General who shall send a copy of the request to the other party.

(2) The request shall contain information concerning the issues in dispute, the identity of the parties and their consent to conciliation in accordance with the rules of procedure for the institution of conciliation and arbitration proceedings.

(3) The Secretary-General shall register the request unless he finds, on the basis of the information contained in the request, that the dispute is manifestly outside the jurisdiction of the Centre. He shall forthwith notify the parties of registration or refusal to register.

Section 2. Constitution of the Conciliation Commission

Article 29

(1) The Conciliation Commission (hereinafter called the Commission) shall be constituted as soon as possible after registration of a request pursuant to Article 28.

(2) (a) The Commission shall consist of a sole conciliator or any uneven number of conciliators appointed as the parties shall agree.

(b) Where the parties do not agree upon the number of conciliators and the method of their appointment, the Commission shall consist of three conciliators, one conciliator appointed by each party and the third, who shall be the president of the Commission, appointed by agreement of the parties.

Article 30

If the Commission shall not have been constituted within 90 days after notice of registration of the request has been dispatched by the Secretary-General in accordance with paragraph (3) of Article 28, or such other period as the parties may agree, the Chairman shall, at the request of either party and after consulting both parties as far as possible, appoint the conciliator or conciliators not yet appointed.

Article 31

(1) Conciliators may be appointed from outside the Panel of Conciliators, except in the case of appointments by the Chairman pursuant to Article 30.

(2) Conciliators appointed from outside the Panel of Conciliators shall possess the qualities stated in paragraph (1) of Article 14.

Section 3. Conciliation Proceedings

Article 32

(1) The Commission shall be the judge of its own competence.

(2) Any objection by a party to the dispute that that dispute is not within the jurisdiction of the Centre, or for other reasons is not within the competence of the Commission, shall be considered by the Commission which shall determine whether to deal with it as a preliminary question or to join it to the merits of the dispute.

Article 33

Any conciliation proceeding shall be conducted in accordance with the provisions of this Section and, except as the parties otherwise agree, in accordance with the Conciliation Rules in effect on the date on which the parties consented to conciliation. If any question of procedure arises which is not covered by this Section or the Conciliation Rules or any rules agreed by the parties, the Commission shall decide the question.

Article 34

(1) It shall be the duty of the Commission to clarify the issues in dispute between the parties and to endeavour to bring about agreement between them upon mutually acceptable terms. To that end, the Commission may at any stage of the proceedings and from time to time recommend terms of settlement to the parties. The parties shall cooperate in good faith with the Commission in order to enable the Commission to carry out its functions, and shall give their most serious consideration to its recommendations.

(2) If the parties reach agreement, the Commission shall draw up a report noting the issues in dispute and recording that the parties have reached agreement. If, at any stage of the proceedings, it appears to the Commission that there is no likelihood of agreement between the parties, it shall close the proceedings and shall draw up a report noting the submission of the dispute and recording the failure of the parties to reach agreement. If one party fails to appear or participate in the proceedings, the Commission shall close the proceedings and shall draw up a report noting that party's failure to appear or participate.

Article 35

Except as the parties to the dispute shall otherwise agree, neither party to a conciliation proceeding shall be entitled in any other proceeding, whether before arbitrators or in a court of law or otherwise, to invoke or rely on any views expressed or statements or admissions or offers of settlement made by the other party in the conciliation proceedings, or the report or any recommendations made by the Commission.

Chapter IV. Arbitration

Section 1. Request for Arbitration

Article 36

(1) Any Contracting State or any national of a Contracting State wishing to institute arbitration proceedings shall address a request to that effect in writing to the Secretary-General who shall send a copy of the request to the other party.

(2) The request shall contain information concerning the issues in dispute, the identity of the parties and their consent to arbitration in accordance with the rules of procedure for the institution of conciliation and arbitration proceedings.

(3) The Secretary-General shall register the request unless he finds, on the basis of the information contained in the request, that the dispute is manifestly outside the jurisdiction of the Centre. He shall forthwith notify the parties of registration or refusal to register.

Section 2. Constitution of the Tribunal

Article 37

(1) The Arbitral Tribunal (hereinafter called the Tribunal) shall be constituted as soon as possible after registration of a request pursuant to Article 36.

(2) (a) The Tribunal shall consist of a sole arbitrator or any uneven number of arbitrators appointed as the parties shall agree.

(b) Where the parties do not agree upon the number of arbitrators and the method of their appointment, the Tribunal shall consist of three arbitrators, one arbitrator appointed by each party and the third, who shall be the president of the Tribunal, appointed by agreement of the parties.

Article 38

If the Tribunal shall not have been constituted within 90 days after notice of registration of the request has been dispatched by the Secretary-General in accordance with paragraph (3) of Article 36, or such other period as the parties may agree, the Chairman shall, at the request of either party and after consulting both parties as far as possible, appoint the arbitrator or arbitrators not yet appointed. Arbitrators appointed by the Chairman pursuant to this Article shall not be nationals of the Contracting State party to the dispute or of the Contracting State whose national is a party to the dispute.

Article 39

The majority of the arbitrators shall be nationals of States other than the Contracting State party to the dispute and the Contracting State whose national is a party to the dispute; provided, however, that the foregoing provisions of this Article shall not apply if the sole arbitrator or each individual member of the Tribunal has been appointed by agreement of the parties.

Article 40

(1) Arbitrators may be appointed from outside the Panel of Arbitrators, except in the case of appointments by the Chairman pursuant to Article 38.

(2) Arbitrators appointed from outside the Panel of Arbitrators shall possess the qualities stated in paragraph (1) of Article 14.

SECTION 3. POWERS AND FUNCTIONS OF THE TRIBUNAL

Article 41

(1) The Tribunal shall be the judge of its own competence.

(2) Any objection by a party to the dispute that that dispute is not within the jurisdiction of the Centre, or for other reasons is not within the competence of the Tribunal, shall be considered by the Tribunal which shall determine whether to deal with it as a preliminary question or to join it to the merits of the dispute.

Article 42

(1) The Tribunal shall decide a dispute in accordance with such rules of law as may be agreed by the parties. In the absence of such agreement, the Tribunal shall apply the law of the Contracting State party to the dispute (including its rules on the conflict of laws) and such rules of international law as may be applicable.

(2) The Tribunal may not bring in a finding of *non liquet* on the ground of silence or obscurity of the law.

(3) The provisions of paragraphs (1) and (2) shall not prejudice the power of the Tribunal to decide a dispute *ex aequo et bono* if the parties so agree.

Article 43

Except as the parties otherwise agree, the Tribunal may, if it deems it necessary at any stage of the proceedings,
  (a) call upon the parties to produce documents or other evidence, and
  (b) visit the scene connected with the dispute, and conduct such inquiries there as it may deem appropriate.

Article 44

Any arbitration proceeding shall be conducted in accordance with the provisions of this Section and, except as the parties otherwise agree, in accordance with the Arbitration Rules in effect on the date on which the parties consented to arbitration. If any question of procedure arises which is not covered by this Section or the Arbitration Rules or any rules agreed by the parties, the Tribunal shall decide the question.

Article 45

(1) Failure of a party to appear or to present his case shall not be deemed an admission of the other party's assertions.

(2) If a party fails to appear or to present his case at any stage of the proceedings the other party may request the Tribunal to deal with the questions submitted to it and to render an award. Before rendering an award, the Tribunal shall notify, and grant a period of grace to, the party failing to appear or to present its case, unless it is satisfied that that party does not intend to do so.

Article 46

Except as the parties otherwise agree, the Tribunal shall, if requested by a party, determine any incidental or additional claims or counter-claims arising directly out of the subject-matter of the dispute provided that they are within the scope of the consent of the parties and are otherwise within the jurisdiction of the Centre.

Article 47

Except as the parties otherwise agree, the Tribunal may, if it considers that the circumstances so require, recommend any provisional measures which should be taken to preserve the respective rights of either party.

Section 4. The Award

Article 48

(1) The Tribunal shall decide questions by a majority of the votes of all its members.

(2) The award of the Tribunal shall be in writing and shall be signed by the members of the Tribunal who voted for it.

(3) The award shall deal with every question submitted to the Tribunal, and shall state the reasons upon which it is based.

(4) Any member of the Tribunal may attach his individual opinion to the award, whether he dissents from the majority or not, or a statement of his dissent.

(5) The Centre shall not publish the award without the consent of the parties.

Article 49

(1) The Secretary-General shall promptly dispatch certified copies of the award to the parties. The award shall be deemed to have been rendered on the date on which the certified copies were dispatched.

(2) The Tribunal upon the request of a party made within 45 days after the date on which the award was rendered may after notice to the other party decide any question which it had omitted to decide in the award, and shall rectify any clerical, arithmetical or similar error in the award. Its decision shall become part of the award and shall be notified to the parties in the same manner as the award. The periods of time provided for under paragraph (2) of Article 51 and paragraph (2) of Article 52 shall run from the date on which the decision was rendered.

Section 5. Interpretation, Revision and Annulment of the Award

Article 50

(1) If any dispute shall arise between the parties as to the meaning or scope of an award, either party may request interpretation of the award by an application in writing addressed to the Secretary-General.

(2) The request shall, if possible, be submitted to the Tribunal which rendered the award. If this shall not be possible, a new Tribunal shall be constituted in accordance with Section 2 of this Chapter. The Tribunal may, if it considers that the circumstances so require, stay enforcement of the award pending its decision.

Article 51

(1) Either party may request revision of the award by an application in writing addressed to the Secretary-General on the ground of discovery of some fact of such a nature as decisively to affect the award, provided that when the award was rendered that fact was unknown to the Tribunal and to the applicant and that the applicant's ignorance of that fact was not due to negligence.

(2) The application shall be made within 90 days after the discovery of such fact and in any event within three years after the date on which the award was rendered.

(3) The request shall, if possible, be submitted to the Tribunal which rendered the award. If this shall not be possible, a new Tribunal shall be constituted in accordance with Section 2 of this Chapter.

(4) The Tribunal may, if it considers that the circumstances so require, stay enforcement of the award pending its decision. If the applicant requests a stay of enforcement of the award in his application, enforcement shall be stayed provisionally until the Tribunal rules on such request.

Article 52

(1) Either party may request annulment of the award by an application in writing addressed to the Secretary-General on one or more of the following grounds:
  (a) that the Tribunal was not properly constituted;
  (b) that the Tribunal has manifestly exceeded its powers;

(c) that there was corruption on the part of a member of the Tribunal;

(d) that there has been a serious departure from a fundamental rule of procedure; or

(e) that the award has failed to state the reasons on which it is based.

(2) The application shall be made within 120 days after the date on which the award was rendered except that when annulment is requested on the ground of corruption such application shall be made within 120 days after discovery of the corruption and in any event within three years after the date on which the award was rendered.

(3) On receipt of the request the Chairman shall forthwith appoint from the Panel of Arbitrators an *ad hoc* Committee of three persons. None of the members of the Committee shall have been a member of the Tribunal which rendered the award, shall be of the same nationality as any such member, shall be a national of the State party to the dispute or of the State whose national is a party to the dispute, shall have been designated to the Panel of Arbitrators by either of those States, or shall have acted as a conciliator in the same dispute. The Committee shall have the authority to annul the award or any part thereof on any of the grounds set forth in paragraph (1).

(4) The provisions of Articles 41-45, 48, 49, 53 and 54, and of Chapters VI and VII shall apply *mutatis mutandis* to proceedings before the Committee.

(5) The Committee may, if it considers that the circumstances so require, stay enforcement of the award pending its decision. If the applicant requests a stay of enforcement of the award in his application, enforcement shall be stayed provisionally until the Committee rules on such request.

(6) If the award is annulled the dispute shall, at the request of either party, be submitted to a new Tribunal constituted in accordance with Section 2 of this Chapter.

Section 6. Recognition and Enforcement of the Award

Article 53

(1) The award shall be binding on the parties and shall not be subject to any appeal or to any other remedy except those provided for in this Convention. Each party shall abide by and comply with the terms of the award except to the extent that enforcement shall have been stayed pursuant to the relevant provisions of this Convention.

(2) For the purposes of this Section, "award" shall include any decision interpreting, revising or annulling such award pursuant to Articles 50, 51, or 52.

Article 54

(1) Each Contracting State shall recognize an award rendered pursuant to this Convention as binding and enforce the pecuniary obligations imposed by that award within its territories as if it were a final judgment of a court in that State. A Contracting State with a federal constitution may enforce such an award in or through its federal courts and may provide that

such courts shall treat the award as if it were a final judgment of the courts of a constituent state.

(2) A party seeking recognition or enforcement in the territories of a Contracting State shall furnish to a competent court or other authority which such State shall have designated for this purpose a copy of the award certified by the Secretary-General. Each Contracting State shall notify the Secretary-General of the designation of the competent court or other authority for this purpose and of any subsequent change in such designation.

(3) Execution of the award shall be governed by the laws concerning the execution of judgments in force in the State in whose territories such execution is sought.

Article 55

Nothing in Article 54 shall be construed as derogating from the law in force in any Contracting State relating to immunity of that State or of any foreign State from execution.

Chapter V. Replacement and Disqualification of Conciliators and Arbitrators

Article 56

(1) After a Commission or a Tribunal has been constituted and proceedings have begun, its composition shall remain unchanged; provided, however, that if a conciliator or an arbitrator should die, become incapacitated, or resign, the resulting vacancy shall be filled in accordance with the provisions of Section 2 of Chapter III or Section 2 of Chapter IV.

(2) A member of a Commission or Tribunal shall continue to serve in that capacity notwithstanding that he shall have ceased to be a member of the Panel.

(3) If a conciliator or arbitrator appointed by a party shall have resigned without the consent of the Commission or Tribunal of which he was a member, the Chairman shall appoint a person from the appropriate Panel to fill the resulting vacancy.

Article 57

A party may propose to a Commission or Tribunal the disqualification of any of its members on account of any fact indicating a manifest lack of the qualities required by paragraph (1) of Article 14. A party to arbitration proceedings may, in addition, propose the disqualification of an arbitrator on the ground that he was ineligible for appointment to the Tribunal under Section 2 of Chapter IV.

Article 58

The decision on any proposal to disqualify a conciliator or arbitrator shall be taken by the other members of the Commission or Tribunal as the case may be, provided that where those members are equally divided, or in the case of a proposal to disqualify a sole conciliator or arbitrator, or a majority of the conciliators or arbitrators, the Chairman shall take that decision. If it is decided that the proposal is well-founded the conciliator or arbitrator to whom the decision relates shall be replaced in accordance with the provisions of Section 2 of Chapter III or Section 2 of Chapter IV.

Chapter VI. Cost of Proceedings

Article 59

The charges payable by the parties for the use of the facilities of the Centre shall be determined by the Secretary-General in accordance with the regulations adopted by the Administrative Council.

Article 60

(1) Each Commission and each Tribunal shall determine the fees and expenses of its members within limits established from time to time by the Administrative Council and after consultation with the Secretary-General.

(2) Nothing in paragraph (1) of this Article shall preclude the parties from agreeing in advance with the Commission or Tribunal concerned upon the fees and expenses of its members.

Article 61

(1) In the case of conciliation proceedings the fees and expenses of members of the Commission as well as the charges for the use of the facilities of the Centre, shall be borne equally by the parties. Each party shall bear any other expenses it incurs in connection with the proceedings.

(2) In the case of arbitration proceedings the Tribunal shall, except as the parties otherwise agree, assess the expenses incurred by the parties in connection with the proceedings, and shall decide how and by whom those expenses, the fees and expenses of the members of the Tribunal and the charges for the use of the facilities of the Centre shall be paid. Such decision shall form part of the award.

Chapter VII. Place of Proceedings

Article 62

Conciliation and arbitration proceedings shall be held at the seat of the Centre except as hereinafter provided.

Article 63

Conciliation and arbitration proceedings may be held, if the parties so agree,

(a) at the seat of the Permanent Court of Arbitration or of any other appropriate institution, whether private or public, with which the Centre may make arrangements for that purpose; or

(b) at any other place approved by the Commission or Tribunal after consultation with the Secretary-General.

Chapter VIII. Disputes Between Contracting States

Article 64

Any dispute arising between Contracting States concerning the interpretation or application of this Convention which is not settled by negotiation shall be referred to the International Court of Justice by the application of any party to such dispute, unless the States concerned agree to another method of settlement. . . .

CANADA-UNITED STATES FREE TRADE AGREEMENT*

27 I.L.M. 281 (1988)

Index

Preamble

Part One: Objectives and Scope
    Chapter One: Objectives and Scope
        Article 101   Establishment of the Free-Trade Area
        Article 102   Objectives
        Article 103   Extent of Obligations
        Article 104   Affirmation and Precedence
        Article 105   National Treatment
    Chapter Two: General Definitions
        Article 201   Definitions of General Application

Part Two: Trade in Goods
    Chapter Three: Rules of Origin
        Article 301   General Rules
        Article 302   Transshipment
        Article 303   Consultation and Revision
        Article 304   Definitions
        Annexes
    Chapter Four: Border Measures
        Article 401   Tariff Elimination
        Article 402   Rounding of Interim Rates
        Article 403   Customs User Fees
        Article 404   Drawback
        Article 405   Duty Waivers
        Article 406   Customs Administration
        Article 407   Import and Export Restrictions
        Article 408   Export Taxes
        Article 409   Other Export Measures
        Article 410   Definitions
        Annexes
    Chapter Five: National Treatment
        Article 501   Incorporation of GATT Rule
        Article 502   Provincial and State Measures

*Signed at Ottawa, Washington, and Palm Springs, December 22 and 23, 1987, and January 2, 1988. Entered into force January 1, 1989.

Chapter Six: Technical Standards
- Article 601 Scope
- Article 602 Affirmation of GATT Agreement
- Article 603 No Disguised Barriers to Trade
- Article 604 Compatibility
- Article 605 Accreditation
- Article 606 Mutual Acceptance of Test Data
- Article 607 Information Exchange
- Article 608 Further Implementation
- Article 609 Definitions

Chapter Seven: Agriculture
- Article 701 Agricultural Subsidies
- Article 702 Special Provisions for Fresh Fruits and Vegetables
- Article 703 Market Access for Agriculture
- Article 704 Market Access for Meat
- Article 705 Market Access for Grain and Grain Products
- Article 706 Market Access for Poultry and Eggs
- Article 707 Market Access for Sugar-Containing Products
- Article 708 Technical Regulations and Standards for Agricultural, Food, Beverage, and Certain Related Goods
- Article 709 Consultations
- Article 710 International Obligations
- Article 711 Definitions
- Annexes

Chapter Eight: Wine and Distilled Spirits
- Article 801 Coverage
- Article 802 Listing
- Article 803 Pricing
- Article 804 Distribution
- Article 805 Blending Requirement
- Article 806 Distinctive Products
- Article 807 International Obligation
- Article 808 Definitions

Chapter Nine: Energy
- Article 901 Scope
- Article 902 Import and Export Restrictions
- Article 903 Export Taxes
- Article 904 Other Export Measures
- Article 905 Regulatory and Other Measures
- Article 906 Government Incentives for Energy Resource Development
- Article 907 National Security Measures
- Article 908 International Obligations
- Article 909 Definitions
- Annexes

Chapter Ten: Trade in Automotive Goods
- Article 1001 Existing Arrangement
- Article 1002 Waiver of Customs Duties
- Article 1003 Import Restrictions
- Article 1004 Select Panel

4. International Dispute Resolution

   Article 1005 Relationship to Other Chapters
   Article 1006 Definitions
   Annex
  Chapter Eleven: Emergency Action
   Article 1101 Bilateral Actions
   Article 1102 Global Actions
   Article 1103 Arbitration
   Article 1104 Definitions
  Chapter Twelve: Exceptions for Trade in Goods
   Article 1201 GATT Exceptions
   Article 1202 Protocol of Provisional Application
   Article 1203 Miscellaneous Exceptions
   Article 1204 Beer and Malt Containing Beverages
   Article 1205 GATT Rights

Part Three: Government Procurement
  Chapter Thirteen: Government Procurement
   Article 1301 Objective
   Article 1302 Reaffirmation of Existing Obligations
   Article 1303 Scope
   Article 1304 Coverage
   Article 1305 Expanded Procedural Obligations
   Article 1306 Monitoring and Exchange of Information
   Article 1307 Further Negotiations
   Article 1308 National Security
   Article 1309 Definitions
   Annexes

Part Four: Services, Investment and Temporary Entry
  Chapter Fourteen: Services
   Article 1401 Scope and Coverage
   Article 1402 Rights and Obligations
   Article 1403 Licensing and Certification
   Article 1404 Sectoral Annexes
   Article 1405 Future Implementation
   Article 1406 Denial of Benefits
   Article 1407 Definition
   Annexes
  Chapter Fifteen: Temporary Entry for Business Persons
   Article 1501 General Principle
   Article 1502 Obligations
   Article 1503 Consultation
   Article 1504 Dispute Settlement
   Article 1505 Relationship to Other Chapters
   Article 1506 Definitions
   Annex
  Chapter Sixteen: Investment
   Article 1601 Scope and Coverage
   Article 1602 National Treatment
   Article 1603 Performance Requirements
   Article 1604 Monitoring
   Article 1605 Expropriation
   Article 1606 Transfers
   Article 1607 Existing Legislation

Article 1608 Disputes
Article 1609 Taxation
Article 1610 International Agreements
Article 1611 Definitions
Annex

Part Five: Financial Services
    Chapter Seventeen: Financial Services
        Article 1701 Scope and Coverage
        Article 1702 Commitments of the United States
        Article 1703 Commitments of Canada
        Article 1704 Notification and Consultation
        Article 1705 General Provisions
        Article 1706 Definitions

Part Six: Institutional Provisions
    Chapter Eighteen: Institutional Provisions
        Article 1801 Application
        Article 1802 The Commission
        Article 1803 Notification
        Article 1804 Consultation
        Article 1805 Initiation of Procedures
        Article 1806 Arbitration
        Article 1807 Panel Procedures
        Article 1808 Referrals of Matters from Judicial or Administrative Proceedings
    Chapter Nineteen: Binational Dispute Settlement in Antidumping and Countervailing Duty Cases
        Article 1901 General Provisions
        Article 1902 Retention of Domestic Antidumping Law and Countervailing Duty Law
        Article 1903 Review of Statutory Amendments
        Article 1904 Review of Final Antidumping and Countervailing Duty Determinations
        Article 1905 Prospective Application
        Article 1906 Duration
        Article 1907 Working Group
        Article 1908 Consultations
        Article 1909 Establishment of Secretariat
        Article 1910 Code of Conduct
        Article 1911 Definitions
        Annexes

Part Seven: Other Provisions
    Chapter Twenty: Other Provisions
        Article 2001 Tax Convention
        Article 2002 Balance of Payments
        Article 2003 National Security
        Article 2004 Intellectual Property
        Article 2005 Cultural Industries
        Article 2006 Retransmission Rights
        Article 2007 Print-in-Canada Requirement
        Article 2008 Plywood Standards

                Article 2009 Softwood Lumber
                Article 2010 Monopolies
                Article 2011 Nullification and Impairment
                Article 2012 Definitions
Part Eight: Final Provisions
    Chapter Twenty-One: Final Provisions
                Article 2101 Statistical Requirements
                Article 2102 Publication of Measures
                Article 2103 Annexes
                Article 2104 Amendments
                Article 2105 Entry into Force
                Article 2106 Duration and Termination
    Letters
        Standstill
        Implementation of Harmonized System
        Plywood Standards

PREAMBLE

The Government of Canada and the Government of the United States of America, resolved:

> To strengthen the unique and enduring friendship between their two nations;
> To promote productivity, full employment, and a steady improvement of living standards in their respective countries;
> To create an expanded and secure market for the goods and services produced in their territories;
> To adopt clear and mutually advantageous rules governing their trade;
> To ensure a predictable commercial environment for business planning and investment;
> To strengthen the competitiveness of the United States and Canadian firms in global markets;
> To reduce government-created trade distortions while preserving the Parties' flexibility to safeguard the public welfare;
> To build on their mutual rights and obligations under the *General Agreement on Tariffs and Trade* and other multilateral and bilateral instruments of cooperation; and
> To contribute to the harmonious development and expansion of world trade and to provide a catalyst to broader international cooperation;

Have agreed as follows:

Part One. Objectives and Scope

CHAPTER ONE. OBJECTIVES AND SCOPE

Article 101. Establishment of the Free-Trade Area

The Government of Canada and the Government of the United States of America, consistent with Article XXIV of the *General Agreement on Tariffs and Trade,* hereby establish a free-trade area.

Article 102. Objectives

The objectives of this Agreement, as elaborated more specifically in its provisions, are to:

a) eliminate barriers to trade in goods and services between the territories of the Parties;

b) facilitate conditions of fair competition within the free-trade area;

c) liberalize significantly conditions for investment within this free-trade area;

d) establish effective procedures for the joint administration of this Agreement and the resolution of disputes; and

e) lay the foundation for further bilateral and multilateral cooperation to expand and enhance the benefits of this Agreement.

Article 103. Extent of Obligations

The Parties to this Agreement shall ensure that all necessary measures are taken in order to give effect to its provisions, including their observance, except as otherwise provided in this Agreement, by state, provincial and local governments.

Article 104. Affirmation and Precedence

1. The Parties affirm their existing rights and obligations with respect to each other, as they exist at the time of entry into force of this Agreement, under bilateral and multilateral agreements to which both are party.

2. In the event of any inconsistency between the provisions of this Agreement and such other agreements, the provisions of this Agreement shall prevail to the extent of the inconsistency, except as otherwise provided in this Agreement.

Article 105. National Treatment

Each Party shall, to the extent provided in this Agreement, accord national treatment with respect to investment and to trade in goods and services. . . .

Part Six. Institutional Provisions

CHAPTER EIGHTEEN. INSTITUTIONAL PROVISIONS

Article 1801. Application

1. Except for the matters covered in Chapter Seventeen (Financial Services) and Chapter Nineteen (Binational Dispute Settlement in Antidumping and Countervailing Duty Cases), the provisions of this Part shall apply with respect to the avoidance or settlement of all disputes regarding the interpretation or application of this Agreement or whenever a Party considers that an actual or proposed measure of the other Party is or would be inconsistent with the obligations of this Agreement or cause nullification or impairment in the sense of Article 2011, unless the Parties agree to use another procedure in any particular case.

2. Disputes arising under both this Agreement and the *General Agreement on Tariffs and Trade,* and agreements negotiated thereunder (GATT), may be settled in either forum, according to the rules of that forum, at the discretion of the complaining Party.

3. Once the dispute settlement provisions of this Agreement or the GATT have been initiated pursuant to Article 1805 or the GATT with respect to any matter, the procedure initiated shall be used to the exclusion of any other.

Article 1802. The Commission

1. The Parties hereby establish the Canada-United States Trade Commission (the Commission) to supervise the implementation of this Agreement, to resolve disputes that may arise over its interpretation and application, to oversee its further elaboration, and to consider any other matter that may affect its operation.

2. The Commission shall be composed of representatives of both Parties. The principal representative of each Party shall be the cabinet-level officer or Minister primarily responsible for international trade, or their designees.

3. The Commission shall convene at least once a year in regular session to review the functioning of this Agreement. Regular sessions of the Commission shall be held alternately in the two countries.

4. The Commission may establish, and delegate responsibilities to, ad hoc or standing committees or working groups and seek the advice of non-governmental individuals or groups.

5. The Commission shall establish its rules and procedures. All decisions of the Commission shall be taken by consensus.

Article 1803. Notification

1. Each Party shall provide written notice to the other Party of any proposed or actual measure that it considers might materially affect the operation of this Agreement. The notice shall include, whenever appropriate, a description of the reasons for the proposed or actual measure.

2. The written notice shall be given as far in advance as possible of the implementation of the measure. If prior notice is not possible, the Party implementing the measure shall provide written notice to the other Party as soon as possible after implementation.

3. Upon request of the other Party, a Party shall promptly provide information and respond to questions pertaining to any actual or proposed measure, whether or not previously notified.

4. The provision of written notice shall be without prejudice as to whether the measure is consistent with this Agreement.

Article 1804. Consultations

1. Either Party may request consultations regarding any actual or proposed measure or any other matter that it considers affects the operation of this Agreement, whether or not the matter has been notified in accordance with Article 1803.

2. The Parties shall make every attempt to arrive at a mutually satisfactory resolution of any matter through consultations under this Article or other consultative provisions in this Agreement.

3. Each Party shall treat any confidential or proprietary information exchanged in the course of consultations on the same basis as the Party providing the information.

Article 1805. Initiation of Procedures

1. If the Parties fail to resolve a matter through consultations within 30 days of a request for consultations under Article 1804, either Party may request in writing a meeting of the Commission. The request shall state the matter complained of, and shall indicate what provisions of this Agreement are considered relevant. Unless otherwise agreed, the Commission shall convene within 10 days and shall endeavour to resolve the dispute promptly.

2. The Commission may call on such technical advisors as it deems necessary, or on the assistance of a mediator acceptable to both Parties, in an effort to reach a mutually satisfactory resolution of the dispute.

Article 1806. Arbitration

1. If a dispute has been referred to the Commission under Article 1805 and has not been resolved within a period of 30 days after such referral, the Commission:

    a) shall refer a dispute regarding actions taken pursuant to Chapter Eleven (Emergency Action); and

    b) may refer any other dispute,

to binding arbitration on such terms as the Commission may adopt.

2. Unless the Commission directs otherwise, an arbitration panel shall be established and perform its functions in a manner consistent with the provisions of paragraphs 1, 3 and 4 of Article 1807.

3. If a Party fails to implement in a timely fashion the findings of a binding arbitration panel and the Parties are unable to agree on appropriate compensation or remedial action, then the other Party shall have the right

to suspend the application of equivalent benefits of this Agreement to the non-complying Party.

Article 1807. Panel Procedures

1. The Commission shall develop and maintain a roster of individuals who are willing and able to serve as panelists. Wherever possible, panelists shall be chosen from this roster. In all cases, panelists shall be chosen strictly on the basis of objectivity, reliability and sound judgment and, where appropriate, have expertise in the particular matter under consideration. Panelists shall not be affiliated with or take instructions from either Party.

2. If a dispute has been referred to the Commission under Article 1805 and has not been resolved within a period of 30 days after such referral, or within such other period as the Commission has agreed upon, or has not been referred to arbitration pursuant to Article 1806, the Commission, upon request of either Party, shall establish a panel of experts to consider the matter. A panel shall be deemed to be established from the date of the request of a Party.

3. The panel shall be composed of five members, at least two of whom shall be citizens of Canada and at least two of whom shall be citizens of the United States. Within 15 days of establishment of the panel, each Party, in consultation with the other Party, shall choose two members of the panel and the Commission shall endeavour to agree on the fifth who shall chair the panel. If a Party fails to appoint its panelists within 15 days, such panelists shall be selected by lot from among its citizens on the roster described in paragraph 1. If the Commission is unable to agree on the fifth panelist within such period, then, at the request of either Party, the four appointed panelists shall decide on the fifth panelist within 30 days of establishment of the panel. If no agreement is possible, the fifth panelist shall be selected by lot from the roster described in paragraph 1.

4. The panel shall establish its rules of procedure, unless the Commission has agreed otherwise. The procedures shall assure a right to at least one hearing before the panel as well as the opportunity to provide written submissions and rebuttal arguments. The proceedings of the panel shall be confidential. Unless otherwise agreed by the Parties, the panel shall base its decision on the arguments and submissions of the Parties.

5. Unless the Parties otherwise agree, the panel shall, within three months after its chairman is appointed, present to the Parties an initial report containing findings of fact, its determination as to whether the measure at issue is or would be inconsistent with the obligations of this Agreement or cause nullification and impairment in the sense of Article 2011, and its recommendations, if any, for resolution of the dispute. Where feasible, the panel shall afford the Parties opportunity to comment on its preliminary findings of fact prior to completion of its report. If requested by either Party at the time of establishment of the panel, the panel shall also present findings as to the degree of adverse trade effect on the other Party of any measure found not to conform with the obligations of the Agreement. Panelists may furnish separate opinions on matters not unanimously agreed.

6. Within 14 days of issuance of the initial report of the panel, a Party

disagreeing in whole or in part shall present a written statement of its objections and the reasons for those objections to the Commission and the panel. In such an event, the panel on its own motion or at the request of the Commission or either Party may request the views of both Parties, reconsider its report, make any further examination that it deems appropriate and issue a final report, together with any separate opinions, within 30 days of issuance of the initial report.

7. Unless the Commission agrees otherwise, the final report of the panel shall be published along with any separate opinions, and any written views that either Party desires to be published.

8. Upon receipt of the final report of the panel, the Commission shall agree on the resolution of the dispute, which normally shall conform with the recommendation of the panel. Whenever possible, the resolution shall be non-implementation or removal of a measure not conforming with this Agreement or causing nullification or impairment in the sense of Article 2011 or, failing such a resolution, compensation.

9. If the Commission has not reached agreement on a mutually satisfactory resolution under paragraph 8 within 30 days of receiving the final report of the panel (or such other date as the Commission may decide), and a Party considers that its fundamental rights (under this Agreement) or benefits (anticipated under this Agreement) are or would be impaired by the implementation or maintenance of the measure at issue, the Party shall be free to suspend the application to the other Party of benefits of equivalent effect until such time as the Parties have reached agreement on a resolution of the dispute.

Article 1808. Referrals of Matters from Judicial or Administrative Proceedings

1. In the event an issue of interpretation of this Agreement arises in any domestic judicial or administrative proceeding of a Party which either Party considers would merit its intervention, or if a court or administrative body solicits the views of a Party, the Parties shall endeavour to agree on the interpretation of the applicable provisions of this Agreement.

2. The Party in whose territory the court or administrative body is located shall submit any agreed interpretation to the court or administrative body in accordance with the rules of that forum. If the Parties are unable to reach agreement on the interpretation of the provision of this Agreement at issue, either Party may submit its own views to the court or administrative body in accordance with the rules of that forum.

CHAPTER NINETEEN. BINATIONAL PANEL DISPUTE SETTLEMENT IN ANTIDUMPING AND COUNTERVAILING DUTY CASES

Article 1901. General Provisions

1. The provisions of Article 1904 shall apply only with respect to goods that the competent investigating authority of the importing Party, applying the importing Party's antidumping or countervailing duty law to the facts of a specific case, determines are goods of the other Party.

2. For the purposes of Articles 1903 and 1904, panels shall be established in accordance with the provisions of Annex 1901.2.

Article 1902. Retention of Domestic Antidumping Law and Countervailing Duty Law

1. Each Party reserves the right to apply its antidumping law and countervailing duty law to goods imported from the territory of the other Party. Antidumping law and countervailing duty law include, as appropriate for each Party, relevant statutes, legislative history, regulations, administrative practice, and judicial precedents.

2. Each Party reserves the right to change or modify its antidumping law or countervailing duty law, provided that in the case of an amendment to a Party's antidumping or countervailing duty statute:

   a) such amendment shall apply to goods from the other Party only if such application is specified in the amending statute;

   b) the amending Party notifies the other Party in writing of the amending statute as far in advance as possible of the date of enactment of such statute;

   c) following notification, the amending Party, upon request of the other Party, consults with the other Party prior to the enactment of the amending statute; and

   d) such amendment, as applicable to the other Party, is not inconsistent with

   i) the *General Agreement on Tariffs and Trade* (GATT), *the Agreement on Implementation of Article VI of the General Agreement on Tariffs and Trade* (the Antidumping Code), or the *Agreement on the Interpretation and Application of Articles VI, XVI and XXIII of the General Agreement on Tariffs and Trade* (the Subsidies Code), or

   ii) the object and purpose of this Agreement and this Chapter, which is to establish fair and predictable conditions for the progressive liberalization of trade between the two countries while maintaining effective disciplines on unfair trade practices, such object and purpose to be ascertained from the provisions of this Agreement, its preamble and objectives, and the practices of the Parties.

Article 1903. Review of Statutory Amendments

1. A Party may request in writing that an amendment to the other Party's antidumping statute or countervailing duty statute be referred to a panel for a declaratory opinion as to whether:

   a) the amendment does not conform to the provisions of subparagraph (d)(i) or (d)(ii) of paragraph 2 of Article 1902; or

   b) such amendment has the function and effect of overturning a prior decision of a panel made pursuant to Article 1904 and does not conform to the provisions of subparagraph (d)(i) or (d)(ii) of paragraph 2 of Article 1902.

Such declaratory opinion shall have force or effect only as provided in this Article.

2. The panel shall conduct its review in accordance with the procedures of Annex 1903.2.

3. In the event that the panel recommends modifications to the amending statute to remedy a non-conformity that it has identified in its opinion:

   a) the Parties shall immediately begin consultations and shall seek to achieve a mutually satisfactory solution to the matter within 90 days of the issuance of the panel's final declaratory opinion. Such solution may include seeking remedial legislation with respect to the statute of the amending Party;

   b) if remedial legislation is not enacted within nine months from the end of the 90-day consultation period referred to in subparagraph (a) and no other agreement has been reached, the Party that requested the panel may

   i) take comparable legislative or equivalent executive action, or

   ii) terminate the Agreement upon 60-day written notice to the other Party.

Article 1904. Review of Final Antidumping and Countervailing Duty Determinations

1. As provided in this Article, the Parties shall replace judicial review of final antidumping and countervailing duty determinations with binational panel review.

2. Either Party may request that a panel review, based upon the administrative record, a final antidumping or countervailing duty determination of a competent investigating authority of either Party to determine whether such determination was in accordance with the antidumping or countervailing duty law of the importing Party. For this purpose, the antidumping or countervailing duty law consists of the relevant statutes, legislative history, regulations, administrative practice, and judicial precedents to the extent that a court of the importing Party would rely on such materials in reviewing a final determination of the competent investigating authority. Solely for purposes of the panel review provided for in this Article, the antidumping and countervailing duty statutes of the Parties, as those statutes may be amended from time to time, are incorporated into this Agreement.

3. The panel shall apply the standard of review described in Article 1911 and the general legal principles that a court of the importing Party otherwise would apply to a review of a determination of the competent investigating authority.

4. A request for a panel shall be made in writing to the other Party within 30 days following the date of publication of the final determination in question in the *Federal Register* or the *Canada Gazette*. In the case of final determinations that are not published in the *Federal Register* or the *Canada Gazette,* the importing Party shall immediately notify the other Party of such final determination where it involves a good from the other Party, and the other Party may request a panel within 30 days of receipt of such notice. Where the competent investigating authority of the importing Party has imposed provisional measures in an investigation, the other Party may provide notice of its intention to request a panel under this Article, and the Parties shall begin to establish a panel at that time. Failure to request a panel within the time specified in this paragraph shall preclude review by a panel.

5. Either Party on its own initiative may request review of a final de-

termination by a panel and shall, upon request of a person who would otherwise be entitled under the law of the importing Party to commence domestic procedures for judicial review of a final determination, request such review.

6. The panel shall conduct its review in accordance with the procedures established by the Parties pursuant to paragraph 14. Where both Parties request a panel to review a final determination, a single panel shall review that determination.

7. The competent investigating authority that issued the final determination in question shall have the right to appear and be represented by counsel before the panel. Each Party shall provide that other persons who, pursuant to the law of the importing Party, otherwise would have had standing to appear and be represented in a domestic judicial review proceeding concerning the determination of the competent investigating authority, shall have the right to appear and be represented by counsel before the panel.

8. The panel may uphold a final determination, or remand it for action not inconsistent with the panel's decision. Where the panel remands a final determination, the panel shall establish as brief a time as is reasonable for compliance with the remand, taking into account the complexity of the facts and legal issues involved and the nature of the panel's decision. In no event shall the time permitted for compliance with a remand exceed an amount of time equal to the maximum amount of time (counted from the date of the filing of a petition, complaint or application) permitted by statute for the competent investigating authority in question to make a final determination in an investigation. If review of the action taken by the competent investigating authority on remand is needed, such review shall be before the same panel, which shall issue a final decision within 90 days of the date on which such remand action is submitted to it.

9. The decision of a panel under this Article shall be binding on the Parties with respect to the particular matter between the Parties that is before the panel.

10. This Agreement shall not affect:

   a) the judicial review procedures of either Party, or

   b) cases appealed under those procedures,

with respect to determinations other than final determinations.

11. A final determination shall not be reviewed under any judicial review procedures of the importing Party if either Party requests a panel with respect to that determination within the time limits set forth in this Article. Neither Party shall provide in its domestic legislation for an appeal from a panel decision to its domestic courts.

12. The provisions of this Article shall not apply where:

   a) neither Party seeks panel review of a final determination;

   b) a revised final determination is issued as a direct result of judicial review of the original final determination by a court of the importing Party in cases where neither Party sought panel review of that original final determination; or

   c) a final determination is issued as a direct result of judicial review that was commenced in a court of the importing Party before the entry into force of this Agreement.

13. Where, within a reasonable time after the panel decision is issued, a Party alleges that:

a) i) a member of the panel was guilty of gross misconduct, bias, or a serious conflict of interest, or otherwise materially violated the rules of conduct,

ii) the panel seriously departed from a fundamental rule of procedure, or

iii) the panel manifestly exceeded its powers, authority or jurisdiction set forth in this Article, and

b) any of the actions set out in subparagraph (a) has materially affected the panel's decision and threatens the integrity of the binational panel review process,

that Party may avail itself of the extraordinary challenge procedure set out in Annex 1904.13.

14. To implement the provisions of this Article, the Parties shall adopt rules of procedure by January 1, 1989. Such rules shall be based, where appropriate, upon judicial rules of appellate procedure, and shall include rules concerning the content and service of requests for panels, a requirement that the competent investigating authority transmit to the panel the administrative record of the proceeding, the protection of business proprietary and other privileged information (including sanctions against persons participating before panels for improper release of such information), participation by private persons, limits on panel review to errors alleged by the Parties or private persons, filing and service, computation and extensions of time, the form and content of briefs and other papers, pre- and post-hearing conferences, oral argument, requests for rehearing, and voluntary terminations of panel reviews. The rules shall be designed to result in final decisions within 315 days of the date on which a request for a panel is made, and shall allow:

a) 30 days for the filing of the complaint;

b) 30 days for designation or certification of the administrative record and its filing with the panel;

c) 60 days for the complainant to file its brief;

d) 60 days for the respondent to file its brief;

e) 15 days for the filing of reply briefs;

f) 15 to 30 days for the panel to convene and hear oral argument; and

g) 90 days for the panel to issue its written decision.

15. The Parties shall, in order to achieve the objectives of this Article, amend their statutes and regulations, as necessary, with respect to antidumping or countervailing duty proceedings involving goods of the other Party. In particular, without limiting the generality of the foregoing: . . .

Article 1905. *Prospective Application*

The provisions of this Chapter shall apply only prospectively to:

a) final determinations of a competent investigating authority made after the entry into force of this Agreement; and

b) with respect to declaratory opinions under Article 1903, amendments to antidumping or countervailing duty statutes enacted after the entry into force of this Agreement.

Article 1906. Duration

The provisions of this Chapter shall be in effect for five years pending the development of a substitute system of rules in both countries for antidumping and countervailing duties as applied to their bilateral trade. If no such system of rules is agreed and implemented at the end of five years, the provisions of this Chapter shall be extended for a further two years. Failure to agree to implement a new regime at the end of the two-year extension shall allow either Party to terminate the Agreement on six-month notice.

Article 1907. Working Group

1. The Parties shall establish a Working Group that shall:
    a) seek to develop more effective rules and disciplines concerning the use of government subsidies;
    b) seek to develop a substitute system of rules for dealing with unfair pricing and government subsidization; and
    c) consider any problems that may arise with respect to the implementation of this Chapter and recommend solutions, where appropriate.
2. The Working Group shall report to the Parties as soon as possible. The Parties shall use their best efforts to develop and implement the substitute system of rules within the time limits established in Article 1906.

Article 1908. Consultations

The Parties shall each designate one or more officials to be responsible for ensuring that consultations take place, where required, so that the provisions of this Chapter are carried out expeditiously.

Article 1909. Establishment of Secretariat

1. The Parties shall establish permanent Secretariat offices to facilitate the operation of this Chapter and the work of panels or committees that may be convened pursuant to this Chapter.
2. The permanent offices of the Secretariat shall be in Washington, District of Columbia, and in the National Capital Region of Canada.
3. Each Party shall be responsible for the operating cost of its Secretariat office.
4. The United States of America shall appoint an individual to serve as secretary of the United States section of the Secretariat who shall be responsible for all administrative matters involving the Secretariat in the United States of America.
5. Canada shall appoint an individual to serve as secretary of the Canadian section of the Secretariat who shall be responsible for all administrative matters involving the Secretariat in Canada.
6. The secretaries of the United States and Canadian sections of the Secretariat shall manage their respective Secretariat offices.
7. The Secretariat may provide support for the Commission established pursuant to Article 1802 if so directed by the Commission.
8. The secretaries shall act jointly to service all meetings of panels or committees established pursuant to this Chapter. The secretary of the coun-

try in which a panel or committee proceeding is held shall prepare a record thereof and each secretary shall preserve an authentic copy of the same in the permanent offices.

9. Each secretary shall receive and file all requests, briefs and other papers properly presented to a panel or committee in any proceeding before it that is instituted pursuant to this Chapter and shall number in numerical order all requests for a panel or committee. The number given to a request shall be the primary file number for briefs and other papers relating to such request.

10. Each secretary shall forward to the other copies of all official letters, documents, records or other papers received or filed with the Secretariat office pertaining to any proceeding before a panel or committee, so that there shall be on file in each office of the Secretariat either the original or a copy of all official letters and other papers relating to the proceeding.

Article 1910. Code of Conduct

The Parties shall, by the date of the entry into force of this Agreement, exchange letters establishing a code of conduct for panelists and members of committees established pursuant to Articles 1903 and 1904.

Article 1911. Definitions

For purposes of this Chapter,

administrative record means, unless otherwise agreed by the Parties and the other persons appearing before a panel:

a) all documentary or other information presented to or obtained by the competent investigating authority in the course of the administrative proceeding, including any governmental memoranda pertaining to the case, and including any record of ex parte meetings as may be required to be kept;

b) a copy of the final determination of the competent investigating authority, including reasons for the determination;

c) all transcripts or records of conferences or hearings before the competent investigating authority; and

d) all notices published in the *Canada Gazette* or the *Federal Register* in connection with the administrative proceeding.

antidumping statute as referred to in Articles 1902 and 1903 means:

a) in the case of Canada, the relevant provisions of the *Special Import Measures Act,* as amended, and any successor statutes;

b) in the case of the United States of America, the relevant provisions of Title VII of the *Tariff Act of 1930,* as amended, and any successor statutes; and

c) the provisions of any other statute that provides for judicial review of final determinations under subparagraph (a) or (b) or indicates the standard of review to be applied.

competent investigating authority means:

a) in the case of Canada,

i) the Canadian Import Tribunal, or its successor, or

ii) the Deputy Minister of National Revenue for Customs and

Excise as defined in the *Special Import Measures Act,* or his successor; and

 b) in the case of the United States of America,

  i) the International Trade Administration of the United States Department of Commerce, or its successor, or

  ii) the United States International Trade Commission, or its successor.

countervailing duty statute as referred to in Articles 1902 and 1903 means:

 a) in the case of Canada, the relevant provisions of the *Special Import Measures Act,* as amended, and any successor statutes;

 b) in the case of the United States of America, section 303 and the relevant provisions of Title VII of the *Tariff Act of 1930,* as amended, and any successor statutes; and

 c) the provisions of any other statute that provides for judicial review of final determinations under subparagraph (a) or (b) or indicates the standard of review to be applied.

final determination means:

 a) in the case of Canada,

  i) an order or finding of the Canadian Import Tribunal under subsection 43(1) of the *Special Import Measures Act,*

  ii) an order by the Canadian Import Tribunal under subsection 76(4) of the *Special Import Measures Act,* continuing an order or finding made under subsection 43(1) of the Act with or without amendment,

  iii) a determination by the Deputy Minister of National Revenue for Customs and Excise pursuant to section 41 of the *Special Import Measures Act,*

  iv) a re-determination by the Deputy Minister pursuant to section 59 of the *Special Import Measures Act,*

  v) a decision by the Canadian Import Tribunal pursuant to subsection 76(3) of the *Special Import Measures Act* not to initiate a review,

  vi) a reconsideration by the Canadian Import Tribunal pursuant to subsection 91(3) of the *Special Import Measures Act,* and

  vii) a review by the Deputy Minister of an undertaking pursuant to section 53(1) of the *Special Import Measures Act;* and

 b) in the case of the United States of America,

  i) a final affirmative determination by the International Trade Administration of the United States Department of Commerce or by the United States International Trade Commission under section 705 or 735 of the *Tariff Act of 1930,* as amended, including any negative part of such a determination,

  ii) a final negative determination by the International Trade Administration of the United States Department of Commerce or by the United States International Trade Commission under section 705 or 735 of the *Tariff Act of 1930,* as amended, including any affirmative part of such a determination,

  iii) a final determination, other than a determination in (iv), under section 751 of the *Tariff Act of 1930,* as amended,

iv) a determination by the United States International Trade Commission under section 751(b) of the *Tariff Act of 1930,* as amended, not to review a determination based upon changed circumstances, and

v) a determination by the International Trade Administration of the United States Department of Commerce as to whether a particular type of merchandise is within the class or kind of merchandise described in an existing finding of dumping or antidumping or countervailing duty order.

general legal principles includes principles such as standing, due process, rules of statutory construction, mootness, and exhaustion of administrative remedies.

remand means a referral back for a determination not inconsistent with the panel or committee decision.

standard of review means the following standards, as may be amended from time to time by a Party:

a) in the case of Canada, the grounds set forth in section 28(1) of the *Federal Court Act* with respect to all final determinations; and

b) in the case of the United States of America,

i) the standard set forth in section 516A(b)(1)(b) of the *Tariff Act of 1930,* as amended, with the exception of a determination referred to in (ii), and

ii) the standard set forth in section 516A(b)(1)(A) of the *Tariff Act of 1930,* as amended, with respect to a determination by the United States International Trade Commission not to initiate a review pursuant to section 751(b) of the *Tariff Act of 1930,* as amended.

Annex 1901.2. Establishment of Binational Panels

1. Prior to the entry into force of the Agreement, the Parties shall develop a roster of individuals to serve as panelists in disputes under this Chapter. The Parties shall consult in developing the roster, which shall include 50 candidates. Each Party shall select 25 candidates, and all candidates shall be citizens of Canada or the United States of America. Candidates shall be of good character, high standing and repute, and shall be chosen strictly on the basis of objectivity, reliability, sound judgment, and general familiarity with international trade law. Candidates shall not be affiliated with either Party, and in no event shall a candidate take instructions from either Party. Judges shall not be considered to be affiliated with either Party. The Parties shall maintain the roster, and may amend it, when necessary, after consultations.

2. A majority of the panelists on each panel shall be lawyers in good standing. Within 30 days of a request for a panel, each Party shall appoint two panelists, in consultation with the other Party. The Parties normally shall appoint panelists from the roster. If a panelist is not selected from the roster, the panelist shall be chosen in accordance with and be subject to the criteria of paragraph 1. Each Party shall have the right to exercise four peremptory challenges, to be exercised simultaneously and in confidence, disqualifying from appointment to the panel up to four candidates proposed

by the other Party. Peremptory challenges and the selection of alternative panelists shall occur within 45 days of the request for the panel. If a Party fails to appoint its members to a panel within 30 days or if a panelist is struck and no alternative panelist is selected within 45 days, such panelist shall be selected by lot on the 31st or 46th day, as the case may be, from that Party's candidates on the roster.

3. Within 55 days of the request for a panel, the Parties shall agree on the selection of a fifth panelist. If the Parties are unable to agree, the four appointed panelists shall select, by agreement, from the roster the fifth panelist within 60 days of the request for a panel. If there is no agreement among the four appointed panelists, the fifth panelist shall be selected by lot on the 61st day from the roster, excluding candidates eliminated by peremptory challenges.

4. Upon appointment of the fifth panelist, the panelists shall promptly appoint a chairman from among the lawyers on the panel by majority vote of the panelists. If there is no majority vote, the chairman shall be appointed by lot from among the lawyers on the panel.

5. Decisions of the panel shall be by majority vote and be based upon the votes of all members of the panel. The panel shall issue a written decision with reasons, together with any dissenting or concurring opinions of panelists.

6. Panelists shall be subject to the code of conduct established pursuant to Article 1910. If a Party believes that a panelist is in violation of the code of conduct, the Parties shall consult and if the Parties agree, the panelist shall be removed and a new panelist shall be selected in accordance with the procedures of this Annex.

7. When a panel is convened pursuant to Article 1904, each panelist shall be required to sign:

   a) a protective order for information supplied by the United States of America or its persons covering business proprietary and other privileged information; and

   b) an undertaking for information supplied by Canada or its persons covering confidential, personal, business proprietary and other privileged information.

8. The United States of America shall establish appropriate sanctions for violations of protective orders issued by it and of undertakings given to Canada. Canada shall establish appropriate sanctions for violations of undertakings given to it and protective orders issued by the United States of America. Each Party shall enforce such sanctions with respect to any person within its jurisdiction. Failure by a panelist to sign a protective order or undertaking shall result in disqualification of the panelist.

9. If a panelist becomes unable to fulfill panel duties or is disqualified, proceedings of the panel shall be suspended pending the selection of a substitute panelist in accordance with the procedures of this Annex.

10. Subject to the code of conduct established by the Parties, and provided that it does not interfere with the performance of the duties of such panelist, a panelist may engage in other business during the term of the panel.

11. While acting as a panelist, a panelist may not appear as counsel before another panel.

12. With the exception of violations of protective orders or undertakings signed pursuant to paragraph 7, panelists shall be immune from suit and legal process relating to acts performed by them in their official capacity.

13. The remuneration of panelists, their travel and lodging expenses, and all general expenses of the panel shall be borne equally by the Parties. Each panelist shall keep a record and render a final account of his time and expenses, and the panel shall keep a record and render a final account of all general expenses. The Commission shall establish amounts of remuneration and expenses that will be paid to the panelists.

Annex 1903.2. Panel Procedures Under Article 1903

1. The panel shall establish its own rules of procedure unless the Parties otherwise agree prior to the establishment of that panel. The procedures shall ensure a right to at least one hearing before the panel, as well as the opportunity to provide written submissions and rebuttal arguments. The proceedings of the panel shall be confidential, unless the Parties otherwise agree. The panel shall base its decisions solely upon the arguments and submissions of the Parties.

2. Unless the Parties otherwise agree, the panel shall, within 90 days after its chairman is appointed, present to the Parties an initial written declaratory opinion containing findings of fact and its determination pursuant to Article 1903.

3. If the findings of the panel are affirmative, the panel may include in its report its recommendations as to the means by which the amending statute could be brought into conformity with the provisions of subparagraph 2(d) of Article 1902. In determining what, if any, recommendations are appropriate, the panel shall consider the extent to which the amending statute affects interests under this Agreement. Individual panelists may provide separate opinions on matters not unanimously agreed. The initial opinion of the panel shall become the final declaratory opinion, unless a Party requests a reconsideration of the initial opinion pursuant to paragraph 4.

4. Within 14 days of the issuance of the initial declaratory opinion, a Party disagreeing in whole or in part with the opinion may present a written statement of its objections and the reasons for those objections to the panel. In such event, the panel shall request the views of both Parties and shall reconsider its initial opinion. The panel shall conduct any further examination that it deems appropriate, and shall issue a final written opinion, together with dissenting or concurring views of individual panelists, within 30 days of the request for reconsideration.

5. Unless the Parties otherwise agree, the final declaratory opinion of the panel shall be published, along with any separate opinions of individual panelists and any written views that either Party may wish to be published.

6. Unless the Parties otherwise agree, meetings and hearings of the panel shall take place at the office of the amending Party's section of the Secretariat.

Annex 1904.13. Extraordinary Challenge Procedure

1. The Parties shall establish an extraordinary challenge committee, comprised of three members, within fifteen days of a request pursuant to paragraph 13 of Article 1904. The members shall be selected from a ten-person roster comprised of judges or former judges of a federal court of the United States of America or a court of superior jurisdiction of Canada. Each Party shall name five persons to this roster. Each Party shall select one member from this roster and the third shall be selected from the roster by the two members chosen by the Parties or, if necessary, by lot from the roster.

2. The Parties shall establish by January 1, 1989 rules of procedure for committees. The rules shall provide for a decision of a committee typically within 30 days of its establishment.

3. Committee decisions shall be binding on the Parties with respect to the particular matter between the Parties that was before the panel. Upon finding that one of the grounds set out in paragraph 13 of Article 1904 has been established, the committee shall vacate the original panel decision or remand it to the original panel for action not inconsistent with the committee's decision; if the grounds are not established, it shall affirm the original panel decision. If the original decision is vacated, a new panel shall be established pursuant to Annex 1901.2. . . .

Article 2003. National Security

Subject to Articles 907 and 1308, nothing in this Agreement shall be construed:

a) to require any Party to furnish or allow access to any information the disclosure of which it considers contrary to its essential security interests;

b) to prevent any Party from taking any action which it considers necessary for the protection of its essential security interests,

    i) relating to the traffic in arms, ammunition and implements of war and to such traffic in other goods, materials and services as is carried on directly or indirectly for the purpose of supplying a military establishment,

    ii) taken in time of war or other emergency in international relations, or

    iii) relating to the implementation of national policies or international agreements relating to the non-proliferation of nuclear weapons or other nuclear explosive devices; or

c) to prevent any Party from taking action in pursuance of its obligations under the United Nations Charter for the maintenance of international peace and security. . . .

Article 2103. Annexes

The Annexes to this Agreement constitute an integral part of this Agreement.

Article 2104. Amendments

1. The Parties may agree upon any modification of or addition to this Agreement.

2. When so agreed and approved in accordance with the applicable domestic legal procedures of each Party, such modifications or additions shall constitute an integral part of this Agreement.

Article 2105. Entry into Force

This Agreement shall enter into force on January 1, 1989 upon an exchange of diplomatic notes certifying the completion of necessary legal procedures by each Party.

Article 2106. Duration and Termination

This Agreement shall remain in force unless terminated by either Party upon six-month notice to the other Party.

5

States and Other Major International Entities

**TREATY OF ROME (1958), as amended by
THE SINGLE EUROPEAN ACT (SEA) (1987)
(SEA amendments identified by brackets)**
Office for Official Publications of the European Communities (1988)*

Contents

I — Text of the Treaty
Preamble
Part One — Principles
Part Two — Foundations of the Community
  Title I — Free movement of goods
    Chapter 1: The Customs Union
      Section 1: Elimination of customs duties between Member States
      Section 2: Setting up of the common customs tariff
    Chapter 2: Elimination of quantitative restrictions between Member States
  Title II — Agriculture
  Title III — Free movement of persons, services and capital
    Chapter 1: Workers
    Chapter 2: Right of establishment

---

*The Treaty of Rome was signed on March 25, 1957, and entered into force on January 1, 1958. The Single European Act was signed in February 1986 and came into force on July 1, 1987. The Treaty of Rome created the European Economic Community, which is one of the three European Communities or an integral part of the European Community. See Chapter 5, Section 3 of the casebook. As of November 1990, the 12 Member States of the European Economic Community and of the European Community were: Belgium, Denmark, the Federal Republic of Germany, France, Greece, Ireland, Italy, Luxembourg, Netherlands, Portugal, Spain, and the United Kingdom.

Chapter 3: Services
Chapter 4: Capital
Title IV — Transport
Part Three — Policy of the Community
Title I — Common rules
Chapter 1: Rules on competition
Section 1: Rules applying to undertakings
Section 2: Dumping
Section 3: Aids granted by States
Chapter 2: Tax provisions
Chapter 3: Approximation of laws
Title II — Economic policy
Chapter 1: Cooperation in economic and monetary policy (Economic and monetary union)
Chapter 2: Conjunctural policy
Chapter 3: Balance of payments
Chapter 4: Commercial policy
Title III — Social policy
Chapter 1: Social provisions
Chapter 2: The European Social Fund
Title IV — The European Investment Bank
Title V — Economic and social cohesion
Title VI — Research and technological development
Title VII — Environment
Part Four — Association of the Overseas Countries and Territories
Part Five — Institutions of the Community
Title I — Provisions governing the institutions
Chapter 1: The institutions
Section 1: The European Parliament
Section 2: The Council
Section 3: The Commission
Section 4: The Court of Justice
Chapter 2: Provisions common to several institutions
Chapter 3: The Economic and Social Committee
Title II — Financial provisions
Part Six — General and final provisions
Setting up of the institutions
Final provisions
Annexes
Annex I — Lists A to G referred to in Articles 19 and 20 of this Treaty
Annex II — List referred to in Article 38 of this Treaty
Annex III — List of invisible transactions referred to in Article 106 of this Treaty
Annex IV — Overseas Countries and Territories to which the provisions of Part IV of this Treaty apply

II — Protocols
Protocol on the Statute of the European Investment Bank
Protocol on German internal trade and connected problems
Protocol on certain provisions relating to France
Protocol on Italy
Protocol on the Grand Duchy of Luxembourg

Protocol on goods originating in and coming from certain
  countries and enjoying special treatment when imported into a
  Member State
Protocol on the treatment to be applied to products within the
  province of the European Coal and Steel Community in respect
  of Algeria and the Overseas Departments of the French
  Republic

Part One. Principles

Article 1

By this Treaty, the High Contracting Parties establish among themselves a European Economic Community.

Article 2

The Community shall have as its task, by establishing a common market and progressively approximating the economic policies of Member States, to promote throughout the Community a harmonious development of economic activities, a continuous and balanced expansion, an increase in stability, an accelerated raising of the standard of living and closer relations between the States belonging to it.

Article 3

For the purposes set out in Article 2, the activities of the Community shall include, as provided in this Treaty and in accordance with the timetable set out therein

(a) the elimination, as between Member States, of customs duties and of quantitative restrictions on the import and export of goods, and of all other measures having equivalent effect;

(b) the establishment of a common customs tariff and of a common commercial policy towards third countries;

(c) the abolition, as between Member States, of obstacles to freedom of movement for persons, services and capital;

(d) the adoption of a common policy in the sphere of agriculture;

(e) the adoption of a common policy in the sphere of transport;

(f) the institution of a system ensuring that competition in the common market is not distorted;

(g) the application of procedures by which the economic policies of Member States can be coordinated and disequilibria in their balances of payments remedied;

(h) the approximation of the laws of Member States to the extent required for the proper functioning of the common market;

(i) the creation of a European Social Fund in order to improve employment opportunities for workers and to contribute to the raising of their standard of living;

(j) the establishment of a European Investment Bank to facilitate the economic expansion of the Community by opening up fresh resources;

(k) the association of the overseas countries and territories in order to increase trade and to promote jointly economic and social development.

Article 4

1. The tasks entrusted to the Community shall be carried out by the following institutions:

a European Parliament,
a Council,
a Commission,
a Court of Justice.

Each institution shall act within the limits of the powers conferred upon it by this Treaty.
2. The Council and the Commission shall be assisted by an Economic and Social Committee acting in an advisory capacity.
[*3.* The audit shall be carried out by a Court of Auditors acting within the limits of the powers conferred upon it by this Treaty.]

Article 5

Member States shall take all appropriate measures, whether general or particular, to ensure fulfilment of the obligations arising out of this Treaty or resulting from action taken by the institutions of the Community. They shall facilitate the achievement of the Community's tasks.

They shall abstain from any measure which could jeopardize the attainment of the objectives of this Treaty.

Article 6

1. Member States shall, in close cooperation with the institutions of the Community, coordinate their respective economic policies to the extent necessary to attain the objectives of this Treaty.
2. The institutions of the Community shall take care not to prejudice the internal and external financial stability of the Member States.

Article 7

Within the scope of application of this Treaty, and without prejudice to any special provisions contained therein, any discrimination on grounds of nationality shall be prohibited.

[The Council may, on a proposal from the Commission and in cooperation with the European Parliament, adopt, by a qualified majority, rules designed to prohibit such discrimination.]

Article 8

1. The common market shall be progressively established during a transitional period of twelve years. . . .

[*Article 8a*

The Community shall adopt measures with the aim of progressively establishing the internal market over a period expiring on 31 December 1992, in accordance with the provisions of this Article and of Articles 8b, 8c, 28, 57 (2), 59, 70 (1), 84, 99, 100a and 100b and without prejudice to the other provisions of this Treaty.

The internal market shall comprise an area without internal frontiers in which the free movement of goods, persons, services and capital is ensured in accordance with the provisions of this Treaty.]

[*Article 8b*

The Commission shall report to the Council before 31 December 1988 and again before 31 December 1990 on the progress made towards achieving the internal market within the time limit fixed in Article 8a.

The Council, acting by a qualified majority on a proposal from the Commission, shall determine the guidelines and conditions necessary to ensure balanced progress in all the sectors concerned.]

[*Article 8c*

When drawing up its proposals with a view to achieving the objectives set out in Article 8a, the Commission shall take into account the extent of the effort that certain economies showing differences in development will have to sustain during the period of establishment of the internal market and it may propose appropriate provisions.

If these provisions take the form of derogations, they must be of a temporary nature and must cause the least possible disturbance to the functioning of the common market.]

Part Two. Foundations of the Community

Title I. Free Movement of Goods

Article 9

1. The Community shall be based upon a customs union which shall cover all trade in goods and which shall involve the prohibition between Member States of customs duties on imports and exports and of all charges having equivalent effect, and the adoption of a common customs tariff in their relations with third countries.

2. The provisions of Chapter 1, Section 1, and of Chapter 2 of this Title shall apply to products originating in Member States and to products coming from third countries which are in free circulation in Member States.

Article 10

1. Products coming from a third country shall be considered to be in free circulation in a Member State if the import formalities have been complied with and any customs duties or charges having equivalent effect which are payable have been levied in that Member State, and if they have not benefited from a total or partial drawback of such duties or charges. . . .

CHAPTER 1. THE CUSTOMS UNION

Section 1. Elimination of Customs Duties Between Member States

Article 12

Member States shall refrain from introducing between themselves any new customs duties on imports or exports or any charges having equivalent effect, and from increasing those which they already apply in their trade with each other.

Article 13

1. Customs duties on imports in force between Member States shall be progressively abolished by them during the transitional period in accordance with Articles 14 and 15.
2. Charges having an effect equivalent to customs duties on imports, in force between Member States shall be progressively abolished by them during the transitional period. . . .

Article 14

1. For each product, the basic duty to which the successive reductions shall be applied shall be the duty applied on 1 January 1957. . . .

Section 2. Setting Up of the Common Customs Tariff

Article 18

The Member States declare their readiness to contribute to the development of international trade and the lowering of barriers to trade by entering into agreements designed, on a basis of reciprocity and mutual advantage, to reduce customs duties below the general level of which they could avail themselves as a result of the establishment of a customs union between them.

Article 19

1. Subject to the conditions and within the limits provided for hereinafter, duties in the common customs tariff shall be at the level of the arithmetical average of the duties applied in the four customs territories comprised in the Community.
2. The duties taken as the basis for calculating this average shall be those applied by Member States on 1 January 1957. . . .

CHAPTER 2. ELIMINATION OF QUANTITATIVE RESTRICTIONS BETWEEN MEMBER STATES

Article 30

Quantitative restrictions on imports and all measures having equivalent effect shall, without prejudice to the following provisions, be prohibited between Member States.

Article 31

Member States shall refrain from introducing between themselves any new quantitative restrictions or measures having equivalent effect. . . .

Article 32

In their trade with one another Member States shall refrain from making more restrictive the quotas and measures having equivalent effect existing at the date of the entry into force of this Treaty.

These quotas shall be abolished by the end of the transitional period at the latest. During that period, they shall be progressively abolished in accordance with the following provisions. . . .

Article 34

1. Quantitative restrictions on exports, and all measures having equivalent effect, shall be prohibited between Member States.

2. Member States shall, by the end of the first stage at the latest, abolish all quantitative restrictions on exports and any measures having equivalent effect which are in existence when this Treaty enters into force. . . .

Article 36

The provisions of Articles 30 to 34 shall not preclude prohibitions or restrictions on imports, exports or goods in transit justified on grounds of public morality, public policy or public security; the protection of health and life of humans, animals or plants; the protection of national treasures possessing artistic, historic or archaeological value; or the protection of industrial and commercial property. Such prohibitions or restrictions shall not, however, constitute a means of arbitrary discrimination or a disguised restriction on trade between Member States. . . .

TITLE II. AGRICULTURE

Article 38

1. The common market shall extend to agriculture and trade in agricultural products. 'Agricultural products' means the products of the soil, of stockfarming and of fisheries and products of first-stage processing directly related to these products.

2. Save as otherwise provided in Articles 39 to 46, the rules laid down for the establishment of the common market shall apply to agricultural products.

3. The products subject to the provisions of Articles 39 to 46 are listed in Annex II to this Treaty. Within two years of the entry into force of this Treaty, however, the Council shall, acting by a qualified majority on a proposal from the Commission, decide what products are to be added to this list.

4. The operation and development of the common market for agricultural products must be accompanied by the establishment of a common agricultural policy among the Member States.

Article 39

1. The objectives of the common agricultural policy shall be:

(a) to increase agricultural productivity by promoting technical progress and by ensuring the rational development of agricultural production and the optimum utilization of the factors of production, in particular labour;

(b) thus to ensure a fair standard of living for the agricultural community, in particular by increasing the individual earnings of persons engaged in agriculture;

(c) to stabilize markets;

(d) to assure the availability of supplies;

(e) to ensure that supplies reach consumers at reasonable prices.

2. In working out the common agricultural policy and the special methods for its application, account shall be taken of:

(a) the particular nature of agricultural activity, which results from the social structure of agriculture and from structural and natural disparities between the various agricultural regions;

(b) the need to effect the appropriate adjustments by degrees;

(c) the fact that in the Member States agriculture constitutes a sector closely linked with the economy as a whole.

Article 40

1. Member States shall develop the common agricultural policy by degrees during the transitional period and shall bring it into force by the end of that period at the latest.

2. In order to attain the objectives set out in Article 39 a common organization of agricultural markets shall be established.

This organization shall take one of the following forms, depending on the product concerned:

(a) common rules on competition;

(b) compulsory coordination of the various national market organizations;

(c) a European market organization.

3. The common organization established in accordance with paragraph 2 may include all measures required to attain the objectives set out in Article 39, in particular regulation of prices, aids for the production and marketing of the various products, storage and carryover arrangements and common machinery for stabilizing imports or exports.

The common organization shall be limited to pursuit of the objectives set out in Article 39 and shall exclude any discrimination between producers or consumers within the Community.

Any common price policy shall be based on common criteria and uniform methods of calculation.

4. In order to enable the common organization referred to in paragraph 2 to attain its objectives, one or more agricultural guidance and guarantee funds may be set up.

Article 41

To enable the objectives set out in Article 39 to be attained, provision may be made within the framework of the common agricultural policy for measures such as:

(a) an effective coordination of efforts in the spheres of vocational training, of research and of the dissemination of agricultural knowledge; this may include joint financing of projects or institutions;

(b) joint measures to promote consumption of certain products.

Article 42

The provisions of the Chapter relating to rules on competition shall apply to production of and trade in agricultural products only to the extent determined by the Council within the framework of Article 43 (2) and (3) and in accordance with the procedure laid down therein, account being taken of the objectives set out in Article 39.

The Council may, in particular, authorize the granting of aid:

(a) for the protection of enterprises handicapped by structural or natural conditions;

(b) within the framework of economic development programmes....

TITLE III. FREE MOVEMENT OF PERSONS, SERVICES AND CAPITAL

CHAPTER 1. WORKERS

Article 48

1. Freedom of movement for workers shall be secured within the Community by the end of the transitional period at the latest.

2. Such freedom of movement shall entail the abolition of any discrimination based on nationality between workers of the Member States as regards employment, remuneration and other conditions of work and employment.

3. It shall entail the right, subject to limitations justified on grounds of public policy, public security or public health:

(a) to accept offers of employment actually made;

(b) to move freely within the territory of Member States for this purpose;

(c) to stay in a Member State for the purpose of employment in accordance with the provisions governing the employment of nationals of that State laid down by law, regulation or administrative action;

(d) to remain in the territory of a Member State after having been employed in that State, subject to conditions which shall be embodied in implementing regulations to be drawn up by the Commission.

4. The provisions of this Article shall not apply to employment in the public service.

Article 49

[As soon as this Treaty enters into force, the Council shall, acting by a qualified majority on a proposal from the Commission, in cooperation with the European Parliament and after consulting the Economic and Social Committee, issue directives or make regulations setting out the measures required to bring about, by progressive stages, freedom of movement for workers, as defined in Article 48, in particular:]

(a) by ensuring close cooperation between national employment services;

(b) by systematically and progressively abolishing those administrative procedures and practices and those qualifying periods in respect of eligibility for available employment, whether resulting from national legislation or from agreements previously concluded between Member States, the maintenance of which would form an obstacle to liberalization of the movement of workers;

(c) by systematically and progressively abolishing all such qualifying periods and other restrictions provided for either under national legislation or under agreements previously concluded between Member States as imposed on workers of other Member States conditions regarding the free choice of employment other than those imposed on workers of the State concerned;

(d) by setting up appropriate machinery to bring offers of employment into touch with applications for employment and to facilitate the achievement of a balance between supply and demand in the employment market in such a way as to avoid serious threats to the standard of living and level of employment in the various regions and industries.

Article 50

Member States shall, within the framework of a joint programme, encourage the exchange of young workers. . . .

CHAPTER 2. RIGHT OF ESTABLISHMENT

Article 52

Within the framework of the provisions set out below, restrictions on the freedom of establishment of nationals of a Member State in the territory of another Member State shall be abolished by progressive stages in the course of the transitional period. Such progressive abolition shall also apply to restrictions on the setting up of agencies, branches or subsidiaries by nationals of any Member State established in the territory of any Member State.

Freedom of establishment shall include the right to take up and pursue activities as self-employed persons and to set up and manage undertakings, in particular companies or firms within the meaning of the second paragraph of Article 58, under the conditions laid down for its own nationals by the law of the country where such establishment is effected, subject to the provisions of the Chapter relating to capital.

Article 53

Member States shall not introduce any new restrictions on the right of establishment in their territories of nationals of other Member States, save as otherwise provided in this Treaty.

Article 54

1. Before the end of the first stage, the Council shall, acting unanimously from the Commission and after consulting the Economic and Social Committee and the European Parliament, draw up a general programme for the abolition of existing restrictions on freedom of establishment within the Community. The Commission shall submit its proposal to the Council during the first two years of the first stage.

The programme shall set out the general conditions under which freedom of establishment is to be attained in the case of each type of activity and in particular the stages by which it is to be attained.

[2. In order to implement this general programme or, in the absence of such programme, in order to achieve a stage in attaining freedom of establishment as regards a particular activity, the Council shall, acting on a proposal from the Commission, in cooperation with the European Parliament and after consulting the Economic and Social Committee, issue directives, acting unanimously until the end of the first stage and by a qualified majority thereafter.] . .

Article 56

1. The provisions of this Chapter and measures taken in pursuance thereof shall not prejudice the applicability of provisions laid down by law, regulation or administrative action providing for special treatment for foreign nationals on grounds of public policy, public security or public health.

2. Before the end of the transitional period, the Council shall, acting unanimously on a proposal from the Commission and after consulting the European Parliament, issue directives for the coordination of the aforementioned provisions laid down by law, regulation or administrative action. [After the end of the second stage, however, the Council shall, acting by a qualified majority on a proposal from the Commission and in cooperation with the European Parliament, issue directives for the coordination of such

provisions as, in each Member State, are a matter for regulation or administrative action.]

Article 57

1. [In order to make it easier for persons to take up and pursue activities as self-employed persons, the Council shall, on a proposal from the Commission and in cooperation with the European Parliament, acting unanimously during the first stage and by a qualified majority thereafter, issue directives for the mutual recognition of diplomas, certificates and other evidence of formal qualifications.] . . .

3. In the case of the medical and allied and pharmaceutical professions, the progressive abolition of restrictions shall be dependent upon coordination of the conditions for their exercise in the various Member States.

Article 58

Companies or firms formed in accordance with the law of a Member State and having their registered office, central administration or principal place of business within the Community shall, for the purposes of this Chapter, be treated in the same way as natural persons who are nationals of Member States.

"Companies or firms" means companies or firms constituted under civil or commercial law, including cooperative societies, and other legal persons governed by public or private law, save for those which are non-profit-making.

CHAPTER 3. SERVICES

Article 59

Within the framework of the provisions set out below, restrictions on freedom to provide services within the Community shall be progressively abolished during the transitional period in respect of nationals of Member States who are established in a State of the Community other than that of the person for whom the services are intended.

[The Council may, acting by a qualified majority on a proposal from the Commission, extend the provisions of the Chapter to nationals of a third country who provide services and who are established within the Community.]

Article 60

Services shall be considered to be 'services' within the meaning of this Treaty where they are normally provided for remuneration, in so far as they are not governed by the provisions relating to freedom of movement for goods, capital and persons.

"Services" shall in particular include:
(a) activities of an industrial character;
(b) activities of a commercial character;

(c) activities of craftsmen;
(d) activities of the professions.

Without prejudice to the provisions of the Chapter relating to the right of establishment, the person providing a service may, in order to do so, temporarily pursue his activity in the State where the service is provided, under the same conditions as are imposed by that State on its own nationals.

Article 61

1. Freedom to provide services in the field of transport shall be governed by the provisions of the Title relating to transport.
2. The liberalization of banking and insurance services connected with movements of capital shall be effected in step with the progressive liberalization of movement of capital.

Article 62

Save as otherwise provided in this Treaty, Member States shall not introduce any new restrictions on the freedom to provide services which have in fact been attained at the date of the entry into force of this Treaty. . . .

CHAPTER 4. CAPITAL

Article 67

1. During the transitional period and to the extent necessary to ensure the proper functioning of the common market, Member States shall progressively abolish between themselves all restrictions on the movement of capital belonging to persons resident in Member States and any discrimination based on the nationality or on the place of residence of the parties or on the place where such capital is invested.
2. Current payments connected with the movement of capital between Member States shall be freed from all restrictions by the end of the first stage at the latest.

Article 68

1. Member States shall, as regards the matters dealt with in this Chapter, be as liberal as possible in granting such exchange authorizations as are still necessary after the entry into force of this Treaty.
2. Where a Member State applies to the movements of capital liberalized in accordance with the provisions of this Chapter the domestic rules governing the capital market and the credit system, it shall do so in a non-discriminatory manner. . . .

Title IV. Transport

Article 74

The objectives of this Treaty shall, in matters governed by this Title, be pursued by Member States within the framework of a common transport policy.

Article 75

1. For the purpose of implementing Article 74, and taking into account the distinctive features of transport, the Council shall, acting unanimously until the end of the second stage and by a qualified majority thereafter, lay down, on a proposal from the Commission and after consulting the Economic and Social Committee and the European Parliament:

(a) common rules applicable to international transport to or from the territory of a Member State or passing across the territory of one or more Member States;

(b) the conditions under which non-resident carriers may operate transport services within a Member State;

(c) any other appropriate provisions.

2. The provisions referred to in *(a)* and *(b)* of paragraph 1 shall be laid down during the transitional period.

3. By way of derogation from the procedure provided for in paragraph 1, where the application of provisions concerning the principles of the regulatory system for transport would be liable to have a serious effect on the standard of living and on employment in certain areas and on the operation of transport facilities, they shall be laid down by the Council acting unanimously. In so doing, the Council shall take into account the need for adaptation to the economic development which will result from establishing the common market. . . .

Part Three. Policy of the Community

Title I. Common Rules

Chapter 1. Rules on Competition

Section 1. Rules Applying to Undertakings

Article 85

1. The following shall be prohibited as incompatible with the common market: all agreements between undertakings, decisions by associations of undertakings and concerted practices which may affect trade between Member States and which have as their object or effect the prevention, restriction or distortion of competition within the common market, and in particular those which:

(a) directly or indirectly fix purchase or selling prices or any other trading conditions;
(b) limit or control production, markets, technical development, or investment;
(c) share markets or sources of supply;
(d) apply dissimilar conditions to equivalent transactions with other trading parties, thereby placing them at a competitive disadvantage;
(e) make the conclusion of contracts subject to acceptance by the other parties of supplementary obligations which, by their nature or according to commercial usage, have no connection with the subject of such contracts.

2. Any agreements or decisions prohibited pursuant to this Article shall be automatically void.

3. The provisions of paragraph 1 may, however, be declared inapplicable in the case of:
— any agreement or category of agreements between undertakings;
— any decision or category of decisions by associations of undertakings;
— any concerted practice or category of concerted practices;
which contributes to improving the production or distribution of goods or to promoting technical or economic progress, while allowing consumers a fair share of the resulting benefit, and which does not:
(a) impose on the undertakings concerned restrictions which are not indispensable to the attainment of these objectives;
(b) afford such undertakings the possibility of eliminating competition in respect of a substantial part of the products in question.

Article 86

Any abuse by one or more undertakings of a dominant position within the common market or in a substantial part of it shall be prohibited as incompatible with the common market in so far as it may affect trade between Member States.

Such abuse may, in particular, consist in:
(a) directly or indirectly imposing unfair purchase or selling prices or other unfair trading conditions;
(b) limiting production, markets or technical development to the prejudice of consumers;
(c) applying dissimilar conditions to equivalent transactions with other trading parties, thereby placing them at a competitive disadvantage;
(d) making the conclusion of contracts subject to acceptance by the other parties of supplementary obligations which, by their nature or according to commercial usage, have no connection with the subject of such contracts.

Article 87

1. Within three years of the entry into force of this Treaty the Council shall, acting unanimously on a proposal from the Commission and after consulting the European Parliament, adopt any appropriate regulations or directives to give effect to the principles set out in Articles 85 and 86.

If such provisions have not been adopted within the period mentioned, they shall be laid down by the Council, acting by a qualified majority on a proposal from the Commission and after consulting the European Parliament.

2. The regulations or directives referred to in paragraph 1 shall be designed in particular:

(a) to ensure compliance with the prohibitions laid down in Article 85 *(1)* and in Article 86 by making provision for fines and periodic penalty payments;

(b) to lay down detailed rules for the application of Article 85 *(3)*, taking into account the need to ensure effective supervision on the one hand, and to simplify administration to the greatest possible extent on the other;

(c) to define, if need be, in the various branches of the economy, the scope of the provisions of Articles 85 and 86;

(d) to define the respective functions of the Commission and of the Court of Justice in applying the provisions laid down in this paragraph;

(e) to determine the relationship between national laws and the provisions contained in this Section or adopted pursuant to this Article. . . .

CHAPTER 2. TAX PROVISIONS

Article 95

No Member State shall impose, directly or indirectly, on the products of other Member States any internal taxation of any kind in excess of that imposed directly or indirectly on similar domestic products.

Furthermore, no Member State shall impose on the products of other Member States any internal taxation of such a nature as to afford indirect protection to other products.

Member States shall, not later than at the beginning of the second stage, repeal or amend any provisions existing when this Treaty enters into force which conflict with the preceding rules.

Article 96

Where products are exported to the territory of any Member State, any repayment of internal taxation shall not exceed the internal taxation imposed on them whether directly or indirectly. . . .

Article 99

[The Council shall, acting unanimously on a proposal from the Commission and after consulting the European Parliament, adopt provisions for the harmonization of legislation concerning turnover taxes, excise duties and other forms of indirect taxation to the extent that such harmonization is necessary to ensure the establishment and the functioning of the internal market within the time-limit laid down in Article 8a.]

CHAPTER 3. APPROXIMATION OF LAWS

Article 100

The Council shall, acting unanimously on a proposal from the Commission, issue directives for the approximation of such provisions laid down by law, regulation or administrative action in Member States as directly affect the establishment or functioning of the common market.

The European Parliament and the Economic and Social Committee shall be consulted in the case of directives whose implementation would, in one or more Member States, involve the amendment of legislation.

[Article 100a

1. By way of derogation from Article 100 and save where otherwise provided in this Treaty, the following provisions shall apply for the achievement of the objectives set out in Article 8a. The Council shall, acting by a qualified majority on a proposal from the Commission in cooperation with the European Parliament and after consulting the Economic and Social Committee, adopt the measures for the approximation of the provisions laid down by law, regulation or administrative action in Member States which have as their object the establishment and functioning of the internal market.

2. Paragraph 1 shall not apply to fiscal provisions, to those relating to the free movement of persons nor to those relating to the rights and interests of employed persons.

3. The Commission, in its proposals envisaged in paragraph 1 concerning health, safety, environmental protection and consumer protection, will take as a base a high level of protection.

4. If, after the adoption of a harmonization measure by the Council acting by a qualified majority, a Member State deems it necessary to apply national provisions on grounds of major needs referred to in Article 36, or relating to protection of the environment or the working environment, it shall notify the Commission of these provisions.

The Commission shall confirm the provisions involved after having verified that they are not a means of arbitrary discrimination or a disguised restriction on trade between Member States.

By way of derogation from the procedure laid down in Articles 169 and 170, the Commission or any Member State may bring the matter directly before the Court of Justice if it considers that another Member State is making improper use of the powers provided for in this Article.

5. The harmonization measures referred to above shall, in appropriate cases, include a safeguard clause authorizing the Member States to take, for one or more of the non-economic reasons referred to in Article 36, provisional measures subject to a Community control procedure.]

[Article 100b

1. During 1992, the Commission shall, together with each Member State, draw up an inventory of national laws, regulations and administrative provisions which fall under Article 100a and which have not been harmonized pursuant to that Article.

The Council, acting in accordance with the provisions of Article 100a, may decide that the provisions in force in a Member State must be recognized as being equivalent to those applied by another Member State.

2. The provisions of Article 100a(4) shall apply by analogy.

3. The Commission shall draw up the inventory referred to in the first subparagraph of paragraph 1 and shall submit appropriate proposals in good time to allow the Council to act before the end of 1992.]

Article 101

Where the Commission finds that a difference between the provisions laid down by law, regulation or administrative action in Member States is distorting the conditions of competition in the common market and that the resultant distortion needs to be eliminated, it shall consult the Member States concerned.

If such consultation does not result in an agreement eliminating the distortion in question, the Council shall, on a proposal from the Commission, acting unanimously during the first stage and by a qualified majority thereafter, issue the necessary directives. The Commission and the Council may take any other appropriate measures provided for in this Treaty.

Article 102

1. Where there is reason to fear that the adoption or amendment of a provision laid down by law, regulation or administrative action may cause distortion within the meaning of Article 101, a Member State desiring to proceed therewith shall consult the Commission. After consulting the Member States, the Commission shall recommend to the States concerned such measures as may be appropriate to avoid the distortion in question.

2. If a State desiring to introduce or amend its own provisions does not comply with the recommendation addressed to it by the Commission, other Member States shall not be required, in pursuance of Article 101, to amend their own provisions in order to eliminate such distortion. If the Member State which has ignored the recommendation of the Commission causes distortion detrimental only to itself, the provisions of Article 101 shall not apply.

Title II. Economic Policy

[Chapter 1. Cooperation in Economic and Monetary Policy (Economic and Monetary Union)

Article 102a

1. In order to ensure the convergence of economic and monetary policies which is necessary for the further development of the Community, Member States shall cooperate in accordance with the objectives of Article

104. In so doing, they shall take account of the experience acquired in cooperation within the framework of the European Monetary System (EMS) and in developing the ECU, and shall respect existing powers in this field.

2. Insofar as further development in the field of economic and monetary policy necessitates institutional changes, the provisions of Article 236 shall be applicable. The Monetary Committee and the Committee of Governors of the Central Banks shall also be consulted regarding institutional changes in the monetary area.]

CHAPTER 2. CONJUNCTURAL POLICY

Article 103

1. Member States shall regard their conjunctural policies as a matter of common concern. They shall consult each other and the Commission on the measures to be taken in the light of the prevailing circumstances.

2. Without prejudice to any other procedures provided for in this Treaty, the Council may, acting unanimously on a proposal from the Commission, decide upon the measures appropriate to the situation.

3. Acting by a qualified majority on a proposal from the Commission, the Council shall, where required, issue any directives needed to give effect to the measures decided upon under paragraph 2.

4. The procedures provided for in this Article shall also apply if any difficulty should arise in the supply of certain products.

CHAPTER 3. BALANCE OF PAYMENTS

Article 104

Each Member State shall pursue the economic policy needed to ensure the equilibrium of its overall balance of payments and to maintain confidence in its currency, while taking care to ensure a high level of employment and a stable level of prices. . . .

Article 105

1. In order to facilitate attainment of the objectives set out in Article 104, Member States shall coordinate their economic policies. They shall for this purpose provide for cooperation between their appropriate administrative departments and between their central banks.

The Commission shall submit to the Council recommendations on how to achieve such cooperation. . . .

Article 107

1. Each Member State shall treat its policy with regard to rates of exchange as a matter of common concern.

2. If a Member State makes an alteration in its rate of exchange which is inconsistent with the objectives set out in Article 104 and which seriously distorts conditions of competition, the Commission may, after consulting the Monetary Committee, authorize other Member States to take for a strictly limited period the necessary measures, the conditions and details of which it shall determine, in order to counter the consequences of such alteration. . . .

CHAPTER 4. COMMERCIAL POLICY

Article 110

By establishing a customs union between themselves Member States aim to contribute, in the common interest, to the harmonious development of world trade, the progressive abolition of restrictions on international trade and the lowering of customs barriers.

The common commercial policy shall take into account the favourable effect which the abolition of customs duties between Member States may have on the increase in the competitive strength of undertakings in those States.

Article 111

The following provisions shall, without prejudice to Articles 115 and 116, apply during the transitional period:

1. Member States shall coordinate their trade relations with third countries so as to bring about, by the end of the transitional period, the conditions needed for implementing a common policy in the field of external trade.

The Commission shall submit to the Council proposals regarding the procedure for common action to be followed during the transitional period and regarding the achievement of uniformity in their commercial policies.

2. The Commission shall submit to the Council recommendations for tariff negotiations with third countries in respect of the common customs tariff.

The Council shall authorize the Commission to open such negotiations.

The Commission shall conduct these negotiations in consultation with a special committee appointed by the Council to assist the Commission in this task and within the framework of such directives as the Council may issue to it.

3. In exercising the powers conferred upon it by this Article, the Council shall act unanimously during the first two stages and by a qualified majority thereafter. . . .

Article 113

1. After the transitional period has ended, the common commercial policy shall be based on uniform principles, particularly in regard to changes in tariff rates, the conclusion of tariff and trade agreements, the achievement of uniformity in measures of liberalization, export policy and measures to protect trade such as those to be taken in case of dumping or subsidies.

2. The Commission shall submit proposals to the Council for implementing the common commercial policy.

3. Where agreements with third countries need to be negotiated, the Commission shall make recommendations to the Council, which shall authorize the Commission to open the necessary negotiations.

The Commission shall conduct these negotiations in consultation with a special committee appointed by the Council to assist the Commission in this task and within the framework of such directives as the Council may issue to it.

4. In exercising the powers conferred upon it by this Article, the Council shall act by a qualified majority.

Article 114

The agreements referred to in Article 111(2) and in Article 113 shall be concluded by the Council on behalf of the Community, acting unanimously during the first two stages and by a qualified majority thereafter.

Article 115

In order to ensure that the execution of measures of commercial policy taken in accordance with this Treaty by any Member State is not obstructed by deflection of trade, or where differences between such measures lead to economic difficulties in one or more of the Member States, the Commission shall recommend the methods for the requisite cooperation between Member States. Failing this, the Commission shall authorize Member States to take the necessary protective measures, the conditions and details of which it shall determine. . . .

Article 116

From the end of the transitional period onwards, Member States shall, in respect of all matters of particular interest to the common market, proceed within the framework of international organizations of an economic character only by common action. To this end, the Commission shall submit to the Council, which shall act by a qualified majority, proposals concerning the scope and implementation of such common action. . . .

Title III. Social Policy

Chapter 1. Social Provisions

Article 117

Member States agree upon the need to promote improved working conditions and an improved standard of living for workers, so as to make possible their harmonization while the improvement is being maintained.

They believe that such a development will ensue not only from the functioning of the common market, which will favour the harmonization of social systems, but also from the procedures provided for in this Treaty and from the approximation of provisions laid down by law, regulation or administrative action.

Article 118

Without prejudice to the other provisions of this Treaty and in conformity with its general objectives, the Commission shall have the task of promoting close cooperation between Member States in the social field, particularly in matters relating to:
— employment;
— labour law and working conditions;
— basic and advanced vocational training;
— social security;
— prevention of occupational accidents and diseases;
— occupational hygiene;
— the right of association, and collective bargaining between employers and workers.

To this end, the Commission shall act in close contact with Member States by making studies, delivering opinions and arranging consultations both on problems arising at national level and on those of concern to international organizations.

Before delivering the opinions provided for in this Article, the Commission shall consult the Economic and Social Committee.

[Article 118a

1. Member States shall pay particular attention to encouraging improvements, especially in the working environment, as regards the health and safety of workers, and shall set as their objective the harmonization of conditions in this area, while maintaining the improvements made.

2. In order to help achieve the objective laid down in the first paragraph, the Council, acting by a qualified majority on a proposal from the Commission, in cooperation with the European Parliament and after consulting the Economic and Social Committee, shall adopt, by means of directives, minimum requirements for gradual implementation, having regard to the conditions and technical rules obtaining in each of the Member States.

Such directives shall avoid imposing administrative, financial and legal constraints in a way which would hold back the creation and development of small and medium-sized undertakings.

3. The provisions adopted pursuant to this Article shall not prevent any Member State from maintaining or introducing more stringent measures for the protection of working conditions compatible with this Treaty.]

[Article 118b

The Commission shall endeavour to develop the dialogue between management and labour at European level which could, if the two sides consider it desirable, lead to relations based on agreement.]

Article 119

Each Member State shall during the first stage ensure and subsequently maintain the application of the principle that men and women should receive equal pay for equal work.

For the purpose of this Article, 'pay' means the ordinary basic or minimum wage or salary and any other consideration, whether in cash or in kind, which the worker receives, directly or indirectly, in respect of his employment from his employer.

Equal pay without discrimination based on sex means:

(a) that pay for the same work at piece rates shall be calculated on the basis of the same unit of measurement;

(b) that pay for work at time rates shall be the same for the same job. . . .

[TITLE V. ECONOMIC AND SOCIAL COHESION

Article 130a

In order to promote its overall harmonious development, the Community shall develop and pursue its actions leading to the strengthening of its economic and social cohesion.

In particular the Community shall aim at reducing disparities between the various regions and the backwardness of the least-favoured regions.

Article 130b

Member States shall conduct their economic policies, and shall coordinate them, in such a way as, in addition, to attain the objectives set out in Article 130a. The implementation of the common policies and of the internal market shall take into account the objectives set out in Article 130a and in Article 130c and shall contribute to their achievement. The Community shall support the achievement of these objectives by the action it takes through the structural Funds (European Agricultural Guidance and Guarantee Fund, Guidance Section, European Social Fund, European Regional Development Fund), the European Investment Bank and the other existing financial instruments. . . .]

[TITLE VI. RESEARCH AND TECHNOLOGICAL DEVELOPMENT

Article 130f

1. The Community's aim shall be to strengthen the scientific and technological basis of European industry and to encourage it to become more competitive at international level.

2. In order to achieve this, it shall encourage undertakings including small and medium-sized undertakings, research centres and universities in their research and technological development activities; it shall support their efforts to cooperate with one another, aiming, notably, at enabling undertakings to exploit the Community's internal market potential to the full, in particular through the opening up of national public contracts, the definition of common standards and the removal of legal and fiscal barriers to that cooperation.

3. In the achievement of these aims, special account shall be taken of the connection between the common research and technological development effort, the establishment of the internal market and the implementation of common policies, particularly as regards competition and trade.

Article 130g

In pursuing these objectives the Community shall carry out the following activities, complementing the activites carried out in the Member States:

(a) implementation of research, technological development and demonstration programmes, by promoting cooperation with undertakings, research centres and universities;

(b) promotion of cooperation in the field of Community research, technological development, and demonstration with third countries and international organizations;

(c) dissemination and optimization of the results of activities in Community research, technological development, and demonstration;

(d) stimulation of the training and mobility of researchers in the Community.

Article 130h

Member States shall, in liaison with the Commission, coordinate among themselves the policies and programmes carried out at national level. In close contact with the Member States, the Commission may take any useful initiative to promote such coordination.

Article 130i

1. The Community shall adopt a multiannual framework programme setting out all its activities. The framework programme shall lay down the scientific and technical objectives, define their respective priorities, set out the main lines of the activities envisaged and fix the amount deemed necessary, the detailed rules for financial participation by the Community in the programme as a whole and the breakdown of this amount between the various activities envisaged.

2. The framework programme may be adapted or supplemented, as the situation changes. . . .]

[TITLE VII. ENVIRONMENT

Article 130r

1. Action by the Community relating to the environment shall have the following objectives:

(i) to preserve, protect and improve the quality of the environment;
(ii) to contribute towards protecting human health;
(iii) to ensure a prudent and rational utilization of natural resources.

2. Action by the Community relating to the environment shall be based on the principles that preventive action should be taken, that environmental damage should as a priority be rectified at source, and that the polluter should pay. Environmental protection requirements shall be a component of the Community's other policies.

3. In preparing its action relating to the environment, the Community shall take account of:

(i) available scientific and technical data;

(ii) environmental conditions in the various regions of the Community;

(iii) the potential benefits and costs of action or of lack of action;

(iv) the economic and social development of the Community as a whole and the balanced development of its regions.

4. The Community shall take action relating to the environment to the extent to which the objectives referred to in paragraph 1 can be attained better at Community level than at the level of the individual Member States. Without prejudice to certain measures of a Community nature, the Member States shall finance and implement the other measures.

5. Within their respective spheres of competence, the Community and the Member States shall cooperate with third countries and with the relevant international organizations. The arrangements for Community cooperation may be the subject of agreements between the Community and the third parties concerned, which shall be negotiated and concluded in accordance with Article 228.

The previous paragraph shall be without prejudice to Member States' competence to negotiate in international bodies and to conclude international agreements.

Article 130s

The Council, acting unanimously on a proposal from the Commission and after consulting the European Parliament and the Economic and Social Committee, shall decide what action is to be taken by the Community.

The Council shall, under the conditions laid down in the preceding subparagraph, define those matters on which decisions are to be taken by a qualified majority.

Article 130t

The protective measures adopted in common pursuant to Article 130s shall not prevent any Member State from maintaining or introducing more stringent protective measures compatible with this Treaty.]

Part Four. Association of the Overseas Countries and Territories

Article 131

The Member States agree to associate with the Community the non-European countries and territories which have special relations with Belgium, Denmark, France, Italy, the Netherlands and the United Kingdom. These countries and territories (hereinafter called the 'countries and territories') are listed in Annex IV to this Treaty.

The purpose of association shall be to promote the economic and social development of the countries and territories and to establish close economic relations between them and the Community as a whole.

In accordance with the principles set out in the Preamble to this Treaty, association shall serve primarily to further the interests and prosperity of the inhabitants of these countries and territories in order to lead them to the economic, social and cultural development to which they aspire.

Article 132

Association shall have the following objectives:

1. Member States shall apply to their trade with the countries and territories the same treatment as they accord each other pursuant to this Treaty.

2. Each country or territory shall apply to its trade with Member States and with the other countries and territories the same treatment as that which it applies to the European State with which it has special relations.

3. The Member States shall contribute to the investments required for the progressive development of these countries and territories.

4. For investments financed by the Community, participation in tenders and supplies shall be open on equal terms to all natural and legal persons who are nationals of a Member State or of one of the countries and territories.

5. In relations between Member States and the countries and territories the right of establishment of nationals and companies or firms shall be regulated in accordance with the provisions and procedures laid down in the Chapter relating to the right of establishment and on a non-discriminatory basis, subject to any special provisions laid down pursuant to Article 136.

Article 133

1. Customs duties on imports into the Member States of goods originating in the countries and territories shall be completely abolished in conformity with the progressive abolition of customs duties between Member States in accordance with the provisions of this Treaty.

2. Customs duties on imports into each country or territory from Member States or from the other countries or territories shall be progressively abolished in accordance with the provisions of Articles 12, 13, 14, 15 and 17.

3. The countries and territories may, however, levy customs duties which meet the needs of their development and industrialization or produce revenue for their budgets.

The duties referred to in the preceding subparagraph shall nevertheless be progressively reduced to the level of those imposed on imports of products from the Member State with which each country or territory has special relations. The percentages and the timetable of the reductions provided for under this Treaty shall apply to the difference between the duty imposed on a product coming from the Member State which has special relations with the country or territory concerned and the duty imposed on the same product coming from within the Community on entry into the importing country or territory.

4. Paragraph 2 shall not apply to countries and territories which, by reason of the particular international obligations by which they are bound, already apply a non-discriminatory customs tariff when this Treaty enters into force.

5. The introduction of or any change in customs duties imposed on goods imported into the countries and territories shall not, either in law or in fact, give rise to any direct or indirect discrimination between imports from the various Member States. . . .

Article 135

Subject to the provisions relating to public health, public security or public policy, freedom of movement within Member States for workers from the countries and territories, and within the countries and territories for workers from Member States, shall be governed by agreements to be concluded subsequently with the unanimous approval of Member States.

Part Five. Institutions of the Community

TITLE I. PROVISIONS GOVERNING THE INSTITUTIONS

CHAPTER 1. THE INSTITUTIONS

Section 1. The European Parliament

Article 137

The European Parliament, which shall consist of representatives of the peoples of the States brought together in the Community, shall exercise the advisory and supervisory powers which are conferred upon it by this Treaty.

Article 138

(Paragraphs 1 and 2 Lapsed on 17 July 1979 in Accordance with Article 14 of the Act Concerning the Election of the Representatives of the European Parliament)

[*See Article 1 of that Act which reads as follows:*

1. The representatives in the European Parliament of the peoples of the States brought together in the Community shall be elected by direct universal suffrage.]

[*See Article 2 of that Act which reads as follows:*

2. The number of representatives elected in each Member State is as follows:

Belgium	24
Denmark	16
Germany	81
Greece	24
Spain	60
France	81
Ireland	15
Italy	81
Luxembourg	6
Netherlands	25
Portugal	24
United Kingdom	81.]

3. The European Parliament shall draw up proposals for elections by direct universal suffrage in accordance with a uniform procedure in all Member States.

The Council shall, acting unanimously, lay down the appropriate provisions, which it shall recommend to Member States for adoption in accordance with their respective constitutional requirements.

Article 139

The European Parliament shall hold an annual session. It shall meet, without requiring to be convened, on the second Tuesday in March.

The European Parliament may meet in extraordinary session at the request of a majority of its members or at the request of the Council or of the Commission.

Article 140

The European Parliament shall elect its President and its officers from among its members.

Members of the Commission may attend all meetings and shall, at their request, be heard on behalf of the Commission.

The Commission shall reply orally or in writing to questions put to it by the European Parliament or by its members.

The Council shall be heard by the European Parliament in accordance with the conditions laid down by the Council in its rules of procedure.

Article 141

Save as otherwise provided in this Treaty, the European Parliament shall act by an absolute majority of the votes cast.

The rules of procedure shall determine the quorum.

Article 142

The European Parliament shall adopt its rules of procedure, acting by a majority of its members.

The proceedings of the European Parliament shall be published in the manner laid down in its rules of procedure.

Article 143

The European Parliament shall discuss in open session the annual general report submitted to it by the Commission.

Article 144

If a motion of censure on the activities of the Commission is tabled before it, the European Parliament shall not vote thereon until at least three days after the motion has been tabled and only by open vote.

If the motion of censure is carried by a two-third majority of the votes cast, representing a majority of the members of the European Parliament, the members of the Commission shall resign as a body. They shall continue to deal with current business until they are replaced in accordance with Article 158.

Section 2. The Council

Article 145

To ensure that the objectives set out in this Treaty are attained, the Council shall, in accordance with the provisions of this Treaty:

— ensure coordination of the general economic policies of the Member States;

— have power to take decisions.

[— confer on the Commission, in the acts which the Council adopts, powers for the implementation of the rules which the Council lays down. The Council may impose certain requirements in respect of the exercise of these powers. The Council may also reserve the right, in specific cases, to exercise directly implementing powers itself. The procedures referred to above must be consonant with principles and rules to be laid down in advance by the Council, acting unanimously on a proposal from the Commission and after obtaining the Opinion of the European Parliament.]

Article 146

(Article Repealed by Article 7 of the Merger Treaty)

[See Article 2 of the Merger Treaty, which reads as follows:

The Council shall consist of representatives of the Member States. Each Government shall delegate to it one of its members.

The office of President shall be held for a term of six months by each member of the Council in turn, in the following order of Member States:

— for a first cycle of six years: Belgium, Denmark, Germany, Greece, Spain, France, Ireland, Italy, Luxembourg, Netherlands, Portugal, United Kingdom,
— for the following cycle of six years: Denmark, Belgium, Greece, Germany, France, Spain, Italy, Ireland, Netherlands, Luxembourg, United Kingdom, Portugal.]

Article 147

(Article Repealed by Article 7 of the Merger Treaty)

[See Article 3 of the Merger Treaty, which reads as follows:

The Council shall meet when convened by its President on his own initiative or at the request of one of its members or of the Commission.]

Article 148

1. Save as otherwise provided in this Treaty, the Council shall act by a majority of its members.

2. Where the Council is required to act by a qualified majority, the votes of its members shall be weighted as follows:

Belgium	5
Denmark	3
Germany	10
Greece	5
Spain	8
France	10
Ireland	3
Italy	10
Luxembourg	2
Netherlands	5
Portugal	5
United Kingdom	10

For their adoption, acts of the Council shall require at least:
— fifty-four votes in favour where this Treaty requires them to be adopted on a proposal from the Commission,
— fifty-four votes in favour, cast by at least eight members, in other cases.

3. Abstentions by members present in person or represented shall not prevent the adoption by the Council of acts which require unanimity.

[Article 149

1. Where, in pursuance of this Treaty, the Council acts on a proposal from the Commission, unanimity shall be required for an act constituting an amendment to that proposal.

2. Where, in pursuance of this Treaty, the Council acts in cooperation with the European Parliament, the following procedure shall apply:

(a) The Council, acting by a qualified majority under the conditions of paragraph 1, on a proposal from the Commission and after obtaining the Opinion of the European Parliament, shall adopt a common position.

(b) The Council's common position shall be communicated to the European Parliament. The Council and the Commission shall inform the European Parliament fully of the reasons which led the Council to adopt its common position and also of the Commission's position.

If, within three months of such communication, the European Parliament approves this common position or has not taken a decision within that period, the Council shall definitively adopt the act in question in accordance with the common position.

(c) The European Parliament may within the period of three months referred to in point *(b)*, by an absolute majority of its component members, propose amendments to the Council's common position. The European Parliament may also, by the same majority, reject the Council's common position. The result of the proceedings shall be transmitted to the Council and the Commission.

If the European Parliament has rejected the Council's common position, unanimity shall be required for the Council to act on a second reading.

(d) The Commission shall, within a period of one month, re-examine the proposal on the basis of which the Council adopted its common position, by taking into account the amendments proposed by the European Parliament.

The Commission shall forward to the Council, at the same time as its re-examined proposal, the amendments of the European Parliament which it has not accepted, and shall express its opinion on them. The Council may adopt these amendments unanimously.

(e) The Council, acting by a qualified majority, shall adopt the proposal as re-examined by the Commission.

Unanimity shall be required for the Council to amend the proposal as re-examined by the Commission.

(f) In the cases referred to in points *(c)*, *(d)* and *(e)*, the Council shall be required to act within a period of three months. If no decision is taken within this period, the Commission proposal shall be deemed not to have been adopted.

(g) The periods referred to in points *(b)* and *(f)* may be extended by a maximum of one month by common accord between the Council and the European Parliament.

3. As long as the Council has not acted, the Commission may alter its proposal at any time during the procedures mentioned in paragraphs 1 and 2.]

Article 150

Where a vote is taken, any member of the Council may also act on behalf of not more than one other member.

Article 151

(Article Repealed by Article 7 of the Merger Treaty)

[*See Articles 5 and 4 of the Merger Treaty, which read as follows:*

Article 5:

The Council shall adopt its rules of procedure.

Article 4:

A committee consisting of the Permanent Representatives of the Member States shall be responsible for preparing the work of the Council and for carrying out the tasks assigned to it by the Council.]

Article 152

The Council may request the Commission to undertake any studies the Council considers desirable for the attainment of the common objectives, and to submit to it any appropriate proposals.

Article 153

The Council shall, after receiving an opinion from the Commission, determine the rules governing the committees provided for in this Treaty.

Article 154

(Article Repealed by Article 7 of the Merger Treaty)

[*See Article 6 of the Merger Treaty, which reads as follows:*

The Council shall, acting by a qualified majority, determine the salaries, allowances and pensions of the President and members of the Commission, and of the President, Judges, Advocates-General and Registrar of the Court of Justice. It shall also, again by a qualified majority, determine any payment to be made instead of remuneration.]

Section 3. The Commission

Article 155

In order to ensure the proper functioning and development of the common market, the Commission shall:
— ensure that the provisions of this Treaty and the measures taken by the institutions pursuant thereto are applied;
— formulate recommendations or deliver opinions on matters dealt with in this Treaty, if it expressly so provides or if the Commission considers it necessary;

— have its own power of decision and participate in the shaping of measures taken by the Council and by the European Parliament in the manner provided for in this Treaty;

— exercise the powers conferred on it by the Council for the implementation of the rules laid down by the latter.

Article 156

(Article Repealed by Article 19 of the Merger Treaty)

[See Article 18 of the Merger Treaty, which reads as follows:

The Commission shall publish annually, not later than one month before the opening of the session of the European Parliament, a general report on the activities of the Communities.]

Article 157

(Article Repealed by Article 19 of the Merger Treaty)

[See Article 10 of the Merger Treaty, which reads as follows:

1. The Commission shall consist of seventeen members, who shall be chosen on the grounds of their general competence and whose independence is beyond doubt.

The number of members of the Commission may be altered by the Council, acting unanimously.

Only nationals of Member States may be members of the Commission.

The Commission must include at least one national of each of the Member States, but may not include more than two members having the nationality of the same State.

2. The members of the Commission shall, in the general interest of the Communities, be completely independent in the performance of their duties.

In the performance of these duties, they shall neither seek nor take instructions from any Government or from any other body.

They shall refrain from any action incompatible with their duties.

Each Member State undertakes to respect this principle and not to seek to influence the members of the Commission in the performance of their tasks.

The members of the Commission may not, during their term of office, engage in any other occupation, whether gainful or not. When entering upon their duties they shall give a solemn undertaking that, both during and after their term of office, they will respect the obligations arising therefrom and in particular their duty to behave with integrity and discretion as regards the acceptance, after they have ceased to hold office, of certain appointments or benefits. In the event of any breach of these obligations, the Court of Justice may, on application by the Council or the Commission, rule that the member concerned be, according to the circumstances, either compulsorily retired in accordance with the provisions of Article 13 or deprived of his right to a pension or other benefits in its stead.]

Article 158

(Article Repealed by Article 19 of the Merger Treaty)

[*See Article 11 of the Merger Treaty, which reads as follows:*

The members of the Commission shall be appointed by common accord of the Governments of the Member States.

Their term of office shall be four years. It shall be renewable.]

Article 159

(Article Repealed by Article 19 of the Merger Treaty)

[*See Article 12 of the Merger Treaty, which reads as follows:*

Apart from normal replacement, or death, the duties of a member of the Commission shall end when he resigns or is compulsorily retired.

The vacancy thus caused shall be filled for the remainder of the member's term of office. The Council may, acting unanimously, decide that such a vacancy need not be filled.

Save in the case of compulsory retirement under the provisions of Article 13, members of the Commission shall remain in office until they have been replaced.]

Article 160

(Article Repealed by Article 19 of the Merger Treaty)

[*See Article 13 of the Merger Treaty, which reads as follows:*

If any member of the Commission no longer fulfils the conditions required for the performance of his duties or if he has been guilty of serious misconduct, the Court of Justice may, on application by the Council or the Commission, compulsorily retire him.]

Article 161

(Article Repealed by Article 19 of the Merger Treaty)

[*See Article 14 of the Merger Treaty, which reads as follows:*

The President and the six Vice-Presidents of the Commission shall be appointed from among its members for a term of two years in accordance with the same procedure as that laid down for the appointment of members of the Commission. Their appointments may be renewed.

The Council, acting unanimously, may amend the provisions concerning Vice-Presidents.

Save where the entire Commission is replaced, such appointments shall be made after the Commission has been consulted.

In the event of retirement or death, the President and the Vice-Presidents shall be replaced for the remainder of their term of office in accordance with the preceding provisions.]

Article 162

(Article Repealed by Article 19 of the Merger Treaty)

[*See Articles 15 and 16 of the Merger Treaty, which read as follows:*

Article 15:

The Council and the Commission shall consult each other and shall settle by common accord their methods of cooperation.

Article 16:

The Commission shall adopt its rules of procedure so as to ensure that both it and its departments operate in accordance with the provisions of the Treaties establishing the European Coal and Steel Community, the European Economic Community and the European Atomic Energy Community, and of this Treaty. It shall ensure that these rules are published.]

Article 163

(Article Repealed by Article 19 of the Merger Treaty)

[*See Article 17 of the Merger Treaty, which reads as follows:*

The Commission shall act by a majority of the number of members provided for in Article 10.*

A meeting of the Commission shall be valid only if the number of members laid down in its rules of procedure is present.]

Section 4. The Court of Justice

Article 164

The Court of Justice shall ensure that in the interpretation and application of this Treaty the law is observed.

---

*Article 10 of the Merger Treaty. See Article 157 above.

Article 165

The Court of Justice shall consist of thirteen Judges.

The Court of Justice shall sit in plenary session. It may, however, form Chambers, each consisting of three or five Judges, either to undertake certain preparatory inquiries or to adjudicate on particular categories of cases in accordance with rules laid down for these purposes.

Whenever the Court of Justice hears cases brought before it by a Member State or by one of the institutions of the Community or, to the extent that the Chambers of the Court do not have the requisite jurisdiction under the Rules of Procedure, has to give preliminary rulings on questions submitted to it pursuant to Article 177, it shall sit in plenary session.

Should the Court of Justice so request, the Council may, acting unanimously, increase the number of Judges and make the necessary adjustments to the second and third paragraphs of this Article and to the second paragraph of Article 167.

Article 166

The Court of Justice shall be assisted by six Advocates-General.

It shall be the duty of the Advocate-General, acting with complete impartiality and independence, to make, in open court, reasoned submissions on cases brought before the Court of Justice, in order to assist the Court in the performance of the task assigned to it in Article 164.

Should the Court of Justice so request, the Council may, acting unanimously, increase the number of Advocates-General and make the necessary adjustments to the third paragraph of Article 167.

Article 167

The Judges and Advocates-General shall be chosen from persons whose independence is beyond doubt and who possess the qualifications required for appointment to the highest judicial offices in their respective countries or who are jurisconsults of recognized competence; they shall be appointed by common accord of the Governments of the Member States for a term of six years.

Every three years there shall be a partial replacement of the Judges. Seven and six Judges shall be replaced alternately.

Every three years there shall be a partial replacement of the Advocates-General. Three Advocates-General shall be replaced on each occasion.

Retiring Judges and Advocates-General shall be eligible for reappointment.

The Judges shall elect the President of the Court of Justice from among their number for a term of three years. He may be re-elected.

Article 168

The Court of Justice shall appoint its Registrar and lay down the rules governing his service.

[*Article 168a*

1. At the request of the Court of Justice and after consulting the Commission and the European Parliament, the Council may, acting unanimously, attach to the Court of Justice a court with jurisdiction to hear and determine at first instance, subject to a right of appeal to the Court of Justice on points of law only and in accordance with the conditions laid down by the Statute, certain classes of action or proceeding brought by natural or legal persons. That court shall not be competent to hear and determine actions brought by Member States or by Community institutions or questions referred for a preliminary ruling under Article 177.

2. The Council, following the procedure laid down in paragraph 1, shall determine the composition of that court and adopt the necessary adjustments and additional provisions to the Statute of the Court of Justice. Unless the Council decides otherwise, the provisions of this Treaty relating to the Court of Justice, in particular the provisions of the Protocol on the Statute of the Court of Justice, shall apply to that court.

3. The members of that court shall be chosen from persons whose independence is beyond doubt and who possess the ability required for appointment to judicial office; they shall be appointed by common accord of the Governments of the Member States for a term of six years. The membership shall be partially renewed every three years. Retiring members shall be eligible for reappointment.

4. That court shall establish its rules of procedure in agreement with the Court of Justice. Those rules shall require the unanimous approval of the Council.]

Article 169

If the Commission considers that a Member State has failed to fulfil an obligation under this Treaty, it shall deliver a reasoned opinion on the matter after giving the State concerned the opportunity to submit its observations.

If the State concerned does not comply with the opinion within the period laid down by the Commission, the latter may bring the matter before the Court of Justice.

Article 170

A Member State which considers that another Member State has failed to fulfil an obligation under this Treaty may bring the matter before the Court of Justice.

Before a Member State brings an action against another Member State for an alleged infringement of an obligation under this Treaty, it shall bring the matter before the Commission.

The Commission shall deliver a reasoned opinion after each of the States concerned has been given the opportunity to submit its own case and its observations on the other party's case both orally and in writing.

If the Commission has not delivered an opinion within three months of the date on which the matter was brought before it, the absence of such opinion shall not prevent the matter from being brought before the Court of Justice.

Article 171

If the Court of Justice finds that a Member State has failed to fulfil an obligation under this Treaty, the State shall be required to take the necessary measures to comply with the judgment of the Court of Justice.

Article 172

Regulations made by the Council pursuant to the provisions of this Treaty may give the Court of Justice unlimited jurisdiction in regard to the penalties provided for in such regulations.

Article 173

The Court of Justice shall review the legality of acts of the Council and the Commission other than recommendations or opinions. It shall for this purpose have jurisdiction in actions brought by a Member State, the Council or the Commission on grounds of lack of competence, infringement of an essential procedural requirement, infringement of this Treaty or of any rule of law relating to its application, or misuse of powers.

Any natural or legal person may, under the same conditions, institute proceedings against a decision addressed to that person or against a decision which, although in the form of a regulation or a decision addressed to another person, is of direct and individual concern to the former.

The proceedings provided for in this Article shall be instituted within two months of the publication of the measure, or of its notification to the plaintiff, or, in the absence thereof, of the day on which it came to the knowledge of the latter, as the case may be.

Article 174

If the action is well founded, the Court of Justice shall declare the act concerned to be void.

In the case of a regulation, however, the Court of Justice shall, if it considers this necessary, state which of the effects of the regulation which it has declared void shall be considered as definitive.

Article 175

Should the Council or the Commission, in infringement of this Treaty, fail to act, the Member States and the other institutions of the Community may bring an action before the Court of Justice to have the infringement established.

The action shall be admissible only if the institution concerned has first been called upon to act. If, within two months of being so called upon, the institution concerned has not defined its position, the action may be brought within a further period of two months.

Any natural or legal person may, under the conditions laid down in the preceding paragraphs, complain to the Court of Justice that an institution of the Community has failed to address to that person any act other than a recommendation or an opinion.

Article 176

The institution whose act has been declared void or whose failure to act has been declared contrary to this Treaty shall be required to take the necessary measures to comply with the judgment of the Court of Justice.

This obligation shall not affect any obligation which may result from the application of the second paragraph of Article 215.

Article 177

The Court of Justice shall have jurisdiction to give preliminary rulings concerning:

(a) the interpretation of this Treaty;

(b) the validity and interpretation of acts of the institutions of the Community;

(c) the interpretation of the statutes of bodies established by an act of the Council, where those statutes so provide.

Where such a question is raised before any court or tribunal of a Member State, that court or tribunal may, if it considers that a decision on the question is necessary to enable it to give judgment, request the Court of Justice to give a ruling thereon.

Where any such question is raised in a case pending before a court or tribunal of a Member State, against whose decisions there is no judicial remedy under national law, that court or tribunal shall bring the matter before the Court of Justice.

Article 178

The Court of Justice shall have jurisdiction in disputes relating to compensation for damage provided for in the second paragraph of Article 215.

Article 179

The Court of Justice shall have jurisdiction in any dispute between the Community and its servants within the limits and under the conditions laid down in the Staff Regulations or the Conditions of Employment.

Article 180

The Court of Justice shall, within the limits hereinafter laid down, have jurisdiction in disputes concerning:

(a) the fulfilment by Member States of obligations under the Statute of the European Investment Bank. In this connection, the Board of Directors of the Bank shall enjoy the powers conferred upon the Commission by Article 169;

(b) measures adopted by the Board of Governors of the Bank. In this connection, any Member State, the Commission or the Board of Directors of the Bank may institute proceedings under the conditions laid down in Article 173;

(c) measures adopted by the Board of Directors of the Bank. Proceedings against such measures may be instituted only by Member States or by the Commission, under the conditions laid down in Article 173, and solely on the grounds of non-compliance with the procedure provided for in Article 21 (2), (5), (6) and (7) of the Statute of the Bank.

Article 181

The Court of Justice shall have jurisdiction to give judgment pursuant to any arbitration clause contained in a contract concluded by or on behalf of the Community, whether that contract be governed by public or private law.

Article 182

The Court of Justice shall have jurisdiction in any dispute between Member States which relates to the subject matter of this Treaty if the dispute is submitted to it under a special agreement between the parties.

Article 183

Save where jurisdiction is conferred on the Court of Justice by this Treaty, disputes to which the Community is a party shall not on that ground be excluded from the jurisdiction of the courts or tribunals of the Member States.

Article 184

Notwithstanding the expiry of the period laid down in the third paragraph of Article 173, any party may, in proceedings in which a regulation of the Council or of the Commission is in issue, plead the grounds specified in the first paragraph of Article 173, in order to invoke before the Court of Justice the inapplicability of that regulation.

Article 185

Actions brought before the Court of Justice shall not have suspensory effect. The Court of Justice may, however, if it considers that circumstances so require, order that application of the contested act be suspended.

Article 186

The Court of Justice may in any cases before it prescribe any necessary interim measures.

Article 187

The judgments of the Court of Justice shall be enforceable under the conditions laid down in Article 192.

Article 188

The Statute of the Court of Justice is laid down in a separate Protocol.

[The Council may, acting unanimously at the request of the Court of Justice and after consulting the Commission and the European Parliament, amend the provisions of Title III of the Statute.]

The Court of Justice shall adopt its rules of procedure. These shall require the unanimous approval of the Council.

CHAPTER 2. PROVISIONS COMMON TO SEVERAL INSTITUTIONS

Article 189

In order to carry out their task the Council and the Commission shall, in accordance with the provisions of this Treaty, make regulations, issue directives, take decisions, make recommendations or deliver opinions.

A regulation shall have general application. It shall be binding in its entirety and directly applicable in all Member States.

A directive shall be binding, as to the result to be achieved, upon each Member State to which it is addressed, but shall leave to the national authorities the choice of form and methods.

A decision shall be binding in its entirety upon those to whom it is addressed.

Recommendations and opinions shall have no binding force.

Article 190

Regulations, directives and decisions of the Council and of the Commission shall state the reasons on which they are based and shall refer to any proposals or opinions which were required to be obtained pursuant to this Treaty.

Article 191

Regulations shall be published in the Official Journal of the Community. They shall enter into force on the date specified in them or, in the absence thereof, on the twentieth day following their publication.

Directives and decisions shall be notified to those to whom they are addressed and shall take effect upon such notification.

Article 192

Decisions of the Council or of the Commission which impose a pecuniary obligation on persons other than States, shall be enforceable.

Enforcement shall be governed by the rules of civil procedure in force in the State in the territory of which it is carried out. The order for its enforcement shall be appended to the decision, without other formality than verification of the authenticity of the decision, by the national authority which the Government of each Member State shall designate for this purpose and shall make known to the Commission and to the Court of Justice.

When these formalities have been completed on application by the party concerned, the latter may proceed to enforcement in accordance with the national law, by bringing the matter directly before the competent authority.

Enforcement may be suspended only by a decision of the Court of Justice. However, the courts of the country concerned shall have jurisdiction over complaints that enforcement is being carried out in an irregular manner.

CHAPTER 3. THE ECONOMIC AND SOCIAL COMMITTEE

Article 193

An Economic and Social Committee is hereby established. It shall have advisory status.

The Committee shall consist of representatives of the various categories of economic and social activity, in particular, representatives of producers, farmers, carriers, workers, dealers, craftsmen, professional occupations and representatives of the general public.

Article 194

The number of members of the Committee shall be as follows:

Belgium	12
Denmark	9
Germany	24
Greece	12
Spain	21
France	24
Ireland	9
Italy	24
Luxembourg	6
Netherlands	12
Portugal	12
United Kingdom	24

The members of the Committee shall be appointed by the Council, acting unanimously, for four years. Their appointments shall be renewable.

The members of the Committee shall be appointed in their personal capacity and may not be bound by any mandatory instructions.

Article 195

1. For the appointment of the members of the Committee, each Member State shall provide the Council with a list containing twice as many candidates as there are seats allotted to its nationals.

The composition of the Committee shall take account of the need to ensure adequate representation of the various categories of economic and social activity.

2. The Council shall consult the Commission. It may obtain the opinion of European bodies which are representative of the various economic and social sectors to which the activities of the Community are of concern.

Article 196

The Committee shall elect its chairman and officers from among its members for a term of two years.

It shall adopt its rules of procedure and shall submit them to the Council for its approval, which must be unanimous.

The Committee shall be convened by its chairman at the request of the Council or of the Commission.

Article 197

The Committee shall include specialized sections for the principal fields covered by this Treaty.

In particular, it shall contain an agricultural section and a transport section, which are the subject of special provisions in the Titles relating to agriculture and transport.

These specialized sections shall operate within the general terms of reference of the Committee. They may not be consulted independently of the Committee.

Sub-committees may also be established within the Committee to prepare on specific questions or in specific fields, draft opinions to be submitted to the Committee for its consideration.

The rules of procedure shall lay down the methods of composition and the terms of reference of the specialized sections and of the sub-committees.

Article 198

The Committee must be consulted by the Council or by the Commission where this Treaty so provides. The Committee may be consulted by these institutions in all cases in which they consider it appropriate.

The Council or the Commission shall, if it considers it necessary, set the Committee, for the submission of its opinion, a time limit which may not be less than ten days from the date which the chairman receives notification to this effect. Upon expiry of the time limit, the absence of an opinion shall not prevent further action.

The opinion of the Committee and that of the specialized section, together with a record of the proceedings, shall be forwarded to the Council and to the Commission.

TITLE II. FINANCIAL PROVISIONS

Article 199

All items of revenue and expenditure of the Community, including those relating to the European Social Fund, shall be included in estimates to be drawn up for each financial year and shall be shown in the budget.

The revenue and expenditure shown in the budget shall be in balance. . . .

Article 203

1. The financial year shall run from 1 January to 31 December.

2. Each institution of the Community shall, before 1 July, draw up estimates of its expenditure. The Commission shall consolidate these estimates in a preliminary draft budget. It shall attach thereto an opinion which may contain different estimates.

The preliminary draft budget shall contain an estimate of revenue and an estimate of expenditure.

3. The Commission shall place the preliminary draft budget before the Council not later than 1 September of the year preceding that in which the budget is to be implemented.

The Council shall consult the Commission and, where appropriate, the other institutions concerned whenever it intends to depart from the preliminary draft budget.

The Council, acting by a qualified majority, shall establish the draft budget and forward it to the European Parliament.

4. The draft budget shall be placed before the European Parliament not later than 5 October of the year preceding that in which the budget is to be implemented.

The European Parliament shall have the right to amend the draft budget, acting by a majority of its members, and to propose to the Council, acting by an absolute majority of the votes cast, modifications to the draft budget relating to expenditure necessarily resulting from this Treaty or from acts adopted in accordance therewith.

If, within 45 days of the draft budget being placed before it, the European Parliament has given its approval, the budget shall stand as finally adopted. If within this period the European Parliament has not amended the draft budget nor proposed any modifications thereto, the budget shall be deemed to be finally adopted.

If within this period the European Parliament has adopted amendments or proposed modifications, the draft budget together with the amendments or proposed modifications shall be forwarded to the Council.

5. After discussing the draft budget with the Commission and, where appropriate, with the other institutions concerned, the Council shall act under the following conditions:

(a) The Council may, acting by a qualified majority, modify any of the amendments adopted by the European Parliament;

(b) With regard to the proposed modifications:

— where a modification proposed by the European Parliament does not have the effect of increasing the total amount of the expenditure of an institution, owing in particular to the fact that the increase in expenditure which it would involve would be expressly compensated by one or more proposed modifications correspondingly reducing expenditure, the Council may, acting by a qualified majority, reject the proposed modification. In the absence of a decision to reject it, the proposed modification shall stand as accepted;

— where a modification proposed by the European Parliament has the effect of increasing the total amount of the expenditure of an institution, the Council may, acting by a qualified majority, accept this proposed modification. In the absence of a decision to accept it, the proposed modification shall stand as rejected:

— where, in pursuance of one of the two preceding subparagraphs, the Council has rejected a proposed modification, it may, acting by a qualified majority, either retain the amount shown in the draft budget or fix another amount.

The draft budget shall be modified on the basis of the proposed modifications accepted by the Council.

If, within 15 days of the draft being placed before it, the Council has not modified any of the amendments adopted by the European Parliament and if the modifications proposed by the latter have been accepted, the budget shall be deemed to be finally adopted. The Council shall inform the European Parliament that it has not modified any of the amendments and that the proposed modifications have been accepted.

If within this period the Council has modified one or more of the amendments adopted by the European Parliament or if the modifications proposed by the latter have been rejected or modified, the modified draft budget shall again be forwarded to the European Parliament. The Council shall inform the European Parliament of the results of its deliberations.

6. Within 15 days of the draft budget being placed before it, the European Parliament, which shall have been notified of the action taken on its proposed modifications, may, acting by a majority of its members and three-fifths of the votes cast, amend or reject the modifications to its amendments made by the Council and shall adopt the budget accordingly. If within this period the European Parliament has not acted, the budget shall be deemed to be finally adopted.

7. When the procedure provided for in this Article has been completed, the President of the European Parliament shall declare that the budget has been finally adopted.

8. However, the European Parliament, acting by a majority of its members and two-thirds of the votes cast, may, if there are important reasons, reject the draft budget and ask for a new draft to be submitted to it. . . .

Part Six. General and Final Provisions

Article 210

The Community shall have legal personality.

Article 211

In each of the Member States, the Community shall enjoy the most extensive legal capacity accorded to legal persons under their laws; it may, in particular, acquire or dispose of movable and immovable property and may be a party to legal proceedings. To this end, the Community shall be represented by the Commission.

Article 212

(Article Repealed by Article 24 of the Merger Treaty)

[*See Article 24 (1) of the Merger Treaty, which reads as follows:*

1. The officials and other servants of the European Coal and Steel Community, the European Economic Community and the European Atomic Energy Community shall, at the date of entry into force of this Treaty, become officials and other servants of the European Communities and form part of the single administration of those Communities.

The Council shall, acting by a qualified majority on a proposal from the Commission and after consulting the other institutions concerned, lay down the Staff Regulations of officials of the European Communities and the Conditions of Employment of other servants of those Communities.]

Article 213

The Commission may, within the limits and under conditions laid down by the Council in accordance with the provisions of this Treaty, collect any information and carry out any checks required for the performance of the tasks entrusted to it.

Article 214

The members of the institutions of the Community, the members of committees, and the officials and other servants of the Community shall be required, even after their duties have ceased, not to disclose information of the kind covered by the obligation of professional secrecy, in particular information about undertakings, their business relations or their cost components.

Article 215

The contractual liability of the Community shall be governed by the law applicable to the contract in question.

In the case of non-contractual liability, the Community shall, in accordance with the general principles common to the laws of the Member States, make good any damage caused by its institutions or by its servants in the performance of their duties.

The personal liability of its servants towards the Community shall be governed by the provisions laid down in their Staff Regulations or in the Conditions of Employment applicable to them.

Article 216

The seat of the institutions of the Community shall be determined by common accord of the Governments of the Member States.

Article 217

The rules governing the languages of the institutions of the Community shall, without prejudice to the provisions contained in the rules of procedure of the Court of Justice, be determined by the Council, acting unanimously.

Article 218

(*Article Repealed by the Second Paragraph of Article 28 of the Merger Treaty*)

[*See the first paragraph of Article 28 of the Merger Treaty, which reads as follows:*

The European Communities shall enjoy in the territories of the Member States such privileges and immunities as are necessary for the performance of their tasks, under the conditions laid down in the Protocol annexed to this Treaty. The same shall apply to the European Investment Bank.]

Article 219

Member States undertake not to submit a dispute concerning the interpretation or application of this Treaty to any method of settlement other than those provided for therein.

Article 220

Member States shall, so far as is necessary, enter into negotiations with each other with a view to securing for the benefit of their nationals:
— the protection of persons and the enjoyment and protection of rights under the same conditions as those accorded by each State to its own nationals;
— the abolition of double taxation within the Community;
— the mutual recognition of companies or firms within the meaning of the second paragraph of Article 48, the retention of legal personality in the event of transfer of their seat from one country to another, and the possibility of mergers between companies or firms governed by the laws of different countries;
— the simplification of formalities governing the reciprocal recognition and enforcement of judgments of courts or tribunals and of arbitration awards.

Article 221

Within three years of the entry into force of this Treaty, Member States shall accord nationals of the other Member States the same treatment as their own nationals as regards participation in the capital of companies or firms within the meaning of Article 58, without prejudice to the application of the other provisions of this Treaty.

Article 222

This Treaty shall in no way prejudice the rules in Member States governing the system of property ownership.

Article 223

1. The provisions of this Treaty shall not preclude the application of the following rules:

(a) No Member State shall be obliged to supply information the disclosure of which it considers contrary to the essential interests of its security;

(b) Any Member State may take such measures as it considers necessary for the protection of the essential interests of its security which are connected with the production of or trade in arms, munitions and war material; such measures shall not adversely affect the conditions of competition in the common market regarding products which are not intended for specifically military purposes.

2. During the first year after the entry into force of this Treaty, the Council shall, acting unanimously, draw up a list of products to which the provisions of paragraph 1 (b) shall apply.

3. The Council may, acting unanimously on a proposal from the Commission, make changes in this list.

Article 224

Member States shall consult each other with a view to taking together the steps needed to prevent the functioning of the common market being affected by measures which a Member State may be called upon to take in the event of serious internal disturbances affecting the maintenance of law and order, in the event of war, serious international tension constituting a threat of war, or in order to carry out obligations it has accepted for the purpose of maintaining peace and international security.

Article 225

If measures taken in the circumstances referred to in Articles 223 and 224 have the effect of distorting the conditions of competition in the common market, the Commission shall, together with the State concerned, examine how these measures can be adjusted to the rules laid down in this Treaty.

By way of derogation from the procedure laid down in Articles 169 and 170, the Commission or any Member State may bring the matter directly before the Court of Justice if it considers that another Member State is making improper use of the powers provided for in Articles 223 and 224. The Court of Justice shall give its ruling *in camera*. . . .

Article 227

1. This Treaty shall apply to the Kingdom of Belgium, the Kingdom of Denmark, the Federal Republic of Germany, the Hellenic Republic, the Kingdom of Spain, the French Republic, Ireland, the Italian Republic, the Grand Duchy of Luxembourg, the Kingdom of the Netherlands, the Por-

tuguese Republic and the United Kingdom of Great Britain and Northern Ireland.

2. With regard to Algeria and the French overseas departments, the general and particular provisions of this Treaty relating to:
— the free movement of goods;
— agriculture, save for Article 40(4);
— the liberalization of services;
— the rules on competition;
— the protective measures provided for in Articles 108, 109, and 226;
— the institutions,
shall apply as soon as this Treaty enters into force.

The conditions under which the other provisions of this Treaty are to apply shall be determined, within two years of the entry into force of this Treaty, by decisions of the Council, acting unanimously on a proposal from the Commission.

The institutions of the Community will, within the framework of the procedures provided for in this Treaty, in particular Article 226, take care that the economic and social development of these areas is made possible.

3. The special arrangements for association set out in Part Four of this Treaty shall apply to the overseas countries and territories listed in Annex IV to this Treaty.

This Treaty shall not apply to those overseas countries and territories having special relations with the United Kingdom of Great Britain and Northern Ireland which are not included in the aforementioned list.

4. The provisions of this Treaty shall apply to the European territories for whose external relations a Member State is responsible. . . .

Article 228

1. Where this Treaty provides for the conclusion of agreements between the Community and one or more States or an international organization, such agreements shall be negotiated by the Commission. Subject to the powers vested in the Commission in this field, such agreements shall be concluded by the Council, after consulting the European Parliament where required by this Treaty.

The Council, the Commission or a Member State may obtain beforehand the opinion of the Court of Justice as to whether an agreement envisaged is compatible with the provisions of this Treaty. Where the opinion of the Court of Justice is adverse, the agreement may enter into force only in accordance with Article 236.

2. Agreements concluded under these conditions shall be binding on the institutions of the Community and on Member States.

Article 229

It shall be for the Commission to ensure the maintenance of all appropriate relations with the organs of the United Nations, of its specialized agencies and of the General Agreement on Tariffs and Trade.

The Commission shall also maintain such relations as are appropriate with all international organizations.

Article 230

The Community shall establish all appropriate forms of cooperation with the Council of Europe.

Article 231

The Community shall establish close cooperation with the Organization for European Economic Cooperation, the details to be determined by common accord.

Article 232

1. The provisions of this Treaty shall not affect the provisions of the Treaty establishing the European Coal and Steel Community, in particular as regards the rights and obligations of Member States, the powers of the institutions of that Community and the rules laid down by that Treaty for the functioning of the common market in coal and steel.

2. The provisions of this Treaty shall not derogate from those of the Treaty establishing the European Atomic Energy Community.

Article 233

The provisions of this Treaty shall not preclude the existence or completion of regional unions between Belgium and Luxembourg, or between Belgium, Luxembourg and the Netherlands, to the extent that the objectives of these regional unions are not attained by application of this Treaty.

Article 234

The rights and obligations arising from agreements concluded before the entry into force of this Treaty between one or more Member States on the one hand, and one or more third countries on the other, shall not be affected by the provisions of this Treaty.

To the extent that such agreements are not compatible with this Treaty, the Member State or States concerned shall take all appropriate steps to eliminate the incompatibilities established. Member States shall, where necessary, assist each other to this end and shall, where appropriate, adopt a common attitude.

In applying the agreements referred to in the first paragraph, Member States shall take into account the fact that the advantages accorded under this Treaty by each Member State form an integral part of the establishment of the Community and are thereby inseparably linked with the creation of common institutions, the conferring of powers upon them and the granting of the same advantages by all the other Member States.

Article 235

If action by the Community should prove necessary to attain, in the course of the operation of the common market, one of the objectives of the Community and this Treaty has not provided the necessary powers, the Council shall, acting unanimously on a proposal from the Commission and after consulting the European Parliament, take the appropriate measures.

Article 236

The Government of any Member State or the Commission may submit to the Council proposals for the amendment of this Treaty.

If the Council, after consulting the European Parliament and, where appropriate, the Commission, delivers an opinion in favour of calling a conference of representatives of the Governments of the Member States, the conference shall be convened by the President of the Council for the purpose of determining by common accord the amendments to be made to this Treaty.

The amendments shall enter into force after being ratified by all the Member States in accordance with their respective constitutional requirements.

Article 237

[Any European State may apply to become a member of the Community. It shall address its application to the Council, which shall act unanimously after consulting the Commission and after receiving the assent of the European Parliament which shall act by an absolute majority of its component members.]

The conditions of admission and the adjustments to this Treaty necessitated thereby shall be the subject of an agreement between the Member States and the applicant State. This agreement shall be submitted for ratification by all the Contracting States in accordance with their respective constitutional requirements.

Article 238

The Community may conclude with a third State, a union of States or an international organization agreements establishing an association involving reciprocal rights and obligations, common action and special procedures.

[These agreements shall be concluded by the Council, acting unanimously and after receiving the assent of the European Parliament which shall act by an absolute majority of its component members.]

Where such agreements call for amendments to this Treaty, these amendments shall first be adopted in accordance with the procedure laid down in Article 236.

Article 239

The Protocols annexed to this Treaty by common accord of the Member States shall form an integral part thereof.

Article 240

This Treaty is concluded for an unlimited period.

TITLE III OF THE SINGLE EUROPEAN ACT (SEA) (1987), EUROPEAN COOPERATION IN THE SPHERE OF FOREIGN POLICY*

Article 30

European Cooperation in the sphere of foreign policy shall be governed by the following provisions:

1. The High Contracting Parties, being members of the European Communities, shall endeavour jointly to formulate and implement a European foreign policy.

2. (a) The High Contracting Parties undertake to inform and consult each other on any foreign policy matters of general interest so as to ensure that their combined influence is exercised as effectively as possible through coordination, the convergence of their positions and the implementation of joint action.

(b) Consultations shall take place before the High Contracting Parties decide on their final position.

(c) In adopting its positions and in its national measures each High Contracting Party shall take full account of the positions of the other partners and shall give due consideration to the desirability of adopting and implementing common European positions.

In order to increase their capacity for joint action in the foreign policy field, the High Contracting Parties shall ensure that common principles and objectives are gradually developed and defined.

The determination of common positions shall constitute a point of reference for the policies of the High Contracting Parties.

(d) The High Contracting Parties shall endeavour to avoid any action or position which impairs their effectiveness as a cohesive force in international relations or within international organizations.

3. (a) The Ministers for Foreign Affairs and a member of the Commission shall meet at least four times a year within the framework of European Political Cooperation. They may also discuss foreign policy matters within the framework of Political Cooperation on the occasion of meetings of the Council of the European Communities.

*The Single European Act was signed in February 1986 and came into force in the European Community on July 1, 1987. For further information, see the footnote to the preceding document, the Treaty of Rome.

(b) The Commission shall be fully associated with the proceedings of Political Cooperation.

(c) In order to ensure the swift adoption of common positions and the implementation of joint action, the High Contracting Parties shall, as far as possible, refrain from impeding the formation of a consensus and the joint action which this could produce.

4. The High Contracting Parties shall ensure that the European Parliament is closely associated with European Political Cooperation. To that end the Presidency shall regularly inform the European Parliament of the foreign policy issues which are being examined within the framework of Political Cooperation and shall ensure that the views of the European Parliament are duly taken into consideration.

5. The external policies of the European Community and the policies agreed in European Political Cooperation must be consistent.

The Presidency and the Commission, each within its own sphere of competence, shall have special responsibility for ensuring that such consistency is sought and maintained.

6. (a) The High Contracting Parties consider that closer cooperation on questions of European security would contribute in an essential way to the development of a European identity in external policy matters. They are ready to coordinate their positions more closely on the political and economic aspects of security.

(b) The High Contracting Parties are determined to maintain the technological and industrial conditions necessary for their security. They shall work to that end both at national level and, where appropriate, within the framework of the competent institutions and bodies.

(c) Nothing in this Title shall impede closer cooperation in the field of security between certain of the High Contracting Parties within the framework of the Western European Union or the Atlantic Alliance.

7. (a) In international institutions and at international conferences which they attend, the High Contracting Parties shall endeavour to adopt common positions on the subjects covered by this Title.

(b) In international institutions and at international conferences in which not all the High Contracting Parties participate, those who do participate shall take full account of positions agreed in European Political Cooperation.

8. The High Contracting Parties shall organize a political dialogue with third countries and regional groupings whenever they deem it necessary.

9. The High Contracting Parties and the Commission, through mutual assistance and information, shall intensify cooperation between their representations accredited to third countries and to international organizations.

10. (a) The Presidency of European Political Cooperation shall be held by the High Contracting Party which holds the Presidency of the Council of the European Communities.

(b) The Presidency shall be responsible for initiating action and coordinating and representing the positions of the Member States in relations with third countries in respect of European Political Cooperation activities. It shall also be responsible for the management of Political Cooperation and in particular for drawing up the timetable of meetings and for convening and organizing meetings.

(c) The Political Directors shall meet regularly in the Political Committee in order to give the necessary impetus, maintain the continuity of European Political Cooperation and prepare Ministers' discussions.

(d) The Political Committee or, if necessary, a ministerial meeting shall convene within forty-eight hours at the request of at least three Member States.

(e) The European Correspondents' Group shall be responsible, under the direction of the Political Committee, for monitoring the implementation of European Political Cooperation and for studying general organizational problems.

(f) Working Groups shall meet as directed by the Political Committee.

(g) A Secretariat based in Brussels shall assist the Presidency in preparing and implementing the activities of European Political Cooperation and in administrative matters. It shall carry out its duties under the authority of the Presidency.

11. As regards privileges and immunities, the members of the European Political Cooperation Secretariat shall be treated in the same way as members of the diplomatic missions of the High Contracting Parties based in the same place as the Secretariat.

12. Five years after the entry into force of this Act the High Contracting Parties shall examine whether any revision of Title III is required.

INTER-AMERICAN TREATY OF RECIPROCAL ASSISTANCE (RIO TREATY)

September 2, 1947, 62 Stat. 1681, T.I.A.S. No. 1838*

In the name of their Peoples, the Governments represented at the Inter-American Conference for the Maintenance of Continental Peace and Security, desirous of consolidating and strengthening their relations of friendship and good neighborliness, and

Considering:

That Resolution VIII of the Inter-American Conference on Problems of War and Peace, which met in Mexico City, recommended the conclusion of a treaty to prevent and repel threats and acts of aggression against any of the countries of America;

That the High Contracting Parties reiterate their will to remain united in an inter-American system consistent with the purposes and principles of the United Nations, and reaffirm the existence of the agreement which they have concluded concerning those matters relating to the maintenance of international peace and security which are appropriate for regional action;

That the High Contracting Parties reaffirm their adherence to the principles of inter-American solidarity and cooperation, and especially to those set forth in the preamble and declarations of the Act of Chapultepec, all of which should be understood to be accepted as standards of their mutual relations and as the juridical basis of the Inter-American System;

That the American States propose, in order to improve the procedures for the pacific settlement of their controversies, to conclude the treaty concerning the "Inter-American Peace System" envisaged in Resolutions IX and XXXIX of the Inter-American Conference on Problems of War and Peace,

That the obligation of mutual assistance and common defense of the American Republics is essentially related to their democratic ideals and to their will to cooperate permanently in the fulfillment of the principles and purposes of a policy of peace;

That the American regional community affirms as a manifest truth that juridical organization is a necessary prerequisite of security and peace, and

---

*Done at Rio de Janeiro on September 2, 1947. Entered into force December 3, 1948. The 23 parties to the treaty are: Argentina, Bahamas, Bolivia, Brazil, Chile, Colombia, Costa Rica, Cuba, Dominican Republic, Ecuador, El Salvador, Guatemala, Haiti, Honduras, Mexico, Nicaragua, Panama, Paraguay, Peru, Trinidad & Tobago, United States, Uruguay, and Venezuela.

that peace is founded on justice and moral order and, consequently, on the international recognition and protection of human rights and freedoms, on the indispensable well-being of the people, and on the effectiveness of democracy for the international realization of justice and security,

Have resolved, in conformity with the objectives stated above, to conclude the following Treaty, in order to assure peace, through adequate means, to provide for effective reciprocal assistance to meet armed attacks against any American State, and in order to deal with threats of aggression against any of them:

Article 1

The High Contracting Parties formally condemn war and undertake in their international relations not to resort to the threat or the use of force in any manner inconsistent with the provisions of the Charter of the United Nations or of this Treaty.

Article 2

As a consequence of the principle set forth in the preceding Article, the High Contracting Parties undertake to submit every controversy which may arise between them to methods of peaceful settlement and to endeavor to settle any such controversy among themselves by means of the procedures in force in the Inter-American System before referring it to the General Assembly or the Security Council of the United Nations.

Article 3

1. The High Contracting Parties agree that an armed attack by any State against an American State shall be considered as an attack against all the American States and, consequently, each one of the said Contracting Parties undertakes to assist in meeting the attack in the exercise of the inherent right of individual or collective self-defense recognized by Article 51 of the Charter of the United Nations.

2. On the request of the State or States directly attacked and until the decision of the Organ of Consultation of the Inter-American System, each one of the Contracting Parties may determine the immediate measures which it may individually take in fulfillment of the obligation contained in the preceding paragraph and in accordance with the principle of continental solidarity. The Organ of Consultation shall meet without delay for the purpose of examining those measures and agreeing upon the measures of a collective character that should be taken.

3. The provisions of this Article shall be applied in case of any armed attack which takes place within the region described in Article 4 or within the territory of an American State. When the attack takes place outside of the said areas, the provisions of Article 6 shall be applied.

4. Measures of self-defense provided for under this Article may be taken until the Security Council of the United Nations has taken the measures necessary to maintain international peace and security.

Article 4

The region to which this Treaty refers is bounded as follows: beginning at the North Pole; thence due south to a point 74 degrees north latitude, 10 degrees west longitude; thence by a rhumb line to a point 47 degrees 30 minutes north latitude, 50 degrees west longitude; thence by a rhumb line to a point 35 degrees north latitude, 60 degrees west longitude; thence due south to a point in 20 degrees north latitude; thence by a rhumb line to a point 5 degrees north latitude, 24 degrees west longitude; thence due south to the South Pole; thence due north to a point 30 degrees south latitude, 90 degrees west longitude; thence by a rhumb line to a point on the Equator at 97 degrees west longitude; thence by a rhumb line to a point 15 degrees north latitude, 120 degrees west longitude; thence by a rhumb line to a point 50 degrees north latitude, 170 degrees east longitude; thence due north to a point in 54 degrees north latitude; thence by a thumb line to a point 65 degrees 30 minutes north latitude, 168 degrees 58 minutes 5 seconds west longitude; thence due north to the North Pole.

Article 5

The High Contracting Parties shall immediately send to the Security Council of the United Nations, in conformity with Articles 51 and 54 of the Charter of the United Nations, complete information concerning the activities undertaken or in contemplation in the exercise of the right of self-defense or for the purpose of maintaining inter-American peace and security.

Article 6

If the inviolability or the integrity of the territory or the sovereignty or political independence of any American State should be affected by an aggression which is not an armed attack or by an extra-continental or intra-continental conflict, or by any other fact or situation that might endanger the peace of America, the Organ of Consultation shall meet immediately in order to agree on the measures which must be taken in case of aggression to assist the victim of the aggression or, in any case, the measures which should be taken for the common defense and for the maintenance of the peace and security of the Continent.

Article 7

In the case of a conflict between two or more American States, without prejudice to the right of self-defense in conformity with Article 51 of the Charter of the United Nations, the High Contracting Parties, meeting in consultation shall call upon the contending States to suspend hostilities and restore matters to the *statu quo ante bellum,* and shall take in addition all other necessary measures to reestablish or maintain inter-American peace and security and for the solution of the conflict by peaceful means. The rejection of the pacifying action will be considered in the determination of the aggressor and in the application of the measures which the consultative meeting may agree upon.

Article 8

For the purposes of this Treaty, the measures on which the Organ of Consultation may agree will comprise one or more of the following: recall of chiefs of diplomatic missions; breaking of diplomatic relations; breaking of consular relations; partial or complete interruption of economic relations or of rail, sea, air, postal, telegraphic, telephonic, and radiotelephonic or radio-telegraphic communications; and use of armed force.

Article 9

In addition to other acts which the Organ of Consultation may characterize as aggression, the following shall be considered as such:

a. Unprovoked armed attack by a State against the territory, the people, or the land, sea or air forces of another State;

b. Invasion, by the armed forces of a State, of the territory of an American State, through the trespassing of boundaries demarcated in accordance with a treaty, judicial decision, or arbitral award, or, in the absence of frontiers thus demarcated, invasion affecting a region which is under the effective jurisdiction of another State.

Article 10

None of the provisions of this Treaty shall be construed as impairing the rights and obligations of the High Contracting Parties under the Charter of the United Nations.

Article 11

The consultations to which this Treaty refers shall be carried out by means of the Meetings of Ministers of Foreign Affairs of the American Republics which have ratified the Treaty, or in the manner or by the organ which in the future may be agreed upon.

Article 12

The Governing Board of the Pan American Union may act provisionally as an organ of consultation until the meeting of the Organ of Consultation referred to in the preceding Article takes place.

Article 13

The consultations shall be initiated at the request addressed to the Governing Board of the Pan American Union by any of the Signatory States which has ratified the Treaty.

Article 14

In the voting referred to in this Treaty only the representatives of the Signatory States which have ratified the Treaty may take part.

Article 15

The Governing Board of the Pan American Union shall act in all matters concerning this Treaty as an organ of liaison among the Signatory States which have ratified this Treaty and between these States and the United Nations.

Article 16

The decisions of the Governing Board of the Pan American Union referred to in Articles 13 and 15 above shall be taken by an absolute majority of the Members entitled to vote.

Article 17

The Organ of Consultation shall take its decisions by a vote of two-thirds of the Signatory States which have ratified the Treaty.

Article 18

In the case of a situation or dispute between American States, the parties directly interested shall be excluded from the voting referred to in two preceding Articles.

Article 19

To constitute a quorum in all the meetings referred to in the previous Articles, it shall be necessary that the number of States represented shall be at least equal to the number of votes necessary for the taking of the decision.

Article 20

Decisions which require the application of the measures specified in Article 8 shall be binding upon all the Signatory States which have ratified this Treaty, with the sole exception that no State shall be required to use armed force without its consent.

Article 21

The measures agreed upon by the Organ of Consultation shall be executed through the procedures and agencies now existing or those which may in the future be established.

Article 22

This Treaty shall come into effect between the States which ratify it as soon as the ratifications of two-thirds of the Signatory States have been deposited.

Article 23

This Treaty is open for signature by the American States at the city of Rio de Janeiro, and shall be ratified by the Signatory States as soon as possible in accordance with their respective constitutional processes. The ratifications shall be deposited with the Pan American Union, which shall notify the Signatory States of each deposit. Such notification shall be considered as an exchange of ratifications.

Article 24

The present Treaty shall be registered with the Secretariat of the United Nations through the Pan American Union, when two-thirds of the Signatory States have deposited their ratifications.

Article 25

This Treaty shall remain in force indefinitely, but may be denounced by any High Contracting Party by a notification in writing to the Pan American Union, which shall inform all the other High Contracting Parties of each notification of denunciation received. After the expiration of two years from the date of the receipt by the Pan American Union of a notification of denunciation by any High Contracting Party, the present Treaty shall cease to be in force and* with respect to such State, but shall remain in full force and effect with respect to all the other High Contracting Parties.

Article 26

The principles and fundamental provisions of this Treaty shall be incorporated in the Organic Pact of the Inter-American System. . . .

---

*The equivalent of the word "and" does not appear in the French, Portuguese, or Spanish texts.

CHARTER OF THE ORGANIZATION OF AMERICAN STATES (as amended)

April 30, 1948, 2 U.S.T. 2394, T.I.A.S. No. 2361; amended effective 1970, 21 U.S.T. 607, T.I.A.S. No. 6847*

In the Name of Their Peoples, the States Represented at the Ninth International Conference of American States,

Convinced that the historic mission of America is to offer to man a land of liberty, and a favorable environment for the development of his personality and the realization of his just aspirations;

Conscious that that mission has already inspired numerous agreements, whose essential value lies in the desire of the American peoples to live together in peace, and, through their mutual understanding and respect for the sovereignty of each one, to provide for the betterment of all, in independence, in equality and under law;

Confident that the true significance of American solidarity and good neighborliness can only mean the consolidation on this continent, within the framework of democratic institutions, of a system of individual liberty and social justice based on respect for the essential rights of man;

Persuaded that their welfare and their contribution to the progress and the civilization of the world will increasingly require intensive continental co-operation;

Resolved to persevere in the noble undertaking that humanity has conferred upon the United Nations, whose principles and purposes they solemnly reaffirm;

Convinced that juridical organization is a necessary condition for security and peace founded on moral order and on justice; and

---

*Done at Bogota on April 30, 1948. Entered into force on December 13, 1951. The 1967 Protocol of Amendment came into force on February 27, 1970. The 33 parties to the charter are: Antigua & Barbuda, Argentina, Bahamas, Barbados, Bolivia, Brazil, Canada, Chile, Colombia, Costa Rica, Cuba, Dominica, Dominican Republic, Ecuador, El Salvador, Grenada, Guatemala, Haiti, Honduras, Jamaica, Mexico, Nicaragua, Panama, Paraguay, Peru, St. Kitts & Nevis, Saint Lucia, Saint Vincent & the Grenadines, Suriname, Trinidad & Tobago, United States, Uruguay, and Venezuela. Cuba was suspended from the OAS in January 1962, on the grounds that adoption of a Marxist-Leninist form of government was not compatible with OAS membership.

A 1985 Protocol, 25 I.L.M. 529 (1986), is in force for many of the parties. The 1985 Protocol, however, is not provided here because it has not been ratified by the United States and several other parties — Canada, Chile, Costa Rica, Ecuador, Guatemala, Haiti, Panama, Peru, Uruguay, and Venezuela.

In accordance with Resolution IX of the Inter-American Conference on Problems of War and Peace, held at Mexico City,

Have Agreed upon the following.

Part One

CHAPTER I. NATURE AND PURPOSES

Article 1

The American States establish by this Charter the international organization that they have developed to achieve an order of peace and justice, to promote their solidarity, to strengthen their collaboration, and to defend their sovereignty, their territorial integrity, and their independence. Within the United Nations, the Organization of American States is a regional agency.

Article 2

The Organization of American States, in order to put into practice the principles on which it is founded and to fulfill its regional obligations under the Charter of the United Nations, proclaims the following essential purposes:

(a) To strengthen the peace and security of the continent;

(b) To prevent possible causes of difficulties and to ensure the pacific settlement of disputes that may arise among the Member States;

(c) To provide for common action on the part of those States in the event of agression;

(d) To seek the solution of political, juridical, and economic problems that may arise among them; and

(e) To promote, by co-operative action, their economic, social, and cultural development.

CHAPTER II. PRINCIPLES

Article 3

The American States reaffirm the following principles:

(a) International law is the standard of conduct of States in their reciprocal relations;

(b) International order consists essentially of respect for the personality, sovereignty, and independence of States, and the faithful fulfilment of obligations derived from treaties and other sources of international law;

(c) Good faith shall govern the relations between States;

(d) The solidarity of the American States and the high aims which are sought through it require the political organization of those States on the basis of the effective exercise of representative democracy;

(e) The American States condemn wars of aggression: victory does not give rights;

(f) An act of aggression against one American State is an act of aggression against all the other American States;

(g) Controversies of an international character arising between two or more American States shall be settled by peaceful procedures;

(h) Social justice and social security are bases of lasting peace;

(i) Economic co-operation is essential to the common welfare and prosperity of the peoples of the continent;

(j) The American States proclaim the fundamental rights of the individual without distinction as to race, nationality, creed, or sex;

(k) The spiritual unity of the continent is based on respect for the cultural values of the American countries and requires their close co-operation for the high purposes of civilization;

(l) The education of peoples should be directed toward justice, freedom, and peace.

Chapter III. Members

Article 4

All American States that ratify the present Charter are Members of the Organization.

Article 5

Any new political entity that arises from the union of several Member States and that, as such, ratifies the present Charter, shall become a Member of the Organization. The entry of the new political entity into the Organization shall result in the loss of membership of each one of the States which constitute it.

Article 6

Any other independent American State that desires to become a Member of the Organization should so indicate by means of a note addressed to the Secretary-General, in which it declares that it is willing to sign and ratify the Charter of the Organization and to accept all the obligations inherent in membership, especially those relating to collective security expressly set forth in Articles 27 and 28 of the Charter.

Article 7

The General Assembly, upon the recommendation of the Permanent Council of the Organization, shall determine whether it is appropriate that the Secretary-General be authorized to permit the applicant State to sign the Charter and to accept the deposit of the Permanent Council and the decision of the General Assembly shall require the affirmative vote of two thirds of the Member States.

Article 8

The Permanent Council shall not make any recommendation nor shall the General Assembly take any decision with respect to a request for admission on the part of a political entity whose territory became subject, in whole or in part, prior to December 18, 1964, the date set by the First Special Inter-American Conference, to litigation or claim between an extracontinental country and one or more Member States of the Organization, until the dispute has been ended by some peaceful procedure.

CHAPTER IV. FUNDAMENTAL RIGHTS AND DUTIES OF STATES

Article 9

States are juridically equal, enjoy equal rights and equal capacity to exercise these rights, and have equal duties. The rights of each State depend not upon its power to ensure the exercise thereof, but upon the mere fact of its existence as a person under international law.

Article 10

Every American State has the duty to respect the rights enjoyed by every other State in accordance with international law.

Article 11

The fundamental rights of States may not be impaired in any manner whatsoever.

Article 12

The political existence of the State is independent of recognition by other States. Even before being recognized, the State has the right to defend its integrity and independence, to provide for its preservation and prosperity, and consequently to organize itself as it sees fit, to legislate concerning its interests, to administer its services, and to determine the jurisdiction and competence of its courts. The exercise of these rights is limited only by the exercise of the rights of other States in accordance with international law.

Article 13

Recognition implies that the State granting it accepts the personability of the new State, with all the rights and duties that international law prescribes for the two States.

Article 14

The right of each State to protect itself and to live its own life does not authorize it to commit unjust acts against another State.

Article 15

The jurisdiction of States within the limits of their national territory is exercised equally over all the inhabitants, whether nationals or aliens.

Article 16

Each State has the right to develop its cultural, political, and economic life freely and naturally. In this free development, the State shall respect the rights of the individual and the principles of universal morality.

Article 17

Respect for and the faithful observance of treaties constitute standards for the development of peaceful relations among States. International treaties and agreements should be public.

Article 18

No State or group of States has the right to intervene, directly or indirectly, for any reason whatever, in the internal or external affairs of any other State. The foregoing principle prohibits not only armed force but also any other form of interference or attempted threat against the personality of the State or against its political, economic, and cultural elements.

Article 19

No State may use or encourage the use of coercive measures of an economic or political character in order to force the sovereign will of another State and obtain from it advantages of any kind.

Article 20

The territory of a State is inviolable; it may not be the object, even temporarily, of military occupation or of other measures of force taken by another State, directly or indirectly, on any grounds whatever. No territorial acquisitions or special advantages obtained either by force or by other means of coercion shall be recognized.

Article 21

The American States bind themselves in their international relations not to have recourse to the use of force, except in the case of self-defense in accordance with existing treaties or in fulfillment thereof.

Article 22

Measures adopted for the maintenance of peace and security in accordance with existing treaties do not constitute a violation of the principles set forth in Articles 18 and 20.

Chapter V. Pacific Settlement of Disputes

Article 23

All international disputes that may arise between American States shall be submitted to the peaceful procedures set forth in this Charter, before being referred to the Security Council of the United Nations.

Article 24

The following are peaceful procedures: direct negotiation, good offices, mediation, investigation and conciliation, judicial settlement, arbitration, and those which the parties to the dispute may especially agree upon at any time.

Article 25

In the event that a dispute arises between two or more American States which, in the opinion of one of them, cannot be settled through the usual diplomatic channels, the parties shall agree on some other peaceful procedure that will enable them to reach a solution.

Article 26

A special treaty will establish adequate procedures for the pacific settlement of disputes and will determine the appropriate means for their application, so that no dispute between American States shall fail of definitive settlement within a reasonable period.

Chapter VI. Collective Security

Article 27

Every act of aggression by a State against the territorial integrity or the inviolability of the territory or against the sovereignty or political independence of an American State shall be considered an act of aggression against the other American States.

Article 28

If the inviolability or the integrity of the territory or the sovereignty or political independence of any American State should be affected by an armed attack or by an act of aggression that is not an armed attack, or by an extra-continental conflict, or by a conflict between two or more American States, or by any other fact or situation that might endanger the peace of America, the American States, in furtherance of the principles of continental solidarity or collective self-defense, shall apply the measures and procedures established in the special treaties on the subject.

Chapter VII. Economic Standards

Article 29

The Member States, inspired by the principles of inter-American solidarity and co-operation, pledge themselves to a united effort to ensure social justice in the Hemisphere and dynamic and balanced economic development for their peoples, as conditions essential to peace and security.

Article 30

The Member States pledge themselves to mobilize their own national human and material resources through suitable programs, and recognize the importance of operating within an efficient domestic structure, as fundamental conditions for their economic and social progress and for assuring effective inter-American cooperation.

Article 31

To accelerate their economic and social development, in accordance with their own methods and procedures and within the framework of the democratic principles and the institutions of the inter-American system, the Member States agree to dedicate every effort to achieve the following basic goals:

(a) Substantial and self-sustained increase in the per capita national product;

(b) Equitable distribution of national income;

(c) Adequate and equitable systems of taxation;

(d) Modernization of rural life and reforms leading to equitable and efficient land-tenure systems, increased agricultural productivity, expanded use of undeveloped land, diversification of production; and improved processing and marketing systems for agricultural products; and the strengthening and expansion of facilities to attain these ends;

(e) Accelerated and diversified industrialization, especially of capital and intermediate goods;

(f) Stability in the domestic price levels, compatible with sustained economic development and the attainment of social justice;

(g) Fair wages, employment opportunities, and acceptable working conditions for all;

(h) Rapid eradication of illiteracy and expansion of educational opportunities for all;

(i) Protection of man's potential through the extension and application of modern medical science;

(j) Proper nutrition, especially through the acceleration of national efforts to increase the production and availability of food;

(k) Adequate housing for all sectors of the population;

(l) Urban conditions that offer the opportunity for a healthful, productive, and full life;

(m) Promotion of private initiative and investment in harmony with action in the public sector; and

(n) Expansion and diversification of exports.

Article 32

In order to attain the objectives set forth in this Chapter, the Member States agree to co-operate with one another, in the broadest spirit of inter-American solidarity, as far as their resources may permit and their laws may provide. . . .

Article 37

The Member States, recognizing the close interdependence between foreign trade and economic and social development, should make individual and united efforts to bring about the following:

(a) Reduction or elimination, by importing countries, of tariff and non-tariff barriers that affect the exports of the Members of the Organization, except when such barriers are applied in order to diversify the economic structure, to speed up the development of the less-developed Member States, or to intensify their process of economic integration, or when they are related to national security or to the needs for economic balance;

(b) Maintenance of continuity in their economic and social development by means of:

(i) Improved conditions for trade in basic commodities through international agreements, where appropriate; orderly marketing procedures that avoid the disruption of markets; and other measures designed to promote the expansion of markets; and to obtain dependable incomes for producers, adequate and dependable supplies for consumers, and stable prices that are both remunerative to producers and fair to consumers;

(ii) Improved international financial co-operation and the adoption of other means for lessening the adverse impact of sharp fluctuations in export earnings experienced by the countries exporting basic commodities; and

(iii) Diversification of exports and expansion of export opportunities for manufactured and semimanufactured products from the developing countries by promoting and strengthening national and multinational institutions and arrangements established for these purposes.

Article 38

The Member States reaffirm the principle that when the more-developed countries grant concessions in international trade agreements that lower or eliminate tariffs or other barriers to foreign trade so that they benefit the less-developed countries, they should not expect reciprocal concessions from those countries that are incompatible with their economic development, financial, and trade needs.

Article 39

The Member States, in order to accelerate their economic development, regional integration, and the expansion and improvement of the conditions of their commerce, shall promote improvement and coordination of transportation and communication in the developing countries and among the Member States.

Article 40

The Member States recognize that integration of the developing countries of the Hemisphere is one of the objectives of the inter-American system and, therefore, shall orient their efforts and take the necessary measures to accelerate the integration process, with a view to establishing a Latin American common market in the shortest possible time.

Article 41

In order to strengthen and accelerate integration in all its aspects, the Member States agree to give adequate priority to the preparation and carrying out of multinational projects and to their financing, as well as to encourage economic and financial institutions of the inter-American system to continue giving their broadest support to regional integration institutions and programs.

Article 42

The Member States agree that technical and financial cooperation that seeks to promote regional economic integration should be based on the principle of harmonious, balanced, and efficient development, with particular attention to the relatively less-developed countries, so that it may be a decisive factor that will enable them to promote, with their own efforts, the improved development of their infrastructure programs, new lines of production, and export diversification.

CHAPTER VIII. SOCIAL STANDARDS

Article 43

The Member States, convinced that man can only achieve the full realization of his aspirations within a just social order, along with economic development and true peace, agree to dedicate every effort to the application of the following principles and mechanisms:

(a) All human beings, without distinction as to race, sex, nationality, creed, or social condition, have a right to material well-being and to their spiritual development, under circumstances of liberty, dignity, equality of opportunity, and economic security;

(b) Work is a right and a social duty, it gives dignity to the one who performs it, and it should be performed under conditions, including a system of fair wages, that ensure life, health, and a decent standard of living for the worker and his family, both during his working years and in his old age, or when any circumstance deprives him of the possibility of working;

(c) Employers and workers, both rural and urban, have the right to associate themselves freely for the defense and promotion of their interests, including the right to collective bargaining and the workers' right to strike, and recognition of the juridical personality of associations and the protection of their freedom and independence, all in accordance with applicable laws;

(d) Fair and efficient systems and procedures for consultation and collaboration among the sectors of production, with due regard for safeguarding the interests of the entire society;

(e) The operation of systems of public administration, banking and credit, enterprise, and distribution and sales, in such a way, in harmony with the private sector, as to meet the requirements and interests of the community;

(f) The incorporation and increasing participation of the marginal sectors of the population, in both rural and urban areas, in the economic, social, civic, cultural, and political life of the nation, in order to achieve the full integration of the national community, acceleration of the process of social mobility, and the consolidation of the democratic system. The encouragement of all efforts of popular promotion and co-operation that have as their purpose the development and progress of the community;

(g) Recognition of the importance of the contribution of organizations such as labor unions, co-operatives, and cultural, professional, business, neighborhood, and community associations to the life of the society and to the development process;

(h) Development of an efficient social security policy; and

(i) Adequate provision for all persons to have due legal aid in order to secure their rights.

Article 44

The Member States recognize that, in order to facilitate the process of Latin American regional integration, it is necessary to harmonize the social legislation of the developing countries, especially in the labor and social security fields, so that the rights of the workers shall be equally protected, and they agree to make the greatest efforts possible to achieve this goal.

CHAPTER IX. EDUCATIONAL, SCIENTIFIC, AND CULTURAL STANDARDS

Article 45

The Member States will give primary importance within their development plans to the encouragement of education, science, and culture, oriented toward the over-all improvement of the individual, and as a foundation for democracy, social justice, and progress.

Article 46

The Member States will co-operate with one another to meet their educational needs, to promote scientific research, and to encourage technological progress. They consider themselves individually and jointly bound to preserve and enrich the cultural heritage of the American peoples.

Article 47

The Member States will exert the greatest efforts, in accordance with their constitutional processes, to ensure the effective exercise of the right to education, on the following bases:

(a) Elementary education, compulsory for children of school age, shall also be offered to all others who can benefit from it. When provided by the State it shall be without charge;

(b) Middle-level education shall be extended progressively to as much of the population as possible, with a view to social improvement. It shall be diversified in such a way that it meets the development needs of each country without prejudice to providing a general education; and

(c) Higher education shall be available to all, provided that, in order to maintain its high level, the corresponding regulatory or academic standards are met.

Article 48

The Member States will give special attention to the eradication of illiteracy, will strengthen adult and vocational education systems, and will ensure that the benefits of culture will be available to the entire population. They will promote the use of all information media to fulfil these aims. . . .

Part Two

Chapter X. The Organs

Article 51

The Organization of American States accomplishes its purposes by means of:
(a) The General Assembly;
(b) The Meeting of Consultation of Ministers of Foreign Affairs;
(c) The Councils;
(d) The Inter-American Juridical Committee;
(e) The Inter-American Commission on Human Rights;
(f) The General Secretariat;
(g) The Specialized Conferences; and
(h) The Specialized Organizations.

There may be established, in addition to those provided for in the Charter and in accordance with the provisions thereof, such subsidiary organs, agencies, and other entities as are considered necessary.

Chapter XI. The General Assembly

Article 52

The General Assembly is the supreme organ of the Organization of American States. It has as its principal powers, in addition to such others as are assigned to it by the Charter, the following:

(a) To decide the general action and policy of the Organization, determine the structure and functions of its organs, and consider any matter relating to friendly relations among the American States;

(b) To establish measures for coordinating the activities of the organs, agencies, and entities of the Organization among themselves and such activities with those of the other institutions of the inter-American system;

(c) To strengthen and coordinate co-operation with the United Nations and its specialized agencies;

(d) To promote collaboration, especially in the economic, social, and cultural fields, with other international organizations whose purposes are similar to those of the Organization of American States;

(e) To approve the program-budget of the Organization and determine the quotas of the Member States;

(f) To consider the annual and special reports that shall be presented to it by the organs, agencies, and entities of the inter-American system;

(g) To adopt general standards to govern the operations of the General Secretariat; and

(h) To adopt its own rules of procedure and, by a two-thirds vote, its agenda.

The General Assembly shall exercise its powers in accordance with the provisions of the Charter and of other inter-American treaties.

Article 53

The General Assembly shall establish the bases for fixing the quota that each Government is to contribute to the maintenance of the Organization, taking into account the ability to pay of the respective countries and their determination to contribute in an equitable manner. Decisions on budgetary matters require the approval of two thirds of the Member States.

Article 54

All Member States have the right to be represented in the General Assembly. Each State has the right to one vote.

Article 55

The General Assembly shall convene annually during the period determined by the rules of procedure and at a place selected in accordance with the principle of rotation. At each regular session the date and place of the next regular session shall be determined, in accordance with the rules of procedure.

If for any reason the General Assembly cannot be held at the place chosen, it shall meet at the General Secretariat, unless one of the Member States should make a timely offer of a site in its territory, in which case the Permanent Council of the Organization may agree that the General Assembly will meet in that place.

Article 56

In Special circumstances and with the approval of two thirds of the Member States, the Permanent Council shall convoke a special session of the General Assembly.

Article 57

Decisions of the General Assembly shall be adopted by the affirmative vote of an absolute majority of the Member States, except in those cases that require a two-thirds vote as provided in the Charter or as may be provided by the General Assembly in its rules of procedure.

Article 58

There shall be a Preparatory Committee of the General Assembly, composed of representatives of all the Member States, which shall:
 (a) Prepare the draft agenda of each session of the General Assembly;
 (b) Review the proposed program-budget and the draft resolution on quotas, and present to the General Assembly a report thereon containing the recommendations it considers appropriate; and
 (c) Carry out such other functions as the General Assembly may assign to it.
 The draft agenda and the report shall, in due course, be transmitted to the Governments of the Member States.

CHAPTER XII. THE MEETING OF CONSULTATION OF MINISTERS OF FOREIGN AFFAIRS

Article 59

The Meeting of Consultation of Ministers of Foreign Affairs shall be held in order to consider problems of an urgent nature and of common interest to the American States, and to serve as the Organ of Consultation.

Article 60

Any Member State may request that a Meeting of Consultation be called. The request shall be addressed to the Permanent Council of the Organization, which shall decide by an absolute majority whether a meeting should be held.

Article 61

The agenda and regulations of the Meeting of Consultation shall be prepared by the Permanent Council of the Organization and submitted to the Member States for consideration.

Article 62

If, for exceptional reasons, a Minister of Foreign Affairs is unable to attend the meeting, he shall be represented by a special delegate.

Article 63

In case of an armed attack within the territory of an American State or within the region of security delimited by treaties in force, a Meeting of

Consultation shall be held without delay. Such Meeting shall be called immediately by the Chairman of the Permanent Council of the Organization, who shall at the same time call a meeting of the Council itself.

Article 64

An Advisory Defense Committee shall be established to advise the Organ of Consultation on problems of military co-operation that may arise in connection with the application of existing special treaties on collective security.

Article 65

The Advisory Defense Committee shall be composed of the highest military authorities of the American States participating in the Meeting of Consultation. Under exceptional circumstances the Governments may appoint substitutes. Each State shall be entitled to one vote.

Article 66

The Advisory Defense Committee shall be convoked under the same conditions as the Organ of Consultation, when the latter deals with matters relating to defense against agression.

Article 67

The Committee shall also meet when the General Assembly or the Meeting of Consultation or the Governments, by a two-thirds majority of the Member States, assign to it technical studies or reports on specific subjects.

Chapter XIII. The Councils of the Organization

COMMON PROVISIONS

Article 68

The Permanent Council of the Organization, the Inter-American Economic and Social Council, and the Inter-American Council for Education, Science, and Culture are directly responsible to the General Assembly and each has the authority granted to it in the Charter and other inter-American instruments, as well as the functions assigned to it by the General Assembly and the Meeting of Consultation of Ministers of Foreign Affairs.

Article 69

All Member States have the right to be represented on each of the Councils. Each State has the right to one vote.

Article 70

The Councils may, within the limits of the Charter and other inter-American instruments, make recommendations on matters within their authority.

Article 71

The Councils, on matters within their respective competence, may present to the General Assembly studies and proposals, drafts of international instruments, and proposals on the holding of specialized conferences, on the creation, modification, or elimination of specialized organizations and other inter-American agencies, as well as on the coordination of their activities. The Councils may also present studies, proposals, and drafts of international instruments to the Specialized Conferences.

Article 72

Each Council may, in urgent cases, convoke Specialized Conferences on matters within its competence, after consulting with the Member States and without having to resort to the procedure provided for in Article 128.

Article 73

The Councils, to the extent of their ability, and with the co-operation of the General Secretariat, shall render to the Governments such specialized services as the latter may request.

Article 74

Each Council has the authority to require the other Councils, as well as the subsidiary organs and agencies responsible to them, to provide it with information and advisory services on matters within their respective spheres of competence. The Councils may also request the same services from the other agencies of the inter-American system.

Article 75

With the prior approval of the General Assembly, the Councils may establish the subsidiary organs and the agencies that they consider advisable for the better performance of their duties. When the General Assembly is not in session, the aforesaid organs or agencies may be established provisionally by the corresponding Council. In constituting the membership of these bodies, the Councils, insofar as possible, shall follow the criteria of rotation and equitable geographic representation.

Article 76

The Councils may hold meetings in any Member State, when they find it advisable and with the prior consent of the Government concerned.

Article 77

Each Council shall prepare its own statutes and submit them to the General Assembly for approval. It shall approve its own rules of procedure and those of its subsidiary organs, agencies, and committees.

CHAPTER XIV. THE PERMANENT COUNCIL OF THE ORGANIZATION

Article 78

The Permanent Council of the Organization is composed of one representative of each Member State, especially appointed by the respective Government, with the rank of ambassador. Each Government may accredit an acting representative, as well as such alternates and advisers as it considers necessary.

Article 79

The office of Chairman of the Permanent Council shall be held by each of the representatives, in turn, following the alphabetic order in Spanish of the names of their respective countries. The office of Vice-Chairman shall be filled in the same way, following reverse alphabetic order.

The Chairman and the Vice-Chairman shall hold office for a term of not more than six months, which shall be determined by the statutes.

Article 80

Within the limits of the Charter and of inter-American treaties and agreements, the Permanent Council takes cognizance of any matter referred to it by the General Assembly or the Meeting of Consultation of Ministers of Foreign Affairs.

Article 81

The Permanent Council shall serve provisionally as the Organ of Consultation when the circumstances contemplated in Article 63 of this Charter arise.

Article 82

The Permanent Council shall keep vigilance over the maintenance of friendly relations among the Member States, and for that purpose shall effectively assist them in the peaceful settlement of their disputes, in accordance with the following provisions.

Article 83

To assist the Permanent Council in the exercise of these powers, an Inter-American Committee on Peaceful Settlement shall be established, which shall function as a subsidiary organ of the Council. The statutes of the Committee shall be prepared by the Council and approved by the General Assembly.

Article 84

The parties to a dispute may resort to the Permanent Council to obtain its good offices. In such a case the Council shall have authority to assist the parties and to recommend the procedures it considers suitable for the peaceful settlement of the dispute.

If the parties so wish, the Chairman of the Council shall refer the dispute directly to the Inter-American Committee on Peaceful Settlement.

Article 85

In the exercise of these powers, the Permanent Council, through the Inter-American Committee on Peaceful Settlement or by any other means, may ascertain the facts in the dispute, and may do so in the territory of any of the parties with the consent of the Government concerned.

Article 86

Any party to a dispute in which none of the peaceful procedures set forth in Article 24 of the Charter is being followed may appeal to the Permanent Council to take cognizance of the dispute.

The Council shall immediately refer the request to the Inter-American Committee on Peaceful Settlement, which shall consider whether or not the matter is within its competence and, if it deems it appropriate, shall offer its good offices to the other party or parties. Once these are accepted, the Inter-American Committee on Peaceful Settlement may assist the parties and recommend the procedures that it considers suitable for the peaceful settlement of the dispute.

In the exercise of these powers, the Committee may carry out an investigation of the facts in the dispute, and may do so in the territory of any of the parties with the consent of the Government concerned.

Article 87

If one of the parties should refuse the offer, the Inter-American Committee on Peaceful Settlement shall limit itself to informing the Permanent Council, without prejudice to its taking steps to restore relations between the parties, if they were interrupted, or to reestablish harmony between them.

Article 88

Once such a report is received, the Permanent Council may make suggestions for bringing the parties together for the purpose of Article 87 and, if it considers it necessary, it may urge the parties to avoid any action that might aggravate the dispute.

If one of the parties should continue to refuse the good offices of the Inter-American Committee on Peaceful Settlement or of the Council, the Council shall limit itself to submitting a report to the General Assembly.

Article 89

The Permanent Council, in the exercise of these functions, shall take its decisions by an affirmative vote of two thirds of its members, excluding the parties to the dispute, except for such decisions as the rules of procedure provide shall be adopted by a simple majority.

Article 90

In performing their functions with respect to the peaceful settlement of disputes, the Permanent Council and the Inter-American Committee on Peaceful Settlement shall observe the provisions of the Charter and the principles and standards of international law, as well as take into account the existence of treaties in force between the parties.

Article 91

The Permanent Council shall also:

(a) Carry out those decisions of the General Assembly or of the Meeting of Consultation of Ministers of Foreign Affairs the implementation of which has not been assigned to any other body;

(b) Watch over the observance of the standards governing the operation of the General Secretariat and, when the General Assembly is not in session, adopt provisions of a regulatory nature that enable the General Secretariat to carry out its administrative functions;

(c) Act as the Preparatory Committee of the General Assembly, in accordance with the terms of Article 58 of the Charter, unless the General Assembly should decide otherwise;

(d) Prepare, at the request of the Member States and with the co-operation of the appropriate organs of the Organization, draft agreements to promote and facilitate co-operation between the Organization of American States and the United Nations or between the Organization and other American agencies of recognized international standing. These draft agreements shall be submitted to the General Assembly for approval;

(e) Submit recommendations to the General Assembly with regard to the functioning of the Organization and the coordination of its subsidiary organs, agencies, and committees;

(f) Present to the General Assembly any observations it may have regarding the reports of the Inter-American Juridical Committee and the Inter-American Commission on Human Rights; and

(g) Perform the other functions assigned to it in the Charter.

Article 92

The Permanent Council and the General Secretariat shall have the same seat.

Chapter XV. The Inter-American Economic and Social Council

Article 93

The Inter-American Economic and Social Council is composed of one principal representative, of the highest rank, of each Member State, especially appointed by the respective Government.

Article 94

The purpose of the Inter-American Economic and Social Council is to promote co-operation among the American countries in order to attain accelerated economic and social development, in accordance with the standards set forth in Chapters VII and VIII. . . .

Article 96

The Inter-American Economic and Social Council shall hold at least one meeting each year at the ministerial level. It shall also meet when convoked by the General Assembly, the Meeting of Consultation of Ministers of Foreign Affairs, at its own initiative, or for the cases contemplated in Article 35 of the Charter.

Article 97

The Inter-American Economic and Social Council shall have a Permanent Executive Committee, composed of a Chairman and no less than seven other members, elected by the Council for terms to be established in the statutes of the Council. Each member shall have the right to one vote. The principles of equitable geographic representation and of rotation shall be taken into account, insofar as possible, in the election of members. The Permanent Executive Committee represents all of the Member States of the Organization. . . .

Chapter XVI. The Inter-American Council for Education, Science, and Culture

Article 99

The Inter-American Council for Education, Science, and Culture is composed of one principal representative, of the highest rank, of each Member State, especially appointed by the respective Government.

Article 100

The purpose of the Inter-American Council for Education, Science, and Culture is to promote friendly relations and mutual understanding between the peoples of the Americas through educational, scientific, and cultural co-operation and exchange between Member States, in order to raise the cultural level of the peoples, reaffirm their dignity as individuals, prepare them fully for the tasks of progress, and strengthen the devotion to peace, democracy, and social justice that has characterized their evolution. . . .

Article 102

The Inter-American Council for Education, Science, and Culture shall hold at least one meeting each year at the ministerial level. It shall also meet when convoked by the General Assembly, by the Meeting of Consultation of Ministers of Foreign Affairs, or at its own initiative.

Article 103

The Inter-American Council for Education, Science, and Culture shall have a Permanent Executive Committee, composed of a Chairman and no less than seven other members, elected by the Council for terms to be established in the statutes of the Council. Each member shall have the right to one vote. The principles of equitable geographic representation and of rotation shall be taken into account, insofar as possible, in the election of members. The Permanent Executive Committee represents all of the Member States of the Organization. . . .

CHAPTER XVII. THE INTER-AMERICAN JURIDICAL COMMITTEE

Article 105

The purpose of the Inter-American Juridical Committee is to serve the Organization as an advisory body on juridical matters; to promote the progressive development and the codification of international law; and to study juridical problems related to the integration of the developing countries of the Hemisphere and, insofar as may appear desirable, the possibility of attaining uniformity in their legislation.

Article 106

The Inter-American Juridical Committee shall undertake the studies and preparatory work assigned to it by the General Assembly, the Meeting of Consultation of Ministers of Foreign Affairs, or the Councils of the Organization. It may also, on its own initiative, undertake such studies and preparatory work as it considers advisable, and suggest the holding of specialized juridical conferences.

Article 107

The Inter-American Juridical Committee shall be composed of eleven jurists, nationals of Member States, elected by the General Assembly for a period of four years from panels of three candidates presented by Member States. In the election, a system shall be used that takes into account partial replacement of membership and, insofar as possible, equitable geographic representation. No two members of the Committee may be nationals of the same State. Vacancies that occur shall be filled in the manner set forth above. . . .

Chapter XVIII. The Inter-American Commission on Human Rights

Article 112

There shall be an Inter-American Commission on Human Rights, whose principal function shall be to promote the observance and protection of human rights and to serve as a consultative organ of the Organization in these matters.

An inter-American convention on human rights shall determine the structure, competence, and procedure of this Commission, as well as those of other organs responsible for these matters.

Chapter XIX. The General Secretariat

Article 113

The General Secretariat is the central and permanent organ of the Organization of American States. It shall perform the functions assigned to it in the Charter, in other inter-American treaties and agreements, and by the General Assembly, and shall carry out the duties entrusted to it by the General Assembly, the Meeting of Consultation of Ministers of Foreign Affairs, or the Councils.

Article 114

The Secretary-General of the Organization shall be elected by the General Assembly for a five-year term and may not be reelected more than once or succeeded by a person of the same nationality. In the event that the office of Secretary-General becomes vacant, the Assistant Secretary-General shall assume his duties until the General Assembly shall elect a new Secretary-General for a full term.

Article 115

The Secretary-General shall direct the General Secretariat, be the legal representative thereof, and, notwithstanding the provisions of Article 91 (b), be responsible to the General Assembly for the proper fulfillment of the obligations and functions of the General Secretariat.

Article 116

The Secretary-General, or his representative, participates with voice but without vote in all meetings of the Organization.

Article 117

The General Secretariat shall promote economic, social, juridical, educational, scientific, and cultural relations among all the Member States of the Organization, in keeping with the actions and policies decided upon by the General Assembly and with the pertinent decisions of the Councils.

Article 118

The General Secretariat shall also perform the following functions:

(a) Transmit *ex officio* to the Member States notice of the convocation of the General Assembly, the Meeting of Consultation of Ministers of Foreign Affairs, the Inter-American Economic and Social Council, the Inter-American Council for Education, Science, and Culture, and the Specialized Conferences;

(b) Advise the other organs, when appropriate, in the preparation of agenda and rules of procedure;

(c) Prepare the proposed program-budget of the Organization on the basis of programs adopted by the Councils, agencies, and entities whose expenses should be included in the program-budget and, after consultation with the Councils or their permanent committees, submit it to the Preparatory Committee of the General Assembly and then to the Assembly itself;

(d) Provide, on a permanent basis, adequate secretariat services for the General Assembly and the other organs, and carry out their directives and assignments. To the extent of its ability, provide services for the other meetings of the Organization;

(e) Serve as custodian of the documents and archives of the Inter-American Conferences, the General Assembly, the Meetings of Consultation of Ministers of Foreign Affairs, the Councils, and the Specialized Conferences;

(f) Serve as depository of inter-American treaties and agreements, as well as of the instruments of ratification thereof;

(g) Submit to the General Assembly at each regular session an annual report on the activities of the Organization and its financial condition; and

(h) Establish relations of co-operation, in accordance with decisions reached by the General Assembly or the Councils, with the Specialized Organizations as well as other national and international organizations.

Article 119

The Secretary-General shall:

(a) Establish such offices of the General Secretariat as are necessary to accomplish its purposes; and

(b) Determine the number of officers and employees of the General Secretariat, appoint them, regulate their powers and duties, and fix their remuneration.

The Secretary-General shall exercise this authority in accordance with such general standards and budgetary provisions as may be established by the General Assembly.

Article 120

The Assistant Secretary-General shall be elected by the General Assembly for a five-year term and may not be reelected more than once or succeeded by a person of the same nationality. In the event that the office of Assistant Secretary-General becomes vacant, the Permanent Council shall elect a substitute to hold that office until the General Assembly shall elect a new Assistant Secretary-General for a full term.

Article 121

The Assistant Secretary-General shall be the Secretary of the Permanent Council. He shall serve as advisory officer to the Secretary-General and shall act as his delegate in all matters that the Secretary-General may entrust to him. During the temporary absence or disability of the Secretary-General, the Assistant Secretary-General shall perform his functions.

The Secretary-General and the Assistant Secretary-General shall be of different nationalities.

Article 122

The General Assembly, by a two-thirds vote of the Member States, may remove the Secretary-General or the Assistant Secretary-General, or both, whenever the proper functioning of the Organization so demands.

Article 123

The Secretary-General shall appoint, with the approval of the respective Council, the Executive Secretary for Economic and Social Affairs and the Executive Secretary for Education, Science, and Culture, who shall also be the secretaries of the respective Councils.

Article 124

In the performance of their duties, the Secretary-General and the personnel of the Secretariat shall not seek or receive instructions from any Government or from any authority outside the Organization, and shall refrain from any action that may be incompatible with their position as international officers responsible only to the Organization.

Article 125

The Member States pledge themselves to respect the exclusively international character of the responsibilities of the Secretary-General and the personnel of the General Secretariat, and not to seek to influence them in the discharge of their duties.

Article 126

In selecting the personnel of the General Secretariat, first consideration shall be given to efficiency, competence, and integrity; but at the same time, in the recruitment of personnel of all ranks, importance shall be given to the necessity of obtaining as wide a geographic representation as possible.

Article 127

The seat of the General Secretariat is the city of Washington.

Chapter XX. The Specialized Conferences

Article 128

The Specialized Conferences are inter-governmental meetings to deal with special technical matters or to develop specific aspects of inter-American co-operation. They shall be held when either the General Assembly or the Meeting of Consultation of Ministers of Foreign Affairs so decides, on its own initiative or at the request of one of the Councils or Specialized Organizations.

Article 129

The agenda and rules of procedure of the Specialized Conferences shall be prepared by the Councils or Specialized Organizations concerned and shall be submitted to the Governments of the Member States for consideration.

Chapter XXI. The Specialized Organizations

Article 130

For the purposes of the present Charter, Inter-American Specialized Organizations are the intergovernmental organizations established by multilateral agreements and having specific functions with respect to technical matters of common interest to the American States. . . .

Article 134

Relations that should exist between the Specialized Organizations and the Organization shall be defined by means of agreements concluded between each organization and the Secretary-General, with the authorization of the General Assembly. . . .

Part Three

Chapter XXII. The United Nations

Article 137

None of the provisions of this Charter shall be construed as impairing the rights and obligations of the Member States under the Charter of the United Nations.

Chapter XXIII. Miscellaneous Provisions

Article 138

Attendance at meetings of the permanent organs of the Organization of American States or at the conferences and meetings provided for in the

Charter, or held under the auspices of the Organization, shall be in accordance with the multilateral character of the aforesaid organs, conferences, and meetings and shall not depend on the bilateral relations between the Government of any Member State and the Government of the host country.

Article 139

The Organization of American States shall enjoy in the territory of each Member such legal capacity, privileges, and immunities as are necessary for the exercise of its functions and the accomplishment of its purposes.

Article 140

The representatives of the Member States on the organs of the Organization, the personnel of their delegations, as well as the Secretary-General and the Assistant Secretary-General shall enjoy the privileges and immunities corresponding to their positions and necessary for the independent performance of their duties. . . .

CHAPTER XXIV. RATIFICATION AND ENTRY INTO FORCE . . .

Article 147

Amendments to the present Charter may be adopted only at a General Assembly convened for that purpose. Amendments shall enter into force in accordance with the terms and the procedure set forth in Article 145.

Article 148

The present Charter shall remain in force indefinitely, but may be denounced by any Member State upon written notification to the General Secretariat, which shall communicate to all the others each notice of denunciation received. After two years from the date on which the General Secretariat receives a notice of denunciation, the present Charter shall cease to be in force with respect to the denouncing State, which shall cease to belong to the Organization after it has fulfilled the obligations arising from the present Charter. . . .

Reservations Made at the Time of Ratifying the Charter of 1948 . . .

UNITED STATES

That the Senate give its advice and consent to ratification of the Charter with the reservation that none of its provisions shall be considered as enlarging the powers of the Federal Government of the United States or limiting the powers of the several states of the Federal Union with respect to any matters recognized under the Constitution as being within the reserved powers of the several states. . . .

6

Foreign Sovereign Immunity and the Act of State Doctrine

U.S. FOREIGN SOVEREIGN IMMUNITIES ACT OF 1976
(as codified and amended)

28 U.S.C. §§1330, 1332, 1391(f), 1441(d), 1602-1611

§1330. Actions against Foreign States

(a) The district courts shall have original jurisdiction without regard to amount in controversy of any nonjury civil action against a foreign state as defined in section 1603(a) of this title as to any claim for relief in personam with respect to which the foreign state is not entitled to immunity either under sections 1605–1607 of this title or under any applicable international agreement.

(b) Personal jurisdiction over a foreign state shall exist as to every claim for relief over which the district courts have jurisdiction under subsection (a) where service has been made under section 1608 of this title.

(c) For purposes of subsection (b), an appearance by a foreign state does not confer personal jurisdiction with respect to any claim for relief not arising out of any transaction or occurrence enumerated in sections 1605-1607 of this title.

(Added Pub. L. 94-583, §2(a), Oct. 21, 1976, 90 Stat. 2891.)

§1332. Diversity of Citizenship; Amount in Controversy; Costs

(a) The district courts shall have original jurisdiction of all civil actions where the matter in controversy exceeds the sum or value of $50,000, exclusive of interest and costs, and is between —

(1) citizens of different States;

(2) citizens of a State and citizens or subjects of a foreign state;

(3) citizens of different States and in which citizens or subjects of a foreign state are additional parties; and

(4) a foreign state, defined in section 1603(a) of this title, as plaintiff and citizens of a State or of different States.

For the purposes of this section, section 1335, and section 1441, an alien admitted to the United States for permanent residence shall be deemed a citizen of the State in which such alien is domiciled.

(b) Except when express provision therefor is otherwise made in a statute of the United States, where the plaintiff who files the case originally in the Federal courts is finally adjudged to be entitled to recover less than the sum or value of $50,000, computed without regard to any setoff or counterclaim to which the defendant may be adjudged to be entitled, and exclusive of interest and costs, the district court may deny costs to the plaintiff and, in addition, may impose costs on the plaintiff.

(c) For the purposes of this section and section 1441 of this title —

(1) a corporation shall be deemed to be a citizen of any State by which it has been incorporated and of the State where it has its principal place of business, except that in any direct action against the insurer of a policy or contract of liability insurance, whether incorporated or unincorporated, to which action the insured is not joined as a party-defendant, such insurer shall be deemed a citizen of the State of which the insured is a citizen, as well as of any State by which the insurer has been incorporated and of the State where it has its principal place of business; and . . .

(As amended Oct. 21, 1976, Pub. L. 94-583, §3, 90 Stat. 2891; Nov. 19, 1988, Pub. L. 100-702, Title II, §§201 to 203, 102 Stat. 4646.)

(d) The word "States," as used in this section, includes the Territories, the District of Columbia, and the Commonwealth of Puerto Rico.

§1391. Venue Generally

(f) A civil action against a foreign state as defined in section 1603(a) of this title may be brought —

(1) in any judicial district in which a substantial part of the events or omissions giving rise to the claim occurred, or a substantial part of property that is the subject of the action is situated;

(2) in any judicial district in which the vessel or cargo of a foreign state is situated, if the claim is asserted under section 1605(b) of this title;

(3) in any judicial district in which the agency or instrumentality is licensed to do business or is doing business, if the action is brought against an agency or instrumentality of a foreign state as defined in section 1603(b) of this title; or

(4) in the United States District Court for the District of Columbia if the action is brought against a foreign state or political subdivision thereof.

§1441. Actions Removable Generally

(d) Any civil action brought in a State court against a foreign state as defined in section 1603(a) of this title may be removed by the foreign state to the district court of the United States for the district and division embracing the place where such action is pending. Upon removal the action shall be tried by the court without jury. Where removal is based upon this subsection, the time limitations of section 1446(b) of this chapter may be enlarged at any time for cause shown.

CHAPTER 97 — JURISDICTIONAL IMMUNITIES OF FOREIGN STATES

Sec.
1602. Findings and declaration of purpose.
1603. Definitions.
1604. Immunity of a foreign state from jurisdiction.
1605. General exceptions to the jurisdictional immunity of a foreign state.
1606. Extent of liability.
1607. Counterclaims.
1608. Service; time to answer default.
1609. Immunity from attachment and execution of property of a foreign state.
1610. Exceptions to the immunity from attachment or execution.
1611. Certain types of property immune from execution.

§1602. Findings and Declaration of Purpose

The Congress finds that the determination by United States courts of the claims of foreign states to immunity from the jurisdiction of such courts would serve the interests of justice and would protect the rights of both foreign states and litigants in United States courts. Under international law, states are not immune from the jurisdiction of foreign courts insofar as their commercial activities are concerned, and their commercial property may be levied upon for the satisfaction of judgments rendered against them in connection with their commercial activities. Claims of foreign states to immunity should henceforth be decided by courts of the United States and of the States in conformity with the principles set forth in this chapter.

(Added Pub. L. 94-583, §4(a), Oct. 21, 1976, 90 Stat. 2892.)

§1603. Definitions

For purposes of this chapter —
(a) A "foreign state", except as used in section 1608 of this title, includes a political subdivision of a foreign state or an agency or instrumentality of a foreign state as defined in subsection (b).

(b) An "agency or instrumentality of a foreign state" means any entity —
(1) which is a separate legal person, corporate or otherwise, and
(2) which is an organ of a foreign state or political subdivision thereof, or a majority of whose shares or other ownership interest is owned by a foreign state or political subdivision thereof, and
(3) which is neither a citizen of a State of the United States as defined in section 1332(c) and (d) of this title, nor created under the laws of any third country.
(c) The "United States" includes all territory and waters, continental or insular, subject to the jurisdiction of the United States.
(d) A "commercial activity" means either a regular course of commercial conduct or a particular commercial transaction or act. The commercial character of an activity shall be determined by reference to the nature of the course of conduct or particular transaction or act, rather than by reference to its purpose.
(e) A "commercial activity carried on in the United States by a foreign state" means commercial activity carried on by such state and having substantial contact with the United States.

(Added Pub. L. 94-583.)

§1604. Immunity of a Foreign State from Jurisdiction

Subject to existing international agreements to which the United States is a party at the time of enactment of this Act a foreign state shall be immune from the jurisdiction of the courts of the United States and of the States except as provided in sections 1605 to 1607 of this chapter.

(Added Pub. L. 94-583.)

§1605. General Exceptions to the Jurisdictional Immunity of a Foreign State

(a) A foreign state shall not be immune from the jurisdiction of courts of the United States or of the States in any case —
(1) in which the foreign state has waived its immunity either explicitly or by implication, notwithstanding any withdrawal of the waiver which the foreign state may purport to effect except in accordance with the terms of the waiver;
(2) in which the action is based upon a commercial activity carried on in the United States by the foreign state; or upon an act performed in the United States in connection with a commercial activity of the foreign state elsewhere; or upon an act outside the territory of the United States in connection with a commercial activity of the foreign state elsewhere and that act causes a direct effect in the United States;

(3) in which rights in property taken in violation of international law are in issue and that property or any property exchanged for such property is present in the United States in connection with a commercial activity carried on in the United States by the foreign state; or that property or any property exchanged for such property is owned or operated by an agency or instrumentality of the foreign state and that agency or instrumentality is engaged in a commercial activity in the United States;

(4) in which rights in property in the United States acquired by succession or gift or rights in immovable property situated in the United States are in issue; or

(5) not otherwise encompassed in paragraph (2) above, in which money damages are sought against a foreign state for personal injury or death, or damage to or loss of property, occurring in the United States and caused by the tortious act or omission of that foreign state or of any official or employee of that foreign state while acting within the scope of his office or employment; except this paragraph shall not apply to —

(A) any claim based upon the exercise or performance or the failure to exercise or perform a discretionary function regardless of whether the discretion be abused, or

(B) any claim arising out of malicious prosecution, abuse of process, libel, slander, misrepresentation, deceit, or interference with contract rights; or

(6) in which the action is brought, either to enforce an agreement made by the foreign State with or for the benefit of a private party to submit to arbitration all or any differences which have arisen or which may arise between the parties with respect to a defined legal relationship, whether contractual or not, concerning a subject matter capable of settlement by arbitration under the laws of the United States, or to confirm an award made pursuant to such an agreement to arbitrate, if (A) the arbitration takes place or is intended to take place in the United States, (B) the agreement or award is or may be governed by a treaty or other international agreement in force for the United States calling for the recognition and enforcement of arbitral awards, (C) the underlying claim, save for the agreement to arbitrate, could have been brought in a United States court under this section or section 1607, or (D) paragraph (1) of this subsection is otherwise applicable.

(b) A foreign state shall not be immune from the jurisdiction of the courts of the United States in any case in which a suit in admiralty is brought to enforce a maritime lien against a vessel or cargo of the foreign state, which maritime lien is based upon a commercial activity of the foreign state: *Provided*, That —

(1) notice of the suit is given by delivery of a copy of the summons and of the complaint to the person, or his agent, having possession of the vessel or cargo against which the maritime lien is asserted; and if the vessel or cargo is arrested pursuant to process obtained on behalf of the party bringing the suit, the service of process of arrest shall be deemed to constitute valid delivery of such notice, but the party bringing the suit shall be liable for any damages sustained by the foreign state as a result of the arrest if the party bringing the suit had actual or constructive knowledge that the vessel or cargo of a foreign state was involved; and

(2) notice to the foreign state of the commencement of suit as provided in section 1608 of this title is initiated within ten days either of the delivery of notice as provided in paragraph (1) of this subsection or, in the case of a party who was unaware that the vessel or cargo of a foreign state was involved, of the date such party determined the existence of the foreign state's interest.

(c) Whenever notice is delivered under subsection (b)(1), the suit to enforce a maritime lien shall thereafter proceed and shall be heard and determined according to the principles of law and rules of practice of suits in rem whenever it appears that, had the vessel been privately owned and possessed, a suit in rem might have been maintained. A decree against the foreign state may include costs of the suit and, if the decree is for a money judgment, interest as ordered by the court, except that the court may not award judgment against the foreign state in an amount greater than the value of the vessel or cargo upon which the maritime lien arose. Such value shall be determined as of the time notice is served under subsection (b)(1). Decrees shall be subject to appeal and revision as provided in other cases of admiralty and maritime jurisdiction. Nothing shall preclude the plaintiff in any proper case from seeking relief in personam in the same action brought to enforce a maritime lien as provided in this section.

(d) A foreign state shall not be immune from the jurisdiction of the courts of the United States in any action brought to foreclose a preferred mortgage, as defined in the Ship Mortgage Act, 1920 (46 U.S.C. 911 and following). Such action shall be brought, heard, and determined in accordance with the provisions of that Act and in accordance with the principles of law and rules of practice of suits in rem, whenever it appears that had the vessel been privately owned and possessed a suit in rem might have been maintained.

(Added Pub. L. 94-583, §4(a), Oct. 21, 1976, 90 Stat. 2892; and amended Pub. L. 100-640, §1, Nov. 19, 1988, 102 Stat. 3333; Pub. L. 100-669, §2, Nov. 16, 1988, 102 Stat. 3969.)

§1606. Extent of Liability

As to any claim for relief with respect to which a foreign state is not entitled to immunity under section 1605 or 1607 of this chapter, the foreign state shall be liable in the same manner and to the same extent as a private individual under like circumstances; but a foreign state except for an agency or instrumentality thereof shall not be liable for punitive damages; if, however, in any case wherein death was caused, the law of the place where the action or omission occurred provides, or has been construed to provide, for damages only punitive in nature, the foreign state shall be liable for actual or compensatory damages measured by the pecuniary injuries resulting from such death which were incurred by the persons for whose benefit the action was brought.

§1607. Counterclaims

In any action brought by a foreign state, or in which a foreign state intervenes, in a court of the United States or of a State, the foreign state shall not be accorded immunity with respect to any counterclaim —

(a) for which a foreign state would not be entitled to immunity under section 1605 of this chapter had such claim been brought in a separate action against the foreign state; or

(b) arising out of the transaction or occurrence that is the subject matter of the claim of the foreign state; or

(c) to the extent that the counterclaim does not seek relief exceeding in amount or differing in kind from that sought by the foreign state.

§1608. Service; Time to Answer; Default

(a) Service in the courts of the United States and of the States shall be made upon a foreign state or political subdivision of a foreign state:

(1) by delivery of a copy of the summons and complaint in accordance with any special arrangement for service between the plaintiff and the foreign state or political subdivision; or

(2) if no special arrangement exists, by delivery of a copy of the summons and complaint in accordance with an applicable international convention on service of judicial documents; or

(3) if service cannot be made under paragraphs (1) or (2), by sending a copy of the summons and complaint and a notice of suit, together with a translation of each into the official language of the foreign state, by any form of mail requiring a signed receipt, to be addressed and dispatched by the clerk of the court to the head of the ministry of foreign affairs of the foreign state concerned, or

(4) if service cannot be made within 30 days under paragraph (3), by sending two copies of the summons and complaint and a notice of suit, together with a translation of each into the official language of the foreign state, by any form of mail requiring a signed receipt, to be addressed and dispatched by the clerk of the court to the Secretary of State in Washington, District of Columbia, to the attention of the Director of Special Consular Services — and the Secretary shall transmit one copy of the papers through diplomatic channels to the foreign state and shall send to the clerk of the court a certified copy of the diplomatic note indicating when the papers were transmitted.

As used in this subsection, a "notice of suit" shall mean a notice addressed to a foreign state and in a form prescribed by the Secretary of State by regulation.

(b) Service in the courts of the United States and of the States shall be made upon an agency or instrumentality of a foreign state:

(1) by delivery of a copy of the summons and complaint in accordance with any special arrangement for service between the plaintiff and the agency or instrumentality; or

(2) if no special arrangement exists, by delivery of a copy of the summons and complaint either to an officer, a managing or general agent, or to any other agent authorized by appointment or by law to receive service of process in the United States; or in accordance with an applicable international convention on service of judicial documents; or

(3) if service cannot be made under paragraphs (1) or (2), and if reasonably calculated to give actual notice, by delivery of a copy of the summons and complaint, together with a translation of each into the official language of the foreign state —

(A) as directed by an authority of the foreign state or political subdivision in response to a letter rogatory or request or

(B) by any form of mail requiring a signed receipt, to be addressed and dispatched by the clerk of the court to the agency or instrumentality to be served, or

(C) as directed by order of the court consistent with the law of the place where service is to be made.

(c) Service shall be deemed to have been made —

(1) in the case of service under subsection (a)(4), as of the date of transmittal indicated in the certified copy of the diplomatic note; and

(2) in any other case under this section, as of the date of receipt indicated in the certification, signed and returned postal receipt, or other proof of service applicable to the method of service employed.

(d) In any action brought in a court of the United States or of a State, a foreign state, a political subdivision thereof, or an agency or instrumentality of a foreign state shall serve an answer or other responsive pleading to the complaint within sixty days after service has been made under this section.

(e) No judgment by default shall be entered by a court of the United States or of a State against a foreign state, a political subdivision thereof, or an agency or instrumentality of a foreign state, unless the claimant establishes his claim or right to relief by evidence satisfactory to the court. A copy of any such default judgment shall be sent to the foreign state or political subdivision in the manner prescribed for service in this section.

§1609. Immunity from Attachment and Execution of Property of a Foreign State

Subject to existing international agreements to which the United States is a party at the time of enactment of this Act the property in the United States of a foreign state shall be immune from attachment arrest and execution except as provided in sections 1610 and 1611 of this chapter.

(Added Pub. L. 94-583.)

§1610. Exceptions to the Immunity from Attachment or Execution

(a) The property in the United States of a foreign state, as defined in section 1603(a) of this chapter, used for a commercial activity in the United States, shall not be immune from attachment in aid of execution, or from execution, upon a judgment entered by a court of the United States or of a State after the effective date of this Act, if —

(1) the foreign state has waived its immunity from attachment in aid of execution or from execution either explicitly or by implication, notwithstanding any withdrawal of the waiver the foreign state may purport to effect except in accordance with the terms of the waiver, or

(2) the property is or was used for the commercial activity upon which the claim is based, or

(3) the execution relates to a judgment establishing rights in property which has been taken in violation of international law or which has been exchanged for property taken in violation of international law, or

(4) the execution relates to a judgment establishing rights in property —

(A) which is acquired by succession or gift, or

(B) which is immovable and situated in the United States: *Provided,* That such property is not used for purposes of maintaining a diplomatic or consular mission or the residence of the Chief of such mission, or

(5) the property consists of any contractual obligation or any proceeds from such a contractual obligation to indemnify or hold harmless the foreign state or its employees under a policy of automobile or other liability or casualty insurance covering the claim which merged into the judgment, or

(6) the judgment is based on an order confirming an arbitral award rendered against the foreign State, provided that attachment in aid of execution, or execution, would not be inconsistent with any provision in the arbitral agreement.

(b) In addition to subsection (a), any property in the United States of an agency or instrumentality of a foreign state engaged in commercial activity in the United States shall not be immune from attachment in aid of execution, or from execution, upon a judgment entered by a court of the United States or of a State after the effective date of this Act if —

(1) the agency or instrumentality has waived its immunity from attachment in aid of execution or from execution either explicitly or implicitly, notwithstanding any withdrawal of the waiver the agency or instrumentality may purport to effect except in accordance with the terms of the waiver, or

(2) the judgment relates to a claim for which the agency or instrumentality is not immune by virtue of section 1605(a) (2), (3), or (5), or 1605(b) of this chapter, regardless of whether the property is or was used for the activity upon which the claim is based.

(c) No attachment or execution referred to in subsections (a) and (b) of this section shall be permitted until the court has ordered such attachment and execution after having determined that a reasonable period of time has elapsed following the entry of judgment and the giving of any notice required under section 1608(e) of this chapter.

(d) The property of a foreign state, as defined in section 1603(a) of this chapter, used for a commercial activity in the United States, shall not be immune from attachment prior to the entry of judgment in any action brought in a court of the United States or of a State, or prior to the elapse of the period of time provided in subsection (c) of this section, if —

(1) the foreign state has explicitly waived its immunity from attachment prior to judgment, notwithstanding any withdrawal of the waiver the foreign state may purport to effect except in accordance with the terms of the waiver, and

(2) the purpose of the attachment is to secure satisfaction of a judgment that has been or may ultimately be entered against the foreign state, and not to obtain jurisdiction.

(e) The vessels of a foreign State shall not be immune from arrest in rem, interlocutory sale, and execution in actions brought to foreclose a preferred mortgage as provided in section 1605(d).

(Added Pub. L. 94-583, §4(a), Oct. 21, 1976, 90 Stat. 2896, and amended Pub. L. 100-640, §2, Nov. 9, 1988, 102 Stat. 3334; Pub. L. 100-669, §3, Nov. 16, 1988, 102 Stat. 3969.)

§1611. Certain Types of Property Immune from Execution

(a) Notwithstanding the provisions of section 1610 of this chapter, the property of those organizations designated by the President as being entitled to enjoy the privileges, exemptions, and immunities provided by the International Organizations Immunities Act shall not be subject to attachment or any other judicial process impeding the disbursement of funds to, or on the order of, a foreign state as the result of an action brought in the courts of the United States or of the States.

(b) Notwithstanding the provisions of section 1610 of this chapter, the property of a foreign state shall be immune from attachment and from execution, if —

(1) the property is that of a foreign central bank or monetary authority held for its own account, unless such bank or authority, or its parent foreign government, has explicitly waived its immunity from attachment in aid of execution, or from execution, notwithstanding any withdrawal of the waiver which the bank, authority or government may purport to effect except in accordance with the terms of the waiver; or

(2) the property is, or is intended to be, used in connection with a military activity and

    (A) is of a military character, or

    (B) is under the control of a military authority or defense agency.

(Added Pub. L. 94-583.)

VIENNA CONVENTION ON DIPLOMATIC RELATIONS

April 18, 1961, 23 U.S.T. 3227, T.I.A.S. No. 7502, 500 U.N.T.S. 95*

The States Parties to the present Convention,
Recalling that peoples of all nations from ancient times have recognized the status of diplomatic agents,

Having in mind the purposes and principles of the Charter of the United Nations concerning the sovereign equality of States, the maintenance of international peace and security, and the promotion of friendly relations among nations,

Believing that an international convention on diplomatic intercourse, privileges and immunities would contribute to the development of friendly relations among nations, irrespective of their differing constitutional and social systems,

Realizing that the purpose of such privileges and immunities is not to benefit individuals but to ensure the efficient performance of the functions of diplomatic missions as representing States,

Affirming that the rules of customary international law should continue to govern questions not expressly regulated by the provisions of the present Convention,

Have agreed as follows:

---

*Adopted at Vienna on April 14, 1961. Entered into force on April 24, 1964. The United States ratified the convention on November 13, 1972.

The other 152 parties to the convention are: Afghanistan, Albania, Algeria, Argentina, Australia, Austria, Bahamas, Bahrain, Bangladesh, Barbados, Belgium, Benin, Bhutan, Bolivia, Botswana, Brazil, Bulgaria, Burkina Faso, Burundi, Byelorussian SSR, Cameroon, Canada, Cape Verde, Central African Republic, Chad, Chile, China, Colombia, Congo, Costa Rica, Cote d'Ivoire, Cuba, Cyprus, Czechoslovakia, Democratic Kampuchea, Democratic People's Republic of Korea, Democratic Yemen, Denmark, Djibouti, Dominica, Dominican Republic, Ecuador, Egypt, El Salvador, Equatorial Guinea, Ethiopia, Fiji, Finland, France, Gabon, German Democratic Republic, Germany (Federal Republic), Ghana, Greece, Guatemala, Guinea, Guyana, Haiti, Holy See, Honduras, Hungary, Iceland, India, Indonesia, Iran (Islamic Republic), Iraq, Ireland, Israel, Italy, Jamaica, Japan, Jordan, Kenya, Kiribati, Kuwait, Lao People's Democratic Republic, Lebanon, Lesotho, Liberia, Libyan Arab Jamahiriya, Liechtenstein, Luxembourg, Madagascar, Malawi, Malaysia, Mali, Malta, Mauritania, Mauritius, Mexico, Mongolia, Morocco, Mozambique, Myanmar, Nauru, Nepal, Netherlands, New Zealand, Nicaragua, Niger, Nigeria, Norway, Oman, Pakistan, Panama, Papua New Guinea, Paraguay, Peru, Philippines, Poland, Portugal, Qatar, Republic of Korea, Romania, Rwanda, Saint Lucia, Samoa, San Marino, Sao Tome and Principe, Saudi Arabia, Senegal, Seychelles, Sierra Leone, Somalia, South Africa, Spain, Sri Lanka, Sudan, Swaziland, Sweden, Switzerland, Syrian Arab Republic, Thailand, Togo, Tonga, Trinidad & Tobago, Tunisia, Turkey, Tuvalu, Uganda, Ukranian SSR, Union of Soviet Socialist Republics, United Arab Emirates, United Kingdom, United Republic of Tanzania, Uruguay, Venezuela, Viet Nam, Western Samoa, Yemen, Yugoslavia, Zaire, and Zambia.

Article 1

For the purpose of the present Convention, the following expressions shall have the meanings hereunder assigned to them:

(a) the "head of the mission" is the person charged by the sending State with the duty of acting in that capacity;

(b) the "members of the mission" are the head of the mission and the members of the staff of the mission;

(c) the "members of the staff of the mission" are the members of the diplomatic staff, of the administrative and technical staff and of the service staff of the mission;

(d) the "members of the diplomatic staff" are the members of the staff of the mission having diplomatic rank;

(e) a "diplomatic agent" is the head of the mission or a member of the diplomatic staff of the mission;

(f) the "members of the administrative and technical staff" are the members of the staff of the mission employed in the administrative and technical service of the mission;

(g) the "members of the service staff" are the members of the staff of the mission in the domestic service of the mission;

(h) a "private servant" is a person who is in the domestic service of a member of the mission and who is not an employee of the sending State;

(i) the "premises of the mission" are the buildings or parts of buildings and the land ancillary thereto, irrespective of ownership, used for the purposes of the mission including the residence of the head of the mission.

Article 2

The establishment of diplomatic relations between States, and of permanent diplomatic missions, takes place by mutual consent.

Article 3

1. The functions of a diplomatic mission consist *inter alia* in:

(a) representing the sending State in the receiving State;

(b) protecting in the receiving State the interests of the sending State and of its nationals, within the limits permitted by international law;

(c) negotiating with the Government of the receiving State;

(d) ascertaining by all lawful means conditions and developments in the receiving State, and reporting thereon to the Government of the sending State;

(e) promoting friendly relations between the sending State and the receiving State, and developing their economic, cultural and scientific relations.

2. Nothing in the present Convention shall be construed as preventing the performance of consular functions by a diplomatic mission.

Article 4

1. The sending State must make certain that the *agrément* of the receiving State has been given for the person it proposes to accredit as head of the mission to that State.

2. The receiving State is not obliged to give reasons to the sending State for a refusal of *agrément*.

Article 5

1. The sending State may, after it has given due notification to the receiving States concerned, accredit a head of mission or assign any member of the diplomatic staff, as the case may be, to more than one State, unless there is express objection by any of the receiving States.

2. If the sending State accredits a head of mission to one or more other States it may establish a diplomatic mission headed by a *chargé d'affaires ad interim* in each State where the head of mission has not his permanent seat.

3. A head of mission or any member of the diplomatic staff of the mission may act as representative of the sending State to any international organization.

Article 6

Two or more States may accredit the same person as head of mission to another State, unless objection is offered by the receiving State.

Article 7

Subject to the provisions of Articles 5, 8, 9 and 11, the sending State may freely appoint the members of the staff of the mission. In the case of military, naval or air attachés, the receiving State may require their names to be submitted beforehand, for its approval.

Article 8

1. Members of the diplomatic staff of the mission should in principle be of the nationality of the sending State.

2. Members of the diplomatic staff of the mission may not be appointed from among persons having the nationality of the receiving State, except with the consent of that State which may be withdrawn at any time.

3. The receiving State may reserve the same right with regard to nationals of a third State who are not also nationals of the sending State.

Article 9

1. The receiving State may at any time and without having to explain its decision, notify the sending State that the head of the mission or any member of the diplomatic staff of the mission is *persona non grata* or that any other member of the staff of the mission is not acceptable. In any such case, the sending State shall, as appropriate, either recall the person concerned or terminate his functions with the mission. A person may be declared *non grata* or not acceptable before arriving in the territory of the receiving State.

2. If the sending State refuses or fails within a reasonable period to carry out its obligations under paragraph 1 of this Article, the receiving State may refuse to recognize the person concerned as a member of the mission.

Article 10

1. The Ministry for Foreign Affairs of the receiving State, or such other ministry as may be agreed, shall be notified of:

(*a*) the appointment of members of the mission, their arrival and their final departure or the termination of their functions with the mission;

(*b*) the arrival and final departure of a person belonging to the family of a member of the mission and, where appropriate, the fact that a person becomes or ceases to be a member of the family of a member of the mission;

(*c*) the arrival and final departure of private servants in the employ of persons referred to in sub-paragraph (*a*) of this paragraph and, where appropriate, the fact that they are leaving the employ of such persons;

(*d*) the engagement and discharge of persons resident in the receiving State as members of the mission or private servants entitled to privileges and immunities.

2. Where possible, prior notification of arrival and final departure shall also be given.

Article 11

1. In the absence of specific agreement as to the size of the mission, the receiving State may require that the size of a mission be kept within limits considered by it to be reasonable and normal, having regard to circumstances and conditions in the receiving State and to the needs of the particular mission.

2. The receiving State may equally, within similar bounds and on a non-discriminatory basis, refuse to accept officials of a particular category.

Article 12

The sending State may not, without the prior express consent of the receiving State, establish offices forming part of the mission in localities other than those in which the mission itself is established.

Article 13

1. The head of the mission is considered as having taken up his functions in the receiving State either when he has presented his credentials or when he has notified his arrival and a true copy of his credentials has been presented to the Ministry for Foreign Affairs of the receiving State, or such other ministry as may be agreed, in accordance with the practice prevailing in the receiving State which shall be applied in a uniform manner.

2. The order of presentation of credentials or of a true copy thereof will be determined by the date and time of the arrival of the head of the mission.

Article 14

1. Heads of mission are divided into three classes, namely:

(*a*) that of ambassadors or nuncios accredited to Heads of State, and other heads of mission of equivalent rank;

(*b*) that of envoys, ministers and internuncios accredited to Heads of State;

(c) that of *chargés d'affaires* accredited to Ministers for Foreign Affairs.

2. Except as concerns precedence and etiquette, there shall be no differentiation between heads of mission by reason of their class.

Article 15

The class to which the heads of their missions are to be assigned shall be agreed between States.

Article 16

1. Heads of mission shall take precedence in their respective classes in the order of the date and time of taking up their functions in accordance with Article 13.

2. Alterations in the credentials of a head of mission not involving any change of class shall not affect his precedence.

3. This article is without prejudice to any practice accepted by the receiving State regarding the precedence of the representative of the Holy See.

Article 17

The precedence of the members of the diplomatic staff of the mission shall be notified by the head of the mission to the Ministry for Foreign Affairs or such other ministry as may be agreed.

Article 18

The procedure to be observed in each State for the reception of heads of mission shall be uniform in respect of each class.

Article 19

1. If the post of head of the mission is vacant, or if the head of the mission is unable to perform his functions, a *chargé d'affaires ad interim* shall act provisionally as head of the mission. The name of the *chargé d'affaires ad interim* shall be notified, either by the head of the mission or, in case he is unable to do so, by the Ministry for Foreign Affairs of the sending State to the Ministry for Foreign Affairs of the receiving State or such other ministry as may be agreed.

2. In cases where no member of the diplomatic staff of the mission is present in the receiving State, a member of the administrative and technical staff may, with the consent of the receiving State, be designated by the sending State to be in charge of the current administrative affairs of the mission.

Article 20

The mission and its head shall have the right to use the flag and emblem of the sending State on the premises of the mission, including the residence of the head of the mission, and on his means of transport.

Article 21

1. The receiving State shall either facilitate the acquisition on its territory, in accordance with its laws, by the sending State of premises necessary for its mission or assist the latter in obtaining accommodation in some other way.

2. It shall also, where necessary, assist missions in obtaining suitable accommodation for their members.

Article 22

1. The premises of the mission shall be inviolable. The agents of the receiving State may not enter them, except with the consent of the head of the mission.

2. The receiving State is under a special duty to take all appropriate steps to protect the premises of the mission against any intrusion or damage and to prevent any disturbance of the peace of the mission or impairment of its dignity.

3. The premises of the mission, their furnishings and other property thereon and the means of transport of the mission shall be immune from search, requisition, attachment or execution.

Article 23

1. The sending State and the head of the mission shall be exempt from all national, regional or municipal dues and taxes in respect of the premises of the mission, whether owned or leased, other than such as represent payment for specific services rendered.

2. The exemption from taxation referred to in this Article shall not apply to such dues and taxes payable under the law of the receiving State by persons contracting with the sending State or the head of the mission.

Article 24

The archives and documents of the mission shall be inviolable at any time and wherever they may be.

Article 25

The receiving State shall accord full facilities for the performance of the functions of the mission.

Article 26

Subject to its laws and regulations concerning zones entry into which is prohibited or regulated for reasons of national security, the receiving State shall ensure to all members of the mission freedom of movement and travel in its territory.

Article 27

1. The receiving State shall permit and protect free communication on the part of the mission for all official purposes. In communicating with the Government and the other missions and consulates of the sending State,

wherever situated, the mission may employ all appropriate means, including diplomatic couriers and messages in code or cipher. However, the mission may install and use a wireless transmitter only with the consent of the receiving State.

2. The official correspondence of the mission shall be inviolable. Official correspondence means all correspondence relating to the mission and its functions.

3. The diplomatic bag shall not be opened or detained.

4. The packages constituting the diplomatic bag must bear visible external marks of their character and may contain only diplomatic documents or articles intended for official use.

5. The diplomatic courier, who shall be provided with an official document indicating his status and the number of packages constituting the diplomatic bag, shall be protected by the receiving State in the performance of his functions. He shall enjoy personal inviolability and shall not be liable to any form of arrest or detention.

6. The sending State or the mission may designate diplomatic couriers *ad hoc*. In such cases the provisions of paragraph 5 of this Article shall also apply, except that the immunities therein mentioned shall cease to apply when such a courier has delivered to the consignee the diplomatic bag in his charge.

7. A diplomatic bag may be entrusted to the captain of a commercial aircraft scheduled to land at an authorized port of entry. He shall be provided with an official document indicating the number of packages constituting the bag but he shall not be considered to be a diplomatic courier. The mission may send one of its members to take possession of the diplomatic bag directly and freely from the captain of the aircraft.

Article 28

The fees and charges levied by the mission in the course of its official duties shall be exempt from all dues and taxes.

Article 29

The person of a diplomatic agent shall be inviolable. He shall not be liable to any form of arrest or detention. The receiving State shall treat him with due respect and shall take all appropriate steps to prevent any attack on his person, freedom or dignity.

Article 30

1. The private residence of a diplomatic agent shall enjoy the same inviolability and protection as the premises of the mission.

2. His papers, correspondence and, except as provided in paragraph 3 of Article 31, his property, shall likewise enjoy inviolability.

Article 31

1. A diplomatic agent shall enjoy immunity from the criminal jurisdiction of the receiving State. He shall also enjoy immunity from its civil and administrative jurisdiction, except in the case of:

(a) a real action relating to private immovable property situated in the territory of the receiving State, unless he holds it on behalf of the sending State for the purpose of the mission;

(b) an action relating to succession in which the diplomatic agent is involved as executor, administrator, heir or legatee as a private person and not on behalf of the sending State;

(c) an action relating to any professional or commercial activity exercised by the diplomatic agent in the receiving State outside his official functions.

2. A diplomatic agent is not obliged to give evidence as a witness.

3. No measures of execution may be taken in respect of a diplomatic agent except in the cases coming under sub-paragraphs (a), (b) and (c) of paragraph 1 of this Article, and provided that the measures concerned can be taken without infringing the inviolability of his person or of his residence.

4. The immunity of a diplomatic agent from the jurisdiction of the receiving State does not exempt him from the jurisdiction of the sending State.

Article 32

1. The immunity from jurisdiction of diplomatic agents and of persons enjoying immunity under Article 37 may be waived by the sending State.

2. Waiver must always be express.

3. The initiation of proceedings by a diplomatic agent or by a person enjoying immunity from jurisdiction under Article 37 shall preclude him from invoking immunity from jurisdiction in respect of any counter-claim directly connected with the principal claim.

4. Waiver of immunity from jurisdiction in respect of civil or administrative proceedings shall not be held to imply waiver of immunity in respect of the execution of the judgment, for which a separate waiver shall be necessary.

Article 33

1. Subject to the provisions of paragraph 3 of this Article, a diplomatic agent shall with respect to services rendered for the sending State be exempt from social security provisions which may be in force in the receiving State.

2. The exemption provided for in paragraph 1 of this Article shall also apply to private servants who are in the sole employ of a diplomatic agent, on condition:

(a) that they are not nationals of or permanently resident in the receiving State; and

(b) that they are covered by the social security provisions which may be in force in the sending State or a third State.

3. A diplomatic agent who employs persons to whom the exemption provided for in paragraph 2 of this Article does not apply shall observe the obligations which the social security provisions of the receiving State impose upon employers.

4. The exemption provided for in paragraphs 1 and 2 of this Article

shall not preclude voluntary participation in the social security system of the receiving State provided that such participation is permitted by that State.

5. The provisions of this Article shall not affect bilateral or multilateral agreements concerning social security concluded previously and shall not prevent the conclusion of such agreements in the future.

Article 34

A diplomatic agent shall be exempt from all dues and taxes, personal or real, national, regional or municipal, except:

(a) indirect taxes of a kind which are normally incorporated in the price of goods or services;

(b) dues and taxes on private immovable property situated in the territory of the receiving State, unless he holds it on behalf of the sending State for the purposes of the mission;

(c) estate, succession or inheritance duties levied by the receiving State, subject to the provisions of paragraph 4 of Article 39;

(d) dues and taxes on private income having its source in the receiving State and capital taxes on investments made in commercial undertakings in the receiving State;

(e) charges levied for specific services rendered;

(f) registration, court or record fees, mortgage dues and stamp duty, with respect to immovable property, subject to the provisions of Article 23.

Article 35

The receiving State shall exempt diplomatic agents from all personal services, from all public service of any kind whatsoever, and from military obligations such as those connected with requisitioning, military contributions and billeting.

Article 36

1. The receiving State shall, in accordance with such laws and regulations as it may adopt, permit entry of and grant exemption from all customs duties, taxes, and related charges other than charges for storage, cartage and similar services, on:

(a) articles for the official use of the mission;

(b) articles for the personal use of a diplomatic agent or members of his family forming part of his household, including articles intended for his establishment.

2. The personal baggage of a diplomatic agent shall be exempt from inspection, unless there are serious grounds for presuming that it contains articles not covered by the exemptions mentioned in paragraph 1 of this Article, or articles the import or export of which is prohibited by the law or controlled by the quarantine regulations of the receiving State. Such inspection shall be conducted only in the presence of the diplomatic agent or of his authorized representative.

Article 37

1. The members of the family of a diplomatic agent forming part of his household shall, if they are not nationals of the receiving State, enjoy the privileges and immunities specified in Articles 29 to 36.

2. Members of the administrative and technical staff of the mission, together with members of their families forming part of their respective households, shall, if they are not nationals of or permanently resident in the receiving State, enjoy the privileges and immunities specified in Articles 29 to 35, except that the immunity from civil and administrative jurisdiction of the receiving State specified in paragraph 1 of Article 31 shall not extend to acts performed outside the course of their duties. They shall also enjoy the privileges specified in Article 36, paragraph 1, in respect of articles imported at the time of first installation.

3. Members of the service staff of the mission who are not nationals of or permanently resident in the receiving State shall enjoy immunity in respect of acts performed in the course of their duties, exemption from dues and taxes on the emoluments they receive by reason of their employment and the exemption contained in Article 33.

4. Private servants of members of the mission shall, if they are not nationals of or permanently resident in the receiving State, be exempt from dues and taxes on the emoluments they receive by reason of their employment. In other respects, they may enjoy privileges and immunities only to the extent admitted by the receiving State. However, the receiving State must exercise its jurisdiction over those persons in such a manner as not to interfere unduly with the performance of the functions of the mission.

Article 38

1. Except insofar as additional privileges and immunities may be granted by the receiving State, a diplomatic agent who is a national of or permanently resident in that State shall enjoy only immunity from jurisdiction, and inviolability, in respect of official acts performed in the exercise of his functions.

2. Other members of the staff of the mission and private servants who are nationals of or permanently resident in the receiving State shall enjoy privileges and immunities only to the extent admitted by the receiving State. However, the receiving State must exercise its jurisdiction over those persons in such a manner as not to interfere unduly with the performance of the functions of the mission.

Article 39

1. Every person entitled to privileges and immunities shall enjoy them from the moment he enters the territory of the receiving State on proceeding to take up his post or, if already in its territory, from the moment when his appointment is notified to the Ministry for Foreign Affairs or such other ministry as may be agreed.

2. When the functions of a person enjoying privileges and immunities have come to an end, such privileges and immunities shall normally cease

at the moment when he leaves the country, or on expiry of a reasonable period in which to do so, but shall subsist until that time, even in case of armed conflict. However, with respect to acts performed by such a person in the exercise of his functions as a member of the mission, immunity shall continue to subsist.

3. In case of the death of a member of the mission, the members of his family shall continue to enjoy the privileges and immunities to which they are entitled until the expiry of a reasonable period in which to leave the country.

4. In the event of the death of a member of the mission not a national of or permanently resident in the receiving State or a member of his family forming part of his household, the receiving State shall permit the withdrawal of the movable property of the deceased, with the exception of any property acquired in the country the export of which was prohibited at the time of his death. Estate, succession and inheritance duties shall not be levied on movable property the presence of which in the receiving State was due solely to the presence there of the deceased as a member of the mission or as a member of the family of a member of the mission.

Article 40

1. If a diplomatic agent passes through or is in the territory of a third State, which has granted him a passport visa if such visa was necessary, while proceeding to take up or to return to his post, or when returning to his own country, the third State shall accord him inviolability and such other immunities as may be required to ensure his transit or return. The same shall apply in the case of any members of his family enjoying privileges or immunities who are accompanying the diplomatic agent, or travelling separately to join him or to return to their country.

2. In circumstances similar to those specified in paragraph 1 of this Article, third States shall not hinder the passage of members of the administrative and technical or service staff of a mission, and of members of their families, through their territories.

3. Third States shall accord to official correspondence and other official communications in transit, including messages in code or cipher, the same freedom and protection as is accorded by the receiving State. They shall accord to diplomatic couriers, who have been granted a passport visa if such visa was necessary, and diplomatic bags in transit the same inviolability and protection as the receiving State is bound to accord.

4. The obligations of third States under paragraphs 1, 2 and 3 of this Article shall also apply to the persons mentioned respectively in those paragraphs, and to official communications and diplomatic bags, whose presence in the territory of the third State is due to *force majeure*.

Article 41

1. Without prejudice to their privileges and immunities, it is the duty of all persons enjoying such privileges and immunities to respect the laws and regulations of the receiving State. They also have a duty not to interfere in the internal affairs of that State.

2. All official business with the receiving State entrusted to the mission by the sending State shall be conducted with or through the Ministry for Foreign Affairs of the receiving State or such other ministry as may be agreed.

3. The premises of the mission must not be used in any manner incompatible with the functions of the mission as laid down in the present Convention or by other rules of general international law or by any special agreements in force between the sending and the receiving State.

Article 42

A diplomatic agent shall not in the receiving State practice for personal profit any professional or commercial activity.

Article 43

The function of a diplomatic agent comes to an end, *inter alia:*

(*a*) on notification by the sending State to the receiving State that the function of the diplomatic agent has come to an end;

(*b*) on notification by the receiving State to the sending State that, in accordance with paragraph 2 of Article 9, it refuses to recognize the diplomatic agent as a member of the mission.

Article 44

The receiving State must, even in case of armed conflict, grant facilities in order to enable persons enjoying privileges and immunities, other than nationals of the receiving State, and members of the families of such persons irrespective of their nationality, to leave at the earliest possible moment. It must, in particular, in case of need, place at their disposal the necessary means of transport for themselves and their property.

Article 45

If diplomatic relations are broken off between two States, or if a mission is permanently or temporarily recalled:

(*a*) the receiving State must, even in case of armed conflict, respect and protect the premises of the mission, together with its property and archives;

(*b*) the sending State may entrust the custody of the premises of the mission, together with its property and archives, to a third State acceptable to the receiving State;

(*c*) the sending State may entrust the protection of its interests and those of its nationals to a third State acceptable to the receiving State.

Article 46

A sending State may with the prior consent of a receiving State, and at the request of a third State not represented in the receiving State, undertake the temporary protection of the interests of the third State and of its nationals.

Article 47

1. In the application of the provisions of the present Convention, the receiving State shall not discriminate as between States.

2. However, discrimination shall not be regarded as taking place:

(*a*) where the receiving State applies any of the provisions of the present Convention restrictively because of a restrictive application of that provision to its mission in the sending State;

(*b*) where by custom or agreement States extend to each other more favourable treatment than is required by the provisions of the present Convention.

Article 48

The present Convention shall be open for signature by all States Members of the United Nations or of any of the specialized agencies or Parties to the Statute of the International Court of Justice, and by any other State invited by the General Assembly of the United Nations to become a Party to the Convention. . . .

Article 49

The present Convention is subject to ratification. The instruments of ratification shall be deposited with the Secretary-General of the United Nations.

Article 50

The present Convention shall remain open for accession by any State belonging to any of the four categories mentioned in Article 48. The instruments of accession shall be deposited with the Secretary-General of the United Nations.

Article 51

1. The present Convention shall enter into force on the thirtieth day following the date of deposit of the twenty-second instrument of ratification or accession with the Secretary-General of the United Nations.

2. For each State ratifying or acceding to the Convention after the deposit of the twenty-second instrument of ratification or accession, the Convention shall enter into force on the thirtieth day after deposit by such State of its instrument of ratification or accession. . . .

7

Allocation of Legal Authority Among States

U.S.-U.K. TREATY OF EXTRADITION
June 8, 1972, 28 U.S.T. 227, T.I.A.S. No. 8468*

The Government of the United States of America and the Government of the United Kingdom of Great Britain and Northern Ireland;
Desiring to make provision for the reciprocal extradition of offenders;
Have agreed as follows:

Article I

Each Contracting Party undertakes to extradite to the other, in the circumstances and subject to the conditions specified in this Treaty, any person found in its territory who has been accused or convicted of any offense within Article III, committed within the jurisdiction of the other Party.

Article II

(1) This Treaty shall apply:

(*a*) in relation to the United Kingdom: to Great Britain and Northern Ireland, the Channel Islands, the Isle of Man, and any territory for the international relations of which the United Kingdom is responsible and to which the Treaty shall have been extended by agreement between the Contracting Parties embodied in an Exchange of Notes; and

(*b*) to the United States of America;

and references to the territory of a Contracting Party shall be construed accordingly.

(2) The application of this Treaty to any territory in respect of which

---

*Signed in London on June 8, 1972. Entered into force on January 21, 1977. See also the U.S.-U.K. Supplementary Treaty Concerning the Extradition Treaty (1985), the next document below.

extension has been made in accordance with paragraph (1) of this Article may be terminated by either Contracting Party giving six months' written notice to the other through the diplomatic channel.

Article III

(1) Extradition shall be granted for an act or omission the facts of which disclose an offense within any of the descriptions listed in the Schedule annexed to this Treaty, which is an integral part of the Treaty, or any other offense, if:

(a) the offense is punishable under the laws of both Parties by imprisonment or other form of detention for more than one year or by the death penalty;

(b) the offense is extraditable under the relevant law, being the law of the United Kingdom or other territory to which this Treaty applies by virtue of sub-paragraph (1)(a) of Article II; and

(c) the offense constitutes a felony under the law of the United States of America.

(2) Extradition shall be granted for any attempt or conspiracy to commit an offense within paragraph (1) of this Article if such attempt or conspiracy is one for which extradition may be granted under the laws of both Parties and is punishable under the laws of both Parties by imprisonment or other form of detention for more than one year or by the death penalty.

(3) Extradition shall also be granted for the offense of impeding the arrest or prosecution of a person who has committed an offense for which extradition may be granted under this Article and which is punishable under the laws of both Parties by imprisonment or other form of detention for a period of five years or more.

(4) A person convicted of and sentenced for an offense shall not be extradited therefor unless he was sentenced to imprisonment or other form of detention for a period of four months or more or, subject to the provisions of Article IV, to the death penalty.

Article IV

If the offense for which extradition is requested is punishable by death under the relevant law of the requesting Party, but the relevant law of the requested Party does not provide for the death penalty in a similar case, extradition may be refused unless the requesting Party gives assurances satisfactory to the requested Party that the death penalty will not be carried out.

Article V

(1) Extradition shall not be granted if:

(a) the person sought would, if proceeded against in the territory of the requested Party for the offense for which his extradition is requested, be entitled to be discharged on the grounds of a previous acquittal or conviction in the territory of the requesting or requested Party or of a third State; or

(b) the prosecution for the offense for which extradition is requested has become barred by lapse of time according to the law of the requesting or requested Party; or

(c) (i) the offense for which extradition is requested is regarded by the requested Party as one of a political character; or

(ii) the person sought proves that the request for his extradition has in fact been made with a view to try or punish him for an offense of a political character.

(2) Extradition may be refused on any other ground which is specified by the law of the requested Party.

Article VI

If the person sought should be under examination or under punishment in the territory of the requested Party for any other offense, his extradition shall be deferred until the conclusion of the trial and the full execution of any punishment awarded to him.

Article VII

(1) The request for extradition shall be made through the diplomatic channel, except as otherwise provided in Article XV.

(2) The request shall be accompanied by:

(a) a description of the person sought, his nationality, if known, and any other information which would help to establish his identity;

(b) a statement of the facts of the offense for which extradition is requested;

(c) the text, if any, of the law
  (i) defining that offense;
  (ii) prescribing the maximum punishment for that offense; and
  (iii) imposing any time limit on the institution of proceedings for that offense;
and

(d) (i) where the requesting Party is the United Kingdom, a statement of the legal provisions which establish the extraditable character of the offense for which extradition is requested under the relevant law, being the law of the United Kingdom or other territory to which this Treaty applies by virtue of sub-paragraph (1)(a) of Article II;

(ii) where the requesting Party is the United States of America, a statement that the offense for which extradition is requested, constitutes a felony under the law of the United States of America.

(3) If the request relates to an accused person, it must also be accompanied by a warrant of arrest issued by a judge, magistrate or other competent authority in the territory of the requesting Party and by such evidence as, according to the law of the requested Party, would justify his committal for trial if the offense had been committed in the territory of the requested Party, including evidence that the person requested is the person to whom the warrant of arrest refers.

(4) If the request relates to a convicted person, it must be accompanied by a certificate or the judgment of conviction imposed in the territory of the

requesting Party and by evidence that the person requested is the person to whom the conviction refers and, if the person was sentenced, by evidence of the sentence imposed and a statement showing to what extent the sentence has not been carried out.

(5) The warrant of arrest, or the judicial document establishing the existence of the conviction, and any deposition or statement or other evidence given on oath or affirmed, or any certified copy thereof shall be received in evidence in any proceedings for extradition:

> (a) if it is authenticated in the case of a warrant by being signed, or in the case of any other original document by being certified, by a judge, magistrate or other competent authority of the requesting Party, or in the case of a copy by being so certified to be a true copy of the original; and

> (b) where the requesting Party is the United Kingdom, by being sealed with the official seal of the appropriate Minister and certified by the principal diplomatic or consular officer of the United States of America in the United Kingdom; and where the requesting Party is the United States of America, by being sealed with the official seal of the Department of State for the Secretary of State; or

> (c) if it is authenticated in such other manner as may be permitted by the law of the requested Party.

Article VIII

(1) In urgent cases the person sought may, in accordance with the law of the requested Party, be provisionally arrested on application through the diplomatic channel by the competent authorities of the requesting Party. The application shall contain an indication of intention to request the extradition of the person sought and a statement of the existence of a warrant of arrest or a conviction against that person, and, if available, a description of the person sought, and such further information, if any, as would be necessary to justify the issue of a warrant of arrest had the offense been committed, or the person sought been convicted, in the territory of the requested Party.

(2) A person arrested upon such an application shall be set at liberty upon the expiration of forty-five days from the date of his arrest if a request for his extradition shall not have been received. This provision shall not prevent the institution of further proceedings for the extradition of the person sought if a request is subsequently received.

Article IX

(1) Extradition shall be granted only if the evidence be found sufficient according to the law of the requested Party either to justify the committal for trial of the person sought if the offense of which he is accused had been committed in the territory of the requested Party or to prove that he is the identical person convicted by the courts of the requesting Party.

(2) If the requested Party requires additional evidence or information to enable a decision to be taken on the request for extradition, such evidence or information shall be submitted within such time as that Party shall require.

Article X

If the extradition of a person is requested concurrently by one of the Contracting Parties and by another State or States, either for the same offense or for different offenses, the requested Party shall make its decision in so far as its law allows, having regard to all the circumstances, including the provisions in this regard in any Agreements in force between the requested Party and the requesting States, the relative seriousness and place of commission of the offenses, the respective dates of the requests, the nationality of the person sought and the possibility of subsequent extradition to another State.

Article XI

(1) The requested Party shall promptly communicate to the requesting Party through the diplomatic channel the decision on the request for extradition.

(2) If a warrant or order for the extradition of a person sought has been issued by the competent authority and he is not removed from the territory of the requested Party within such time as may be required under the law of that Party, he may be set at liberty and the requested Party may subsequently refuse to extradite him for the same offense.

Article XII

(1) A person extradited shall not be detained or proceeded against in the territory of the requesting Party for any offense other than an extraditable offense established by the facts in respect of which his extradition has been granted, or on account of any other matters, nor be extradited by that Party to a third State —

(*a*) until after he has returned to the territory of the requested Party; or

(*b*) until the expiration of thirty days after he has been free to return to the territory of the requested Party.

(2) The provisions of paragraph (1) of this Article shall not apply to offenses committed, or matters arising, after the extradition.

Article XIII

When a request for extradition is granted, the requested Party shall, so far as its law allows and subject to such conditions as it may impose having regard to the rights of other claimants, furnish the requesting Party with all sums of money and other articles —

(*a*) which may serve as proof of the offense to which the request relates; or

(*b*) which may have been acquired by the person sought as a result of the offense and are in his possession.

Article XIV

(1) The requested Party shall make all necessary arrangements for and meet the cost of the representation of the requesting Party in any proceedings arising out of a request for extradition.

(2) Expenses relating to the transportation of a person sought shall be paid by the requesting Party. No pecuniary claim arising out of the arrest, detention, examination and surrender of a person sought under the provisions of this Treaty shall be made by the requested Party against the requesting Party.

Article XV

A request on the part of the Government of the United States of America for the extradition of an offender who is found in any of the territories to which this Treaty has been extended in accordance with paragraph (1) of Article II may be made to the Governor or other competent authority of that territory, who may take the decision himself or refer the matter to the Government of the United Kingdom for their decision.

Article XVI

(1) This Treaty shall be ratified, and the instruments of ratification shall be exchanged at Washington as soon as possible. It shall come into force three months after the date of the exchange of instruments of ratification.

(2) This Treaty shall apply to any offense listed in the annexed Schedule committed before or after this Treaty enters into force, provided that extradition shall not be granted for an offense committed before this Treaty enters into force which was not an offense under the laws of both Contracting Parties at the time of its commission.

(3) On the entry into force of this Treaty the provisions of the Extradition Treaty of December 22, 1931 shall cease to have effect as between the United Kingdom and the United States of America.

(4) Either of the Contracting Parties may terminate this Treaty at any time by giving notice to the other through the diplomatic channel. In that event the Treaty shall cease to have effect six months after the receipt of the notice. . . .

SCHEDULE. LIST OF OFFENSES REFERRED TO IN ARTICLE III

1. Murder; attempt to murder, including assault with intent to murder.
2. Manslaughter.
3. Maliciously wounding or inflicting grievous bodily harm.
4. Unlawful throwing or application of any corrosive or injurious substance upon the person of another.
5. Rape; unlawful sexual intercourse with a female; indecent assault.
6. Gross indecency or unlawful sexual acts with a child under the age of fourteen years.
7. Procuring a woman or young person for immoral purposes; living on the earnings of prostitution.
8. Unlawfully administering drugs or using instruments with intent to procure the miscarriage of a woman.
9. Bigamy.
10. Kidnapping, abduction, false imprisonment.

11. Neglecting, ill-treating, abandoning, exposing or stealing a child.
12. An offense against the law relating to narcotic drugs, cannabis sativa L, hallucinogenic drugs, cocaine and its derivatives, and other dangerous drugs.
13. Theft; larceny; embezzlement.
14. Robbery; assault with intent to rob.
15. Burglary or housebreaking or shopbreaking.
16. Receiving or otherwise handling any goods, money, valuable securities or other property, knowing the same to have been stolen or unlawfully obtained.
17. Obtaining property, money or valuable securities by false pretenses or other form of deception.
18. Blackmail or extortion.
19. False accounting.
20. Fraud or false statements by company directors and other officers.
21. An offense against the bankruptcy laws.
22. An offense relating to counterfeiting or forgery.
23. Bribery, including soliciting, offering or accepting bribes.
24. Perjury; subornation of perjury.
25. Arson.
26. Malicious damage to property.
27. Any malicious act done with intent to endanger the safety of persons travelling or being upon a railway.
28. Piracy, involving ships or aircraft, according to international law.
29. Unlawful seizure of an aircraft.

U.S.-U.K. SUPPLEMENTARY TREATY CONCERNING THE EXTRADITION TREATY

June 25, 1985, 24 I.L.M. 1105 (1985)*

The Government of the United States of America and the Government of the United Kingdom of Great Britain and Northern Ireland;

Desiring to make more effective the Extradition Treaty between the Contracting Parties, signed at London on 8 June 1972 (hereinafter referred to as "the Extradition Treaty");

Have resolved to conclude a Supplementary Treaty and have agreed as follows:

Article 1

For the purposes of the Extradition Treaty, none of the following offenses shall be regarded as an offense of a political character:

(a) an offense within the scope of the Convention for the Suppression of Unlawful Seizure of Aircraft, opened for signature at The Hague on 16 December 1970;

(b) an offense within the scope of the Convention for the Suppression of Unlawful Acts against the Safety of Civil Aviation, opened for signature at Montreal on 23 September 1971;

(c) an offense within the scope of the Convention on the Prevention and Punishment of Crimes against Internationally Protected Persons, including Diplomatic Agents, opened for signature at New York on 14 December 1973;

(d) an offense within the scope of the International Convention against the Taking of Hostages, opened for signature at New York on 18 December 1979;

(e) murder;

(f) manslaughter;

(g) maliciously wounding or inflicting grievous bodily harm;

(h) kidnapping, abduction, false imprisonment or unlawful detention, including the taking of a hostage;

(i) the following offenses relating to explosives:

(1) the causing of an explosion likely to endanger life or cause serious damage to property; or

(2) conspiracy to cause such an explosion; or

(3) the making or possession of an explosive substance by a person

*Signed in Washington on June 25, 1985. Entered into force on December 23, 1986.

who intends either himself or through another person to endanger life or cause serious damage to property;

(j) the following offenses relating to firearms or ammunition:

(1) the possession of a firearm or ammunition by a person who intends either himself or through another person to endanger life; or

(2) the use of a firearm by a person with intent to resist or prevent the arrest or detention of himself or another person;

(k) damaging property with intent to endanger life or with reckless disregard as to whether the life of another would thereby be endangered;

(l) an attempt to commit any of the foregoing offenses.

Article 2

Article V, paragraph (1)(b) of the Extradition Treaty is amended to read as follows:

"(b) the prosecution for the offense for which extradition is requested has become barred by lapse of time according to the law of the requesting Party; or"

Article 3

Article VIII, paragraph (2) of the Extradition Treaty is amended to read as follows:

"(2) A person arrested upon such an application shall be set at liberty upon the expiration of sixty days from the date of his arrest if a request for his extradition shall not have been received. This provision shall not prevent the institution of further proceedings for the extradition of the person sought if a request for extradition is subsequently received."

Article 4

This Supplementary Treaty shall apply to any offense committed before or after this Supplementary Treaty enters into force, provided that this Supplementary Treaty shall not apply to an offense committed before this Supplementary Treaty enters into force which was not an offense under the laws of both Contracting Parties at the time of its commission.

Article 5

This Supplementary Treaty shall form an integral part of the Extradition Treaty and shall apply:

(a) in relation to the United Kingdom: to Great Britain and Northern Ireland, the Channel Islands, the Isle of Man and the territories for whose international relations the United Kingdom is responsible which are listed in the Annex to this Supplementary Treaty;

(b) to the United States of America;

and references to the territory of a Contracting Party shall be construed accordingly.

Article 6

This Supplementary Treaty shall be subject to ratification and the instruments of ratification shall be exchanged at London as soon as possible. It shall enter into force upon the exchange of instruments of ratification. It shall be subject to termination in the same manner as the Extradition Treaty. . . .

Annex

Anguilla
Bermuda
British Indian Ocean Territory
British Virgin Islands
Cayman Islands
Falkland Islands
Falkland Islands Dependencies
Gibraltar
Hong Kong
Montserrat
Pitcairn, Henderson, Ducie and Oeno Islands
St. Helena
St. Helena Dependencies
The Sovereign Base Areas of Akrotiri and Dhekelia in the Island of Cyprus
Turks and Caicos Islands

U.S.-U.K. TREATY CONCERNING THE GRAND CAYMAN ISLANDS RELATING TO MUTUAL LEGAL ASSISTANCE IN CRIMINAL MATTERS

July 3, 1986, S. Treaty Doc. 8, 100th Cong. 1st Sess. (1987)*

The Government of the United States of America and the Government of the United Kingdom of Great Britain and Northern Ireland, including the Government of the Cayman Islands;

Desiring to improve the effectiveness of the law enforcement authorities of both the United States of America and the Cayman Islands in the investigation, prosecution, and suppression of crime through cooperation and mutual legal assistance in criminal matters;

Have agreed as follows:

Article 1. Scope of Assistance

1. The Parties shall provide mutual assistance, in accordance with the provisions of this Treaty, for the investigation, prosecution, and suppression of criminal offenses of the nature and in the circumstances set out in this Treaty, including the civil and administrative proceedings referred to in paragraph 3(c) of Article 19.

2. For the purposes of paragraph 1, assistance shall include:
   (a) taking the testimony or statements of persons;
   (b) providing documents, records, and articles of evidence;
   (c) serving documents;
   (d) locating persons;
   (e) transferring persons in custody for testimony;
   (f) executing requests for searches and seizures;
   (g) immobilizing criminally obtained assets;
   (h) assistance in proceedings related to forfeiture, restitution and collection of fines; and
   (i) any other steps deemed appropriate by both Central Authorities.

3. This Treaty is intended solely for mutual legal assistance between the Parties. The provisions of this Treaty shall not create any right on the part of any private person to obtain, suppress, or exclude any evidence, or to impede the execution of a request.

---

*Signed at Grand Cayman, Cayman Islands on July 3, 1986. Entered into force on March 19, 1990.

Article 2. Central Authorities

1. A Central Authority shall be established by each Party.

2. For the United States of America, the Central Authority shall be the Attorney General or a person designated by him. For the Cayman Islands, the Central Authority shall be the Cayman Mutual Legal Assistance Authority or a person designated by it.

3. Requests under this Treaty shall be made by the Central Authority of the Requesting Part to the Central Authority of the Requested Party.

Article 3. Limitations on Assistance

1. The assistance afforded by this Treaty shall not extend to:

(a) any matter which relates directly or indirectly to the regulation, including the imposition, calculation, and collection, of taxes, except for any matter falling within sub-paragraphs 3(d) and 3(e) of Article 19; or

(b) any conduct not punishable by imprisonment of more than one year.

2. The Central Authority of the Requested Party may deny assistance where:

(a) the request is not made in conformity with the provisions of this Treaty;

(b) the request relates to a political offense or to an offense under military law which would not be an offense under ordinary criminal law; or

(c) the request does not establish that there are reasonable grounds for believing:

(i) that the criminal offense specified in the request has been committed; and

(ii) that the information sought relates to the offense and is located in the territory of the Requested Party.

3. The Central Authority shall deny assistance where the Attorney General of the Requested Party has issued a certificate to the effect that the execution of the request is contrary to the public interest of the Requested Party.

4. Before denying assistance pursuant to this Article the Central Authority of the Requested Party shall consult with the Central Authority of the Requesting Party to consider whether assistance can be given subject to such conditions as it deems necessary. If the Requesting Party accepts assistance subject to these conditions, it shall comply with the conditions.

Article 4. Form and Contents of Requests

1. Requests shall be submitted in writing by the Central Authority of the Requesting Party in such form as may from time to time be agreed between the Central Authorities.

2. The request shall include the following:

(a) the name of the authority conducting the investigation or proceeding to which the request relates;

(b) the subject matter and nature of the investigation or proceeding for the purposes of which the request is made and in particular the criminal offense or offenses for the investigation, prosecution or suppression of which the assistance is requested;

(c) information concerning the persons involved including, where available, their full names, dates of birth, and addresses;

(d) the information relied upon in support of the request;

(e) a description of the evidence, information or other assistance sought; such description shall specify where possible the time period to which any such evidence or information relates;

(f) the purpose for which the evidence or information or other assistance is sought; and

(g) the identity and presumed location, where known, of any person from whom evidence is sought.

3. To the extent necessary and possible, a request shall also include:

(a) the identity and location of a person to be served, that person's relationship to the proceedings, and the manner in which service is to be made;

(b) available information on the identity and whereabouts of a person to be located;

(c) a precise description of the place or person to be searched and of the articles to be seized;

(d) a description of the manner in which any testimony or statement is to be taken and recorded;

(e) a list of questions to be asked of a witness;

(f) a description of any particular procedure to be followed in executing the request;

(g) information as to the allowances and expenses to which a person asked to appear in the territory of the Requesting Party will be entitled; and

(h) any other information which may be brought to the attention of the Requested Party to facilitate its execution of the request.

Article 5. Execution of Requests

1. The Central Authority of the Requested Party shall promptly execute any request or, when appropriate, shall transmit it to the authority having jurisdiction to do so. The competent authorities of the Requested Party shall do everything in their power to execute the request. The Courts of the Requested Party shall have jurisdiction to issue subpoenas, search warrants, or other orders necessary to execute the request.

2. When execution of the request requires judicial or administrative action, the request shall be presented to the appropriate authority by the persons designated by the Central Authority of the Requested Party.

3. Requests shall be executed in accordance with the laws of the Requested Party except to the extent that this Treaty provides otherwise. However, the method of execution specified in the request shall be followed except insofar as it is prohibited by the laws of the Requested Party.

4. If execution of the request would interfere with an ongoing criminal investigation or proceeding in the territory of the Requested Party, the

Central Authority of that Party may postpone execution or make execution subject to conditions determined necessary after consultations with the Requesting Party. If the Requesting Party accepts the assistance subject to the conditions it shall comply with the conditions.

5. The Central Authority of the Requested Party shall promptly inform the Central Authority of the Requesting Party of the outcome of the execution of the request. If the request is denied, the Central Authority of the Requested Party shall inform the Central Authority of the Requesting Party of the reasons for the denial.

Article 6. Costs

1. The following expenses, and none other, incurred in executing a request shall be reimbursed by the Requesting Party upon application of the Central Authority of the Requested Party:

(a) travel expenses of a witness presenting testimony in the territory of the Requesting Party;

(b) fees of expert witnesses retained with the approval of the Central Authority of the Requesting Party;

(c) fees of counsel appointed or retained with the approval of the Central Authority of the Requesting Party for a witness giving testimony;

(d) reasonable costs of locating, reproducing, and transporting to the Central Authority of the Requesting Party documents or records specified in a request;

(e) costs of stenographic reports requested by the Central Authority of the Requesting Party, other than reports prepared by a salaried government employee; and

(f) reasonable costs of interpreters or translators.

2. A witness who appears in the territory of the Requesting Party pursuant to Article 10 shall be entitled to the same fees and allowances ordinarily accorded to a witness in the territory of the Requesting Party.

3. A witness who appears in the territory of the Requested Party pursuant to Article 8 shall be entitled to such fees and allowances as shall be agreed between the Central Authorities.

Article 7. Limitations on Use

1. The Requesting Party shall not use any information or evidence obtained under this Treaty for any purposes other than for the investigation, prosecution or suppression in the territory of the Requesting Party of those criminal offenses stated in the request without the prior consent of the Requested Party.

2. Unless otherwise agreed by both Central Authorities, information or evidence furnished under this Treaty shall be kept confidential, except to the extent that the information or evidence is needed for investigations or proceedings forming part of the prosecution of a criminal offense described in the request.

3. The Central Authority of the Requesting Party may request that the application for assistance, its contents and related documents, and the granting of assistance be kept confidential. If the request cannot be executed without breaking confidentiality, the Central Authority of the Re-

quested Party shall so inform the Central Authority of the Requesting Party which shall then determine whether the request should nevertheless be executed.

4. Except as may be permitted under paragraph 1, any information or evidence obtained under this Treaty which has been made public in the territory of the Requesting Party in a proceeding forming part of the prosecution of a criminal offense described in the request may be used only for the following additional purposes:

(a) where a trial results in a conviction for any criminal offense within the scope of this Treaty, for any purpose against the person(s) convicted;

(b) whether or not a trial results in the conviction of any person, in the prosecution of any person for any criminal offense within the scope of this Treaty; and

(c) in civil or administrative proceedings, only if and to the extent that such proceedings relate to:

(i) the recovery of the unlawful proceeds of a criminal offense within the scope of this Treaty from a person who has knowingly received them;

(ii) the collection of tax or enforcement of tax penalties resulting from the knowing receipt of the unlawful proceeds of a criminal offense within the scope of this Treaty; or

(iii) the recovery in rem of the unlawful proceeds or instrumentalities of a criminal offense within the scope of this Treaty.

Article 8. Taking Testimony and Producing Evidence in the Territory of the Requested Party

1. A person requested to testify or to produce documentary information or articles in the territory of the Requested Party may be compelled to do so in accordance with the requirements of the law of the Requested Party.

2. If the person referred to in paragraph 1 asserts a claim of immunity, incapacity, or privilege under the laws of the Requesting Party, the evidence shall nonetheless be taken and the claim made known to the Requesting Party for resolution by the authorities of that Party.

3. The Requesting Party shall furnish information in advance about the date and place of the taking of the evidence pursuant to this Article.

4. The Requested Party shall authorize the presence of such persons as are specified in the request during the taking of any evidence in the territory of the Requested Party and shall allow persons designated in the request to question the person whose testimony or evidence is being taken.

5. Documentary information other than official records produced in the territory of the Requested Party pursuant to this Article shall be authenticated by the attestation of a person competent to do so in the manner indicated in Form A appended to this Treaty. [Form A is not included in this Documentary Supplement.]

Article 9. Providing Records of Government Agencies

1. The Requested Party shall provide the Requesting Party with copies of publicly available records of government departments and agencies in the territory of the Requested Party.

2. The Requested Party may provide copies of any record or information in the possession of a government department or agency in the territory of that Party but not publicly available to the same extent and under the same conditions as it would be available to its own law enforcement or judicial authorities.

3. Official records produced pursuant to this Article shall be authenticated by the attestation of an authorized person in the manner in Form B appended to this Treaty. The attestation shall be signed by, and state the official position of, the attesting person, and the seal of the authority executing the request shall be affixed thereto. . . . [Form B omitted.]

Article 10. Appearance in the Territory of the Requesting Party

1. When the appearance of a person who is in the territory of the Requested Party is needed in the territory of the Requesting Party for the purpose of the execution of a request under this Treaty, the Central Authority of the Requesting Party may request that the Central Authority of the other party invite the person to appear before the appropriate authority in the territory of the Requesting Party. The response of the person shall be communicated promptly to the Central Authority of the Requesting Party. Such a person shall be under no compulsion to accept such an invitation.

2. A person appearing in the territory of the Requesting Party pursuant to this Article shall not be subject to service of process or be detained or subjected to any restriction of personal liberty by reason of any acts or convictions in either the territory of the Requesting or Requested Party which preceded his departure from the territory of the Requested Party.

3. The safe conduct provided for by this Article shall cease ten days after the person has been notified in writing by the appropriate authorities that his presence is no longer required, or if the person has left the territory of the Requesting Party and voluntarily returned to it.

Article 11. Transferring Persons in Custody for Testimonial Purposes

1. A person in the custody of the Requested Party who is needed as a witness in connection with the execution of a request in the territory of the Requesting Party shall be transported to the territory of that Party if the person and the Requested Party consent.

2. A person in the custody of the Requesting Party whose presence in the territory of the Requested Party is needed in connection with the execution of a request under this Treaty may be transported to the territory of the Requested Party if the person and both Parties consent.

3. For the purpose of this Article:

(a) the Receiving Party shall be responsible for the safety and health of the person transferred and have the authority and obligation to keep the person transferred in custody unless otherwise authorized by the Sending Party;

(b) the Receiving Party shall return the person transferred to the custody of the Sending Party as soon as circumstances permit or as otherwise agreed and in any event no later than the date upon which he would have been released from custody in the territory of the Sending Party; and

(c) the person transferred shall receive credit for service of the sentence imposed in the territory of the Sending Party for time served in the custody of the Receiving Party.

Article 12. Location of Persons

1. The Requested Party shall take all necessary measures to locate or identify persons who are believed to be in the territory of that Party and who are needed in connection with the investigation, prosecution or suppression of a criminal offense in the territory of the Requesting Party.

2. The Requested Party shall promptly communicate the results of its inquiries to the Requesting Party.

Article 13. Service of Documents

1. The Requested Party shall effect service of any document relating to or forming part of any request for assistance properly made under the provisions of this Treaty transmitted to it for this purpose by the Requesting Party, provided that the Requested Party shall not be obliged to serve any subpoena or other process requiring the attendance of any person before any authority or tribunal in the territory of the Requesting Party.

2. The Requesting Party shall transmit any such request for the service of a document inviting the appearance of a person before an authority in the territory of the Requesting Party to the Requested Party a reasonable time before the scheduled appearance.

3. The Requested Party shall return a proof of service in the manner specified in the request.

Article 14. Search and Seizure

1. A request for assistance pursuant to Article 1 involving the search, seizure and delivery of an article to the Requesting Party shall be executed if it includes the information justifying such action under the laws of the Requested Party.

2. Every official who has custody of a seized article shall certify the continuity of custody, the identity, and the integrity of its condition. No further certification shall be required. The certificates shall be admissible in evidence in the territory of the Requesting Party as evidence of the truth of the matters set forth therein.

3. The Requested Party shall not be obliged to provide any item seized to the Requesting Party unless that Party has agreed to such terms and conditions as may be required by the Requested Party to protect third party interests in the item to be transferred.

Article 15. Return of Documents and Articles

The Requesting Party shall return any documents or articles furnished to it in the execution of a request under this Treaty as soon as possible unless the Requested Party waives the return of the documents or articles.

Article 16. Proceeds of Crime

1. The Central Authority of one Party may notify the Central Authority of the other Party when it has reason to believe that proceeds of a criminal offense are located in the territory of the other Party.

2. The Parties shall assist each other to the extent permitted by their respective laws in proceedings related to:
   (a) the forfeiture of the proceeds of criminal offenses;
   (b) restitution to the victims of criminal offenses; and
   (c) the collection of fines imposed as a sentence for a criminal offense.

Article 17. Exclusivity

1. Assistance and procedures set forth in this Treaty shall not prevent one Party from granting assistance to the other Party through the provisions of other international agreements or arrangements which may be applicable.

2. Subject to the terms of paragraph 1, a Party needing assistance as provided in Article 1 in the investigation, prosecution or suppression of a criminal offense as defined in Article 19 shall request assistance pursuant to this Treaty.

3. No Party shall enforce any compulsory measure, including a grand jury subpoena, for the production of documents located in the territory of the other Party with respect to any criminal offense within the scope of this Treaty, unless its obligations under the Treaty have first been fulfilled pursuant to paragraph 4 of this Article with respect to a request concerning those documents.

4. Where denial for a request or unreasonable delay in its execution may be jeopardizing the successful completion of an investigation, prosecution or other proceeding, the Central Authority of the Requesting Party shall so inform the Central Authority of the Requested Party in writing. Thereafter, either Contracting Party may give at least 45 days' notice in writing to the other Contracting Party that, unless otherwise agreed, the Parties' obligations under this Article shall be deemed to have been fulfilled; provided that in no case shall the obligations under this Article be deemed to have been fulfilled sooner than 90 days after the date of receipt of the request for assistance.

Article 18. Consultations

1. The Central Authorities will consult, at times mutually agreed by them, to enable the most effective use to be made of this Treaty. Such consultations shall include such information as may be lawfully disclosed concerning the status and disposition of proceedings utilizing documentary information and other evidence secured pursuant to this Treaty.

2. In any case of difficulty either Central Authority may request the assistance of the Contracting Parties to resolve the difficulty by way of consultation.

Article 19. Definitions

For the purpose of this Treaty:

1. "The Contracting Parties" means the Government of the United States and the Government of the United Kingdom.

2. "The Parties" means the Government of the United States and the Government of the Cayman Islands.

3. "Criminal offense" which, except in the case of any matter falling within sub-paragraphs (d) and (e) of this definition, does not include any conduct or matter which relates directly or indirectly to the regulation, imposition, calculation or collection of taxes, but subject always to those exclusions, means:

(a) Any conduct punishable by more than one year's imprisonment under the laws of both the Requesting and Requested Parties:

(b) "Racketeering" which means:

(i) the use or investment, directly or indirectly, knowingly by any person of any part of racketeering income, or the proceeds of such income, in the acquisition of any interest in, or the establishment or operation of, any enterprise which is engaged in, or the activities of which affect commerce, including interstate or foreign commerce;

(ii) the acquisition or maintenance knowingly by any person through a pattern of racketeering activity or through collection of an unlawful debt, directly or indirectly, of any interest in or control of any enterprise which is engaged in, or the activities of which affect commerce, including interstate or foreign commerce; or

(iii) where any person is employed by or associated with any enterprise engaged in, or the activities of which affect commerce, including interstate or foreign commerce, the conduct or participation in the conduct, directly or indirectly, knowingly by that person of the affairs of the enterprise through a pattern of racketeering activity or collection of unlawful debt; . . .

(c) "Narcotics trafficking" which means all offenses or ancillary civil or administrative proceedings taken by either of the Parties or their agencies connected with, arising from, related to, resulting from any narcotics activity covered by the Single Convention on Narcotic Drugs, 1961, or the Protocol Amending the Single Convention on Narcotics Drugs, 1961, or any other international agreements or arrangements binding upon both the Parties;

(d) Willfully or dishonestly obtaining money, property or valuable securities from other persons by means of false or fraudulent pretenses or statements, whether oral or written, regarding or affecting benefits available in connection with the laws and regulations relating to income or other taxes;

(e) Willfully or dishonestly making false statements whether oral or written, to government tax authorities (e.g., willfully or dishonestly submitting a false income tax return) with respect to any tax matter arising from the unlawful proceeds of any criminal offense covered by any other provision of this definition, except sub-paragraph (f), or willfully or dishonestly failing to make a report to government tax authorities as required by law in respect of, or to pay the tax due on, any such unlawful proceeds;

(*f*) Willfully or dishonestly failing to make to the Government a report which is required by law to be made to it in respect of an international transfer of currency or other financial transactions connected with, arising from or related to the unlawful proceeds of any criminal offense falling within any provision of this Article, except this sub-paragraph or sub-paragraph (*e*) above:

(*g*) "Insider trading" which means the offer, purchase, or sale of securities by any person while in possession of material non-public information directly or indirectly relating to the securities offered, purchased, or sold, in breach of a legally binding duty of trust or confidence;

(*h*) Fraudulent securities practices, which means the use by any person willfully or dishonestly of any means, directly or indirectly, in connection with the offer, purchase or sale of any security:

(i) to employ any device, scheme, or artifice to defraud;

(ii) dishonestly to make any untrue statement of a material fact or to omit to state a material fact necessary in order to make the statement made, in light of the circumstances under which it was made, not misleading; or

(iii) dishonestly to engage in any act, practice, or course of business which operates or would operate as a fraud or deceit upon any person;

(*i*) "Foreign corrupt practices" which means the corrupt offering, paying, or making of inducements by any person to any foreign official or foreign political party, official thereof or candidate for foreign official office in order to assist such person in obtaining or retaining business for himself or in directing business to any other person;

(*j*) Any of the above defined criminal offenses, where United States federal jurisdiction is based upon interstate transport, use of the mails, telecommunications or other interstate facilities;

(*k*) Such further offenses as may from time to time be agreed upon by exchange of diplomatic notes between the United States and the United Kingdom, including the Cayman Islands; and

(*l*) Any attempt or conspiracy to commit, or participation as accessory after the fact to, any of the above defined criminal offenses.

Article 20. *Ratification, Entry into Force, and Termination . . .*

3. The Government of either the United States or the United Kingdom, including the Cayman Islands, may terminate this Treaty by giving three months' notice in writing to the other Government at any time. . . .

HAGUE CONVENTION ON THE TAKING OF EVIDENCE

March 18, 1970, 23 U.S.T. 2555, T.I.A.S. No. 7444, 847 U.N.T.S. 231*

The States signatory to the present Convention,
Desiring to facilitate the transmission and execution of Letters of Request and to further the accommodation of the different methods which they use for this purpose,
Desiring to improve mutual judicial co-operation in civil or commercial matters,
Have resolved to conclude a Convention to this effect and have agreed upon the following provisions —

Chapter I — Letters of Request

Article 1

In civil or commercial matters a judicial authority of a Contracting State may, in accordance with the provisions of the law of that State, request the competent authority of another Contracting State, by means of a Letter of Request, to obtain evidence, or to perform some other judicial act.

A Letter shall not be used to obtain evidence which is not intended for use in judicial proceedings, commenced or contemplated.

The expression "other judicial act" does not cover the service of judicial documents or the issuance of any process by which judgments or orders are executed or enforced, or orders for provisional or protective measures.

Article 2

A Contracting State shall designate a Central Authority which will undertake to receive Letters of Request coming from a judicial authority of another Contracting State and to transmit them to the authority competent to execute them. Each State shall organize the Central Authority in accordance with its own law.

Letters shall be sent to the Central Authority of the State of execution without being transmitted through any other authority of that State.

---

*Done at The Hague on March 18, 1970. Entered into force on October 7, 1972. The 21 parties to the convention are: Argentina, Barbados, Cyprus, Czechoslovakia, Denmark, Finland, France, Germany (Federal Republic), Israel, Italy, Luxembourg, Mexico, Monaco, Netherlands, Norway, Portugal, Singapore, Spain, Sweden, United Kingdom, and the United States.

Article 3

A Letter of Request shall specify —
(a) the authority requesting its execution and the authority requested to execute it, if known to the requesting authority;
(b) the names and addresses of the parties to the proceedings and their representatives, if any;
(c) the nature of the proceedings for which the evidence is required, giving all necessary information in regard thereto;
(d) the evidence to be obtained or other judicial act to be performed.
Where appropriate, the Letter shall specify, inter alia —
(e) the names and addresses of the persons to be examined;
(f) the questions to be put to the persons to be examined or a statement of the subject-matter about which they are to be examined;
(g) the documents or other property, real or personal, to be inspected;
(h) any requirement that the evidence is to be given on oath or affirmation, and any special form to be used;
(i) any special method or procedure to be followed under Article 9.

A Letter may also mention any information necessary for the application of Article 11.

No legalization or other like formality may be required.

Article 4

A Letter of Request shall be in the language of the authority requested to execute it or be accompanied by a translation into that language.

Nevertheless, a Contracting State shall accept a Letter in either English or French, or a translation into one of these languages, unless it has made the reservation authorized by Article 33.

A Contracting State which has more than one official language and cannot, for reasons of internal law, accept Letters in one of these languages for the whole of its territory, shall, by declaration, specify the language in which the Letter or translation thereof shall be expressed for execution in the specified parts of its territory. In case of failure to comply with this declaration, without justifiable excuse, the costs of translation into the required language shall be borne by the State of origin.

A Contracting State may, by declaration, specify the language or languages other than those referred to in the preceding paragraphs, in which a Letter may be sent to its Central Authority.

Any translation accompanying a Letter shall be certified as correct, either by a diplomatic officer or consular agent or by a sworn translator or by any other person so authorized in either State.

Article 5

If the Central Authority considers that the request does not comply with the provisions of the present Convention, it shall promptly inform the authority of the State of origin which transmitted the Letter of Request, specifying the objections to the Letter.

Article 6

If the authority to whom a Letter of Request has been transmitted is not competent to execute it, the Letter shall be sent forthwith to the authority in the same State which is competent to execute it in accordance with the provisions of its own law.

Article 7

The requesting authority shall, if it so desires, be informed of the time when, and the place where, the proceedings will take place, in order that the parties concerned, and their representatives, if any, may be present. This information shall be sent directly to the parties or their representatives when the authority of the State of origin so requests.

Article 8

A Contracting State may declare that members of the judicial personnel of the requesting authority of another Contracting State may be present at the execution of a Letter of Request. Prior authorization by the competent authority designated by the declaring State may be required.

Article 9

The judicial authority which executes a Letter of Request shall apply its own law as to the methods and procedures to be followed.

However, it will follow a request of the requesting authority that a special method or procedure be followed, unless this is incompatible with the internal law of the State of execution or is impossible of performance by reason of its internal practice and procedure or by reason of practical difficulties.

A Letter of Request shall be executed expeditiously.

Article 10

In executing a Letter of Request the requested authority shall apply the appropriate measures of compulsion in the instances and to the same extent as are provided by its internal law for the execution of orders issued by the authorities of its own country or of requests made by parties in internal proceedings.

Article 11

In the execution of a Letter of Request the person concerned may refuse to give evidence in so far as he has a privilege or duty to refuse to give the evidence —

(a) under the law of the State of execution; or

(b) under the law of the State of origin, and the privilege or duty has been specified in the Letter, or, at the instance of the requested authority, has been otherwise confirmed to that authority by the requesting authority.

A Contracting State may declare that, in addition, it will respect privileges and duties existing under the law of States other than the State of origin and the State of execution, to the extent specified in that declaration.

Article 12

The execution of a Letter of Request may be refused only to the extent that —

(a) in the State of execution the execution of the Letter does not fall within the functions of the judiciary; or

(b) the State addressed considers that its sovereignty or security would be prejudiced thereby.

Execution may not be refused solely on the ground that under its internal law the State of execution claims exclusive jurisdiction over the subject-matter of the action or that its internal law would not admit a right of action on it.

Article 13

The documents establishing the execution of the Letter of Request shall be sent by the requested authority to the requesting authority by the same channel which was used by the latter.

In every instance where the Letter is not executed in whole or in part, the requesting authority shall be informed immediately through the same channel and advised of the reasons.

Article 14

The execution of the Letter of Request shall not give rise to any reimbursement of taxes or costs of any nature.

Nevertheless, the State of execution has the right to require the State of origin to reimburse the fees paid to experts and interpreters and the costs occasioned by the use of a special procedure requested by the State of origin under Article 9, paragraph 2.

The requested authority whose law obliges the parties themselves to secure evidence, and which is not able itself to execute the Letter, may, after having obtained the consent of the requesting authority, appoint a suitable person to do so. When seeking this consent the requested authority shall indicate the approximate costs which would result from this procedure. If the requesting authority gives its consent it shall reimburse any costs incurred; without such consent the requesting authority shall not be liable for the costs.

Chapter II — Taking of Evidence by Diplomatic Officers, Consular Agents and Commissioners

Article 15

In a civil or commercial matter, a diplomatic officer or consular agent of a Contracting State may, in the territory of another Contracting State and within the area where he exercises his functions, take the evidence without compulsion of nationals of a State which he represents in aid of proceedings commenced in the courts of a State which he represents.

A Contracting State may declare that evidence may be taken by a diplomatic officer or consular agent only if permission to that effect is given upon application made by him or on his behalf to the appropriate authority designated by the declaring State.

Article 16

A diplomatic officer or consular agent of a Contracting State may, in the territory of another Contracting State and within the area where he exercises his functions, also take the evidence, without compulsion, of nationals of the State in which he exercises his functions or of a third State, in aid of proceedings commenced in the courts of a State which he represents, if —

(a) a competent authority designated by the State in which he exercises his functions has given its permission either generally or in the particular case, and

(b) he complies with the conditions which the competent authority has specified in the permission.

A Contracting State may declare that evidence may be taken under this Article without its prior permission.

Article 17

In a civil or commercial matter, a person duly appointed as a commissioner for the purpose may, without compulsion, take evidence in the territory of a Contracting State in aid of proceedings commenced in the courts of another Contracting State if —

(a) a competent authority designated by the State where the evidence is to be taken has given its permission either generally or in the particular case; and

(b) he complies with the conditions which the competent authority has specified in the permission.

A Contracting State may declare that evidence may be taken under this Article without its prior permission.

Article 18

A Contracting State may declare that a diplomatic officer, consular agent or commissioner authorized to take evidence under Articles 15, 16 or 17, may apply to the competent authority designated by the declaring State for appropriate assistance to obtain the evidence by compulsion. The declaration may contain such conditions as the declaring State may see fit to impose.

If the authority grants the application it shall apply any measures of compulsion which are appropriate and are prescribed by its law for use in internal proceedings.

Article 19

The competent authority, in giving the permission referred to in Articles 15, 16 or 17, or in granting the application referred to in Article 18, may lay down such conditions as it deems fit, *inter alia,* as to the time and place of the taking of the evidence. Similarly it may require that it be given reasonable advance notice of the time, date and place of the taking of the evidence; in such a case a representative of the authority shall be entitled to be present at the taking of the evidence.

Article 20

In the taking of evidence under any Article of this Chapter persons concerned may be legally represented.

Article 21

Where a diplomatic officer, consular agent or commissioner is authorized under Articles 15, 16 or 17 to take evidence —

(a) he may take all kinds of evidence which are not incompatible with the law of the State where the evidence is taken or contrary to any permission granted pursuant to the above Articles, and shall have power within such limits to administer an oath or take an affirmation;

(b) a request to a person to appear or to give evidence shall, unless the recipient is a national of the State where the action is pending, be drawn up in the language of the place where the evidence is taken or be accompanied by a translation into such language;

(c) the request shall inform the person that he may be legally represented and, in any State that has not filed a declaration under Article 18, shall also inform him that he is not compelled to appear or to give evidence;

(d) the evidence may be taken in the manner provided by the law applicable to the court in which the action is pending provided that such manner is not forbidden by the law of the State where the evidence is taken;

(e) a person requested to give evidence may invoke the privileges and duties to refuse to give the evidence contained in Article 11.

Article 22

The fact that an attempt to take evidence under the procedure laid down in this Chapter has failed, owing to the refusal of a person to give evidence, shall not prevent an application being subsequently made to take the evidence in accordance with Chapter I.

Chapter III — General Clauses

Article 23

A Contracting State may at the time of signature, ratification or accession, declare that it will not execute Letters of Request issued for the purpose of obtaining pre-trial discovery of documents as known in Common Law countries.

Article 24

A Contracting State may designate other authorities in addition to the Central Authority and shall determine the extent of their competence. However, Letters of Request may in all cases be sent to the Central Authority.

Federal States shall be free to designate more than one Central Authority.

Article 25

A Contracting State which has more than one legal system may designate the authorities of one of such systems, which shall have exclusive competence to execute Letters of Request pursuant to this Convention.

Article 26

A Contracting State, if required to do so because of constitutional limitations, may request the reimbursement by the State of origin of fees and costs, in connection with the execution of Letters of Request, for the service of process necessary to compel the appearance of a person to give evidence, the costs of attendance of such persons, and the cost of any transcript of the evidence.

Where a State has made a request pursuant to the above paragraph, any other Contracting State may request from that State the reimbursement of similar fees and costs.

Article 27

The provisions of the present Convention shall not prevent a Contracting State from —

(a) declaring that Letters of Request may be transmitted to its judicial authorities through channels other than those provided for in Article 2;

(b) permitting, by internal law or practice, any act provided for in this Convention to be performed upon less restrictive conditions;

(c) permitting, by internal law or practice, methods of taking evidence other than those provided for in this Convention.

Article 28

The present Convention shall not prevent an agreement between any two or more Contracting States to derogate from —

(a) the provisions of Article 2 with respect to methods of transmitting Letters of Request;

(b) the provisions of Article 4 with respect to the languages which may be used;

(c) the provisions of Article 8 with respect to the presence of judicial personnel at the execution of Letters;

(d) the provisions of Article 11 with respect to the privileges and duties of witnesses to refuse to give evidence;

(e) the provisions of Article 13 with respect to the methods of returning executed Letters to the requesting authority;

(f) the provisions of Article 14 with respect to fees and costs;

(g) the provisions of Chapter II.

Article 29

Between Parties to the present Convention who are also Parties to one or both of the Conventions on Civil Procedure signed at the Hague on the 17th of July 1905 and the 1st of March 1954, this Convention shall replace Articles 8-16 of the earlier Conventions.

Article 30

The present Convention shall not affect the application of Article 23 of the Convention of 1905, or of Article 24 of the Convention of 1954.

Article 31

Supplementary Agreements between Parties to the Conventions of 1905 and 1954 shall be considered as equally applicable to the present Convention unless the Parties have otherwise agreed.

Article 32

Without prejudice to the provisions of Articles 29 and 31, the present Convention shall not derogate from conventions containing provisions on the matters covered by this Convention to which the Contracting States are, or shall become Parties.

Article 33

A State may, at the time of signature, ratification or accession exclude, in whole or in part, the application of the provisions of paragraph 2 of Article 4 and of Chapter II. No other reservation shall be permitted.

Each Contracting State may at any time withdraw a reservation it has made; the reservation shall cease to have effect on the sixtieth day after notification of the withdrawal.

When a State has made a reservation, any other State affected thereby may apply the same rule against the reserving State.

Article 34

A State may at any time withdraw or modify a declaration.

Article 35

A Contracting State shall, at the time of the deposit of its instrument of ratification or accession, or at a later date, inform the Ministry of Foreign Affairs of the Netherlands of the designation of authorities, pursuant to Articles 2, 8, 24 and 25.

A Contracting State shall likewise inform the Ministry, where appropriate, of the following —

(a) the designation of the authorities to whom notice must be given, whose permission may be required, and whose assistance may be invoked in the taking of evidence by diplomatic officers and consular agents, pursuant to Articles 15, 16 and 18 respectively;

(b) the designation of the authorities whose permission may be required in the taking of evidence by commissioners pursuant to Article 17 and of those who may grant the assistance provided for in Article 18;

(c) declarations pursuant to Articles 4, 8, 11, 15, 16, 17, 18, 23 and 27;

(d) any withdrawal or modification of the above designations and declarations;

(e) the withdrawal of any reservation.

Article 36

Any difficulties which may arise between Contracting States in connection with the operation of this Convention shall be settled through diplomatic channels. . . .

Article 41

The present Convention shall remain in force for five years from the date of its entry into force. . . .

If there has been no denunciation, it shall be renewed tacitly every five years. . . .

8

State Responsibility — Injuries to Aliens and International Human Rights

U.S.-EGYPT TREATY CONCERNING THE RECIPROCAL ENCOURAGEMENT AND PROTECTION OF INVESTMENTS
September 29, 1982, 21 I.L.M. 927 (1982)*

Whereas, each agrees that economic cooperation through the pursuit of policies and practices which foster bilateral trade and investment, will contribute substantially to the long-term benefit and welfare of the peoples of each Party, and

Recognizing that agreement on a general framework for the encouragement and nondiscriminatory treatment of investments will stimulate the flow of productive capital and technology and thereby provide for a more effective use of capital and technical resources for development needs, further promoting economic stability and durable peace. . . .

Article I. Definitions

1. For the purposes of this Treaty,

(a) "company" means any kind of juridical entity; including any corporation, company, association, or other organization, that is duly incorporated, constituted, or otherwise duly organized, regardless of whether or not the entity is duly organized for pecuniary gain, privately or publicly owned, or organized with limited or unlimited liability.

(b) "company of a Party" means a company duly incorporated, constituted, or otherwise duly organized under the applicable laws and regulations of a Party or a political or administrative subdivision thereof in which

(i) natural persons who are nationals of such Party, or

---

*Signed in Washington, D.C., on September 29, 1982. Ratified by the United States on December 6, 1988. Not yet in force as of June 1990. Resubmitted to the Egyptian Parliament.

(ii) such Party or a political or administrative subdivision thereof or their agencies or instrumentalities

have a substantial interest.

Each Party reserves the right to deny to any of its own companies or to a company of the other Party the advantages of this Treaty, if nationals of any third country own or control such company; provided that whenever one Party believes that the benefits of this Treaty should not be extended to a company of the other Party for this reason, it shall first consult with the other Party to seek a mutually satisfactory resolution of this matter.

The juridical status of a company of a Party shall be recognized by the other Party and its political or administrative subdivisions.

(c) "investment" means every kind of investment, owned or controlled, including equity, debt, service and investment contracts; and includes, but is not limited to:

(i) tangible and intangible property, including rights, such as mortgages, liens and pledges;

(ii) a company or shares of stock in a company or interests in the assets thereof;

(iii) a claim to money or a claim to performance having economic value due under an investment agreement;

(iv) valid intellectual and industrial property rights, including, but not limited to, rights with respect to copyrights, patents, trademarks, trade names, industrial designs, trade secrets and know-how, and goodwill;

(v) licenses and permits issued pursuant to law, including those issued for manufacture and sale of products;

(vi) any right conferred by law or contract including, but not limited to, rights, within the confines of law, to search for or utilize natural resources, and rights to manufacture, use and sell products;

(vii) returns which are reinvested.

(d) "own or control" means ownership or control that is direct or indirect, including ownership or control exercised through subsidiaries or affiliates, wherever located.

(e) "national" of a Party means a natural person who is a national of a Party under its applicable law.

(f) "return" means an amount derived from an investment, including but not limited to, profit; dividend; interest; royalty payment; management, technical assistance or other fee; and payment in kind.

Article II. *Encouragement and Promotion of Investments*

1. Each Party undertakes to provide and maintain a favorable environment for investments in its territory by nationals and companies of the other Party and shall, in applying its laws, regulations, administrative practices and procedures, permit such investments to be established and acquired on terms and conditions that accord treatment no less favorable than the treatment it accords to investments of its own nationals or companies or to nationals and companies of any third country, whichever is the most favorable.

2. (a) Each Party shall accord investments in its territory, and associated activities related to these investments, of nationals or companies of the other Party treatment no less favorable than that which it accords in like situations to investments and associated activities of its own nationals or companies, or nationals or companies of any third country, whichever is the most favorable. Associated activities related to an investment include, but are not limited to:

(i) the establishment, control and maintenance of branches, agencies, offices, factories or other facilities for the conduct of business;

(ii) the organization of companies under applicable laws and regulations; the acquisition of companies or interests in companies or in their property; and the management, control, maintenance, use, enjoyment and expansion, and the sale, liquidation, dissolution or other disposition, of companies organized or acquired;

(iii) the making, performance and enforcement of contracts related to investment;

(iv) the acquisition (whether by purchase, lease or any other legal means), ownership and disposition (whether by sale, testament or any other legal means) of personal property of all kinds, both tangible and intangible;

(v) the leasing of real property appropriate for the conduct of business;

(vi) the acquisition, maintenance and protection of copyrights, patents, trademarks, trade secrets, trade names, licenses and other approvals of products and manufacturing processes, and other industrial property rights; and,

(vii) the borrowing of funds at market terms and conditions from local financial institutions, as well as the purchase and issuance of equity shares in the local financial markets, and, in accordance with national regulations and practices, the purchase of foreign exchange for the operation of the enterprise.

2. (b) Consistent with paragraph 4 of this Article, each Party shall apply the present Treaty to investments in its territory by nationals or companies of the other Party made prior to the entry into force of this Treaty provided such application is not inconsistent with agreements, contractual arrangements, investment authorizations and licenses made under legislation existing at the time the concerned investments were made.

3. Notwithstanding the preceding provisions of this Article, each Party reserves the right to maintain limited exceptions to the standard of national treatment otherwise required concerning investments or associated activities if such exceptions fall within one of the sectors listed in the Annex to this Treaty. Both Parties hereby agree to maintain the number of such exceptions to a minimum. In addition, each Party shall notify the other Party of any specific measures which constitute exceptions to the standard of national treatment provided herein. In no event, however, shall the treatment to be accorded pursuant to any exception be less favorable than that accorded in like situations to investments and associated activities of nationals or companies of any third country. Moreover, no exception, within the sectors contained in the Annex, introduced after the date of entry into force

of this Treaty shall apply to investments of nationals or companies of the other Party existing in that sector at the time the exception becomes effective.

4. The treatment, protection and security of investments shall never be less than that required by international law and national legislation.

5. (a) Subject to the laws relating to the entry and sojourn of aliens, nationals of either Party shall be permitted to enter and to remain in the territory of the other Party for the purpose of establishing, developing, directing, administering or advising on the operations of an investment to which they or the companies that employ them have committed or are in the process of committing a substantial amount of capital or other resources.

(b) Nationals and companies of either Party, and their companies which they own or control in the territory of the other Party, shall be able to engage the managing director of their choice. Further, subject to employment laws of each Party, nationals and companies of either Party shall be permitted to engage, within the territory of the other Party, professional and technical personnel of their choice, for the particular purpose of rendering professional, technical and managerial assistance necessary for the planning and operation of investments.

6. In the context of national economic policies and the desire to promote investment of all types, both private and public, the Parties recognize that conditions of competitive equality should be maintained where investments owned or controlled by a Party or its agencies or instrumentalities, within the territory of such Party, are in competition under similar conditions and situations with privately owned or controlled investments of nationals or companies of the other Party.

7. In the context of its national economic policies and objectives, each Party shall seek to avoid the imposition of performance requirements on the investments of nationals and companies of the other Party.

8. Each Party recognizes that in order to maintain a favorable environment for investments in its territory by nationals or companies of the other Party, it should provide effective means of asserting claims and enforcing rights with respect to investment agreements, investment authorizations and properties. Each Party shall grant to nationals or companies of the other Party, on terms and conditions no less favorable than those which it grants in like situations to its own nationals or companies or to nationals or companies of any third country, whichever is the most favorable treatment, the right of access to its courts of justice, administrative tribunals and agencies, and all other bodies exercising adjudicatory authority, and the right to employ persons of their choice, who otherwise qualify under applicable laws and regulations of the forum for the purpose of asserting claims, and enforcing rights, with respect to their investments.

9. Each Party and its political or administrative subdivisions shall make public all laws, regulations, administrative practices and procedures, and adjudicatory decisions that pertain to or affect investments in its territory of nationals or companies of the other Party.

Article III. Compensation for Expropriation

1. No investment or any part of an investment of a national or a company of either Party shall be expropriated or nationalized by the other Party or a political or administrative subdivision thereof — or subjected to any other measure, direct or indirect (including, for example, the levying of taxation, the compulsory sale of all or part of such an investment, or impairment or deprivation of management, control or economic value of such an investment by the national or company concerned), if the effect of such other measure, or a series of such other measures, would be tantamount to expropriation or nationalization (all expropriations, all nationalizations and all such other measures hereinafter referred to as "expropriation") — unless the expropriation

(a) is done for a public purpose;

(b) is accomplished under due process of law;

(c) is not discriminatory;

(d) is accompanied by prompt and adequate compensation, freely realizable; and

(e) does not violate any specific provision on contractual stability or expropriation contained in an investment agreement between the national or company concerned and the Party making the expropriation.

Compensation shall be equivalent to the fair market value of the expropriated investment on the date of expropriation. The calculation of such compensation shall not reflect any reduction in such fair market value due to either prior public notice or announcement of the expropriatory action, or the occurrence of the events that constituted or resulted in the expropriatory action. Such compensation shall include payments for delay as may be considered appropriate under international law, and shall be freely transferable at the prevailing rate of exchange for current transactions on the date of the expropriatory action.

2. If either Party or a political or administrative subdivision thereof expropriates the investment of any company duly incorporated, constituted or otherwise duly organized in its territory, and if nationals or companies of the other Party, directly or indirectly, own, hold or have other rights with respect to the equity of such company, then the Party within whose territory the expropriation occurs shall ensure that such nationals or companies of the other Party receive compensation in accordance with the provisions of the preceding paragraph.

3. Except as otherwise provided in an agreement between the Parties, or between a Party and a national or company of the other Party, a national or company of either Party that asserts that all or part of its investment in the territory of the other Party has been expropriated shall have a right to prompt review by the appropriate judicial or administrative authorities of such other Party to determine whether any such expropriation has occurred and, if so, whether such expropriation, and any compensation thereof, conforms to the principles of international law as set forth in this Article. . . .

Article V. Transfers

1. Either Party shall in respect to investments by nationals or companies of the other Party grant to those nationals or companies the free transfer of:

   a. returns.

   b. royalties and other payments deriving from licenses, franchises and other similar grants or rights.

   c. installments in repayment of loans.

   d. amounts spent for the management of the investment in the territory of the other Party or a third country.

   e. Additional funds necessary for the maintenance of the investment.

   f. the proceeds of partial or total sale or liquidation of the investment, including a liquidation effected as a result of [war or any similar] event . . . ; and

   g. compensation payments pursuant to Article III.

2. To the extent a national or company of either Party has not made another arrangement with the appropriate authorities of the other Party in whose territory the investment of such national or company is situated, currency transfers made pursuant to Paragraph 1 of this Article shall be permitted in the currency of the original investment or in any other freely convertible currency. Such transfers shall be made at the prevailing rate of exchange on the date of transfer with respect to current transactions in the currency to be transferred.

3. Notwithstanding the preceding paragraphs, either Party may maintain laws and regulations: (a) requiring reports of currency transfer; and (b) imposing income taxes by such means as a withholding tax applicable to dividends or other transfers. Furthermore, either Party may protect the rights of creditors, or ensure the satisfaction of judgments in adjudicatory proceedings, through the equitable, nondiscriminatory and good faith application of its law.

Article VI. Consultations and Exchange of Information

1. The Parties shall, upon the written request of either of them, promptly hold consultations to discuss the interpretation or application of this Treaty or to resolve any disputes in connection therewith. Consultations shall be held should one Party request consultations to discuss the effects on its national interests of laws, regulations, decisions, administrative practices or procedures, or policies of the other Party that pertain to or affect investments of its nationals or companies in the territory of such other Party, including conditions imposed on establishment of investments. The consultations will seek to avoid or ameliorate the adverse effects that these laws, regulations, decisions, administrative practices or procedures, or policies may have on the Party requesting the consultations.

2. Further, for the purpose of reviewing the operation of this Treaty in encouraging investments, consultations should be held biennially between the two Parties. Those consultations should aim at exchanging information and views on the progress regarding investments.

3. If one Party requests in writing that the other Party supply informa-

tion in its possession concerning investments in its territory by nationals or companies of the Party making the request, then the other Party shall, consistent with its applicable laws and regulations and with due regard for business confidentiality, endeavor to establish appropriate procedures and arrangements for the provision of any such information.

Article VII. Settlement of Legal Investment Disputes Between One Party and a National or Company of the Other Party

1. For purposes of this Article, a legal investment dispute is defined as a dispute involving (i) the interpretation or application of an investment agreement between a Party and a national or company of the other Party; or (ii) an alleged breach of any right conferred or created by this Treaty with respect to an investment.

2. In the event of a legal investment dispute between a Party and a national or company of the other Party with respect to an investment of such national or company in the territory of such Party, the parties shall initially seek to resolve the dispute by consultation and negotiation. The Parties may, upon the initiative of either of them and as a part of their consultation and negotiation, agree to rely upon non-binding, third-Party procedures. If the dispute cannot be resolved through consultation and negotiation, then the dispute shall be submitted for settlement in accordance with the applicable dispute-settlement procedures upon which a Party and national or company of the other Party have previously agreed. With respect to expropriation by either Party, any dispute-settlement procedures specified in an investment agreement between such Party and such national or company shall remain binding and shall be enforceable in accordance with the terms of the investment agreement and relevant provisions of domestic laws of such Party and treaties and other international agreements regarding enforcement of arbitral awards to which such Party has subscribed.

3. (a) In the event that the legal investment dispute is not resolved under procedures specified above, the national or company concerned may choose to submit the dispute to the International Centre for the Settlement of Investment Disputes ("Centre") for settlement by conciliation or binding arbitration, if, within six (6) months of the date upon which it arose: (i) the dispute has not been settled through consultation and negotiation; or (ii) the dispute has not, for any good faith reason, been submitted for resolution in accordance with any applicable dispute-settlement procedures previously agreed to by the Parties to the dispute; or (iii) the national or company concerned has not brought the dispute before the courts of justice or administrative tribunals or agencies of competent jurisdiction of the Party that is a Party to the dispute.

(b) Each Party hereby consents to the submission of an investment dispute to the Centre for settlement by conciliation or binding arbitration.

(c) Conciliation or binding arbitration of such disputes shall be done in accordance with the provisions of the Convention on the Settlement of Investment Disputes Between States and Nationals of Other States ("Convention") and the Regulations and Rules of the Centre.

4. In any proceeding, judicial, arbitral or otherwise, concerning a legal

investment dispute between it and a national or company of the other Party, a Party shall not assert, as a defense, counter-claim, right of set-off or otherwise, that the national or company concerned has received or will receive, pursuant to an insurance contract, indemnification or other compensation for all or part of its alleged damages from any third Party whatsoever, whether public or private, including such other Party and its political or administrative subdivisions, agencies and instrumentalities. Notwithstanding the foregoing, a national or company of the other Party shall not be entitled to compensation for more than the value of its affected assets, taking into account all sources of compensation within the territory of the Party liable for the compensation.

5. For the purpose of any proceedings initiated before the Centre in accordance with this Article, any company that, immediately prior to the occurrence of the event or events giving rise to the dispute, was a company of the other Party, shall be treated as a national or company of such other Party.

6. The provisions of this Article shall not apply to a dispute arising under an official export credit, guarantee, or insurance arrangement, pursuant to which the Parties have agreed to other means of settling disputes.

Article VIII. Settlement of Disputes Between the Parties Concerning Interpretation or Application of this Treaty

1. Any dispute between the Parties concerning the interpretation or application of this Treaty should, if possible, be resolved through diplomatic channels.

2. If the dispute cannot be resolved through diplomatic channels, it shall, upon the agreement of the Parties, be submitted to the International Court of Justice.

3. (a) In the absence of such agreement, the dispute shall, upon the written request of either Party, be submitted to an arbitral tribunal for binding decision in accordance with the applicable rules and principles of international law.

(b) The Tribunal shall consist of three arbitrators, one appointed by each Party, and a Chairman appointed by agreement of the other two arbitrators. The Chairman shall not be a national of either Party. Each Party shall appoint an arbitrator within 60 days, and the Chairman shall be appointed within 90 days, after a Party has requested arbitration of a dispute.

(c) If the periods set forth in (b) above are not met, and in the absence of some other arrangement between the Parties, either Party may invite the President of the International Court of Justice to make the necessary appointment. If the President is a national of either of the Parties or is unable to act for any reason, either Party may invite the Vice President, or if he is also a national of either Party or otherwise unable to act, the next most senior member of the International Court of Justice, to make the appointment.

(d) In the event that an arbitrator is for any reason unable to perform his duties, a replacement shall be appointed within thirty (30) days of determination thereof, utilizing the same method by which the arbitrator being replaced was appointed. If a replacement is not appointed within the time limit specified above, either Party may invite the President of the International Court of Justice to make the necessary appointment. If the President is a national of either of the Parties or is unable to act for any reason, either Party may invite the Vice President, or if he is also a national of either Party or otherwise unable to act, the next most senior member of the International Court of Justice, to make the appointment.

(e) Unless otherwise agreed to by the Parties to the dispute, all submissions shall be made and all hearings shall be completed within one hundred and twenty (120) days of the date of the selection of the third arbitrator, and the Tribunal shall render its decision within thirty (30) days of the date of the final submissions or the date of the closing of the hearings, whichever is later, and such decision shall be binding on each Party.

(f) Except as otherwise agreed to by the Parties, arbitration proceedings shall be governed by the Model Rules on Arbitral Procedure adopted by the United Nations International Law Commission in 1958 ("Model Rules") and commended to Member States by the United Nations General Assembly in Resolution 1262 (XIII). To the extent that procedural questions are not resolved by this Article or the Model Rules they shall be resolved by the Tribunal. Notwithstanding any other provision of this Treaty or the Model Rules, the Tribunal shall in all cases act by majority vote.

(g) Each Party shall bear the costs of its own arbitrator and counsel in the arbitral proceeding. The cost of the Chairman and remaining expenses shall be borne in equal parts by the Parties.

4. The provisions of this Article shall not apply to a dispute arising under an official export credit, guarantee, or insurance arrangement, pursuant to which the Parties have agreed to other means of settling disputes.

Article IX. Preservation of Rights

1. This Treaty shall not supersede, prejudice, or otherwise derogate from (a) laws, regulations, administrative practices or procedures, or adjudicatory decisions of either Party, (b) international legal obligations, or (c) obligations assumed by either Party, including those contained in an investment agreement or an investment authorization, whether extant at the time of entry into force of this Treaty or thereafter, that entitle investments or associated activities of nationals or companies of the other Party to treatment more favorable than that accorded by this Treaty in like situations.

2. This Treaty shall not derogate from or terminate any other agreement entered into by the two Parties and in force as between the two Parties on the date on which this Treaty enters into force.

Article X. Measures Not Precluded by Treaty

1. This Treaty shall not preclude the application by either Party or any political or administrative subdivision thereof of any and all measures necessary for the maintenance of public order and morals, the fulfillment of its existing international obligations, the protection of its own security interests, or such measures deemed appropriate by the Parties to fulfill future international obligations.

2. This Treaty shall not preclude either Party from prescribing special formalities in connection with the establishment of investments in its territory of nationals and companies of the other Party, but such formalities shall not impair the substance of any of the rights set forth in this Treaty.

Article XI. Taxation

With respect to its tax policies, each Party should strive to accord fairness and equity in the treatment of investments of nationals or companies of the other Party. Nevertheless, all matters relating to the taxation of nationals or companies of a Party, or their investments in the territories of the other Party or a political or administrative subdivision thereof shall be excluded from this Treaty, subject, however, to specific provisions of Articles III and V.

Article XII. Application of Treaty to Political or Administrative Subdivisions of the Parties

This Treaty shall apply to the political and/or administrative subdivisions of each Party.

Article XIII. Entry into Force and Duration and Termination . . .

3. Either Party may, by giving one (1) year's written notice to the other Party, terminate this Treaty at the end of the initial ten (10) year period or at any time thereafter.

4. With respect to investments made or acquired prior to the date of termination of this Treaty and to which this Treaty otherwise applies, the provisions of all of the other Articles of this Treaty shall continue to be effective for a further period of ten (10) years from such date of termination.

5. The attached Annex and Protocol are integral parts of this Treaty. . . .

Annex

Consistent with Article II paragraph 3, each Party reserves the right to maintain limited exceptions in the sectors it has indicated below:

The United States of America

Air transportation, ocean and coastal shipping; banking; insurance; government grants; government insurance and loan programs; energy and power production; use of land and natural resources; custom house brokers; ownership of real estate; radio and television broadcasting; telephone and telegraph services; submarine cable services; satellite communications.

The Arab Republic of Egypt

Air and sea transportation; maritime agencies; land transportation other than that of tourism; mail, telecommunication, telegraph services and other public services which are state monopolies; banking and insurance; commercial activity such as distribution, wholesaling, retailing, import and export activities; commercial agency and broker activities; ownership of real estate; use of land; natural resources; national loans; radio, television, and the issuance of newspapers and magazines.

Protocol

On signing the Treaty concerning the Reciprocal Encouragement and protection of Investments, the United States of America and the Arab Republic of Egypt have, in addition, agreed on the following provisions which should be regarded as an integral part of this Treaty:

1. The term "substantial interest" as used in the provisions of Article I of the Agreement means such extent of interest as to permit the exercise of control or significant influence on the company. In cases where there is a difference of views as to the existence of substantial interest, both Parties shall consult promptly to make a determination.

2. With regard to Article I, paragraph 1(c)(iv), in specific cases of disagreement as to the existence or validity of an intellectual or industrial property right, either Party may require substantiation of such validity in the form of a written agreement, or other instrument, or evidence of registration pursuant to international conventions.

3. The provisions of Article II, Paragraph 3, shall not apply to advantages accorded by either Party to nationals or companies of a third country by virtue of a special security or regional arrangement, including regional customs unions or free trade areas. Furthermore, these provisions do not apply to the ownership of real estate or to rights to engage in mining on government-owned lands.

4. This Treaty, and, in particular, the provisions of Article II, paragraph 5 (b) shall be subject to the provisions of Article X.

5. With regard to Article III, Paragraph 1 (d) the term "prompt" does not necessarily mean instantaneous. The intent is that the Party diligently and expeditiously carry out any necessary formalities.

6. The Parties recognize that restrictions on transfers abroad of sales or liquidation proceeds of an investment will adversely affect future capital inflows, contrary to the spirit of this Treaty and the interests of the Party imposing those restrictions. Nevertheless, the Parties recognize that it is possible that the Arab Republic of Egypt may find its foreign exchange reserves at a very low level. In these circumstances, the Arab Republic of Egypt may temporarily delay transfers required under Article V, Paragraph 1 (f), but only: (i) in a manner not less favorable than that accorded to comparable transfers to investors of third countries; (ii) to the extent and for the time period necessary to restore its reserves to a minimally acceptable level, but in no case for periods of time longer than that permitted by the provisions of Law 43 in force on the date of signature of this Treaty; and (iii) after providing the investor an opportunity to invest the sales or liquidation proceeds in a manner which will preserve their real value free of exchange risk until transfer occurs.

7. With regard to the Annex, the exceptions noted by the Arab Republic

of Egypt under "commercial activity" do not include integrated operations which combine production and sales activities for their products.

8. Recognizing that international financial markets and institutions further stimulate the process of economic development through the international transmission of investment and associated technology, each Party undertakes to maintain a favorable environment for investment by nationals or companies of the other Party in the insurance and banking sectors. Therefore, each Party accords to investments by nationals or companies of the other Party in investment banks, merchant-banks and reinsurance companies whose activities are confined to transactions in foreign currencies treatment no less favorable than that accorded under existing laws and regulations to investments by its own nationals and companies or to investments by nationals or companies of any third country, whichever is the more favorable. Both Parties agree to hold future discussions concerning the expansion of investment possibilities in these sectors by nationals or companies of either Party in the territory of the other Party.

OECD DECLARATION ON INTERNATIONAL INVESTMENT AND MULTINATIONAL ENTERPRISES

June 21, 1976, 15 I.L.M. 967 (1976)*

The governments of OECD member countries considering

that international investment has assumed increased importance in the world economy and has considerably contributed to the development of their countries;

that multinational enterprises play an important role in this investment process;

that co-operation by Member countries can improve the foreign investment climate, encourage the positive contribution which multinational enterprises can make to economic and social progress, and minimise and resolve difficulties which may arise from their various operations;

that, while continuing endeavours within the OECD may lead to further international arrangements and agreements in this field, it seems appropriate at this stage to intensify their co-operation and consultation on issues relating to international investment and multinational enterprises through inter-related instruments each of which deals with a different aspect of the matter and together constitute a framework within which the OECD will consider these issues:

DECLARE:

Guidelines for MNE's   I.   that they jointly recommend to multinational enterprises operating in their territories the observance of the Guidelines as set forth in the Annex hereto having regard to the considerations and understandings which introduce the Guidelines and are an integral part of them.

National Treatment   II.1   that Member countries should, consistent with their needs to maintain public order, to protect their essential security interests and to fulfil commitments relating to international peace and security, accord to enterprises operating in

---

*This declaration was adopted on June 21, 1976, by the governments of the states in the Organization of Economic Cooperation and Development (OECD), except for the Turkish government. The 24 members of the OECD in 1976 and still as of October 1990 are Australia, Austria, Belgium, Canada, Denmark, Finland, France, Germany (Federal Republic), Greece, Iceland, Ireland, Italy, Japan, Luxembourg, Netherlands, New Zealand, Norway, Portugal, Spain, Sweden, Switzerland, Turkey, United Kingdom, and United States.

their territories and owned or controlled directly or indirectly by nationals of another Member country (hereinafter referred to as "Foreign-Controlled Enterprises") treatment under their laws, regulations and administrative practices, consistent with international law and no less favourable than that accorded in like situations to domestic enterprises (hereinafter referred to as "National Treatment").

2   that Member countries will consider applying "National Treatment" in respect of countries other than Member countries.

3   that Member countries will endeavour to ensure that their territorial subdivisions apply "National Treatment".

4   that this Declaration does not deal with the right of Member countries to regulate the entry of foreign investment or the conditions of establishment of foreign enterprises.

International Investment Incentives and Disincentives

III.1   that they recognise the need to strengthen their co-operation in the field of international direct investment.

2   that they thus recognise the need to give due weight to the interests of Member countries affected by specific laws, regulations and administrative practices in this field (hereinafter called "measures") providing official incentives and disincentives to international direct investment.

3   that Member countries will endeavour to make such measures as transparent as possible, so that their importance and purpose can be ascertained and that information on them can be readily available.

Consultation Procedures

IV   that they are prepared to consult one another on the above matters in conformity with the Decisions of the Council relating to Inter-Governmental Consultation Procedures on the Guidelines for Multinational Enterprises, on National Treatment and on International Investment Incentives and Disincentives.

Review

V   that they will review the above matters within three years with a view to improving the effectiveness of international economic co-operation among Member countries on issues relating to international investment and multinational enterprises.

Annex to the Declaration of 21st June, 1976 by Governments of OECD Member Countries on International Investment and Multinational Enterprises

Guidelines for Multinational Enterprises

1. Multinational enterprises now play an important part in the economies of Member countries and in international economic relations, which is of increasing interest to governments. Through international direct investment, such enterprises can bring substantial benefits to home and host countries by contributing to the efficient utilisation of capital, technology and human resources between countries and can thus fulfil an important role in the promotion of economic and social welfare. But the advances made by multinational enterprises in organising their operations beyond the national framework may lead to abuse of concentrations of economic power and to conflicts with national policy objectives. In addition, the complexity of these multinational enterprises and the difficulty of clearly perceiving their diverse structures, operations and policies sometimes give rise to concern.

2. The common aim of the Member countries is to encourage the positive contributions which multinational enterprises can make to economic and social progress and to minimise and resolve the difficulties to which their various operations may give rise. In view of the transnational structure of such enterprises, this aim will be furthered by co-operation among the OECD countries where the headquarters of most of the multinational enterprises are established and which are the location of a substantial part of their operations. The guidelines set out hereafter are designed to assist in the achievement of this common aim and to contribute to improving the foreign investment climate.

3. Since the operations of multinational enterprises extend throughout the world, including countries that are not Members of the Organisation, international co-operation in this field should extend to all States. Member countries will give their full support to efforts undertaken in co-operation with non-Member countries, and in particular with developing countries, with a view to improving the welfare and living standards of all people both by encouraging the positive contributions which multinational enterprises can make and by minimising and resolving the problems which may arise in connection with their activities.

4. Within the Organisation, the programme of co-operation to attain these ends will be a continuing, pragmatic and balanced one. It comes within the general aims of the Convention on the Organisation for Economic Co-operation and Development (O.E.C.D.) and makes full use of the various specialised bodies of the Organisation, whose terms of reference already cover many aspects of the role of multinational enterprises, notably in matters of international trade and payments, competition, taxation, manpower, industrial development, science and technology. In these bodies,

work is being carried out on the identification of issues, the improvement of relevant qualitative and statistical information and the elaboration of proposals for action designed to strengthen inter-governmental co-operation. In some of these areas procedures already exist through which issues related to the operations of multinational enterprises can be taken up. This work could result in the conclusion of further and complementary agreements and arrangements between governments.

5. The initial phase of the co-operation programme is composed of a Declaration and three Decisions promulgated simultaneously as they are complementary and inter-connected, in respect of guidelines for multinational enterprises, national treatment for foreign-controlled enterprises and international investment incentives and disincentives.

6. The guidelines set out below are recommendations jointly addressed by Member countries to multinational enterprises operating in their territories. These guidelines, which take into account the problems which can arise because of the international structure of these enterprises, lay down standards for the activities of these enterprises in the different Member countries. Observance of the guidelines is voluntary and not legally enforceable. However, they should help to ensure that the operations of these enterprises are in harmony with national policies of the countries where they operate and to strengthen the basis of mutual confidence between enterprises and States.

7. Every State has the right to prescribe the conditions under which multinational enterprises operate within its national jurisdiction, subject to international law and to the international agreements to which it has subscribed. The entities of a multinational enterprise located in various countries are subject to the laws of these countries.

8. A precise legal definition of multinational enterprises is not required for the purposes of the guidelines. These usually comprise companies or other entities whose ownership is private, state or mixed, established in different countries and so linked that one or more of them may be able to exercise a significant influence over the activities of others and, in particular, to share knowledge and resources with the others. The degree of autonomy of each entity in relation to the others varies widely from one multinational enterprise to another, depending on the nature of the links between such entities and the fields of activity concerned. For these reasons, the guidelines are addressed to the various entities within the multinational enterprise (parent companies and/or local entities) according to the actual distribution of responsibilities among them on the understanding that they will co-operate and provide assistance to one another as necessary to facilitate observance of the guidelines. The word "enterprise" as used in these guidelines refers to these various entities in accordance with their responsibilities.

9. The guidelines are not aimed at introducing differences of treatment between multinational and domestic enterprises; wherever relevant they reflect good practice for all. Accordingly, multinational and domestic enterprises are subject to the same expectations in respect of their conduct wherever the guidelines are relevant to both.

10. The use of appropriate international dispute settlement mechanisms, including arbitration, should be encouraged as a means of facilitating the resolution of problems arising between enterprises and Member countries.

11. Member countries have agreed to establish appropriate review and consultation procedures concerning issues arising in respect of the guidelines. When multinational enterprises are made subject to conflicting requirements by Member countries, the governments concerned will co-operate in good faith with a view to resolving such problems either within the Committee on International Investment and Multinational Enterprises established by the OECD Council on 21st January, 1975 or through other mutually acceptable arrangements.

HAVING REGARD to the foregoing considerations, the Member countries set forth the following guidelines for multinational enterprises with the understanding that Member countries will fulfil their responsibilities to treat enterprises equitably and in accordance with international law and international agreements, as well as contractual obligations to which they have subscribed:

General Policies

Enterprises should

(1) take fully into account established general policy objectives of the Member countries in which they operate;

(2) in particular, give due consideration to those countries' aims and priorities with regard to economic and social progress, including industrial and regional development, the protection of the environment, the creation of employment opportunities, the promotion of innovation and the transfer of technology,

(3) while observing their legal obligations concerning information, supply their entities with supplementary information the latter may need in order to meet requests by the authorities of the countries in which those entities are located for information relevant to the activities of those entities, taking into account legitimate requirements of business confidentiality;

(4) favour close co-operation with the local community and business interests;

(5) allow their component entities freedom to develop their activities and to exploit their competitive advantage in domestic and foreign markets, consistent with the need for specialisation and sound commercial practice;

(6) when filling responsible posts in each country of operation, take due account of individual qualifications without discrimination as to nationality, subject to particular national requirements in this respect;

(7) not render — and they should not be solicited or expected to

render — any bribe or other improper benefit, direct or indirect, to any public servant or holder of public office;
(8) unless legally permissible, not make contributions to candidates for public office or to political parties or other political organisations;
(9) abstain from any improper involvement in local political activities.

Disclosure of Information

Enterprises should, having due regard to their nature and relative size in the economic context of their operations and to requirements of business confidentiality and to cost, publish in a form suited to improve public understanding a sufficient body of factual information on the structure, activities and policies of the enterprise as a whole, as a supplement, in so far as is necessary for this purpose, to information to be disclosed under the national law of the individual countries in which they operate. To this end, they should publish within reasonable time limits, on a regular basis, but at least annually, financial statements and other pertinent information relating to the enterprise as a whole, comprising in particular:

(i) the structure of the enterprise, showing the name and location of the parent company, its main affiliates, its percentage ownership, direct and indirect, in these affiliates, including shareholdings between them;
(ii) the geographical areas* where operations are carried out and the principal activities carried on therein by the parent company and the main affiliates;
(iii) the operating results and sales by geographical area and the sales in the major lines of business for the enterprise as a whole;
(iv) significant new capital investment by geographical area and, as far as practicable, by major lines of business for the enterprise as a whole;
(v) a statement of the sources and uses of funds by the enterprise as a whole;
(vi) the average number of employees in each geographical area;
(vii) research and development expenditure for the enterprise as a whole;
(viii) the policies followed in respect of intra-group pricing;
(ix) the accounting policies, including those on consolidation, observed in compiling the published information.

*For the purposes of the guidelines on disclosure of information the term "geographical area" means groups of countries or individual countries as each enterprise determines it appropriate in its particular circumstances. While no single method of grouping is appropriate for all enterprises, or for all purposes, the factors to be considered by an enterprise would include the significance of operations carried out in individual countries or areas as well as the effects on its competitiveness, geographic proximity, economic affinity, similarities in business environments and the nature, scale and degree of interrelationship of the enterprises' operations in the various countries.

Competition

Enterprises should while conforming to official competition rules and established policies of the countries in which they operate,

(1) refrain from actions which would adversely affect competition in the relevant market by abusing a dominant position of market power, by means of, for example,

    (a) anti-competitive acquisitions,
    (b) predatory behaviour toward competitors,
    (c) unreasonable refusal to deal,
    (d) anti-competitive abuse of industrial property rights,
    (e) discriminatory (i.e. unreasonably differentiated) pricing and using such pricing transactions between affiliated enterprises as a means of affecting adversely competition outside these enterprises;

(2) allow purchasers, distributors and licensees freedom to resell, export, purchase and develop their operations consistent with law, trade conditions, the need for specialisation and sound commercial practice;

(3) refrain from participating in or otherwise purposely strengthening the restrictive effects of international or domestic cartels or restrictive agreements which adversely affect or eliminate competition and which are not generally or specifically accepted under applicable national or international legislation;

(4) be ready to consult and co-operate, including the provision of information, with competent authorities of countries whose interests are directly affected in regard to competition issues or investigations. Provision of information should be in accordance with safeguards normally applicable in this field.

Financing

Enterprises should, in managing the financial and commercial operations of their activities, and especially their liquid foreign assets and liabilities, take into consideration the established objectives of the countries in which they operate regarding balance of payments and credit policies.

Taxation

Enterprises should

(1) upon request of the taxation authorities of the countries in which they operate, provide, in accordance with the safeguards and relevant procedures of the national laws of these countries, the information necessary to determine correctly the taxes to be assessed in connection with their operations, including relevant information concerning their operations in other countries;

(2) refrain from making use of the particular facilities available to them, such as transfer pricing which does not conform to an arm's length

standard, for modifying in ways contrary to national laws the tax base on which members of the group are assessed.

Employment and Industrial Relations

Enterprises should within the framework of law, regulations and prevailing labour relations and employment practices, in each of the countries in which they operate,

(1) respect the right of their employees to be represented by trade unions and other bona fide organisations of employees, and engage in constructive negotiations, either individually or through employers' associations, with such employee organisations with a view to reaching agreements on employment conditions, which should include provisions for dealing with disputes arising over the interpretation of such agreements, and for ensuring mutually respected rights and responsibilities;

(2) (a) provide such facilities to representatives of the employees as may be necessary to assist in the development of effective collective agreements;

(b) provide to representatives of employees information which is needed for meaningful negotiations on conditions of employment;

(3) provide to representatives of employees where this accords with local law and practice, information which enables them to obtain a true and fair view of the performance of the entity or, where appropriate, the enterprise as a whole;

(4) observe standards of employment and industrial relations not less favourable than those observed by comparable employers in the host country;

(5) in their operations, to the greatest extent practicable, utilise, train and prepare for upgrading members of the local labour force in co-operation with representatives of their employees and, where appropriate, the relevant governmental authorities;

(6) in considering changes in their operations which would have major effects upon the livelihood of their employees, in particular in the case of the closure of an entity involving collective lay-offs or dismissals; provide reasonable notice of such changes to representatives of their employees, and where appropriate to the relevant governmental authorities, and co-operate with the employee representative and appropriate governmental authorities so as to mitigate to the maximum extent practicable adverse effects;

(7) implement their employment policies including hiring, discharge, pay, promotion and training without discrimination unless selectivity in respect of employee characteristics is in furtherance of established governmental policies which specifically promote greater equality of employment opportunity;

(8) in the context of bona fide negotiations* with representatives of

---

*Bona fide negotiations may include labour disputes as part of the process of negotiation. Whether or not labour disputes are so included will be determined by the law and prevailing employment practices of particular countries.

employees on conditions of employment or while employees are exercising a right to organise, not threaten to utilise a capacity to transfer the whole or part of an operating unit from the country concerned in order to influence unfairly those negotiations or to hinder the exercise of a right to organise;

(9) enable authorised representatives of their employees to conduct negotiations on collective bargaining or labour management relations issues with representatives of management who are authorised to take decisions on the matters under negotiation.

Science and Technology

Enterprises should

(1) endeavour to ensure that their activities fit satisfactorily into the scientific and technological policies and plans of the countries in which they operate, and contribute to the development of national scientific and technological capacities, including as far as appropriate the establishment and improvement in host countries of their capacity to innovate;

(2) to the fullest extent practicable, adopt in the course of their business activities practices which permit the rapid diffusion of technologies with due regard to the protection of industrial and intellectual property rights;

(3) when granting licenses for the use of industrial property rights or when otherwise transferring technology do so on reasonable terms and conditions.

CODE OF CONDUCT ON TRANSNATIONAL CORPORATIONS, AS PROPOSED BY THE U.N. SECRETARY-GENERAL

February 1, 1988, U.N. E/1988/39/Add.1*

Preamble

The General Assembly,

Recalling Economic and Social Council resolutions 1908 (LVII) of 2 August 1974 and 1913 (LVII) of 5 December 1974, establishing the Commission on Transnational Corporations and the United Nations Centre on Transnational Corporations with the mandate, as their highest priority of work, of concluding a Code of Conduct on Transnational Corporations,

Convinced that a universally accepted, comprehensive and effective Code of Conduct on Transnational Corporations is an essential element in the strengthening of international economic and social co-operation and, in particular, in achieving one of the main goals and objectives in that co-operation, namely, to maximize the contributions of transnational corporations to economic development and growth and to minimize the negative effects of the activities of these corporations.

Decides to adopt the following Code of Conduct on Transnational Corporations:

Definitions and Scope of Application

1. (a) This Code is universally applicable to enterprises, irrespective of their country of origin and their ownership, including private, public or mixed, comprising entities in two or more countries, regardless of the legal form and fields of activity of these entities, which operate under a system of decision-making, permitting coherent policies and a common strategy through one or more decision-making centres, in which the entities are so linked, by ownership or otherwise, that one or more of them may be able to exercise a significant influence over the activities of others and, in particular, to share knowledge, resources and responsibilities with the others. Such enterprises are referred to in this Code as transnational corporations.

(b) The term "entities" in the Code refers to both parent entities

---

*A draft Code is still under consideration by the U.N. Economic and Social Council and has not been formally acted on by the U.N. General Assembly.

— that is, entities which are the main source of influence over others — and other entities, unless otherwise specified in the Code.

(c) The term "transnational corporation" in the Code refers to the enterprise as a whole or its various entities.

(d) The term "home country" means the country in which the parent entity is located. The term "host country" means a country other than the home country in which an entity other than the parent entity is located.

(e) The term "country in which a transnational corporation operates" refers to a home or host country in which an entity of a transnational corporation conducts operations.

2. For the application of this Code, it is irrelevant whether or not enterprises as described in paragraph 1 (a) above are referred to in any country as transnational corporations.

3. The Code is universally applicable in all States, regardless of their political and economic systems or their level of development.

4. The provisions of the Code addressed to transnational corporations reflect good practice for all enterprises. Subject to the provisions of paragraph 52, wherever the provisions of the Code are relevant to both, transnational corporations and domestic enterprises shall be subject to the same expectations with regard to their conduct.

5. Subject to the relevant constitutions, charters or other fundamental laws of the regional groupings of States concerned, any reference in this Code to States, countries or Governments, also includes regional groupings of States, to the extent that the provisions of this Code relate to matters within these groupings' own competence, with respect to such competence.

6. In their interpretation and application the provisions of this Code are interrelated and each provision should be construed in the context of the other provisions.

Activities of Transnational Corporations

A. General

Respect for National Sovereignty and Observance of Domestic Laws, Regulations and Administrative Practices

7. Transnational corporations shall respect the national sovereignty of the countries in which they operate and the right of each State to exercise its permanent sovereignty over its natural wealth and resources.

8. An entity of a transnational corporation is subject to the laws, regulations and established administrative practices of the country in which it operates.

9. Transnational corporations shall respect the right of each State to regulate and monitor accordingly the activities of their entities operating within its territory.

Adherence to Economic Goals and Development Objectives, Policies and Priorities

10. Transnational corporations should carry out their activities in conformity with the development policies, objectives and priorities set out by the Governments of the countries in which they operate and work seriously towards making a positive contribution to the achievement of such goals at the national and, as appropriate, the regional level, within the framework of regional integration programmes. Transnational corporations should co-operate with the Governments of the countries in which they operate with a view to contributing to the development process and should be responsive to requests for consultation in this respect, thereby establishing mutually beneficial relations with these countries.

11. Transnational corporations should carry out their operations in conformity with applicable intergovernmental co-operative arrangements concluded by the countries in which they operate.

Review and Renegotiation of Contracts and Agreements

12. (a) Contracts or agreements between Governments and transnational corporations should be negotiated and implemented in good faith. In such contracts or agreements, especially long-term ones, review or renegotiation clauses should normally be included.

(b) In the absence of such clauses and where there has been a fundamental change of the circumstances on which the contract or agreement was based, transnational corporations, acting in good faith, should co-operate with Governments for the review or renegotiation of such contract or agreement.

Adherence to Socio-Cultural Objectives and Values

13. Transnational corporations should respect the social and cultural objectives, values and traditions of the countries in which they operate. While economic and technological development is normally accompanied by social change, transnational corporations should avoid practices, products or services which cause detrimental effects on cultural patterns and socio-cultural objectives as determined by Governments. For this purpose, transnational corporations should respond positively to requests for consultations from Governments concerned.

Respect for Human Rights and Fundamental Freedoms

14. Transnational corporations shall respect human rights and fundamental freedoms in the countries in which they operate. In their social and industrial relations, transnational corporations shall not discriminate on the basis of race, colour, sex, religion, language, social, national and ethnic origin or political or other opinion. Transnational corporations shall conform to government policies designed to extend equality of opportunity and treatment.

Non-Collaboration by Transnational Corporations with Racist Minority Régimes in Southern Africa

15. In accordance with the efforts of the international community towards the elimination of *apartheid* in South Africa and its continued illegal occupation of Namibia,

(a) Transnational corporations shall refrain from operations and activities supporting and sustaining the racist minority régime of South Africa in maintaining the system of *apartheid* and the illegal occupation of Namibia;

(b) Transnational corporations shall engage in appropriate activities within their competence with a view to eliminating racial discrimination and all other aspects of the system of *apartheid;*

(c) Transnational corporations shall comply strictly with obligations resulting from Security Council decisions and shall fully respect those resulting from all relevant United Nations resolutions;

(d) With regard to investment in Namibia, transnational corporations shall comply strictly with obligations resulting from Security Council resolution 283 (1970) and other relevant Security Council decisions and shall fully respect those resulting from all relevant United Nations resolutions.

Non-interference in Internal Affairs of Host Countries

16. Transnational corporations shall not interfere in the internal affairs of host countries, without prejudice to their participation in activities that are permitted by the laws, regulations or established administrative practices of host countries.

17. Transnational corporations shall not engage in activities of a political nature which are not permitted by the laws and established policies and administrative practices of the countries in which they operate.

Non-Interference in Intergovernmental Relations

18. Transnational corporations shall not interfere in intergovernmental relations provided that this provision shall not preclude such activities as are sanctioned within the framework of bilateral or multilateral co-operation.

19. Transnational corporations should not request Governments acting on their behalf to take the measures referred to in the second sentence of paragraph 67.

20. With respect to the exhaustion of local remedies, transnational corporations should not request Governments to act on their behalf in any manner inconsistent with paragraph 67.

Abstention from Corrupt Practices

21. (a) Transnational corporations shall refrain, in their transactions, from the offering, promising or giving of any payment, gift or other advantage to or for the benefit of a public official as consideration for performing or refraining from the performance of his duties in connection with those transactions.

(b) Transnational corporations shall maintain accurate records of any payments made by them to any public official or intermediary. They shall make available these records to the competent authorities of the countries in which they operate, upon request, for investigations and proceedings concerning those payments.

B. Economic, Financial and Social

Ownership and Control

22. Transnational corporations should make every effort so to allocate their decision-making powers among their entities as to enable them to contribute to the economic and social development of the countries in which they operate.

23. To the extent permitted by national laws, policies and established administrative practices of the country in which it operates, each entity of a transnational corporation should co-operate with the other entities, in accordance with the actual distribution of responsibilities among them and consistent with paragraph 22, so as to enable each entity to meet effectively the requirements established by the laws, policies and regulations of the country in which it operates.

24. Transnational corporations should co-operate with Governments and nationals of the countries in which they operate in the implementation of national objectives for local equity participation and for the effective exercise of control by local partners as determined by equity, contractual terms in non-equity arrangements or the laws of such countries.

25. Transnational corporations should carry out their personnel policies in accordance with the national policies of each of the countries in which they operate which give priority to the employment and promotion of its nationals at all levels of management and direction of the affairs of each entity so as to enhance the effective participation of its nationals in the decision-making process.

26. Transnational corporations should contribute to the managerial and technical training of nationals of the countries in which they operate and facilitate their employment at all levels of management of the entities and enterprises as a whole.

Employment Conditions and Industrial Relations

27. For the purposes of this Code, the principles set out in the Tripartite Declaration of Principles concerning Multinational Enterprises and Social Policy, adopted by the Governing Body of the International Labour Office, should apply in the field of employment, training, conditions of work and life and industrial relations.

Balance of Payments and Financing

28. Transnational corporations shall carry out their operations in conformity with laws and regulations and with full regard to the policy objec-

tives set out by the countries in which they operate, particularly developing countries, relating to balance of payments, financial transactions and other issues dealt with in the subsequent paragraphs of this section.

29. Transnational corporations should respond positively to requests for consultation on their activities from the Governments of the countries in which they operate, with a view to contributing to the alleviation of pressing problems of balance of payments and finance of such countries.

30. As required by government regulations and in furtherance of government policies, and consistent with the purpose, nature and extent of their operations, transnational corporations should contribute to the promotion of exports and the diversification of exports and, where appropriate, imports in the countries in which they operate and to an increased utilization of goods, services and other resources which are available in these countries.

31. Transnational corporations should be responsive to requests by Governments of the countries in which they operate, particularly developing countries, concerning the phasing over a limited period of time of the repatriation of capital in case of disinvestment or remittances of accumulated profits, when the size and timing of such transfers would cause serious balance-of-payments difficulties for such countries.

32. Transnational corporations should not, contrary to generally accepted financial practices prevailing in the countries in which they operate, engage in short-term financial operations or transfers or defer or advance foreign exchange payments, including intra-corporate payments, in a manner which would increase currency instability and thereby cause serious balance-of-payments difficulties for the countries concerned.

33. Transnational corporations should not impose restrictions on their entities, beyond generally accepted commercial practices prevailing in the countries in which they operate, regarding the transfer of goods, services and funds which would cause serious balance-of-payments difficulties for the countries in which they operate.

34. When having recourse to the money and capital markets of the countries in which they operate, transnational corporations should not, beyond generally accepted financial practices prevailing in such countries, engage in activities which would have a significant adverse impact on the working of local markets, particularly by restricting the availability of funds to other enterprises. When issuing shares with the objective of increasing local equity participation in an entity operating in such a country, or engaging in long-term borrowing in the local market, transnational corporations should consult with the Government of the country concerned upon its request on the effects of such transactions on the local money and capital markets.

Transfer Pricing

35. In respect of their intra-corporate transactions, transnational corporations should not use pricing policies that are not based on relevant market prices, or, in the absence of such prices, the arm's length principle, which have the effect of adversely affecting the tax revenues, the foreign

exchange resources or other aspects of the economy of the countries in which they operate.

Taxation

36. Transnational corporations shall not, contrary to the laws and regulations of the countries in which they operate, use their corporate structure and modes of operation, such as the use of intra-corporate pricing which is not based on the arm's length principle, or other means, to modify the tax base on which their entities are assessed.

Competition and Restrictive Business Practices

37. For the purposes of this Code, the relevant provisions of the Set of Multilaterally Agreed Equitable Principles and Rules for the Control of Restrictive Business Practices adopted by the General Assembly in its resolution 35/63 of 5 December 1980 shall also apply in the field of restrictive business practices.

Transfer of Technology

38. (a) Transnational corporations shall conform to the transfer of technology laws and regulations of the countries in which they operate. They shall co-operate with the competent authorities of those countries in assessing the impact of international transfers of technology in their economies and consult with them regarding the various technological options which might help those countries, particularly developing countries, to attain their economic and social development.

(b) Transnational corporations in their transfer of technology transactions, including intra-corporate transactions, should avoid practices which adversely affect the international flow of technology, or otherwise hinder the economic and technological development of countries, particularly developing countries.

(c) Transnational corporations should contribute to the strengthening of the scientific and technological capacities of developing countries, in accordance with the science and technology established policies and priorities of those countries. Transnational corporations should undertake substantial research and development activities in developing countries and should make full use of local resources and personnel in this process.

Consumer Protection

39. Transnational corporations shall carry out their operations, in particular production and marketing, in accordance with national laws, regulations, administrative practices and policies concerning consumer protection of the countries in which they operate. Transnational corporations shall also perform their activities with due regard to relevant international standards, so that they do not cause injury to the health or endanger the safety of

consumers or bring about variations in the quality of products in each market which would have detrimental effects on consumers.

40. Transnational corporations shall, in respect of the products and services which they produce or market or propose to produce or market in any country, supply to the competent authorities of that country on request or on a regular basis, as specified by these authorities, all relevant information concerning:

> Characteristics of these products or services which may be injurious to the health and safety of consumers including experimental uses and related aspects;
> Prohibitions, restrictions, warnings and other public regulatory measures imposed in other countries on grounds of health and safety protection on these products or services.

41. Transnational corporations should disclose to the public in the countries in which they operate all appropriate information on the contents and, to the extent known, on possible hazardous effects of the products they produce or market in the countries concerned by means of proper labelling, informative and accurate advertising or other appropriate methods. Packaging of their products should be safe and the contents of the product should not be misrepresented.

42. Transnational corporations should be responsive to requests from Governments of the countries in which they operate and be prepared to co-operate with international organizations in their efforts to develop and promote national and international standards for the protection of the health and safety of consumers and to meet the basic needs of consumers.

Environmental Protection

43. Transnational corporations shall carry out their activities in accordance with national laws, regulations, established administrative practices and policies relating to the preservation of the environment of the countries in which they operate and with due regard to relevant international standards. Transnational corporations should, in performing their activities, take steps to protect the environment and where damaged to rehabilitate it and should make efforts to develop and apply adequate technologies for this purpose.

44. Transnational corporations shall, in respect to the products, processes and services they have introduced or propose to introduce in any country, supply to the competent authorities of that country on request or on a regular basis, as specified by these authorities, all relevant information concerning:

> Characteristics of these products, processes and other activities including experimental uses and related aspects which may harm the environment and the measures and costs necessary to avoid or at least to mitigate their harmful effects;

Prohibitions, restrictions, warnings and other public regulatory measures imposed in other countries on grounds of protection of the environment on these products, processes and services.

45. Transnational corporations should be responsive to requests from Governments of the countries in which they operate and be prepared where appropriate to co-operate with international organizations in their efforts to develop and promote national and international standards for the protection of the environment.

C. Disclosure of Information

46. Transnational corporations should disclose to the public in the countries in which they operate, by appropriate means of communication, clear, full and comprehensible information on the structure, policies, activities and operations of the transnational corporation as a whole. The information should include financial as well as non-financial items and should be made available on a regular annual basis, normally within six months and in any case not later than 12 months from the end of the financial year of the corporation. In addition, during the financial year, transnational corporations should wherever appropriate make available a semi-annual summary of financial information.

The financial information to be disclosed annually should be provided where appropriate on a consolidated basis, together with suitable explanatory notes and should include, *inter alia,* the following:

(a) A balance sheet;
(b) An income statement, including operating results and sales;
(c) A statement of allocation of net profits or net income;
(d) A statement of the sources and uses of funds;
(e) Significant new long-term capital investment;
(f) Research and development expenditure.

The non-financial information referred to in the first subparagraph should include, *inter alia:*

(a) The structure of the transnational corporation, showing the name and location of the parent company, its main entities, its percentage ownership, direct and indirect, in these entities, including shareholdings between them;
(b) The main activity of its entities;
(c) Employment information including average number of employees;
(d) Accounting policies used in compiling and consolidating the information published;
(e) Policies applied in respect of transfer pricing.

The information provided for the transnational corporation as a whole should as far as practicable be broken down:

By geographical area or country, as appropriate, with regard to the activities of its main entities, sales, operating results, significant new investments and number of employees;

By major line of business as regards sales and significant new investment.

The method of breakdown as well as details of information provided shall be determined by the nature, scale and interrelationships of the transnational corporation's operations, with due regard to their significance for the areas or countries concerned.

The extent, detail and frequency of the information provided should take into account the nature and size of the transnational corporation as a whole, the requirements of confidentiality and effects on the transnational corporation's competitive position as well as the cost involved in producing the information.

The information herein required should, as necessary, be in addition to information required by national laws, regulations and established administrative practices of the countries in which transnational corporations operate.

47. (a) Transnational corporations shall supply to the competent authorities in each of the countries in which they operate, upon request or on a regular basis as specified by those authorities, and in accordance with national legislation, all information required for legislative and administrative purposes relevant to the activities and policies of their entities in the country concerned.

(b) Transnational corporations shall, to the extent permitted by the provisions of the relevant national laws, regulations, established administrative practices and policies of the countries concerned, supply to competent authorities in the countries in which they operate information held in other countries needed to enable them to obtain a true and fair view of the operations of the transnational corporation concerned as a whole in so far as the information requested relates to the activities of the entities in the countries seeking such information.

(c) The provisions of paragraph 54 concerning confidentiality shall apply to information supplied under the provisions of this paragraph.

48. (a) With due regard to the relevant provisions of the ILO Tripartite Declaration of Principles concerning Multinational Enterprises and Social Policy and in accordance with national laws, regulations and practices in the field of labour relations, transnational corporations shall provide to trade unions or other representatives of employees in their entities in each of the countries in which they operate, by appropriate means of communication, the necessary information on the activities dealt with in this Code to enable them to obtain a true and fair view of the performance of the local entity and, where appropriate, the corporation as a whole. Such information shall include, where provided for by national law and practices, *inter alia,* prospects or plans for future development having major economic and social effects on the employees concerned.

(b) Procedures for consultation on matters of mutual concern should be worked out by mutual agreement between entities of transnational corporations and trade unions or other representatives of employees in accordance with national law and practice.

(c) Information made available pursuant to the provisions of this paragraph should be subject to appropriate safeguards for confidentiality so that no damage is caused to the parties concerned.

Treatment of Transnational Corporations

A. General Provisions Relating to the Treatment of Transnational Corporations

49. In all matters relating to the Code, States shall fulfil, in good faith, their international obligations, including generally recognized and accepted international legal rules and principles.

50. States have the right to regulate the entry and establishment of transnational corporations including determining the role that such corporations may play in economic and social development and prohibiting or limiting the extent of their presence in specific sectors.

51. Transnational corporations should receive fair and equitable treatment in the countries in which they operate.

52. Subject to national requirements for maintaining public order and protecting national security and consistent with national constitutions and laws, and without prejudice to measures specified in legislation relating to the declared development objectives of the developing countries, entities of transnational corporations should be given treatment accorded to domestic enterprises in similar circumstances. Nothing in this paragraph should be construed as excluding the right of the host country to grant such special incentives and facilities to transnational corporations as may be considered necessary in its national interest.

53. The importance of endeavouring to assure the clarity and stability of national policies, laws, regulations and established administrative practices is acknowledged. Laws and regulations affecting transnational corporations should be publicly and readily available. To the extent appropriate, relevant information regarding decisions of competent administrative bodies relating to transnational corporations should be disseminated.

54. Information furnished by transnational corporations to the authorities in each of the countries in which they operate containing confidential business information shall be accorded reasonable safeguards normally applicable in the area in which the information is provided, particularly to protect its confidentiality.

55. In order to achieve the purposes of paragraph 26 relating to managerial and technical training and employment of nationals of the countries in which transnational corporations operate, the transfer of those nationals between the entities of a transnational corporation should, subject to the laws and regulations of the countries concerned, be facilitated.

56. Transnational corporations are entitled to transfer all payments

legally due. Such transfers are subject to the relevant legislation of host countries, such as foreign exchange laws, and to restrictions emanating from exceptional balance of payment difficulties.

B. Nationalization and Compensation

57. It is acknowledged that States have the right to nationalize or expropriate the assets of a transnational corporation operating in their territory, and that appropriate compensation is to be paid by the State concerned, in accordance with the applicable legal rules and principles.

C. Jurisdiction

58. An entity of a transnational corporation is subject to the jurisdiction of the country in which it operates.

D. Dispute Settlement

59. Disputes between States and entities of transnational corporations, which are not amicably settled between the parties, shall be submitted to competent national courts or authorities. Where the parties so agree, or have agreed, such disputes may be referred to other mutually acceptable dispute settlement procedures.

60. Where the exercise of jurisdiction over transnational corporations and their entities by more than one State may lead to conflicts of jurisdiction, States concerned should endeavour to avoid such conflicts, in particular by seeking to avoid the exercise of jurisdiction by one State where jurisdiction more properly appertains to another State, and should endeavour to adopt mutually acceptable principles and procedures, bilaterally and multilaterally, for the settlement of such conflicts on the basis of respect for the principle of sovereign equality and for their mutual interests.

Intergovernmental Co-Operation

61. States agree that intergovernmental co-operation is essential in accomplishing the objectives of the Code.

62. States agree that intergovernmental co-operation should be established or strengthened at the international level and, where appropriate, at the bilateral, regional and interregional levels.

63. States agree to exchange information on the measures they have taken to give effect to the Code and on their experience with the Code.

64. States agree to consult on a bilateral or multilateral basis, as appropriate, on matters relating to the Code and its application and with respect to the development of international agreements and arrangements on issues related to the Code.

65. States agree to take into consideration the objectives of the Code

as reflected in its provisions when negotiating bilateral or multilateral agreements concerning transnational corporations.

66. States agree not to use transnational corporations as instruments to intervene in the internal or external affairs of other States and agree to take appropriate action within their jurisdiction to prevent transnational corporations from engaging in activities referred to in paragraphs 16 to 18 of this Code.

67. Government action on behalf of a transnational corporation operating in another country shall be subject to the principle of exhaustion of local remedies provided in such a country and, when agreed among the Governments concerned, to procedures for dealing with international legal claims. Such action should not in any event amount to the use of any type of coercive measures not consistent with the Charter of the United Nations and the Declaration on Principles of International Law concerning Friendly Relations and Co-operation among States in accordance with the Charter of the United Nations.

Implementation of the Code of Conduct

A. Action at the National Level

68. In order to ensure and promote the implementation of the Code at the national level, States should, *inter alia:*

(a) Publicize and disseminate the Code;
(b) Follow the implementation of the Code within their territories;
(c) Report to the United Nations Commission on Transnational Corporations on the action taken at the national level to promote the Code and on the experience gained from its implementation;
(d) Take action to reflect their support for the Code and take into account the objectives of the Code as reflected in its provisions when introducing, implementing and reviewing laws, regulations and administrative practices on matters dealt with in the Code.

B. International Institutional Machinery

69. The United Nations Commission on Transnational Corporations shall assume the functions of the international institutional machinery for the implementation of the Code. In this capacity, the Commission shall be open to the participation of all States. It may establish the subsidiary bodies and specific procedures it deems necessary for the effective discharge of its functions. The United Nations Centre on Transnational Corporations shall act as the secretariat to the Commission.

70. The Commission shall act as the international body within the United Nations system for all matters related to the Code. It shall establish and maintain close contacts with other United Nations organizations and specialized agencies dealing with matters related to the Code and its implementation with a view to co-ordinating work related to the Code. When

matters covered by international agreements or arrangements, specifically referred to in the Code, which have been worked out in other United Nations forums, arise, the Commission shall forward such matters to the competent bodies concerned with such agreements or arrangements.

71. The Commission shall have the following functions:

(a) To discuss at its annual sessions matters related to the Code. If agreed by the Governments engaged in consultations on specific issues related to the Code, the Commission shall facilitate such intergovernmental consultations to the extent possible. Representatives of trade unions, business, consumer and other relevant groups may express their views on matters related to the Code through the non-governmental organizations represented in the Commission.

(b) Periodically to assess the implementation of the Code, such assessments being based on reports submitted by Governments and, as appropriate, on documentation from United Nations organizations and specialized agencies performing work relevant to the Code and non-governmental organizations represented in the Commission. The first assessment shall take place not earlier than two years and not later than three years after the adoption of the Code. The second assessment shall take place two years after the first one. The Commission shall determine whether a periodicity of two years is to be maintained or modified for subsequent assessments. The format of assessments shall be determined by the Commission.

(c) To provide, upon the request of a Government, clarification of the provisions of the Code in the light of actual situations in which the applicability and implications of the Code have been the subject of intergovernmental consultations. In clarifying the provisions of the Code, the Commission shall not draw conclusions concerning the conduct of the parties involved in the situation which led to the request for clarification. The clarification is to be restricted to issues illustrated by such a situation. The detailed procedures regarding clarification are to be determined by the Commission.

(d) To report annually to the General Assembly through the Economic and Social Council on its activities regarding the implementation of the Code.

(e) To facilitate intergovernmental arrangements or agreements on specific aspects relating to transnational corporations upon request of the Governments concerned.

72. The United Nations Centre on Transnational Corporations shall provide assistance relating to the implementation of the Code, *inter alia,* by collecting, analysing and disseminating information and conducting research and surveys, as required and specified by the Commission.

C. Review Procedure

73. The Commission shall make recommendations to the General Assembly through the Economic and Social Council for the purpose of reviewing the Code. The first review shall take place not later than six years after the adoption of the Code. The General Assembly shall establish, as appropriate, the modalities for reviewing the Code.

UNIVERSAL DECLARATION OF HUMAN RIGHTS

December 10, 1948, U.N. G.A. Res. 217 (III 1948)*

The General Assembly,

Proclaims this Universal Declaration of Human Rights as a common standard of achievement for all peoples and all nations, to the end that every individual and every organ of society, keeping this Declaration constantly in mind, shall strive by teaching and education to promote respect for these rights and freedoms and by progressive measures, national and international, to secure their universal and effective recognition and observance, both among the peoples of Member States themselves and among the peoples of territories under their jurisdiction.

Article 1

All human beings are born free and equal in dignity and rights. They are endowed with reason and conscience and should act towards one another in a spirit of brotherhood.

Article 2

Everyone is entitled to all the rights and freedoms set forth in this declaration, without discrimination of any kind, such as race, colour, sex, language, religion, political or other opinion, national or social origin, property, birth or other status.

Furthermore, no distinction shall be made on the basis of the political, jurisdictional or international status of the country or territory to which a person belongs, whether it be independent, trust, non-self-governing or under any other limitation of sovereignty.

Article 3

Everyone has the right to life, liberty and the security of person.

Article 4

No one shall be held in slavery or servitude; slavery and the slave trade shall be prohibited in all their forms.

---

*The declaration was adopted by the U.N. General Assembly on December 10, 1948. Forty-eight states voted in favor, none against, and eight abstained (including Saudi Arabia, South Africa, Union of Soviet Socialist Republics, and Yugoslavia).

Article 5

No one shall be subjected to torture or to cruel, inhuman or degrading treatment or punishment.

Article 6

Everyone has the right to recognition everywhere as a person before the law.

Article 7

All are equal before the law and are entitled without any discrimination to equal protection of the law. All are entitled to equal protection against any discrimination in violation of this Declaration and against any incitement to such discrimination.

Article 8

Everyone has the right to an effective remedy by the competent national tribunals for acts violating the fundamental rights granted him by the constitution or by law.

Article 9

No one shall be subjected to arbitrary arrest, detention or exile.

Article 10

Everyone is entitled in full equality to a fair and public hearing by an independent and impartial tribunal, in the determination of his rights and obligations and of any criminal charge against him.

Article 11

1. Everyone charged with a penal offence has the right to be presumed innocent until proved guilty according to law in a public trial at which he has had all the guarantees necessary for his defence.
2. No one shall be held guilty of any penal offence on account of any act or omission which did not constitute a penal offence, under national or international law, at the time when it was committed. Nor shall a heavier penalty be imposed than the one that was applicable at the time the penal offence was committed.

Article 12

No one shall be subjected to arbitrary interference with his privacy, family, home or correspondence, nor to attacks upon his honour and reputation. Everyone has the right to the protection of the law against such interference or attacks.

Article 13

1. Everyone has the right to freedom of movement and residence within the borders of each State.
2. Everyone has the right to leave any country, including his own, and to return to his country.

Article 14

1. Everyone has the right to seek and to enjoy in other countries asylum from persecution.
2. This right may not be invoked in the case of prosecutions genuinely arising from non-political crimes or from acts contrary to the purposes and principles of the United Nations.

Article 15

1. Everyone has the right to a nationality.
2. No one shall be arbitrarily deprived of his nationality nor denied the right to change his nationality.

Article 16

1. Men and women of full age, without any limitation due to race, nationality or religion, have the right to marry and to found a family. They are entitled to equal rights as to marriage, during marriage and at its dissolution.
2. Marriage shall be entered into only with the free and full consent of the intending spouses.
3. The family is the natural and fundamental group unit of society and is entitled to protection by society and the State.

Article 17

1. Everyone has the right to own property alone as well as in association with others.
2. No one shall be arbitrarily deprived of his property.

Article 18

Everyone has the right to freedom of thought, conscience and religion; this right includes freedom to change his religion or belief, and freedom, either alone or in community with others and in public or private, to manifest his religion or belief in teaching, practice, worship and observance.

Article 19

Everyone has the right to freedom of opinion and expression; this right includes freedom to hold opinions without interference and to seek, receive and impart information and ideas through any media and regardless of frontiers.

Article 20

1. Everyone has the right to freedom of peaceful assembly and association.
2. No one may be compelled to belong to an association.

Article 21

1. Everyone has the right to take part in the government of his country, directly or through freely chosen representatives.
2. Everyone has the right of equal access to public service in his country.
3. The will of the people shall be the basis of the authority of government; this will shall be expressed in periodic and genuine elections which shall be by universal and equal suffrage and shall be held by secret vote or by equivalent free voting procedures.

Article 22

Everyone, as a member of society, has the right to social security and is entitled to realization, through national effort and international cooperation and in accordance with the organization and resources of each State, of the economic, social and cultural rights indispensable for his dignity and the free development of his personality.

Article 23

1. Everyone has the right to work, to free choice of employment, to just and favorable conditions of work and to protection against unemployment.
2. Everyone, without any discrimination, has the right to equal pay for equal work.
3. Everyone who works has the right to just and favourable remuneration ensuring for himself and his family and existence worthy of human dignity, and supplemented, if necessary, by other means of social protection.
4. Everyone has the right to form and to join trade unions for the protection of his interests.

Article 24

Everyone has the right to rest and leisure, including reasonable limitation of working hours and periodic holidays with pay.

Article 25

1. Everyone has the right to a standard of living adequate for the health and well-being of himself and of his family, including food, clothing, housing and medical care and necessary social services, and the right to security in the event of unemployment, sickness, disability, widowhood, old age or other lack of livelihood in circumstances beyond his control.
2. Motherhood and childhood are entitled to special care and assistance. All children, whether born in or out of wedlock, shall enjoy the same social protection.

Article 26

1. Everyone has the right to education. Education shall be free, at least in the elementary and fundamental stages. Elementary education shall be compulsory. Technical and professional education shall be made generally available and higher education shall be equally accessible to all on the basis of merit.

2. Education shall be directed to the full development of the human personality and to the strengthening of respect for human rights and fundamental freedoms. It shall promote understanding, tolerance and friendship among all nations, racial or religious groups, and shall further the activities of the United Nations for the maintenance of peace.

3. Parents have a right to choose the kind of education that shall be given to their children.

Article 27

1. Everyone has the right freely to participate in the cultural life of the community, to enjoy the arts and to share in scientific advancement and its benefits.

2. Everyone has the right to the protection of the moral and material interests resulting from any scientific, literary or artistic production of which he is the author.

Article 28

Everyone is entitled to a social and international order in which the rights and freedoms set forth in this Declaration can be fully realized.

Article 29

1. Everyone has duties to the community in which alone the free and full development of his personality is possible.

2. In the exercise of his rights and freedoms, everyone shall be subject only to such limitations as are determined by law solely for the purpose of securing due recognition and respect for the rights and freedoms of others and of meeting the just requirements of morality, public order and the general welfare in a democratic society.

3. These rights and freedoms may in no case be exercised contrary to the purposes and principles of the United Nations.

Article 30

Nothing in this Declaration may be interpreted as implying for any States, group or person any right to engage in any activity or to perform any act aimed at the destruction of any of the rights and freedoms set forth herein.

INTERNATIONAL COVENANT ON CIVIL AND POLITICAL RIGHTS

December 16, 1966, 999 U.N.T.S. 171*

Recognizing that these rights derive from the inherent dignity of the human person,

Recognizing that, in accordance with the Universal Declaration of Human Rights, the ideal of free human beings enjoying civil and political freedom and freedom from fear and want can only be achieved if conditions are created whereby everyone may enjoy his civil and political rights, as well as his economic, social and cultural rights,

Considering the obligation of States under the Charter of the United Nations to promote universal respect for, and observance of, human rights and freedoms,

Realizing that the individual, having duties to other individuals and to the community to which he belongs, is under a responsibility to strive for the promotion and observance of the rights recognized in the present Covenant,

Agree upon the following articles:

Part I

Article 1

1. All peoples have the right of self-determination. By virtue of that right they freely determine their political status and freely pursue their economic, social and cultural development.

2. All peoples may, for their own ends, freely dispose of their natural wealth and resources without prejudice to any obligations arising out of

---

*Adopted by the U.N. General Assembly at New York on December 16, 1966. G.A. Res. 2200. Entered into force on March 23, 1976. The United States has not ratified the covenant.

The 89 parties to the covenant are: Afghanistan, Algeria, Argentina, Australia, Austria, Barbados, Belgium, Bolivia, Bulgaria, Byelorussian SSR, Cameroon, Canada, Central African Republic, Chile, Colombia, Congo, Costa Rica, Cyprus, Czechoslovakia, Democratic People's Republic of Korea, Democratic Yemen, Denmark, Dominican Republic, Ecuador, Egypt, El Salvador, Equatorial Guinea, Finland, France, Gabon, Gambia, German Democratic Republic, Germany (Federal Republic), Guinea, Guyana, Hungary, Iceland, India, Iran (Islamic Republic), Iraq, Ireland, Italy, Jamaica, Japan, Jordan, Kenya, Lebanon, Libyan Arab Jamahiriya, Luxembourg, Madagascar, Mali, Mauritius, Mexico, Mongolia, Morocco, Netherlands, New Zealand, Nicaragua, Niger, Norway, Panama, Peru, Philippines, Poland, Portugal, Romania, Rwanda, Saint Vincent & the Grenadines, San Marino, Senegal, Spain, Sri Lanka, Sudan, Suriname, Sweden, Syrian Arab Republic, Togo, Trinidad & Tobago, Tunisia, Ukrainian SSR, Union of Soviet Socialist Republics, United Kingdom, United Republic of Tanzania, Uruguay, Venezuela, Viet Nam, Yugoslavia, Zaire, and Zambia.

international economic co-operation, based upon the principle of mutual benefit, and international law. In no case may a people be deprived of its own means of subsistence.

3. The States Parties to the present Covenant, including those having responsibility for the administration of Non-Self-Governing and Trust Territories, shall promote the realization of the right of self-determination, and shall respect that right, in conformity with the provisions of the Charter of the United Nations.

Part II

Article 2

1. Each State Party to the present Covenant undertakes to respect and to ensure to all individuals within its territory and subject to its jurisdiction the rights recognized in the present Covenant, without distinction of any kind, such as race, colour, sex, language, religion, political or other opinion, national or social origin, property, birth or other status.

2. Where not already provided for by existing legislative or other measures, each State Party to the present Covenant undertakes to take the necessary steps, in accordance with its constitutional processes and with the provisions of the present Covenant, to adopt such legislative or other measures as may be necessary to give effect to the rights recognized in the present Covenant.

3. Each State Party to the present Covenant undertakes:

(*a*) To ensure that any person whose rights or freedoms as herein recognized are violated shall have an effective remedy, notwithstanding that the violation has been committed by persons acting in an official capacity;

(*b*) To ensure that any person claiming such a remedy shall have his right thereto determined by competent judicial, administrative or legislative authorities, or by any other competent authority provided for by the legal system of the State, and to develop the possibilities of judicial remedy;

(*c*) To ensure that the competent authorities shall enforce such remedies when granted.

Article 3

The States Parties to the present Covenant undertake to ensure the equal right of men and women to the enjoyment of all civil and political rights set forth in the present Covenant.

Article 4

1. In time of public emergency which threatens the life of the nation and the existence of which is officially proclaimed, the States Parties to the present Covenant may take measures derogating from their obligations under the present Covenant to the extent strictly required by the exigencies

of the situation, provided that such measures are not inconsistent with their other obligations under international law and do not involve discrimination solely on the ground of race, color, sex, language, religion or social origin.

2. No derogation from articles 6, 7, 8 (paragraphs 1 and 2), 11, 15, 16 and 18 may be made under this provision.

3. Any State Party to the present Covenant availing itself of the right of derogation shall immediately inform the other States Parties to the present Covenant, through the intermediary of the Secretary-General of the United Nations, of the provisions from which it has derogated and of the reasons by which it was actuated. A further communication shall be made, through the same intermediary, on the date on which it terminates such derogation.

Article 5

1. Nothing in the present Covenant may be interpreted as implying for any State, group or person any right to engage in any activity or perform any act aimed at the destruction of any of the rights and freedoms recognized herein or at their limitation to a greater extent than is provided for in the present Covenant.

2. There shall be no restriction upon or derogation from any of the fundamental human rights recognized or existing in any State Party to the present Covenant pursuant to law, conventions, regulations or custom on the pretext that the present Covenant does not recognize such rights or that it recognizes them to a lesser extent.

Part III

Article 6

1. Every human being has the inherent right to life. This right shall be protected by law. No one shall be arbitrarily deprived of his life.

2. In countries which have not abolished the death penalty, sentence of death may be imposed only for the most serious crimes in accordance with the law in force at the time of the commission of the crime and not contrary to the provisions of the present Covenant and to the Convention on the Prevention and Punishment of the Crime of Genocide. This penalty can only be carried out pursuant to a final judgement rendered by a competent court.

3. When deprivation of life constitutes the crime of genocide, it is understood that nothing in this article shall authorize any State Party to the present Covenant to derogate in any way from any obligation assumed under the provisions of the Convention on the Prevention and Punishment of the Crime of Genocide.

4. Anyone sentenced to death shall have the right to seek pardon or commutation of the sentence. Amnesty, pardon or commutation of the sentence of death may be granted in all cases.

5. Sentence of death shall not be imposed for crimes committed by persons below eighteen years of age and shall not be carried out on pregnant women.

6. Nothing in this article shall be invoked to delay or to prevent the abolition of capital punishment by any State Party to the present Covenant.

Article 7

No one shall be subjected to torture or to cruel, inhuman or degrading treatment or punishment. In particular, no one shall be subjected without his free consent to medical or scientific experimentation.

Article 8

1. No one shall be held in slavery; slavery and the slave-trade in all their forms shall be prohibited.
2. No one shall be held in servitude.
3. (*a*) No one shall be required to perform forced or compulsory labour.

(*b*) Paragraph 3 (*a*) shall not be held to preclude, in countries where imprisonment with hard labour may be imposed as a punishment for a crime, the performance of hard labour in pursuance of a sentence to such punishment by a competent court.

(*c*) For the purpose of this paragraph the term "forced or compulsory labour" shall not include:

(i) Any work or service, not referred to in sub-paragraph (*b*), normally required of a person who is under detention in consequence of a lawful order of a court, or of a person during conditional release from such detention;

(ii) Any service of a military character and, in countries where conscientious objection is recognized, any national service required by law of conscientious objectors;

(iii) Any service exacted in cases of emergency or calamity threatening the life or well-being of the community;

(iv) Any work or service which forms part of normal civil obligations.

Article 9

1. Everyone has the right to liberty and security of person. No one shall be subjected to arbitrary arrest or detention. No one shall be deprived of his liberty except on such grounds and in accordance with such procedure as are established by law.

2. Anyone who is arrested shall be informed, at the time of arrest, of the reasons for his arrest and shall be promptly informed of any charges against him.

3. Anyone arrested or detained on a criminal charge shall be brought promptly before a judge or other officer authorized by law to exercise judicial power and shall be entitled to trial within a reasonable time or to release. It shall not be the general rule that persons awaiting trial shall be detained in custody, but release may be subject to guarantees to appear for trial, at any other stage of the judicial proceedings, and, should occasion arise, for execution of the judgement.

4. Anyone who is deprived of his liberty by arrest or detention shall be entitled to take proceedings before a court, in order that that court may decide without delay on the lawfulness of his detention and order his release if the detention is not lawful.

5. Anyone who has been the victim of unlawful arrest or detention shall have an enforceable right to compensation.

Article 10

1. All persons deprived of their liberty shall be treated with humanity and with respect for the inherent dignity of the human person.

2. (*a*) Accused persons shall, save in exceptional circumstances, be segregated from convicted persons and shall be subject to separate treatment appropriate to their status as unconvicted persons.

(*b*) Accused juvenile persons shall be separated from adults and brought as speedily as possible for adjudication.

3. The penitentiary system shall comprise treatment of prisoners the essential aim of which shall be their reformation and social rehabilitation. Juvenile offenders shall be segregated from adults and be accorded treatment appropriate to their age and legal status.

Article 11

No one shall be imprisoned merely on the ground of inability to fulfil a contractual obligation.

Article 12

1. Everyone lawfully within the territory of a State shall, within that territory, have the right to liberty of movement and freedom to choose his residence.

2. Everyone shall be free to leave any country, including his own.

3. The above-mentioned rights shall not be subject to any restrictions except those which are provided by law, are necessary to protect national security, public order (*ordre public*), public health or morals or the rights and freedoms of others, and are consistent with the other rights recognized in the present Covenant.

4. No one shall be arbitrarily deprived of the right to enter his own country.

Article 13

An alien lawfully in the territory of a State Party to the present Covenant may be expelled therefrom only in pursuance of a decision reached in accordance with law and shall, except where compelling reasons of national security otherwise require, be allowed to submit the reasons against his explusion and to have his case reviewed by, and be represented for the purpose before, the competent authority or a person or persons especially designated by the competent authority.

Article 14

1. All persons shall be equal before the courts and tribunals. In the determination of any criminal charge against him, or of his rights and obligations in a suit at law, everyone shall be entitled to a fair and public hearing by a competent, independent and impartial tribunal established by law. The Press and the public may be excluded from all or part of a trial for reasons of morals, public order (*ordre public*) or national security in a democratic society, or when the interest of the private lives of the parties so requires, or to the extent strictly necessary in the opinion of the court in special circumstances where publicity would prejudice the interests of justice; but any judgement rendered in a criminal case or in a suit at law shall be made public except where the interest of juvenile persons otherwise requires or the proceedings concern matrimonial disputes or the guardianship of children.

2. Everyone charged with a criminal offence shall have the right to be presumed innocent until proved guilty according to law.

3. In the determination of any criminal charge against him, everyone shall be entitled to the following minimum guarantees, in full equality:

(*a*) To be informed promptly and in detail in a language which he understands of the nature and cause of the charge against him;

(*b*) To have adequate time and facilities for the preparation of his defence and to communicate with counsel of his own choosing;

(*c*) To be tried without undue delay;

(*d*) To be tried in his presence, and to defend himself in person or through legal assistance of his own choosing; to be informed, if he does not have legal assistance, of this right; and to have legal assistance assigned to him, in any case where the interests of justice so require, and without payment by him in any such case if he does not have sufficient means to pay for it;

(*e*) To examine, or have examined, the witnesses against him and to obtain the attendance and examination of witnesses on his behalf under the same conditions as witnesses against him;

(*f*) To have the free assistance of an interpreter if he cannot understand or speak the language used in court;

(*g*) Not to be compelled to testify against himself or to confess guilt.

4. In the case of juvenile persons, the procedure shall be such as will take account of their age and the desirability of promoting their rehabilitation.

5. Everyone convicted of a crime shall have the right to his conviction and sentence being reviewed by a higher tribunal according to law.

6. When a person has by a final decision been convicted of a criminal offence and when subsequently his conviction has been reversed or he has been pardoned on the ground that a new or newly discovered fact shows conclusively that there has been a miscarriage of justice, the person who has suffered punishment as a result of such conviction shall be compensated according to law, unless it is proved that the non-disclosure of the unknown fact in time is wholly or partly attributable to him.

7. No one shall be liable to be tried or punished again for an offence

for which he has already been finally convicted or acquitted in accordance with the law and penal procedure of each country.

Article 15

1. No one shall be held guilty of any criminal offence on account of any act or omission which did not constitute a criminal offence, under national or international law, at the time when it was committed. Nor shall a heavier penalty be imposed than the one that was applicable at the time when the criminal offence was committed. If, subsequent to the commission of the offence, provision is made by law for the imposition of a lighter penalty, the offender shall benefit thereby.

2. Nothing in this article shall prejudice the trial and punishment of any person for any act or omission which, at the time when it was committed, was criminal according to the general principles of law recognized by the community of nations.

Article 16

Everyone shall have the right to recognition everywhere as a person before the law.

Article 17

1. No one shall be subjected to arbitrary or unlawful interference with his privacy, family, home or correspondence, nor to unlawful attacks on his honour and reputation.

2. Everyone has the right to the protection of the law against such interference or attacks.

Article 18

1. Everyone shall have the right to freedom of thought, conscience and religion. This right shall include freedom to have or to adopt a religion or belief of his choice, and freedom, either individually or in community with others and in public or private, to manifest his religion or belief in worship, observance, practice and teaching.

2. No one shall be subject to coercion which would impair his freedom to have or to adopt a religion or belief of his choice.

3. Freedom to manifest one's religion or beliefs may be subject only to such limitations as are prescribed by law and are necessary to protect public safety, order, health, or morals or the fundamental rights and freedoms of others.

4. The States Parties to the present Covenant undertake to have respect for the liberty of parents and, when applicable, legal guardians to ensure the religious and moral education of their children in conformity with their own convictions.

Article 19

1. Everyone shall have the right to hold opinions without interference.

2. Everyone shall have the right to freedom of expression; this right

shall include freedom to seek, receive and impart information and ideas of all kinds, regardless of frontiers, either orally, in writing or in print, in the form of art, or through any other media of his choice.

3. The exercise of the rights provided for in paragraph 2 of this article carries with it special duties and responsibilities. It may therefore be subject to certain restrictions, but these shall only be such as are provided by law and are necessary:

(a) For respect of the rights or reputations of others;

(b) For the protection of national security or of public order (*ordre public*), or of public health or morals.

Article 20

1. Any propaganda for war shall be prohibited by law.

2. Any advocacy of national, racial or religious hatred that constitutes incitement to discrimination, hostility or violence shall be prohibited by law.

Article 21

The right of peaceful assembly shall be recognized. No restrictions may be placed on the exercise of this right other than those imposed in conformity with the law and which are necessary in a democratic society in the interests of national security or public safety, public order (*ordre public*), the protection of public health or morals or the protection of the rights and freedoms of others.

Article 22

1. Everyone shall have the right to freedom of association with others, including the right to form and join trade unions for the protection of his interests.

2. No restrictions may be placed on the exercise of this right other than those which are prescribed by law and which are necessary in a democratic society in the interests of national security or public safety, public order (*ordre public*), the protection of public health or morals or the protection of the rights and freedoms of others. This article shall not prevent the imposition of lawful restrictions on members of the armed forces and of the police in their exercise of this right.

3. Nothing in this article shall authorize States Parties to the International Labour Organisation Convention of 1948 concerning freedom of association and protection of the right to organize to take legislative measures which would prejudice, or to apply the law in such a manner as to prejudice, the guarantees provided for in that Convention.

Article 23

1. The family is the natural and fundamental group unit of society and is entitled to protection by society and the State.

2. The right of men and women of marriageable age to marry and to found a family shall be recognized.

3. No marriage shall be entered into without the free and full consent of the intending spouses.

4. States Parties to the present Covenant shall take appropriate steps to ensure equality of rights and responsibilities of spouses as to marriage, during marriage and at its dissolution. In the case of dissolution, provision shall be made for the necessary protection of any children.

Article 24

1. Every child shall have, without any discrimination as to race, colour, sex, language, religion, national or social origin, property or birth, the right to such measures of protection as are required by his status as a minor, on the part of his family, society and the State.
2. Every child shall be registered immediately after birth and shall have a name.
3. Every child has the right to acquire a nationality.

Article 25

Every citizen shall have the right and the opportunity, without any of the distinctions mentioned in article 2 and without unreasonable restrictions:

(*a*) To take part in the conduct of public affairs, directly or through freely chosen representatives;

(*b*) To vote and to be elected at genuine periodic elections which shall be by universal and equal suffrage and shall be held by secret ballot, guaranteeing the free expression of the will of the electors;

(*c*) To have access, on general terms of equality, to public service in his country.

Article 26

All persons are equal before the law and are entitled without any discrimination to the equal protection of the law. In this respect, the law shall prohibit any discrimination and guarantee to all persons equal and effective protection against discrimination on any ground such as race, colour, sex, language, religion, political or other opinion, national or social origin, property, birth or other status.

Article 27

In those States in which ethnic, religious or linguistic minorities exist, persons belonging to such minorities shall not be denied the right, in community with the other members of their group, to enjoy their own culture, to profess and practise their own religion, or to use their own language.

Part IV

Article 28

1. There shall be established a Human Rights Committee (hereafter referred to in the present Covenant as the Committee). It shall consist of eighteen members and shall carry out the functions hereinafter provided.

2. The Committee shall be composed of nationals of the States Parties to the present Covenant who shall be persons of high moral character and recognized competence in the field of human rights, consideration being given to the usefulness of the participation of some persons having legal experience.

3. The members of the Committee shall be elected and shall serve in their personal capacity.

Article 29

1. The members of the Committee shall be elected by secret ballot from a list of persons possessing the qualifications prescribed in article 28 and nominated for the purpose by the States Parties to the present Covenant.

2. Each State Party to the present Covenant may nominate not more than two persons. These persons shall be nationals of the nominating State.

3. A person shall be eligible for renomination.

Article 30

1. The initial election shall be held no later than six months after the date of the entry into force of the present Covenant.

2. At least four months before the date of each election to the Committee, other than an election to fill a vacancy declared in accordance with article 34, the Secretary-General of the United Nations shall address a written invitation to the States Parties to the present Covenant to submit their nominations for membership of the Committee within three months.

3. The Secretary-General of the United Nations shall prepare a list in alphabetical order of all the persons thus nominated, with an indication of the States Parties which have nominated them, and shall submit it to the States Parties to the present Covenant no later than one month before the date of each election.

4. Elections of the members of the Committee shall be held at a meeting of the States Parties to the present Covenant convened by the Secretary-General of the United Nations at the Headquarters of the United Nations. At that meeting, for which two thirds of the States Parties to the present Covenant shall constitute a quorum, the persons elected to the Committee shall be those nominees who obtain the largest number of votes and an absolute majority of the votes of the representatives of States Parties present and voting.

Article 31

1. The Committee may not include more than one national of the same State.

2. In the election of the Committee, consideration shall be given to equitable geographical distribution of membership and to the representation of the different forms of civilization and of the principal legal systems.

Article 32

1. The members of the Committee shall be elected for a term of four years. They shall be eligible for re-election if renominated. However, the

terms of nine of the members elected at the first election shall expire at the end of two years; immediately after the first election, the names of these nine members shall be chosen by lot by the Chairman of the meeting referred to in article 30, paragraph 4.

2. Elections at the expiry of office shall be held in accordance with the preceding articles of this part of the present Covenant.

Article 33

1. If, in the unanimous opinion of the other members, a member of the Committee has ceased to carry out his functions for any cause other than absence of a temporary character, the Chairman of the Committee shall notify the Secretary-General of the United Nations, who shall then declare the seat of that member to be vacant.

2. In the event of the death or the resignation of a member of the Committee, the Chairman shall immediately notify the Secretary-General of the United Nations, who shall declare the seat vacant from the date of death or the date on which the resignation takes effect.

Article 34

1. When a vacancy is declared in accordance with article 33 and if the term of office of the member to be replaced does not expire within six months of the declaration of the vacancy, the Secretary-General of the United Nations shall notify each of the States Parties to the present Covenant, which may within two months submit nominations in accordance with article 29 for the purpose of filling the vacancy.

2. The Secretary-General of the United Nations shall prepare a list in alphabetical order of the persons thus nominated and shall submit it to the States Parties to the present Covenant. The election to fill the vacancy shall then take place in accordance with the relevant provisions of this part of the present Covenant.

3. A member of the Committee elected to fill a vacancy declared in accordance with article 33 shall hold office for the remainder of the term of the member who vacated the seat on the Committee under the provisions of that article.

Article 35

The members of the Committee shall, with the approval of the General Assembly of the United Nations, receive emoluments from United Nations resources on such terms and conditions as the General Assembly may decide, having regard to the importance of the Committee's responsibilities.

Article 36

The Secretary-General of the United Nations shall provide the necessary staff and facilities for the effective performance of the functions of the Committee under the present Covenant.

Article 37

1. The Secretary-General of the United Nations shall convene the initial meeting of the Committee at the Headquarters of the United Nations.

2. After its initial meeting, the Committee shall meet at such times as shall be provided in its rules of procedure.

3. The Committee shall normally meet at the Headquarters of the United Nations or at the United Nations Office at Geneva.

Article 38

Every member of the Committee shall, before taking up his duties, make a solemn declaration in open committee that he will perform his functions impartially and conscientiously.

Article 39

1. The Committee shall elect its officers for a term of two years. They may be re-elected.

2. The Committee shall establish its own rules of procedure, but these rules shall provide, *inter alia,* that:

(*a*) Twelve members shall constitute a quorum;

(*b*) Decisions of the Committee shall be made by a majority vote of the members present.

Article 40

1. The States Parties to the present Covenant undertake to submit reports on the measures they have adopted which give effect to the rights recognized herein and on the progress made in the enjoyment of those rights:

(*a*) Within one year of the entry into force of the present Covenant for the States Parties concerned;

(*b*) Thereafter whenever the Committee so requests.

2. All reports shall be submitted to the Secretary-General of the United Nations, who shall transmit them to the Committee for consideration. Reports shall indicate the factors and difficulties, if any, affecting the implementation of the present Covenant.

3. The Secretary-General of the United Nations may, after consultation with the Committee, transmit to the specialized agencies concerned copies of such parts of the reports as may fall within their field of competence.

4. The Committee shall study the reports submitted by the States Parties to the present Covenant. It shall transmit its reports, and such general comments as it may consider appropriate, to the States Parties. The Committee may also transmit to the Economic and Social Council these comments along with the copies of the reports it has received from States Parties to the present Covenant.

5. The States Parties to the present Covenant may submit to the Committee observations on any comments that may be made in accordance with paragraph 4 of this article.

Article 41

1. A State Party to the present Covenant may at any time declare under this article that it recognizes the competence of the Committee to receive and consider communications to the effect that a State Party claims that another State Party is not fulfilling its obligations under the present Covenant. Communications under this article may be received and considered only if submitted by a State Party which has made a declaration recognizing in regard to itself the competence of the Committee. No communication shall be received by the Committee if it concerns a State Party which has not made such a declaration. Communications received under this article shall be dealt with in accordance with the following procedure:

(a) If a State Party to the present Covenant considers that another State Party is not giving effect to the provisions of the present Covenant, it may, by written communication, bring the matter to the attention of that State Party. Within three months after the receipt of the communication, the receiving State shall afford the State which sent the communication an explanation or any other statement in writing clarifying the matter, which should include, to the extent possible and pertinent, reference to domestic procedures and remedies taken, pending, or available in the matter.

(b) If the matter is not adjusted to the satisfaction of both States Parties concerned within six months after the receipt by the receiving State of the initial communication, either State shall have the right to refer the matter to the Committee, by notice given to the Committee and to the other State.

(c) The Committee shall deal with a matter referred to it only after it has ascertained that all available domestic remedies have been invoked and exhausted in the matter, in conformity with the generally recognized principles of international law. This shall not be the rule where the application of the remedies is unreasonably prolonged.

(d) The Committee shall hold closed meetings when examining communications under this article.

(e) Subject to the provisions of sub-paragraph (c), the Committee shall make available its good offices to the States Parties concerned with a view to a friendly solution of the matter on the basis of respect for human rights and fundamental freedoms as recognized in the present Covenant.

(f) In any matter referred to it, the Committee may call upon the States Parties concerned, referred to in sub-paragraph (b), to supply any relevant information.

(g) The States Parties concerned, referred to in sub-paragraph (b), shall have the right to be represented when the matter is being considered in the Committee and to make submissions orally and/or in writing.

(h) The Committee shall, within twelve months after the date of receipt of notice under sub-paragraph (b), submit a report:

    (i) If a solution within the terms of sub-paragraph (e) is reached, the Committee shall confine its report to a brief statement of the facts and of the solution reached;

(ii) If a solution within the terms of sub-paragraph (*e*) is not reached, the Committee shall confine its report to a brief statement of the facts; the written submissions and record of the oral submissions made by the States Parties concerned shall be attached to the report.

In every matter, the report shall be communicated to the States Parties concerned.

2. The provisions of this article shall come into force when ten States Parties to the present Covenant have made declarations under paragraph 1 of this article. Such declarations shall be deposited by the States Parties with the Secretary-General of the United Nations, who shall transmit copies thereof to the other States Parties. A declaration may be withdrawn at any time by notification to the Secretary-General. Such a withdrawal shall not prejudice the consideration of any matter which is the subject of a communication already transmitted under this article; no further communication by any State Party shall be received after the notification of withdrawal of the declaration has been received by the Secretary-General, unless the State Party concerned has made a new declaration.

Article 42

1. (*a*) If a matter referred to the Committee in accordance with article 41 is not resolved to the satisfaction of the States Parties concerned, the Committee may, with the prior consent of the States Parties concerned, appoint an *ad hoc* Conciliation Commission (hereinafter referred to as the Commission). The good offices of the Commission shall be made available to the States Parties concerned with a view to an amicable solution of the matter on the basis of respect for the present Covenant.

(*b*) The Commission shall consist of five persons acceptable to the States Parties concerned. If the States Parties concerned fail to reach agreement within three months on all or part of the composition of the Commission the members of the Commission concerning whom no agreement has been reached shall be elected by secret ballot by a two-thirds majority vote of the Committee from among its members.

2. The members of the Commission shall serve in their personal capacity. They shall not be nationals of the States Parties concerned, or of a State not party to the present Covenant, or of a State Party which has not made a declaration under article 41.

3. The Commission shall elect its own Chairman and adopt its own rules of procedure.

4. The meetings of the Commission shall normally be held at the Headquarters of the United Nations or at the United Nations Office at Geneva. However, they may be held at such other convenient places as the Commission may determine in consultation with the Secretary-General of the United Nations and the States Parties concerned.

5. The secretariat provided in accordance with article 36 shall also service the commissions appointed under this article.

6. The information received and collated by the Committee shall be made available to the Commission and the Commission may call upon

the States Parties concerned to supply any other relevant information.

7. When the Commission has fully considered the matter, but in any event not later than twelve months after having been seized of the matter, it shall submit to the Chairman of the Committee a report for communication to the States Parties concerned.

(*a*) If the Commission is unable to complete its consideration of the matter within twelve months, it shall confine its report to a brief statement of the status of its consideration of the matter.

(*b*) If an amicable solution to the matter on the basis of respect for human rights as recognized in the present Covenant is reached, the Commission shall confine its report to a brief statement of the facts and of the solution reached.

(*c*) If a solution within the terms of sub-paragraph (*b*) is not reached, the Commission's report shall embody its findings on all questions of fact relevant to the issues between the States Parties concerned, and its views on the possibilities of an amicable solution of the matter. This report shall also contain the written submissions and a record of the oral submissions made by the States Parties concerned.

(*d*) If the Commission's report is submitted under sub-paragraph (*c*), the States Parties concerned shall, within three months of the receipt of the report, notify the Chairman of the Committee whether or not they accept the contents of the report of the Commission.

8. The provisions of this article are without prejudice to the responsibilities of the Committee under article 41.

9. The States Parties concerned shall share equally all the expenses of the members of the Commission in accordance with estimates to be provided by the Secretary-General of the United Nations.

10. The Secretary-General of the United Nations shall be empowered to pay the expenses of the members of the Commission, if necessary, before reimbursement by the States Parties concerned, in accordance with paragraph 9 of this article.

Article 43

The members of the Committee, and of the *ad hoc* conciliation commissions which may be appointed under article 42, shall be entitled to the facilities, privileges and immunities of experts on mission for the United Nations as laid down in the relevant sections of the Convention on the Privileges and Immunities of the United Nations.

Article 44

The provisions for the implementation of the present Covenant shall apply without prejudice to the procedures prescribed in the field of human rights by or under the constituent instruments and the conventions of the United Nations and of the specialized agencies and shall not prevent the States Parties to the present Covenant from having recourse to other procedures for settling a dispute in accordance with general or special international agreements in force between them.

Article 45

The Committee shall submit to the General Assembly of the United Nations through the Economic and Social Council, an annual report on its activities.

Part V

Article 46

Nothing in the present Covenant shall be interpreted as impairing the provisions of the Charter of the United Nations and of the constitutions of the specialized agencies which define the respective responsibilities of the various organs of the United Nations and of the specialized agencies in regard to the matters dealt with in the present Covenant.

Article 47

Nothing in the present Covenant shall be interpreted as impairing the inherent right of all peoples to enjoy and utilize fully and freely their natural wealth and resources. . . .

OPTIONAL PROTOCOL TO THE INTERNATIONAL COVENANT ON CIVIL AND POLITICAL RIGHTS

999 U.N.T.S. 171, 6 I.L.M. 383 (1967)*

The States Parties to the present Protocol,
Considering that in order further to achieve the purposes of the Covenant on Civil and Political Rights (hereinafter referred to as the Covenant) and the implementation of its provisions it would be appropriate to enable the Human Rights Committee set up in part IV of the Covenant (hereinafter referred to as the Committee) to receive and consider, as provided in the present Protocol, communications from individuals claiming to be victims of violations of any of the rights set forth in the Covenant,
Have agreed as follows:

Article 1

A State Party to the Covenant that becomes a party to the present Protocol recognizes the competence of the Committee to receive and consider communications from individuals subject to its jurisdiction who claim to be victims of a violation by that State Party of any of the rights set forth in the Covenant. No communication shall be received by the Committee if it concerns a State Party to the Covenant which is not a party to the present Protocol.

Article 2

Subject to the provisions of article 1, individuals who claim that any of their rights enumerated in the Covenant have been violated and who have exhausted all available domestic remedies may submit a written communication to the Committee for consideration.

Article 3

The Committee shall consider inadmissible any communication under the present Protocol which is anonymous, or which it considers to be an

---

*Adopted by the U.N. General Assembly at New York on December 16, 1966 G.A. Res. 2200. Entered into force on March 23, 1976. The United States has not ratified the optional protocol.

The 48 parties to the optional protocol are: Algeria, Argentina, Austria, Barbados, Bolivia, Cameroon, Canada, Central African Republic, Colombia, Congo, Costa Rica, Denmark, Dominican Republic, Ecuador, Equatorial Guinea, Finland, France, Gambia, Hungary, Iceland, Ireland, Italy, Jamaica, Luxembourg, Libyan Arab Jamahiriya, Madagascar, Mauritius, Netherlands, New Zealand, Nicaragua, Niger, Norway, Panama, Peru, Philippines, Portugal, Saint Vincent & the Grenadines, San Marino, Senegal, Spain, Suriname, Sweden, Trinidad & Tobago, Togo, Uruguay, Venezuela, Zaire, and Zambia.

abuse of the right of submission of such communications or to be incompatible with the provisions of the Covenant.

Article 4

1. Subject to the provisions of article 3, the Committee shall bring any communications submitted to it under the present Protocol to the attention of the State Party to the present Protocol alleged to be violating any provision of the Covenant.

2. Within six months, the receiving State shall submit to the Committee written explanations or statements clarifying the matter and the remedy, if any, that may have been taken by that State.

Article 5

1. The Committee shall consider communications received under the present Protocol in the light of all written information made available to it by the individual and by the State Party concerned.

2. The Committee shall not consider any communication from an individual unless it has ascertained that:

(a) The same matter is not being examined under another procedure of international investigation or settlement;

(b) The individual has exhausted all available domestic remedies.

This shall not be the rule where the application of the remedies is unreasonably prolonged.

3. The Committee shall hold closed meetings when examining communications under the present Protocol.

4. The Committee shall forward its views to the State Party concerned and to the individual.

Article 6

The Committee shall include in its annual report under article 45 of the Covenant a summary of its activities under the present Protocol.

Article 7

Pending the achievement of the objectives of resolution 1514 (XV) adopted by the General Assembly of the United Nations on 14 December 1960 concerning the Declaration on the Granting of Independence to Colonial Countries and Peoples, the provisions of the present Protocol shall in no way limit the right of petition granted to these peoples by the Charter of the United Nations and other international conventions and instruments under the United Nations and its specialized agencies. . . .

Article 10

The provisions of the present Protocol shall extend to all parts of federal States without any limitations or exceptions.

Article 11

1. Any State Party to the present Protocol may propose an amendment and file it with the Secretary-General of the United Nations. The Secretary-General shall thereupon communicate any proposed amendments to the States Parties to the present Protocol with a request that they notify him whether they favour a conference of States Parties for the purpose of considering and voting upon the proposal. In the event that at least one third of the States Parties favours such a conference, the Secretary-General shall convene the conference under the auspices of the United Nations. Any amendment adopted by a majority of the States Parties present and voting at the conference shall be submitted to the General Assembly of the United Nations for approval.

2. Amendments shall come into force when they have been approved by the General Assembly of the United Nations and accepted by a two-thirds majority of the States Parties to the present Protocol in accordance with their respective constitutional processes.

3. When amendments come into force, they shall be binding on those States Parties which have accepted them, other States Parties still being bound by the provisions of the present Protocol and any earlier amendment which they have accepted. . . .

INTERNATIONAL COVENANT ON ECONOMIC, SOCIAL AND CULTURAL RIGHTS

December 16, 1966, 993 U.N.T.S. 3*

The States Parties to the present Covenant,

Considering that, in accordance with the principles proclaimed in the Charter of the United Nations, recognition of the inherent dignity and of the equal and inalienable rights of all members of the human family is the foundation of freedom, justice and peace in the world,

Recognizing that these rights derive from the inherent dignity of the human person,

Recognizing that, in accordance with the Universal Declaration of Human Rights, the ideal of free human beings enjoying freedom from fear and want can only be achieved if conditions are created whereby everyone may enjoy his economic, social and cultural rights, as well as his civil and political rights,

Considering the obligation of States under the Charter of the United Nations to promote universal respect for, and observance of, human rights and freedoms,

Realizing that the individual, having duties to other individuals and to the community to which he belongs, is under a responsibility to strive for the promotion and observance of the rights recognized in the present Covenant,

Agree upon the following articles:

---

*Adopted by the U.N. General Assembly at New York on December 16, 1966. Annex to G.A. Res. 2200. Entered into force on January 3, 1976. The United States has not ratified the covenant.

The 92 parties to the covenant are: Afghanistan, Algeria, Argentina, Australia, Austria, Barbados, Belgium, Bolivia, Bulgaria, Byelorussian SSR, Cameroon, Canada, Central African Republic, Chile, Colombia, Congo, Costa Rica, Cyprus, Czechoslovakia, Democratic People's Republic of Korea, Democratic Yemen, Denmark, Dominican Republic, Ecuador, Egypt, El Salvador, Equatorial Guinea, Finland, France, Gabon, Gambia, German Democratic Republic, Germany (Federal Republic), Greece, Guatemala, Guinea, Guyana, Honduras, Hungary, Iceland, India, Iran (Islamic Republic), Iraq, Ireland, Italy, Jamaica, Japan, Jordan, Kenya, Lebanon, Libyan Arab Jamahiriya, Luxembourg, Madagascar, Mali, Mauritius, Mexico, Mongolia, Morocco, Netherlands, New Zealand, Nicaragua, Niger, Norway, Panama, Peru, Philippines, Poland, Portugal, Romania, Rwanda, Saint Vincent & the Grenadines, San Marino, Senegal, Solomon Islands, Spain, Sri Lanka, Sudan, Suriname, Sweden, Syrian Arab Republic, Togo, Trinidad & Tobago, Tunisia, Uganda, Ukrainian SSR, Union of Soviet Socialist Republics, United Kingdom, United Republic of Tanzania, Uruguay, Venezuela, Viet Nam, Yugoslavia, Zaire, and Zambia.

Part I

Article 1

1. All peoples have the right of self-determination. By virtue of that right they freely determine their political status and freely pursue their economic, social and cultural development.

2. All peoples may, for their own ends, freely dispose of their natural wealth and resources without prejudice to any obligations arising out of international economic co-operation, based upon the principle of mutual benefit, and international law. In no case may a people be deprived of its own means of subsistence.

3. The States Parties to the present Covenant, including those having responsibility for the administration of Non-Self-Governing and Trust Territories, shall promote the realization of the right of self-determination, and shall respect that right, in conformity with the provisions of the Charter of the United Nations.

Part II

Article 2

1. Each State Party to the present Covenant undertakes to take steps, individually and through international assistance and co-operation, especially economic and technical, to the maximum of its available resources, with a view to achieving progressively the full realization of the rights recognized in the present Covenant by all appropriate means, including particularly the adoption of legislative measures.

2. The States Parties to the present Covenant undertake to guarantee that the rights enunciated in the present Covenant will be exercised without discrimination of any kind as to race, colour, sex, language, religion, political or other opinion, national or social origin, property, birth or other status.

3. Developing countries, with due regard to human rights and their national economy, may determine to what extent they would guarantee the economic rights recognized in the present Covenant to non-nationals.

Article 3

The States Parties to the present Covenant undertake to ensure the equal right of men and women to the enjoyment of all economic, social and cultural rights set forth in the present Covenant.

Article 4

The States Parties to the present Covenant recognize that, in the enjoyment of those rights provided by the State in conformity with the present Covenant, the State may subject such rights only to such limitations as are determined by law only in so far as this may be compatible with the nature of these rights and solely for the purpose of promoting the general welfare in a democratic society.

Article 5

1. Nothing in the present Covenant may be interpreted as implying for any State, group or person any right to engage in any activity or to perform any act aimed at the destruction of any of the rights or freedoms recognized herein, or at their limitation to a greater extent than is provided for in the present Covenant.

2. No restriction upon or derogation from any of the fundamental human rights recognized or existing in any country in virtue of law, conventions, regulations or custom shall be admitted on the pretext that the present Covenant does not recognize such rights or that it recognizes them to a lesser extent.

Part III

Article 6

1. The States Parties to the present Covenant recognize the right to work, which includes the right of everyone to the opportunity to gain his living by work which he freely chooses or accepts, and will take appropriate steps to safeguard this right.

2. The steps to be taken by a State Party to the present Covenant to achieve the full realization of this right shall include technical and vocational guidance and training programmes, policies and techniques to achieve steady economic, social and cultural development and full and productive employment under conditions safeguarding fundamental political and economic freedoms to the individual.

Article 7

The States Parties to the present Covenant recognize the right of everyone to the enjoyment of just and favourable conditions of work, which ensure, in particular:

(*a*) remuneration which provides all workers, as a minimum, with:

(i) fair wages and equal remuneration for work of equal value without distinction of any kind, in particular women being guaranteed conditions of work not inferior to those enjoyed by men, with equal pay for equal work;

(ii) a decent living for themselves and their families in accordance with the provisions of the present Covenant;

(*b*) safe and healthy working conditions;

(*c*) equal opportunity for everyone to be promoted in his employment to an appropriate higher level, subject to no considerations other than those of seniority and competence;

(*d*) rest, leisure and reasonable limitation of working hours and periodic holidays with pay, as well as remuneration for public holidays.

Article 8

1. The States Parties to the present Covenant undertake to ensure:

(*a*) the right of everyone to form trade unions and join the trade union of his choice, subject only to the rules of the organization concerned, for the promotion and protection of his economic and social interests. No restrictions may be placed on the exercise of this right other than those prescribed by law and which are necessary in a democratic society in the interests of national security or public order or for the protection of the rights and freedoms of others;

(*b*) the right of trade unions to establish national federations or confederations and the right of the latter to form or join international trade-union organizations;

(*c*) the right of trade unions to function freely subject to no limitations other than those prescribed by law and which are necessary in a democratic society in the interests of national security or public order or for the protection of the rights and freedoms of others;

(*d*) the right to strike, provided that it is exercised in conformity with the laws of the particular country.

2. This article shall not prevent the imposition of lawful restrictions on the exercise of these rights by members of the armed forces or of the police or of the administration of the State.

3. Nothing in this article shall authorize States Parties to the International Labour Organisation Convention of 1948 concerning Freedom of Association and Protection of the Right to Organize to take legislative measures which would prejudice, or apply the law in such a manner as would prejudice, the guarantees provided for in that Convention.

Article 9

The States Parties to the present Covenant recognize the right of everyone to social security, including social insurance.

Article 10

The States Parties to the present Covenant recognize that:

1. The widest possible protection and assistance should be accorded to the family, which is the natural and fundamental group unit of society, particularly for its establishment and while it is responsible for the care and education of dependent children. Marriage must be entered into with the free consent of the intending spouses.

2. Special protection should be accorded to mothers during a reasonable period before and after childbirth. During such period working mothers should be accorded paid leave or leave with adequate social security benefits.

3. Special measures of protection and assistance should be taken on behalf of all children and young persons without any discrimination for reasons of parentage or other conditions. Children and young persons should be protected from economic and social exploitation. Their employment in work harmful to their morals or health or dangerous to life or likely

to hamper their normal development should be punishable by law. States should also set age limits below which the paid employment of child labour should be prohibited and punishable by law.

Article 11

1. The States Parties to the present Covenant recognize the right of everyone to an adequate standard of living for himself and his family, including adequate food, clothing and housing, and to the continuous improvement of living conditions. The States Parties will take appropriate steps to ensure the realization of this right, recognizing to this effect the essential importance of international co-operation based on free consent.

2. The States Parties to the present Covenant, recognizing the fundamental right of everyone to be free from hunger, shall take, individually and through international co-operation, the measures, including specific programmes, which are needed:

(*a*) to improve methods of production, conservation and distribution of food by making full use of technical and scientific knowledge, by disseminating knowledge of the principles of nutrition and by developing or reforming agrarian systems in such a way as to achieve the most efficient development and utilization of natural resources;

(*b*) taking into account the problems of both food-importing and food-exporting countries, to ensure an equitable distribution of world food supplies in relation to need.

Article 12

1. The States Parties to the present Covenant recognize the right of everyone to the enjoyment of the highest attainable standard of physical and mental health.

2. The steps to be taken by the States Parties to the present Covenant to achieve the full realization of this right shall include those necessary for:

(*a*) the provision for the reduction of the stillbirth-rate and of infant mortality and for the healthy development of the child;

(*b*) the improvement of all aspects of environmental and industrial hygiene;

(*c*) the prevention, treatment and control of epidemic, endemic, occupational and other diseases;

(*d*) the creation of conditions which would assure to all medical service and medical attention in the event of sickness.

Article 13

1. The States Parties to the present Covenant recognize the right of everyone to education. They agree that education shall be directed to the full development of the human personality and the sense of its dignity, and shall strengthen the respect for human rights and fundamental freedoms. They further agree that education shall enable all persons to participate effectively in a free society, promote understanding, tolerance and friendship among all nations and all racial, ethnic or religious groups, and further the activities of the United Nations for the maintenance of peace.

2. The States Parties to the present Covenant recognize that, with a view to achieving the full realization of this right:

(a) primary education shall be compulsory and available free to all;

(b) secondary education in its different forms, including technical and vocational secondary education, shall be made generally available and accessible to all by every appropriate means, and in particular by the progressive introduction of free education;

(c) higher education shall be made equally accessible to all, on the basis of capacity, by every appropriate means, and in particular by the progressive introduction of free education;

(d) fundamental education shall be encouraged or intensified as far as possible for those persons who have not received or completed the whole period of their primary education;

(e) the development of a system of schools at all levels shall be actively pursued, an adequate fellowship system shall be established, and the material conditions of teaching staff shall be continuously improved.

3. The States Parties to the present Covenant undertake to have respect for the liberty of parents and, when applicable, legal guardians, to choose for their children schools, other than those established by the public authorities, which conform to such minimum educational standards as may be laid down or approved by the State and to ensure the religious and moral education of their children in conformity with their own convictions.

4. No part of this article shall be construed so as to interfere with the liberty of individuals and bodies to establish and direct educational institutions, subject always to the observance of the principles set forth in paragraph 1 of this article and to the requirement that the education given in such institutions shall conform to such minimum standards as may be laid down by the State.

Article 14

Each State Party to the present Covenant which, at the time of becoming a Party, has not been able to secure in its metropolitan territory or other territories under its jurisdiction compulsory primary education, free of charge, undertakes, within two years, to work out and adopt a detailed plan of action for the progressive implementation, within a reasonable number of years, to be fixed in the plan, of the principle of compulsory education free of charge for all.

Article 15

1. The States Parties to the present Covenant recognize the right of everyone:

(a) to take part in cultural life;

(b) to enjoy the benefits of scientific progress and its applications;

(c) to benefit from the protection of the moral and material interests resulting from any scientific, literary or artistic production of which he is the author.

2. The steps to be taken by the States Parties to the present Covenant to achieve the full realization of this right shall include those necessary for the conservation, the development and the diffusion of science and culture.

3. The States Parties to the present Covenant undertake to respect the freedom indispensable for scientific research and creative activity.

4. The States Parties to the present Covenant recognize the benefits to be derived from the encouragement and development of international contacts and cooperation in the scientific and cultural fields.

Part IV

Article 16

1. The States Parties to the present Covenant undertake to submit in conformity with this part of the Covenant reports on the measures which they have adopted and the progress made in achieving the observance of the rights recognized herein.

2. (*a*) All reports shall be submitted to the Secretary-General of the United Nations, who shall transmit copies to the Economic and Social Council for consideration in accordance with the provisions of the present Covenant.

(*b*) The Secretary-General of the United Nations shall also transmit to the specialized agencies copies of the reports, or any relevant parts therefrom, from States Parties to the present Covenant which are also members of these specialized agencies in so far as these reports, or parts therefrom, relate to any matters which fall within the responsibilities of the said agencies in accordance with their constitutional instruments.

Article 17

1. The States Parties to the present Covenant shall furnish their reports in stages, in accordance with a programme to be established by the Economic and Social Council within one year of the entry into force of the present Covenant after consultation with the States Parties and the specialized agencies concerned.

2. Reports may indicate factors and difficulties affecting the degree of fulfilment of obligations under the present Covenant.

3. Where relevant information has previously been furnished to the United Nations or to any specialized agency by any State Party to the present Covenant, it will not be necessary to reproduce that information, but a precise reference to the information so furnished will suffice.

Article 18

Pursuant to its responsibilities under the Charter of the United Nations in the field of human rights and fundamental freedoms, the Economic and Social Council may make arrangements with the specialized agencies in respect of their reporting to it on the progress made in achieving the observance of the provisions of the present Covenant falling within the scope of their activities. These reports may include particulars of decisions and recommendations on such implementation adopted by their competent organs.

Article 19

The Economic and Social Council may transmit to the Commission on Human Rights for study and general recommendation or as appropriate for information the reports concerning human rights submitted by States in accordance with articles 16 and 17, and those concerning human rights submitted by the specialized agencies in accordance with article 18.

Article 20

The States Parties to the present Covenant and the specialized agencies concerned may submit comments to the Economic and Social Council on any general recommendation under article 19 or reference to such general recommendation in any report of the Commission on Human Rights or any documentation referred to therein.

Article 21

The Economic and Social Council may submit from time to time to the General Assembly reports with recommendations of a general nature and a summary of the information received from the States Parties to the present Covenant and the specialized agencies on the measures taken and the progress made in achieving general observance of the rights recognized in the present Covenant.

Article 22

The Economic and Social Council may bring to the attention of other organs of the United Nations, their subsidiary organs and specialized agencies concerned with furnishing technical assistance any matters arising out of the reports referred to in this part of the present Covenant which may assist such bodies in deciding, each within its field of competence, on the advisability of international measures likely to contribute to the effective progressive implementation of the present Covenant.

Article 23

The States Parties to the present Covenant agree that international action for the achievement of the rights recognized in the present Covenant includes such methods as the conclusion of conventions, the adoption of recommendations, the furnishing of technical assistance and the holding of regional meetings and technical meetings for the purpose of consultation and study organized in conjunction with the Governments concerned.

Article 24

Nothing in the present Covenant shall be interpreted as impairing the provisions of the Charter of the United Nations and of the constitutions of the specialized agencies which define the respective responsibilities of the various organs of the United Nations and of the specialized agencies in regard to the matters dealt with in the present Covenant.

Article 25

Nothing in the present Covenant shall be interpreted as impairing the inherent right of all peoples to enjoy and utilize fully and freely their natural wealth and resources. . . .

INTERNATIONAL CONVENTION ON THE ELIMINATION OF ALL FORMS OF RACIAL DISCRIMINATION

March 7, 1966, 660 U.N.T.S. 195*

The States Parties to this Convention,

Considering that the Charter of the United Nations is based on the principles of the dignity and equality inherent in all human beings, and that all Member States have pledged themselves to take joint and separate action, in co-operation with the Organization, for the achievement of one of the purposes of the United Nations which is to promote and encourage universal respect for and observance of human rights and fundamental freedoms for all, without distinction as to race, sex, language or religion,

Considering that the Universal Declaration of Human Rights proclaims that all human beings are born free and equal in dignity and rights and that everyone is entitled to all the rights and freedoms set out therein, without distinction of any kind, in particular as to race, colour or national origin,

Considering that all human beings are equal before the law and are entitled to equal protection of the law against any discrimination and against any incitement to discrimination, . . .

Convinced that any doctrine of superiority based on racial differentiation is scientifically false, morally condemnable, socially unjust and dangerous, and that there is no justification for racial discrimination, in theory or in practice, anywhere,

Reaffirming that discrimination between human beings on the grounds of race, colour or ethnic origin in an obstacle to friendly and peaceful

---

*Adopted by the U.N. General Assembly at New York on December 21, 1965. G.A. Res. 2106. Entered into force on January 4, 1969. The United States has not ratified the convention.

The 125 parties to the convention are: Algeria, Afghanistan, Antigua and Barbuda, Argentina, Australia, Austria, The Bahamas, Bangladesh, Barbados, Belgium, Bolivia, Botswana, Brazil, Bulgaria, Burkina Faso, Burundi, Byelorussian SSR, Cameroon, Canada, Cape Verde, Central African Republic, Chad, Chile, China, Colombia, Costa Rica, Cote d'Ivoire, Congo, Cuba, Cyprus, Czechoslovakia, Democratic Kampuchea, Democratic Yemen, Denmark, Dominican Republic, Ecuador, Egypt, El Salvador, Ethiopia, Fiji, Finland, France, Gabon, Gambia, German Democratic Republic, Germany (Federal Republic), Ghana, Greece, Guatemala, Guinea, Guyana, Haiti, Holy See, Hungary, Iceland, India, Iran (Islamic Republic), Iraq, Israel, Italy, Jamaica, Jordan, Kuwait, Lao People's Democratic Republic, Lebanon, Lesotho, Liberia, Libyan Arab Jamahiriya, Luxembourg, Madagascar, Maldives, Mali, Malta, Mauritania, Mauritius, Mexico, Mongolia, Morocco, Mozambique, Namibia, Nepal, Netherlands, New Zealand, Nicaragua, Niger, Nigeria, Norway, Pakistan, Panama, Papua New Guinea, Peru, Philippines, Poland, Portugal, Qatar, Republic of Korea, Romania, Rwanda, Saint Vincent & the Grenadines, Senegal, Seychelles, Sierra Leone, Solomon Islands, Somalia, Spain, Sri Lanka, Sudan, Suriname, Swaziland, Sweden, Syrian Arab Republic, Togo, Tonga, Trinidad & Tobago, Tunisia, Uganda, Ukrainian SSR, Union of Soviet Socialist Republics, United Arab Emirates, United Kingdom, United Republic of Tanzania, Uruguay, Venezuela, Vietnam, Yemen, Yugoslavia, Zaire, and Zambia.

relations among nations and is capable of disturbing peace and security among peoples and the harmony of persons living side by side even within one and the same State,

Convinced that the existence of racial barriers is repugnant to the ideals of any human society,

Alarmed by manifestations of racial discrimination still in evidence in some areas of the world and by governmental policies based on racial superiority or hatred, such as policies of *apartheid,* segregation or separation,

Resolved to adopt all necessary measures for speedily eliminating racial discrimination in all its forms and manifestations, and to prevent and combat racist doctrines and practices in order to promote understanding between races and to build an international community free from all forms of racial segregation and racial discrimination, . . .

Have agreed as follows:

Part I

Article 1

1. In this Convention, the term "racial discrimination" shall mean any distinction, exclusion, restriction or preference based on race, colour, descent, or national or ethnic origin which has the purpose or effect of nullifying or impairing the recognition, enjoyment or exercise, on an equal footing, of human rights and fundamental freedoms in the political, economic, social, cultural or any other field of public life.

2. This Convention shall not apply to distinctions, exclusions, restrictions or preferences made by a State Party to this Convention between citizens and non-citizens.

3. Nothing in this Convention may be interpreted as affecting in any way the legal provisions of States Parties concerning nationality, citizenship or naturalization, provided that such provisions do not discriminate against any particular nationality.

4. Special measures taken for the sole purpose of securing adequate advancement of certain racial or ethnic groups or individuals requiring such protection as may be necessary in order to ensure such groups or individuals equal enjoyment or exercise of human rights and fundamental freedoms shall not be deemed racial discrimination, provided, however, that such measures do not, as a consequence, lead to the maintenance of separate rights for different racial groups and that they shall not be continued after the objectives for which they were taken have been achieved.

Article 2

1. States Parties condemn racial discrimination and undertake to pursue by all appropriate means and without delay a policy of eliminating racial discrimination in all its forms and promoting understanding among all races, and, to this end:

(a) Each State Party undertakes to engage in no act or practice of racial discrimination against persons, groups of persons or institutions and to ensure that all public authorities and public institutions, national and local, shall act in conformity with this obligation;

(b) Each State Party undertakes not to sponsor, defend or support racial discrimination by any persons or organizations;

(c) Each State Party shall take effective measures to review governmental, national and local policies, and to amend, rescind or nullify any laws and regulations which have the effect of creating or perpetuating racial discrimination wherever it exists;

(d) Each State Party shall prohibit and bring to an end, by all appropriate means, including legislation as required by circumstances, racial discrimination by any persons, group or organization;

(e) Each State Party undertakes to encourage, where appropriate, integrationist multi-racial organizations and movements and other means of eliminating barriers between races, and to discourage anything which tends to strengthen racial division.

2. States Parties shall, when the circumstances so warrant, take, in the social, economic, cultural and other fields, special and concrete measures to ensure the adequate development and protection of certain racial groups or individuals belonging to them, for the purpose of guaranteeing them the full and equal enjoyment of human rights and fundamental freedoms. These measures shall in no case entail as a consequence the maintenance of unequal or separate rights for different racial groups after the objectives for which they were taken have been achieved.

Article 3

States Parties particularly condemn racial segregation and *apartheid* and undertake to prevent, prohibit and eradicate all practices of this nature in territories under their jurisdiction.

Article 4

States Parties condemn all propaganda and all organizations which are based on ideas or theories of superiority of one race or group of persons of one colour or ethnic origin, or which attempt to justify or promote racial hatred and discrimination in any form, and undertake to adopt immediate and positive measures designed to eradicate all incitement to, or acts of, such discrimination and, to this end, with due regard to the principles embodied in the Universal Declaration of Human Rights and the rights expressly set forth in article 5 of this Convention, *inter alia:*

(a) Shall declare an offence punishable by law all dissemination of ideas based on racial superiority or hatred, incitement to racial discrimination, as well as all acts of violence or incitement to such acts against any race or group of persons of another colour or ethnic origin, and also the provision of any assistance to racist activities, including the financing thereof;

(b) Shall declare illegal and prohibit organizations, and also organized and all other propaganda activities, which promote and incite racial discrimination, and shall recognize participation in such organizations or activities as an offence punishable by law;

(c) Shall not permit public authorities or public institutions, national or local, to promote or incite racial discrimination.

Article 5

In compliance with the fundamental obligations laid down in article 2 of this Convention, States Parties undertake to prohibit and to eliminate racial discrimination in all its forms and to guarantee the right of everyone, without distinction as to race, colour, or national or ethnic origin, to equality before the law, notably in the enjoyment of the following rights:

(a) The right to equal treatment before the tribunals and all other organs administering justice;

(b) The right to security of person and protection by the State against violence or bodily harm, whether inflicted by government officials or by any individual, group or institution;

(c) Political rights, in particular the rights to participate in elections — to vote and to stand for election — on the basis of universal and equal suffrage, to take part in the Government as well as in the conduct of public affairs at any level and to have equal access to public service;

(d) Other civil rights, in particular:

(i) The right to freedom of movement and residence within the border of the State;

(ii) The right to leave any country, including one's own, and to return to one's country;

(iii) The right to nationality;

(iv) The right to marriage and choice of spouse;

(v) The right to own property alone as well as in association with others;

(vi) The right to inherit;

(vii) The right to freedom of thought, conscience and religion;

(viii) The right to freedom of opinion and expression;

(ix) The right to freedom of peaceful assembly and association;

(e) Economic, social and cultural rights, in particular:

(i) The rights to work, to free choice of employment, to just and favourable conditions of work, to protection against unemployment, to equal pay for equal work, to just and favourable remuneration;

(ii) The right to form and join trade unions;

(iii) The right to housing;

(iv) The right to public health, medical care, social security and social services;

(v) The right to education and training;

(vi) The right to equal participation in cultural activities;

(f) The right of access to any place or service intended for use by the general public, such as transport, hotels, restaurants, cafés, theatres and parks.

Article 6

States Parties shall assure to everyone within their jurisdiction effective protection and remedies, through the competent national tribunals and other State institutions, against any acts of racial discrimination which violate his human rights and fundamental freedoms contrary to this Convention, as well as the right to seek from such tribunals just and adequate reparation or satisfaction for any damage suffered as a result of such discrimination.

Article 7

States Parties undertake to adopt immediate and effective measures, particularly in the fields of teaching, education, culture and information, with a view to combating prejudices which lead to racial discrimination and to promoting understanding, tolerance and friendship among nations and racial or ethnical groups, as well as to propagating the purposes and principles of the Charter of the United Nations, the Universal Declaration of Human Rights, the United Nations Declaration on the Elimination of All Forms of Racial Discrimination, and this Convention.

Part II

Article 8

1. There shall be established a Committee on the Elimination of Racial Discrimination (hereinafter referred to as the Committee) consisting of eighteen experts of high moral standing and acknowledged impartiality elected by States Parties from among their nationals, who shall serve in their personal capacity, consideration being given to equitable geographical distribution and to the representation of the different forms of civilization as well as of the principal legal systems.

2. The members of the Committee shall be elected by secret ballot from a list of persons nominated by the States Parties. Each State Party may nominate one person from among its own nationals.

3. The initial election shall be held six months after the date of the entry into force of this Convention. At least three months before the date of each election the Secretary-General of the United Nations shall address a letter to the States Parties inviting them to submit their nominations within two months. The Secretary-General shall prepare a list in alphabetical order of all persons thus nominated, indicating the States Parties which have nominated them, and shall submit it to the States Parties.

4. Elections of the members of the Committee shall be held at a meeting of States Parties convened by the Secretary-General at United Nations Headquarters. At that meeting, for which two-thirds of the States Parties shall constitute a quorum, the persons elected to the Committee shall be those nominees who obtain the largest number of votes and an absolute majority of the votes of the representatives of States Parties present and voting.

5. (*a*) The members of the Committee shall be elected for a term of four years. However, the terms of nine of the members elected at the first election shall expire at the end of two years; immediately after the first election the names of these nine members shall be chosen by lot by the Chairman of the Committee.

(*b*) For the filling of casual vacancies, the State Party whose expert has ceased to function as a member of the Committee shall appoint another expert from among its nationals, subject to the approval of the Committee.

6. States Parties shall be responsible for the expenses of the members of the Committee while they are in performance of Committee duties.

Article 9

1. States Parties undertake to submit to the Secretary-General of the United Nations, for consideration by the Committee, a report on the legislative, judicial, administrative or other measures which they have adopted and which give effect to the provisions of this Convention: (*a*) within one year after the entry into force of the Convention for the State concerned; and (*b*) thereafter every two years and whenever the Committee so requests. The Committee may request further information from the States Parties.

2. The Committee shall report annually, through the Secretary-General, to the General Assembly of the United Nations on its activities and may make suggestions and general recommendations based on the examination of the reports and information received from the States Parties. Such suggestions and general recommendations shall be reported to the General Assembly together with comments, if any, from States Parties.

Article 10

1. The Committee shall adopt its own rules of procedure.
2. The Committee shall elect its officers for a term of two years.
3. The secretariat of the Committee shall be provided by the Secretary-General of the United Nations.
4. The meetings of the Committee shall normally be held at United Nations Headquarters.

Article 11

1. If a State Party considers that another State Party is not giving effect to the provisions of this Convention, it may bring the matter to the attention of the Committee. The Committee shall then transmit the communication to the State Party concerned. Within three months, the receiving State shall submit to the Committee written explanations or statements clarifying the matter and the remedy, if any, that may have been taken by that State.

2. If the matter is not adjusted to the satisfaction of both parties, either by bilateral negotiations or by any other procedure open to them, within six months after the receipt by the receiving State of the initial communication, either State shall have the right to refer the matter again to the Committee by notifying the Committee and also the other State.

3. The Committee shall deal with a matter referred to it in accordance with paragraph 2 of this article after it has ascertained that all available domestic remedies have been invoked and exhausted in the case, in conformity with the generally recognized principles of international law. This shall not be the rule where the application of the remedies is unreasonably prolonged.

4. In any matter referred to it, the Committee may call upon the States Parties concerned to supply any other relevant information.

5. When any matter arising out of this article is being considered by the Committee, the States Parties concerned shall be entitled to send a representative to take part in the proceedings of the Committee, without voting rights, while the matter is under consideration.

Article 12

1. (*a*) After the Committee has obtained and collated all the information it deems necessary, the Chairman shall appoint an *ad hoc* Conciliation Commission (hereinafter referred to as the Commission) comprising five persons who may or may not be members of the Committee. The members of the Commission shall be appointed with the unanimous consent of the parties to the dispute, and its good offices shall be made available to the States concerned with a view to an amicable solution of the matter on the basis of respect for this Convention.

(*b*) If the States parties to the dispute fail to reach agreement within three months on all or part of the composition of the Commission, the members of the Commission not agreed upon by the States parties to the dispute shall be elected by secret ballot by a two-thirds majority vote of the Committee from among its own members.

2. The members of the Commission shall serve in their personal capacity. They shall not be nationals of the States parties to the dispute or of a State not Party to this Convention.

3. The Commission shall elect its own Chairman and adopt its own rules of procedure.

4. The meetings of the Commission shall normally be held at United Nations Headquarters or at any other convenient place as determined by the Commission.

5. The secretariat provided in accordance with article 10, paragraph 3, of this Convention shall also service the Commission whenever a dispute among States Parties brings the Commission into being.

6. The States parties to the dispute shall share equally all the expenses of the members of the Commission in accordance with estimates to be provided by the Secretary-General of the United Nations.

7. The Secretary-General shall be empowered to pay the expenses of the members of the Commission, if necessary, before reimbursement by the States parties to the dispute in accordance with paragraph 6 of this article.

8. The information obtained and collated by the Committee shall be made available to the Commission, and the Commission may call upon the States concerned to supply any other relevant information.

Article 13

1. When the Commission has fully considered the matter, it shall prepare and submit to the Chairman of the Committee a report embodying its findings on all questions of fact relevant to the issue between the parties and containing such recommendations as it may think proper for the amicable solution of the dispute.

2. The Chairman of the Committee shall communicate the report of the Commission to each of the States parties to the dispute. These States shall, within three months, inform the Chairman of the Committee whether or not they accept the recommendations contained in the report of the Commission.

3. After the period provided for in paragraph 2 of this article, the Chairman of the Committee shall communicate the report of the Commission and the declarations of the States Parties concerned to the other States Parties to this Convention.

Article 14

1. A State Party may at any time declare that it recognizes the competence of the Committee to receive and consider communications from individuals or groups of individuals within its jurisdiction claiming to be victims of a violation by that State Party of any of the rights set forth in this Convention. No communication shall be received by the Committee if it concerns a State Party which has not made such a declaration.

2. Any State Party which makes a declaration as provided for in paragraph 1 of this article may establish or indicate a body within its national legal order which shall be competent to receive and consider petitions from individuals and groups of individuals within its jurisdiction who claim to be victims of a violation of any of the rights set forth in this Convention and who have exhausted other available local remedies.

3. A declaration made in accordance with paragraph 1 of this article and the name of any body established or indicated in accordance with paragraph 2 of this article shall be deposited by the State Party concerned with the Secretary-General of the United Nations, who shall transmit copies thereof to the other States Parties. A declaration may be withdrawn at any time by notification to the Secretary-General, but such a withdrawal shall not affect communications pending before the Committee.

4. A register of petitions shall be kept by the body established or indicated in accordance with paragraph 2 of this article, and certified copies of the register shall be filed annually through appropriate channels with the Secretary-General on the understanding that the contents shall not be publicly disclosed.

5. In the event of failure to obtain satisfaction from the body established or indicated in accordance with paragraph 2 of this article, the petitioner shall have the right to communicate the matter to the Committee within six months.

6. (*a*) The Committee shall confidentially bring any communication referred to it to the attention of the State Party alleged to be violating any provision of this Convention, but the identity of the individual or groups of

individuals concerned shall not be revealed without his or their express consent. The Committee shall not receive anonymous communications.

(b) Within three months, the receiving State shall submit to the Committee written explanations or statements clarifying the matter and the remedy, if any, that may have been taken by that State.

7. (a) The Committee shall consider communications in the light of all information made available to it by the State Party concerned and by the petitioner. The Committee shall not consider any communication from a petitioner unless it has ascertained that the petitioner has exhausted all available domestic remedies. However, this shall not be the rule where the application of the remedies is unreasonably prolonged.

(b) The Committee shall forward its suggestions and recommendations, if any, to the State Party concerned and to the petitioner.

8. The Committee shall include in its annual report a summary of such communications and, where appropriate, a summary of the explanations and statements of the States Parties concerned and of its own suggestions and recommendations.

9. The Committee shall be competent to exercise the functions provided for in this article only when at least ten States Parties to this Convention are bound by declarations in accordance with paragraph 1 of this article.

Article 15

1. Pending the achievement of the objectives of the Declaration on the Granting of Independence to Colonial Countries and Peoples, contained in General Assembly resolution 1514 (XV) of 14 December 1960, the provisions of this Convention shall in no way limit the right of petition granted to these peoples by other international instruments or by the United Nations and its specialized agencies.

2. (a) The Committee established under article 8, paragraph 1, of this Convention shall receive copies of the petitions from, and submit expressions of opinion and recommendations on these petitions to, the bodies of the United Nations which deal with matters directly related to the principles and objectives of this Convention in their consideration of petitions from the inhabitants of Trust and Non-Self-Governing Territories and all other territories to which General Assembly resolution 1514 (XV) applies, relating to matters covered by this Convention which are before these bodies.

(b) The Committee shall receive from the competent bodies of the United Nations copies of the reports concerning the legislative, judicial, administrative or other measures directly related to the principles and objectives of this Convention applied by the administering Powers within the Territories mentioned in sub-paragraph (a) of this paragraph, and shall express opinions and make recommendations to these bodies.

3. The Committee shall include in its report to the General Assembly a summary of the petitions and reports it has received from United Nations bodies, and the expressions of opinion and recommendations of the Committee relating to the said petitions and reports.

4. The Committee shall request from the Secretary-General of the

United Nations all information relevant to the objectives of this Convention and available to him regarding the Territories mentioned in paragraph 2 (*a*) of this article.

Article 16

The provisions of this Convention concerning the settlement of disputes or complaints shall be applied without prejudice to other procedures for settling disputes or complaints in the field of discrimination laid down in the constituent instruments of, or in conventions adopted by, the United Nations and its specialized agencies, and shall not prevent the States Parties from having recourse to other procedures for settling a dispute in accordance with general or special international agreements in force between them.

Part III . . .

Article 20

1. The Secretary-General of the United Nations shall receive and circulate to all States which are or may become Parties to this Convention reservations made by States at the time of ratification or accession. Any State which objects to the reservation shall, within a period of ninety days from the date of the said communication, notify the Secretary-General that it does not accept it.

2. A reservation incompatible with the object and purpose of this Convention shall not be permitted, nor shall a reservation the effect of which would inhibit the operation of any of the bodies established by this Convention be allowed. A reservation shall be considered incompatible or inhibitive if at least two-thirds of the States Parties to this Convention object to it.

3. Reservations may be withdrawn at any time by notification to this effect addressed to the Secretary-General. Such notification shall take effect on the date on which it is received. . . .

Article 22

Any dispute between two or more States Parties with respect to the interpretation or application of this Convention, which is not settled by negotiation or by the procedures expressly provided for in this Convention, shall, at the request of any of the parties to the dispute, be referred to the International Court of Justice for decision, unless the disputants agree to another mode of settlement. . . .

CONVENTION ON THE PREVENTION AND PUNISHMENT OF THE CRIME OF GENOCIDE

December 9, 1948, 78 U.N.T.S. 277*

The Contracting Parties,
Having considered the declaration made by the General Assembly of the United Nations in its resolution 96 (I) dated 11 December 1946 that genocide is a crime under international law, contrary to the spirit and aims of the United Nations and condemned by the civilized world;
Recognizing that at all periods of history genocide has inflicted great losses on humanity; and
Being convinced that, in order to liberate mankind from such an odious scourge, international co-operation is required,
Hereby agree as hereinafter provided:

Article I

The Contracting Parties confirm that genocide, whether committed in time of peace or in time of war, is a crime under international law which they undertake to prevent and to punish.

Article II

In the present Convention, genocide means any of the following acts committed with intent to destroy, in whole or in part, a national, ethnical, racial or religious group, as such:

  (a) Killing members of the group;
  (b) Causing serious bodily or mental harm to members of the group;

---

*Adopted by the U.N. General Assembly at New York on December 9, 1948. G.A. Res. 2670. Entered into force on January 12, 1951. The United States ratified the convention on November 25, 1988. See the U. S. reservations next.

The other 101 parties to the convention are: Afghanistan, Albania, Algeria, Antigua and Barbuda, Argentina, Australia, Austria, The Bahamas, Barbados, Belgium, Brazil, Bulgaria, Burkina Faso, Burma, Byelorussian SSR, Canada, Chile, China, Colombia, Costa Rica, Cuba, Cyprus, Czechoslovakia, Democratic Kampuchea, Democratic Yemen, Denmark, Ecuador, Egypt, El Salvador, Ethiopia, Fiji, Finland, France, Gabon, German Democratic Republic, Germany (Federal Republic), Ghana, Greece, Guatemala, Haiti, Honduras, Hungary, Iceland, India, Iran (Islamic Republic), Iraq, Ireland, Israel, Italy, Jamaica, Jordan, Korea (Democratic People's Republic), Lao People's Democratic Republic, Lebanon, Lesotho, Liberia, Luxembourg, Libyan Arab Jamahiriya, Maldives, Mali, Mexico, Monaco, Mongolia, Morocco, Mozambique, Nepal, Netherlands, New Zealand, Nicaragua, Norway, Pakistan, Panama, Papua New Guinea, Peru, Philippines, Poland, Republic of Korea, Romania, Rwanda, Saint Vincent and the Grenadines, Saudi Arabia, Senegal, Spain, Sri Lanka, Sweden, Syrian Arab Republic, Togo, Tonga, Tunisia, Turkey, Ukranian SSR, Union of Soviet Socialist Republics, United Kingdom, United Republic of Tanzania, Uruguay, Venezuela, Viet Nam, Yemen, Yugoslavia, and Zaire.

(c) Deliberately inflicting on the group conditions of life calculated to bring about its physical destruction in whole or in part;
(d) Imposing measures intended to prevent births within the group;
(e) Forcibly transferring children of the group to another group.

Article III

The following acts shall be punishable:

(a) Genocide;
(b) Conspiracy to commit genocide;
(c) Direct and public incitement to commit genocide;
(d) Attempt to commit genocide;
(e) Complicity in genocide.

Article IV

Persons committing genocide or any of the other acts enumerated in article III shall be punished, whether they are constitutionally responsible rulers, public officials or private individuals.

Article V

The Contracting Parties undertake to enact, in accordance with their respective Constitutions, the necessary legislation to give effect to the provisions of the present Convention and, in particular, to provide effective penalties for persons guilty of genocide or of any of the other acts enumerated in article III.

Article VI

Persons charged with genocide or any of the other acts enumerated in article III shall be tried by a competent tribunal of the State in the territory of which the act was committed, or by such international penal tribunal as may have jurisdiction with respect to those Contracting Parties which shall have accepted its jurisdiction.

Article VII

Genocide and the other acts enumerated in article III shall not be considered as political crimes for the purpose of extradition.

The Contracting Parties pledge themselves in such cases to grant extradition in accordance with their laws and treaties in force.

Article VIII

Any Contracting Party may call upon the competent organs of the United Nations to take such action under the Charter of the United Nations as they consider appropriate for the prevention and suppression of acts of genocide or any of the other acts enumerated in article III.

Article IX

Disputes between the Contracting Parties relating to the interpretation, application or fulfilment of the present Convention, including those relating to the responsibility of a State for genocide or for any of the other acts enumerated in article III, shall be submitted to the International Court of Justice at the request of any of the parties to the dispute. . . .

Article XIV

The present Convention shall remain in effect for a period of ten years as from the date of its coming into force.

It shall thereafter remain in force for successive periods of five years for such Contracting Parties as have not denounced it at least six months before the expiration of the current period.

Denunciation shall be effected by a written notification addressed to the Secretary-General of the United Nations. . . .

U.S. RESERVATIONS AND UNDERSTANDINGS TO THE GENOCIDE CONVENTION

28 I.L.M. 782 (1989)*

Reservations:

(1) That with reference to article IX of the Convention, before any dispute to which the United States is a party may be submitted to the jurisdiction of the International Court of Justice under this article, the specific consent of the United States is required in each case.

(2) That nothing in the Convention requires or authorizes legislation or other action by the United States of America prohibited by the Constitution of the United States as interpreted by the United States.

Understandings:

(1) That the term "intent to destroy, in whole or in part, a national, ethnical, racial, or religious group as such" appearing in article II means the specific intent to destroy, in whole or in substantial part, a national, ethnical, racial or religious group as such by the acts specified in article II.

(2) That the term "mental harm" in article II(b) means permanent impairment of mental faculties through drugs, torture or similar techniques.

(3) That the pledge to grant extradition in accordance with a state's laws and treaties in force found in article VII extends only to acts which are criminal under the laws of both the requesting and the requested state and nothing in article VI affects the right of any state to bring to trial before its own tribunals any of its nationals for acts committed outside a state.

(4) That acts in the course of armed conflicts committed without the specific intent required by article II are not sufficient to constitute genocide as defined by this Convention.

(5) That with regard to the reference to an international penal tribunal in article VI of the Convention, the United States declares that it reserves the right to effect its participation in any such tribunal only by a treaty entered into specifically for that purpose with the advice and consent of the Senate.

*The United States ratified the Genocide Convention on November 25, 1988, subject to the following reservations and understandings.

CONVENTION ON THE ELIMINATION OF ALL FORMS OF DISCRIMINATION AGAINST WOMEN

December 18, 1979, 19 I.L.M. 33 (1980)*

The States Parties to the present Convention,

Noting that the Charter of the United Nations reaffirms faith in fundamental human rights, in the dignity and worth of the human person and in the equal rights of men and women,

Noting that the Universal Declaration of Human Rights affirms the principle of the inadmissibility of discrimination and proclaims that all human beings are born free and equal in dignity and rights and that everyone is entitled to all the rights and freedoms set forth therein, without distinction of any kind including distinction based on sex,

Noting that States Parties to the International Covenant on Human Rights have the obligation to secure the equal rights of men and women to enjoy all economic, social, cultural, civil and political rights,

Considering the international conventions concluded under the auspices of the United Nations and the specialized agencies promoting equality of rights of men and women, . . .

Concerned, however, that despite these various instruments extensive discrimination against women continues to exist,

Recalling that discrimination against women violates the principles of equality of rights and respect for human dignity, is an obstacle to the participation of women, on equal terms with men, in the political, social, economic and cultural life of their countries, hampers the growth of the prosperity of society and the family, and makes more difficult the full development of the potentialities of women in the service of their countries and of humanity,

---

*Adopted by the General Assembly of the United Nations on December 18, 1979. G.A. Res. 280. Entered into force on September 3, 1981. The United States has not ratified the convention.

The 100 parties to the convention are: Angola, Antigua & Barbuda, Argentina, Australia, Austria, Bangladesh, Barbados, Belgium, Bhutan, Brazil, Bulgaria, Burkina Faso, Byelorussian SSR, Canada, Cape Verde, Chile, China, Colombia, Congo, Costa Rica, Cuba, Cyprus, Czechoslovakia, Democratic Yemen, Denmark, Dominica, Dominican Republic, Ecuador, Egypt, El Salvador, Equatorial Guinea, Ethiopia, Finland, France, Gabon, German Democratic Republic, Germany (Federal Republic), Ghana, Greece, Guatemala, Guinea, Guinea-Bissau, Guyana, Haiti, Honduras, Hungary, Iceland, Indonesia, Iraq, Ireland, Italy, Jamaica, Japan, Kenya, Lao People's Democratic Republic, Liberia, Libyan Arab Jamahiriya, Luxembourg, Madagascar, Malawi, Mali, Mauritius, Mexico, Mongolia, New Zealand, Nicaragua, Nigeria, Norway, Panama, Paraguay, Peru, Philippines, Poland, Portugal, Republic of Korea, Romania, Rwanda, Saint Kitts and Nevis, Saint-Lucia, Saint Vincent & the Grenadines, Senegal, Sierra Leone, Spain, Sri Lanka, Sweden, Switzerland, Thailand, Togo, Tunisia, Turkey, Uganda, Ukrainian SSR, Union of Soviet Socialist Republics, United Kingdom, United Republic of Tanzania, Uruguay, Venezuela, Viet Nam, Yugoslavia, Zaire, and Zambia.

Concerned that in situations of poverty women have the least access to food, health, education, training and opportunities for employment and other needs,

Convinced that the establishment of the new international economic order based on equity and justice will contribute significantly towards the promotion of equality between men and women,

Emphasizing that the eradication of *apartheid,* of all forms of racism, racial discrimination, colonialism, neo-colonialism, aggression, foreign occupation and domination and interference in the internal affairs of States is essential to the full enjoyment of the rights of men and women,

Convinced that the full and complete development of a country, the welfare of the world and the cause of peace require the maximum participation of women on equal terms with men in all fields,

Bearing in mind the great contribution of women to the welfare of the family and to the development of society, so far not fully recognized, the social significance of maternity and the role of both parents in the family and in the upbringing of children, and aware that the role of women in procreation should not be a basis for discrimination but that the upbringing of children requires a sharing of responsibility between men and women and society as a whole,

Aware that a change in the traditional role of men as well as the role of women in society and in the family is needed to achieve full equality between men and women,

Determined to implement the principles set forth in the Declaration on the Elimination of Discrimination against Women and, for that purpose, to adopt the measures required for the elimination of such discrimination in all its forms and manifestations,

Have agreed on the following:

Part I

Article 1

For the purposes of the present Convention, the term "discrimination against women" shall mean any distinction, exclusion or restriction made on the basis of sex which has the effect or purpose of impairing or nullifying the recognition, enjoyment or exercise by women, irrespective of their marital status, on a basis of equality of men and women, of human rights and fundamental freedoms in the political, economic, social, cultural, civil or any other field.

Article 2

States Parties condemn discrimination against women in all its forms, agree to pursue, by all appropriate means and without delay, a policy of eliminating discrimination against women and, to this end, undertake:

(a) To embody the principle of the equality of men and women in their national Constitutions or other appropriate legislation if not yet incorporated therein, and to ensure, through law and other appropriate means, the practical realization of this principle;

(b) To adopt appropriate legislative and other measures, including sanctions where appropriate, prohibiting all discrimination against women;

(c) To establish legal protection of the rights of women on an equal basis with men and to ensure through competent national tribunals and other public institutions the effective protection of women against any act of discrimination;

(d) To refrain from engaging in any act or practice of discrimination against women and to ensure that public authorities and institutions shall act in conformity with this obligation;

(e) To take all appropriate measures to eliminate discrimination against women by any person, organization or enterprise;

(f) To take all appropriate measures, including legislation, to modify or abolish existing laws, regulations, customs and practices which constitute discrimination against women;

(g) To repeal all national penal provisions which constitute discrimination against women.

Article 3

States Parties shall take in all fields, in particular in the political, social, economic and cultural fields, all appropriate measures, including legislation, to ensure the full development and advancement of women, for the purpose of guaranteeing them the exercise and enjoyment of human rights and fundamental freedoms on a basis of equality with men.

Article 4

1. Adoption by States Parties of temporary special measures aimed at accelerating *de facto* equality between men and women shall not be considered discrimination as defined in this Convention, but shall in no way entail, as a consequence, the maintenance of unequal or separate standards; these measures shall be discontinued when the objectives of equality of opportunity and treatment have been achieved.

2. Adoption by States Parties of special measures, including those measures contained in the present Convention, aimed at protecting maternity, shall not be considered discriminatory.

Article 5

States Parties shall take all appropriate measures:

(a) To modify the social and cultural patterns of conduct of men and women, with a view to achieving the elimination of prejudices and customary and all other practices which are based on the idea of the inferiority or the superiority of either of the sexes or on stereotyped roles for men and women;

(b) To ensure that family education includes a proper understanding of maternity as a social function and the recognition of the common responsibility of men and women in the upbringing and development of their children, it being understood that the interest of the children is the primordial consideration in all cases.

Article 6

States Parties shall take all appropriate measures, including legislation, to suppress all forms of traffic in women and exploitation of prostitution of women.

Part II

Article 7

States Parties shall take all appropriate measures to eliminate discrimination against women in the political and public life of the country and, in particular, shall ensure, on equal terms with men, the right:

(a) To vote in all elections and public referenda and to be eligible for election to all publicly elected bodies;

(b) To participate in the formulation of government policy and the implementation thereof and to hold public office and perform all public functions at all levels of government;

(c) To participate in non-governmental organizations and associations concerned with the public and political life of the country.

Article 8

States Parties shall take all appropriate measures to ensure to women on equal terms with men and, without any discrimination, the opportunity to represent their Governments at the international level and to participate in the work of international organizations.

Article 9

1. States Parties shall grant women equal rights with men to acquire, change or retain their nationality. They shall ensure in particular that neither marriage to an alien nor change of nationality by the husband during marriage shall automatically change the nationality of the wife, render her stateless or force upon her the nationality of the husband.

2. States Parties shall grant women equal rights with men with respect to the nationality of their children.

Part III

Article 10

States Parties shall take all appropriate measures to eliminate discrimination against women in order to ensure to them equal rights with men in the field of education and in particular to ensure, on a basis of equality of men and women:

(a) The same conditions for career and vocational guidance, for access to studies and for the achievement of diplomas in educational establishments of all categories in rural as well as in urban areas; this equality shall be ensured in pre-school, general, technical, professional and higher technical education, as well as in all types of vocational training;

(b) Access to the same curricula, the same examinations, teaching staff with qualifications of the same standard and school premises and equipment of the same quality;

(c) The elimination of any stereotyped concept of the roles of men and women at all levels and in all forms of education by encouraging coeducation and other types of education which will help to achieve this aim and, in particular, by the revision of textbooks and school programmes and the adaptation of teaching methods;

(d) The same opportunities to benefit from scholarships and other study grants;

(e) The same opportunities for access to programmes of continuing education, including adult and functional literacy programmes, particularly those aimed at reducing, at the earliest possible time, any gap in education existing between men and women;

(f) The reduction of female student drop-out rates and the organization of programmes for girls and women who have left school prematurely;

(g) The same opportunities to participate actively in sports and physical education;

(h) Access to specific educational information to help to ensure the health and well-being of families, including information and advice on family planning.

Article 11

1. States Parties shall take all appropriate measures to eliminate discrimination against women in the field of employment in order to ensure, on a basis of equality of men and women, the same rights, in particular:

(a) The right to work as an inalienable right of all human beings;

(b) The right to the same employment opportunities, including the application of the same criteria for selection in matters of employment;

(c) The right to free choice of profession and employment, the right to promotion, job security and all benefits and conditions of service and the right to receive vocational training and retraining, including apprenticeships, advanced vocational training and recurrent training;

(d) The right to equal remuneration, including benefits, and to equal treatment in respect of work of equal value, as well as equality of treatment in the evaluation of the quality of work;

(e) The right to social security, particularly in cases of retirement, unemployment, sickness, invalidity and old age and other incapacity to work, as well as the right to paid leave;

(f) The right to protection of health and to safety in working conditions, including the safeguarding of the function of reproduction.

2. In order to prevent discrimination against women on the grounds of marriage or maternity and to ensure their effective right to work, States Parties shall take appropriate measures:

(a) To prohibit, subject to the imposition of sanctions, dismissal on the grounds of pregnancy or of maternity leave and discrimination in dismissals on the basis of marital status;

(b) To introduce maternity leave with pay or with comparable social benefits without loss of former employment, seniority or social allowances;

(c) To encourage the provision of the necessary supporting social services to enable parents to combine family obligations with work responsibilities and participation in public life, in particular through promoting the establishment and development of a network of childcare facilities;

(d) To provide special protection to women during pregnancy in types of work proved to be harmful to them.

3. Protective legislation relating to matters covered in this article shall be reviewed periodically in the light of scientific and technological knowledge and shall be revised, repealed or extended as necessary.

Article 12

1. States Parties shall take all appropriate measures to eliminate discrimination against women in the field of health care in order to ensure, on a basis of equality of men and women, access to health care services, including those related to family planning.

2. Notwithstanding the provisions of paragraph 1 above, States Parties shall ensure to women appropriate services in connexion with pregnancy, confinement and the post-natal period, granting free services where necessary, as well as adequate nutrition during pregnancy and lactation.

Article 13

States Parties shall take all appropriate measures to eliminate discrimination against women in other areas of economic and social life in order to ensure, on a basis of equality of men and women, the same rights, in particular:

(a) The right to family benefits;

(b) The right to bank loans, mortgages and other forms of financial credit;

(c) The right to participate in recreational activities, sports and in all aspects of cultural life.

Article 14

1. States Parties shall take into account the particular problems faced by rural women and the significant roles which they play in the economic survival of their families, including their work in the nonmonetized sectors of the economy, and shall take all appropriate measures to ensure the application of the provisions of this Convention to women in rural areas.

2. States Parties shall take all appropriate measures to eliminate discrimination against women in rural areas in order to ensure, on a basis of equality of men and women, that they participate in and benefit from rural development and, in particular, shall ensure to such women the right:

(a) To participate in the elaboration and implementation of development planning at all levels;

(b) To have access to adequate health care facilities, including information, counselling and services in family planning;

(c) To benefit directly from social security programmes;

(d) To obtain all types of training and education, formal and nonformal, including that relating to functional literacy, as well as the benefit of all community and extension services, *inter alia,* in order to increase their technical proficiency;

(e) To organize self-help groups and co-operatives in order to obtain equal access to economic opportunities through employment or self-employment;

(f) To participate in all community activities;

(g) To have access to agricultural credit and loans, marketing facilities, appropriate technology and equal treatment in land and agrarian reform as well as in land resettlement schemes;

(h) To enjoy adequate living conditions, particularly in relation to housing, sanitation, electricity and water supply, transport and communications.

Part IV

Article 15

1. States Parties shall accord to women equality with men before the law.

2. States Parties shall accord to women, in civil matters, a legal capacity identical to that of men and the same opportunities to exercise that capacity. They shall in particular give women equal rights to conclude contracts and to administer property and treat them equally in all stages of procedure in courts and tribunals.

3. States Parties agree that all contract and all other private instruments of any kind with a legal effect which is directed at restricting the legal capacity of women shall be deemed null and void.

4. States Parties shall accord to men and women the same rights with regard to the law relating to the movement of persons and the freedom to choose their residence and domicile.

Article 16

1. States Parties shall take all appropriate measures to eliminate discrimination against women in all matters relating to marriage and family relations and in particular shall ensure, on a basis of equality of men and women;

(a) The same right to enter into marriage;

(b) The same right freely to choose a spouse and to enter into marriage only with their free and full consent;

(c) The same rights and responsibilities during marriage and at its dissolution;

(d) The same rights and responsibilities as parents, irrespective of their marital status, in matters relating to their children. In all cases the interests of the children shall be paramount;

(e) The same rights to decide freely and responsibly on the number and spacing of their children and to have access to the information, education and means to enable them to exercise these rights;

(f) The same rights and responsibilities with regard to guardianship, wardship, trusteeship and adoption of children, or similar institutions where these concepts exist in national legislation. In all cases the interest of the children shall be paramount;

(g) The same personal rights as husband and wife, including the right to choose a family name, a profession and an occupation;

(h) The same rights for both spouses in respect of the ownership, acquisition, management, administration, enjoyment and disposition of property, whether free of charge or for a valuable consideration.

2. The betrothal and the marriage of a child shall have no legal effect and all necessary action, including legislation, shall be taken to specify a minimum age for marriage and to make the registration of marriages in an official registry compulsory.

Part V

Article 17

1. For the purpose of considering the progress made in the implementation of present Convention, there shall be established a Committee on the Elimination of Discrimination against Women (hereinafter referred to as the Committee) consisting, at the time of entry into force of the Convention, of 18 and, after its ratification or accession by the thirty-fifth State Party, of 23 experts of high moral standing and competence in the field covered by the Convention. The experts shall be elected by States Parties from among their nationals and shall serve in their personal capacity, consideration being given to equitable geographical distribution and to the representation of the different forms of civilization as well as the principal legal systems.

2. The members of the Committee shall be elected by secret ballot from a list of persons nominated by States Parties. Each State Party may nominate one person from among its own nationals.

3. The initial election shall be held six months after the date of the entry into force of the present Convention. At least three months before the date of each election the Secretary-General of the United Nations shall address a letter to the States Parties inviting them to submit their nominations within two months. The Secretary-General shall prepare a list in alphabetical order of all persons thus nominated, indicating the States Parties which have nominated them, and shall submit it to the States Parties.

4. Elections of the members of the Committee shall be held at a meeting of States Parties convened by the Secretary-General at United Nations Headquarters. At that meeting, for which two thirds of the States Parties shall constitute a quorum, the persons elected to the Committee shall be those nominees who obtain the largest number of votes and an absolute majority of the votes of the representatives of States Parties present and voting.

5. The members of the Committee shall be elected for a term of four years. However, the terms of nine of the members elected at the first election shall expire at the end of two years; immediately after the first election the names of these nine members shall be chosen by lot by the Chairman of the Committee.

6. The election of the five additional members of the Committee shall be held in accordance with the provisions of paragraphs 2, 3 and 4 of the present article following the thirty-fifth ratification or accession. The terms of two of the additional members elected on this occasion shall expire at the end of two years, the names of these two members having been chosen by lot by the Chairman of the Committee.

7. For the filling of casual vacancies, the State Party whose expert has ceased to function as a member of the Committee shall appoint another expert from among its nationals, subject to the approval of the Committee.

8. The members of the Committee shall, with the approval of the General Assembly, receive emoluments from United Nations resources on such terms and conditions as the General Assembly may decide, having regard to the importance of the Committee's responsibilities.

9. The Secretary-General of the United Nations shall provide the necessary staff and facilities for the effective performance of the functions of the Committee under the present Convention.

Article 18

1. States Parties undertake to submit to the Secretary-General of the United Nations, for consideration by the Committee, a report on the legislative, judicial, administrative or other measures which they have adopted to give effect to the provisions of the Convention and on the progress made in this respect:

(a) Within one year after the entry into force for the State concerned;

(b) Thereafter at least every four years and further whenever the Committee so requests.

2. Reports may indicate factors and difficulties affecting the degree of fulfillment of obligations under the present Convention.

Article 19

1. The Committee shall adopt its own rules of procedure.
2. The Committee shall elect its officers for a term of two years.

Article 20

1. The Committee shall normally meet for a period of not more than two weeks annually in order to consider the reports submitted in accordance with article 18 of the present Convention.

2. The meetings of the Committee shall normally be held at United Nations Headquarters or at any other convenient place as determined by the Committee.

Article 21

1. The Committee shall, through the Economic and Social Council, report annually to the General Assembly on its activities and may make suggestions and general recommendations based on the examination of reports and information received from the States Parties. Such suggestions and general recommendations shall be included in the report of the Committee together with comments, if any, from States Parties.

2. The Secretary-General shall transmit the reports of the Committee to the Commission on the Status of Women for its information.

Article 22

Specialized agencies shall be entitled to be represented at the consideration of the implementation of such provisions of the present Convention as fall within the scope of their activities. The Committee may invite the specialized agencies to submit reports on the implementation of the Convention in areas falling within the scope of their activities.

Part VI

Article 23

Nothing in this Convention shall affect any provisions that are more conducive to the achievement of equality between men and women which may be contained:
(a) in the legislation of a State Party; or
(b) in any other international convention, treaty or agreement in force for that State.

Article 24

States Parties undertake to adopt all necessary measures at the national level aimed at achieving the full realization of the rights recognized in the present Convention. . . .

Article 28

1. The Secretary-General of the United Nations shall receive and circulate to all States the text of reservations made by States at the time of ratification or accession.

2. A reservation incompatible with the object and purpose of the present Convention shall not be permitted.

3. Reservations may be withdrawn at any time by notification to this effect addressed to the Secretary-General of the United Nations who shall then inform all States thereof. Such notification shall take effect on the date on which it is received.

Article 29

1. Any dispute between two or more States Parties concerning the interpretation or application of the present Convention which is not settled by negotiation shall, at the request of one of them, be submitted to arbitration. If within six months from the date of the request for arbitration the parties are unable to agree on the organization of the arbitration, any one of those parties may refer the dispute to the International Court of Justice by request in conformity with the Statute of the Court.

2. Each State Party may at the time of signature or ratification of this Convention or accession thereto declare that it does not consider itself bound by paragraph 1 of this article. The other States Parties shall not be bound by paragraph 1 of this article with respect to any State Party which has made such a reservation.

3. Any State Party which has made a reservation in accordance with paragraph 2 of this article may at any time withdraw that reservation by notification to the Secretary-General of the United Nations. . . .

CONVENTION AGAINST TORTURE AND OTHER CRUEL, INHUMAN, OR DEGRADING TREATMENT OR PUNISHMENT

December 10, 1984, 23 I.L.M. 1027 (1984), as modified, 24 I.L.M. 535 (1985)*

The States Parties to this Convention,
Considering that, in accordance with the principles proclaimed in the Charter of the United Nations, recognition of the equal and inalienable rights of all members of the human family is the foundation of freedom, justice and peace in the world,

Recognizing that those rights derive from the inherent dignity of the human person,

Considering the obligation of States under the Charter, in particular Article 55, to promote universal respect for, and observance of, human rights and fundamental freedoms,

Having regard to article 5 of the Universal Declaration of Human Rights and article 7 of the International Covenant on Civil and Political Rights, both of which provide that no one shall be subjected to torture or to cruel, inhuman or degrading treatment or punishment,

Having regard also to the Declaration on the Protection of All Persons from Being Subjected to Torture and Other Cruel, Inhuman or Degrading Treatment or Punishment, adopted by the General Assembly on 9 December 1975,

Desiring to make more effective the struggle against torture and other cruel, inhuman or degrading treatment or punishment throughout the world,

Have agreed as follows:

---

*Adopted, without a vote, by the General Assembly of the United Nations on December 10, 1984. Entered into force on June 26, 1987. The U.S. Senate advised and consented, with reservations, to the convention on October 29, 1990. U.S. ratification is expected.

The 50 parties to the convention are: Afghanistan, Algeria, Argentina, Austria, Australia, Belize, Brazil, Bulgaria, Byelorussian SSR, Cameroon, Canada, Chile, China, Colombia, Czechoslovakia, Denmark, Ecuador, Egypt, Finland, France, German Democratic Republic, Greece, Guinea, Guyana, Hungary, Italy, Luxembourg, Libya, Mexico, Netherlands, New Zealand, Norway, Panama, Peru, Philippines, Poland, Portugal, Senegal, Spain, Sweden, Switzerland, Togo, Tunisia, Turkey, Uganda, Ukrainian SSR, Union of Soviet Socialist Republics, United Kingdom, Uruguay, and Yugoslavia.

Part I

Article 1

1. For the purposes of this Convention, the term "torture" means any act by which severe pain or suffering, whether physical or mental, is intentionally inflicted on a person for such purposes as obtaining from him or a third person information or a confession, punishing him for an act he or a third person has committed or is suspected of having committed, or intimidating or coercing him or a third person, or for any reason based on discrimination of any kind, when such pain or suffering is inflicted by or at the instigation of or with the consent or acquiescence of a public official or other person acting in an official capacity. It does not include pain or suffering arising only from, inherent in or incidental to lawful sanctions.

2. This article is without prejudice to any international instrument or national legislation which does or may contain provisions of wider application.

Article 2

1. Each State Party shall take effective legislative, administrative, judicial or other measures to prevent acts of torture in any territory under its jurisdiction.

2. No exceptional circumstances whatsoever, whether a state of war or a threat of war, internal political instability or any other public emergency, may be invoked as a justification of torture.

3. An order from a superior officer or a public authority may not be invoked as a justification of torture.

Article 3

1. No State Party shall expel, return or extradite a person to another State where there are substantial grounds for believing that he would be in danger of being subjected to torture.

2. For the purpose of determining whether there are such grounds, the competent authorities shall take into account all relevant considerations including, where applicable, the existence in the State concerned of a consistent pattern of gross, flagrant or mass violations of human rights.

Article 4

1. Each State Party shall ensure that all acts of torture are offences under its criminal law. The same shall apply to an attempt to commit torture and to an act by any person which constitutes complicity or participation in torture.

2. Each State Party shall make these offences punishable by appropriate penalties which take into account their grave nature.

Article 5

1. Each State Party shall take such measures as may be necessary to establish its jurisdiction over the offences referred to in article 4 in the following cases:

(a) When the offences are committed in any territory under its jurisdiction or on board a ship or aircraft registered in that State;

(b) When the alleged offender is a national of that State;

(c) When the victim is a national of that State if that State considers it appropriate.

2. Each State Party shall likewise take such measures as may be necessary to establish its jurisdiction over such offences in cases where the alleged offender is present in any territory under its jurisdiction and it does not extradite him pursuant to article 8 to any of the States mentioned in paragraph 1 of this article.

3. This Convention does not exclude any criminal jurisdiction exercised in accordance with internal law.

Article 6

1. Upon being satisfied, after an examination of information available to it, that the circumstances so warrant, any State Party in whose territory a person alleged to have committed any offence referred to in article 4 is present shall take him into custody or take other legal measures to ensure his presence. The custody and other legal measures shall be as provided in the law of that State but may be continued only for such time as is necessary to enable any criminal or extradition proceedings to be instituted.

2. Such State shall immediately make a preliminary inquiry into the facts.

3. Any person in custody pursuant to paragraph 1 of this article shall be assisted in communicating immediately with the nearest appropriate representative of the State of which he is a national, or, if he is a stateless person, with the representative of the State where he usually resides.

4. When a State, pursuant to this article, has taken a person into custody, it shall immediately notify the States referred to in article 5, paragraph 1, of the fact that such person is in custody and of the circumstances which warrant his detention. The State which makes the preliminary inquiry contemplated in paragraph 2 of this article shall promptly report its findings to the said States and shall indicate whether it intends to exercise jurisdiction.

Article 7

1. The State Party in the territory under whose jurisdiction a person alleged to have committed any offence referred to in article 4 is found shall in the cases contemplated in article 5, if it does not extradite him, submit the case to its competent authorities for the purpose of prosecution.

2. These authorities shall take their decision in the same manner as in the case of any ordinary offence of a serious nature under the law of that State. In the cases referred to in article 5, paragraph 2, the standards of evidence required for prosecution and conviction shall in no way be less

stringent than those which apply in the cases referred to in article 5, paragraph 1.

3. Any person regarding whom proceedings are brought in connection with any of the offences referred to in article 4 shall be guaranteed fair treatment at all stages of the proceedings.

Article 8

1. The offences referred to in article 4 shall be deemed to be included as extraditable offences in any extradition treaty existing between States Parties. States Parties undertake to include such offences as extraditable offences in every extradition treaty to be concluded between them.

2. If a State Party which makes extradition conditional on the existence of a treaty receives a request for extradition from another State Party with which it has no extradition treaty, it may consider this Convention as the legal basis for extradition in respect of such offences. Extradition shall be subject to the other conditions provided by the law of the requested State.

3. States Parties which do not make extradition conditional on the existence of a treaty shall recognize such offences as extraditable offences between themselves subject to the conditions provided by the law of the requested State.

4. Such offences shall be treated, for the purpose of extradition between States Parties, as if they had been committed not only in the place in which they occurred but also in the territories of the States required to establish their jurisdiction in accordance with article 5, paragraph 1.

Article 9

1. States Parties shall afford one another the greatest measure of assistance in connection with criminal proceedings brought in respect of any of the offences referred to in article 4, including the supply of all evidence at their disposal necessary for the proceedings.

2. States Parties shall carry out their obligations under paragraph 1 of this article in conformity with any treaties on mutual judicial assistance that may exist between them.

Article 10

1. Each State Party shall ensure that education and information regarding the prohibition against torture are fully included in the training of law enforcement personnel, civil or military, medical personnel, public officials and other persons who may be involved in the custody, interrogation or treatment of any individual subjected to any form of arrest, detention or imprisonment.

2. Each State Party shall include this prohibition in the rules or instructions issued in regard to the duties and functions of any such persons.

Article 11

Each State Party shall keep under systematic review interrogation rules, instructions, methods and practices as well as arrangements for the custody and treatment of persons subjected to any form of arrest, detention or imprisonment in any territory under its jurisdiction, with a view to preventing any cases of torture.

Article 12

Each State Party shall ensure that its competent authorities proceed to a prompt and impartial investigation, wherever there is reasonable ground to believe that an act of torture has been committed in any territory under its jurisdiction.

Article 13

Each State Party shall ensure that any individual who alleges he has been subjected to torture in any territory under its jurisdiction has the right to complain to, and to have his case promptly and impartially examined by, its competent authorities. Steps shall be taken to ensure that the complainant and witnesses are protected against all ill-treatment or intimidation as a consequence of his complaint or any evidence given.

Article 14

1. Each State Party shall ensure in its legal system that the victim of an act of torture obtains redress and has an enforceable right to fair and adequate compensation, including the means for as full rehabilitation as possible. In the event of the death of the victim as a result of an act of torture, his dependents shall be entitled to compensation.

2. Nothing in this article shall affect any right of the victim or other persons to compensation which may exist under national law.

Article 15

Each State Party shall ensure that any statement which is established to have been made as a result of torture shall not be invoked as evidence in any proceedings, except against a person accused of torture as evidence that the statement was made.

Article 16

1. Each State Party shall undertake to prevent in any territory under its jurisdiction other acts of cruel, inhuman or degrading treatment or punishment which do not amount to torture as defined in article 1, when such acts are committed by or at the instigation of or with the consent or acquiescence of a public official or other person acting in an official capacity. In particular, the obligations contained in articles 10, 11, 12 and 13 shall apply with the substitution for references to torture of references to other forms of cruel, inhuman or degrading treatment or punishment.

2. The provisions of this Convention are without prejudice to the provisions of any other international instrument or national law which prohibits cruel, inhuman or degrading treatment or punishment or which relates to extradition or expulsion.

Part II

Article 17

1. There shall be established a Committee against Torture (hereinafter referred to as the Committee) which shall carry out the functions hereinafter provided. The Committee shall consist of ten experts of high moral standing and recognized competence in the field of human rights, who shall serve in their personal capacity. The experts shall be elected by the States Parties, consideration being given to equitable geographical distribution and to the usefulness of the participation of some persons having legal experience.

2. The members of the Committee shall be elected by secret ballot from a list of persons nominated by States Parties. Each State Party may nominate one person from among its own nationals. States Parties shall bear in mind the usefulness of nominating persons who are also members of the Human Rights Committee established under the International Covenant on Civil and Political Rights and who are willing to serve on the Committee against Torture. . . .

5. The members of the Committee shall be elected for a term of four years. They shall be eligible for re-election if renominated. . . .

Article 18

1. The Committee shall elect its officers for a term of two years. They may be re-elected.

2. The Committee shall establish its own rules of procedure, but these rules shall provide, *inter alia,* that:

(a) Six members shall constitute a quorum;

(b) Decisions of the Committee shall be made by a majority vote of the members present.

3. The Secretary-General of the United Nations shall provide the necessary staff and facilities for the effective performance of the functions of the Committee under this Convention. . . .

5. The States Parties shall be responsible for expenses incurred in connection with the holding of meetings of the States Parties and of the Committee, including reimbursement to the United Nations for any expenses, such as the cost of staff and facilities, incurred by the United Nations pursuant to paragraph 3 of this article.

Article 19

1. The States Parties shall submit to the Committee, through the Secretary-General of the United Nations, reports on the measures they have taken to give effect to their undertakings under this Convention, within one year after the entry into force of the Convention for the State Party concerned. Thereafter the States Parties shall submit supplementary reports every four years on any new measures taken and such other reports as the Committee may request.

2. The Secretary-General of the United Nations shall transmit the reports to all States Parties.

3. Each report shall be considered by the Committee which may make such general comments on the report as it may consider appropriate and shall forward these to the State Party concerned. That State Party may respond with any observations it chooses to the Committee.

4. The Committee may, at its discretion, decide to include any comments made by it in accordance with paragraph 3 of this article, together with the observations thereon received from the State Party concerned, in its annual report made in accordance with article 24. If so requested by the State Party concerned, the Committee may also include a copy of the report submitted under paragraph 1 of this article.

Article 20

1. If the Committee receives reliable information which appears to it to contain well-founded indications that torture is being systematically practised in the territory of a State Party, the Committee shall invite that State Party to co-operate in the examination of the information and to this end to submit observations with regard to the information concerned.

2. Taking into account any observations which may have been submitted by the State Party concerned, as well as any other relevant information available to it, the Committee may, if it decides that this is warranted, designate one or more of its members to make a confidential inquiry and to report to the Committee urgently.

3. If any inquiry is made in accordance with paragraph 2 of this article, the Committee shall seek the co-operation of the State Party concerned. In agreement with that State Party, such an inquiry may include a visit to its territory.

4. After examining the findings of its member or members submitted in accordance with paragraph 2 of this article, the Committee shall transmit these findings to the State Party concerned together with any comments or suggestions which seem appropriate in view of the situation.

5. All the proceedings of the Committee referred to in paragraphs 1 to 4 of this article shall be confidential, and at all stages of the proceedings the co-operation of the State Party shall be sought. After such proceedings have been completed with regard to an inquiry made in accordance with paragraph 2, the Committee may, after consultations with the State Party concerned, decide to include a summary account of the results of the proceedings in its annual report made in accordance with article 24.

Article 21

1. A State Party to this Convention may at any time declare under this article that it recognizes the competence of the Committee to receive and consider communications to the effect that a State Party claims that another State Party is not fulfilling its obligations under this Convention. Such communications may be received and considered according to the procedures laid down in this article only if submitted by a State Party which has made a declaration recognizing in regard to itself the competence of the Committee. No communication shall be dealt with by the Committee under this article if it concerns a State Party which has not made such a declaration.

Communications received under this article shall be dealt with in accordance with the following procedure:

(a) If a State Party considers that another State Party is not giving effect to the provisions of this Convention, it may, by written communication, bring the matter to the attention of that State Party. Within three months after the receipt of the communication the receiving State shall afford the State which sent the communication an explanation or any other statement in writing clarifying the matter, which should include, to the extent possible and pertinent, reference to domestic procedures and remedies taken, pending or available in the matter;

(b) If the matter is not adjusted to the satisfaction of both States Parties concerned within six months after the receipt by the receiving State of the initial communication, either State shall have the right to refer the matter to the Committee, by notice given to the Committee and to the other State;

(c) The Committee shall deal with a matter referred to it under this article only after it has ascertained that all domestic remedies have been invoked and exhausted in the matter, in conformity with the generally recognized principles of international law. This shall not be the rule where the application of the remedies is unreasonably prolonged or is unlikely to bring effective relief to the person who is the victim of the violation of this Convention;

(d) The Committee shall hold closed meetings when examining communications under this article;

(e) Subject to the provisions of subparagraph (c), the Committee shall make available its good offices to the States Parties concerned with a view to a friendly solution of the matter on the basis of respect for the obligations provided for in this Convention. For this purpose, the Committee may, when appropriate, set up an *ad hoc* conciliation commission;

(f) In any matter referred to it under this article, the Committee may call upon the States Parties concerned, referred to in subparagraph (b), to supply any relevant information;

(g) The States Parties concerned, referred to in subparagraph (b), shall have the right to be represented when the matter is being considered by the Committee and to make submissions orally and/or in writing;

(h) The Committee shall, within twelve months after the date of receipt of notice under subparagraph (b), submit a report:

(i) If a solution within the terms of subparagraph (e) is reached, the Committee shall confine its report to a brief statement of the facts and of the solution reached;

(ii) If a solution within the terms of subparagraph (e) is not reached, the Committee shall confine its report to a brief statement of the facts; the written submissions and record of the oral submissions made by the States Parties concerned shall be attached to the report. In every matter, the report shall be communicated to the States Parties concerned.

2. The provisions of this article shall come into force when five States Parties to this Convention have made declarations under paragraph 1 of this article. Such declarations shall be deposited by the States Parties with the Secretary-General of the United Nations, who shall transmit copies thereof to the other States Parties. A declaration may be withdrawn at any time by

notification to the Secretary-General. Such a withdrawal shall not prejudice the consideration of any matter which is the subject of a communication already transmitted under this article; no further communication by any State Party shall be received under this article after the notification of withdrawal of the declaration has been received by the Secretary-General, unless the State Party concerned has made a new declaration.

Article 22

1. A State Party to this Convention may at any time declare under this article that it recognizes the competence of the Committee to receive and consider communications from or on behalf of individuals subject to its jurisdiction who claim to be victims of a violation by a State Party of the provisions of the Convention. No communication shall be received by the Committee if it concerns a State Party which has not made such a declaration.

2. The Committee shall consider inadmissible any communication under this article which is anonymous or which it considers to be an abuse of the right of submission of such communications or to be incompatible with the provisions of this Convention.

3. Subject to the provisions of paragraph 2, the Committee shall bring any communications submitted to it under this article to the attention of the State Party to this Convention which has made a declaration under paragraph 1 and is alleged to be violating any provisions of the Convention. Within six months, the receiving State shall submit to the Committee written explanations or statements clarifying the matter and the remedy, if any, that may have been taken by that State.

4. The Committee shall consider communications received under this article in the light of all information made available to it by or on behalf of the individual and by the State Party concerned.

5. The Committee shall not consider any communications from an individual under this article unless it has ascertained that:

(a) The same matter has not been, and is not being, examined under another procedure of international investigation or settlement;

(b) The individual has exhausted all available domestic remedies; this shall not be the rule where the application of the remedies is unreasonably prolonged or is unlikely to bring effective relief to the person who is the victim of the violation of this Convention.

6. The Committee shall hold closed meetings when examining communications under this article.

7. The Committee shall forward its views to the State Party concerned and to the individual.

8. The provisions of this article shall come into force when five States Parties to this Convention have made declarations under paragraph 1 of this article. . . .

Article 23

The members of the Committee and of the ad hoc conciliation commissions which may be appointed under article 21, paragraph 1(e), shall be entitled to the facilities, privileges and immunities of experts on mission for the United Nations as laid down in the relevant sections of the Convention on the Privileges and Immunities of the United Nations.

Article 24

The Committee shall submit an annual report on its activities under this Convention to the States Parties and to the General Assembly of the United Nations.

Part III . . .

Article 30

1. Any dispute between two or more States Parties concerning the interpretation or application of this Convention which cannot be settled through negotiation shall, at the request of one of them, be submitted to arbitration. If within six months from the date of the request for arbitration the Parties are unable to agree on the organization of the arbitration, any one of those Parties may refer the dispute to the International Court of Justice by request in conformity with the Statute of the Court.

2. Each State may, at the time of signature or ratification of this Convention or accession thereto, declare that it does not consider itself bound by paragraph 1 of this article. The other States Parties shall not be bound by paragraph 1 of this article with respect to any State Party having made such a reservation.

3. Any State Party having made a reservation in accordance with paragraph 2 of this article may at any time withdraw this reservation by notification to the Secretary-General of the United Nations. . . .

CONVENTION ON THE RIGHTS OF THE CHILD

November 20, 1989, 28 I.L.M. 1448 (1989)*

Preamble

The States Parties to the present Convention,
Considering that, in accordance with the principles proclaimed in the Charter of the United Nations, recognition of the inherent dignity and of the equal and inalienable rights of all members of the human family is the foundation of freedom, justice and peace in the world,

Bearing in mind, that the peoples of the United Nations have, in the Charter, reaffirmed their faith in fundamental human rights and in the dignity and worth of the human person, and have determined to promote social progress and better standards of life in larger freedom,

Recognizing that the United Nations has, in the Universal Declaration of Human Rights and in the International Covenants on Human Rights, proclaimed and agreed that everyone is entitled to all the rights and freedoms set forth therein, without distinction of any kind, such as race, colour, sex, language, religion, political or other opinion, national or social origin, property, birth or other status,

Recalling that, in the Universal Declaration of Human Rights, the United Nations has proclaimed that childhood is entitled to special care and assistance,

Convinced that the family, as the fundamental group of society and the natural environment for the growth and well-being of all its members and particularly children, should be afforded the necessary protection and assistance so that it can fully assume its responsibilities within the community,

Recognizing that the child, for the full and harmonious development of his or her personality, should grow up in a family environment, in an atmosphere of happiness, love and understanding,

Considering that the child should be fully prepared to live an individual life in society, and brought up in the spirit of the ideals proclaimed in the

---

*Adopted by the U.N. General Assembly at New York on November 28, 1989. Entered into force on September 2, 1990. The United States has not ratified the convention as of October 1990.

As of September 27, 1990, the 45 parties to the convention were: Bangladesh, Belize, Benin, Bhutan, Bolivia, Brazil, Burkina Faso, Chile, Costa Rica, Ecuador, Egypt, El Salvador, France, Gambia, Ghana, Guatemala, Guinea, Guinea-Bissau, Holy See, Honduras, Indonesia, Kenya, People's Democratic Republic of Korea, Mali, Mauritius, Mexico, Mongolia, Nepal, Paraguay, Peru, Philippines, Portugal, Senegal, Seychelles, Sierra Leone, St. Kitts & Nevis, Sudan, Sweden, Togo, Uganda, U.S.S.R., Venezuela, Viet Nam, Zaire, and Zimbabwe.

Charter of the United Nations, and in particular in the spirit of peace, dignity, tolerance, freedom, equality and solidarity,

Bearing in mind that the need to extend particular care to the child has been stated in the Geneva Declaration of the Rights of the Child of 1924 and in the Declaration of the Rights of the Child adopted by the General Assembly on 20 November 1959 and recognized in the Universal Declaration of Human Rights, in the International Covenant on Civil and Political Rights (in particular in articles 23 and 24), in the International Covenant on Economic, Social and Cultural Rights (in particular in article 10) and in the statutes and relevant instruments of specialized agencies and international organizations concerned with the welfare of children, . . .

Taking due account of the importance of the traditions and cultural values of each people for the protection and harmonious development of the child,

Recognizing the importance of international co-operation for improving the living conditions of children in every country, in particular in the developing countries,

Have agreed as follows:

Part I

Article 1

For the purposes of the present Convention, a child means every human being below the age of eighteen years unless, under the law applicable to the child, majority is attained earlier.

Article 2

1. States Parties shall respect and ensure the rights set forth in the present Convention to each child within their jurisdiction without discrimination of any kind, irrespective of the child's or his or her parent's or legal guardian's race, colour, sex, language, religion, political or other opinion, national, ethnic or social origin, property, disability, birth or other status.

2. States Parties shall take all appropriate measures to ensure that the child is protected against all forms of discrimination or punishment on the basis of the status, activities, expressed opinions, or beliefs of the child's parents, legal guardians, or family members.

Article 3

1. In all actions concerning children, whether undertaken by public or private social welfare institutions, courts of law, administrative authorities or legislative bodies, the best interests of the child shall be a primary consideration.

2. States Parties undertake to ensure the child such protection and care as is necessary for his or her well-being, taking into account the rights and duties of his or her parents, legal guardians, or other individuals legally responsible for him or her, and, to this end, shall take all appropriate legislative and administrative measures.

3. States Parties shall ensure that the institutions, services and facilities responsible for the care or protection of children shall conform with the standards established by competent authorities, particularly in the areas of safety, health, in the number and suitability of their staff, as well as competent supervision.

Article 4

States Parties shall undertake all appropriate legislative, administrative, and other measures for the implementation of the rights recognized in the present Convention. With regard to economic, social and cultural rights, States Parties shall undertake such measures to the maximum extent of their available resources and, where needed, within the framework of international co-operation.

Article 5

States Parties shall respect the responsibilities, rights and duties of parents or, where applicable, the members of the extended family or community as provided for by local custom, legal guardians or other persons legally responsible for the child, to provide, in a manner consistent with the evolving capacities of the child, appropriate direction and guidance in the exercise by the child of the rights recognized in the present Convention.

Article 6

1. States Parties recognize that every child has the inherent right to life.
2. States Parties shall ensure to the maximum extent possible the survival and development of the child.

Article 7

1. The child shall be registered immediately after birth and shall have the right from birth to a name, the right to acquire a nationality and, as far as possible, the right to know and be cared for by his or her parents.
2. States Parties shall ensure the implementation of these rights in accordance with their national law and their obligations under the relevant international instruments in this field, in particular where the child would otherwise be stateless.

Article 8

1. States Parties undertake to respect the right of the child to preserve his or her identity, including nationality, name and family relations as recognized by law without unlawful interference.
2. Where a child is illegally deprived of some or all of the elements of his or her identity, States Parties shall provide appropriate assistance and protection, with a view to speedily re-establishing his or her identity.

Article 9

1. States Parties shall ensure that a child shall not be separated from his or her parents against their will, except when competent authorities

subject to judicial review determine, in accordance with applicable law and procedures, that such separation is necessary for the best interests of the child. Such determination may be necessary in a particular case such as one involving abuse or neglect of the child by the parents, or one where the parents are living separately and a decision must be made as to the child's place of residence.

2. In any proceedings pursuant to paragraph 1 of the present article, all interested parties shall be given an opportunity to participate in the proceedings and make their views known.

3. States Parties shall respect the right of the child who is separated from one or both parents to maintain personal relations and direct contact with both parents on a regular basis, except if it is contrary to the child's best interests.

4. Where such separation results from any action initiated by a State Party, such as the detention, imprisonment, exile, deportation or death (including death arising from any cause while the person is in the custody of the State) of one or both parents or of the child, that State Party shall, upon request, provide the parents, the child or, if appropriate, another member of the family with the essential information concerning the whereabouts of the absent member(s) of the family unless the provision of the information would be detrimental to the well-being of the child. States Parties shall further ensure that the submission of such a request shall of itself entail no adverse consequences for the person(s) concerned. . . .

Article 11

1. States Parties shall take measures to combat the illicit transfer and non-return of children abroad.

2. To this end, States Parties shall promote the conclusion of bilateral or multilateral agreements or accession to existing agreements.

Article 12

1. States Parties shall assure to the child who is capable of forming his or her own views the right to express those views freely in all matters affecting the child, the views of the child being given due weight in accordance with the age and maturity of the child.

2. For this purpose, the child shall in particular be provided the opportunity to be heard in any judicial and administrative proceedings affecting the child, either directly, or through a representative or an appropriate body, in a manner consistent with the procedural rules of national law.

Article 13

1. The child shall have the right to freedom of expression; this right shall include freedom to seek, receive and impart information and ideas of all kinds, regardless of frontiers, either orally, in writing or in print, in the form of art, or through any other media of the child's choice.

2. The exercise of this right may be subject to certain restrictions, but these shall only be such as are provided by law and are necessary:

(*a*) For respect of the rights or reputations of others; or

(b) For the protection of national security or of public order (*ordre public*), or of public health or morals.

Article 14

1. States Parties shall respect the right of the child to freedom of thought, conscience and religion.

2. States Parties shall respect the rights and duties of the parents and, when applicable, legal guardians, to provide direction to the child in the exercise of his or her right in a manner consistent with the evolving capacities of the child.

3. Freedom to manifest one's religion or beliefs may be subject only to such limitations as are prescribed by law and are necessary to protect public safety, order, health or morals, or the fundamental rights and freedoms of others.

Article 15

1. States Parties recognize the rights of the child to freedom of association and to freedom of peaceful assembly.

2. No restrictions may be placed on the exercise of these rights other than those imposed in conformity with the law and which are necessary in a democratic society in the interests of national security or public safety, public order (*ordre public*), the protection of public health or morals or the protection of the rights and freedoms of others.

Article 16

1. No child shall be subjected to arbitrary or unlawful interference with his or her privacy, family, home or correspondence, nor to unlawful attacks on his or her honour and reputation.

2. The child has the right to the protection of the law against such interference or attacks.

Article 17

States Parties recognize the important function performed by the mass media and shall ensure that the child has access to information and material from a diversity of national and international sources, especially those aimed at the promotion of his or her social, spiritual and moral well-being and physical and mental health. To this end, States Parties shall:

(a) Encourage the mass media to disseminate information and material of social and cultural benefit to the child and in accordance with the spirit of article 29;

(b) Encourage international co-operation in the production, exchange and dissemination of such information and material from a diversity of cultural, national and international sources;

(c) Encourage the production and dissemination of children's books;

(d) Encourage the mass media to have particular regard to the linguistic needs of the child who belongs to a minority group or who is indigenous;

(e) Encourage the development of appropriate guidelines for the protection of the child from information and material injurious to his or her well-being, bearing in mind the provisions of articles 13 and 18.

Article 18

1. States Parties shall use their best efforts to ensure recognition of the principle that both parents have common responsibilities for the upbringing and development of the child. Parents or, as the case may be, legal guardians, have the primary responsibility for the upbringing and development of the child. The best interests of the child will be their basic concern.

2. For the purpose of guaranteeing and promoting the rights set forth in the present Convention, States Parties shall render appropriate assistance to parents and legal guardians in the performance of their child-rearing responsibilities and shall ensure the development of institutions, facilities and services for the care of children.

3. States Parties shall take all appropriate measures to ensure that children of working parents have the right to benefit from child-care services and facilities for which they are eligible.

Article 19

1. States Parties shall take all appropriate legislative, administrative, social and educational measures to protect the child from all forms of physical or mental violence, injury or abuse, neglect or negligent treatment, maltreatment or exploitation, including sexual abuse, while in the care of parent(s), legal guardian(s) or any other person who has the care of the child. . . .

Article 27

1. States Parties recognize the right of every child to a standard of living adequate for the child's physical, mental, spiritual, moral and social development. . . .

Article 28

1. States Parties recognize the right of the child to education, and with a view to achieving this right progressively and on the basis of equal opportunity, they shall, in particular:

(*a*) Make primary education compulsory and available free to all;

(*b*) Encourage the development of different forms of secondary education, including general and vocational education, make them available and accessible to every child, and take appropriate measures such as the introduction of free education and offering financial assistance in case of need;

(*c*) Make higher education accessible to all on the basis of capacity by every appropriate means;

(*d*) Make educational and vocational information and guidance available and accessible to all children;

(*e*) Take measures to encourage regular attendance at schools and the reduction of drop-out rates. . . .

Article 30

In those States in which ethnic, religious or linguistic minorities or persons of indigenous origin exist, a child belonging to such a minority or who is indigenous shall not be denied the right, in community with other members of his or her group, to enjoy his or her own culture, to profess and practise his or her own religion, or to use his or her own language. . . .

Article 40

1. States Parties recognize the right of every child alleged as, accused of, or recognized as having infringed the penal law to be treated in a manner consistent with the promotion of the child's sense of dignity and worth, which reinforces the child's respect for the human rights and fundamental freedoms of others and which takes into account the child's age and the desirability of promoting the child's reintegration and the child's assuming a constructive role in society.

2. To this end, and having regard to the relevant provisions of international instruments, States Parties shall, in particular, ensure that:

(*a*) No child shall be alleged as, be accused of, or recognized as having infringed the penal law by reason of acts or omissions that were not prohibited by national or international law at the time they were committed;

(*b*) Every child alleged as or accused of having infringed the penal law has at least the following guarantees:

(i) To be presumed innocent until proven guilty according to law;

(ii) To be informed promptly and directly of the charges against him or her, and, if appropriate, through his or her parents or legal guardians, and to have legal or other appropriate assistance in the preparation and presentation of his or her defence;

(iii) To have the matter determined without delay by a competent, independent and impartial authority or judicial body in a fair hearing according to law, in the presence of legal or other appropriate assistance and, unless it is considered not to be in the best interest of the child, in particular, taking into account his or her age or situation, his or her parents or legal guardians;

(iv) Not to be compelled to give testimony or to confess guilt; to examine or have examined adverse witnesses and to obtain the participation and examination of witnesses on his or her behalf under conditions of equality;

(v) If considered to have infringed the penal law, to have this decision and any measures imposed in consequence thereof reviewed by a higher competent, independent and impartial authority or judicial body according to law;

(vi) To have the free assistance of an interpreter if the child cannot understand or speak the language used;

(vii) To have his or her privacy fully respected at all stages of the proceedings.

3. States Parties shall seek to promote the establishment of laws, procedures, authorities and institutions specifically applicable to children alleged as, accused of, or recognized as having infringed the penal law, and, in particular:

(a) The establishment of a minimum age below which children shall be presumed not to have the capacity to infringe the penal law;

(b) Whenever appropriate and desirable, measures for dealing with such children without resorting to judicial proceedings, providing that human rights and legal safeguards are fully respected. . . .

Article 41

Nothing in the present Convention shall affect any provisions which are more conducive to the realization of the rights of the child and which may be contained in:

(a) The law of a State Party; or

(b) International law in force for that State.

Part II

Article 42

States Parties undertake to make the principles and provisions of the Convention widely known, by appropriate and active means, to adults and children alike.

Article 43

1. For the purpose of examining the progress made by States Parties in achieving the realization of the obligations undertaken in the present Convention, there shall be established a Committee on the Rights of the Child, which shall carry out the functions hereinafter provided.

2. The Committee shall consist of ten experts of high moral standing and recognized competence in the field covered by this Convention. The members of the Committee shall be elected by States Parties from among their nationals and shall serve in their personal capacity, consideration being given to equitable geographical distribution, as well as to the principal legal systems.

3. The members of the Committee shall be elected by secret ballot from a list of persons nominated by States Parties. Each State Party may nominate one person from among its own nationals. . . .

6. The members of the Committee shall be elected for a term of four years. They shall be eligible for re-election if renominated. . . .

10. The meetings of the Committee shall normally be held at United Nations Headquarters or at any other convenient place as determined by the Committee. The Committee shall normally meet annually. . . .

Article 44

1. States Parties undertake to submit to the Committee, through the Secretary-General of the United Nations, reports on the measures they have adopted which give effect to the rights recognized herein and on the progress made on the enjoyment of those rights:

(a) Within two years of the entry into force of the Convention for the State Party concerned;

(*b*) Thereafter every five years.

2. Reports made under the present article shall indicate factors and difficulties, if any, affecting the degree of fulfillment of the obligations under the present Convention. Reports shall also contain sufficient information to provide the Committee with a comprehensive understanding of the implementation of the Convention in the country concerned.

3. A State Party which has submitted a comprehensive initial report to the Committee need not, in its subsequent reports submitted in accordance with paragraph 1 (*b*) of the present article, repeat basic information previously provided.

4. The Committee may request from States Parties further information relevant to the implementation of the Convention.

5. The Committee shall submit to the General Assembly, through the Economic and Social Council, every two years, reports on its activities.

6. States Parties shall make their reports widely available to the public in their own countries. . . .

EUROPEAN CONVENTION FOR THE PROTECTION OF HUMAN RIGHTS AND FUNDAMENTAL FREEDOMS

November 4, 1950, 312 U.N.T.S. 221, E.T.S. 5, as amended by Protocol No. 3, E.T.S. 45, Protocol No. 5, E.T.S. 55, and Protocol No. 8, E.T.S. 118*

The Governments signatory hereto, being Members of the Council of Europe,

Considering the Universal Declaration of Human Rights proclaimed by the General Assembly of the United Nations on 10th December 1948;

Considering that this Declaration aims at securing the universal and effective recognition and observance of the Rights therein declared;

Considering that the aim of the Council of Europe is the achievement of greater unity between its Members and that one of the methods by which that aim is to be pursued is the maintenance and further realisation of Human Rights and Fundamental Freedoms;

Reaffirming their profound belief in those Fundamental Freedoms which are the foundation of justice and peace in the world and are best maintained on the one hand by an effective political democracy and on the other by a common understanding and observance of the Human Rights upon which they depend;

Being resolved, as the Governments of European countries which are likeminded and have a common heritage of political traditions, ideals, freedom and the rule of law to take the first steps for the collective enforcement of certain of the Rights stated in the Universal Declaration,

Have agreed as follows;

Article 1

The High Contracting Parties shall secure to everyone within their jurisdiction the rights and freedoms defined in Section 1 of this Convention.

---

*The European Convention was signed at Rome on November 4, 1950. Entered into force on September 3, 1953. The convention was amended by Protocols Nos. 3, 5, and 8, which entered into force on September 21, 1970, on December 20, 1971, and on January 1, 1990, respectively. The convention, as amended, is provided here.

The 23 parties to the convention are: Austria, Belgium, Cyprus, Denmark, Finland, France, Germany (Federal Republic), Greece, Iceland, Italy, Ireland, Liechtenstein, Luxembourg, Malta, Netherlands, Norway, Portugal, San Marino, Spain, Sweden, Switzerland, Turkey, and the United Kingdom. In October 1990, Hungary became the first East European member of the Council of Europe. Its ratification of the European Convention was likely to occur soon. Czechoslovakia, Poland, and Yugoslavia were expected to join the Council in 1991.

Section 1

Article 2

1. Everyone's right to life shall be protected by law. No one shall be deprived of his life intentionally save in the execution of a sentence of a court following his conviction of a crime for which this penalty is provided by law.

2. Deprivation of life shall not be regarded as inflicted in contravention of this Article when it results from the use of force which is no more than absolutely necessary:

(a) in defence of any person from unlawful violence;

(b) in order to effect a lawful arrest or prevent the escape of a person lawfully detained;

(c) in action lawfully taken for the purpose of quelling a riot or insurrection.

Article 3

No one shall be subjected to torture or inhuman or degrading treatment or punishment.

Article 4

1. No one shall be held in slavery or servitude.

2. No one shall be required to perform forced or compulsory labour.

3. For the purpose of this Article the term 'forced or compulsory labour' shall not include:

(a) any work required to be done in the ordinary course of detention imposed according to the provisions of Article 5 of this Convention or during conditional release from such detention;

(b) any service of a military character or, in case of conscientious objectors in countries where they are recognised, service exacted instead of compulsory military service;

(c) any service exacted in case of an emergency or calamity threatening the life or well-being of the community;

(d) any work or service which forms part of normal civic obligations.

Article 5

1. Everyone has the right to liberty and security of person. No one shall be deprived of his liberty save in the following cases and in accordance with a procedure prescribed by law:

(a) the lawful detention of a person after conviction by a competent court;

(b) the lawful arrest or detention of a person for non-compliance with the lawful order of a court or in order to secure the fulfilment of any obligation prescribed by law;

(c) the lawful arrest or detention of a person effected for the purpose of bringing him before the competent legal authority on a reasonable suspicion of having committed an offence or when it is reasonably considered necessary to prevent his committing an offence or fleeing after having done so;

(d) the detention of a minor by lawful order for the purpose of educational supervision or his lawful detention for the purpose of bringing him before the competent legal authority;

(e) the lawful detention of persons for the prevention of the spreading of infectious diseases, of persons of unsound mind, alcoholics or drug addicts or vagrants;

(f) the lawful arrest or detention of a person to prevent his effecting an unauthorised entry into the country or of a person against whom action is being taken with a view to deportation or extradition.

2. Everyone who is arrested shall be informed promptly, in a language which he understands, of the reasons for his arrest and of any charge against him.

3. Everyone arrested or detained in accordance with the provisions of paragraph 1 (c) of this Article shall be brought promptly before a judge or other officer authorized by law to exercise judicial power and shall be entitled to trial within a reasonable time or to release pending trial. Release may be conditioned by guarantee to appear for trial.

4. Everyone who is deprived of his liberty by arrest or detention shall be entitled to take proceedings by which the lawfulness of his detention shall be decided speedily by a court and his release ordered if the detention is not lawful.

5. Everyone who has been the victim of arrest or detention in contravention of the provisions of this Article shall have an enforceable right to compensation.

Article 6

1. In the determination of his civil rights and obligations or of any criminal charge against him, everyone is entitled to a fair and public hearing within a reasonable time by an independent and impartial tribunal established by law. Judgment shall be pronounced publicly but the press and public may be excluded from all or part of the trial in the interests of morals, public order or national security in a democratic society, where the interests of juveniles or the protection of the private life of the parties so require, or to the extent strictly necessary in the opinion of the court in special circumstances where publicity would prejudice the interests of justice.

2. Everyone charged with a criminal offence shall be presumed innocent until proved guilty according to the law.

3. Everyone charged with a criminal offence has the following minimum rights:

(a) to be informed promptly, in a language which he understands and in detail, of the nature and cause of the accusation against him;

(b) to have adequate time and facilities for the preparation of his defence;

(c) to defend himself in person or through legal assistance of his own choosing or, if he has not sufficient means to pay for legal assistance, to be given it free when the interests of justice so require;

(d) to examine or have examined witnesses against him and to obtain the attendance and examination of witnesses on his behalf under the same conditions as witnesses against him;

(e) to have the free assistance of an interpreter if he cannot understand or speak the language used in court.

Article 7

1. No one shall be held guilty of any criminal offence on account of any act or omission which did not constitute a criminal offence under national or international law at the time when it was committed. Nor shall a heavier penalty be imposed than the one that was applicable at the time the criminal offence was committed.

2. This Article shall not prejudice the trial and punishment of any person for any act or omission which, at the time when it was committed, was criminal according to the general principles of law recognised by civilised nations.

Article 8

1. Everyone has the right to respect for his private and family life, his home and his correspondence.

2. There shall be no interference by a public authority with the exercise of this right except such as is in accordance with the law and is necessary in a democratic society in the interests of national security, public safety or the economic well-being of the country, for the prevention of disorder or crime, for the protection of health or morals, or for the protection of the rights and freedoms of others.

Article 9

1. Everyone has the right to freedom of thought, conscience and religion; this right includes freedom to change his religion or belief and freedom, either alone or in community with others and in public or private, to manifest his religion or belief, in worship, teaching, practice and observance.

2. Freedom to manifest one's religion or belief shall be subject only to such limitations as are prescribed by law and are necessary in a democratic society in the interests of public safety, for the protection of public order, health or morals, or for the protection of the rights and freedoms of others.

Article 10

1. Everyone has the right to freedom of expression. This right shall include freedom to hold opinions and to receive and impart information and ideas without interference by public authority and regardless of frontiers. This article shall not prevent States from requiring the licensing of broadcasting, television or cinema enterprises.

2. The exercise of these freedoms, since it carries with it duties and responsibilities, may be subject to such formalities, conditions, restrictions or penalties as are prescribed by law and are necessary in a democratic society, in the interests of national security, territorial integrity or public safety, for the prevention of disorder or crime, for the protection of health or morals, for the protection of the reputation or rights of others, for preventing the disclosure of information received in confidence, or for maintaining the authority and impartiality of the judiciary.

Article 11

1. Everyone has the right to freedom of peaceful assembly and freedom of association with others, including the right to form and join trade unions for the protection of his interests.

2. No restrictions shall be placed on the exercise of these rights other than such as are prescribed by law and are necessary in a democratic society in the interests of national security or public safety, for the prevention of disorder or crime, for the protection of health or morals or for the protection of the rights and freedoms of others. This article shall not prevent the imposition of lawful restrictions on the exercise of these rights by members of the armed forces, of the police or of the administration of the State.

Article 12

Men and women of marriageable age have the right to marry and found a family, according to the national laws governing the exercise of this right.

Article 13

Everyone whose rights and freedoms as set forth in this Convention are violated shall have an effective remedy before a national authority notwithstanding that the violation has been committed by persons acting in an official capacity.

Article 14

The enjoyment of the rights and freedoms set forth in this Convention shall be secured without discrimination on any ground such as sex, race, colour, language, religion, political or other opinion, national or social origin, association with a national minority, property, birth or other status.

Article 15

1. In time of war or other public emergency threatening the life of the nation, any High Contracting Party may take measures derogating from its obligations under this Convention to the extent strictly required by the exigencies of the situation, provided that such measures are not inconsistent with its other obligations under international law.

2. No derogation from Article 2, except in respect of deaths resulting from lawful acts of war, or from Articles 3, 4 (paragraph 1) and 7 shall be made under this provision.

3. Any High Contracting Party availing itself of this right of derogation shall keep the Secretary General of the Council of Europe fully informed of the measures which it has taken and the reasons therefor. It shall also inform the Secretary General of the Council of Europe when such measures have ceased to operate and provisions of the Convention are again being fully executed.

Article 16

Nothing in Articles 10, 11 and 14 shall be regarded as preventing the High Contracting Parties from imposing restrictions on the political activity of aliens.

Article 17

Nothing in this Convention may be interpreted as implying for any State, group or person any right to engage in any activity or perform any act aimed at the destruction of any of the rights and freedoms set forth herein or at their limitation to a greater extent than is provided for in the Convention.

Article 18

The restrictions permitted under this Convention to the said rights and freedoms shall not be applied for any purpose other than those for which they have been prescribed.

Section II

Article 19

To ensure the observance of the engagements undertaken by the High Contracting Parties in the present Convention, there shall be set up:
(a) A European Commission of Human Rights, hereinafter referred to as "the Commission";
(b) A European Court of Human Rights, hereinafter referred to as 'the Court'.

Section III

Article 20

1. The Commission shall consist of a number of members equal to that of the High Contracting Parties. No two members of the Commission may be nationals of the same State.
2. The Commission shall sit in plenary sessions. It may, however, set up Chambers, each composed of at least seven members. The Chambers may examine petitions submitted under Article 25 of this Convention which can be dealt with on the basis of established case law or which raise no

serious question affecting the interpretation or application of the Convention. Subject to this restriction and to the provisions of paragraph 5 of this Article, the Chambers shall exercise all the powers conferred on the Commission by the Convention.

The member of the Commission elected in respect of a High Contracting Party against which a petition has been lodged shall have the right to sit on a Chamber to which that petition has been referred.

3. The Commission may set up committees, each composed of at least three members, with the power, exercisable by a unanimous vote, to declare inadmissible or strike from its list of cases a petition submitted under Article 25, when such a decision can be taken without further examination.

4. A Chamber or committee may at any time relinquish jurisdiction in favour of the plenary Commission, which may also order the transfer to it of any petition referred to a Chamber or committee.

5. Only the plenary Commission can exercise the following powers:

a. the examination of applications submitted under Article 24;

b. the bringing of a case before the Court in accordance with Article 48a.

c. the drawing up of rules of procedure in accordance with Article 36.

Article 21

1. The members of the Commission shall be elected by the Committee of Ministers by an absolute majority of votes, from a list of names drawn up by the Bureau of the Consultative Assembly; each group of the Representatives of the High Contracting Parties in the Consultative Assembly shall put forward three candidates, of whom two at least shall be its nationals.

2. As far as applicable, the same procedure shall be followed to complete the Commission in the event of other States subsequently becoming Parties to this Convention, and in filling casual vacancies.

3. The candidates shall be of high moral character and must either possess the qualifications required for appointment to high judicial office or be persons of recognised competence in national or international law.

Article 22

1. The members of the Commission shall be elected for a period of six years. They may be re-elected. However, of the members elected at the first election, the terms of seven members shall expire at the end of three years.

2. The members whose terms are to expire at the end of the initial period of three years shall be chosen by lot by the Secretary General of the Council of Europe immediately after the first election has been completed.

3. In order to ensure that, as far as possible, one half of the membership of the Commission shall be renewed every three years, the Committee of Ministers may decide, before proceeding to any subsequent election, that the term or terms of office of one or more members to be elected shall be for a period other than six years but not more than nine and not less than three years.

4. In cases where more than one term of office is involved and the Committee of Ministers applies the preceding paragraph, the allocation of

the terms of office shall be effected by the drawing of lots by the Secretary General, immediately after the election.

5. A member of the Commission elected to replace a member whose term of office has not expired shall hold office for the remainder of his predecessor's term.

6. The members of the Commission shall hold office until replaced. After having been replaced, they shall continue to deal with such cases as they already have under consideration.

Article 23

The members of the Commission shall sit on the Commission in their individual capacity.

During their term of office they shall not hold any position which is incompatible with their independence and impartiality as members of the Commission or the demands of this office.

Article 24

Any High Contracting Party may refer to the Commission, through the Secretary General of the Council of Europe, any alleged breach of the provisions of the Convention by another High Contracting Party.

Article 25

1. The Commission may receive petitions addressed to the Secretary General of the Council of Europe from any person, non-governmental organisation or group of individuals claiming to be the victim of a violation by one of the High Contracting Parties of the rights set forth in this Convention, provided that the High Contracting Party against which the complaint has been lodged has declared that it recognises the competence of the Commission to receive such petitions. Those of the High Contracting Parties who have made such a declaration undertake not to hinder in any way the effective exercise of this right.

2. Such declarations may be made for a specific period.

3. The declarations shall be deposited with the Secretary General of the Council of Europe who shall transmit copies thereof to the High Contracting Parties and publish them.

4. The Commission shall only exercise the powers provided for in this Article when at least six High Contracting Parties are bound by declarations made in accordance with the preceding paragraphs.

Article 26

The Commission may only deal with the matter after all domestic remedies have been exhausted, according to the generally recognised rules of international law, and within a period of six months from the date on which the final decision was taken.

Article 27

1. The Commission shall not deal with any petition submitted under Article 25 which:

(a) is anonymous, or

(b) is substantially the same as a matter which has already been examined by the Commission or has already been submitted to another procedure of international investigation or settlement and if it contains no relevant new information.

2. The Commission shall consider inadmissible any petition submitted under Article 25, which it considers incompatible with the provisions of the present Convention, manifestly ill-founded, or an abuse of the right of petition.

3. The Commission shall reject any petition referred to it which it considers inadmissible under Article 26.

Article 28

1. In the event of the Commission accepting a petition referred to it:

a. it shall, with a view to ascertaining the facts, undertake together with the representatives of the parties an examination of the petition and, if need be, an investigation, for the effective conduct of which the States concerned shall furnish all necessary facilities, after an exchange of views with the Commission;

b. it shall at the same time place itself at the disposal of the parties concerned with a view to securing a friendly settlement of the matter on the basis of respect for human rights as defined in this Convention.

2. If the Commission succeeds in effecting a friendly settlement, it shall draw up a Report which shall be sent to the States concerned, to the Committee of Ministers and to the Secretary General of the Council of Europe for publication. This Report shall be confined by brief statements of the facts and of the solution reached.

Article 29

After it has accepted a petition submitted under Article 25, the Commission may nevertheless decide by a majority of two-thirds of its members to reject the petition if, in the course of its examination, it finds that the existence of one of the grounds for non-acceptance provided for in Article 27 has been established.

In such a case, the decision shall be communicated to the parties.

Article 30

1. The Commission may at any stage of the proceedings decide to strike a petition out of its list of cases where the circumstances lead to the conclusion that:

a. the applicant does not intend to pursue his petition, or

b. the matter has been resolved, or

c. for any other reason established by the Commission, it is no longer justified to continue the examination of the petition.

However, the Commission shall continue the examination of a petition if respect for human rights as defined in this Convention so requires.

2. If the Commission decides to strike a petition out of its list after having accepted it, it shall draw up a Report which shall contain a statement of the facts and the decision striking out the petition together with the reasons therefor. The Report shall be transmitted to the parties as well as to the Committee of Ministers for information. The Commission may publish it.

3. The Commission may decide to restore a petition to its list of cases if it considers that the circumstances justify such a course.

Article 31

1. If the examination of the petition has not been completed in accordance with Article 28 (paragraph 2), 29 or 30, the Commission shall draw up a Report on the facts and state its opinion as to whether the facts found disclose a breach by the State concerned of its obligations under the Convention. The individual opinions of members of the Commission on this point may be stated in the Report.

2. The report shall be transmitted to the Committee of Ministers. It shall also be transmitted to the States concerned, who shall be at a liberty to publish it.

3. In transmitting the report to the Committee of Ministers the Commission may make such proposals as it thinks fit.

Article 32

1. If the question is not referred to the Court in accordance with Article 48 of this Convention within a period of three months from the date of the transmission of the report to the Committee of Ministers, the Committee of Ministers shall decide by a majority of two-thirds of the members entitled to sit on the Committee whether there has been a violation of the Convention.

2. In the affirmative case the Committee of Ministers shall prescribe a period during which the High Contracting Party concerned must take the measures required by the decision of the Committee of Ministers.

3. If the High Contracting Party concerned has not taken satisfactory measures within the prescribed period, the Committee of Ministers shall decide by the majority provided for in paragraph 1 above what effect shall be given to its original decision and shall publish the report.

4. The High Contracting Parties undertake to regard as binding on them any decision which the Committee of Ministers may take in application of the preceding paragraphs.

Article 33

The Commission shall meet in camera.

Article 34

Subject to the provisions of Articles 20 (paragraph 3) and 29, the Commission shall take its decisions by a majority of the members present and voting.

Article 35

The Commission shall meet as the circumstances require. The meetings shall be convened by the Secretary General of the Council of Europe.

Article 36

The Commission shall draw up its own rules of procedure.

Article 37

The secretariat of the Commission shall be provided by the Secretary General of the Council of Europe.

Section IV

Article 38

The European Court of Human Rights shall consist of a number of judges equal to that of the Members of the Council of Europe. No two judges may be nationals of the same State.

Article 39

1. The members of the Court shall be elected by the Consultative Assembly by a majority of the votes cast from a list of persons nominated by the Members of the Council of Europe; each Member shall nominate three candidates, of whom two at least shall be its nationals.
2. As far as applicable, the same procedure shall be followed to complete the Court in the event of the admission of new Members of the Council of Europe, and in filling casual vacancies.
3. The candidates shall be of high moral character and must either possess the qualifications required for appointment to high judicial office or be jurisconsults of recognised competence.

Article 40

1. The members of the Court shall be elected for a period of nine years. They may be re-elected. . . .

3. In order to ensure that, as far as possible, one third of the membership of the Court shall be renewed every three years, the Consultative Assembly may decide, before proceeding to any subsequent election, that the term or terms of office of one or more members to be elected shall be for a period other than nine years but not more than twelve and not less than six years.

4. In cases where more than one term of office is involved and the Consultative Assembly applies the preceding paragraph, the allocation of the terms of office shall be effected by the drawing of lots by the Secretary General immediately after the election.

5. A member of the Court elected to replace a member whose term of office has not expired shall hold office for the remainder of his predecessor's term.

6. The members of the Court shall hold office until replaced. After having been replaced, they shall continue to deal with such cases as they already have under consideration.

7. The members of the Court shall sit on the Court in their individual capacity. During their term of office, they shall not hold any position which is incompatible with their independence and impartiality as members of the Court or the demands of this office.

Article 41

The Court shall elect its President and one or two Vice-Presidents for a period of three years. They may be re-elected.

Article 42

The members of the Court shall receive for each day of duty a compensation to be determined by the Committee of Ministers.

Article 43

For the consideration of each case brought before it the Court shall consist of a Chamber composed of nine judges. There shall sit as an ex officio member of the Chamber the judge who is a national of any State Party concerned, or, if there is none, a person of its choice who shall sit in the capacity of judge; the names of the other judges shall be chosen by lot by the President before the opening of the case.

Article 44

Only the High Contracting Parties and the Commission shall have the right to bring a case before the Court.

Article 45

The jurisdiction of the Court shall extend to all cases concerning the interpretation and application of the present Convention which the High Contracting Parties or the Commission shall refer to in accordance with Article 48.

Article 46

1. Any of the High Contracting Parties may at any time declare that it recognises as compulsory *ipso facto* and without special agreement the jurisdiction of the Court in all matters concerning the interpretation and application of the present Convention.

2. The declarations referred to above may be made unconditionally or on condition of reciprocity on the part of several or certain other High Contracting Parties or for a specified period.

3. These declarations shall be deposited with the Secretary General of the Council of Europe who shall transmit copies thereof to the High Contracting Parties.

Article 47

The Court may only deal with a case after the Commission has acknowledged the failure of efforts for a friendly settlement and within the period of three months provided for in Article 32.

Article 48

The following may bring a case before the Court, provided that the High Contracting Party concerned, if there is only one, or the High Contracting Parties concerned, if there is more than one, are subject to the compulsory jurisdiction of the Court or, failing that, with the consent of the High Contracting Party concerned, if there is only one, or of the High Contracting Parties concerned if there is more than one:

(a) the Commission;

(b) a High Contracting Party whose national is alleged to be a victim;

(c) a High Contracting Party which referred the case to the Commission;

(d) a High Contracting Party against which the complaint has been lodged.

Article 49

In the event of dispute as to whether the Court has jurisdiction, the matter shall be settled by decision of the Court.

Article 50

If the Court finds that a decision or a measure taken by a legal authority or any other authority of a High Contracting Party is completely or partially in conflict with the obligations arising from the present Convention, and if the internal law of the said Party allows only partial reparation to be made for the consequences of this decision or measure, the decision of the Court shall, if necessary, afford just satisfaction to the injured party.

Article 51

1. Reasons shall be given for the judgment of the Court.

2. If the judgment does not represent in whole or in part the unanimous opinion of the judges, any judge shall be entitled to deliver a separate opinion.

Article 52

The judgment of the Court shall be final.

Article 53

The High Contracting Parties undertake to abide by the decision of the Court in any case to which they are parties.

Article 54

The judgment of the Court shall be transmitted to the Committee of Ministers which shall supervise its execution.

Article 55

The Court shall draw up its own rules and shall determine its own procedure.

Article 56

1. The first election of the members of the Court shall take place after the declarations by the High Contracting Parties mentioned in Article 46 have reached a total of eight. . . .

Section V

Article 57

On receipt of a request from the Secretary General of the Council of Europe any High Contracting Party shall furnish an explanation of the manner in which its internal law ensures the effective implementation of any of the provision of this Convention.

Article 58

The expenses of the Commission and the Court shall be borne by the Council of Europe.

Article 59

The members of the Commission and the Court shall be entitled, during the discharge of their functions, to the privileges and immunities provided for in Article 40 of the Statute of the Council of Europe and in the agreements made thereunder.

Article 60

Nothing in this Convention shall be construed as limiting or derogating from any of the human rights and fundamental freedoms which may be ensured under the laws of any High Contracting Party or under any other agreement to which it is a Party.

Article 61

Nothing in this Convention shall prejudice the powers conferred on the Committee of Ministers by the Statute of the Council of Europe.

Article 62

The High Contracting Parties agree that, except by special agreement, they will not avail themselves of treaties, conventions or declarations in force between them for the purpose of submitting, by way of petition, a dispute arising out of the interpretation or application of this Convention to a means of settlement other than those provided for in this Convention.

Article 63

1. Any State may at the time of its ratification or at any time thereafter declare by notification addressed to the Secretary General of the Council of Europe that the present Convention shall extend to all or any of the territories for whose international relations it is responsible.

2. The Convention shall extend to the territory or territories named in the notification as from the thirtieth day after the receipt of this notification by the Secretary General of the Council of Europe.

3. The provisions of this Convention shall be applied in such territories with due regard, however, to local requirements.

4. Any State which has made a declaration in accordance with paragraph 1 of this Article may at any time thereafter declare on behalf of one or more of the territories to which the declaration relates that it accepts the competence of the Commission to receive petitions from individuals, non-governmental organisations or groups of individuals in accordance with Article 25 of the present Convention.

Article 64

1. Any State may, when signing this Convention or when depositing its instrument of ratification, make a reservation in respect of any particular provision of the Convention to the extent that any law then in force in its territory is not in conformity with the provision. Reservations of a general character shall not be permitted under this Article.

2. Any reservation made under this Article shall contain a brief statement of the law concerned.

Article 65

1. A High Contracting Party may denounce the present Convention only after the expiry of five years from the date on which it became a Party to it and after six months' notice contained in a notification addressed to the Secretary General of the Council of Europe, who shall inform the other High Contracting Parties.

2. Such a denunciation shall not have the effect of releasing the High Contracting Party concerned from its obligations under this Convention in respect of any act which, being capable of constituting a violation of such obligations, may have been performed by it before the date at which the denunciation became effective.

3. Any High Contracting Party which shall cease to be a member of the Council of Europe shall cease to be a Party to this Convention under the same conditions.

4. The Convention may be denounced in accordance with the provi-

sions of the preceding paragraphs in respect of any territory to which it has been declared to extend under the terms of Article 63.

Article 66

1. This Convention shall be open to the signature of the Members of the Council of Europe. It shall be ratified. Ratifications shall be deposited with the Secretary General of the Council of Europe.

2. The present Convention shall come into force after the deposit of ten instruments of ratification.

3. As regards any signatory ratifying subsequently, the Convention shall come into force at the date of the deposit of its instrument of ratification.

4. The Secretary General of the Council of Europe shall notify all Members of the Council of Europe of the entry into force of the Convention, the names of the High Contracting Parties who have ratified it, and the deposit of all instruments of ratification which may be effected subsequently.

PROTOCOLS TO THE EUROPEAN CONVENTION FOR THE PROTECTION OF HUMAN RIGHTS AND FUNDAMENTAL FREEDOMS

PROTOCOL NO. 1
March 20, 1952, 213 U.N.T.S. 262, E.T.S. 9*

The Governments signatory hereto, being Members of the Council of Europe,

Being resolved to take steps to ensure the collective enforcement of certain rights and freedoms other than those already included in Section I of the Convention for the Protection of Human Rights and Fundamental Freedoms signed at Rome on 4th November, 1950 (hereinafter referred to as "the Convention"),

Have agreed as follows:

Article 1

Every natural or legal person is entitled to the peaceful enjoyment of his possessions. No one shall be deprived of his possessions except in the public interest and subject to the conditions provided for by law and by the general principles of international law.

The preceding provisions shall not, however, in any way impair the right of a State to enforce such laws as it deems necessary to control the use of property in accordance with the general interest or to secure the payment of taxes or other contributions or penalties.

Article 2

No person shall be denied the right to education. In the exercise of any functions which it assumes in relation to education and to teaching, the State shall respect the right of parents to ensure such education and teaching in conformity with their own religious and philosophical convictions.

Article 3

The High Contracting Parties undertake to hold free elections at reasonable intervals by secret ballot, under conditions which will ensure the free expression of the opinion of the people in the choice of the legislature.

---

*Done at Paris on March 20, 1952. Entered into force on May 18, 1954. The parties to the protocol include all the parties to the European Convention, except for Liechtenstein, Spain, and Switzerland.

Article 4

Any High Contracting Party may at the time of signature or ratification or at any time thereafter communicate to the Secretary-General of the Council of Europe a declaration stating the extent to which it undertakes that the provisions of the present Protocol shall apply to such of the territories for the international relations of which it is responsible as are named therein.

Any High Contracting Party which has communicated a declaration in virtue of the preceding paragraph may from time to time communicate a further declaration modifying the terms of any former declaration or terminating the application of the provisions of this Protocol in respect of any territory.

A declaration made in accordance with this Article shall be deemed to have been made in accordance with Paragraph (1) of Article 63 of the Convention.

Article 5

As between the High Contracting Parties the provisions of Articles 1, 2, 3 and 4 of this Protocol shall be regarded as additional Articles to the Convention and all the provisions of the Convention shall apply accordingly. . . .

PROTOCOL NO. 2
May 6, 1963, E.T.S. 44, 58 A.J.I.L. 331 (1964)*

Conferring upon the European Court of Human Rights Competence to Give Advisory Opinions . . .

Article 1

1. The Court may, at the request of the Committee of Ministers, give advisory opinions on legal questions concerning the interpretation of the Convention and the Protocols thereto.

2. Such opinions shall not deal with any question relating to the content or scope of the rights or freedoms defined in Section 1 of the Convention and in the Protocols thereto, or with any other questions which the Commission, the Court or the Committee of Ministers might have to consider in consequence of any such proceedings as could be instituted in accordance with the Convention.

3. Decisions of the Committee of Ministers to request an advisory opinion of the Court shall require a two-thirds majority vote of the representatives entitled to sit on the Committee.

*Done at Strasbourg, France, on May 6, 1963. Entered into force on September 21, 1970. The parties to the protocol include all the parties to the European Convention.

Article 2

The Court shall decide whether a request for an advisory opinion submitted by the Committee of Ministers is within its consultative competence as defined in Article 1 of this Protocol.

Article 3

1. For the consideration of requests for an advisory opinion, the Court shall sit in plenary session.
2. Reasons shall be given for advisory opinions of the Court.
3. If the advisory opinion does not represent in whole or in part the unanimous opinion of the judges, any judge shall be entitled to deliver a separate opinion.
4. Advisory opinions of the Court shall be communicated to the Committee of Ministers.

Article 4

The powers of the Court under Article 55 of the Convention shall extend to the drawing up of such rules and the determination of such procedure as the Court may think necessary for the purposes of this Protocol.

Article 5

1. . . .
2. This Protocol shall enter into force as soon as all States Parties to the Convention shall have become Parties to the Protocol, in accordance with the provisions of paragraph 1 of this article.
3. From the date of the entry into force of this Protocol, Articles 1 to 4 shall be considered an integral part of the Convention. . . .

PROTOCOL NO. 4
September 16, 1963, E.T.S. 46, 7 I.L.M. 978 (1986)*

Securing Certain Rights and Freedoms Other Than Those Already Included in the Convention and in the First Protocol Thereto

PREAMBLE . . .

Article 1

No one shall be deprived of his liberty merely on the ground of inability to fulfil a contractual obligation.

---

*Done at Strasbourg on September 16, 1963. Entered into force on May 2, 1968. The parties to the protocol include all the parties to the European Convention except Cyprus, Greece, Liechtenstein, Malta, Spain, Switzerland, Turkey, and the United Kingdom.

Article 2

1. Everyone lawfully within the territory of a state shall, within that territory, have the right to liberty of movement and freedom to choose his residence.

2. Everyone shall be free to leave any country, including his own.

3. No restrictions shall be placed on the exercise of these rights other than such as are in accordance with law and are necessary in a democratic society in the interests of national security or public safety, for the maintenance of "ordre public," for the prevention of crime, for the protection of health or morals, or for the protection of the rights and freedoms of others.

4. The rights set forth in paragraph 1 may also be subject, in particular areas, to restrictions imposed in accordance with law and justified by the public interest in a democratic society.

Article 3

1. No one shall be expelled, by means either of an individual or of a collective measure, from the territory of the state of which he is a national.

2. No one shall be deprived of the right to enter the territory of the state of which he is a national.

Article 4

Collective expulsion of aliens is prohibited. . . .

Article 6

1. As between the High Contracting Parties the provisions of Articles 1 to 5 of this Protocol shall be regarded as additional articles to the Convention, and all the provisions of the Convention shall apply accordingly.

2. Nevertheless, the right of individual recourse recognised by a declaration made under Article 25 of the Convention, or the acceptance of the compulsory jurisdiction of the Court by a declaration made under Article 46 of the Convention, shall not be effective in relation to this Protocol unless the High Contracting Party concerned has made a statement recognising such right, or accepting such jurisdiction, in respect of all or any of Articles 1 to 4 of the Protocol. . . .

PROTOCOL NO. 6
April 28, 1983, 22 I.L.M. 538 (1963)*

Article 1

The death penalty shall be abolished. No one shall be condemned to such penalty or executed.

---

*Done at Strasbourg on April 28, 1983. Entered into force on March 1, 1985. The parties to the protocol include all the parties to the European Convention except Cyprus, Ireland, Liechtenstein, Malta, Turkey, and the United Kingdom.

Article 2

A State may make provision in its law for the death penalty in respect of acts committed in time of war or of imminent threat of war; such penalty shall be applied only in the instances laid down in the law and in accordance with its provisions. The State shall communicate to the Secretary General of the Council of Europe the relevant provisions of that law.

Article 3

No derogation from the provisions of this Protocol shall be made under Article 15 of the Convention.

Article 4

No reservation may be made under Article 64 of the Convention in respect of the provisions of this Protocol. . . .

Article 6

As between the States Parties the provisions of Articles 1 to 5 of this Protocol shall be regarded as additional articles to the Convention and all the provisions of the Convention shall apply accordingly. . . .

PROTOCOL NO. 7
November 22, 1984, 24 I.L.M. 535*

Article 1

1. An alien lawfully resident in the territory of a State shall not be expelled therefrom except in pursuance of a decision reached in accordance with law and shall be allowed:
   a. to submit reasons against his expulsion,
   b. to have his case reviewed, and
   c. to be represented for these purposes before the competent authority or a person or persons designated by that authority.
2. An alien may be expelled before the exercise of his rights under paragraph 1. a, b and c of this Article, when such expulsion is necessary in the interests of public order or is grounded on reasons of national security.

Article 2

1. Everyone convicted of a criminal offence by a tribunal shall have the right to have conviction or sentence reviewed by a higher tribunal. The exercise of this right, including the grounds on which it may be exercised, shall be governed by law.

---

*Done at Strasbourg on November 22, 1984. Entered into force on November 1, 1988. The parties to the protocol include all the parties to the European Convention, except for Belgium, Cyprus, the Federal Republic of Germany, Ireland, Italy, Liechtenstein, Malta, Netherlands, Portugal, Spain, Turkey, and the United Kingdom.

2. This right may be subject to exceptions in regard to offences of a minor character, as prescribed by law, or in cases in which the person concerned was tried in the first instance by the highest tribunal or was convicted following an appeal against acquittal.

Article 3

When a person has by a final decision been convicted of a criminal offence and when subsequently his conviction has been reversed, or he has been pardoned, on the ground that a new or newly discovered fact shows conclusively that there has been a miscarriage of justice, the person who has suffered punishment as a result of such conviction shall be compensated according to the law or the practice of the State concerned, unless it is proved that the nondisclosure of the unknown fact in time is wholly or partly attributable to him.

Article 4

1. No one shall be liable to be tried or punished again in criminal proceedings under the jurisdiction of the same State for an offence for which he has already been finally acquitted or convicted in accordance with the law and penal procedure of that State.

2. The provisions of the preceding paragraph shall not prevent the reopening of the case in accordance with the law and penal procedure of the State concerned, if there is evidence of new or newly discovered facts, or if there has been a fundamental defect in the previous proceedings, which could affect the outcome of the case.

3. No derogation from this Article shall be made under Article 15 of the Convention.

Article 5

Spouses shall enjoy equality of rights and responsibilities of a private law character between them, and in their relations with their children, as to marriage, during marriage and in the event of its dissolution. This Article shall not prevent States from taking such measures as are necessary in the interests of the children. . . .

Article 7

1. As between the States Parties, the provisions of Articles 1 to 6 of this Protocol shall be regarded as additional Articles to the Convention, and all the provisions of the Convention shall apply accordingly.

2. Nevertheless, the right of individual recourse recognised by a declaration made under Article 25 of the Convention, or the acceptance of the compulsory jurisdiction of the Court by a declaration made under Article 46 of the Convention, shall not be effective in relation to this Protocol unless the State concerned has made a statement recognising such right, or accepting such jurisdiction in respect of Articles 1 to 5 of this Protocol. . . .

AMERICAN CONVENTION ON HUMAN RIGHTS

November 22, 1969, 9 I.L.M. 673 (1970)*

Preamble

The American states signatory to the present Convention,

Reaffirming their intention to consolidate in this hemisphere, within the framework of democratic institutions, a system of personal liberty and social justice based on respect for the essential rights of man;

Recognizing that the essential rights of man are not derived from one's being a national of a certain state, but are based upon attributes of the human personality, and that they therefore justify international protection in the form of a convention reinforcing or complementing the protection provided by the domestic law of the American states;

Considering that these principles have been set forth in the Charter of the Organization of American States, in the American Declaration of the Rights and Duties of Man, and in the Universal Declaration of Human Rights, and that they have been reaffirmed and refined in other international instruments, worldwide as well as regional in scope;

Reiterating that, in accordance with the Universal Declaration of Human Rights, the ideal of free men enjoying freedom from fear and want can be achieved only if conditions are created whereby everyone may enjoy his economic, social, and cultural rights, as well as his civil and political rights; . . .

Have agreed upon the following:

Part I — State Obligations and Rights Protected

CHAPTER I — GENERAL OBLIGATIONS

Article 1. Obligation to Respect Rights

1. The States Parties to this Convention undertake to respect the rights and freedoms recognized herein and to ensure to all persons subject to their jurisdiction the free and full exercise of those rights and freedoms, without

---

*Signed at San Jose, Costa Rica on November 22, 1969. Entered into force on July 18, 1978. The United States has not ratified the convention.

The 20 parties to the convention are: Argentina, Barbados, Bolivia, Colombia, Costa Rica, Dominican Republic, Ecuador, El Salvador, Grenada, Guatemala, Haiti, Honduras, Jamaica, Mexico, Nicaragua, Panama, Peru, Suriname, Uruguay, and Venezuela.

any discrimination for reasons of race, color, sex, language, religion, political or other opinion, national or social origin, economic status, birth, or any other social condition.

2. For the purposes of this Convention, "person" means every human being.

Article 2. Domestic Legal Effects

Where the exercise of any of the rights or freedoms referred to in Article 1 is not already ensured by legislative or other provisions, the States Parties undertake to adopt, in accordance with their constitutional processes and the provisions of this Convention, such legislative or other measures as may be necessary to give effect to those rights or freedoms.

CHAPTER II — CIVIL AND POLITICAL RIGHTS

Article 3. Right to Juridical Personality

Every person has the right to recognition as a person before the law.

Article 4. Right to Life

1. Every person has the right to have his life respected. This right shall be protected by law and, in general, from the moment of conception. No one shall be arbitrarily deprived of his life.

2. In countries that have not abolished the death penalty, it may be imposed only for the most serious crimes and pursuant to a final judgment rendered by a competent court and in accordance with a law establishing such punishment, enacted prior to the commission of the crime. The application of such punishment shall not be extended to crimes to which it does not presently apply.

3. The death penalty shall not be reestablished in states that have abolished it.

4. In no case shall capital punishment be inflicted for political offenses or related common crimes.

5. Capital punishment shall not be imposed upon persons who, at the time the crime was committed, were under 18 years of age or over 70 years of age; nor shall it be applied to pregnant women.

6. Every person condemned to death shall have the right to apply for amnesty, pardon, or commutation of sentence, which may be granted in all cases. Capital punishment shall not be imposed while such a petition is pending decision by the competent authority.

Article 5. Right to Humane Treatment

1. Every person has the right to have his physical, mental, and moral integrity respected.

2. No one shall be subjected to torture or to cruel, inhuman, or degrading punishment or treatment. All persons deprived of their liberty shall be treated with respect for the inherent dignity of the human person.

3. Punishment shall not be extended to any person other than the criminal.

4. Accused persons shall, save in exceptional circumstances, be segregated from convicted persons, and shall be subject to separate treatment appropriate to their status as unconvicted persons.

5. Minors while subject to criminal proceedings shall be separated from adults and brought before specialized tribunals, as speedily as possible, so that they may be treated in accordance with their status as minors.

6. Punishments consisting of deprivation of liberty shall have as an essential aim the reform and social readaptation of the prisoners.

Article 6. *Freedom from Slavery*

1. No one shall be subject to slavery or to involuntary servitude, which are prohibited in all their forms, as are the slave trade and traffic in women.

2. No one shall be required to perform forced or compulsory labor. This provision shall not be interpreted to mean that, in those countries in which the penalty established for certain crimes is deprivation of liberty at forced labor, the carrying out of such a sentence imposed by a competent court is prohibited. Forced labor shall not adversely affect the dignity or the physical or intellectual capacity of the prisoner.

3. For the purposes of this article, the following do not constitute forced or compulsory labor:

   a. work or service normally required of a person imprisoned in execution of a sentence or formal decision passed by the competent judicial authority. Such work or service shall be carried out under the supervision and control of public authorities, and any persons performing such work or service shall not be placed at the disposal of any private party, company, or juridical person;

   b. military service and, in countries in which conscientious objectors are recognized, national service that the law may provide for in lieu of military service;

   c. service exacted in time of danger or calamity that threatens the existence or the well-being of the community; or

   d. work or service that forms part of normal civic obligations.

Article 7. *Right to Personal Liberty*

1. Every person has the right to personal liberty and security.

2. No one shall be deprived of his physical liberty except for the reasons and under the conditions established beforehand by the constitution of the State Party concerned or by a law established pursuant thereto.

3. No one shall be subject to arbitrary arrest or imprisonment.

4. Anyone who is detained shall be informed of the reasons for his detention and shall be promptly notified of the charge or charges against him.

5. Any person detained shall be brought promptly before a judge or other officer authorized by law to exercise judicial power and shall be entitled to trial within a reasonable time or to be released without prejudice to

the continuation of the proceedings. His release may be subject to guarantees to assure his appearance for trial.

6. Anyone who is deprived of his liberty shall be entitled to recourse to a competent court, in order that the court may decide without delay on the lawfulness of his arrest or detention order his release if the arrest or detention is unlawful. In States Parties whose laws provide that anyone who believes himself to be threatened with deprivation of his liberty is entitled to recourse to a competent court in order that it may decide on the lawfulness of such threat, this remedy may not be restricted or abolished. The interested party or another person in his behalf is entitled to seek these remedies.

7. No one shall be detained for debt. This principle shall not limit the orders of a competent judicial authority issued for nonfulfillment of duties of support.

Article 8. Right to a Fair Trial

1. Every person has the right to a hearing, with due guarantees and within a reasonable time, by a competent, independent, and impartial tribunal, previously established by law, in the substantiation of any accusation of a criminal nature made against him or for the determination of his rights and obligations of a civil, labor, fiscal, or any other nature.

2. Every person accused of a criminal offense has the right to be presumed innocent so long as his guilt has not been proven according to law. During the proceedings, every person is entitled, with full equality, to the following minimum guarantees:

    a. the right of the accused to be assisted without charge by a translator or interpreter, if he does not understand or does not speak the language of the tribunal or court;

    b. prior notification in detail to the accused of the charges against him;

    c. adequate time and means for the preparation of his defense;

    d. the right of the accused to defend himself personally or to be assisted by legal counsel of his own choosing, and to communicate freely and privately with his counsel;

    e. the inalienable right to be assisted by counsel provided by the state, paid or not as the domestic law provides, if the accused does not defend himself personally or engage his own counsel within the time period established by law;

    f. the right of the defense to examine witnesses present in the court and to obtain the appearance, as witnesses, of experts or other persons who may throw light on the facts;

    g. the right not to be compelled to be a witness against himself or to plead guilty; and

    h. the right to appeal the judgment to a higher court.

3. A confession of guilt by the accused shall be valid only if it is made without coercion of any kind.

4. An accused person acquitted by a nonappealable judgment shall not be subjected to a new trial for the same cause.

5. Criminal proceedings shall be public, except insofar as may be necessary to protect the interests of justice.

Article 9. Freedom from Ex Post Facto Laws

No one shall be convicted of any act or omission that did not constitute a criminal offense, under the applicable law, at the time it was committed. A heavier penalty shall not be imposed than the one that was applicable at the time the criminal offense was committed. If subsequent to the commission of the offense the law provides for the imposition of a lighter punishment, the guilty person shall benefit therefrom.

Article 10. Right to Compensation

Every person has the right to be compensated in accordance with the law in the event he has been sentenced by a final judgment through a miscarriage of justice.

Article 11. Right to Privacy

1. Everyone has the right to have his honor respected and his dignity recognized.
2. No one may be the object of arbitrary or abusive interference with his private life, his family, his home, or his correspondence, or of unlawful attacks on his honor or reputation.
3. Everyone has the right to the protection of the law against such interference or attacks.

Article 12. Freedom of Conscience and Religion

1. Everyone has the right to freedom of conscience and of religion. This right includes freedom to maintain or to change one's religion or beliefs, and freedom to profess or disseminate one's religion or beliefs, either individually or together with others, in public or in private.
2. No one shall be subject to restrictions that might impair his freedom to maintain or to change his religion or beliefs.
3. Freedom to manifest one's religion and beliefs may be subject only to the limitations prescribed by law that are necessary to protect public safety, order, health, or morals, or the rights or freedoms of others.
4. Parents or guardians, as the case may be, have the right to provide for the religious and moral education of their children or wards that is in accord with their own convictions.

Article 13. Freedom of Thought and Expression

1. Everyone has the right to freedom of thought and expression. This right includes freedom to seek, receive, and impart information and ideas of all kinds, regardless of frontiers, either orally, in writing, in print, in the form of art, or through any other medium of one's choice.
2. The exercise of the right provided for in the foregoing paragraph shall not be subject to prior censorship but shall be subject to subsequent

imposition of liability, which shall be expressly established by law to the extent necessary to ensure:

    a. respect for the rights or reputations of others; or

    b. the protection of national security, public order, or public health or morals.

3. The right of expression may not be restricted by indirect methods or means, such as the abuse of government or private controls over newsprint, radio broadcasting frequencies, or equipment used in the dissemination of information, or by any other means tending to impede the communication and circulation of ideas and opinions.

4. Notwithstanding the provisions of paragraph 2 above, public entertainments may be subject by law to prior censorship for the sole purpose of regulating access to them for the moral protection of childhood and adolescence.

5. Any propaganda for war and any advocacy of national, racial, or religious hatred that constitute incitements to lawless violence or to any other similar illegal action against any person or group of persons on any grounds including those of race, color, religion, language, or national origin shall be considered as offenses punishable by law.

Article 14. *Right of Reply*

1. Anyone injured by inaccurate or offensive statements or ideas disseminated to the public in general by a legally regulated medium of communication has the right to reply or to make a correction using the same communications outlet, under such conditions as the law may establish.

2. The correction or reply shall not in any case remit other legal liabilities that may have been incurred.

3. For the effective protection of honor and reputation, every publisher, and every newspaper, motion picture, radio, and television company, shall have a person responsible who is not protected by immunities or special privileges.

Article 15. *Right of Assembly*

The right of peaceful assembly, without arms, is recognized. No restrictions may be placed on the exercise of this right other than those imposed in conformity with the law and necessary in a democratic society in the interest of national security, public safety or public order, or to protect public health or morals or the rights or freedoms of others.

Article 16. *Freedom of Association*

1. Everyone has the right to associate freely for ideological, religious, political, economic, labor, social, cultural, sports, or other purposes.

2. The exercise of this right shall be subject only to such restrictions established by law as may be necessary in a democratic society, in the interest of national security, public safety or public order, or to protect public health or morals or the rights and freedoms of others.

3. The provisions of this article do not bar the imposition of legal

restrictions, including even deprivation of the exercise of the right of association, on members of the armed forces and the police.

Article 17. Rights of the Family

1. The family is the natural and fundamental group unit of society and is entitled to protection by society and the state.
2. The right of men and women of marriageable age to marry and to raise a family shall be recognized, if they meet the conditions required by domestic laws, insofar as such conditions do not affect the principle of nondiscrimination established in this Convention.
3. No marriage shall be entered into without the free and full consent of the intending spouses.
4. The States Parties shall take appropriate steps to ensure the equality of rights and the adequate balancing of responsibilities of the spouses as to marriage, during marriage, and in the event of its dissolution. In case of dissolution, provision shall be made for the necessary protection of any children solely on the basis of their own best interests.
5. The law shall recognize equal rights for children born out of wedlock and those born in wedlock.

Article 18. Right to a Name

Every person has the right to a given name and to the surnames of his parents or that of one of them. The law shall regulate the manner in which this right shall be ensured for all, by the use of assumed names if necessary.

Article 19. Rights of the Child

Every minor child has the right to the measures of protection required by his condition as a minor on the part of his family, society, and the state.

Article 20. Right to Nationality

1. Every person has the right to a nationality.
2. Every person has the right to the nationality of the state in whose territory he was born if he does not have the right to any other nationality.
3. No one shall be arbitrarily deprived of his nationality or of the right to change it.

Article 21. Right to Property

1. Everyone has the right to the use and enjoyment of his property. The law may subordinate such use and enjoyment to the interest of society.
2. No one shall be deprived of his property except upon payment of just compensation, for reasons of public utility or social interest, and in the cases and according to the forms established by law.
3. Usury and any other form of exploitation of man by man shall be prohibited by law.

Article 22. Freedom of Movement and Residence

1. Every person lawfully in the territory of a State Party has the right to move about in it, and to reside in it subject to the provisions of the law.

2. Every person has the right to leave any country freely, including his own.

3. The exercise of the foregoing rights may be restricted only pursuant to a law to the extent necessary in a democratic society to prevent crime or to protect national security, public safety, public order, public morals, public health, or the rights or freedoms of others.

4. The exercise of the rights recognized in paragraph 1 may also be restricted by law in designated zones for reasons of public interest.

5. No one can be expelled from the territory of the state of which he is a national or be deprived of the right to enter it.

6. An alien lawfully in the territory of a State Party to this Convention may be expelled from it only pursuant to a decision reached in accordance with law.

7. Every person has the right to seek and be granted asylum in a foreign territory, in accordance with the legislation of the state and international conventions, in the event he is being pursued for political offenses or related common crimes.

8. In no case may an alien be deported or returned to a country, regardless of whether or not it is his country of origin, if in that country his right to life or personal freedom is in danger of being violated because of his race, nationality, religion, social status, or political opinions.

9. The collective expulsion of aliens is prohibited.

Article 23. Right to Participate in Government

1. Every citizen shall enjoy the following rights and opportunities:

   a. to take part in the conduct of public affairs, directly or through freely chosen representatives;

   b. to vote and to be elected in genuine periodic elections, which shall be by universal and equal suffrage and by secret ballot that guarantees the free expression of the will of the voters; and

   c. to have access, under general conditions of equality, to the public service of his country.

2. The law may regulate the exercise of the rights and opportunities referred to in the preceding paragraph only on the basis of age, nationality, residence, language, education, civil and mental capacity, or sentencing by a competent court in criminal proceedings.

Article 24. Right to Equal Protection

All persons are equal before the law. Consequently, they are entitled, without discrimination, to equal protection of the law.

Article 25. Right to Judicial Protection

1. Everyone has the right to simple and prompt recourse, or any other effective recourse, to a competent court or tribunal for protection against

acts that violate his fundamental rights recognized by the constitution or laws of the state concerned or by this Convention, even though such violation may have been committed by persons acting in the course of their official duties.

2. The States Parties undertake:

    a. to ensure that any person claiming such remedy shall have his rights determined by the competent authority provided for by the legal system of the state;

    b. to develop the possibilities of judicial remedy; and

    c. to ensure that the competent authorities shall enforce such remedies when granted.

CHAPTER III — ECONOMIC, SOCIAL, AND CULTURAL RIGHTS

Article 26. Progressive Development

The States Parties undertake to adopt measures, both internally and through international cooperation, especially those of an economic and technical nature, with a view to achieving progressively, by legislation or other appropriate means, the full realization of the rights implicit in the economic, social, educational, scientific, and cultural standards set forth in the Charter of the Organization of American States as amended by the Protocol of Buenos Aires.

CHAPTER IV — SUSPENSION OF GUARANTEES, INTERPRETATION, AND APPLICATION

Article 27. Suspension of Guarantees

1. In time of war, public danger, or other emergency that threatens the independence or security of a State Party, it may take measures derogating from its obligations under the present Convention to the extent and for the period of time strictly required by the exigencies of the situation, provided that such measures are not inconsistent with its other obligations under international law and do not involve discrimination on the ground of race, color, sex, language, religion, or social origin.

2. The foregoing provision does not authorize any suspension of the following articles: Article 3 (Right to Juridical Personality), Article 4 (Right to Life), Article 5 (Right to Humane Treatment), Article 6 (Freedom from Slavery), Article 9 (Freedom from *Ex Post Facto* Laws), Article 12 (Freedom of Conscience and Religion), Article 17 (Rights of the Family), Article 18 (Right to a Name), Article 19 (Rights of the Child), Article 20 (Right to Nationality), and Article 23 (Right to Participate in Government), or of the judicial guarantees essential for the protection of such rights.

3. Any State Party availing itself of the right of suspension shall immediately inform the other States Parties, through the Secretary General of the Organization of American States, of the provisions the application of which it has suspended, the reasons that gave rise to the suspension, and the date set for the termination of such suspension.

Article 28. Federal Clause

1. Where a State Party is constituted as a federal state, the national government of such State Party shall implement all the provisions of the Convention over whose subject matter it exercises legislative and judicial jurisdiction.

2. With respect to the provisions over whose subject matter the constituent units of the federal state have jurisdiction, the national government shall immediately take suitable measures, in accordance with its constitution and its laws, to the end that the competent authorities of the constituent units may adopt appropriate provisions for the fulfillment of this Convention.

3. Whenever two or more States Parties agree to form a federation or other type of association, they shall take care that the resulting federal or other compact contains the provisions necessary for continuing and rendering effective the standards of this Convention in the new state that is organized.

Article 29. Restrictions Regarding Interpretation

No provision of this Convention shall be interpreted as:

a. permitting any State Party, group, or person to suppress the enjoyment or exercise of the rights and freedoms recognized in this Convention or to restrict them to a greater extent than is provided for herein;

b. restricting the enjoyment or exercise of any right or freedom recognized by virtue of the laws of any State Party or by virtue of another convention to which one of the said states is a party;

c. precluding other rights or guarantees that are inherent in the human personality or derived from representative democracy as a form of government; or

d. excluding or limiting the effect that the American Declaration of the Rights and Duties of Man and other international acts of the same nature may have.

Article 30. Scope of Restrictions

The restrictions that, pursuant to this Convention, may be placed on the enjoyment or exercise of the rights or freedoms recognized herein may not be applied except in accordance with laws enacted for reasons of general interest and in accordance with the purpose for which such restrictions have been established.

Article 31. Recognition of Other Rights

Other rights and freedoms recognized in accordance with the procedures established in Articles 76 and 77 may be included in the system of protection of this Convention.

Chapter V — Personal Responsibilities

Article 32. Relationship between Duties and Rights

1. Every person has responsibilities to his family, his community, and mankind.

2. The rights of each person are limited by the rights of others, by the security of all, and by the just demands of the general welfare, in a democratic society.

Part II — Means of Protection

Chapter VI — Competent Organs

Article 33

The following organs shall have competence with respect to matters relating to the fulfillment of the commitments made by the States Parties to this Convention:

    a. the Inter-American Commission on Human Rights, referred to as "The Commission"; and

    b. the Inter-American Court of Human Rights, referred to as "The Court."

Chapter VII — Inter-American Commission on Human Rights

Section 1. Organization

Article 34

The Inter-American Commission on Human Rights shall be composed of seven members, who shall be persons of high moral character and recognized competence in the field of human rights.

Article 35

The Commission shall represent all the member countries of the Organization of American States.

Article 36

1. The members of the Commission shall be elected in a personal capacity by the General Assembly of the Organization from a list of candidates proposed by the governments of the member states.

2. Each of those governments may propose up to three candidates, who may be nationals of the states proposing them or of any other member state of the Organization of American States. When a slate of three is proposed, at least one of the candidates shall be a national of a state other than the one proposing the slate.

Article 37

1. The members of the Commission shall be elected for a term of four years and may be reelected only once, but the terms of three of the members chosen in the first election shall expire at the end of two years. Immediately following that election the General Assembly shall determine the names of those three members by lot.

2. No two nationals of the same state may be members of the Commission.

Article 38

Vacancies that may occur on the Commission for reasons other than the normal expiration of a term shall be filled by the Permanent Council of the Organization in accordance with the provisions of the Statute of the Commission.

Article 39

The Commission shall prepare its Statute, which it shall submit to the General Assembly for approval. It shall establish its own Regulations.

Article 40

Secretariat services for the Commission shall be furnished by the appropriate specialized unit of the General Secretariat of the Organization. This unit shall be provided with the resources required to accomplish the tasks assigned to it by the Commission.

SECTION 2. FUNCTIONS

Article 41

The main function of the Commission shall be to promote respect for and defense of human rights. In the exercise of its mandate, it shall have the following functions and powers:

  a. to develop an awareness of human rights among the peoples of America;

  b. to make recommendations to the governments of the member states, when it considers such action advisable, for the adoption of progressive measures in favor of human rights within the framework of their domestic law and constitutional provisions as well as appropriate measures to further the observance of those rights;

  c. to prepare such studies or reports as it considers advisable in the performance of its duties;

  d. to request the governments of the member states to supply it with information on the measures adopted by them in matters of human rights;

  e. to respond, through the General Secretariat of the Organization of American States, to inquiries made by the member states on matters related to human rights and, within the limits of its possibilities, to provide those states with the advisory services they request;

f. to take action on petitions and other communications pursuant to its authority under the provisions of Articles 44 through 51 of this Convention; and

g. to submit an annual report to the General Assembly of the Organization of American States.

Article 42

The States Parties shall transmit to the Commission a copy of each of the reports and studies that they submit annually to the Executive Committees of the Inter-American Economic and Social Council and the Inter-American Council for Education, Science, and Culture, in their respective fields, so that the Commission may watch over the promotion of the rights implicit in the economic, social, educational, scientific, and cultural standards set forth in the Charter of the Organization of American States as amended by the Protocol of Buenos Aires.

Article 43

The States Parties undertake to provide the Commission with such information as it may request of them as to the manner in which their domestic law ensures the effective application of any provisions of this Convention.

SECTION 3. COMPETENCE

Article 44

Any person or group of persons, or any nongovernmental entity legally recognized in one or more member states of the Organization, may lodge petitions with the Commission containing denunciations or complaints of violation of this Convention by a State Party.

Article 45

1. Any State Party may, when it deposits its instrument of ratification of or adherence to this Convention, or at any later time, declare that it recognizes the competence of the Commission to receive and examine communications in which a State Party alleges that another State Party has committed a violation of a human right set forth in this Convention.

2. Communications presented by virtue of this article may be admitted and examined only if they are presented by a State Party that has made a declaration recognizing the aforementioned competence of the Commission. The Commission shall not admit any communication against a State Party that has not made such a declaration.

3. A declaration concerning recognition of competence may be made to be valid for an indefinite time, for a specified period, or for a specific case. . . .

Article 46

1. Admission by the Commission of a petition or communication lodged in accordance with Articles 44 or 45 shall be subject to the following requirements:

    a. that the remedies under domestic law have been pursued and exhausted in accordance with generally recognized principles of international law;

    b. that the petition or communication is lodged within a period of six months from the date on which the party alleging violation of his rights was notified of the final judgment;

    c. that the subject of the petition or communication is not pending in another international proceeding for settlement; and

    d. that, in the case of Article 44, the petition contains the name, nationality, profession, domicile, and signature of the person or persons or of the legal representative of the entity lodging the petition.

2. The provisions of paragraphs 1.a and 1.b of this article shall not be applicable when:

    a. the domestic legislation of the state concerned does not afford due process of law for the protection of the right or rights that have allegedly been violated;

    b. the party alleging violation of his rights has been denied access to the remedies under domestic law or has been prevented from exhausting them; or

    c. there has been unwarranted delay in rendering a final judgment under the aforementioned remedies.

Article 47

The Commission shall consider inadmissible any petition or communication submitted under Articles 44 or 45 if:

    a. any of the requirements indicated in Article 46 has not been met;

    b. the petition or communication does not state facts that tend to establish a violation of the rights guaranteed by this Convention;

    c. the statements of the petitioner or of the state indicate that the petition or communication is manifestly groundless or obviously out of order; or

    d. the petition or communication is substantially the same as one previously studied by the Commission or by another international organization.

SECTION 4. PROCEDURE

Article 48

1. When the Commission receives a petition or communication alleging violation of any of the rights protected by this Convention, it shall proceed as follows:

    a. If it considers the petition or communication admissible, it shall request information from the government of the state indicated as being responsible for the alleged violations and shall furnish that government a transcript of the pertinent portions of the petition or communication. This information shall be submitted within a reasonable period to be determined by the Commission in accordance with the circumstances of each case.

b. After the information has been received, or after the period established has elapsed and the information has not been received, the Commission shall ascertain whether the grounds for the petition or communication still exist. If they do not, the Commission shall order the record to be closed.

c. The Commission may also declare the petition or communication inadmissible or out of order on the basis of information or evidence subsequently received.

d. If the record has not been closed, the Commission shall, with the knowledge of the parties, examine the matter set forth in the petition or communication in order to verify the facts. If necessary and advisable, the Commission shall carry out an investigation, for the effective conduct of which it shall request, and the states concerned shall furnish to it, all necessary facilities.

e. The Commission may request the states concerned to furnish any pertinent information and, if so requested, shall hear oral statements or receive written statements from the parties concerned.

f. The Commission shall place itself at the disposal of the parties concerned with a view to reaching a friendly settlement of the matter on the basis of respect for the human rights recognized in this Convention.

2. However, in serious and urgent cases, only the presentation of a petition or communication that fulfills all the formal requirements of admissibility shall be necessary in order for the Commission to conduct an investigation with the prior consent of the state in whose territory a violation has allegedly been committed.

Article 49

If a friendly settlement has been reached in accordance with paragraph 1.f of Article 48, the Commission shall draw up a report, which shall be transmitted to the petitioner and to the States Parties to this Convention, and shall then be communicated to the Secretary General of the Organization of American States for publication. This report shall contain a brief statement of the facts and of the solution reached. If any party in the case so requests, the fullest possible information shall be provided to it.

Article 50

1. If a settlement is not reached, the Commission shall, within the time limit established by its Statute, draw up a report setting forth the facts and stating its conclusions. If the report, in whole or in part, does not represent the unanimous agreement of the members of the Commission, any member may attach to it a separate opinion. The written and oral statements made by the parties in accordance with paragraph 1.e of Article 48 shall also be attached to the report.

2. The report shall be transmitted to the states concerned, which shall not be at liberty to publish it.

3. In transmitting the report, the Committee may make such proposals and recommendations as it sees fit.

Article 51

1. If, within a period of three months from the date of the transmittal of the report of the Commission to the states concerned, the matter has not either been settled or submitted by the Commission or by the state concerned to the Court and its jurisdiction accepted, the Commission may, by the vote of an absolute majority of its members, set forth its opinion and conclusions concerning the question submitted for its consideration.

2. Where appropriate, the Commission shall make pertinent recommendations and shall prescribe a period within which the state is to take the measures that are incumbent upon it to remedy the situation examined.

3. When the prescribed period has expired, the Commission shall decide by the vote of an absolute majority of its members whether the state has taken adequate measures and whether to publish its report.

CHAPTER VIII — INTER-AMERICAN COURT OF HUMAN RIGHTS

SECTION 1. ORGANIZATION

Article 52

1. The Court shall consist of seven judges, nationals of the member states of the Organization, elected in an individual capacity from among jurists of the highest moral authority and of recognized competence in the field of human rights, who possess the qualifications required for the exercise of the highest judicial functions in conformity with the law of the state of which they are nationals or of the state that proposes them as candidates.

2. No two judges may be nationals of the same state.

Article 53

1. The judges of the Court shall be elected by secret ballot by an absolute majority vote of the States Parties to the Convention, in the General Assembly of the Organization, from a panel of candidates proposed by those states.

2. Each of the States Parties may propose up to three candidates, nationals of the state that proposes them or of any other member state of the Organization of American States. When a slate of three is proposed, at least one of the candidates shall be a national of a state other than the one proposing the slate.

Article 54

1. The judges of the Court shall be elected for a term of six years and may be reelected only once. The term of three of the judges chosen in the

first election shall expire at the end of three years. Immediately after the election, the names of the three judges shall be determined by lot in the General Assembly.

2. A judge elected to replace a judge whose term has not expired shall complete the term of the latter.

3. The judges shall continue in office until the expiration of their term. However, they shall continue to serve with regard to cases that they have begun to hear and that are still pending, for which purposes they shall not be replaced by the newly elected judges.

Article 55

1. If a judge is a national of any of the States Parties to a case submitted to the Court, he shall retain his right to hear that case.

2. If one of the judges called upon to hear a case should be a national of one the States Parties to the case, any other State Party in the case may appoint a person of its choice to serve on the Court as an *ad hoc* judge.

3. If among the judges called upon to hear a case none is a national of any of the States Parties to the case, each of the latter may appoint an *ad hoc* judge.

4. An *ad hoc* judge shall possess the qualifications indicated in Article 52.

5. If several States Parties to the Convention should have the same interest in a case, they shall be considered as a single party for purposes of the above provisions. In case of doubt, the Court shall decide.

Article 56

Five judges shall constitute a quorum for the transaction of business by the Court.

Article 57

The Commission shall appear in all cases before the Court.

Article 58

1. The Court shall have its seat at the place determined by the States Parties to the Convention in the General Assembly of the Organization; however, it may convene in the territory of any member state of the Organization of American States when a majority of the Court consider it desirable, and with the prior consent of the state concerned. The seat of the Court may be changed by the States Parties to the Convention in the General Assembly by a two-thirds vote.

2. The Court shall appoint its own Secretary. . . .

Article 59

The Court shall establish its Secretariat, which shall function under the direction of the Secretary of the Court, in accordance with the administrative standards of the General Secretariat of the Organization in all respect not incompatible with the independence of the Court. The staff of the Court's Secretariat shall be appointed by the Secretary General of the Organization, in consultation with the Secretary of the Court.

Article 60

The Court shall draw up its Statute which it shall submit to the General Assembly for approval. It shall adopt its own Rules of Procedure.

SECTION 2. JURISDICTION AND FUNCTIONS

Article 61

1. Only the States Parties and the Commission shall have the right to submit a case to the Court.

2. In order for the Court to hear a case, it is necessary that the procedures set forth in Articles 48 to 50 shall have been completed.

Article 62

1. A State Party may, upon depositing its instrument of ratification or adherence to this Convention, or at any subsequent time, declare that it recognizes as binding, *ipso facto,* and not requiring special agreement, the jurisdiction of the Court on all matters relating to the interpretation or application of this Convention.

2. Such declaration may be made unconditionally, on the condition of reciprocity, for a specified period, or for specific cases. It shall be presented to the Secretary General of the Organization, who shall transmit copies thereof to the other member states of the Organization and to the Secretary of the Court.

3. The jurisdiction of the Court shall comprise all cases concerning the interpretation and application of the provisions of this Convention that are submitted to it, provided that the States Parties to the case recognize or have recognized such jurisdiction, whether by special declaration pursuant to the preceding paragraphs, or by a special agreement.

Article 63

1. If the Court finds that there has been a violation of a right or freedom protected by this Convention, the Court shall rule that the injured party be ensured the enjoyment of his right or freedom that was violated. It shall also rule, if appropriate, that the consequences of the measure or situation that constituted the breach of such right or freedom be remedied and that fair compensation be paid to the injured party.

2. In cases of extreme gravity and urgency, and when necessary to avoid irreparable damage to persons, the Court shall adopt such provisional measures as it deems pertinent in matters it has under consideration. With respect to a case not yet submitted to the Court, it may act at the request of the Commission.

Article 64

1. The member states of the Organization may consult the Court regarding the interpretation of this Convention or of other treaties concerning the protection of human rights in the American states. Within their spheres of competence, the organs listed in Chapter X of the Charter of the Organization of American States, as amended by the Protocol of Buenos Aires, may in like manner consult the Court.

2. The Court, at the request of a member state of the Organization, may provide that state with opinions regarding the compatibility of any of its domestic laws with the aforesaid international instruments.

Article 65

To each regular session of the General Assembly of the Organization of American States the Court shall submit, for the Assembly's consideration, a report on its work during the previous year. It shall specify, in particular, the cases in which a state has not complied with its judgments, making any pertinent recommendations.

SECTION 3. PROCEDURE

Article 66

1. Reasons shall be given for the judgment of the Court.
2. If the judgment does not represent in whole or in part the unanimous opinion of the judges, any judge shall be entitled to have his dissenting or separate opinion attached to the judgment.

Article 67

The judgment of the Court shall be final and not subject to appeal. In case of disagreement as to the meaning or scope of the judgment, the Court shall interpret it at the request of any of the parties, provided the request is made within ninety days from the date of notification of the judgment.

Article 68

1. The States Parties to the Convention undertake to comply with the judgment of the Court in any case to which they are parties.
2. That part of a judgment that stipulates compensatory damages may be executed in the country concerned in accordance with domestic procedure governing the execution of judgments against the state.

Article 69

The parties to the case shall be notified of the judgment of the Court and it shall be transmitted to the States Parties to the Convention.

Chapter IX — Common Provisions

Article 70

1. The judges of the Court and the members of the Commission shall enjoy, from the moment of their election and throughout their term of office, the immunities extended to diplomatic agents in accordance with international law. During the exercise of their official function they shall, in addition, enjoy the diplomatic privileges necessary for the performance of their duties.

2. At no time shall the judges of the Court or the members of the Commission be held liable for any decisions or opinions issued in the exercise of their functions.

Article 71

The position of judge of the Court or member of the Commission is incompatible with any other activity that might affect the independence or impartiality of such judge or member, as determined in the respective statutes.

Article 72

The judges of the Court and the members of the Commission shall receive emoluments and travel allowances in the form and under the conditions set forth in their statutes, with due regard for the importance and independence of their office. Such emoluments and travel allowances shall be determined in the budget of the Organization of American States, which shall also include the expenses of the Court and its Secretariat. To this end, the Court shall draw up its own budget and submit it for approval to the General Assembly through the General Secretariat. The latter may not introduce any changes in it.

Article 73

The General Assembly may, only at the request of the Commission or the Court, as the case may be, determine sanctions to be applied against members of the Commission or judges of the Court when there are justifiable grounds for such action as set forth in the respective statutes. A vote of a two-thirds majority of the member states of the Organization shall be required for a decision in the case of members of the Commission and, in the case of judges of the Court, a two-thirds majority vote of the States Parties to the Convention shall also be required. . . .

AFRICAN CHARTER ON HUMAN AND PEOPLES' RIGHTS (BANJUL CHARTER)
June 27, 1981, 21 I.L.M. 59 (1981)*

Preamble

The African States members of the Organization of African Unity, parties to the present convention entitled "African Charter on Human and Peoples' Rights. . . .

Reaffirming the pledge they solemnly made in Article 2 of the [O.A.U.] Charter to eradicate all forms of colonialism from Africa, to coordinate and intensify their cooperation and efforts to achieve a better life for the peoples of Africa and to promote international cooperation having due regard to the Charter of the United Nations and the Universal Declaration of Human Rights;

Taking into consideration the virtues of their historical tradition and the values of African civilization which should inspire and characterize their reflection on the concept of human and peoples' rights;

Recognizing on the one hand, that fundamental human rights stem from the attributes of human beings, which justifies their national and international protection and on the other hand that the reality and respect of people's rights should necessarily guarantee human rights;

Considering that the enjoyment of rights and freedoms also implies the performance of duties on the part of everyone;

Convinced that it is henceforth essential to pay a particular attention to the right to development and that civil and political rights cannot be dissociated from economic, social and cultural rights in their conception as well as universality and that the satisfaction of economic, social and cultural rights is a guarantee for the enjoyment of civil and political rights;

Conscious of their duty to achieve the total liberation of Africa, the peoples of which are still struggling for their dignity and genuine independence, and undertaking to eliminate colonialism, neo-colonialism, apartheid, zionism and to dismantle aggressive foreign military bases and all forms of discrimination, particularly those based on race, ethnic group, color, sex, language, religion or political opinions; . . .

Have agreed as follows:

*Adopted by the Organization of African Unity at Nairobi, Kenya, on June 27, 1981. Entered into force on Oct. 21, 1986. The United States is not a party to the charter.

The 36 parties to the charter are: Algeria, Benin, Botswana, Burkina Faso, Cape Verde, Central African Republic, Chad, Comoros, Congo, Egypt, Equatorial Guinea, Gabon, Gambia, Ghana, Guinea, Guinea-Bissau, Liberia, Libya, Mali, Mauritania, Mozambique, Niger, Nigeria, Rwanda, Sahrawi Arab Democratic Republic, Sao Tome & Principe, Senegal, Sierra Leone, Somalia, Sudan, Togo, Tunisia, Uganda, Tanzania, Zaire, Zambia, and Zimbabwe.

Part I — Rights and Duties

Chapter I. Human and Peoples' Rights

Article 1

The Member States of the Organization of African Unity parties to the present Charter shall recognize the rights, duties and freedoms enshrined in this Charter and shall undertake to adopt legislative or other measures to give effect to them.

Article 2

Every individual shall be entitled to the enjoyment of the rights and freedoms recognized and guaranteed in the present Charter without distinction of any kind such as race, ethnic group, color, sex, language, religion, political or any other opinion, national and social origin, fortune, birth or other status.

Article 3

1. Every individual shall be equal before the law.
2. Every individual shall be entitled to equal protection of the law.

Article 4

Human beings are inviolable. Every human being shall be entitled to respect for his life and the integrity of his person. No one may be arbitrarily deprived of this right.

Article 5

Every individual shall have the right to the respect of the dignity inherent in a human being and to the recognition of his legal status. All forms of exploitation and degredation of man particularly slavery, slave trade, torture, cruel, inhuman or degrading punishment and treatment shall be prohibited.

Article 6

Every individual shall have the right to liberty and to the security of his person. No one may be deprived of his freedom except for reasons and conditions previously laid down by law. In particular, no one may be arbitrarily arrested or detained.

Article 7

1. Every individual shall have the right to have his cause heard. This comprises:
    a) the right to an appeal to competent national organs against acts of violating his fundamental rights as recognized and guaranteed by conventions, laws, regulations and customs in force;

b) the right to be presumed innocent until proved guilty by a competent court or tribunal;

c) the right to defence, including the right to be defended by counsel of his choice;

d) the right to be tried within a reasonable time by an impartial court or tribunal.

2. No one may be condemned for an act or omission which did not constitute a legally punishable offence at the time it was committed. No penalty may be inflicted for an offence for which no provision was made at the time it was committed. Punishment is personal and can be imposed only on the offender.

Article 8

Freedom of conscience, the profession and free practice of religion shall be guaranteed. No one may, subject to law and order, be submitted to measures restricting the exercise of these freedoms.

Article 9

1. Every individual shall have the right to receive information.
2. Every individual shall have the right to express and disseminate his opinions within the law.

Article 10

1. Every individual shall have the right to free association provided that he abides by the law.
2. Subject to the obligation of solidarity provided for in Article 29 no one may be compelled to join an association.

Article 11

Every individual shall have the right to assemble freely with others. The exercise of this right shall be subject only to necessary restrictions provided for by law in particular those enacted in the interest of national security, the safety, health, ethics and rights and freedoms of others.

Article 12

1. Every individual shall have the right to freedom of movement and residence within the borders of a State provided he abides by the law.
2. Every individual shall have the right to leave any country including his own, and to return to his country. This right may only be subject to restrictions, provided for by law for the protection of national security, law and order, public health or morality.
3. Every individual shall have the right, when persecuted, to seek and obtain asylum in other countries in accordance with laws of those countries and international conventions.
4. A non-national legally admitted in a territory of a State Party to the

present Charter, may only be expelled from it by virtue of a decision taken in accordance with the law.

5. The mass expulsion of non-nationals shall be prohibited. Mass expulsion shall be that which is aimed at national, racial, ethnic or religious groups.

Article 13

1. Every citizen shall have the right to participate freely in the government of his country, either directly or through freely chosen representatives in accordance with the provisions of the law.

2. Every citizen shall have the right of equal access to the public service of his country.

3. Every individual shall have the right of access to public property and services in strict equality of all persons before the law.

Article 14

The right to property shall be guaranteed. It may only be encroached upon in the interest of public need or in the general interest of the community and in accordance with the provisions of appropriate laws.

Article 15

Every individual shall have the right to work under equitable and satisfactory conditions, and shall receive equal pay for equal work.

Article 16

1. Every individual shall have the right to enjoy the best attainable state of physical and mental health.

2. States parties to the present Charter shall take the necessary measures to protect the health of their people and to ensure that they receive medical attention when they are sick.

Article 17

1. Every individual shall have the right to education.

2. Every individual may freely take part in the cultural life of his community.

3. The promotion and protection of morals and traditional values recognized by the community shall be the duty of the State.

Article 18

1. The family shall be the natural unit and basis of society. It shall be protected by the State which shall take care of its physical health and moral.

2. The State shall have the duty to assist the family which is the custodian of morals and traditional values recognized by the community.

3. The State shall ensure the elimination of every discrimination against women and also censure the protection of the rights of the woman and

the child as stipulated in international declarations and conventions.

4. The aged and the disabled shall also have the right to special measures of protection in keeping with their physical or moral needs.

Article 19

All peoples shall be equal; they shall enjoy the same respect and shall have the same rights. Nothing shall justify the domination of a people by another.

Article 20

1. All peoples shall have the right to existence. They shall have the unquestionable and inalienable right to self-determination. They shall freely determine their political status and shall pursue their economic and social development according to the policy they have freely chosen.

2. Colonized or oppressed peoples shall have the right to free themselves from the bonds of domination by resorting to any means recognized by the international community.

3. All peoples shall have the right to the assistance of the States parties to the present Charter in their liberation struggle against foreign domination, be it political, economic or cultural.

Article 21

1. All peoples shall freely dispose of their wealth and natural resources. This right shall be exercised in the exclusive interest of the people. In no case shall a people be deprived of it.

2. In case of spoliation the dispossessed people shall have the right to the lawful recovery of its property as well as to an adequate compensation.

3. The free disposal of wealth and natural resources shall be exercised without prejudice to the obligation of promoting international economic cooperation based on mutual respect, equitable exchange and the principles of international law.

4. States parties to the present Charter shall individually and collectively exercise the right to free disposal of their wealth and natural resources with a view to strengthening African unity and solidarity.

5. States parties to the present Charter shall undertake to eliminate all forms of foreign economic exploitation particularly that practiced by international monopolies so as to enable their peoples to fully benefit from the advantages derived from their national resources.

Article 22

1. All peoples shall have the right to their economic, social and cultural development with due regard to their freedom and identity and in the equal enjoyment of the common heritage of mankind.

2. States shall have the duty, individually or collectively, to ensure the exercise of the right to development.

Article 23

1. All peoples shall have the right to national and international peace and security. The principles of solidarity and friendly relations implicitly affirmed by the Charter of the United Nations and reaffirmed by that of the Organization of African Unity shall govern relations between States.

2. For the purpose of strengthening peace, solidarity and friendly relations, States parties to the present Charter shall ensure that:

(a) any individual enjoying the right of asylum under Article 12 of the present Charter shall not engage in subversive activities against his country of origin or any other State party to the present Charter;

(b) their territories shall not be used as bases for subversive or terrorist activities against the people of any other State party to the present Charter.

Article 24

All peoples shall have the right to a general satisfactory environment favorable to their development.

Article 25

States parties to the present Charter shall have the duty to promote and ensure through teaching, education and publication, the respect of the rights and freedoms contained in the present Charter and to see to it that these freedoms and rights as well as corresponding obligations and duties are understood.

Article 26

States parties to the present Charter shall have the duty to guarantee the independence of the Courts and shall allow the establishment and improvement of appropriate national institutions entrusted with the promotion and protection of the rights and freedoms guaranteed by the present Charter.

CHAPTER II. DUTIES

Article 27

1. Every individual shall have duties towards his family and society, the State and other legally recognized communities and the international community.

2. The rights and freedoms of each individual shall be exercised with due regard to the rights of others, collective security, morality and common interest.

Article 28

Every individual shall have the duty to respect and consider his fellow beings without discrimination, and to maintain relations aimed at promoting, safeguarding and reinforcing mutual respect and tolerance.

Article 29

The individual shall also have the duty:

1. To preserve the harmonious development of the family and to work for the cohesion and respect of the family; to respect his parents at all times, to maintain them in case of need;

2. To serve his national community by placing his physical and intellectual abilities at its service;

3. Not to compromise the security of the State whose national or resident he is;

4. To preserve and strengthen social and national solidarity, particularly when the latter is threatened;

5. To preserve and strengthen the national independence and the territorial integrity of his country and to contribute to its defence in accordance with the law;

6. To work to the best of his abilities and competence, and to pay taxes imposed by law in the interest of the society;

7. To preserve and strengthen positive African cultural values in his relations with other members of the society, in the spirit of tolerance, dialogue and consultation and, in general, to contribute to the promotion of the moral well being of society;

8. To contribute to the best of his abilities, at all times and at all levels, to the promotion and achievement of African unity.

Part II — Measures of Safeguard

CHAPTER I. ESTABLISHMENT AND ORGANIZATION OF THE AFRICAN COMMISSION ON HUMAN AND PEOPLES' RIGHTS

Article 30

An African Commission on Human and Peoples' Rights, hereinafter called "the Commission," shall be established within the Organization of African Unity to promote human and peoples' rights and ensure their protection in Africa.

Article 31

1. The Commission shall consist of eleven members chosen from amongst African personalities of the highest reputation, known for their high morality, integrity, impartiality and competence in matters of human and peoples' rights; particular consideration being given to persons having legal experience.

2. The members of the Commission shall serve in their personal capacity.

Article 32

The Commission shall not include more than one national of the same State.

Article 33

The members of the Commission shall be elected by secret ballot by the Assembly of Heads of State and Government, from a list of persons nominated by the States parties to the present Charter.

Article 34

Each State party to the present Charter may not nominate more than two candidates. The candidates must have the nationality of one of the States parties to the present Charter. When two candidates are nominated by a State, one of them may not be a national of that State.

Article 35

1. The Secretary General of the Organization of African Unity shall invite States parties to the present Charter at least four months before the elections to nominate candidates;
2. The Secretary General of the Organization of African Unity shall make an alphabetical list of the persons thus nominated and communicate it to the Heads of State and Government at least one month before the elections.

Article 36

The members of the Commission shall be elected for a six year period and shall be eligible for re-election. However, the term of office of four of the members elected at the first election shall terminate after two years and the term of office of the three others, at the end of four years. . . .

Article 42

1. The Commission shall elect its Chairman and Vice Chairman for a two year period. They shall be eligible for re-election.
2. The Commission shall lay down its rules of procedure.
3. Seven members shall form a quorum.
4. In case of an equality of votes, the Chairman shall have a casting vote.
5. The Secretary General may attend the meetings of the Commission. He shall neither participate in deliberations nor shall he be entitled to vote. The Chairman of the Commission may, however, invite him to speak. . . .

CHAPTER II. MANDATE OF THE COMMISSION

Article 45

The functions of the Commission shall be:
1. To promote Human and Peoples' Rights and in particular:
   a) to collect documents, undertake studies and researches on African problems in the field of human and peoples' rights, organize seminars, symposia and conferences, disseminate information, encourage national and local institutions concerned with human and peoples' rights, and

should the case arise, give its views or make recommendations to Governments.

b) to formulate and lay down, principles and rules aimed at solving legal problems relating to human and peoples' rights and fundamental freedoms upon which African Governments may base their legislations.

c) co-operate with other African and international institutions concerned with the promotion and protection of human and peoples' rights.

2. Ensure the protection of human and peoples' rights under conditions laid down by the present Charter.

3. Interpret all the provisions of the present Charter at the request of a State party, an institution of the OAU or an African Organization recognized by the OAU.

4. Perform any other tasks which may be entrusted to it by the Assembly of Heads of State and Government.

CHAPTER III. PROCEDURE OF THE COMMISSION

Article 46

The Commission may resort to any appropriate method of investigation; it may hear from the Secretary General of the Organization of African Unity or any other person capable of enlightening it.

COMMUNICATION FROM STATES

Article 47

If a State party to the present Charter has good reasons to believe that another State party to this Charter has violated the provisions of the Charter, it may draw, by written communication, the attention of that State to the matter. This communication shall also be addressed to the Secretary General of the OAU and to the Chairman of the Commission. Within three months of the receipt of the communication, the State to which the communication is addressed shall give the enquiring State written explanation or statement elucidating the matter. This should include as much as possible relevant information relating to the laws and rules of procedure applied and applicable, and the redress already given or course of action available.

Article 48

If within three months from the date on which the original communication is received by the State to which it is addressed, the issue is not settled to the satisfaction of the two States involved through bilateral negotiation or by any other peaceful procedure, either State shall have the right to submit the matter to the Commission through the Chairman and shall notify the other States involved.

Article 49

Notwithstanding the provisions of Article 47, if a State party to the present Charter considers that another State party has violated the provisions of the Charter, it may refer the matter directly to the Commission by addressing a communication to the Chairman, to the Secretary General of the Organization of African Unity and the State concerned.

Article 50

The Commission can only deal with a matter submitted to it after making sure that all local remedies, if they exist, have been exhausted, unless it is obvious to the Commission that the procedure of achieving these remedies would be unduly prolonged.

Article 51

1. The Commission may ask the States concerned to provide it with all relevant information.
2. When the Commission is considering the matter, States concerned may be represented before it and submit written or oral representation.

Article 52

After having obtained from the States concerned and from other sources all the information it deems necessary and after having tried all appropriate means to reach an amicable solution based on the respect of Human and Peoples' Rights, the Commission shall prepare, within a reasonable period of time from the notification referred to in Article 48, a report stating the facts and its findings. This report shall be sent to the States concerned and communicated to the Assembly of Heads of State and Government.

Article 53

While transmitting its report, the Commission may make to the Assembly of Heads of State and Government such recommendations as it deems useful.

Article 54

The Commission shall submit to each ordinary Session of the Assembly of Heads of State and Government a report on its activities.

OTHER COMMUNICATIONS

Article 55

1. Before each Session, the Secretary of the Commission shall make a list of the communications other than those of States parties to the present Charter and transmit them to the members of the Commission, who shall

indicate which communications should be considered by the Commission.

2. A communication shall be considered by the Commission if a simple majority of its members so decide.

Article 56

Communications relating to human and peoples' rights referred to in Article 55 received by the Commission, shall be considered if they:

1. Indicate their authors even if the latter request anonymity,

2. Are compatible with the Charter of the Organization of African Unity or with the present Charter,

3. Are not written in disparaging or insulting language directed against the State concerned and its institutions or to the Organization of African Unity,

4. Are not based exclusively on news disseminated through the mass media,

5. Are sent after exhausting local remedies, if any, unless it is obvious that this procedure is unduly prolonged,

6. Are submitted within a reasonable period from the time local remedies are exhausted or from the date the Commission is seized of the matter, and

7. Do not deal with cases which have been settled by these States involved in accordance with the principles of the Charter of the United Nations, or the Charter of the Organization of African Unity or the provisions of the present Charter.

Article 57

Prior to any substantive consideration, all communications shall be brought to the knowledge of the State concerned by the Chairman of the Commission.

Article 58

1. When it appears after deliberations of the Commission that one or more communications apparently relate to special cases which reveal the existence of a series of serious or massive violations of human and peoples' rights, the Commission shall draw the attention of the Assembly of Heads of State and Government to these special cases.

2. The Assembly of Heads of State and Government may then request the Commission to undertake an in-depth study of these cases and make a factual report, accompanied by its findings and recommendations.

3. A case of emergency duly noticed by the Commission shall be submitted by the latter to the Chairman of the Assembly of Heads of State and Government who may request an in-depth study.

Article 59

1. All measures taken within the provisions of the present Chapter shall remain confidential until such a time as the Assembly of Heads of State and Government shall otherwise decide.

2. However, the report shall be published by the Chairman of the Commission upon the decision of the Assembly of Heads of State and Government.

3. The report on the activities of the Commission shall be published by its Chairman after it has been considered by the Assembly of Heads of State and Government.

Chapter IV. Applicable Principles

Article 60

The Commission shall draw inspiration from international law on human and peoples' rights, particularly from the provisions of various African instruments on human and peoples' rights, the Charter of the United Nations, the Charter of the Organization of African Unity, the Universal Declaration of Human Rights, other instruments adopted by the United Nations and by African countries in the field of human and peoples' rights as well as from the provisions of various instruments adopted within the Specialized Agencies of the United Nations of which the parties to the present Charter are members.

Article 61

The Commission shall also take into consideration, as subsidiary measures to determine the principles of law, other general or special international conventions, laying down rules expressly recognized by member states of the Organization of African Unity, African practices consistent with international norms on human and peoples' rights, customs generally accepted as law, general principles of law recognized by African states as well as legal precedents and doctrine.

Article 62

Each state party shall undertake to submit every two years, from the date the present Charter comes into force, a report on the legislative or other measures taken with a view to giving effect to the rights and freedoms recognized and guaranteed by the present Charter. . . .

"HELSINKI FINAL ACT," CONFERENCE ON SECURITY AND CO-OPERATION IN EUROPE (CSCE)

August 1, 1975, 14 I.L.M. 1292 (1975)*

... Motivated by the political will, in the interest of peoples, to improve and intensify their relations and to contribute in Europe to peace, security, justice and co-operation as well as to rapprochement among themselves and with the other States of the world.

Determined, in consequence, to give full effect to the results of the Conference and to assure, among their States and throughout Europe, the benefits deriving from those results and thus to broaden, deepen and make continuing and lasting the process of détente,

The High Representatives of the participating States have solemnly adopted the following:

Questions relating to Security in Europe . . .

1

(A) DECLARATION ON PRINCIPLES GUIDING RELATIONS BETWEEN PARTICIPATING STATES . . .

I. Sovereign Equality, Respect for the Rights Inherent in Sovereignty

The participating States will respect each other's sovereign equality and individuality as well as all the rights inherent in and encompassed by its sovereignty, including in particular the right of every State to juridical equality, to territorial integrity and to freedom and political independence. They will also respect each other's right freely to choose and develop its political, social, economic and cultural systems as well as its right to determine its laws and regulations.

---

*The Conference on Security and Cooperation in Europe opened in Helsinki on July 3, 1973 and continued at Geneva from September 18, 1973 to July 21, 1975. It was concluded at Helsinki on August 1, 1975 by the High Representatives of Austria, Belgium, Bulgaria, Canada, Cyprus, Czechoslovakia, Denmark, Finland, France, German Democratic Republic, Germany (Federal Republic), Greece, Holy See, Hungary, Iceland, Ireland, Italy, Liechtenstein, Luxembourg, Malta, Monaco, Netherlands, Norway, Poland, Portugal, Romania, San Marino, Spain, Sweden, Switzerland, Turkey, Union of Soviet Socialist Republics, United Kingdom, United States, and Yugoslavia.

The Helsinki Final Act, which was signed by the 35 countries participating in the conference, has no legally binding effect.

Within the framework of international law, all the participating States have equal rights and duties. They will respect each other's right to define and conduct as it wishes its relations with other States in accordance with international law and in the spirit of the present Declaration. They consider that their frontiers can be changed, in accordance with international law, by peaceful means and by agreement. They also have the right to belong or not to belong to international organizations, to be or not to be a party to bilateral or multilateral treaties including the right to be or not to be a party to treaties of alliance; they also have the right to neutrality.

II. *Refraining from the Threat or Use of Force*

The participating States will refrain in their mutual relations, as well as in their international relations in general, from the threat or use of force against the territorial integrity or political independence of any State, or in any other manner inconsistent with the purposes of the United Nations and with the present Declaration. No consideration may be invoked to serve to warrant resort to the threat or use of force in contravention of this principle.

Accordingly, the participating States will refrain from any acts constituting a threat of force or direct or indirect use of force against another participating State. Likewise they will refrain from any manifestation of force for the purpose of inducing another participating State to renounce the full exercise of its sovereign rights. Likewise they will also refrain in their mutual relations from any act of reprisal by force.

No such threat or use of force will be employed as a means of settling disputes, or questions likely to give rise to disputes, between them.

III. *Inviolability of Frontiers*

The participating States regard as inviolable all one another's frontiers as well as the frontiers of all States in Europe and therefore they will refrain now and in the future from assaulting these frontiers.

Accordingly, they will also refrain from any demand for, or act of, seizure and usurpation of part or all of the territory of any participating State.

IV. *Territorial Integrity of States*

The participating States will respect the territorial integrity of each of the participating States.

Accordingly, they will refrain from any action inconsistent with the purpose and principles of the Charter of the United Nations against the territorial integrity, political independence or the unity of any participating State, and in particular from any such action constituting a threat or use of force.

The participating States will likewise refrain from making each other's territory the object of military occupation or other direct or indirect measures of force in contravention of international law, or the object of acquisition by means of such measures or the threat of them. No such occupation or acquisition will be recognized as legal.

V. Peaceful Settlement of Disputes

The participating States will settle disputes among them by peaceful means in such a manner as not to endanger international peace and security, and justice.

They will endeavour in good faith and a spirit of co-operation to reach a rapid and equitable solution on the basis of international law.

For this purpose they will use such means as negotiation, enquiry, mediation, conciliation, arbitration, judicial settlement or other peaceful means of their own choice including any settlement procedure agreed to in advance of disputes to which they are parties.

In the event of failure to reach a solution by any of the above peaceful means, the parties to a dispute will continue to seek a mutually agreed way to settle the dispute peacefully.

Participating States, parties to a dispute among them, as well as other participating States, will refrain from any action which might aggravate the situation to such a degree as to endanger the maintenance of international peace and security and thereby make a peaceful settlement of the dispute more difficult.

VI. Non-Intervention in Internal Affairs

The participating States will refrain from any intervention, direct or indirect, individual or collective, in the internal or external affairs falling within the domestic jurisdiction of another participating State, regardless of their mutual relations.

They will accordingly refrain from any form of armed intervention or threat of such intervention against another participating State.

They will likewise in all circumstances refrain from any other act of military, or of political, economic or other coercion designed to subordinate to their own interest the exercise by another participating State of the rights inherent in its sovereignty and thus to secure advantages of any kind.

Accordingly, they will, inter alia, refrain from direct or indirect assistance to terrorist activities, or to subversive or other activities directed towards the violent overthrow of the regime of another participating State.

VII. Respect for Human Rights and Fundamental Freedoms, Including the Freedom of Thought, Conscience, Religion or Belief

The participating States will respect human rights and fundamental freedoms, including the freedom of thought, conscience, religion or belief, for all without distinction as to race, sex, language or religion.

They will promote and encourage the effective exercise of civil, political, economic, social, cultural and other rights and freedoms all of which derive from the inherent dignity of the human person and are essential for his free and full development.

Within this framework the participating States will recognize and respect the freedom of the individual to profess and practise, alone or in community with others, religion or belief acting in accordance with the dictates of his own conscience.

The participating States on whose territory national minorities exist will respect the right of persons belonging to such minorities to equality before the law, will afford them the full opportunity for the actual enjoyment of human rights and fundamental freedoms and will, in this manner, protect their legitimate interests in this sphere.

The participating States recognize the universal significance of human rights and fundamental freedoms, respect for which is an essential factor for the peace, justice and well-being necessary to ensure the development of friendly relations and co-operation among themselves as among all States.

They will constantly respect these rights and freedoms in their mutual relations and will endeavour jointly and separately, including in co-operation with the United Nations, to promote universal and effective respect for them.

They confirm the right of the individual to know and act upon his rights and duties in this field.

In the field of human rights and fundamental freedoms, the participating States will act in conformity with the purposes and principles of the Charter of the United Nations and with the Universal Declaration of Human Rights. They will also fulfil their obligations as set forth in the international declarations and agreements in this field, including inter alia the International Covenants on Human Rights, by which they may be bound.

VIII. *Equal Rights and Self-Determination of Peoples*

The participating States will respect the equal rights of peoples and their right to self-determination, acting at all times in conformity with the purposes and principles of the Charter of the United Nations and with the relevant norms of international law, including those relating to territorial integrity of States.

By virtue of the principle of equal rights and self-determination of peoples, all peoples always have the right, in full freedom, to determine, when and as they wish, their internal and external political status, without external interference, and to pursue as they wish their political, economic, social and cultural development.

The participating States reaffirm the universal significance of respect for and effective exercise of equal rights and self-determination of peoples for the development of friendly relations among themselves as among all States; they also recall the importance of the elimination of any form of violation of this principle.

IX. *Co-operation among States*

The participating States will develop their co-operation with one another and with all States in all fields in accordance with the purposes and principles of the Charter of the United Nations. In developing their co-operation the participating States will place special emphasis on the fields as set forth within the framework of the Conference on Security and Co-operation in Europe, with each of them making its contribution in conditions of full equality.

They will endeavour, in developing their co-operation as equals, to promote mutual understanding and confidence, friendly and good-neighbourly relations among themselves, international peace, security and justice. They will equally endeavour, in developing their co-operation, to improve the well-being of peoples and contribute to the fulfilment of their aspirations through, inter alia, the benefits resulting from increased mutual knowledge and from progress and achievement in the economic, scientific, technological, social, cultural and humanitarian fields. They will take steps to promote conditions favourable to making these benefits available to all; they will take into account the interest of all in the narrowing of differences in the levels of economic development, and in particular the interest of developing countries throughout the world.

They confirm that governments, institutions, organizations and persons have a relevant and positive role to play in contributing toward the achievement of these aims of their co-operation.

They will strive, in increasing their co-operation as set forth above, to develop closer relations among themselves on an improved and more enduring basis for the benefit of peoples.

X. *Fulfilment in Good Faith of Obligations Under International Law*

The participating States will fulfil in good faith their obligations under international law, both those obligations arising from the generally recognized principles and rules of international law and those obligations arising from treaties or other agreements, in conformity with international law, to which they are parties.

In exercising their sovereign rights, including the right to determine their laws and regulations, they will conform with their legal obligations under international law; they will furthermore pay due regard to and implement the provisions in the Final Act of the Conference on Security and Co-operation in Europe.

The participating States confirm that in the event of a conflict between the obligations of the members of the United Nations under the Charter of the United Nations and their obligations under any treaty or other international agreement, their obligations under the Charter will prevail, in accordance with Article 103 of the Charter of the United Nations.

All the principles set forth above are of primary significance and, accordingly, they will be equally and unreservedly applied, each of them being interpreted taking into account the others.

The participating States express their determination fully to respect and apply these principles, as set forth in the present Declaration, in all aspects, to their mutual relations and co-operation in order to ensure to each participating State the benefits resulting from the respect and application of these principles by all.

The participating States, paying due regard to the principles above and, in particular, to the first sentence of the tenth principle, "Fulfilment in good faith of obligations under international law", note that the present Declaration does not affect their rights and obligations, nor the corresponding treaties and other agreements and arrangements.

The participating States express the conviction that respect for these principles will encourage the development of normal and friendly relations and the progress of co-operation among them in all fields. They also express the conviction that respect for these principles will encourage the development of political contacts among them which in turn would contribute to better mutual understanding of their positions and views.

The participating States declare their intention to conduct their relations with all other States in the spirit of the principles contained in the present Declaration. . . .

CHARTER OF PARIS FOR A NEW EUROPE

November 21, 1990, — I.L.M. — (1990)*

A New Era of Democracy, Peace and Unity

We, the Heads of State or Government of the States participating in the Conference on Security and Co-operation in Europe, have assembled in Paris at a time of profound change and historic expectations. The era of confrontation and division of Europe has ended. We declare that henceforth our relations will be founded on respect and co-operation.

Europe is liberating itself from the legacy of the past. The courage of men and women, the strength of the will of the peoples and the power of the ideas of the Helsinki Final Act have opened a new era of democracy, peace and unity in Europe.

Ours is a time for fulfilling the hopes and expectations our peoples have cherished for decades: steadfast commitment to democracy based on human rights and fundamental freedoms; prosperity through economic liberty and social justice; and equal security for all our countries.

The Ten Principles of the Final Act will guide us towards this ambitious future, just as they have lighted our way towards better relations for the past fifteen years. Full implementation of all CSCE commitments must form the basis for the initiatives we are now taking to enable our nations to live in accordance with their aspirations.

HUMAN RIGHTS, DEMOCRACY AND RULE OF LAW

We undertake to build, consolidate and strengthen democracy as the only system of government of our nations. In this endeavour, we will abide by the following:

Human rights and fundamental freedoms are the birthright of all human beings, are inalienable and are guaranteed by law. Their protection and promotion is the first responsibility of government. Respect for them

---

*Signed in Paris on November 21, 1990, at the conclusion of a three-day summit meeting of the Conference on Security and Cooperation in Europe (CSCE). The heads of state or government of all the nations of Europe, except Albania, plus the United States and Canada, attended the meeting and signed the document. The 34 countries included: Austria, Belgium, Bulgaria, Canada, Cyprus, Czechoslovakia, Denmark, Finland, France, Germany, Greece, Holy See, Hungary, Iceland, Ireland, Italy, Liechtenstein, Luxembourg, Malta, Monaco, Netherlands, Norway, Poland, Portugal, Romania, San Marino, Spain, Sweden, Switzerland, Turkey, Union of Soviet Socialist Republics, United Kingdom, United States, and Yugoslavia.

is an essential safeguard against an over-mighty State. Their observance and full exercise are the foundation of freedom, justice and peace.

Democratic government is based on the will of the people, expressed regularly through free and fair elections. Democracy has as its foundation respect for the human person and the rule of law. Democracy is the best safeguard of freedom of expression, tolerance of all groups of society, and equality of opportunity for each person.

Democracy, with its representative and pluralist character, entails accountability to the electorate, the obligation of public authorities to comply with the law and justice administered impartially. No one will be above the law.

We affirm that, without discrimination,
every individual has the right to:
  freedom of thought, conscience and religion or belief,
  freedom of expression,
  freedom of association and peaceful assembly,
  freedom of movement;
no one will be:
  subject to arbitrary arrest or detention,
  subject to torture or other cruel, inhuman or degrading treatment or punishment;
everyone also has the right:
  to know and act upon his rights,
  to participate in free and fair elections,
  to fair and public trial if charged with an offence,
  to own property alone or in association and to exercise individual enterprise,
  to enjoy his economic, social and cultural rights.

We affirm that the ethnic, cultural, linguistic and religious identity of national minorities will be protected and that persons belonging to national minorities have the right freely to express, preserve and develop that identity without any discrimination and in full equality before the law.

We will ensure that everyone will enjoy recourse to effective remedies, national or international, against any violation of his rights.

Full respect for these precepts is the bedrock on which we will seek to construct the new Europe.

Our States will co-operate and support each other with the aim of making democratic gains irreversible.

ECONOMIC LIBERTY AND RESPONSIBILITY

Economic liberty, social justice and environmental responsibility are indispensable for prosperity.

The free will of the individual, exercised in democracy and protected by the rule of law, forms the necessary basis for successful economic and social development. We will promote economic activity which respects and upholds human dignity.

Freedom and political pluralism are necessary elements in our common objective of developing market economies towards sustainable economic growth, prosperity, social justice, expanding employment and efficient use of economic resources. The success of the transition to market economy by countries making efforts to this effect is important and in the interest of us all. It will enable us to share a higher level of prosperity which is our common objective. We will co-operate to this end.

Preservation of the environment is a shared responsibility of all our nations. While supporting national and regional efforts in this field, we must also look to the pressing need for joint action on a wider scale.

FRIENDLY RELATIONS AMONG PARTICIPATING STATES

Now that a new era is dawning in Europe, we are determined to expand and strengthen friendly relations and co-operation among the States of Europe, the United States of America and Canada, and to promote friendship among our peoples.

To uphold and promote democracy, peace and unity in Europe, we solemnly pledge our full commitment to the Ten Principles of the Helsinki Final Act. We affirm the continuing validity of the Ten Principles and our determination to put them into practice. All the Principles apply equally and unreservedly, each of them being interpreted taking into account the others. They form the basis for our relations.

In accordance with our obligations under the Charter of the United Nations and commitments under the Helsinki Final Act, we renew our pledge to refrain from the threat or use of force against the territorial integrity or political independence of any State, or from acting in any other manner inconsistent with the principles or purposes of those documents. We recall that non-compliance with obligations under the Charter of the United Nations constitutes a violation of international law.

We reaffirm our commitment to settle disputes by peaceful means. We decide to develop mechanisms for the prevention and resolution of conflicts among the participating States.

With the ending of the division of Europe, we will strive for a new quality in our security relations while fully respecting each other's freedom of choice in that respect. Security is indivisible and the security of every participating State is inseparably linked to that of all the others. We therefore pledge to co-operate in strengthening confidence and security among us and in promoting arms control and disarmament.

We welcome the Joint Declaration of Twenty-Two States on the improvement of their relations.

Our relations will rest on our common adherence to democratic values and to human rights and fundamental freedoms. We are convinced that in order to strengthen peace and security among our States, the advancement of democracy, and respect for and effective exercise of human rights, are indispensable. We reaffirm the equal rights of peoples and their right to self-determination in conformity with the Charter of the United Nations and with the relevant norms of international law, including those relating to territorial integrity of States.

We are determined to enhance political consultation and to widen co-operation to solve economic, social, environmental, cultural and humanitarian problems. This common resolve and our growing interdependence will help to overcome the mistrust of decades, to increase stability and to build a united Europe.

We want Europe to be a source of peace, open to dialogue and to co-operation with other countries, welcoming exchanges and involved in the search for common responses to the challenges of the future.

Security

Friendly relations among us will benefit from the consolidation of democracy and improved security.

We welcome the signature of the Treaty on Conventional Armed Forces in Europe by twenty-two participating States, which will lead to lower levels of armed forces. We endorse the adoption of a substantial new set of Confidence- and Security-building Measures which will lead to increased transparency and confidence among all participating States. These are important steps towards enhanced stability and security in Europe.

The unprecedented reduction in armed forces resulting from the Treaty on Conventional Armed Forces in Europe, together with new approaches to security and co-operation within the CSCE process, will lead to a new perception of security in Europe and a new dimension in our relations. In this context we fully recognize the freedom of States to choose their own security arrangements.

Unity

Europe whole and free is calling for a new beginning. We invite our peoples to join in this great endeavour.

We note with great satisfaction the Treaty on the Final Settlement with respect to Germany signed in Moscow on 12 September 1990 and sincerely welcome the fact that the German people have united to become one State in accordance with the principles of the Final Act of the Conference on Security and Co-operation in Europe and in full accord with their neighbours. The establishment of the national unity of Germany is an important contribution to a just and lasting order of peace for a united, democratic Europe aware of its responsibility for stability, peace and co-operation.

The participation of both North American and European States is a fundamental characteristic of the CSCE; it underlies its past achievements and is essential to the future of the CSCE process. An abiding adherence to shared values and our common heritage are the ties which bind us together. With all the rich diversity of our nations, we are united in our commitment to expand our co-operation in all fields. The challenges confronting us can only be met by common action, co-operation and solidarity.

The CSCE and the World

The destiny of our nations is linked to that of all other nations. We support fully the United Nations and the enhancement of its role in promoting international peace, security and justice. We reaffirm our commitment to the principles and purposes of the United Nations as enshrined in the Charter and condemn all violations of these principles. We recognize with satisfaction the growing role of the United Nations in world affairs and its increasing effectiveness, fostered by the improvement in relations among our States.

Aware of the dire needs of a great part of the world, we commit ourselves to solidarity with all other countries. Therefore, we issue a call from Paris today to all the nations of the world. We stand ready to join with any and all States in common efforts to protect and advance the community of fundamental human values.

Guidelines for the Future

Proceeding from our firm commitment to the full implementation of all CSCE principles and provisions, we now resolve to give a new impetus to a balanced and comprehensive development of our co-operation in order to address the needs and aspirations of our peoples.

HUMAN DIMENSION

We declare our respect for human rights and fundamental freedoms to be irrevocable. We will fully implement and build upon the provisions relating to the human dimension of the CSCE.

Proceeding from the Document of the Copenhagen Meeting of the Conference on the Human Dimension, we will co-operate to strengthen democratic institutions and to promote the application of the rule of law. To that end, we decide to convene a seminar of experts in Oslo from 4 to 15 November 1991.

Determined to foster the rich contribution of national minorities to the life of our societies, we undertake further to improve their situation. We reaffirm our deep conviction that friendly relations among our peoples, as well as peace, justice, stability and democracy, require that the ethnic, cultural, linguistic and religious identity of national minorities be protected and conditions for the promotion of that identity be created. We declare that questions related to national minorities can only be satisfactorily resolved in a democratic political framework. We further acknowledge that the rights of persons belonging to national minorities must be fully respected as part of universal human rights. Being aware of the urgent need for increased co-operation on, as well as better protection of, national minorities, we decide to convene a meeting of experts on national minorities to be held in Geneva from 1 to 19 July 1991.

We express our determination to combat all forms of racial and ethnic hatred, anti-semitism, xenophobia and discrimination against anyone as well as persecution on religious and ideological grounds.

In accordance with our CSCE commitments, we stress that free movement and contacts among our citizens as well as the free flow of information and ideas are crucial for the maintenance and development of free societies and flourishing cultures. We welcome increased tourism and visits among our countries.

The human dimension mechanism has proved its usefulness, and we are consequently determined to expand it to include new procedures involving, *inter alia,* the services of experts or a roster of eminent persons experienced in human rights issues which could be raised under the mechanism. We shall provide, in the context of the mechanism, for individuals to be involved in the protection of their rights. Therefore, we undertake to develop further our commitments in this respect, in particular at the Moscow Meeting of the Conference on the Human Dimension, without prejudice to obligations under existing international instruments to which our States may be parties.

We recognize the important contribution of the Council of Europe to the promotion of human rights and the principles of democracy and the rule of law as well as to the development of cultural co-operation. We welcome moves by several participating States to join the Council of Europe and adhere to its European Convention on Human Rights. We welcome as well the readiness of the Council of Europe to make its experience available to the CSCE.

SECURITY

The changing political and military environment in Europe opens new possibilities for common efforts in the field of military security. We will build on the important achievements attained in the Treaty on Conventional Armed Forces in Europe and in the Negotiations on Confidence- and Security-building Measures. We undertake to continue the CSBM negotiations under the same mandate, and to seek to conclude them no later than the Follow-up Meeting of the CSCE to be held in Helsinki in 1992. We also welcome the decision of the participating States concerned to continue the CFE negotiation under the same mandate and to seek to conclude it no later than the Helsinki Follow-up Meeting. Following a period for national preparations we look forward to a more structured co-operation among all participating States on security matters, and to discussions and consultations among the thirty-four participating States aimed at establishing by 1992, from the conclusion of the Helsinki Follow-up Meeting, new negotiations on disarmament and confidence and security building open to all participating States.

We call for the earliest possible conclusion of the Convention on an effectively verifiable, global and comprehensive ban on chemical weapons, and we intend to be original signatories to it.

We reaffirm the importance of the Open Skies initiative and call for the successful conclusion of the negotiations as soon as possible.

Although the threat of conflict in Europe has diminished, other dangers threaten the stability of our societies. We are determined to co-operate in defending democratic institutions against activities which violate the independence, sovereign equality or territorial integrity of the participating States. These include illegal activities involving outside pressure, coercion and subversion.

We unreservedly condemn, as criminal, all acts, methods and practices of terrorism and express our determination to work for its eradication both bilaterally and through multilateral co-operation. We will also join together in combating illicit trafficking in drugs.

Being aware that an essential complement to the duty of States to refrain from the threat or use of force is the peaceful settlement of disputes, both being essential factors for the maintenance and consolidation of international peace and security, we will not only seek effective ways of preventing, through political means, conflicts which may yet emerge, but also define, in conformity with international law, appropriate mechanisms for the peaceful resolution of any disputes which may arise. Accordingly, we undertake to seek new forms of co-operation in this area, in particular a range of methods for the peaceful settlement of disputes, including mandatory third-party involvement. We stress that full use should be made in this context of the opportunity of the Meeting on the Peaceful Settlement of Disputes which will be convened in Valletta at the beginning of 1991. The Council of Ministers for Foreign Affairs will take into account the Report of the Valletta Meeting.

Economic Co-operation

We stress that economic co-operation based on market economy constitutes an essential element of our relations and will be instrumental in the construction of a prosperous and united Europe. Democratic institutions and economic liberty foster economic and social progress, as recognized in the Document of the Bonn Conference on Economic Co-operation, the results of which we strongly support.

We underline that co-operation in the economic field, science and technology is now an important pillar of the CSCE. The participating States should periodically review progress and give new impulses in these fields.

We are convinced that our overall economic co-operation should be expanded, free enterprise encouraged and trade increased and diversified according to GATT rules. We will promote social justice and progress and further the welfare of our peoples. We recognize in this context the importance of effective policies to address the problem of unemployment.

We reaffirm the need to continue to support democratic countries in transition towards the establishment of market economy and the creation of the basis for self-sustained economic and social growth, as already undertaken by the Group of twenty-four countries. We further underline the necessity of their increased integration, involving the acceptance of disciplines as well as benefits, into the international economic and financial system.

We consider that increased emphasis on economic co-operation within the CSCE process should take into account the interests of developing participating States.

We recall the link between respect for and promotion of human rights and fundamental freedoms and scientific progress. Co-operation in the field of science and technology will play an essential role in economic and social development. Therefore, it must evolve towards a greater sharing of appropriate scientific and technological information and knowledge with a view to overcoming the technological gap which exists among the participating

States. We further encourage the participating States to work together in order to develop human potential and the spirit of free enterprise.

We are determined to give the necessary impetus to co-operation among our States in the fields of energy, transport and tourism for economic and social development. We welcome, in particular, practical steps to create optimal conditions for the economic and rational development of energy resources, with due regard for environmental considerations.

We recognize the important role of the European Community in the political and economic development of Europe. International economic organizations such as the Economic Commission for Europe of the United Nations (ECE/UN), the Bretton Woods Institutions, the Organisation for Economic Co-operation and Development (OECD), the European Free Trade Association (EFTA) and the International Chamber of Commerce (ICC) also have a significant task in promoting economic co-operation, which will be further enhanced by the establishment of the European Bank for Reconstruction and Development (EBRD). In order to pursue our objectives, we stress the necessity for effective co-ordination of the activities of these organizations and emphasize the need to find methods for all our States to take part in these activities.

ENVIRONMENT

We recognize the urgent need to tackle the problems of the environment and the importance of individual and co-operative efforts in this area. We pledge to intensify our endeavours to protect and improve our environment in order to restore and maintain a sound ecological balance in air, water and soil. Therefore, we are determined to make full use of the CSCE as a framework for the formulation of common environmental commitments and objectives, and thus to pursue the work reflected in the Report of the Sofia Meeting on the Protection of the Environment.

We emphasize the significant role of a well-informed society in enabling the public and individuals to take initiatives to improve the environment. To this end, we commit ourselves to promoting public awareness and education on the environment as well as the public reporting of the environmental impact of policies, projects and programmes.

We attach priority to the introduction of clean and low-waste technology, being aware of the need to support countries which do not yet have their own means for appropriate measures.

We underline that environmental policies should be supported by appropriate legislative measures and administrative structures to ensure their effective implementation.

We stress the need for new measures providing for the systematic evaluation of compliance with the existing commitments and, moreover, for the development of more ambitious commitments with regard to notification and exchange of information about the state of the environment and potential environmental hazards. We also welcome the creation of the European Environment Agency (EEA).

We welcome the operational activities, problem-oriented studies and policy reviews in various existing international organizations engaged in the protection of the environment, such as the United Nations Environment Programme (UNEP), the Economic Commission for Europe of the United Nations (ECE/UN) and the Organisation for Economic Co-operation and Development (OECD). We emphasize the need for strengthening their co-operation and for their efficient co-ordination.

Culture

We recognize the essential contribution of our common European culture and our shared values in overcoming the division of the continent. Therefore we underline our attachment to creative freedom and to the protection and promotion of our cultural and spiritual heritage, in all its richness and diversity.

In view of the recent changes in Europe, we stress the increased importance of the Cracow Symposium and we look forward to its consideration of guidelines for intensified co-operation in the field of culture. We invite the Council of Europe to contribute to this Symposium.

In order to promote greater familiarity amongst our peoples, we favour the establishment of cultural centres in cities of other participating States as well as increased co-operation in the audio-visual field and wider exchange in music, theatre, literature and the arts.

We resolve to make special efforts in our national policies to promote better understanding, in particular among young people, through cultural exchanges, co-operation in all fields of education and, more specifically, through teaching and training in the languages of other participating States. We intend to consider first results of this action at the Helsinki Follow-up Meeting in 1992.

Migrant Workers

We recognize that the issues of migrant workers and their families legally residing in host countries have economic, cultural and social aspects as well as their human dimension. We reaffirm that the protection and promotion of their rights, as well as the implementation of relevant international obligations, is our common concern.

Mediterranean

We consider that the fundamental political changes that have occurred in Europe have a positive relevance to the Mediterranean region. Thus, we will continue efforts to strengthen security and co-operation in the Mediterranean as an important factor for stability in Europe. We welcome the Report of the Palma de Mallorca Meeting on the Mediterranean, the results of which we all support.

We are concerned with the continuing tensions in the region, and renew our determination to intensify efforts towards finding just, viable and lasting solutions, through peaceful means, to outstanding crucial problems, based on respect for the principles of the Final Act.

We wish to promote favourable conditions for a harmonious development and diversification of relations with the non-participating Mediterranean States. Enhanced co-operation with these States will be pursued with the aim of promoting economic and social development and thereby enhancing stability in the region. To this end, we will strive together with these countries toward a substantial narrowing of the prosperity gap between Europe and its Mediterranean neighbours.

NON-GOVERNMENTAL ORGANIZATIONS

We recall the major role that non-governmental organizations, religious and other groups and individuals have played in the achievement of the objectives of the CSCE and will further facilitate their activities for the implementation of the CSCE commitments by the participating States. These organizations, groups and individuals must be involved in an appropriate way in the activities and new structures of the CSCE in order to fulfil their important tasks.

New Structures and Institutions of the CSCE Process

Our common efforts to consolidate respect for human rights, democracy and the rule of law, to strengthen peace and to promote unity in Europe require a new quality of political dialogue and co-operation and thus development of the structures of the CSCE.

The intensification of our consultations at all levels is of prime importance in shaping our future relations. To this end, we decide on the following:

We, the Heads of State or Government, shall meet next time in Helsinki on the occasion of the CSCE Follow-up Meeting 1992. Thereafter, we will meet on the occasion of subsequent follow-up meetings.

Our Ministers for Foreign Affairs will meet, as a Council, regularly and at least once a year. These meetings will provide the central forum for political consultations within the CSCE process. The Council will consider issues relevant to the Conference on Security and Co-operation in Europe and take appropriate decisions.

The first meeting of the Council will take place in Berlin.

A Committee of Senior Officials will prepare the meetings of the Council and carry out its decisions. The Committee will review current issues and may take appropriate decisions, including in the form of recommendations to the Council.

Additional meetings of the representatives of the participating States may be agreed upon to discuss questions of urgent concern.

The Council will examine the development of provisions for convening meetings of the Committee of Senior Officials in emergency situations.

Meetings of other Ministers may also be agreed by the participating States.

In order to provide administrative support for these consultations we establish a Secretariat in Prague.

Follow-up meetings of the participating States will be held, as a rule, every two years to allow the participating States to take stock of developments, review the implementation of their commitments and consider further steps in the CSCE process.

We decide to create a Conflict Prevention Centre in Vienna to assist the Council in reducing the risk of conflict.

We decide to establish an Office for Free Elections in Warsaw to facilitate contacts and the exchange of information on elections within participating States.

Recognizing the important role parliamentarians can play in the CSCE process, we call for greater parliamentary involvement in the CSCE, in particular through the creation of a CSCE parliamentary assembly, involving members of parliaments from all participating States. To this end, we urge that contacts be pursued at parliamentary level to discuss the field of activities, working methods and rules of procedure of such a CSCE parliamentary structure, drawing on existing experience and work already undertaken in this field.

We ask our Ministers for Foreign Affairs to review this matter on the occasion of their first meeting as a Council.

Procedural and organizational modalities relating to certain provisions contained in the Charter of Paris for a New Europe are set out in the Supplementary Document which is adopted together with the Charter of Paris.

We entrust to the Council the further steps which may be required to ensure the implementation of decisions contained in the present document, as well as in the Supplementary Document, and to consider further efforts for the strengthening of security and co-operation in Europe. The Council may adopt any amendment to the supplementary document which it may deem appropriate. . . .

Wherefore, we, the undersigned High Representatives of the participating States, mindful of the high political significance we attach to the results of the Summit Meeting, and declaring our determination to act in accordance with the provisions we have adopted, have subscribed our signatures below:

Done at Paris, on 21 November 1990, in the name of . . .

9

Law of the Sea

CONVENTION ON THE TERRITORIAL SEA AND CONTIGUOUS ZONE

April 29, 1958, 15 U.S.T. 1606, T.A.I.S. No. 5639, 516 U.N.T.S. 205*

*The States Parties to this Convention
Have agreed* as follows:

Part I. Territorial Sea

Section I. General

Article 1

1. The sovereignty of a State extends, beyond its land territory and its internal waters, to a belt of sea adjacent to its coast, described as the territorial sea.

2. This sovereignty is exercised subject to the provisions of these articles and to other rules of international law.

Article 2

The sovereignty of a coastal State extends to the air space over the territorial sea as well as to its bed and subsoil.

---

*Done at Geneva on April 29, 1958. Entered into force on September 10, 1964. The United States ratified the convention on April 12, 1961.

The other 45 parties to the convention are: Australia, Belgium, Bulgaria, Byelorussian SSR, Czechoslovakia, Democratic Kampuchea, Denmark, Dominican Republic, Fiji, Finland, German Democratic Republic, Haiti, Hungary, Israel, Italy, Jamaica, Japan, Kenya, Lesotho, Madagascar, Malawi, Malaysia, Malta, Mauritius, Mexico, Netherlands, Nigeria, Portugal, Romania, Senegal, Sierra Leone, Solomon Islands, South Africa, Spain, Swaziland, Switzerland, Thailand, Tonga, Trinidad & Tobago, Uganda, Ukrainian SSR, Union of Soviet Socialist Republics, United Kingdom, Venezuela, and Yugoslavia.

Section II. Limits of the Territorial Sea

Article 3

Except where otherwise provided in these articles, the normal baseline for measuring the breadth of the territorial sea is the low-water line along the coast as marked on large-scale charts officially recognized by the coastal State.

Article 4

1. In localities where the coast line is deeply indented and cut into, or if there is a fringe of islands along the coast in its immediate vicinity, the method of straight baselines joining appropriate points may be employed in drawing the baseline from which the breadth of the territorial sea is measured.
2. The drawing of such baselines must not depart to any appreciable extent from the general direction of the coast, and the sea areas lying within the lines must be sufficiently closely linked to the land domain to be subject to the régime of internal waters.
3. Baselines shall not be drawn to and from low-tide elevations, unless lighthouses or similar installations which are permanently above sea level have been built on them.
4. Where the method of straight baselines is applicable under the provisions of paragraph 1, account may be taken, in determining particular baselines, of economic interests peculiar to the region concerned, the reality and the importance of which are clearly evidenced by a long usage.
5. The system of straight baselines may not be applied by a State in such a manner as to cut off from the high seas the territorial sea of another State.
6. The coastal State must clearly indicate straight baselines on charts, to which due publicity must be given.

Article 5

1. Waters on the landward side of the baseline of the territorial sea form part of the internal waters of the State.
2. Where the establishment of a straight baseline in accordance with article 4 has the effect of enclosing as internal waters areas which previously had been considered as part of the territorial sea or of the high seas, a right of innocent passage, as provided in articles 14 to 23, shall exist in those waters.

Article 6

The outer limit of the territorial sea is the line every point of which is at a distance from the nearest point of the baseline equal to the breadth of the territorial sea.

Article 7

1. This article relates only to bays the coasts of which belong to a single State.

2. For the purposes of these articles, a bay is a well-marked indentation whose penetration is in such proportion to the width of its mouth as to contain landlocked waters and constitute more than a mere curvature of the coast. An indentation shall not, however, be regarded as a bay unless its area is as large as, or larger than, that of the semi-circle whose diameter is a line drawn across the mouth of that indentation.

3. For the purpose of measurement, the area of an indentation is that lying between the low-water mark around the shore of the indentation and a line joining the low-water marks of its natural entrance points. Where, because of the presence of islands, an indentation has more than one mouth, the semi-circle shall be drawn on a line as long as the sum total of the lengths of the lines across the different mouths. Islands within an indentation shall be included as if they were part of the water areas of the indentation.

4. If the distance between the low-water marks of the natural entrance points of a bay does not exceed twenty-four miles, a closing line may be drawn between these two low-water marks, and the waters enclosed thereby shall be considered as internal waters.

5. Where the distance between the low-water marks of the natural entrance points of a bay exceeds twenty-four miles, a straight baseline of twenty-four miles shall be drawn within the bay in such a manner as to enclose the maximum area of water that is possible with a line of that length.

6. The foregoing provisions shall not apply to so-called "historic" bays, or in any case where the straight baseline system provided for in article 4 is applied.

Article 8

For the purpose of delimiting the territorial sea, the outermost permanent harbour works which form an integral part of the harbour system shall be regarded as forming part of the coast.

Article 9

Roadsteads which are normally used for the loading, unloading and anchoring of ships, and which would otherwise be situated wholly or partly outside the outer limit of the territorial sea, are included in the territorial sea. The coastal State must clearly demarcate such roadsteads and indicate them on charts together with their boundaries, to which due publicity must be given.

Article 10

1. An island is a naturally-formed area of land, surrounded by water, which is above water at high-tide.

2. The territorial sea of an island is measured in accordance with the provisions of these articles.

Article 11

1. A low-tide elevation is a naturally-formed area of land which is surrounded by and above water at low-tide but submerged at high tide. Where a low-tide elevation is situated wholly or partly at a distance not

exceeding the breadth of the territorial sea from the mainland or an island, the low-water line on that elevation may be used as the baseline for measuring the breadth of the territorial sea.

2. Where a low-tide elevation is wholly situated at a distance exceeding the breadth of the territorial sea from the mainland or an island, it has no territorial sea of its own.

Article 12

1. Where the coasts of two States are opposite or adjacent to each other, neither of the two States is entitled, failing agreement between them to the contrary, to extend its territorial sea beyond the median line every point of which is equidistant from the nearest points on the baselines from which the breadth of the territorial seas of each of the two States is measured. The provisions of this paragraph shall not apply, however, where it is necessary by reason of historic title or other special circumstances to delimit the territorial seas of the two States in a way which is at variance with this provision.

2. The line of delimitation between the territorial seas of two States lying opposite to each other or adjacent to each other shall be marked on large-scale charts officially recognized by the coastal States.

Article 13

If a river flows directly into the sea, the baseline shall be a straight line across the mouth of the river between points on the low-tide line of its banks.

SECTION III. RIGHT OF INNOCENT PASSAGE

SUB-SECTION A. RULES APPLICABLE TO ALL SHIPS

Article 14

1. Subject to the provisions of these articles, ships of all States, whether coastal or not, shall enjoy the right of innocent passage through the territorial sea.

2. Passage means navigation through the territorial sea for the purpose either of traversing that sea without entering internal waters, or of proceeding to internal waters, or of making for the high seas from internal waters.

3. Passage includes stopping and anchoring, but only in so far as the same are incidental to ordinary navigation or are rendered necessary by *force majeure* or by distress.

4. Passage is innocent so long as it is not prejudicial to the peace, good order or security of the coastal State. Such passage shall take place in conformity with these articles and with other rules of international law.

5. Passage of foreign fishing vessels shall not be considered innocent if they do not observe such laws and regulations as the coastal State may make and publish in order to prevent these vessels from fishing in the territorial sea.

6. Submarines are required to navigate on the surface and to show their flag.

Article 15

1. The coastal State must not hamper innocent passage through the territorial sea.
2. The coastal State is required to give appropriate publicity to any dangers to navigation, of which it has knowledge, within its territorial sea.

Article 16

1. The coastal State may take the necessary steps in its territorial sea to prevent passage which is not innocent.
2. In the case of ships proceeding to internal waters, the coastal State shall also have the right to take the necessary steps to prevent any breach of the conditions to which admission of those ships to those waters is subject.
3. Subject to the provisions of paragraph 4, the coastal State may, without discrimination amongst foreign ships, suspend temporarily in specified areas of its territorial sea the innocent passage of foreign ships if such suspension is essential for the protection of its security. Such suspension shall take effect only after having been duly published.
4. There shall be no suspension of the innocent passage of foreign ships through straits which are used for international navigation between one part of the high seas and another part of the high seas or the territorial sea of a foreign State.

Article 17

Foreign ships exercising the right of innocent passage shall comply with the laws and regulations enacted by the coastal State in conformity with these articles and other rules of international law and, in particular, with such laws and regulations relating to transport and navigation.

SUB-SECTION B. RULES APPLICABLE TO MERCHANT SHIPS

Article 18

1. No charge may be levied upon foreign ships by reason only of their passage through the territorial sea.
2. Charges may be levied upon a foreign ship passing through the territorial sea as payment only for specific services rendered to the ship. These charges shall be levied without discrimination.

Article 19

1. The criminal jurisdiction of the coastal State should not be exercised on board a foreign ship passing through the territorial sea to arrest any person or to conduct any investigation in connexion with any crime committed on board the ship during its passage, save only in the following cases:
(*a*) If the consequences of the crime extend to the coastal State; or

(*b*) If the crime is of a kind to disturb the peace of the country or the good order of the territorial sea; or

(*c*) If the assistance of the local authorities has been requested by the captain of the ship or by the consul of the country whose flag the ship flies; or

(*d*) If it is necessary for the suppression of illicit traffic in narcotic drugs.

2. The above provisions do not affect the right of the coastal State to take any steps authorized by its laws for the purpose of an arrest or investigation on board a foreign ship passing through the territorial sea after leaving internal waters.

3. In the cases provided for in paragraphs 1 and 2 of this article, the coastal State shall, if the captain so requests, advise the consular authority of the flag State before taking any steps, and shall facilitate contact between such authority and the ship's crew. In cases of emergency this notification may be communicated while the measures are being taken.

4. In considering whether or how an arrest should be made, the local authorities shall pay due regard to the interests of navigation.

5. The coastal State may not take any steps on board a foreign ship passing through the territorial sea to arrest any person or to conduct any investigation in connexion with any crime committed before the ship entered the territorial sea, if the ship, proceeding from a foreign port, is only passing through the territorial sea without entering internal waters.

Article 20

1. The coastal State should not stop or divert a foreign ship passing through the territorial sea for the purpose of exercising civil jurisdiction in relation to a person on board the ship.

2. The coastal State may not levy execution against or arrest the ship for the purpose of any civil proceedings, save only in respect of obligations or liabilities assumed or incurred by the ship itself in the course or for the purpose of its voyage through the waters of the coastal State.

3. The provisions of the previous paragraph are without prejudice to the right of the coastal State, in accordance with its laws, to levy execution against or to arrest, for the purpose of any civil proceedings, a foreign ship lying in the territorial sea, or passing through the territorial sea after leaving internal waters.

SUB-SECTION C. RULES APPLICABLE TO GOVERNMENT SHIPS OTHER THAN WARSHIPS

Article 21

The rules contained in sub-sections A and B shall also apply to government ships operated for commercial purposes.

Article 22

1. The rules contained in sub-section A and in article 18 shall apply to government ships operated for non-commercial purposes.

2. With such exceptions as are contained in the provisions referred to in the preceding paragraph, nothing in these articles affects the immunities which such ships enjoy under these articles or other rules of international law.

SUB-SECTION D.   RULE APPLICABLE TO WARSHIPS

Article 23

If any warship does not comply with the regulations of the coastal State concerning passage through the territorial sea and disregards any request for compliance which is made to it, the coastal State may require the warship to leave the territorial sea.

Part II.   Contiguous Zone

Article 24

1. In a zone of the high seas contiguous to its territorial sea, the coastal State may exercise the control necessary to:

(*a*) Prevent infringement of its customs, fiscal, immigration or sanitary regulations within its territory or territorial sea;

(*b*) Punish infringement of the above regulations committed within its territory or territorial sea.

2. The contiguous zone may not extend beyond twelve miles from the baseline from which the breadth of the territorial sea is measured.

3. Where the coasts of two States are opposite or adjacent to each other, neither of the two States is entitled, failing agreement between them to the contrary, to extend its contiguous zone beyond the median line every point of which is equidistant from the nearest points on the baselines from which the breadth of the territorial seas of the two States is measured.

Part III.   Final Articles

Article 25

The provisions of this Convention shall not affect conventions or other international agreements already in force, as between States Parties to them. . . .

Article 29

1. This Convention shall come into force on the thirtieth day following the date of deposit of the twenty-second instrument of ratification or accession with the Secretary-General of the United Nations. . . .

Article 30

1. After the expiration of a period of five years from the date on which this Convention shall enter into force, a request for the revision of this

Convention may be made at any time by any Contracting Party by means of a notification in writing addressed to the Secretary-General of the United Nations.

2. The General Assembly of the United Nations shall decide upon the steps, if any, to be taken in respect of such request. . . .

CONVENTION ON THE CONTINENTAL SHELF

April 29, 1958, 15 U.S.T. 471, T.I.A.S. No. 5578, 499 U.N.T.S. 311*

The States Parties to this Convention
Have agreed as follows:

Article 1

For the purpose of these articles, the term "continental shelf" is used as referring (*a*) to the seabed and subsoil of the submarine areas adjacent to the coast but outside the area of the territorial sea, to a depth of 200 metres or, beyond that limit, to where the depth of the superjacent waters admits of the exploitation of the natural resources of the said areas; (*b*) to the seabed and subsoil of similar submarine areas adjacent to the coasts of islands.

Article 2

1. The coastal State exercises over the continental shelf sovereign rights for the purpose of exploring it and exploiting its natural resources.

2. The rights referred to in paragraph 1 of this article are exclusive in the sense that if the coastal State does not explore the continental shelf or exploit its natural resources, no one may undertake these activities, or make a claim to the continental shelf, without the express consent of the coastal State.

3. The rights of the coastal State over the continental shelf do not depend on occupation, effective or notional, or on any express proclamation.

4. The natural resources referred to in these articles consist of the mineral and other non-living resources of the seabed and subsoil together with living organisms belonging to sedentary species, that is to say, organisms which, at the harvestable stage, either are immobile on or under the seabed or are unable to move except in constant physical contact with the seabed or the subsoil.

*Done at Geneva on April 29, 1958. Entered into force on June 10, 1964. The United States ratified the convention on April 12, 1961.

The other 53 parties to the convention are: Albania, Australia, Bulgaria, Byelorussian SSR, Canada, Colombia, Costa Rica, Cyprus, Czechoslovakia, Democratic Kampuchea, Denmark, Dominican Republic, Fiji, Finland, France, German Democratic Republic, Greece, Guatemala, Haiti, Israel, Jamaica, Kenya, Lesotho, Madagascar, Malawi, Malaysia, Malta, Mauritius, Mexico, Netherlands, New Zealand, Nigeria, Norway, Poland, Portugal, Romania, Senegal, Sierra Leone, Solomon Islands, South Africa, Spain, Swaziland, Sweden, Switzerland, Thailand, Tonga, Trinidad & Tobago, Uganda, Ukrainian SSR, Union of Soviet Socialist Republics, United Kingdom, Venezuela, and Yugoslavia.

Article 3

The rights of the coastal State over the continental shelf do not affect the legal status of the superjacent waters as high seas, or that of the airspace above those waters.

Article 4

Subject to its right to take reasonable measures for the exploration of the continental shelf and the exploitation of its natural resources, the coastal State may not impede the laying or maintenance of submarine cables or pipe lines on the continental shelf.

Article 5

1. The exploration of the continental shelf and the exploitation of its natural resources must not result in any unjustifiable interference with navigation, fishing or the conservation of the living resources of the sea, nor result in any interference with fundamental oceanographic or other scientific research carried out with the intention of open publication.

2. Subject to the provisions of paragraphs 1 and 6 of this article, the coastal State is entitled to construct and maintain or operate on the continental shelf installations and other devices necessary for its exploration and the exploitation of its natural resources, and to establish safety zones around such installations and devices and to take in those zones measures necessary for their protection.

3. The safety zones referred to in paragraph 2 of this article may extend to a distance of 500 metres around the installations and other devices which have been erected, measured from each point of their outer edge. Ships of all nationalities must respect these safety zones.

4. Such installations and devices, though under the jurisdiction of the coastal State, do not possess the status of islands. They have no territorial sea of their own, and their presence does not affect the delimitation of the territorial sea of the coastal State.

5. Due notice must be given of the construction of any such installations, and permanent means for giving warning of their presence must be maintained. Any installations which are abandoned or disused must be entirely removed.

6. Neither the installations or devices, nor the safety zones around them, may be established where interference may be caused to the use of recognized sea lanes essential to international navigation.

7. The coastal State is obliged to undertake, in the safety zones, all appropriate measures for the protection of the living resources of the sea from harmful agents.

8. The consent of the coastal State shall be obtained in respect of any research concerning the continental shelf and undertaken there. Nevertheless the coastal State shall not normally withhold its consent if the request is submitted by a qualified institution with a view to purely scientific research into the physical or biological characteristics of the continental shelf, subject to the proviso that the coastal State shall have the right, if it so desires, to

participate or to be represented in the research, and that in any event the results shall be published.

Article 6

1. Where the same continental shelf is adjacent to the territories of two or more States whose coasts are opposite each other, the boundary of the continental shelf appertaining to such States shall be determined by agreement between them. In the absence of agreement, and unless another boundary line is justified by special circumstances, the boundary is the median line, every point of which is equidistant from the nearest points of the baselines from which the breadth of the territorial sea of each State is measured.

2. Where the same continental shelf is adjacent to the territories of two adjacent States, the boundary of the continental shelf shall be determined by agreement between them. In the absence of agreement, and unless another boundary line is justified by special circumstances, the boundary shall be determined by application of the principle of equidistance from the nearest points of the baselines from which the breadth of the territorial sea of each State is measured.

3. In delimiting the boundaries of the continental shelf, any lines which are drawn in accordance with the principles set out in paragraphs 1 and 2 of this article should be defined with reference to charts and geographical features as they exist at a particular date, and reference should be made to fixed permanent identifiable points on the land.

Article 7

The provisions of these articles shall not prejudice the right of the coastal State to exploit the subsoil by means of tunnelling irrespective of the depth of water above the subsoil. . . .

Article 12

1. At the time of signature, ratification or accession, any State may make reservations to articles of the Convention other than to articles 1 to 3 inclusive. . . .

CONVENTION ON THE HIGH SEAS

April 29, 1958, 13 U.S.T. 2312, T.I.A.S. No. 5200, 450 U.N.T.S. 82*

The States Parties to this Convention,
Desiring to codify the rules of international law relating to the high seas, . . .
Have agreed as follows:

Article 1

The term "high seas" means all parts of the sea that are not included in the territorial sea or in the internal waters of a State.

Article 2

The high seas being open to all nations, no State may validly purport to subject any part of them to its sovereignty. Freedom of the high seas is exercised under the conditions laid down by these articles and by the other rules of international law. It comprises, *inter alia,* both for coastal and non-coastal States:

(1) Freedom of navigation;
(2) Freedom of fishing;
(3) Freedom to lay submarine cables and pipelines;
(4) Freedom to fly over the high seas.

These freedoms, and others which are recognized by the general principles of international law, shall be exercised by all States with reasonable regard to the interests of other States in their exercise of the freedom of the high seas.

Article 3

1. In order to enjoy the freedom of the seas on equal terms with coastal States, States having no sea-coast should have free access to the sea. To this

---

*Done at Geneva on April 29, 1958. Entered into force on September 30, 1962. The United States ratified the convention on April 12, 1961.

The other 57 parties to the convention are: Afghanistan, Albania, Australia, Austria, Belgium, Bulgaria, Byelorussian SSR, Central African Republic, Costa Rica, Cyprus, Czechoslovakia, Democratic Kampuchea, Denmark, Dominican Republic, Fiji, Finland, German Democratic Republic, Germany (Federal Republic), Guatemala, Haiti, Hungary, Indonesia, Israel, Italy, Jamaica, Japan, Kenya, Lesotho, Madagascar, Malawi, Malaysia, Mauritius, Mexico, Mongolia, Nepal, Netherlands, Nigeria, Poland, Portugal, Romania, Senegal, Sierra Leone, Solomon Islands, South Africa, Spain, Swaziland, Switzerland, Thailand, Tonga, Trinidad & Tobago, Uganda, Ukrainian SSR, Union of Soviet Socialist Republics, United Kingdom, Upper Volta, Venezuela, and Yugoslavia.

end States situated between the sea and a State having no sea-coast shall by common agreement with the latter and in conformity with existing international convention accord:

(a) To the State having no sea-coast, on a basis of reciprocity, free transit through their territory; and

(b) To ships flying the flag of that State treatment equal to that accorded to their own ships, or to the ships of any other States, as regards access to seaports and the use of such ports.

2. States situated between the sea and a State having no sea-coast shall settle, by mutual agreement with the latter, and taking into account the rights of the coastal State or State of transit and the special conditions of the State having no sea-coast, all matters relating to freedom of transit and equal treatment in ports, in case such States are not already parties to existing international conventions.

Article 4

Every State, whether coastal or not, has the right to sail ships under its flag on the high seas.

Article 5

1. Each State shall fix the conditions for the grant of its nationality to ships, for the registration of ships in its territory, and for the right to fly its flag. Ships have the nationality of the State whose flag they are entitled to fly. There must exist a genuine link between the State and the ship; in particular, the State must effectively exercise its jurisdiction and control in administrative, technical and social matters over ships flying its flag.

2. Each State shall issue to ships to which it has granted the right to fly its flag documents to that effect.

Article 6

1. Ships shall sail under the flag of one State only and, save in exceptional cases expressly provided for in international treaties or in these articles, shall be subject to its exclusive jurisdiction on the high seas. A ship may not change its flag during a voyage or while in a port of call, save in the case of a real transfer of ownership or change of registry.

2. A ship which sails under the flags of two or more States, using them according to convenience, may not claim any of the nationalities in question with respect to any other State, and may be assimilated to a ship without nationality.

Article 7

The provisions of the preceding articles do not prejudice the question of ships employed on the official service of an inter-governmental organization flying the flag of the organization.

Article 8

1. Warships on the high seas have complete immunity from the jurisdiction of any State other than the flag State.

2. For the purposes of these articles, the term "warship" means a ship belonging to the naval forces of a State and bearing the external marks distinguishing warships of its nationality, under the command of an officer duly commissioned by the government and whose name appears in the Navy List, and manned by a crew who are under regular naval discipline.

Article 9

Ships owned or operated by a State and used only on government non-commercial service shall, on the high seas, have complete immunity from the jurisdiction of any State other than the flag State.

Article 10

1. Every State shall take such measures for ships under its flag as are necessary to ensure safety at sea with regard *inter alia* to:

(*a*) The use of signals, the maintenance of communications and the prevention of collisions;

(*b*) The manning of ships and labour conditions for crews taking into account the applicable international labour instruments;

(*c*) The construction, equipment and seaworthiness of ships.

2. In taking such measures each State is required to conform to generally accepted international standards and to take any steps which may be necessary to ensure their observance.

Article 11

1. In the event of a collision or of any other incident of navigation concerning a ship on the high seas, involving the penal or disciplinary responsibility of the master or of any other person in the service of the ship, no penal or disciplinary proceedings may be instituted against such persons except before the judicial or administrative authorities either of the flag State or of the State of which such person is a national.

2. In disciplinary matters, the State which has issued a master's certificate or a certificate of competence or licence shall alone be competent, after due legal process, to pronounce the withdrawal of such certificates, even if the holder is not a national of the State which issued them.

3. No arrest or detention of the ship, even as a measure of investigation, shall be ordered by any authorities other than those of the flag State.

Article 12

1. Every State shall require the master of a ship sailing under its flag, in so far as he can do so without serious danger to the ship, the crew or the passengers,

(*a*) To render assistance to any person found at sea in danger of being lost;

(*b*) To proceed with all possible speed to the rescue of persons in distress if informed of their need of assistance, in so far as such action may reasonably be expected of him;

(c) After a collision, to render assistance to the other ship, her crew and her passengers and, where possible, to inform the other ship of the name of his own ship, her port of registry and the nearest port at which she will call.

2. Every coastal State shall promote the establishment and maintenance of an adequate and effective search and rescue service regarding safety on and over the sea and — where circumstances so require — by way of mutual regional arrangements co-operate with neighbouring States for this purpose.

Article 13

Every State shall adopt effective measures to prevent and punish the transport of slaves in ships authorized to fly its flag, and to prevent the unlawful use of its flag for that purpose. Any slave taking refuge on board any ship, whatever its flag, shall *ipso facto* be free.

Article 14

All States shall co-operate to the fullest possible extent in the repression of piracy on the high seas or in any other place outside the jurisdiction of any State.

Article 15

Piracy consists of any of the following acts:

(1) Any illegal acts of violence, detention or any act of depredation, committed for private ends by the crew or the passengers of a private ship or a private aircraft, and directed:

(a) On the high seas, against another ship or aircraft, or against persons or property on board such ship or aircraft;

(b) Against a ship, aircraft, persons or property in a place outside the jurisdiction of any State;

(2) Any act of voluntary participation in the operation of a ship or of an aircraft with knowledge of facts making it a pirate ship or aircraft;

(3) Any act of inciting or of intentionally facilitating an act described in sub-paragraph 1 or sub-paragraph 2 of this article.

Article 16

The acts of piracy, as defined in article 15, committed by a warship, government ship or government aircraft whose crew has mutinied and taken control of the ship or aircraft are assimilated to acts committed by a private ship.

Article 17

A ship or aircraft is considered a pirate ship or aircraft if it is intended by the persons in dominant control to be used for the purpose of committing one of the acts referred to in article 15. The same applies if the ship or aircraft has been used to commit any such act, so long as it remains under the control of the persons guilty of that act.

Article 18

A ship or aircraft may retain its nationality although it has become a pirate ship or aircraft. The retention or loss of nationality is determined by the law of the State from which such nationality was derived.

Article 19

On the high seas, or in any other place outside the jurisdiction of any State, every State may seize a pirate ship or aircraft, or a ship taken by piracy and under the control of pirates, and arrest the persons and seize the property on board. The courts of the State which carried out the seizure may decide upon the penalties to be imposed, and may also determine the action to be taken with regard to the ships, aircraft or property, subject to the rights of third parties acting in good faith.

Article 20

Where the seizure of a ship or aircraft on suspicion of piracy has been effected without adequate grounds, the State making the seizure shall be liable to the State the nationality of which is possessed by the ship or aircraft, for any loss or damage caused by the seizure.

Article 21

A seizure on account of piracy may only be carried out by warships or military aircraft, or other ships or aircraft on government service authorized to that effect.

Article 22

1. Except where acts of interference derive from powers conferred by treaty, a warship which encounters a foreign merchant ship on the high seas is not justified in boarding her unless there is reasonable ground for suspecting:
   (a) That the ship is engaged in piracy; or
   (b) That the ship is engaged in the slave trade; or
   (c) That, though flying a foreign flag or refusing to show its flag, the ship is, in reality, of the same nationality as the warship.
2. In the cases provided for in sub-paragraphs (a), (b) and (c) above, the warship may proceed to verify the ship's right to fly its flag. To this end, it may send a boat under the command of an officer to the suspected ship. If suspicion remains after the documents have been checked, it may proceed to a further examination on board the ship, which must be carried out with all possible consideration.
3. If the suspicions prove to be unfounded, and provided that the ship boarded has not committed any act justifying them, it shall be compensated for any loss or damage that may have been sustained.

Article 23

1. The hot pursuit of a foreign ship may be undertaken when the competent authorities of the coastal State have good reason to believe that the ship has violated the laws and regulations of that State. Such pursuit must be commenced when the foreign ship or one of its boats is within the internal waters or the territorial sea or the contiguous zone of the pursuing State, and may only be continued outside the territorial sea or the contiguous zone if the pursuit has not been interrupted. It is not necessary that, at the time when the foreign ship within the territorial sea or the contiguous zone receives the order to stop, the ship giving the order should likewise be within the territorial sea or the contiguous zone. If the foreign ship is within a contiguous zone, as defined in article 24 of the Convention on the Territorial Sea and the Contiguous Zone, the pursuit may only be undertaken if there has been a violation of the rights for the protection of which the zone was established.

2. The right of hot pursuit ceases as soon as the ship pursued enters the territorial sea of its own country or of a third State.

3. Hot pursuit is not deemed to have begun unless the pursuing ship has satisfied itself by such practicable means as may be available that the ship pursued or one of its boats or other craft working as a team and using the ship pursued as a mother ship are within the limits of the territorial sea, or as the case may be within the contiguous zone. The pursuit may only be commenced after a visual or auditory signal to stop has been given at a distance which enables it to be seen or heard by the foreign ship.

4. The right of hot pursuit may be exercised only by warships or military aircraft, or other ships or aircraft on government service specially authorized to that effect.

5. Where hot pursuit is effected by an aircraft:

(a) The provisions of paragraph 1 to 3 of this article shall apply *mutatis mutandis;*

(b) The aircraft giving the order to stop must itself actively pursue the ship until a ship or aircraft of the coastal State, summoned by the aircraft, arrives to take over the pursuit, unless the aircraft is itself able to arrest the ship. It does not suffice to justify an arrest on the high seas that the ship was merely sighted by the aircraft as an offender or suspected offender, if it was not both ordered to stop and pursued by the aircraft itself or other aircraft or ships which continue the pursuit without interruption.

6. The release of a ship arrested within the jurisdiction of a State and escorted to a port of that State for the purposes of an enquiry before the competent authorities may not be claimed solely on the ground that the ship, in the course of its voyage, was escorted across a portion of the high seas, if the circumstances rendered this necessary.

7. Where a ship has been stopped or arrested on the high seas in circumstances which do not justify the exercise of the right of hot pursuit, it shall be compensated for any loss or damage that may have been thereby sustained.

Article 24

Every State shall draw up regulations to prevent pollution of the seas by the discharge of oil from ships or pipelines or resulting from the exploitation and exploration of the seabed and its subsoil, taking account of existing treaty provisions on the subject.

Article 25

1. Every State shall take measures to prevent pollution of the seas from the dumping of radioactive waste, taking into account any standards and regulations which may be formulated by the competent international organizations.
2. All States shall co-operate with the competent international organizations in taking measures for the prevention of pollution of the seas or air space above, resulting from any activities with radio-active materials or other harmful agents.

Article 26

1. All States shall be entitled to lay submarine cables and pipelines on the bed of the high seas.
2. Subject to its right to take reasonable measures for the exploration of the continental shelf and the exploitation of its natural resources, the coastal State may not impede the laying or maintenance of such cables or pipelines.
3. When laying such cables or pipelines the State in question shall pay due regard to cables or pipelines already in position on the seabed. In particular, possibilities of repairing existing cables or pipelines shall not be prejudiced.

Article 27

Every State shall take the necessary legislative measures to provide that the breaking or injury by a ship flying its flag or by a person subject to its jurisdiction of a submarine cable beneath the high seas done wilfully or through culpable negligence, in such a manner as to be liable to interrupt or obstruct telegraphic or telephonic communications, and similarly the breaking or injury of a submarine pipeline or high-voltage power cable shall be a punishable offence. This provision shall not apply to any break or injury caused by persons who acted merely with the legitimate object of saving their lives or their ships, after having taken all necessary precautions to avoid such break or injury.

Article 28

Every State shall take the necessary legislative measures to provide that, if persons subject to its jurisdiction who are the owners of a cable or pipeline beneath the high seas, in laying or repairing that cable or pipeline, cause a break in or injury to another cable or pipeline, they shall bear the cost of the repairs.

Article 29

Every State shall take the necessary legislative measures to ensure that the owners of ships who can prove that they have sacrificed an anchor, a net or any other fishing gear, in order to avoid injuring a submarine cable or pipeline, shall be indemnified by the owner of the cable or pipeline, provided that the owner of the ship has taken all reasonable precautionary measures beforehand.

Article 30

The provisions of this Convention shall not affect conventions or other international agreements already in force, as between States Parties to them. . . .

OPTIONAL PROTOCOL OF SIGNATURE CONCERNING THE COMPULSORY SETTLEMENT OF DISPUTES TO THE LAW OF THE SEA CONVENTIONS

April 29, 1958, 450 U.N.T.S. 169*

The States Parties to this Protocol and to any one or more of the Conventions on the Law of the Sea adopted by the United Nations Conference on the Law of the Sea held at Geneva from 24 February to 27 April 1958,

Expressing their wish to resort, in all matters concerning them in respect of any dispute arising out of the interpretation or application of any article of any Convention on the Law of the Sea of 29 April 1958, to the compulsory jurisdiction of the International Court of Justice, unless some other form of settlement is provided in the Convention or has been agreed upon by the Parties within a reasonable period,

Have agreed as follows:

Article I

Disputes arising out of the interpretation or application of any Convention on the Law of the Sea shall lie within the compulsory jurisdiction of the International Court of Justice, and may accordingly be brought before the Court by an application made by any party to the dispute being a Party to this Protocol.

Article II

This undertaking relates to all the provisions of any Convention on the Law of the Sea except, in the Convention on Fishing and Conservation of the Living Resources of the High Seas, articles 4, 5, 6, 7 and 8, to which articles 9, 10, 11 and 12 of that Convention remain applicable.

Article III

The Parties may agree, within a period of two months after one party has notified its opinion to the other that a dispute exists, to resort not to the International Court of Justice but to an arbitral tribunal. After the expiry

---

*Done at Geneva on April 29, 1958. Entered into force on September 30, 1962. The United States has not ratified the optional protocol.

The 38 parties to the optional protocol are: Australia, Belgium, Bolivia, Colombia, Costa Rica, Cuba, Denmark, Dominican Republic, Finland, France, Germany (Federal Republic), Ghana, Haiti, Holy See, Hungary, Liberia, Madagascar, Malawi, Malaysia, Malta, Mauritius, Nepal, Netherlands, New Zealand, Pakistan, Panama, Portugal, Sierra Leone, Solomon Islands, Sri Lanka, Sweden, Switzerland, Uganda, United Kingdom, Uruguay, and Yugoslavia.

of the said period, either Party to this Protocol may bring the dispute before the Court by an application.

Article IV

1. Within the same period of two months, the Parties to this Protocol may agree to adopt a conciliation procedure before resorting to the International Court of Justice.

2. The conciliation commission shall make its recommendations within five months after its appointment. If its recommendations are not accepted by the parties to the dispute within two months after they have been delivered, either party may bring the dispute before the Court by an application. . . .

UNCLOS RESOLUTION I RE: ESTABLISHMENT OF PREPARATORY COMMISSION

April 30, 1982, 21 I.L.M. 1253 (1982)*

Resolution 1. Establishment of the Preparatory Commission for the International Sea-Bed Authority and for the International Tribunal for the Law of the Sea

The Third United Nations Conference on the Law of the Sea,

Having adopted the Convention on the Law of the Sea which provides for the establishment of the International Sea-Bed Authority and the International Tribunal for the Law of the Sea,

Having decided to take all possible measures to ensure the entry into effective operation without undue delay of the Authority and the Tribunal and to make the necessary arrangements for the commencement of their functions,

Having decided that a Preparatory Commission should be established for the fulfilment of these purposes,

Decides as follows:

1. There is hereby established the Preparatory Commission for the International Sea-Bed Authority and for the International Tribunal for the Law of the Sea. Upon signature of or accession to the Convention by 50 States, the Secretary-General of the United Nations shall convene the Commission, and it shall meet no sooner than 60 days and no later than 90 days thereafter.

2. The Commission shall consist of the representatives of States and of Namibia, represented by the United Nations Council for Namibia, which have signed the Convention or acceded to it. The representatives of signatories of the Final Act may participate fully in the deliberations of the Commission as observers but shall not be entitled to participate in the taking of decisions.

3. The Commission shall elect its Chairman and other officers.

4. The Rules of Procedure of the Third United Nations Conference on

---

*Adopted at the Third U.N. Conference on the Law of the Sea (UNCLOS) in a vote that also included the Law of the Sea Convention, *infra*, and three other resolutions. The vote on April 30, 1982 was 130 delegations in favor, 4 against, and 17 abstentions. The convention and the four resolutions, with some drafting changes (included here for Resolution 1), were later annexed to the Final Act, which was done at Montego Bay, Jamaica, on Dec. 10, 1982.

the Law of the Sea shall apply *mutatis mutandis* to the adoption of the rules of procedure of the Commission.

5. The Commission shall:

(a) prepare the provisional agenda for the first session of the Assembly and of the Council and, as appropriate, make recommendations relating to items thereon;

(b) prepare draft rules of procedure of the Assembly and of the Council;

(c) make recommendations concerning the budget for the first financial period of the Authority;

(d) make recommendations concerning the relationship between the Authority and the United Nations and other international organizations;

(e) make recommendations concerning the Secretariat of the Authority in accordance with the relevant provisions of the Convention;

(f) undertake studies, as necessary, concerning the establishment of the headquarters of the Authority, and make recommendations relating thereto;

(g) prepare draft rules, regulations and procedures, as necessary to enable the Authority to commence its functions, including draft regulations concerning the financial management and the internal administration of the Authority;

(h) exercise the powers and functions assigned to it by resolution II of the Third United Nations Conference on the Law of the Sea relating to preparatory investment;

(i) undertake studies on the problems which would be encountered by developing land-based producer States likely to be most seriously affected by the production of minerals derived from the Area with a view to minimizing their difficulties and helping them to make the necessary economic adjustment, including studies on the establishment of a compensation fund, and submit recommendations to the Authority thereon.

6. The Commission shall have such legal capacity as may be necessary for the exercise of its functions and the fulfilment of its purposes as set forth in this resolution.

7. The Commission may establish such subsidiary bodies as are necessary for the exercise of its functions and shall determine their functions and rules of procedure. It may also make use, as appropriate, of outside sources of expertise in accordance with United Nations practice to facilitate the work of bodies so established.

8. The Commission shall establish a special commission for the Enterprise and entrust to it the functions referred to in paragraph 12 of resolution II of the Third United Nations Conference on the Law of the Sea relating to preparatory investment. The special commission shall take all measures necessary for the early entry into effective operation of the Enterprise.

9. The Commission shall establish a special commission on the problems which would be encountered by developing land-based producer States likely to be most seriously affected by the production of minerals derived from the Area and entrust to it the functions referred to in paragraph 5 (i).

10. The Commission shall prepare a report containing recommendations for submission to the meeting of the States Parties to be convened in

accordance with Annex VI, article 4, of the Convention regarding practical arrangements for the establishment of the International Tribunal for the Law of the Sea.

11. The Commission shall prepare a final report on all matters within its mandate, except as provided in paragraph 10, for the presentation to the Assembly at its first session. Any action which may be taken on the basis of the report must be in conformity with the provisions of the Convention concerning the powers and functions entrusted to the respective organs of the Authority.

12. The Commission shall meet at the seat of the Authority if facilities are available; it shall meet as often as necessary for the expeditious exercise of its functions.

13. The Commission shall remain in existence until the conclusion of the first session of the Assembly, at which time its property and records shall be transferred to the Authority.

14. The expenses of the Commission shall be met from the regular budget of the United Nations, subject to the approval of the General Assembly of the United Nations. . . .

CONVENTION ON THE LAW OF THE SEA

December 10, 1982, U.N. A/CONF. 62/122, 21 I.L.M. 1261 (1982)*

Table of Contents

PREAMBLE

PART I. INTRODUCTION
    Article 1.   Use of terms and scope

PART II. TERRITORIAL SEA AND CONTIGUOUS ZONE
    SECTION 1.   GENERAL PROVISIONS
        Article 2.   Legal status of the territorial sea, of the air space over the territorial sea and of its bed and subsoil
    SECTION 2.   LIMITS OF THE TERRITORIAL SEA
        Article 3.   Breadth of the territorial sea
        Article 4.   Outer limit of the territorial sea
        Article 5.   Normal baseline
        Article 6.   Reefs
        Article 7.   Straight baselines
        Article 8.   Internal waters
        Article 9.   Mouths of rivers
        Article 10.   Bays
        Article 11.   Ports
        Article 12.   Roadsteads
        Article 13.   Low-tide elevations
        Article 14.   Combination of methods for determining baselines
        Article 15.   Delimitation of the territorial sea between States with opposite or adjacent coasts
        Article 16.   Charts and lists of geographical co-ordinates
    SECTION 3.   INNOCENT PASSAGE IN THE TERRITORIAL SEA
    SUBSECTION A.   RULES APPLICABLE TO ALL SHIPS
        Article 17.   Right of innocent passage
        Article 18.   Meaning of passage
        Article 19.   Meaning of innocent passage
        Article 20.   Submarines and other underwater vehicles
        Article 21.   Laws and regulations of the coastal State relating to innocent passage

*Done at Montego Bay, Jamaica, on December 10, 1982. Not yet entered into force. The United States has not ratified the convention.

As of November 1990, the 44 parties to the convention were: Angola, Antigua & Barbuda, The Bahamas, Bahrain, Belize, Brazil, Cameroon, Cape Verde, Cote d'Ivoire, Cuba, Cyprus, Democratic Yemen, Egypt, Fiji, Gambia, Ghana, Guinea, Guinea-Bissau, Iceland, Indonesia, Iraq, Jamaica, Kenya, Kuwait, Mali, Mexico, Namibia, Nigeria, Oman, Paraguay, Philippines, Saint Lucia, Sao Tome & Principe, Senegal, Somalia, Sudan, Tanzania, Togo, Trinidad & Tobago, Tunisia, Uganda, Yugoslavia, Zaire, and Zambia. Sixty parties are necessary for the convention to enter into force. (Article 308.)

Article 22. Sea lanes and traffic separation schemes in the territorial sea
Article 23. Foreign nuclear-powered ships and ships carrying nuclear or other inherently dangerous or noxious substances
Article 24. Duties of the coastal State
Article 25. Rights of protection of the coastal State
Article 26. Charges which may be levied upon foreign ships

SUBSECTION B. RULES APPLICABLE TO MERCHANT SHIPS AND GOVERNMENT SHIPS OPERATED FOR COMMERCIAL PURPOSES
Article 27. Criminal jurisdiction on board a foreign ship
Article 28. Civil jurisdiction in relation to foreign ships

SUBSECTION C. RULES APPLICABLE TO WARSHIPS AND OTHER GOVERNMENT SHIPS OPERATED FOR NON-COMMERCIAL PURPOSES
Article 29. Definition of warships
Article 30. Non-compliance by warships with the laws and regulations of the coastal State
Article 31. Responsibility of the flag State for damage caused by a warship or other government ship operated for non-commercial purposes
Article 32. Immunities of warships and other government ships operated for non-commercial purposes

SECTION 4. CONTIGUOUS ZONE
Article 33. Contiguous zone

PART III. STRAITS USED FOR INTERNATIONAL NAVIGATION
SECTION 1. GENERAL PROVISIONS
Article 34. Legal status of waters forming straits used for international navigation
Article 35. Scope of this Part
Article 36. High seas routes or routes through exclusive economic zones through straits used for international navigation

SECTION 2. TRANSIT PASSAGE
Article 37. Scope of this section
Article 38. Right of transit passage
Article 39. Duties of ships and aircraft during transit passage
Article 40. Research and survey activities
Article 41. Sea lanes and traffic separation schemes in straits used for international navigation
Article 42. Laws and regulations of States bordering straits relating to transit passage
Article 43. Navigational and safety aids and other improvements and the prevention, reduction and control of pollution
Article 44. Duties of States bordering straits

SECTION 3. INNOCENT PASSAGE
Article 45. Innocent passage

PART IV. ARCHIPELAGIC STATES
Article 46. Use of terms
Article 47. Archipelagic baselines
Article 48. Measurement of the breadth of the territorial sea, the contiguous zone, the exclusive economic zone and the continental shelf

Article 49. Legal status of archipelagic waters, of the air space over archipelagic waters and of their bed and subsoil
Article 50. Delimitation of internal waters
Article 51. Existing agreements, traditional fishing rights and existing submarine cables
Article 52. Right of innocent passage
Article 53. Right of archipelagic sea lanes passage
Article 54. Duties of ships and aircraft during their passage, research and survey activities, duties of the archipelagic State and laws and regulations of the archipelagic State relating to archipelagic sea lanes passage

PART V. EXCLUSIVE ECONOMIC ZONE
Article 55. Specific legal régime of the exclusive economic zone
Article 56. Rights, jurisdiction and duties of the coastal State in the exclusive economic zone
Article 57. Breadth of the exclusive economic zone
Article 58. Rights and duties of other States in the exclusive economic zone
Article 59. Basis for the resolution of conflicts regarding the attribution of rights and jurisdiction in the exclusive economic zone
Article 60. Artificial islands, installations and structures in the exclusive economic zone
Article 61. Conservation of the living resources
Article 62. Utilization of the living resources
Article 63. Stocks occurring within the exclusive economic zones of two or more coastal States or both within the exclusive economic zone and in an area beyond and adjacent to it
Article 64. Highly migratory species
Article 65. Marine mammals
Article 66. Anadromous stocks
Article 67. Catadromous species
Article 68. Sedentary species
Article 69. Right of land-locked States
Article 70. Right of geographically disadvantaged States
Article 71. Non-applicability of articles 69 and 70
Article 72. Restrictions on transfer of rights
Article 73. Enforcement of laws and regulations of the coastal State
Article 74. Delimitation of the exclusive economic zone between States with opposite or adjacent coasts
Article 75. Charts and lists of geographical co-ordinates

PART VI. CONTINENTAL SHELF
Article 76. Definition of the continental shelf
Article 77. Rights of the coastal State over the continental shelf
Article 78. Legal status of the superjacent waters and air space and the rights and freedoms of other States
Article 79. Submarine cables and pipelines on the continental shelf
Article 80. Artificial islands, installations and structures on the continental shelf
Article 81. Drilling on the continental shelf
Article 82. Payments and contributions with respect to the exploitation of the continental shelf beyond 200 nautical miles

Article 83.   Delimitation of the continental shelf between States with opposite or adjacent coasts
Article 84.   Charts and lists of geographical co-ordinates
Article 85.   Tunnelling

PART VII. HIGH SEAS
  SECTION 1.   GENERAL PROVISIONS
    Article 86.   Application of the provisions of this Part
    Article 87.   Freedom of the high seas
    Article 88.   Reservation of the high seas for peaceful purposes
    Article 89.   Invalidity of claims of sovereignty over the high seas
    Article 90.   Right of navigation
    Article 91.   Nationality of ships
    Article 92.   Status of ships
    Article 93.   Ships flying the flag of the United Nations, its specialized agencies and the International Atomic Energy Agency
    Article 94.   Duties of the flag State
    Article 95.   Immunity of warships on the high seas
    Article 96.   Immunity of ships used only on government non-commercial service
    Article 97.   Penal jurisdiction in matters of collision or any other incident of navigation
    Article 98.   Duty to render assistance
    Article 99.   Prohibition of the transport of slaves
    Article 100. Duty to co-operate in the repression of piracy
    Article 101. Definition of piracy
    Article 102. Piracy by a warship, government ship or government aircraft whose crew has mutinied
    Article 103. Definition of a pirate ship or aircraft
    Article 104. Retention or loss of the nationality of a pirate ship or aircraft
    Article 105. Seizure of a pirate ship or aircraft
    Article 106. Liability for seizure without adequate grounds
    Article 107. Ships and aircraft which are entitled to seize on account of piracy
    Article 108. Illicit traffic in narcotic drugs or psychotropic substances
    Article 109. Unauthorized broadcasting from the high seas
    Article 110. Right of visit
    Article 111. Right of hot pursuit
    Article 112. Right to lay submarine cables and pipelines
    Article 113. Breaking or injury of a submarine cable or pipeline
    Article 114. Breaking or injury by owners of a submarine cable or pipeline of another submarine cable or pipeline
    Article 115. Indemnity for loss incurred in avoiding injury to a submarine cable or pipeline
  SECTION 2.   CONSERVATION AND MANAGEMENT OF THE LIVING RESOURCES OF THE HIGH SEAS
    Article 116. Right to fish on the high seas
    Article 117. Duty of States to adopt with respect to their nationals measures for the conservation of the living resources of the high seas
    Article 118. Co-operation of States in the conservation and management of living resources

Article 119. Conservation of the living resources of the high seas
Article 120. Marine mammals

PART VIII. REGIME OF ISLANDS
Article 121. Régime of islands

PART IX. ENCLOSED OR SEMI-ENCLOSED SEAS
Article 122. Definition
Article 123. Co-operation of States bordering enclosed or semi-enclosed seas

PART X. RIGHT OF ACCESS OF LAND-LOCKED STATES TO AND FROM THE SEA AND FREEDOM OF TRANSIT
Article 124. Use of terms
Article 125. Right of access to and from the sea and freedom of transit
Article 126. Exclusion of application of the most-favoured-nation clause
Article 127. Customs duties, taxes and other charges
Article 128. Free zones and other customs facilities
Article 129. Co-operation in the construction and improvement of means of transport
Article 130. Measures to avoid or eliminate delays or other difficulties of a technical nature in traffic in transit
Article 131. Equal treatment in maritime ports
Article 132. Grant of greater transit facilities

PART XI. THE AREA
SECTION 1. GENERAL PROVISIONS
Article 133. Use of terms
Article 134. Scope of this Part
Article 135. Legal status of the superjacent waters and air space
SECTION 2. PRINCIPLES GOVERNING THE AREA
Article 136. Common heritage of mankind
Article 137. Legal status of the Area and its resources
Article 138. General conduct of States in relation to the Area
Article 139. Responsibility to ensure compliance and liability for damage
Article 140. Benefit of mankind
Article 141. Use of the Area exclusively for peaceful purposes
Article 142. Rights and legitimate interests of coastal States
Article 143. Marine scientific research
Article 144. Transfer of technology
Article 145. Protection of the marine environment
Article 146. Protection of human life
Article 147. Accommodation of activities in the Area and in the marine environment
Article 148. Participation of developing States in activities in the Area
Article 149. Archaeological and historical objects
SECTION 3. DEVELOPMENT OF RESOURCES OF THE AREA
Article 150. Policies relating to activities in the Area
Article 151. Production policies
Article 152. Exercise of powers and functions by the Authority
Article 153. System of exploration and exploitation
Article 154. Periodic review
Article 155. The Review Conference

SECTION 4. THE AUTHORITY
SUBSECTION A. GENERAL PROVISIONS
- Article 156. Establishment of the Authority
- Article 157. Nature and fundamental principles of the Authority
- Article 158. Organs of the Authority

SUBSECTION B. THE ASSEMBLY
- Article 159. Composition, procedure and voting
- Article 160. Powers and functions

SUBSECTION C. THE COUNCIL
- Article 161. Composition, procedure and voting
- Article 162. Powers and functions
- Article 163. Organs of the Council
- Article 164. The Economic Planning Commission
- Article 165. The Legal and Technical Commission

SUBSECTION D. THE SECRETARIAT
- Article 166. The Secretariat
- Article 167. The staff of the Authority
- Article 168. International character of the Secretariat
- Article 169. Consultation and co-operation with international and non-governmental organizations

SUBSECTION E. THE ENTERPRISE
- Article 170. The Enterprise

SUBSECTION F. FINANCIAL ARRANGEMENTS OF THE AUTHORITY
- Article 171. Funds of the Authority
- Article 172. Annual budget of the Authority
- Article 173. Expenses of the Authority
- Article 174. Borrowing power of the Authority
- Article 175. Annual audit

SUBSECTION G. LEGAL STATUS, PRIVILEGES AND IMMUNITIES
- Article 176. Legal status
- Article 177. Privileges and immunities
- Article 178. Immunity from legal process
- Article 179. Immunity from search and any form of seizure
- Article 180. Exemption from restrictions, regulations, controls and moratoria
- Article 181. Archives and official communications of the Authority
- Article 182. Privileges and immunities of certain persons connected with the Authority
- Article 183. Exemption from taxes and customs duties

SUBSECTION H. SUSPENSION OF THE EXERCISE OF RIGHTS AND PRIVILEGES OF MEMBERS
- Article 184. Suspension of the exercise of voting rights
- Article 185. Suspension of exercise of rights and privileges of membership

SECTION 5. SETTLEMENT OF DISPUTES AND ADVISORY OPINIONS
- Article 186. Sea-Bed Disputes Chamber of the International Tribunal for the Law of the Sea
- Article 187. Jurisdiction of the Sea-Bed Disputes Chamber
- Article 188. Submission of disputes to a special chamber of the International Tribunal for the Law of the Sea or an *ad hoc* chamber of the Sea-Bed Disputes Chamber or to binding commercial arbitration
- Article 189. Limitation on jurisdiction with regard to decisions of the Authority

Article 190. Participation and appearance of sponsoring States Parties in proceedings
Article 191. Advisory opinions

PART XII. PROTECTION AND PRESERVATION OF THE MARINE ENVIRONMENT
SECTION 1. GENERAL PROVISIONS
Article 192. General obligation
Article 193. Sovereign right of States to exploit their natural resources
Article 194. Measures to prevent, reduce and control pollution of the marine environment
Article 195. Duty not to transfer damage or hazards or transform one type of pollution into another
Article 196. Use of technologies or introduction of alien or new species
SECTION 2. GLOBAL AND REGIONAL CO-OPERATION
Article 197. Co-operation on a global or regional basis
Article 198. Notification of imminent or actual damage
Article 199. Contingency plans against pollution
Article 200. Studies, research programmes and exchange of information and data
Article 201. Scientific criteria for regulations
SECTION 3. TECHNICAL ASSISTANCE
Article 202. Scientific and technical assistance to developing States
Article 203. Preferential treatment for developing States
SECTION 4. MONITORING AND ENVIRONMENTAL ASSESSMENT
Article 204. Monitoring of the risks or effects of pollution
Article 205. Publication of reports
Article 206. Assessment of potential effects of activities
SECTION 5. INTERNATIONAL RULES AND NATIONAL LEGISLATION TO PREVENT, REDUCE AND CONTROL POLLUTION OF THE MARINE ENVIRONMENT
Article 207. Pollution from land-based sources
Article 208. Pollution from sea-bed activities
Article 209. Pollution from activities in the Area
Article 210. Pollution by dumping
Article 211. Pollution from vessels
Article 212. Pollution from or through the atmosphere
SECTION 6. ENFORCEMENT
Article 213. Enforcement with respect to pollution from land-based sources
Article 214. Enforcement with respect to pollution from sea-bed activities
Article 215. Enforcement with respect to pollution from activities in the Area
Article 216. Enforcement with respect to pollution by dumping
Article 217. Enforcement by flag States
Article 218. Enforcement by port States
Article 219. Measures relating to seaworthiness of vessels to avoid pollution
Article 220. Enforcement by coastal States
Article 221. Measures to avoid pollution arising from maritime casualties
Article 222. Enforcement with respect to pollution from or through the atmosphere

SECTION 7. SAFEGUARDS
- Article 223. Measures to facilitate proceedings
- Article 224. Exercise of powers of enforcement
- Article 225. Duty to avoid adverse consequences in the exercise of the powers of enforcement
- Article 226. Investigation of foreign vessels
- Article 227. Non-discrimination with respect to foreign vessels
- Article 228. Suspension and restrictions on institution of proceedings
- Article 229. Institution of civil proceedings
- Article 230. Monetary penalties and the observance of recognized rights of the accused
- Article 231. Notification to the flag State and other States concerned
- Article 232. Liability of States arising from enforcement measures
- Article 233. Safeguards with respect to straits used for international navigation

SECTION 8. ICE-COVERED AREAS
- Article 234. Ice-covered areas

SECTION 9. RESPONSIBILITY AND LIABILITY
- Article 235. Responsibility and liability

SECTION 10. SOVEREIGN IMMUNITY
- Article 236. Sovereign immunity

SECTION 11. OBLIGATIONS UNDER OTHER CONVENTIONS ON THE PROTECTION AND PRESERVATION OF THE MARINE ENVIRONMENT
- Article 237. Obligations under other conventions on the protection and preservation of the marine environment

PART XIII. MARINE SCIENTIFIC RESEARCH

SECTION 1. GENERAL PROVISIONS
- Article 238. Right to conduct marine scientific research
- Article 239. Promotion of marine scientific research
- Article 240. General principles for the conduct of marine scientific research
- Article 241. Non-recognition of marine scientific research activities as the legal basis for claims

SECTION 2. INTERNATIONAL CO-OPERATION
- Article 242. Promotion of international co-operation
- Article 243. Creation of favourable conditions
- Article 244. Publication and dissemination of information and knowledge

SECTION 3. CONDUCT AND PROMOTION OF MARINE SCIENTIFIC RESEARCH
- Article 245. Marine scientific research in the territorial sea
- Article 246. Marine scientific research in the exclusive economic zone and on the continental shelf
- Article 247. Marine scientific research projects undertaken by or under the auspices of international organizations
- Article 248. Duty to provide information to the coastal State
- Article 249. Duty to comply with certain conditions
- Article 250. Communications concerning marine scientific research projects
- Article 251. General criteria and guidelines

Article 252. Implied consent
Article 253. Suspension or cessation of marine scientific research activities
Article 254. Rights of neighbouring land-locked and geographically disadvantaged States
Article 255. Measures to facilitate marine scientific research and assist research vessels
Article 256. Marine scientific research in the Area
Article 257. Marine scientific research in the water column beyond the exclusive economic zone

SECTION 4. SCIENTIFIC RESEARCH INSTALLATIONS OR EQUIPMENT IN THE MARINE ENVIRONMENT
Article 258. Deployment and use
Article 259. Legal status
Article 260. Safety zones
Article 261. Non-interference with shipping routes
Article 262. Identification markings and warning signals

SECTION 5. RESPONSIBILITY AND LIABILITY
Article 263. Responsibility and liability

SECTION 6. SETTLEMENT OF DISPUTES AND INTERIM MEASURES
Article 264. Settlement of disputes
Article 265. Interim measures

PART XIV. DEVELOPMENT AND TRANSFER OF MARINE TECHNOLOGY
SECTION 1. GENERAL PROVISIONS
Article 266. Promotion of the development and transfer of marine technology
Article 267. Protection of legitimate interests
Article 268. Basic objectives
Article 269. Measures to achieve the basic objectives

SECTION 2. INTERNATIONAL CO-OPERATION
Article 270. Ways and means of international co-operation
Article 271. Guidelines, criteria and standards
Article 272. Co-ordination of international programmes
Article 273. Co-operation with international organizations and the Authority
Article 274. Objectives of the Authority

SECTION 3. NATIONAL AND REGIONAL MARINE SCIENTIFIC AND TECHNOLOGICAL CENTRES
Article 275. Establishment of national centres
Article 276. Establishment of regional centres
Article 277. Functions of regional centres

SECTION 4. CO-OPERATION AMONG INTERNATIONAL ORGANIZATIONS
Article 278. Co-operation among international organizations

PART XV. SETTLEMENT OF DISPUTES
SECTION 1. GENERAL PROVISIONS
Article 279. Obligation to settle disputes by peaceful means
Article 280. Settlement of disputes by any peaceful means chosen by the parties

Article 281. Procedure where no settlement has been reached by the parties
Article 282. Obligations under general, regional or bilateral agreements
Article 283. Obligation to exchange views
Article 284. Conciliation
Article 285. Application of this section to disputes submitted pursuant to Part XI

SECTION 2. COMPULSORY PROCEDURES ENTAILING BINDING DECISIONS
Article 286. Application of procedures under this section
Article 287. Choice of procedure
Article 288. Jurisdiction
Article 289. Experts
Article 290. Provisional measures
Article 291. Access
Article 292. Prompt release of vessels and crews
Article 293. Applicable law
Article 294. Preliminary proceedings
Article 295. Exhaustion of local remedies
Article 296. Finality and binding force of decisions

SECTION 3. LIMITATIONS AND EXCEPTIONS TO APPLICABILITY OF SECTION 2
Article 297. Limitations on applicability of section 2
Article 298. Optional exceptions to applicability of section 2
Article 299. Right of the parties to agree upon a procedure

PART XVI. GENERAL PROVISIONS
Article 300. Good faith and abuse of rights
Article 301. Peaceful uses of the seas
Article 302. Disclosure of information
Article 303. Archaeological and historical objects found at sea
Article 304. Responsibility and liability for damage

PART XVII. FINAL PROVISIONS
Article 305. Signature
Article 306. Ratification and formal confirmation
Article 307. Accession
Article 308. Entry into force
Article 309. Reservations and exceptions
Article 310. Declarations and statements
Article 311. Relation to other conventions and international agreements
Article 312. Amendment
Article 313. Amendment by simplified procedure
Article 314. Amendments to the provisions of this Convention relating exclusively to activities in the Area
Article 315. Signature, ratification of, accession to and authentic texts of amendments
Article 316. Entry into force of amendments
Article 317. Denunciation
Article 318. Status of Annexes
Article 319. Depositary
Article 320. Authentic texts

Law of the Sea Convention (1982)

ANNEX I. HIGHLY MIGRATORY SPECIES

ANNEX II. COMMISSION ON THE LIMITS OF THE CONTINENTAL SHELF

ANNEX III. BASIC CONDITIONS OF PROSPECTING, EXPLORATION AND EXPLOITATION
- Article 1. Title to minerals
- Article 2. Prospecting
- Article 3. Exploration and exploitation
- Article 4. Qualifications of applicants
- Article 5. Transfer of technology
- Article 6. Approval of plans of work
- Article 7. Selection among applicants for production authorizations
- Article 8. Reservation of areas
- Article 9. Activities in reserved areas
- Article 10. Preference and priority among applicants
- Article 11. Joint arrangements
- Article 12. Activities carried out by the Enterprise
- Article 13. Financial terms of contracts
- Article 14. Transfer of data
- Article 15. Training programmes
- Article 16. Exclusive right to explore and exploit
- Article 17. Rules, regulations and procedures of the Authority
- Article 18. Penalties
- Article 19. Revision of contract
- Article 20. Transfer of rights and obligations
- Article 21. Applicable law
- Article 22. Responsibility

ANNEX IV. STATUTE OF THE ENTERPRISE
- Article 1. Purposes
- Article 2. Relationship to the Authority
- Article 3. Limitation of liability
- Article 4. Structure
- Article 5. Governing Board
- Article 6. Powers and functions of the Governing Board
- Article 7. Director-General and staff of the Enterprise
- Article 8. Location
- Article 9. Reports and financial statements
- Article 10. Allocation of net income
- Article 11. Finances
- Article 12. Operations
- Article 13. Legal status, privileges and immunities

ANNEX V. CONCILIATION
- SECTION 1. CONCILIATION PROCEDURE PURSUANT TO SECTION 1 OF PART XV
  - Article 1. Institution of proceedings
  - Article 2. List of conciliators
  - Article 3. Constitution of conciliation commission
  - Article 4. Procedure
  - Article 5. Amicable settlement
  - Article 6. Functions of the commission
  - Article 7. Report

Article 8. Termination
Article 9. Fees and expenses
Article 10. Right of parties to modify procedure
SECTION 2. COMPULSORY SUBMISSION TO CONCILIATION PROCEDURE PURSUANT TO SECTION 3 OF PART XV
Article 11. Institution of proceedings
Article 12. Failure to reply or to submit to conciliation
Article 13. Competence
Article 14. Application of section 1

ANNEX VI. STATUTE OF THE INTERNATIONAL TRIBUNAL FOR THE LAW OF THE SEA
Article 1. General provisions
SECTION 1. ORGANIZATION OF THE TRIBUNAL
Article 2. Composition
Article 3. Membership
Article 4. Nominations and elections
Article 5. Term of office
Article 6. Vacancies
Article 7. Incompatible activities
Article 8. Conditions relating to participation of members in a particular case
Article 9. Consequence of ceasing to fulfil required conditions
Article 10. Privileges and immunities
Article 11. Solemn declaration by members
Article 12. President, Vice-President and Registrar
Article 13. Quorum
Article 14. Sea-Bed Disputes Chamber
Article 15. Special chambers
Article 16. Rules of the Tribunal
Article 17. Nationality of members
Article 18. Remuneration of members
Article 19. Expenses of the Tribunal
SECTION 2. COMPETENCE
Article 20. Access to the Tribunal
Article 21. Jurisdiction
Article 22. Reference of disputes subject to other agreements
Article 23. Applicable law
SECTION 3. PROCEDURE
Article 24. Institution of proceedings
Article 25. Provisional measures
Article 26. Hearing
Article 27. Conduct of case
Article 28. Default
Article 29. Majority for decision
Article 30. Judgment
Article 31. Request to intervene
Article 32. Right to intervene in cases of interpretation or application
Article 33. Finality and binding force of decisions
Article 34. Costs
SECTION 4. SEA-BED DISPUTES CHAMBER
Article 35. Composition
Article 36. Ad Hoc Chambers

Article 37. Access
Article 38. Applicable law
Article 39. Enforcement of decisions of the Chamber
Article 40. Applicability of other sections of this Annex
SECTION 5. AMENDMENTS
Article 41. Amendments

ANNEX VII. ARBITRATION
Article 1. Institution of proceedings
Article 2. List of arbitrators
Article 3. Constitution of arbitral tribunal
Article 4. Functions of arbitral tribunal
Article 5. Procedure
Article 6. Duties of parties to a dispute
Article 7. Expenses
Article 8. Required majority for decisions
Article 9. Default of appearance
Article 10. Award
Article 11. Finality of award
Article 12. Interpretation or implementation of award
Article 13. Application to entities other than States Parties.

ANNEX VIII. SPECIAL ARBITRATION
Article 1. Institution of proceedings
Article 2. Lists of experts
Article 3. Constitution of special arbitral tribunal
Article 4. General provisions
Article 5. Fact finding

ANNEX IX. PARTICIPATION BY INTERNATIONAL ORGANIZATIONS
Article 1. Use of terms
Article 2. Signature
Article 3. Formal confirmation and accession
Article 4. Extent of participation and rights and obligations
Article 5. Declarations, notifications and communications
Article 6. Responsibility and liability
Article 7. Settlement of disputes
Article 8. Applicability of Part XVII

The States Parties to this Convention,

Prompted by the desire to settle, in a spirit of mutual understanding and co-operation, all issues relating to the law of the sea and aware of the historic significance of this Convention as an important contribution to the maintenance of peace, justice and progress for all peoples of the world,

Noting that developments since the United Nations Conferences on the Law of the Sea held at Geneva in 1958 and 1960 have accentuated the need for a new and generally acceptable Convention on the law of the sea,

Conscious that the problems of ocean space are closely interrelated and need to be considered as a whole,

Recognizing the desirability of establishing through this Convention, with due regard for the sovereignty of all States, a legal order for the seas and oceans which will facilitate international communication, and will promote the peaceful uses of the seas and oceans, the equitable and efficient utilization of their resources, the conservation of their living resources, and the study, protection and preservation of the marine environment,

Bearing in mind that the achievement of these goals will contribute to the realization of a just and equitable international economic order which takes into account the interests and needs of mankind as a whole and, in particular, the special interests and needs of developing countries, whether coastal or land-locked,

Desiring by this Convention to develop the principles embodied in resolution 2749 (XXV) of 17 December 1970 in which the General Assembly of the United Nations solemnly declared *inter alia* that the area of the sea-bed and ocean floor and the subsoil thereof, beyond the limits of national jurisdiction, as well as its resources, are the common heritage of mankind, the exploration and exploitation of which shall be carried out for the benefit of mankind as a whole, irrespective of the geographical location of States,

Believing that the codification and progressive development of the law of the sea achieved in this Convention will contribute to the strengthening of peace, security, co-operation and friendly relations among all nations in conformity with the principles of justice and equal rights and will promote the economic and social advancement of all peoples of the world, in accordance with the Purposes and Principles of the United Nations as set forth in the Charter,

Affirming that matters not regulated by this Convention continue to be governed by the rules and principles of general international law,

Have agreed as follows:

Part I. Introduction

Article 1. Use of Terms and Scope

1. For the purposes of this Convention:

(1) "Area" means the sea-bed and ocean floor and subsoil thereof, beyond the limits of national jurisdiction;

(2) "Authority" means the International Sea-Bed Authority;

(3) "activities in the Area" means all activities of exploration for, and exploitation of, the resources of the Area;

(4) "pollution of the marine environment" means the introduction by man, directly or indirectly, of substances or energy into the marine environment, including estuaries, which results or is likely to result in such deleterious effects as harm to living resources and marine life, hazards to human health, hindrance to marine activities, including fishing and other legitimate uses of the sea, impairment of quality for use of sea water and reduction of amenities;

(5) (a) "dumping" means:

(i) any deliberate disposal of wastes or other matter from vessels, aircraft, platforms or other man-made structures at sea;

(ii) any deliberate disposal of vessels, aircraft, platforms or other man-made structures at sea;

(b) "dumping" does not include:

(i) the disposal of wastes or other matter incidental to, or derived from the normal operations of vessels, aircraft, platforms or other man-made structures at sea and their equipment, other than wastes or other matter transported by or to vessels, aircraft, platforms or other man-made structures at sea, operating for the purpose of disposal of such matter or derived from the treatment of such wastes or other matter on such vessels, aircraft, platforms or structures;

(ii) placement of matter for a purpose other than the mere disposal thereof, provided that such placement is not contrary to the aims of this Convention.

2. (1) "States Parties" means States which have consented to be bound by this Convention and for which this Convention is in force.

(2) This Convention applies *mutatis mutandis* to the entities referred to in article 305, paragraph 1(b), (c), (d), (e) and (f), which become Parties to this Convention in accordance with the conditions relevant to each, and to that extent "States Parties" refers to those entities.

Part II. Territorial Sea and Contiguous Zone

Section 1. General Provisions

Article 2. Legal Status of the Territorial Sea, of the Air Space over the Territorial Sea and of Its Bed and Subsoil

1. The sovereignty of a coastal State extends, beyond its land territory and internal waters and, in the case of an archipelagic State, its archipelagic waters, to an adjacent belt of sea, described as the territorial sea.

2. This sovereignty extends to the air space over the territorial sea as well as to its bed and subsoil.

3. The sovereignty over the territorial sea is exercised subject to this Convention and to other rules of international law.

Section 2. Limits of the Territorial Sea

Article 3. Breadth of the Territorial Sea

Every State has the right to establish the breadth of its territorial sea up to a limit not exceeding 12 nautical miles, measured from baselines determined in accordance with this Convention.

Article 4. Outer Limit of the Territorial Sea

The outer limit of the territorial sea is the line every point of which is at a distance from the nearest point of the baseline equal to the breadth of the territorial sea.

Article 5. Normal Baseline

Except where otherwise provided in this Convention, the normal baseline for measuring the breadth of the territorial sea is the low-water line along the coast as marked on large-scale charts officially recognized by the coastal State.

Article 6. Reefs

In the case of islands situated on atolls or of islands having fringing reefs, the baseline for measuring the breadth of the territorial sea is the seaward low-water line of the reef, as shown by the appropriate symbol on charts officially recognized by the coastal State.

Article 7. Straight Baselines

1. In localities where the coastline is deeply indented and cut into, or if there is a fringe of islands along the coast in its immediate vicinity, the method of straight baselines joining appropriate points may be employed in drawing the baseline from which the breadth of the territorial sea is measured.

2. Where because of the presence of a delta and other natural conditions the coastline is highly unstable, the appropriate points may be selected along the furthest seaward extent of the low-water line and, notwithstanding subsequent regression of the low-water line, the straight baselines shall remain effective until changed by the coastal State in accordance with this Convention.

3. The drawing of straight baselines must not depart to any appreciable extent from the general direction of the coast, and the sea areas lying within the lines must be sufficiently closely linked to the land domain to be subject to the régime of internal waters.

4. Straight baselines shall not be drawn to and from low-tide elevations, unless lighthouses or similar installations which are permanently above sea level have been built on them or except in instances where the drawing of baselines to and from such elevations has received general international recognition.

5. Where the method of straight baselines is applicable under paragraph 1, account may be taken, in determining particular baselines, of economic interests peculiar to the region concerned, the reality and the importance of which are clearly evidenced by long usage.

6. The system of straight baselines may not be applied by a State in such a manner as to cut off the territorial sea of another State from the high seas or an exclusive economic zone.

Article 8. Internal Waters

1. Except as provided in Part IV, waters on the landward side of the baseline of the territorial sea form part of the internal waters of the State.

2. Where the establishment of a straight baseline in accordance with the method set forth in article 7 has the effect of enclosing as internal water areas which had not previously been considered as such, a right of innocent passage as provided in this Convention shall exist in those waters.

Article 9. Mouths of Rivers

If a river flows directly into the sea, the baseline shall be a straight line across the mouth of the river between points on the low-water line of its banks.

Article 10. Bays

1. This article relates only to bays the coasts of which belong to a single State.

2. For the purposes of this Convention, a bay is a well-marked indentation whose penetration is in such proportion to the width of its mouth as to contain land-locked waters and constitute more than a mere curvature of the coast. An indentation shall not, however, be regarded as a bay unless its area is as large as, or larger than, that of the semi-circle whose diameter is a line drawn across the mouth of that indentation.

3. For the purpose of measurement, the area of an indentation is that lying between the low-water mark around the shore of the indentation and a line joining the low-water mark of its natural entrance points. Where, because of the presence of islands, an indentation has more than one mouth, the semi-circle shall be drawn on a line as long as the sum total of the lengths of the lines across the different mouths. Islands within an indentation shall be included as if they were part of the water area of the indentation.

4. If the distance between the low-water marks of the natural entrance points of a bay does not exceed 24 nautical miles, a closing line may be drawn between these two low-water marks, and the waters enclosed thereby shall be considered as internal waters.

5. Where the distance between the low-water marks of the natural entrance points of a bay exceeds 24 nautical miles, a straight baseline of 24 nautical miles shall be drawn within the bay in such a manner as to enclose the maximum area of water that is possible with a line of that length.

6. The foregoing provisions do not apply to so-called "historic" bays, or in any case where the system of straight baselines provided for in article 7 is applied.

Article 11. Ports

For the purpose of delimiting the territorial sea, the outermost permanent harbour works which form an integral part of the harbour system are regarded as forming part of the coast. Off-shore installations and artificial islands shall not be considered as permanent harbour works.

Article 12. Roadsteads

Roadsteads which are normally used for the loading, unloading and anchoring of ships, and which would otherwise be situated wholly or partly outside the outer limit of the territorial sea, are included in the territorial sea.

Article 13. Low-Tide Elevations

1. A low-tide elevation is a naturally formed area of land which is surrounded by and above water at low tide but submerged at high tide.

Where a low-tide elevation is situated wholly or partly at a distance not exceeding the breadth of the territorial sea from the mainland or an island, the low-water line on that elevation may be used as the baseline for measuring the breadth of the territorial sea.

2. Where a low-tide elevation is wholly situated at a distance exceeding the breadth of the territorial sea from the mainland or an island, it has no territorial sea of its own.

Article 14. Combination of Methods for Determining Baselines

The coastal State may determine baselines in turn by any of the methods provided for in the foregoing articles to suit different conditions.

Article 15. Delimination of the Territorial Sea Between States with Opposite or Adjacent Coasts

Where the coasts of two States are opposite or adjacent to each other, neither of the two States is entitled, failing agreement between them to the contrary, to extend its territorial sea beyond the median line every point of which is equidistant from the nearest points on the baselines from which the breadth of the territorial seas of each of the two States is measured. The above provision does not apply, however, where it is necessary by reason of historic title or other special circumstances to delimit the territorial seas of the two States in a way which is at variance therewith.

Article 16. Charts and Lists of Geographical Co-ordinates

1. The baselines for measuring the breadth of the territorial sea determined in accordance with articles 7, 9 and 10, or the limits derived therefrom, and the lines of delimitation drawn in accordance with articles 12 and 15 shall be shown on charts of a scale or scales adequate for ascertaining their position. Alternatively, a list of geographical co-ordinates of points, specifying the geodetic datum, may be substituted.

2. The coastal State shall give due publicity to such charts or lists of geographical co-ordinates and shall deposit a copy of each such chart or list with the Secretary-General of the United Nations.

SECTION 3. INNOCENT PASSAGE IN THE TERRITORIAL SEA

SUBSECTION A. RULES APPLICABLE TO ALL SHIPS

Article 17. Right of Innocent Passage

Subject to this Convention, ships of all States, whether coastal or land-locked, enjoy the right of innocent passage through the territorial sea.

Article 18. Meaning of Passage

1. Passage means navigation through the territorial sea for the purpose of:
    (a) traversing that sea without entering internal waters or calling at a roadstead or port facility outside internal waters; or

(b) proceeding to or from internal waters or a call at such roadstead or port facility.

2. Passage shall be continuous and expeditious. However, passage includes stopping and anchoring, but only in so far as the same are incidental to ordinary navigation or are rendered necessary by *force majeure* or distress or for the purpose of rendering assistance to persons, ships or aircraft in danger or distress.

Article 19. Meaning of Innocent Passage

1. Passage is innocent so long as it is not prejudicial to the peace, good order or security of the coastal State. Such passage shall take place in conformity with this Convention and with other rules of international law.

2. Passage of a foreign ship shall be considered to be prejudicial to the peace, good order or security of the coastal State if in the territorial sea it engages in any of the following activities:

(a) any threat or use of force against the sovereignty, territorial integrity or political independence of the coastal State, or in any other manner in violation of the principles of international law embodied in the Charter of the United Nations;

(b) any exercise or practice with weapons of any kind;

(c) any act aimed at collecting information to the prejudice of the defence or security of the coastal State;

(d) any act of propaganda aimed at affecting the defence or security of the coastal State;

(e) the launching, landing or taking on board of any aircraft;

(f) the launching, landing or taking on board of any military device;

(g) the loading or unloading of any commodity, currency or person contrary to the customs, fiscal, immigration or sanitary laws and regulations of the coastal State;

(h) any act of wilful and serious pollution contrary to this Convention;

(i) any fishing activities;

(j) the carrying out of research or survey activities;

(k) any act aimed at interfering with any systems of communication or any other facilities or installations of the coastal State;

(l) any other activity not having a direct bearing on passage.

Article 20. Submarines and Other Underwater Vehicles

In the territorial sea, submarines and other underwater vehicles are required to navigate on the surface and to show their flag.

Article 21. Laws and Regulations of the Coastal State Relating to Innocent Passage

1. The coastal State may adopt laws and regulations, in conformity with the provisions of this Convention and other rules of international law, relating to innocent passage through the territorial sea, in respect of all or any of the following:

(a) the safety of navigation and the regulation of maritime traffic;

(b) the protection of navigational aids and facilities and other facilities or installations;
(c) the protection of cables and pipelines;
(d) the conservation of the living resources of the sea;
(e) the prevention of infringement of the fisheries laws and regulations of the coastal State;
(f) the preservation of the environment of the coastal State and the prevention, reduction and control of pollution thereof;
(g) marine scientific research and hydrographic surveys;
(h) the prevention of infringement of the customs, fiscal, immigration or sanitary laws and regulations of the coastal State.

2. Such laws and regulations shall not apply to the design, construction, manning or equipment of foreign ships unless they are giving effect to generally accepted international rules or standards.

3. The coastal State shall give due publicity to all such laws and regulations.

4. Foreign ships exercising the right of innocent passage through the territorial sea shall comply with all such laws and regulations and all generally accepted international regulations relating to the prevention of collisions at sea.

Article 22. Sea Lanes and Traffic Separation Schemes in the Territorial Sea

1. The coastal State may, where necessary having regard to the safety of navigation, require foreign ships exercising the right of innocent passage through its territorial sea to use such sea lanes and traffic separation schemes as it may designate or prescribe for the regulation of the passage of ships.

2. In particular, tankers, nuclear-powered ships and ships carrying nuclear or other inherently dangerous or noxious substances or materials may be required to confine their passage to such sea lanes.

3. In the designation of sea lanes and the prescription of traffic separation schemes under this article, the coastal State shall take into account:
(a) the recommendations of the competent international organization;
(b) any channels customarily used for international navigation;
(c) the special characteristics of particular ships and channels; and
(d) the density of traffic.

4. The coastal State shall clearly indicate such sea lanes and traffic separation schemes on charts to which due publicity shall be given.

Article 23. Foreign Nuclear-Powered Ships and Ships Carrying Nuclear or Other Inherently Dangerous or Noxious Substances

Foreign nuclear-powered ships and ships carrying nuclear or other inherently dangerous or noxious substances shall, when exercising the right of innocent passage through the territorial sea, carry documents and observe special precautionary measures established for such ships by international agreements.

Article 24. Duties of the Coastal State

1. The coastal State shall not hamper the innocent passage of foreign ships through the territorial sea except in accordance with this Convention. In particular, in the application of this Convention or of any laws or regulations adopted in conformity with this Convention, the coastal State shall not:

   (a) impose requirements on foreign ships which have the practical effect of denying or impairing the right of innocent passage; or

   (b) discriminate in form or in fact against the ships of any State or against ships carrying cargoes to, from or on behalf of any State.

2. The coastal State shall give appropriate publicity to any danger to navigation, of which it has knowledge, within its territorial sea.

Article 25. Rights of Protection of the Coastal State

1. The coastal State may take the necessary steps in its territorial sea to prevent passage which is not innocent.

2. In the case of ships proceeding to internal waters or a call at a port facility outside internal waters, the coastal State also has the right to take the necessary steps to prevent any breach of the conditions to which admission of those ships to internal waters or such a call is subject.

3. The coastal State may, without discrimination in form or in fact among foreign ships, suspend temporarily in specified areas of its territorial sea the innocent passage of foreign ships if such suspension is essential for the protection of its security, including weapons exercises. Such suspension shall take effect only after having been duly published.

Article 26. Charges Which May Be Levied upon Foreign Ships

1. No charge may be levied upon foreign ships by reason only of their passage through the territorial sea.

2. Charges may be levied upon a foreign ship passing through the territorial sea as payment only for specific services rendered to the ship. These charges shall be levied without discrimination.

SUBSECTION B. RULES APPLICABLE TO MERCHANT SHIPS AND GOVERNMENT SHIPS OPERATED FOR COMMERCIAL PURPOSES

Article 27. Criminal Jurisdiction on Board a Foreign Ship

1. The criminal jurisdiction of the coastal State should not be exercised on board a foreign ship passing through the territorial sea to arrest any person or to conduct any investigation in connection with any crime committed on board the ship during its passage, save only in the following cases:

   (a) if the consequences of the crime extend to the coastal State;

   (b) if the crime is of a kind to disturb the peace of the country or the good order of the territorial sea;

   (c) if the assistance of the local authorities has been requested by the master of the ship or by a diplomatic agent or consular officer of the flag State; or

   (d) if such measures are necessary for the suppression of illicit traffic in narcotic drugs or psychotropic substances.

2. The above provisions do not affect the right of the coastal State to take any steps authorized by its laws for the purpose of an arrest or investigation on board a foreign ship passing through the territorial sea after leaving internal waters.

3. In the cases provided for in paragraphs 1 and 2, the coastal State shall, if the master so requests, notify a diplomatic agent or consular officer of the flag State before taking any steps, and shall facilitate contact between such agent or officer and the ship's crew. In cases of emergency this notification may be communicated while the measures are being taken.

4. In considering whether or in what manner an arrest should be made, the local authorities shall have due regard to the interests of navigation.

5. Except as provided in Part XII or with respect to violations of laws and regulations adopted in accordance with Part V, the coastal State may not take any steps on board a foreign ship passing through the territorial sea to arrest any person or to conduct any investigation in connection with any crime committed before the ship entered the territorial sea, if the ship, proceeding from a foreign port, is only passing through the territorial sea without entering internal waters.

Article 28. *Civil Jurisdiction in Relation to Foreign Ships*

1. The coastal State should not stop or divert a foreign ship passing through the territorial sea for the purpose of exercising civil jurisdiction in relation to a person on board the ship.

2. The coastal State may not levy execution against or arrest the ship for the purpose of any civil proceedings, save only in respect of obligations or liabilities assumed or incurred by the ship itself in the course or for the purpose of its voyage through the waters of the coastal State.

3. Paragraph 2 is without prejudice to the right of the coastal State, in accordance with its laws, to levy execution against or to arrest, for the purpose of any civil proceedings, a foreign ship lying in the territorial sea, or passing through the territorial sea after leaving internal waters.

SUBSECTION C. RULES APPLICABLE TO WARSHIPS AND OTHER GOVERNMENT SHIPS OPERATED FOR NON-COMMERCIAL PURPOSES

Article 29. *Definition of Warships*

For the purposes of this Convention, "warship" means a ship belonging to the armed forces of a State bearing the external marks distinguishing such ships of its nationality, under the command of an officer duly commissioned by the government of the State and whose name appears in the appropriate service list or its equivalent, and manned by a crew which is under regular armed forces discipline.

Article 30. *Non-compliance by Warships with the Laws and Regulations of the Coastal State*

If any warship does not comply with the laws and regulations of the coastal State concerning passage through the territorial sea and disregards any request for compliance therewith which is made to it, the coastal State may require it to leave the territorial sea immediately.

Article 31. Responsibility of the Flag State for Damage Caused by a Warship or Other Government Ship Operated For Non-commercial Purposes

The flag State shall bear international responsibility for any loss or damage to the coastal State resulting from the non-compliance by a warship or other government ship operated for non-commercial purposes with the laws and regulations of the coastal State concerning passage through the territorial sea or with the provisions of this Convention or other rules of international law.

Article 32. Immunities of Warships and Other Government Ships Operated for Non-commercial Purposes

With such exceptions as are contained in subsection A and in articles 30 and 31, nothing in this Convention affects the immunities of warships and other government ships operated for non-commercial purposes.

SECTION 4. CONTIGUOUS ZONE

Article 33. Contiguous Zone

1. In a zone contiguous to its territorial sea, described as the contiguous zone, the coastal State may exercise the control necessary to:
    (a) prevent infringement of its customs, fiscal, immigration or sanitary laws and regulations within its territory or territorial sea;
    (b) punish infringement of the above laws and regulations committed within its territory or territorial sea.
2. The contiguous zone may not extend beyond 24 nautical miles from the baselines from which the breadth of the territorial sea is measured.

Part III. Straits Used for International Navigation

SECTION 1. GENERAL PROVISIONS

Article 34. Legal Status of Waters Forming Straits Used for International Navigation

1. The régime of passage through straits used for international navigation established in this Part shall not in other respects affect the legal status of the waters forming such straits or the exercise by the States bordering the straits of their sovereignty or jurisdiction over such waters and their air space, bed and subsoil.
2. The sovereignty or jurisdiction of the States bordering the straits is exercised subject to this Part and to other rules of international law.

Article 35. Scope of This Part

Nothing in this Part affects:

(a) any areas of internal waters within a strait, except where the establishment of a straight baseline in accordance with the method set forth in article 7 has the effect of enclosing as internal waters areas which had not previously been considered as such;

(b) the legal status of the waters beyond the territorial seas of States bordering straits as exclusive economic zones or high seas; or

(c) the legal régime in straits in which passage is regulated in whole or in part by long-standing international conventions in force specifically relating to such straits.

Article 36. High Seas Routes or Routes Through Exclusive Economic Zones Through Straits Used for International Navigation

This Part does not apply to a strait used for international navigation if there exists through the strait a route through the high seas or through an exclusive economic zone of similar convenience with respect to navigational and hydrographical characteristics; in such routes, the other relevant Parts of this Convention, including the provisions regarding the freedoms of navigation and overflight, apply.

SECTION 2. TRANSIT PASSAGE

Article 37. Scope of This Section

This section applies to straits which are used for international navigation between one part of the high seas or an exclusive economic zone and another part of the high seas or an exclusive economic zone.

Article 38. Right of Transit Passage

1. In straits referred to in article 37, all ships and aircraft enjoy the right of transit passage, which shall not be impeded; except that, if the strait is formed by an island of a State bordering the strait and its mainland, transit passage shall not apply if there exists seaward of the island a route through the high seas or through an exclusive economic zone of similar convenience with respect to navigational and hydrographical characteristics.

2. Transit passage means the exercise in accordance with this Part of the freedom of navigation and overflight solely for the purpose of continuous and expeditious transit of the strait between one part of the high seas or an exclusive economic zone and another part of the high seas or an exclusive economic zone. However, the requirement of continuous and expeditious transit does not preclude passage through the strait for the purpose of entering, leaving or returning from a State bordering the strait, subject to the conditions of entry to that State.

3. Any activity which is not an exercise of the right of transit passage through a strait remains subject to the other applicable provisions of this Convention.

Article 39. Duties of Ships and Aircraft During Transit Passage

1. Ships and aircraft, while exercising the right of transit passage, shall:
    (a) proceed without delay through or over the strait;
    (b) refrain from any threat or use of force against the sovereignty, territorial integrity or political independence of States bordering the strait, or in any other manner in violation of the principles of international law embodied in the Charter of the United Nations;
    (c) refrain from any activities other than those incident to their normal modes of continuous and expeditious transit unless rendered necessary by *force majeure* or by distress;
    (d) comply with other relevant provisions of this Part.
2. Ships in transit passage shall:
    (a) comply with generally accepted international regulations, procedures and practices for safety at sea, including the International Regulations for Preventing Collisions at Sea;
    (b) comply with generally accepted international regulations, procedures and practices for the prevention, reduction and control of pollution from ships.
3. Aircraft in transit passage shall:
    (a) observe the Rules of the Air established by the International Civil Aviation Organization as they apply to civil aircraft; state aircraft will normally comply with such safety measures and will at all times operate with due regard for the safety of navigation;
    (b) at all times monitor the radio frequency assigned by the competent internationally designated air traffic control authority or the appropriate international distress radio frequency.

Article 40. Research and Survey Activities

During transit passage, foreign ships, including marine scientific research and hydrographic survey ships, may not carry out any research or survey activities without the prior authorization of the States bordering straits.

Article 41. Sea Lanes and Traffic Separation Schemes in Straits Used for International Navigation

1. In conformity with this Part, States bordering straits may designate sea lanes and prescribe traffic separation schemes for navigation in straits where necessary to promote the safe passage of ships.
2. Such States may, when circumstances require, and after giving due publicity thereto, substitute other sea lanes or traffic separation schemes for any sea lanes or traffic separation schemes previously designated or prescribed by them.
3. Such sea lanes and traffic separation schemes shall conform to generally accepted international regulations.
4. Before designating or substituting sea lanes or prescribing or substituting traffic separation schemes, States bordering straits shall refer proposals to the competent international organization with a view to their

adoption. The organization may adopt only such sea lanes and traffic separation schemes as may be agreed with the States bordering the straits, after which the States may designate, prescribe or substitute them.

5. In respect of a strait where sea lanes or traffic separation schemes through the waters of two or more States bordering the strait are being proposed, the States concerned shall co-operate in formulating proposals in consultation with the competent international organization.

6. States bordering straits shall clearly indicate all sea lanes and traffic separation schemes designated or prescribed by them on charts to which due publicity shall be given.

7. Ships in transit passage shall respect applicable sea lanes and traffic separation schemes established in accordance with this article.

Article 42. Laws and Regulations of States Bordering Straits Relating to Transit Passage

1. Subject to the provisions of this section, States bordering straits may adopt laws and regulations relating to transit passage through straits, in respect of all or any of the following:

   (a) the safety of navigation and the regulation of maritime traffic, as provided in article 41;

   (b) the prevention, reduction and control of pollution, by giving effect to applicable international regulations regarding the discharge of oil, oily wastes and other noxious substances in the strait;

   (c) with respect to fishing vessels, the prevention of fishing, including the stowage of fishing gear;

   (d) the loading or unloading of any commodity, currency or person in contravention of the customs, fiscal, immigration or sanitary laws and regulations of States bordering straits.

2. Such laws and regulations shall not discriminate in form or in fact among foreign ships or in their application have the practical effect of denying, hampering or impairing the right of transit passage as defined in this section.

3. States bordering straits shall give due publicity to all such laws and regulations.

4. Foreign ships exercising the right of transit passage shall comply with such laws and regulations.

5. The flag State of a ship or the State of registry of an aircraft entitled to sovereign immunity which acts in a manner contrary to such laws and regulations or other provisions of this Part shall bear international responsibility for any loss or damage which results to States bordering straits.

Article 43. Navigational and Safety Aids and Other Improvements and the Prevention, Reduction and Control of Pollution

User States and States bordering a strait should by agreement co-operate:

   (a) in the establishment and maintenance in a strait of necessary navigational and safety aids or other improvements in aid of international navigation; and

   (b) for the prevention, reduction and control of pollution from ships.

Article 44. *Duties of States Bordering Straits*

States bordering straits shall not hamper transit passage and shall give appropriate publicity to any danger to navigation or overflight within or over the strait of which they have knowledge. There shall be no suspension of transit passage.

SECTION 3. INNOCENT PASSAGE

Article 45. *Innocent Passage*

1. The régime of innocent passage, in accordance with Part II, section 3, shall apply in straits used for international navigation:
    (a) excluded from the application of the régime of transit passage under article 38, paragraph 1; or
    (b) between a part of the high seas or an exclusive economic zone and the territorial sea of a foreign State.

2. There shall be no suspension of innocent passage through such straits.

Part IV. Archipelagic States

Article 46. *Use of Terms*

For the purposes of this Convention:
    (a) "archipelagic State" means a State constituted wholly by one or more archipelagos and may include other islands;
    (b) "archipelago" means a group of islands, including parts of islands, interconnecting waters and other natural features which are so closely interrelated that such islands, waters and other natural features form an intrinsic geographical, economic and political entity, or which historically have been regarded as such.

Article 47. *Archipelagic Baselines*

1. An archipelagic State may draw straight archipelagic baselines joining the outermost points of the outermost islands and drying reefs of the archipelago provided that within such baselines are included the main islands and an area in which the ratio of the area of the water to the area of the land, including atolls, is between 1 to 1 and 9 to 1.

2. The length of such baselines shall not exceed 100 nautical miles, except that up to 3 per cent of the total number of baselines enclosing any archipelago may exceed that length, up to a maximum length of 125 nautical miles.

3. The drawing of such baselines shall not depart to any appreciable extent from the general configuration of the archipelago.

4. Such baselines shall not be drawn to and from low-tide elevations, unless lighthouses or similar installations which are permanently above sea level have been built on them or where a low-tide elevation is situated wholly or partly at a distance not exceeding the breadth of the territorial sea from the nearest island.

5. The system of such baselines shall not be applied by an archipelagic State in such a manner as to cut off from the high seas or the exclusive economic zone the territorial sea of another State.

6. If a part of the archipelagic waters of an archipelagic State lies between two parts of an immediately adjacent neighbouring State, existing rights and all other legitimate interests which the latter State has traditionally exercised in such waters and all rights stipulated by agreement between those States shall continue and be respected.

7. For the purpose of computing the ratio of water to land under paragraph 1, land areas may include waters lying within the fringing reefs of islands and atolls, including that part of a steep-sided oceanic plateau which is enclosed or nearly enclosed by a chain of limestone islands and drying reefs lying on the perimeter of the plateau.

8. The baselines drawn in accordance with this article shall be shown on charts of a scale or scales adequate for ascertaining their position. Alternatively, lists of geographical co-ordinates of points, specifying the geodetic datum, may be substituted.

9. The archipelagic State shall give due publicity to such charts or lists of geographical co-ordinates and shall deposit a copy of each such chart or list with the Secretary-General of the United Nations.

Article 48. Measurement of the Breadth of the Territorial Sea, the Contiguous Zone, the Exclusive Economic Zone and the Continental Shelf

The breadth of the territorial sea, the contiguous zone, the exclusive economic zone and the continental shelf shall be measured from archipelagic baselines drawn in accordance with article 47.

Article 49. Legal Status of Archipelagic Waters, of the Air Space over Archipelagic Waters and of Their Bed and Subsoil

1. The sovereignty of an archipelagic State extends to the waters enclosed by the archipelagic baselines drawn in accordance with article 47, described as archipelagic waters, regardless of their depth or distance from the coast.

2. This sovereignty extends to the air space over the archipelagic waters, as well as to their bed and subsoil, and the resources contained therein.

3. This sovereignty is exercised subject to this Part.

4. The régime of archipelagic sea lanes passage established in this Part shall not in other respects affect the status of the archipelagic waters, including the sea lanes, or the exercise by the archipelagic State of its sovereignty over such waters and their air space, bed and subsoil, and the resources contained therein.

Article 50. Delimitation of Internal Waters

Within its archipelagic waters, the archipelagic State may draw closing lines for the delimitation of internal waters, in accordance with articles 9, 10 and 11.

Article 51. Existing Agreements, Traditional Fishing Rights and Existing Submarine Cables

1. Without prejudice to article 49, an archipelagic State shall respect existing agreements with other States and shall recognize traditional fishing rights and other legitimate activities of the immediately adjacent neighbouring States in certain areas falling within archipelagic waters. The terms and conditions for the exercise of such rights and activities, including the nature, the extent and the areas to which they apply, shall, at the request of any of the States concerned, be regulated by bilateral agreements between them. Such rights shall not be transferred to or shared with third States or their nationals.

2. An archipelagic State shall respect existing submarine cables laid by other States and passing through its waters without making a landfall. An archipelagic State shall permit the maintenance and replacement of such cables upon receiving due notice of their location and the intention to repair or replace them.

Article 52. Right of Innocent Passage

1. Subject to article 53 and without prejudice to article 50, ships of all States enjoy the right of innocent passage through archipelagic waters, in accordance with Part II, section 3.

2. The archipelagic State may, without discrimination in form or in fact among foreign ships, suspend temporarily in specified areas of its archipelagic waters the innocent passage of foreign ships if such suspension is essential for the protection of its security. Such suspension shall take effect only after having been duly published.

Article 53. Right of Archipelagic Sea Lanes Passage

1. An archipelagic State may designate sea lanes and air routes thereabove, suitable for the continuous and expeditious passage of foreign ships and aircraft through or over its archipelagic waters and the adjacent territorial sea.

2. All ships and aircraft enjoy the right of archipelagic sea lanes passage in such sea lanes and air routes.

3. Archipelagic sea lanes passage means the exercise in accordance with this Convention of the rights of navigation and overflight in the normal mode solely for the purpose of continuous, expeditious and unobstructed transit between one part of the high seas or an exclusive economic zone and another part of the high seas or an exclusive economic zone.

4. Such sea lanes and air routes shall traverse the archipelagic waters and the adjacent territorial sea and shall include all normal passage routes used as routes for international navigation or overflight through or over archipelagic waters and, within such routes, so far as ships are concerned, all normal navigational channels, provided that duplication of routes of similar convenience between the same entry and exit points shall not be necessary.

5. Such sea lanes and air routes shall be defined by a series of continu-

ous axis lines from the entry points of passage routes to the exit points. Ships and aircraft in archipelagic sea lanes passage shall not deviate more than 25 nautical miles to either side of such axis lines during passage, provided that such ships and aircraft shall not navigate closer to the coasts than 10 per cent of the distance between the nearest points on islands bordering the sea lane.

6. An archipelagic State which designates sea lanes under this article may also prescribe traffic separation schemes for the safe passage of ships through narrow channels in such sea lanes.

7. An archipelagic State may, when circumstances require, after giving due publicity thereto, substitute other sea lanes or traffic separation schemes for any sea lanes or traffic separation schemes previously designated or prescribed by it.

8. Such sea lanes and traffic separation schemes shall conform to generally accepted international regulations.

9. In designating or substituting sea lanes or prescribing or substituting traffic separation schemes, an archipelagic State shall refer proposals to the competent international organization with a view to their adoption. The organization may adopt only such sea lanes and traffic separation schemes as may be agreed with the archipelagic State, after which the archipelagic State may designate, prescribe or substitute them.

10. The archipelagic State shall clearly indicate the axis of the sea lanes and the traffic separation schemes designated or prescribed by it on charts to which due publicity shall be given.

11. Ships in archipelagic sea lanes passage shall respect applicable sea lanes and traffic separation schemes established in accordance with this article.

12. If an archipelagic State does not designate sea lanes or air routes, the right of archipelagic sea lanes passage may be exercised through the routes normally used for international navigation.

Article 54. Duties of Ships and Aircraft During Their Passage, Research and Survey Activities, Duties of the Archipelagic State and Laws and Regulations of the Archipelagic State Relating to Archipelagic Sea Lanes Passage

Articles 39, 40, 42 and 44 apply *mutatis mutandis* to archipelagic sea lanes passage.

Part V. Exclusive Economic Zone

Article 55. Specific Legal Régime of the Exclusive Economic Zone

The exclusive economic zone is an area beyond and adjacent to the territorial sea, subject to the specific legal régime established in this Part, under which the rights and jurisdiction of the coastal State and the rights and freedoms of other States are governed by the relevant provisions of this Convention.

Article 56. Rights, Jurisdiction and Duties of the Coastal State in the Exclusive Economic Zone

1. In the exclusive economic zone, the coastal State has:

(a) sovereign rights for the purpose of exploring and exploiting, conserving and managing the natural resources, whether living or non-living, of the waters superjacent to the sea-bed and of the sea-bed and its subsoil, and with regard to other activities for the economic exploitation and exploration of the zone, such as the production of energy from the water, currents and winds;

(b) jurisdiction as provided for in the relevant provisions of this Convention with regard to:

(i) the establishment and use of artificial islands, installations and structures;

(ii) marine scientific research;

(iii) the protection and preservation of the marine environment;

(c) other rights and duties provided for in this Convention.

2. In exercising its rights and performing its duties under this Convention in the exclusive economic zone, the coastal State shall have due regard to the rights and duties of other States and shall act in a manner compatible with the provisions of this Convention.

3. The rights set out in this article with respect to the sea-bed and subsoil shall be exercised in accordance with Part VI.

Article 57. Breadth of the Exclusive Economic Zone

The exclusive economic zone shall not extend beyond 200 nautical miles from the baselines from which the breadth of the territorial sea is measured.

Article 58. Rights and Duties of Other States in the Exclusive Economic Zone

1. In the exclusive economic zone, all States, whether coastal or land-locked, enjoy, subject to the relevant provisions of this Convention, the freedoms referred to in article 87 of navigation and overflight and of the laying of submarine cables and pipelines, and other internationally lawful uses of the sea related to these freedoms, such as those associated with the operation of ships, aircraft and submarine cables and pipelines, and compatible with the other provisions of this Convention.

2. Articles 88 to 115 and other pertinent rules of international law apply to the exclusive economic zone in so far as they are not incompatible with this Part.

3. In exercising their rights and performing their duties under this Convention in the exclusive economic zone, States shall have due regard to the rights and duties of the coastal State and shall comply with the laws and regulations adopted by the coastal State in accordance with the provisions of this Convention and other rules of international law in so far as they are not incompatible with this Part.

Article 59. Basis for the Resolution of Conflicts Regarding the Attribution of Rights and Jurisdiction in the Exclusive Economic Zone

In cases where this Convention does not attribute rights or jurisdiction to the coastal State or to other States within the exclusive economic zone, and a conflict arises between the interests of the coastal State and any other State or States, the conflict should be resolved on the basis of equity and in the light of all the relevant circumstances, taking into account the respective importance of the interests involved to the parties as well as to the international community as a whole.

Article 60. Artificial Islands, Installations and Structures in the Exclusive Economic Zone

1. In the exclusive economic zone, the coastal State shall have the exclusive right to construct and to authorize and regulate the construction, operation and use of:
    (a) artificial islands;
    (b) installations and structures for the purposes provided for in article 56 and other economic purposes;
    (c) installations and structures which may interfere with the exercise of the rights of the coastal State in the zone.
2. The coastal State shall have exclusive jurisdiction over such artificial islands, installations and structures, including jurisdiction with regard to customs, fiscal, health, safety and immigration laws and regulations.
3. Due notice must be given of the construction of such artificial islands, installations or structures, and permanent means for giving warning of their presence must be maintained. Any installations or structures which are abandoned or disused shall be removed to ensure safety of navigation, taking into account any generally accepted international standards established in this regard by the competent international organization. Such removal shall also have due regard to fishing, the protection of the marine environment and the rights and duties of other States. Appropriate publicity shall be given to the depth, position and dimensions of any installations or structures not entirely removed.
4. The coastal State may, where necessary, establish reasonable safety zones around such artificial islands, installations and structures in which it may take appropriate measures to ensure the safety both of navigation and of the artificial islands, installations and structures.
5. The breadth of the safety zones shall be determined by the coastal State, taking into account applicable international standards. Such zones shall be designed to ensure that they are reasonably related to the nature and function of the artificial islands, installations or structures, and shall not exceed a distance of 500 metres around them, measured from each point of their outer edge, except as authorized by generally accepted international standards or as recommended by the competent international organization. Due notice shall be given of the extent of safety zones.
6. All ships must respect these safety zones and shall comply with

generally accepted international standards regarding navigation in the vicinity of artificial islands, installations, structures and safety zones.

7. Artificial islands, installations and structures and the safety zones around them may not be established where interference may be caused to the use of recognized sea lanes essential to international navigation.

8. Artificial islands, installations and structures do not possess the status of islands. They have no territorial sea of their own, and their presence does not affect the delimitation of the territorial sea, the exclusive economic zone or the continental shelf.

Article 61. Conservation of the Living Resources

1. The coastal State shall determine the allowable catch of the living resources in its exclusive economic zone.

2. The coastal State, taking into account the best scientific evidence available to it, shall ensure through proper conservation and management measures that the maintenance of the living resources in the exclusive economic zone is not endangered by over-exploitation. As appropriate, the coastal State and competent international organizations, whether subregional, regional or global, shall co-operate to this end.

3. Such measures shall also be designed to maintain or restore populations of harvested species at levels which can produce the maximum sustainable yield, as qualified by relevant environmental and economic factors, including the economic needs of coastal fishing communities and the special requirements of developing States, and taking into account fishing patterns, the interdependence of stocks and any generally recommended international minimum standards, whether subregional, regional or global.

4. In taking such measures the coastal State shall take into consideration the effects on species associated with or dependent upon harvested species with a view to maintaining or restoring populations of such associated or dependent species above levels at which their reproduction may become seriously threatened.

5. Available scientific information, catch and fishing effort statistics, and other data relevant to the conservation of fish stocks shall be contributed and exchanged on a regular basis through competent international organizations, whether subregional, regional or global, where appropriate and with participation by all States concerned, including States whose nationals are allowed to fish in the exclusive economic zone.

Article 62. Utilization of the Living Resources

1. The coastal State shall promote the objective of optimum utilization of the living resources in the exclusive economic zone without prejudice to article 61.

2. The coastal State shall determine its capacity to harvest the living resources of the exclusive economic zone. Where the coastal State does not have the capacity to harvest the entire allowable catch, it shall, through agreements or other arrangements and pursuant to the terms, conditions,

laws and regulations referred to in paragraph 4, give other States access to the surplus of the allowable catch, having particular regard to the provisions of articles 69 and 70, especially in relation to the developing States mentioned therein.

3. In giving access to other States to its exclusive economic zone under this article, the coastal State shall take into account all relevant factors, including, *inter alia,* the significance of the living resources of the area to the economy of the coastal State concerned and its other national interests, the provisions of articles 69 and 70, the requirements of developing States in the subregion or region in harvesting part of the surplus and the need to minimize economic dislocation in States whose nationals have habitually fished in the zone or which have made substantial efforts in research and identification of stocks.

4. Nationals of other States fishing in the exclusive economic zone shall comply with the conservation measures and with the other terms and conditions established in the laws and regulations of the coastal State. These laws and regulations shall be consistent with this Convention and may relate, *inter alia,* to the following:

(a) licensing of fishermen, fishing vessels and equipment, including payment of fees and other forms of remuneration, which, in the case of developing coastal States, may consist of adequate compensation in the field of financing, equipment and technology relating to the fishing industry;

(b) determining the species which may be caught, and fixing quotas of catch, whether in relation to particular stocks or groups of stocks or catch per vessel over a period of time or to the catch by nationals of any State during a specified period;

(c) regulating seasons and areas of fishing, the types, sizes and amount of gear, and the types, sizes and number of fishing vessels that may be used;

(d) fixing the age and size of fish and other species that may be caught;

(e) specifying information required of fishing vessels, including catch and effort statistics and vessel position reports;

(f) requiring, under the authorization and control of the coastal State, the conduct of specified fisheries research programmes and regulating the conduct of such research, including the sampling of catches, disposition of samples and reporting of associated scientific data;

(g) the placing of observers or trainees on board such vessels by the coastal State;

(h) the landing of all or any part of the catch by such vessels in the ports of the coastal State;

(i) terms and conditions relating to joint ventures or other co-operative arrangements;

(j) requirements for the training of personnel and the transfer of fisheries technology, including enhancement of the coastal State's capability of undertaking fisheries research;

(k) enforcement procedures.

5. Coastal States shall give due notice of conservation and management laws and regulations.

Article 63. Stocks Occurring Within the Exclusive Economic Zones of Two or More Coastal States or Both Within the Exclusive Economic Zone and in an Area Beyond and Adjacent to It

1. Where the same stock or stocks of associated species occur within the exclusive economic zones of two or more coastal States, these States shall seek, either directly or through appropriate subregional or regional organizations, to agree upon the measures necessary to co-ordinate and ensure the conservation and development of such stocks without prejudice to the other provisions of this Part.

2. Where the same stock or stocks of associated species occur both within the exclusive economic zone and in an area beyond and adjacent to the zone, the coastal State and the States fishing for such stocks in the adjacent area shall seek, either directly or through appropriate subregional or regional organizations, to agree upon the measures necessary for the conservation of these stocks in the adjacent area.

Article 64. Highly Migratory Species

1. The coastal State and other States whose nationals fish in the region for the highly migratory species listed in Annex I shall co-operate directly or through appropriate international organizations with a view to ensuring conservation and promoting the objective of optimum utilization of such species throughout the region, both within and beyond the exclusive economic zone. In regions for which no appropriate international organization exists, the coastal State and other States whose nationals harvest these species in the region shall co-operate to establish such an organization and participate in its work.

2. The provisions of paragraph 1 apply in addition to the other provisions of this Part.

Article 65. Marine Mammals

Nothing in this Part restricts the right of a coastal State or the competence of an international organization, as appropriate, to prohibit, limit or regulate the exploitation of marine mammals more strictly than provided for in this Part. States shall co-operate with a view to the conservation of marine mammals and in the case of cetaceans shall in particular work through the appropriate international organizations for their conservation, management and study.

Article 66. Anadromous Stocks

1. States in whose rivers anadromous stocks originate shall have the primary interest in and responsibility for such stocks.

2. The State of origin of anadromous stocks shall ensure their conservation by the establishment of appropriate regulatory measures for fishing in

all waters landward of the outer limits of its exclusive economic zone and for fishing provided for in paragraph 3(b). The State of origin may, after consultations with the other States referred to in paragraphs 3 and 4 fishing these stocks, establish total allowable catches for stocks originating in its rivers.

3. (a) Fisheries for anadromous stocks shall be conducted only in waters landward of the outer limits of exclusive economic zones, except in cases where this provision would result in economic dislocation for a State other than the State of origin. With respect to such fishing beyond the outer limits of the exclusive economic zone, States concerned shall maintain consultations with a view to achieving agreement on terms and conditions of such fishing giving due regard to the conservation requirements and the needs of the State of origin in respect of these stocks.

(b) The State of origin shall co-operate in minimizing economic dislocation in such other States fishing these stocks, taking into account the normal catch and the mode of operations of such States, and all the areas in which such fishing has occurred.

(c) States referred to in subparagraph (b), participating by agreement with the State of origin in measures to renew anadromous stocks, particularly by expenditures for that purpose, shall be given special consideration by the State of origin in the harvesting of stocks originating in its rivers.

(d) Enforcement of regulations regarding anadromous stocks beyond the exclusive economic zone shall be by agreement between the State of origin and the other States concerned.

4. In cases where anadromous stocks migrate into or through the waters landward of the outer limits of the exclusive economic zone of a State other than the State of origin, such State shall co-operate with the State of origin with regard to the conservation and management of such stocks.

5. The State of origin of anadromous stocks and other States fishing these stocks shall make arrangements for the implementation of the provisions of this article, where appropriate, through regional organizations.

Article 67. Catadromous Species

1. A coastal State in whose waters catadromous species spend the greater part of their life cycle shall have responsibility for the management of these species and shall ensure the ingress and egress of migrating fish.

2. Harvesting of catadromous species shall be conducted only in waters landward of the outer limits of exclusive economic zones. When conducted in exclusive economic zones, harvesting shall be subject to this article and the other provisions of this Convention concerning fishing in these zones.

3. In cases where catadromous fish migrate through the exclusive economic zone of another State, whether as juvenile or maturing fish, the management, including harvesting, of such fish shall be regulated by agreement between the State mentioned in paragraph 1 and the other State concerned. Such agreement shall ensure the rational management of the species and take into account the responsibilities of the State mentioned in paragraph 1 for the maintenance of these species.

Article 68. Sedentary Species

This Part does not apply to sedentary species as defined in article 77, paragraph 4.

Article 69. Right of Land-Locked States

1. Land-locked States shall have the right to participate, on an equitable basis, in the exploitation of an appropriate part of the surplus of the living resources of the exclusive economic zones of coastal States of the same subregion or region, taking into account the relevant economic and geographical circumstances of all the States concerned and in conformity with the provisions of this article and of articles 61 and 62.

2. The terms and modalities of such participation shall be established by the States concerned through bilateral, subregional or regional agreements taking into account, *inter alia:*

   (a) the need to avoid effects detrimental to fishing communities or fishing industries of the coastal State;

   (b) the extent to which the land-locked State, in accordance with the provisions of this article, is participating or is entitled to participate under existing bilateral, subregional or regional agreements in the exploitation of living resources of the exclusive economic zones of other coastal States;

   (c) the extent to which other land-locked States and geographically disadvantaged States are participating in the exploitation of the living resources of the exclusive economic zone of the coastal State and the consequent need to avoid a particular burden for any single coastal State or a part of it;

   (d) the nutritional needs of the populations of the respective States.

3. When the harvesting capacity of a coastal State approaches a point which would enable it to harvest the entire allowable catch of the living resources in its exclusive economic zone, the coastal State and other States concerned shall co-operate in the establishment of equitable arrangements on a bilateral, subregional or regional basis to allow for participation of developing land-locked States of the same subregion or region in the exploitation of the living resources of the exclusive economic zones of coastal States of the subregion or region, as may be appropriate in the circumstances and on terms satisfactory to all parties. In the implementation of this provision the factors mentioned in paragraph 2 shall also be taken into account.

4. Developed land-locked States shall, under the provisions of this article, be entitled to participate in the exploitation of living resources only in the exclusive economic zones of developed coastal States of the same subregion or region having regard to the extent to which the coastal State, in giving access to other States to the living resources of its exclusive economic zone, has taken into account the need to minimize detrimental effects on fishing communities and economic dislocation in States whose nationals have habitually fished in the zone.

5. The above provisions are without prejudice to arrangements agreed upon in subregions or regions where the coastal States may grant to land-

locked States of the same subregion or region equal or preferential rights for the exploitation of the living resources in the exclusive economic zones.

Article 70. Right of Geographically Disadvantaged States

1. Geographically disadvantaged States shall have the right to participate, on an equitable basis, in the exploitation of an appropriate part of the surplus of the living resources of the exclusive economic zones of coastal States of the same subregion or region, taking into account the relevant economic and geographical circumstances of all the States concerned and in conformity with the provisions of this article and of articles 61 and 62.

2. For the purposes of this Part, "geographically disadvantaged States" means coastal States, including States bordering enclosed or semi-enclosed seas, whose geographical situation makes them dependent upon the exploitation of the living resources of the exclusive economic zones of other States in the subregion or region for adequate supplies of fish for the nutritional purposes of their populations or parts thereof, and coastal States which can claim no exclusive economic zones of their own.

3. The terms and modalities of such participation shall be established by the States concerned through bilateral, subregional or regional agreements taking into account, *inter alia:*

   (a) the need to avoid effects detrimental to fishing communities or fishing industries of the coastal State;

   (b) the extent to which the geographically disadvantaged State, in accordance with the provisions of this article, is participating or is entitled to participate under existing bilateral, subregional or regional agreements in the exploitation of living resources of the exclusive economic zones of other coastal States;

   (c) the extent to which other geographically disadvantaged States and land-locked States are participating in the exploitation of the living resources of the exclusive economic zone of the coastal State and the consequent need to avoid a particular burden for any single coastal State or a part of it;

   (d) the nutritional needs of the populations of the respective States.

4. When the harvesting capacity of a coastal State approaches a point which would enable it to harvest the entire allowable catch of the living resources in its exclusive economic zone, the coastal State and other States concerned shall co-operate in the establishment of equitable arrangements on a bilateral, subregional or regional basis to allow for participation of developing geographically disadvantaged States of the same subregion or region in the exploitation of the living resources of the exclusive economic zones of coastal States of the subregion or region, as may be appropriate in the circumstances and on terms satisfactory to all parties. In the implementation of this provision the factors mentioned in paragraph 3 shall also be taken into account.

5. Developed geographically disadvantaged States shall, under the provisions of this article, be entitled to participate in the exploitation of living resources only in the exclusive economic zones of developed coastal States of the same subregion or region having regard to the extent to which the

coastal State, in giving access to other States to the living resources of its exclusive economic zone, has taken into account the need to minimize detrimental effects on fishing communities and economic dislocation in States whose nationals have habitually fished in the zone.

6. The above provisions are without prejudice to arrangements agreed upon in subregions or regions where the coastal States may grant to geographically disadvantaged States of the same subregion or region equal or preferential rights for the exploitation of the living resources in the exclusive economic zones.

Article 71. Non-Applicability of Articles 69 and 70

The provisions of articles 69 and 70 do not apply in the case of a coastal State whose economy is overwhelmingly dependent on the exploitation of the living resources of its exclusive economic zone.

Article 72. Restrictions on Transfer of Rights

1. Rights provided under articles 69 and 70 to exploit living resources shall not be directly or indirectly transferred to third States or their nationals by lease or licence, by establishing joint ventures or in any other manner which has the effect of such transfer unless otherwise agreed by the States concerned.

2. The foregoing provision does not preclude the States concerned from obtaining technical or financial assistance from third States or international organizations in order to facilitate the exercise of the rights pursuant to articles 69 and 70, provided that it does not have the effect referred to in paragraph 1.

Article 73. Enforcement of Laws and Regulations of the Coastal State

1. The coastal State may, in the exercise of its sovereign rights to explore, exploit, conserve and manage the living resources in the exclusive economic zone, take such measures, including boarding, inspection, arrest and judicial proceedings, as may be necessary to ensure compliance with the laws and regulations adopted by it in conformity with this Convention.

2. Arrested vessels and their crews shall be promptly released upon the posting of reasonable bond or other security.

3. Coastal State penalties for violations of fisheries laws and regulations in the exclusive economic zone may not include imprisonment, in the absence of agreements to the contrary by the States concerned, or any other form of corporal punishment.

4. In cases of arrest or detention of foreign vessels the coastal State shall promptly notify the flag State, through appropriate channels, of the action taken and of any penalties subsequently imposed.

Article 74. Delimitation of the Exclusive Economic Zone Between States with Opposite or Adjacent Coasts

1. The delimitation of the exclusive economic zone between States with opposite or adjacent coasts shall be effected by agreement on the basis of

international law, as referred to in Article 38 of the Statute of the International Court of Justice, in order to achieve an equitable solution.

2. If no agreement can be reached within a reasonable period of time, the States concerned shall resort to the procedures provided for in Part XV.

3. Pending agreement as provided for in paragraph 1, the States concerned, in a spirit of understanding and co-operation, shall make every effort to enter into provisional arrangements of a practical nature and, during this transitional period, not to jeopardize or hamper the reaching of the final agreement. Such arrangements shall be without prejudice to the final delimitation.

4. Where there is an agreement in force between the States concerned, questions relating to the delimitation of the exclusive economic zone shall be determined in accordance with the provisions of that agreement.

Article 75. Charts and Lists of Geographical Co-ordinates

1. Subject to this Part, the outer limit lines of the exclusive economic zone and the lines of delimitation drawn in accordance with article 74 shall be shown on charts of a scale or scales adequate for ascertaining their position. Where appropriate, lists of geographical co-ordinates of points, specifying the geodetic datum, may be substituted for such outer limit lines or lines of delimitation.

2. The coastal State shall give due publicity to such charts or lists of geographical co-ordinates and shall deposit a copy of each such chart or list with the Secretary-General of the United Nations.

Part VI. Continental Shelf

Article 76. Definition of the Continental Shelf

1. The continental shelf of a coastal State comprises the sea-bed and subsoil of the submarine areas that extend beyond its territorial sea throughout the natural prolongation of its land territory to the outer edge of the continental margin, or to a distance of 200 nautical miles from the baselines from which the breadth of the territorial sea is measured where the outer edge of the continental margin does not extend up to that distance.

2. The continental shelf of a coastal State shall not extend beyond the limits provided for in paragraphs 4 to 6.

3. The continental margin comprises the submerged prolongation of the land mass of the coastal State, and consists of the sea-bed and subsoil of the shelf, the slope and the rise. It does not include the deep ocean floor with its oceanic ridges or the subsoil thereof.

4. (a) For the purposes of this Convention, the coastal State shall establish the outer edge of the continental margin wherever the margin extends beyond 200 nautical miles from the baselines from which the breadth of the territorial sea is measured, by either:

(i) a line delineated in accordance with paragraph 7 by reference to the outermost fixed points at each of which the thickness of sedimentary rocks is at least 1 per cent of the shortest distance from such point to the foot of the continental slope; or

(ii) a line delineated in accordance with paragraph 7 by reference to fixed points not more than 60 nautical miles from the foot of the continental slope.

(b) In the absence of evidence to the contrary, the foot of the continental slope shall be determined as the point of maximum change in the gradient at its base.

5. The fixed points comprising the line of the outer limits of the continental shelf on the sea-bed, drawn in accordance with paragraph 4 (a)(i) and (ii), either shall not exceed 350 nautical miles from the baselines from which the breadth of the territorial sea is measured or shall not exceed 100 nautical miles from the 2,500 metre isobath, which is a line connecting the depth of 2,500 metres.

6. Notwithstanding the provisions of paragraph 5, on submarine ridges, the outer limit of the continental shelf shall not exceed 350 nautical miles from the baselines from which the breadth of the territorial sea is measured. This paragraph does not apply to submarine elevations that are natural components of the continental margin, such as its plateaux, rises, caps, banks and spurs.

7. The coastal State shall delineate the outer limits of its continental shelf, where that shelf extends beyond 200 nautical miles from the baselines from which the breadth of the territorial sea is measured, by straight lines not exceeding 60 nautical miles in length, connecting fixed points, defined by co-ordinates of latitude and longitude.

8. Information on the limits of the continental shelf beyond 200 nautical miles from the baselines from which the breadth of the territorial sea is measured shall be submitted by the coastal State to the Commission on the Limits of the Continental Shelf set up under Annex II on the basis of equitable geographical representation. The Commission shall make recommendations to coastal States on matters related to the establishment of the outer limits of their continental shelf. The limits of the shelf established by a coastal State on the basis of these recommendations shall be final and binding.

9. The coastal State shall deposit with the Secretary-General of the United Nations charts and relevant information, including geodetic data, permanently describing the outer limits of its continental shelf. The Secretary-General shall give due publicity thereto.

10. The provisions of this article are without prejudice to the question of delimitation of the continental shelf between States with opposite or adjacent coasts.

Article 77. *Rights of the Coastal State over the Continental Shelf*

1. The coastal State exercises over the continental shelf sovereign rights for the purpose of exploring it and exploiting its natural resources.

2. The rights referred to in paragraph 1 are exclusive in the sense that if the coastal State does not explore the continental shelf or exploit its

natural resources, no one may undertake these activities without the express consent of the coastal State.

3. The rights of the coastal State over the continental shelf do not depend on occupation, effective or notional, or on any express proclamation.

4. The natural resources referred to in this Part consist of the mineral and other non-living resources of the sea-bed and subsoil together with living organisms belonging to sedentary species, that is to say, organisms which, at the harvestable stage, either are immobile on or under the sea-bed or are unable to move except in constant physical contact with the sea-bed or the subsoil.

Article 78. Legal Status of the Superjacent Waters and Air Space and the Rights and Freedoms of Other States

1. The rights of the coastal State over the continental shelf do not affect the legal status of the superjacent waters or of the air space above those waters.

2. The exercise of the rights of the coastal State over the continental shelf must not infringe or result in any unjustifiable interference with navigation and other rights and freedoms of other States as provided for in this Convention.

Article 79. Submarine Cables and Pipelines on the Continental Shelf

1. All States are entitled to lay submarine cables and pipelines on the continental shelf, in accordance with the provisions of this article.

2. Subject to its right to take reasonable measures for the exploration of the continental shelf, the exploitation of its natural resources and the prevention, reduction and control of pollution from pipelines, the coastal State may not impede the laying or maintenance of such cables or pipelines.

3. The delineation of the course for the laying of such pipelines on the continental shelf is subject to the consent of the coastal State.

4. Nothing in this Part affects the right of the coastal State to establish conditions for cables or pipelines entering its territory or territorial sea, or its jurisdiction over cables and pipelines constructed or used in connection with the exploration of its continental shelf or exploitation of its resources or the operations of artificial islands, installations and structures under its jurisdiction.

5. When laying submarine cables or pipelines, States shall have due regard to cables or pipelines already in position. In particular, possibilities of repairing existing cables or pipelines shall not be prejudiced.

Article 80. Artificial Islands, Installations and Structures on the Continental Shelf

Article 60 applies *mutatis mutandis* to artificial islands, installations and structures on the continental shelf.

Article 81. Drilling on the Continental Shelf

The coastal State shall have the exclusive right to authorize and regulate drilling on the continental shelf for all purposes.

Article 82. Payments and Contributions with Respect to the Exploitation of the Continental Shelf Beyond 200 Nautical Miles

1. The coastal State shall make payments or contributions in kind in respect of the exploitation of the non-living resources of the continental shelf beyond 200 nautical miles from the baselines from which the breadth of the territorial sea is measured.

2. The payments and contributions shall be made annually with respect to all production at a site after the first five years of production at that site. For the sixth year, the rate of payment or contribution shall be 1 per cent of the value or volume of production at the site. The rate shall increase by 1 per cent for each subsequent year until the twelfth year and shall remain at 7 per cent thereafter. Production does not include resources used in connection with exploitation.

3. A developing State which is a net importer of a mineral resource produced from its continental shelf is exempt from making such payments or contributions in respect of that mineral resource.

4. The payments or contributions shall be made through the Authority, which shall distribute them to States Parties to this Convention, on the basis of equitable sharing criteria, taking into account the interests and needs of developing States, particularly the least developed and the land-locked among them.

Article 83. Delimitation of the Continental Shelf Between States with Opposite or Adjacent Coasts

1. The delimitation of the continental shelf between States with opposite or adjacent coasts shall be effected by agreement on the basis of international law, as referred to in Article 38 of the Statute of the International Court of Justice, in order to achieve an equitable solution.

2. If no agreement can be reached within a reasonable period of time, the States concerned shall resort to the procedures provided for in Part XV.

3. Pending agreement as provided for in paragraph 1, the States concerned, in a spirit of understanding and co-operation, shall make every effort to enter into provisional arrangements of a practical nature and, during this transitional period, not to jeopardize or hamper the reaching of the final agreement. Such arrangements shall be without prejudice to the final delimitation.

4. Where there is an agreement in force between the States concerned, questions relating to the delimitation of the continental shelf shall be determined in accordance with the provisions of that agreement.

Article 84. Charts and Lists of Geographical Co-ordinates

1. Subject to this Part, the outer limit lines of the continental shelf and the lines of delimitation drawn in accordance with article 83 shall be shown on charts of a scale or scales adequate for ascertaining their position. Where appropriate, lists of geographical co-ordinates of points, specifying the geodetic datum, may be substituted for such outer limit lines or lines of delimitation.

2. The coastal State shall give due publicity to such charts or lists of

geographical co-ordinates and shall deposit a copy of each such chart or list with the Secretary-General of the United Nations and, in the case of those showing the outer limit lines of the continental shelf, with the Secretary-General of the Authority.

Article 85. *Tunnelling*

This Part does not prejudice the right of the coastal State to exploit the subsoil by means of tunnelling, irrespective of the depth of water above the subsoil.

Part VII. High Seas

SECTION 1. GENERAL PROVISIONS

Article 86. *Application of the Provisions of This Part*

The provisions of this Part apply to all parts of the sea that are not included in the exclusive economic zone, in the territorial sea or in the internal waters of a State, or in the archipelagic waters of an archipelagic State. This article does not entail any abridgement of the freedoms enjoyed by all States in the exclusive economic zone in accordance with article 58.

Article 87. *Freedom of the High Seas*

1. The high seas are open to all States, whether coastal or land-locked. Freedom of the high seas is exercised under the conditions laid down by this Convention and by other rules of international law. It comprises, *inter alia*, both for coastal and land-locked States:
   (a) freedom of navigation;
   (b) freedom of overflight;
   (c) freedom to lay submarine cables and pipelines, subject to Part VI;
   (d) freedom to construct artificial islands and other installations permitted under international law, subject to Part VI;
   (e) freedom of fishing, subject to the conditions laid down in section 2;
   (f) freedom of scientific research, subject to Parts VI and XIII.
2. These freedoms shall be exercised by all States with due regard for the interests of other States in their exercise of the freedom of the high seas, and also with due regard for the rights under this Convention with respect to activities in the Area.

Article 88. *Reservation of the High Seas for Peaceful Purposes*

The high seas shall be reserved for peaceful purposes.

Article 89. *Invalidity of Claims of Sovereignty Over the High Seas*

No State may validly purport to subject any part of the high seas to its sovereignty.

Article 90. Right of Navigation

Every State, whether coastal or land-locked, has the right to sail ships flying its flag on the high seas.

Article 91. Nationality of Ships

1. Every State shall fix the conditions for the grant of its nationality to ships, for the registration of ships in its territory, and for the right to fly its flag. Ships have the nationality of the State whose flag they are entitled to fly. There must exist a genuine link between the State and the ship.

2. Every State shall issue to ships to which it has granted the right to fly its flag documents to that effect.

Article 92. Status of Ships

1. Ships shall sail under the flag of one State only and, save in exceptional cases expressly provided for in international treaties or in this Convention, shall be subject to its exclusive jurisdiction on the high seas. A ship may not change its flag during a voyage or while in a port of call, save in the case of a real transfer of ownership or change of registry.

2. A ship which sails under the flags of two or more States, using them according to convenience, may not claim any of the nationalities in question with respect to any other State, and may be assimilated to a ship without nationality.

Article 93. Ships Flying the Flag of the United Nations, its Specialized Agencies and the International Atomic Energy Agency

The preceding articles do not prejudice the question of ships employed on the official service of the United Nations, its specialized agencies or the International Atomic Energy Agency, flying the flag of the organization.

Article 94. Duties of the Flag State

1. Every State shall effectively exercise its jurisdiction and control in administrative, technical and social matters over ships flying its flag.

2. In particular every State shall:

    (a) maintain a register of ships containing the names and particulars of ships flying its flag, except those which are excluded from generally accepted international regulations on account of their small size; and

    (b) assume jurisdiction under its internal law over each ship flying its flag and its master, officers and crew in respect of administrative, technical and social matters concerning the ship.

3. Every State shall take such measures for ships flying its flag as are necessary to ensure safety at sea with regard, *inter alia,* to:

    (a) the construction, equipment and seaworthiness of ships;

    (b) the manning of ships, labour conditions and the training of crews, taking into account the applicable international instruments;

    (c) the use of signals, the maintenance of communications and the prevention of collisions.

4. Such measures shall include those necessary to ensure:

(a) that each ship, before registration and thereafter at appropriate intervals, is surveyed by a qualified surveyor of ships, and has on board such charts, nautical publications and navigational equipment and instruments as are appropriate for the safe navigation of the ship;

(b) that each ship is in the charge of a master and officers who possess appropriate qualifications, in particular in seamanship, navigation, communications and marine engineering, and that the crew is appropriate in qualification and numbers for the type, size, machinery and equipment of the ship;

(c) that the master, officers and, to the extent appropriate, the crew are fully conversant with and required to observe the applicable international regulations concerning the safety of life at sea, the prevention of collisions, the prevention, reduction and control of marine pollution, and the maintenance of communications by radio.

5. In taking the measures called for in paragraphs 3 and 4 each State is required to conform to generally accepted international regulations, procedures and practices and to take any steps which may be necessary to secure their observance.

6. A State which has clear grounds to believe that proper jurisdiction and control with respect to a ship have not been exercised may report the facts to the flag State. Upon receiving such a report, the flag State shall investigate the matter and, if appropriate, take any action necessary to remedy the situation.

7. Each State shall cause an inquiry to be held by or before a suitably qualified person or persons into every marine casualty or incident of navigation on the high seas involving a ship flying its flag and causing loss of life or serious injury to nationals of another State or serious damage to ships or installations of another State or to the marine environment. The flag State and the other State shall co-operate in the conduct of any inquiry held by that other State into any such marine casualty or incident of navigation.

Article 95. *Immunity of Warships on the High Seas*

Warships on the high seas have complete immunity from the jurisdiction of any State other than the flag State.

Article 96. *Immunity of Ships Used Only on Government Non-commercial Service*

Ships owned or operated by a State and used only on government non-commercial service shall, on the high seas, have complete immunity from the jurisdiction of any State other than the flag State.

Article 97. *Penal Jurisdiction in Matters of Collision or Any Other Incident of Navigation*

1. In the event of a collision or any other incident of navigation concerning a ship on the high seas, involving the penal or disciplinary responsibility of the master or of any other person in the service of the ship, no penal or disciplinary proceedings may be instituted against such person except

before the judicial or administrative authorities either of the flag State or of the State of which such person is a national.

2. In disciplinary matters, the State which has issued a master's certificate or a certificate of competence or licence shall alone be competent, after due legal process, to pronounce the withdrawal of such certificates, even if the holder is not a national of the State which issued them.

3. No arrest or detention of the ship, even as a measure of investigation, shall be ordered by any authorities other than those of the flag State.

Article 98. Duty to Render Assistance

1. Every State shall require the master of a ship flying its flag, in so far as he can do so without serious danger to the ship, the crew or the passengers:

(a) to render assistance to any person found at sea in danger of being lost;

(b) to proceed with all possible speed to the rescue of persons in distress, if informed of their need of assistance, in so far as such action may reasonably be expected of him;

(c) after a collision, to render assistance to the other ship, its crew and its passengers and, where possible, to inform the other ship of the name of his own ship, its port of registry and the nearest port at which it will call.

2. Every coastal State shall promote the establishment, operation and maintenance of an adequate and effective search and rescue service regarding safety on and over the sea and, where circumstances so require, by way of mutual regional arrangements co-operate with neighbouring States for this purpose.

Article 99. Prohibition of the Transport of Slaves

Every State shall take effective measures to prevent and punish the transport of slaves in ships authorized to fly its flag and to prevent the unlawful use of its flag for that purpose. Any slave taking refuge on board any ship, whatever its flag, shall *ipso facto* be free.

Article 100. Duty to Co-operate in the Repression of Piracy

All States shall co-operate to the fullest possible extent in the repression of piracy on the high seas or in any other place outside the jurisdiction of any State.

Article 101. Definition of Piracy

Piracy consists of any of the following acts:

(a) any illegal acts of violence or detention, or any act of depredation, committed for private ends by the crew or the passengers of a private ship or a private aircraft, and directed:

(i) on the high seas, against another ship or aircraft, or against persons or property on board such ship or aircraft;

(ii) against a ship, aircraft, persons or property in a place outside the jurisdiction of any State;

(b) any act of voluntary participation in the operation of a ship or of an aircraft with knowledge of facts making it a pirate-ship or aircraft;

(c) any act of inciting or of intentionally facilitating an act described in subparagraph (a) or (b).

Article 102. Piracy by a Warship, Government Ship or Government Aircraft Whose Crew Has Mutinied

The acts of piracy, as defined in article 101, committed by a warship, government ship or government aircraft whose crew has mutinied and taken control of the ship or aircraft are assimilated to acts committed by a private ship or aircraft.

Article 103. Definition of a Pirate Ship or Aircraft

A ship or aircraft is considered a pirate ship or aircraft if it is intended by the persons in dominant control to be used for the purpose of committing one of the acts referred to in article 101. The same applies if the ship or aircraft has been used to commit any such act, so long as it remains under the control of the persons guilty of that act.

Article 104. Retention or Loss of the Nationality of a Pirate Ship or Aircraft

A ship or aircraft may retain its nationality although it has become a pirate ship or aircraft. The retention or loss of nationality is determined by the law of the State from which such nationality was derived.

Article 105. Seizure of a Pirate Ship or Aircraft

On the high seas, or in any other place outside the jurisdiction of any State, every State may seize a pirate ship or aircraft, or a ship or aircraft taken by piracy and under the control of pirates, and arrest the persons and seize the property on board. The courts of the State which carried out the seizure may decide upon the penalties to be imposed, and may also determine the action to be taken with regard to the ships, aircraft or property, subject to the rights of third parties acting in good faith.

Article 106. Liability for Seizure Without Adequate Grounds

Where the seizure of a ship or aircraft on suspicion of piracy has been effected without adequate grounds, the State making the seizure shall be liable to the State the nationality of which is possessed by the ship or aircraft for any loss or damage caused by the seizure.

Article 107. Ships and Aircraft Which are Entitled to Seize on Account of Piracy

A seizure on account of piracy may be carried out only by warships or military aircraft, or other ships or aircraft clearly marked and identifiable as being on government service and authorized to that effect.

Article 108. Illicit Traffic in Narcotic Drugs or Psychotropic Substances

1. All States shall co-operate in the suppression of illicit traffic in narcotic drugs and psychotropic substances engaged in by ships on the high seas contrary to international conventions.

2. Any State which has reasonable grounds for believing that a ship flying its flag is engaged in illicit traffic in narcotic drugs or psychotropic substances may request the co-operation of other States to suppress such traffic.

Article 109. Unauthorized Broadcasting from the High Seas

1. All States shall co-operate in the suppression of unauthorized broadcasting from the high seas.

2. For the purposes of this Convention, "unauthorized broadcasting" means the transmission of sound radio or television broadcasts from a ship or installation on the high seas intended for reception by the general public contrary to international regulations, but excluding the transmission of distress calls.

3. Any person engaged in unauthorized broadcasting may be prosecuted before the court of:

   (a) the flag State of the ship;
   (b) the State of registry of the installation;
   (c) the State of which the person is a national;
   (d) any State where the transmissions can be received; or
   (e) any State where authorized radio communication is suffering interference.

4. On the high seas, a State having jurisdiction in accordance with paragraph 3 may, in conformity with article 110, arrest any person or ship engaged in unauthorized broadcasting and seize the broadcasting apparatus.

Article 110. Right of Visit

1. Except where acts of interference derive from powers conferred by treaty, a warship which encounters on the high seas a foreign ship, other than a ship entitled to complete immunity in accordance with articles 95 and 96, is not justified in boarding it unless there is reasonable ground for suspecting that:

   (a) the ship is engaged in piracy;
   (b) the ship is engaged in the slave trade;
   (c) the ship is engaged in unauthorized broadcasting and the flag State of the warship has jurisdiction under article 109;
   (d) the ship is without nationality; or
   (e) though flying a foreign flag or refusing to show its flag, the ship is, in reality, of the same nationality as the warship.

2. In the cases provided for in paragraph 1, the warship may proceed to verify the ship's right to fly its flag. To this end, it may send a boat under the command of an officer to the suspected ship. If suspicion remains after the documents have been checked, it may proceed to a further examination on board the ship, which must be carried out with all possible consideration.

3. If the suspicions prove to be unfounded, and provided that the ship boarded has not committed any act justifying them, it shall be compensated for any loss or damage that may have been sustained.

4. These provisions apply *mutatis mutandis* to military aircraft.

5. These provisions also apply to any other duly authorized ships or aircraft clearly marked and identifiable as being on government service.

Article 111. Right of Hot Pursuit

1. The hot pursuit of a foreign ship may be undertaken when the competent authorities of the coastal State have good reason to believe that the ship has violated the laws and regulations of that State. Such pursuit must be commenced when the foreign ship or one of its boats is within the internal waters, the archipelagic waters, the territorial sea or the contiguous zone of the pursuing State, and may only be continued outside the territorial sea or the contiguous zone if the pursuit has not been interrupted. It is not necessary that, at the time when the foreign ship within the territorial sea or the contiguous zone receives the order to stop, the ship giving the order should likewise be within the territorial sea or the contiguous zone. If the foreign ship is within a contiguous zone, as defined in article 33, the pursuit may only be undertaken if there has been a violation of the rights for the protection of which the zone was established.

2. The right of hot pursuit shall apply *mutatis mutandis* to violations in the exclusive economic zone or on the continental shelf, including safety zones around continental shelf installations, of the laws and regulations of the coastal State applicable in accordance with this Convention to the exclusive economic zone or the continental shelf, including such safety zones.

3. The right of hot pursuit ceases as soon as the ship pursued enters the territorial sea of its own State or of a third State.

4. Hot pursuit is not deemed to have begun unless the pursuing ship has satisfied itself by such practicable means as may be available that the ship pursued or one of its boats or other craft working as a team and using the ship pursued as a mother ship is within the limits of the territorial sea, or, as the case may be, within the contiguous zone or the exclusive economic zone or above the continental shelf. The pursuit may only be commenced after a visual or auditory signal to stop has been given at a distance which enables it to be seen or heard by the foreign ship.

5. The right of hot pursuit may be exercised only by warships or military aircraft, or other ships or aircraft clearly marked and identifiable as being on government service and authorized to that effect.

6. Where hot pursuit is effected by an aircraft:

(a) the provisions of paragraphs 1 to 4 shall apply *mutatis mutandis;*

(b) the aircraft giving the order to stop must itself actively pursue the ship until a ship or another aircraft of the coastal State, summoned by the aircraft, arrives to take over the pursuit, unless the aircraft is itself able to arrest the ship. It does not suffice to justify an arrest outside the territorial sea that the ship was merely sighted by the aircraft as an offender or suspected offender, if it was not both ordered to stop and pursued by the aircraft itself or other aircraft or ships which continue the pursuit without interruption.

7. The release of a ship arrested within the jurisdiction of a State and escorted to a port of that State for the purposes of an inquiry before the competent authorities may not be claimed solely on the ground that the ship, in the course of its voyage, was escorted across a portion of the exclusive economic zone or the high seas, if the circumstances rendered this necessary.

8. Where a ship has been stopped or arrested outside the territorial sea in circumstances which do not justify the exercise of the right of hot pursuit, it shall be compensated for any loss or damage that may have been thereby sustained.

Article 112.   Right to Lay Submarine Cables and Pipelines

1. All States are entitled to lay submarine cables and pipelines on the bed of the high seas beyond the continental shelf.

2. Article 79, paragraph 5, applies to such cables and pipelines.

Article 113.   Breaking or Injury of a Submarine Cable or Pipeline

Every State shall adopt the laws and regulations necessary to provide that the breaking or injury by a ship flying its flag or by a person subject to its jurisdiction of a submarine cable beneath the high seas done wilfully or through culpable negligence, in such a manner as to be liable to interrupt or obstruct telegraphic or telephonic communications, and similarly the breaking or injury of a submarine pipeline or high-voltage power cable, shall be a punishable offence. This provision shall apply also to conduct calculated or likely to result in such breaking or injury. However, it shall not apply to any break or injury caused by persons who acted merely with the legitimate object of saving their lives or their ships, after having taken all necessary precautions to avoid such break or injury.

Article 114.   Breaking or Injury by Owners of a Submarine Cable or Pipeline of Another Submarine Cable or Pipeline

Every State shall adopt the laws and regulations necessary to provide that, if persons subject to its jurisdiction who are the owners of a submarine cable or pipeline beneath the high seas, in laying or repairing that cable or pipeline, cause a break in or injury to another cable or pipeline, they shall bear the cost of the repairs.

Article 115.   Indemnity for Loss Incurred in Avoiding Injury to a Submarine Cable or Pipeline

Every State shall adopt the laws and regulations necessary to ensure that the owners of ships who can prove that they have sacrificed an anchor, a net or any other fishing gear, in order to avoid injuring a submarine cable or pipeline, shall be indemnified by the owner of the cable or pipeline, provided that the owner of the ship has taken all reasonable precautionary measures beforehand.

SECTION 2. CONSERVATION AND MANAGEMENT OF THE LIVING
RESOURCES OF THE HIGH SEAS

Article 116. Right to Fish on the High Seas

All States have the right for their nationals to engage in fishing on the high seas subject to:
(a) their treaty obligations;
(b) the rights and duties as well as the interests of coastal States provided for, *inter alia,* in article 63, paragraph 2, and articles 64 to 67; and
(c) the provisions of this section.

Article 117. Duty of States to Adopt with Respect to Their Nationals Measures for the Conservation of the Living Resources of the High Seas

All States have the duty to take, or to co-operate with other States in taking, such measures for their respective nationals as may be necessary for the conservation of the living resources of the high seas.

Article 118. Co-operation of States in the Conservation and Management of Living Resources

States shall co-operate with each other in the conservation and management of living resources in the areas of the high seas. States whose nationals exploit identical living resources, or different living resources in the same area, shall enter into negotiations with a view to taking the measures necessary for the conservation of the living resources concerned. They shall, as appropriate, co-operate to establish subregional or regional fisheries organizations to this end.

Article 119. Conservation of the Living Resources of the High Seas

1. In determining the allowable catch and establishing other conservation measures for the living resources in the high seas, States shall:
(a) take measures which are designed, on the best scientific evidence available to the States concerned, to maintain or restore populations of harvested species at levels which can produce the maximum sustainable yield, as qualified by relevant environmental and economic factors, including the special requirements of developing States, and taking into account fishing patterns, the interdependence of stocks and any generally recommended international minimum standards, whether subregional, regional or global;
(b) take into consideration the effects on species associated with or dependent upon harvested species with a view to maintaining or restoring populations of such associated or dependent species above levels at which their reproduction may become seriously threatened.

2. Available scientific information, catch and fishing effort statistics, and other data relevant to the conservation of fish stocks shall be contributed and exchanged on a regular basis through competent international organi-

zations, whether subregional, regional or global, where appropriate and with participation by all States concerned.

3. States concerned shall ensure that conservation measures and their implementation do not discriminate in form or in fact against the fishermen of any State.

Article 120. Marine Mammals

Article 65 also applies to the conservation and management of marine mammals in the high seas.

Part VIII. Regime of Islands

Article 121. Régime of Islands

1. An island is a naturally formed area of land, surrounded by water, which is above water at high tide.

2. Except as provided for in paragraph 3, the territorial sea, the contiguous zone, the exclusive economic zone and the continental shelf of an island are determined in accordance with the provisions of this Convention applicable to other land territory.

3. Rocks which cannot sustain human habitation or economic life of their own shall have no exclusive economic zone or continental shelf.

Part IX. Enclosed or Semi-Enclosed Seas

Article 122. Definition

For the purposes of this Convention, "enclosed or semi-enclosed sea" means a gulf, basin or sea surrounded by two or more States and connected to another sea or the ocean by a narrow outlet or consisting entirely or primarily of the territorial seas and exclusive economic zones of two or more coastal States.

Article 123. Co-operation of States Bordering Enclosed or Semi-Enclosed Seas

States bordering an enclosed or semi-enclosed sea should co-operate with each other in the exercise of their rights and in the performance of their duties under this Convention. To this end they shall endeavour, directly or through an appropriate regional organization:

(a) to co-ordinate the management, conservation, exploration and exploitation of the living resources of the sea;

(b) to co-ordinate the implementation of their rights and duties with respect to the protection and preservation of the marine environment;

(c) to co-ordinate their scientific research policies and undertake where appropriate joint programmes of scientific research in the area;

(d) to invite, as appropriate, other interested States or international organizations to co-operate with them in furtherance of the provisions of this article.

Part X. Right of Access of Land-Locked States to and from the Sea and Freedom of Transit

Article 124. Use of Terms

1. For the purposes of this Convention:
   (a) "land-locked State" means a State which has no sea-coast;
   (b) "transit State" means a State, with or without a sea-coast, situated between a land-locked State and the sea, through whose territory traffic in transit passes;
   (c) "traffic in transit" means transit of persons, baggage, goods and means of transport across the territory of one or more transit States, when the passage across such territory, with or without trans-shipment, warehousing, breaking bulk or change in the mode of transport, is only a portion of a complete journey which begins or terminates within the territory of the land-locked State;
   (d) "means of transport" means:
      (i) railway rolling stock, sea, lake and river craft and road vehicles;
      (ii) where local conditions so require, porters and pack animals.

2. Land-locked States and transit States may, by agreement between them, include as means of transport pipelines and gas lines and means of transport other than those included in paragraph 1.

Article 125. Right of Access to and from the Sea and Freedom of Transit

1. Land-locked States shall have the right of access to and from the sea for the purpose of exercising the rights provided for in this Convention including those relating to the freedom of the high seas and the common heritage of mankind. To this end, land-locked States shall enjoy freedom of transit through the territory of transit States by all means of transport.

2. The terms and modalities for exercising freedom of transit shall be agreed between the land-locked States and transit States concerned through bilateral, subregional or regional agreements.

3. Transit States, in the exercise of their full sovereignty over their territory, shall have the right to take all measures necessary to ensure that the rights and facilities provided for in this Part for land-locked States shall in no way infringe their legitimate interests.

Article 126. Exclusion of Application of the Most-Favoured-Nation Clause

The provisions of this Convention, as well as special agreements relating to the exercise of the right of access to and from the sea, establishing rights and facilities on account of the special geographical position of land-locked States, are excluded from the application of the most-favoured-nation clause.

Article 127. Customs Duties, Taxes and Other Charges

1. Traffic in transit shall not be subject to any customs duties, taxes or other charges except charges levied for specific services rendered in connection with such traffic.

2. Means of transport in transit and other facilities provided for and used by land-locked States shall not be subject to taxes or charges higher than those levied for the use of means of transport of the transit State.

Article 128. Free Zones and Other Customs Facilities

For the convenience of traffic in transit, free zones or other customs facilities may be provided at the ports of entry and exit in the transit States, by agreement between those States and the land-locked States. . . .

Article 130. Measures to Avoid or Eliminate Delays or Other Difficulties of a Technical Nature in Traffic in Transit

1. Transit States shall take all appropriate measures to avoid delays or other difficulties of a technical nature in traffic in transit. . . .

Article 132. Grant of Greater Transit Facilities

This Convention does not entail in any way the withdrawal of transit facilities which are greater than those provided for in this Convention and which are agreed between States Parties to this Convention or granted by a State Party. This Convention also does not preclude such grant of greater facilities in the future.

Part XI. The Area

Section 1. General Provisions

Article 133. Use of Terms

For the purposes of this Part:
 (a) "resources" means all solid, liquid or gaeous mineral resources *in situ* in the Area at or beneath the sea-bed, including polymetallic nodules;
 (b) resources, when recovered from the Area, are referred to as "minerals".

Article 134. Scope of This Part

1. This Part applies to the Area.
2. Activities in the Area shall be governed by the provisions of this Part.
3. The requirements concerning deposit of, and publicity to be given to, the charts or lists of geographical co-ordinates showing the limits referred to in article 1, paragraph 1(1) are set forth in Part VI.
4. Nothing in this article affects the establishment of the outer limits of

the continental shelf in accordance with Part VI or the validity of agreements relating to delimitation between States with opposite or adjacent coasts.

Article 135. *Legal Status of the Superjacent Waters and Air Space*

Neither this Part nor any rights granted or exercised pursuant thereto shall affect the legal status of the waters superjacent to the Area or that of the air space above those waters.

SECTION 2. PRINCIPLES GOVERNING THE AREA

Article 136. *Common Heritage of Mankind*

The Area and its resources are the common heritage of mankind.

Article 137. *Legal Status of the Area and Its Resources*

1. No State shall claim or exercise sovereignty or sovereign rights over any part of the Area or its resources, nor shall any State or natural or juridical person appropriate any part thereof. No such claim or exercise of sovereignty or sovereign rights nor such appropriation shall be recognized.

2. All rights in the resources of the Area are vested in mankind as a whole, on whose behalf the Authority shall act. These resources are not subject to alienation. The minerals recovered from the Area, however, may only be alienated in accordance with this Part and the rules, regulations and procedures of the Authority.

3. No State or natural or juridical person shall claim, acquire or exercise rights with respect to the minerals recovered from the Area except in accordance with this Part. Otherwise, no such claim, acquisition or exercise of such rights shall be recognized.

Article 138. *General Conduct of States in Relation to the Area*

The general conduct of States in relation to the Area shall be in accordance with the provisions of this Part, the principles embodied in the Charter of the United Nations and other rules of international law in the interests of maintaining peace and security and promoting international co-operation and mutual understanding.

Article 139. *Responsibility to Ensure Compliance and Liability for Damage*

1. States Parties shall have the responsibility to ensure that activities in the Area, whether carried out by States Parties, or state enterprises or natural or juridical persons which possess the nationality of States Parties or are effectively controlled by them or their nationals, shall be carried out in conformity with this Part. The same responsibility applies to international organizations for activities in the Area carried out by such organizations.

2. Without prejudice to the rules of international law and Annex III, article 22, damage caused by the failure of a State Party or international organization to carry out its responsibilities under this Part shall entail liability; States Parties or international organizations acting together shall bear joint and several liability. A State Party shall not however be liable for

damage caused by any failure to comply with this Part by a person whom it has sponsored under article 153, paragraph 2(b), if the State Party has taken all necessary and appropriate measures to secure effective compliance under article 153, paragraph 4, and Annex III, article 4, paragraph 4.

3. States Parties that are members of international organizations shall take appropriate measures to ensure the implementation of this article with respect to such organizations.

Article 140. Benefit of Mankind

1. Activities in the Area shall, as specifically provided for in this Part, be carried out for the benefit of mankind as a whole, irrespective of the geographical location of States, whether coastal or land-locked, and taking into particular consideration the interests and needs of developing States and of peoples who have not attained full independence or other self-governing status recognized by the United Nations in accordance with General Assembly resolution 1514 (XV) and other relevant General Assembly resolutions.

2. The Authority shall provide for the equitable sharing of financial and other economic benefits derived from activities in the Area through any appropriate mechanism, on a non-discriminatory basis, in accordance with article 160, paragraph 2(f)(i).

Article 141. Use of the Area Exclusively for Peaceful Purposes

The Area shall be open to use exclusively for peaceful purposes by all States, whether coastal or land-locked, without discrimination and without prejudice to the other provisions of this Part.

Article 142. Rights and Legitimate Interests of Coastal States

1. Activities in the Area, with respect to resource deposits in the Area which lie across limits of national jurisdiction, shall be conducted with due regard to the rights and legitimate interests of any coastal State across whose jurisdiction such deposits lie.

2. Consultations, including a system of prior notification, shall be maintained with the State concerned, with a view to avoiding infringement of such rights and interests. In cases where activities in the Area may result in the exploitation of resources lying within national jurisdiction, the prior consent of the coastal State concerned shall be required.

3. Neither this Part nor any rights granted or exercised pursuant thereto shall affect the rights of coastal States to take such measures consistent with the relevant provisions of Part XII as may be necessary to prevent, mitigate or eliminate grave and imminent danger to their coastline, or related interests from pollution or threat thereof or from other hazardous occurrences resulting from or caused by any activities in the Area.

Article 143. Marine Scientific Research

1. Marine scientific research in the Area shall be carried out exclusively for peaceful purposes and for the benefit of mankind as a whole, in accordance with Part XIII.

2. The Authority may carry out marine scientific research concerning the Area and its resources, and may enter into contracts for that purpose. The Authority shall promote and encourage the conduct of marine scientific research in the Area, and shall co-ordinate and disseminate the results of such research and analysis when available.

3. States Parties may carry out marine scientific research in the Area. States Parties shall promote international co-operation in marine scientific research in the Area by:

(a) participating in international programmes and encouraging co-operation in marine scientific research by personnel of different countries and of the Authority;

(b) ensuring that programmes are developed through the Authority or other international organizations as appropriate for the benefit of developing States and technologically less developed States with a view to:

(i) strengthening their research capabilities;

(ii) training their personnel and the personnel of the Authority in the techniques and applications of research;

(iii) fostering the employment of their qualified personnel in research in the Area;

(c) effectively disseminating the results of research and analysis when available, through the Authority or other international channels when appropriate.

Article 144. *Transfer of Technology*

1. The Authority shall take measures in accordance with this Convention:

(a) to acquire technology and scientific knowledge relating to activities in the Area; and

(b) to promote and encourage the transfer to developing States of such technology and scientific knowledge so that all States Parties benefit therefrom.

2. To this end the Authority and States Parties shall co-operate in promoting the transfer of technology and scientific knowledge relating to activities in the Area so that the Enterprise and all States Parties may benefit therefrom. In particular they shall initiate and promote:

(a) programmes for the transfer of technology to the Enterprise and to developing States with regard to activities in the Area, including, *inter alia,* facilitating the access of the Enterprise and of developing States to the relevant technology, under fair and reasonable terms and conditions;

(b) measures directed towards the advancement of the technology of the Enterprise and the domestic technology of developing States, particularly by providing opportunities to personnel from the Enterprise and from developing States for training in marine science and technology and for their full participation in activities in the Area.

Article 145. *Protection of the Marine Environment*

Necessary measures shall be taken in accordance with this Convention with respect to activities in the Area to ensure effective protection for the marine environment from harmful effects which may arise from such activities. To this end the Authority shall adopt appropriate rules, regulations and procedures for *inter alia:*

(a) the prevention, reduction and control of pollution and other hazards to the marine environment, including the coastline, and of interference with the ecological balance of the marine environment, particular attention being paid to the need for protection from harmful effects of such activities as drilling, dredging, excavation, disposal of waste, construction and operation or maintenance of installations, pipelines and other devices related to such activities;

(b) the protection and conservation of the natural resources of the Area and the prevention of damage to the flora and fauna of the marine environment.

Article 146. Protection of Human Life

With respect to activities in the Area, necessary measures shall be taken to ensure effective protection of human life. To this end the Authority shall adopt appropriate rules, regulations and procedures to supplement existing international law as embodied in relevant treaties.

Article 147. Accommodation of Activities in the Area and in the Marine Environment

1. Activities in the Area shall be carried out with reasonable regard for other activities in the marine environment.
2. Installations used for carrying out activities in the Area shall be subject to the following conditions:

(a) such installations shall be erected, emplaced and removed solely in accordance with this Part and subject to the rules, regulations and procedures of the Authority. Due notice must be given of the erection, emplacement and removal of such installations, and permanent means for giving warning of their presence must be maintained;

(b) such installations may not be established where interference may be caused to the use of recognized sea lanes essential to international navigation or in areas of intense fishing activity;

(c) safety zones shall be established around such installations with appropriate markings to ensure the safety of both navigation and the installations. The configuration and location of such safety zones shall not be such as to form a belt impeding the lawful access of shipping to particular maritime zones or navigation along international sea lanes;

(d) such installations shall be used exclusively for peaceful purposes;

(e) such installations do not possess the status of islands. They have no territorial sea of their own, and their presence does not affect the delimitation of the territorial sea, the exclusive economic zone or the continental shelf.

3. Other activities in the marine environment shall be conducted with reasonable regard for activities in the Area.

Article 148. Participation of Developing States in Activities in the Area

The effective participation of developing States in activities in the Area shall be promoted as specifically provided for in this Part, having due regard to their special interests and needs, and in particular to the special need of the land-locked and geographically disadvantaged among them to overcome obstacles arising from their disadvantaged location, including remoteness from the Area and difficulty of access to and from it.

Article 149. Archaeological and Historical Objects

All objects of an archaeological and historical nature found in the Area shall be preserved or disposed of for the benefit of mankind as a whole, particular regard being paid to the preferential rights of the State or country of origin, or the State of cultural origin, or the State of historical and archaeological origin.

SECTION 3. DEVELOPMENT OF RESOURCES OF THE AREA

Article 150. Policies Relating to Activities in the Area

Activities in the Area shall, as specifically provided for in this Part, be carried out in such a manner as to foster healthy development of the world economy and balanced growth of international trade, and to promote international co-operation for the over-all development of all countries, especially developing States, and with a view to ensuring:

(a) the development of the resources of the Area;

(b) orderly, safe and rational management of the resources of the Area, including the efficient conduct of activities in the Area and, in accordance with sound principles of conservation, the avoidance of unnecessary waste;

(c) the expansion of opportunities for participation in such activities consistent in particular with articles 144 and 148;

(d) participation in revenues by the Authority and the transfer of technology to the Enterprise and developing States as provided for in this Convention;

(e) increased availability of the minerals derived from the Area as needed in conjunction with minerals derived from other sources, to ensure supplies to consumers of such minerals;

(f) the promotion of just and stable prices remunerative to producers and fair to consumers for minerals derived both from the Area and from other sources, and the promotion of long-term equilibrium between supply and demand;

(g) the enhancement of opportunities for all States Parties, irrespective of their social and economic systems or geographical location, to participate in the development of the resources of the Area and the prevention of monopolization of activities in the Area;

(h) the protection of developing countries from adverse effects on their economies or on their export earnings resulting from a reduction in the price of an affected mineral, or in the volume of exports of that mineral, to the extent that such reduction is caused by activities in the Area, as provided in article 151;

(i) the development of the common heritage for the benefit of mankind as a whole; and

(j) conditions of access to markets for the imports of minerals produced from the resources of the Area and for imports of commodities produced from such minerals shall not be more favourable than the most favourable applied to imports from other sources.

Article 151. Production Policies

1. (a) Without prejudice to the objectives set forth in article 150 and for the purpose of implementing subparagraph (h) of that article, the Authority, acting through existing forums or such new arrangements or agreements as may be appropriate, in which all interested parties, including both producers and consumers, participate, shall take measures necessary to promote the growth, efficiency and stability of markets for those commodities produced from the minerals derived from the Area, at prices remunerative to producers and fair to consumers. All States Parties shall co-operate to this end.

(b) The Authority shall have the right to participate in any commodity conference dealing with those commodities and in which all interested parties including both producers and consumers participate. The Authority shall have the right to become a party to any arrangement or agreement resulting from such conferences. Participation of the Authority in any organs established under those arrangements or agreements shall be in respect of production in the Area and in accordance with the relevant rules of those organs.

(c) The Authority shall carry out its obligations under the arrangements or agreements referred to in this paragraph in a manner which assures a uniform and non-discriminatory implementation in respect of all production in the Area of the minerals concerned. In doing so, the Authority shall act in a manner consistent with the terms of existing contracts and approved plans of work of the Enterprise.

2. (a) During the interim period specified in paragraph 3, commercial production shall not be undertaken pursuant to an approved plan of work until the operator has applied for and has been issued a production authorization by the Authority. Such production authorizations may not be applied for or issued more than five years prior to the planned commencement of commercial production under the plan of work unless, having regard to the nature and timing of project development, the rules, regulations and procedures of the Authority prescribe another period.

(b) In the application for the production authorization, the operator shall specify the annual quantity of nickel expected to be recovered under the approved plan of work. The application shall include a schedule of expenditures to be made by the operator after he has received the authorization which are reasonably calculated to allow him to begin commercial production on the date planned.

(c) For the purposes of subparagraphs (a) and (b), the Authority shall establish appropriate performance requirements in accordance with Annex III, article 17.

(d) The Authority shall issue a production authorization for the level of production applied for unless the sum of that level and the levels already authorized exceeds the nickel production ceiling, as calculated pursuant to paragraph 4 in the year of issuance of the authorization, during any year of planned production falling within the interim period.

(e) When issued, the production authorization and approved application shall become a part of the approved plan of work.

(f) If the operator's application for a production authorization is denied pursuant to subparagraph (d), the operator may apply again to the Authority at any time.

3. The interim period shall begin five years prior to 1 January of the year in which the earliest commercial production is planned to commence under an approved plan of work. If the earliest commercial production is delayed beyond the year originally planned, the beginning of the interim period and the production ceiling originally calculated shall be adjusted accordingly. The interim period shall last 25 years or until the end of the Review Conference referred to in article 155 or until the day when such new arrangements or agreements as are referred to in paragraph 1 enter into force, whichever is earliest. The Authority shall resume the power provided in this article for the remainder of the interim period if the said arrangements or agreements should lapse or become ineffective for any reason whatsoever.

4. (a) The production ceiling for any year of the interim period shall be the sum of:

(i) the difference between the trend line values for nickel consumption, as calculated pursuant to subparagraph (b), for the year immediately prior to the year of the earliest commercial production and the year immediately prior to the commencement of the interim period; and

(ii) sixty per cent of the difference between the trend line values for nickel consumption, as calculated pursuant to subparagraph (b), for the year for which the production authorization is being applied for and the year immediately prior to the year of the earliest commercial production.

(b) For the purposes of subparagraph (a):

(i) trend line values used for computing the nickel production ceiling shall be those annual nickel consumption values on a trend line computed during the year in which a production authorization is issued. The trend line shall be derived from a linear regression of the logarithms of actual nickel consumption for the most recent 15-year period for which such data are available, time being the independent variable. This trend line shall be referred to as the original trend line;

(ii) if the annual rate of increase of the original trend line is less than 3 per cent, then the trend line used to determine the quantities referred to in subparagraph (a) shall instead be one passing through the original trend line at the value for the first year of the relevant 15-year period, and increasing at 3 per cent annually; provided however that the production ceiling established for any year of the interim period may not in any case exceed the difference between the original trend line value for that year and the original trend line value for the year immediately prior to the commencement of the interim period.

5. The Authority shall reserve to the Enterprise for its initial production a quantity of 38,000 metric tonnes of nickel from the available production ceiling calculated pursuant to paragraph 4.

6. (a) An operator may in any year produce less than or up to 8 per cent more than the level of annual production of minerals from polymetallic nodules specified in his production authorization, provided that the over-all amount of production shall not exceed that specified in the authorization. Any excess over 8 per cent and up to 20 per cent in any year, or any excess in the first and subsequent years following two consecutive years in which excesses occur, shall be negotiated with the Authority, which may require the operator to obtain a supplementary production authorization to cover additional production.

(b) Applications for such supplementary production authorizations shall be considered by the Authority only after all pending applications by operators who have not yet received production authorizations have been acted upon and due account has been taken of other likely applicants. The Authority shall be guided by the principle of not exceeding the total production allowed under the production ceiling in any year of the interim period. It shall not authorize the production under any plan of work of a quantity in excess of 46,500 metric tonnes of nickel per year.

7. The levels of production of other metals such as copper, cobalt and manganese extracted from the polymetallic nodules that are recovered pursuant to a production authorization should not be higher than those which would have been produced had the operator produced the maximum level of nickel from those nodules pursuant to this article. The Authority shall establish rules, regulations and procedures pursuant to Annex III, article 17, to implement this paragraph.

8. Rights and obligations relating to unfair economic practices under relevant multilateral trade agreements shall apply to the exploration for and exploitation of minerals from the Area. In the settlement of disputes arising under this provision, States Parties which are Parties to such multilateral trade agreements shall have recourse to the dispute settlement procedures of such agreements.

9. The Authority shall have the power to limit the level of production of minerals from the Area, other than minerals from polymetallic nodules, under such conditions and applying such methods as may be appropriate by adopting regulations in accordance with article 161, paragraph 8.

10. Upon the recommendation of the Council on the basis of advice from the Economic Planning Commission, the Assembly shall establish a system of compensation or take other measures of economic adjustment assistance including co-operation with specialized agencies and other international organizations to assist developing countries which suffer serious adverse effects on their export earnings or economies resulting from a reduction in the price of an affected mineral or in the volume of exports of that mineral, to the extent that such reduction is caused by activities in the Area. The Authority on request shall initiate studies on the problems of

those States which are likely to be most seriously affected with a view to minimizing their difficulties and assisting them in their economic adjustment.

Article 152. *Exercise of Powers and Functions by the Authority*

1. The Authority shall avoid discrimination in the exercise of its powers and functions, including the granting of opportunities for activities in the Area.

2. Nevertheless, special consideration for developing States, including particular consideration for the land-locked and geographically disadvantaged among them, specifically provided for in this Part shall be permitted.

Article 153. *System of Exploration and Exploitation*

1. Activities in the Area shall be organized, carried out and controlled by the Authority on behalf of mankind as a whole in accordance with this article as well as other relevant provisions of this Part and the relevant Annexes, and the rules, regulations and procedures of the Authority.

2. Activities in the Area shall be carried out as prescribed in paragraph 3:

(a) by the Enterprise, and

(b) in association with the Authority by States Parties, or state enterprises or natural or juridical persons which possess the nationality of States Parties or are effectively controlled by them or their nationals, when sponsored by such States, or any group of the foregoing which meets the requirements provided in this Part and in Annex III.

3. Activities in the Area shall be carried out in accordance with a formal written plan of work drawn up in accordance with Annex III and approved by the Council after review by the Legal and Technical Commission. In the case of activities in the Area carried out as authorized by the Authority by the entities specified in paragraph 2(b), the plan of work shall, in accordance with Annex III, article 3, be in the form of a contract. Such contracts may provide for joint arrangements in accordance with Annex III, article 11.

4. The Authority shall exercise such control over activities in the Area as is necessary for the purpose of securing compliance with the relevant provisions of this Part and the Annexes relating thereto, and the rules, regulations and procedures of the Authority, and the plans of work approved in accordance with paragraph 3. States Parties shall assist the Authority by taking all measures necessary to ensure such compliance in accordance with article 139.

5. The Authority shall have the right to take at any time any measures provided for under this Part to ensure compliance with its provisions and the exercise of the functions of control and regulation assigned to it thereunder or under any contract. The Authority shall have the right to inspect all installations in the Area used in connection with activities in the Area.

6. A contract under paragraph 3 shall provide for security of tenure. Accordingly, the contract shall not be revised, suspended or terminated except in accordance with Annex III, articles 18 and 19.

Article 154. Periodic Review

Every five years from the entry into force of this Convention, the Assembly shall undertake a general and systematic review of the manner in which the international régime of the Area established in this Convention has operated in practice. In the light of this review the Assembly may take, or recommend that other organs take, measures in accordance with the provisions and procedures of this Part and the Annexes relating thereto which will lead to the improvement of the operation of the régime.

Article 155. The Review Conference

1. Fifteen years from 1 January of the year in which the earliest commercial production commences under an approved plan of work, the Assembly shall convene a conference for the review of those provisions of this Part and the relevant Annexes which govern the system of exploration and exploitation of the resources of the Area. The Review Conference shall consider in detail, in the light of the experience acquired during that period:

(a) whether the provisions of this Part which govern the system of exploration and exploitation of the resources of the Area have achieved their aims in all respects, including whether they have benefited mankind as a whole;

(b) whether, during the 15-year period, reserved areas have been exploited in an effective and balanced manner in comparison with non-reserved areas;

(c) whether the development and use of the Area and its resources have been undertaken in such a manner as to foster healthy development of the world economy and balanced growth of international trade;

(d) whether monopolization of activities in the Area has been prevented;

(e) whether the policies set forth in articles 150 and 151 have been fulfilled; and

(f) whether the system has resulted in the equitable sharing of benefits derived from activities in the Area, taking into particular consideration the interests and needs of the developing States.

2. The Review Conference shall ensure the maintenance of the principle of the common heritage of mankind, the international régime designed to ensure equitable exploitation of the resources of the Area for the benefit of all countries, especially the developing States, and an Authority to organize, conduct and control activities in the Area. It shall also ensure the maintenance of the principles laid down in this Part with regard to the exclusion of claims or exercise of sovereignty over any part of the Area, the rights of States and their general conduct in relation to the Area, and their participation in activities in the Area in conformity with this Convention, the prevention of monopolization of activities in the Area, the use of the Area exclusively for peaceful purposes, economic aspects of activities in the Area, marine scientific research, transfer of technology, protection of the marine environment, protection of human life, rights of coastal States, the legal status of the waters superjacent to the Area and that of the air space

above those waters and accommodation between activities in the Area and other activities in the marine environment.

3. The decision-making procedure applicable at the Review Conference shall be the same as that applicable at the Third United Nations Conference on the Law of the Sea. The Conference shall make every effort to reach agreement on any amendments by way of consensus and there should be no voting on such matters until all efforts at achieving consensus have been exhausted.

4. If, five years after its commencement, the Review Conference has not reached agreement on the system of exploration and exploitation of the resources of the Area, it may decide during the ensuing 12 months, by a three-fourths majority of the States Parties, to adopt and submit to the States Parties for ratification or accession such amendments changing or modifying the system as it determines necessary and appropriate. Such amendments shall enter into force for all States Parties 12 months after the deposit of instruments of ratification or accession by three fourths of the States Parties.

5. Amendments adopted by the Review Conference pursuant to this article shall not affect rights acquired under existing contracts.

SECTION 4. THE AUTHORITY

SUBSECTION A. GENERAL PROVISIONS

Article 156. Establishment of the Authority

1. There is hereby established the International Sea-Bed Authority, which shall function in accordance with this Part.

2. All States Parties are *ipso facto* members of the Authority.

3. Observers at the Third United Nations Conference on the Law of the Sea who have signed the Final Act and who are not referred to in article 305, paragraph 1(c), (d), (e) or (f), shall have the right to participate in the Authority as observers, in accordance with its rules, regulations and procedures.

4. The seat of the Authority shall be in Jamaica.

5. The Authority may establish such regional centres or offices as it deems necessary for the exercise of its functions.

Article 157. Nature and Fundamental Principles of the Authority

1. The Authority is the organization through which States Parties shall, in accordance with this Part, organize and control activities in the Area, particularly with a view to administering the resources of the Area.

2. The powers and functions of the Authority shall be those expressly conferred upon it by this Convention. The Authority shall have such incidental powers, consistent with this Convention, as are implicit in and necessary for the exercise of those powers and functions with respect to activities in the Area.

3. The Authority is based on the principle of the sovereign equality of all its members.

4. All members of the Authority shall fulfil in good faith the obligations assumed by them in accordance with this Part in order to ensure to all of them the rights and benefits resulting from membership.

Article 158. Organs of the Authority

1. There are hereby established, as the principal organs of the Authority, an Assembly, a Council and a Secretariat.

2. There is hereby established the Enterprise, the organ through which the Authority shall carry out the functions referred to in article 170, paragraph 1.

3. Such subsidiary organs as may be found necessary may be established in accordance with this Part.

4. Each principal organ of the Authority and the Enterprise shall be responsible for exercising those powers and functions which are conferred upon it. In exercising such powers and functions each organ shall avoid taking any action which may derogate from or impede the exercise of specific powers and functions conferred upon another organ.

SUBSECTION B. THE ASSEMBLY

Article 159. Composition, Procedure and Voting

1. The Assembly shall consist of all the members of the Authority. Each member shall have one representative in the Assembly, who may be accompanied by alternates and advisers.

2. The Assembly shall meet in regular annual sessions and in such special sessions as may be decided by the Assembly, or convened by the Secretary-General at the request of the Council or of a majority of the members of the Authority.

3. Sessions shall take place at the seat of the Authority unless otherwise decided by the Assembly.

4. The Assembly shall adopt its rules of procedure. At the beginning of each regular session, it shall elect its President and such other officers as may be required. They shall hold office until a new President and other officers are elected at the next regular session.

5. A majority of the members of the Assembly shall constitute a quorum.

6. Each member of the Assembly shall have one vote.

7. Decisions on questions of procedure, including decisions to convene special sessions of the Assembly, shall be taken by a majority of the members present and voting.

8. Decisions on questions of substance shall be taken by a two-thirds majority of the members present and voting, provided that such majority includes a majority of the members participating in the session. When the issue arises as to whether a question is one of substance or not, that question shall be treated as one of substance unless otherwise decided by the Assembly by the majority required for decisions on questions of substance.

9. When a question of substance comes up for voting for the first time, the President may, and shall, if requested by at least one fifth of the members

of the Assembly, defer the issue of taking a vote on that question for a period not exceeding five calendar days. This rule may be applied only once to any question, and shall not be applied so as to defer the question beyond the end of the session.

10. Upon a written request addressed to the President and sponsored by at least one fourth of the members of the Authority for an advisory opinion on the conformity with this Convention of a proposal before the Assembly on any matter, the Assembly shall request the Sea-Bed Disputes Chamber of the International Tribunal for the Law of the Sea to give an advisory opinion thereon and shall defer voting on that proposal pending receipt of the advisory opinion by the Chamber. If the advisory opinion is not received before the final week of the session in which it is requested, the Assembly shall decide when it will meet to vote upon the deferred proposal.

Article 160. *Powers and Functions*

1. The Assembly, as the sole organ of the Authority consisting of all the members, shall be considered the supreme organ of the Authority to which the other principal organs shall be accountable as specifically provided for in this Convention. The Assembly shall have the power to establish general policies in conformity with the relevant provisions of this Convention on any question or matter within the competence of the Authority.

2. In addition, the powers and functions of the Assembly shall be:

(a) to elect the members of the Council in accordance with article 161;

(b) to elect the Secretary-General from among the candidates proposed by the Council;

(c) to elect, upon the recommendation of the Council, the members of the Governing Board of the Enterprise and the Director-General of the Enterprise;

(d) to establish such subsidiary organs as it finds necessary for the exercise of its functions in accordance with this Part. In the composition of these subsidiary organs due account shall be taken of the principle of equitable geographical distribution and of special interests and the need for members qualified and competent in the relevant technical questions dealt with by such organs;

(e) to assess the contributions of members to the administrative budget of the Authority in accordance with an agreed scale of assessment based upon the scale used for the regular budget of the United Nations until the Authority shall have sufficient income from other sources to meet its administrative expenses;

(f) (i) to consider and approve, upon the recommendation of the Council, the rules, regulations and procedures on the equitable sharing of financial and other economic benefits derived from activities in the Area and the payments and contributions made pursuant to article 82, taking into particular consideration the interests and needs of developing States and peoples who have not attained full independence or other self-governing status. If the Assembly does not approve the recommendations of the Council, the Assembly shall return them to the Council for reconsideration in the light of the views expressed by the Assembly;

(ii) to consider and approve the rules, regulations and procedures of the Authority, and any amendments thereto, provisionally adopted by the Council pursuant to article 162, paragraph 2 (o)(ii). These rules, regulations and procedures shall relate to prospecting, exploration and exploitation in the Area, the financial management and internal administration of the Authority, and, upon the recommendation of the Governing Board of the Enterprise, to the transfer of funds from the Enterprise to the Authority;

(g) to decide upon the equitable sharing of financial and other economic benefits derived from activities in the Area, consistent with this Convention and the rules, regulations and procedures of the Authority;

(h) to consider and approve the proposed annual budget of the Authority submitted by the Council;

(i) to examine periodic reports from the Council and from the Enterprise and special reports requested from the Council or any other organ of the Authority;

(j) to initiate studies and make recommendations for the purpose of promoting international co-operation concerning activities in the Area and encouraging the progressive development of international law relating thereto and its codification;

(k) to consider problems of a general nature in connection with activities in the Area arising in particular for developing States, as well as those problems for States in connection with activities in the Area that are due to their geographical location, particularly for land-locked and geographically disadvantaged States;

(l) to establish, upon the recommendation of the Council, on the basis of advice from the Economic Planning Commission, a system of compensation or other measures of economic adjustment assistance as provided in article 151, paragraph 10;

(m) to suspend the exercise of rights and privileges of membership pursuant to article 185;

(n) to discuss any question or matter within the competence of the Authority and to decide as to which organ of the Authority shall deal with any such question or matter not specifically entrusted to a particular organ, consistent with the distribution of powers and functions among the organs of the Authority.

SUBSECTION C. THE COUNCIL

Article 161. Composition, Procedure and Voting

1. The Council shall consist of 36 members of the Authority elected by the Assembly in the following order:

(a) four members from among those States Parties which, during the last five years for which statistics are available, have either consumed more than 2 per cent of total world consumption or have had net imports of more than 2 per cent of total world imports of the commodities produced from the categories of minerals to be derived from the Area, and in any case one State from the Eastern European (Socialist) region, as well as the largest consumer;

(b) four members from among the eight States Parties which have the largest investments in preparation for and in the conduct of activities in the Area, either directly or through their nationals, including at least one State from the Eastern European (Socialist) region;

(c) four members from among States Parties which on the basis of production in areas under their jurisdiction are major net exporters of the categories of minerals to be derived from the Area, including at least two developing States whose exports of such minerals have a substantial bearing upon their economies;

(d) six members from among developing States Parties, representing special interests. The special interests to be represented shall include those of States with large populations, States which are land-locked or geographically disadvantaged, States which are major importers of the categories of minerals to be derived from the Area, States which are potential producers of such minerals, and least developed States;

(e) eighteen members elected according to the principle of ensuring an equitable geographical distribution of seats in the Council as a whole, provided that each geographical region shall have at least one member elected under this subparagraph. For this purpose, the geographical regions shall be Africa, Asia, Eastern European (Socialist), Latin America and Western European and Others.

2. In electing the members of the Council in accordance with paragraph 1, the Assembly shall ensure that:

(a) land-locked and geographically disadvantaged States are represented to a degree which is reasonably proportionate to their representation in the Assembly;

(b) coastal States, especially developing States, which do not qualify under paragraph 1(a), (b), (c) or (d) are represented to a degree which is reasonably proportionate to their representation in the Assembly;

(c) each group of States Parties to be represented on the Council is represented by those members, if any, which are nominated by that group.

3. Elections shall take place at regular sessions of the Assembly. Each member of the Council shall be elected for four years. At the first election, however, the term of one half of the members of each group referred to in paragraph 1 shall be two years.

4. Members of the Council shall be eligible for re-election, but due regard should be paid to the desirability of rotation of membership.

5. The Council shall function at the seat of the Authority, and shall meet as often as the business of the Authority may require, but not less than three times a year.

6. A majority of the members of the Council shall constitute a quorum.

7. Each member of the Council shall have one vote.

8. (a) Decisions on questions of procedure shall be taken by a majority of the members present and voting.

(b) Decisions on questions of substance arising under the following provisions shall be taken by a two-thirds majority of the members present and voting, provided that such majority includes a majority of the members of the Council: article 162, paragraph 2, subparagraphs (f); (g); (h); (i); (n); (p); (v); article 191.

(c) Decisions on questions of substance arising under the following provisions shall be taken by a three-fourths majority of the members present and voting, provided that such majority includes a majority of the members of the Council: article 162, paragraph 1; article 162, paragraph 2, subparagraphs (a); (b); (c); (d); (e); (l); (q); (r); (s); (t); (u) in cases of non-compliance by a contractor or a sponsor; (w) provided that orders issued thereunder may be binding for not more than 30 days unless confirmed by a decision taken in accordance with subparagraph (d); article 162, paragraph 2, subparagraphs (x); (y); (z); article 163, paragraph 2; article 174, paragraph 3; Annex IV, article 11.

(d) Decisions on questions of substance arising under the following provisions shall be taken by consensus: article 162, paragraph 2(m) and (o); adoption of amendments to Part XI.

(e) For the purposes of subparagraphs (d), (f) and (g), "consensus" means the absence of any formal objection. Within 14 days of the submission of a proposal to the Council, the President of the Council shall determine whether there would be a formal objection to the adoption of the proposal. If the President determines that there would be such an objection, the President shall establish and convene, within three days following such determination, a conciliation committee consisting of not more than nine members of the Council, with the President as chairman, for the purpose of reconciling the differences and producing a proposal which can be adopted by consensus. The committee shall work expeditiously and report to the Council within 14 days following its establishment. If the committee is unable to recommend a proposal which can be adopted by consensus, it shall set out in its report the grounds on which the proposal is being opposed.

(f) Decisions on questions not listed above which the Council is authorized to take by the rules, regulations and procedures of the Authority or otherwise shall be taken pursuant to the subparagraphs of this paragraph specified in the rules, regulations and procedures or, if not specified therein, then pursuant to the subparagraph determined by the Council if possible in advance, by consensus.

(g) When the issue arises as to whether a question is within subparagraph (a), (b), (c) or (d), the question shall be treated as being within the subparagraph requiring the higher or highest majority or consensus as the case may be, unless otherwise decided by the Council by the said majority or by consensus.

9. The Council shall establish a procedure whereby a member of the Authority not represented on the Council may send a representative to attend a meeting of the Council when a request is made by such member, or a matter particularly affecting it is under consideration. Such a representative shall be entitled to participate in the deliberations but not to vote.

Article 162. Powers and Functions

1. The Council is the executive organ of the Authority. The Council shall have the power to establish, in conformity with this Convention and the general policies established by the Assembly, the specific policies to be pursued by the Authority on any question or matter within the competence of the Authority.

2. In addition, the Council shall:

(a) supervise and co-ordinate the implementation of the provisions of this Part on all questions and matters within the competence of the Authority and invite the attention of the Assembly to cases of non-compliance;

(b) propose to the Assembly a list of candidates for the election of the Secretary-General;

(c) recommend to the Assembly candidates for the election of the members of the Governing Board of the Enterprise and the Director-General of the Enterprise;

(d) establish, as appropriate, and with due regard to economy and efficiency, such subsidiary organs as it finds necessary for the exercise of its functions in accordance with this Part. In the composition of subsidiary organs, emphasis shall be placed on the need for members qualified and competent in relevant technical matters dealt with by those organs provided that due account shall be taken of the principle of equitable geographical distribution and of special interests;

(e) adopt its rules of procedure including the method of selecting its president;

(f) enter into agreements with the United Nations or other international organizations on behalf of the Authority and within its competence, subject to approval by the Assembly;

(g) consider the reports of the Enterprise and transmit them to the Assembly with its recommendations;

(h) present to the Assembly annual reports and such special reports as the Assembly may request;

(i) issue directives to the Enterprise in accordance with article 170;

(j) approve plans of work in accordance with Annex III, article 6. The Council shall act upon each plan of work within 60 days of its submission by the Legal and Technical Commission at a session of the Council in accordance with the following procedures:

(i) if the Commission recommends the approval of a plan of work, it shall be deemed to have been approved by the Council if no member of the Council submits in writing to the President within 14 days a specific objection alleging non-compliance with the requirements of Annex III, article 6. If there is an objection, the conciliation procedure set forth in article 161, paragraph 8(e), shall apply. If, at the end of the conciliation procedure, the objection is still maintained, the plan of work shall be deemed to have been approved by the Council unless the Council disapproves it by consensus among its members excluding any State or States making the application or sponsoring the applicant;

(ii) if the Commission recommends the disapproval of a plan of work or does not make a recommendation, the Council may approve the plan of work by a three-fourths majority of the members present and voting, provided that such majority includes a majority of the members participating in the session;

(k) approve plans of work submitted by the Enterprise in accordance with Annex IV, article 12, applying, *mutatis mutandis,* the procedures set forth in subparagraph (j);

(l) exercise control over activities in the Area in accordance with article 153, paragraph 4, and the rules, regulations and procedures of the Authority;

(m) take, upon the recommendation of the Economic Planning Commission, necessary and appropriate measures in accordance with article 150, subparagraph (h), to provide protection from the adverse economic effects specified therein;

(n) make recommendations to the Assembly, on the basis of advice from the Economic Planning Commission, for a system of compensation or other measures of economic adjustment assistance as provided in article 151, paragraph 10;

(o) (i) recommend to the Assembly rules, regulations and procedures on the equitable sharing of financial and other economic benefits derived from activities in the Area and the payments and contributions made pursuant to article 82, taking into particular consideration the interests and needs of the developing States and peoples who have not attained full independence or other self-governing status;

(ii) adopt and apply provisionally, pending approval by the Assembly, the rules, regulations and procedures of the Authority, and any amendments thereto, taking into account the recommendations of the Legal and Technical Commission or other subordinate organ concerned. These rules, regulations and procedures shall relate to prospecting, exploration and exploitation in the Area and the financial management and internal administration of the Authority. Priority shall be given to the adoption of rules, regulations and procedures for the exploration for and exploitation of polymetallic nodules. Rules, regulations and procedures for the exploration for and exploitation of any resource other than polymetallic nodules shall be adopted within three years from the date of a request to the Authority by any of its members to adopt such rules, regulations and procedures in respect of such resource. All rules, regulations and procedures shall remain in effect on a provisional basis until approved by the Assembly or until amended by the Council in the light of any views expressed by the Assembly;

(p) review the collection of all payments to be made by or to the Authority in connection with operations pursuant to this Part;

(q) make the selection from among applicants for production authorizations pursuant to Annex III, article 7, where such selection is required by that provision;

(r) submit the proposed annual budget of the Authority to the Assembly for its approval;

(s) make recommendations to the Assembly concerning policies on any question or matter within the competence of the Authority;

(t) make recommendations to the Assembly concerning suspension of the exercise of the rights and privileges of membership pursuant to article 185;

(u) institute proceedings on behalf of the Authority before the Sea-Bed Disputes Chamber in cases of non-compliance;

(v) notify the Assembly upon a decision by the Sea-Bed Disputes Chamber in proceedings instituted under subparagraph (u), and make any recommendations which it may find appropriate with respect to measures to be taken;

(w) issue emergency orders, which may include orders for the suspension or adjustment of operations, to prevent serious harm to the marine environment arising out of activities in the Area;

(x) disapprove areas for exploitation by contractors or the Enterprise in cases where substantial evidence indicates the risk of serious harm to the marine environment;

(y) establish a subsidiary organ for the elaboration of draft financial rules, regulations and procedures relating to:

(i) financial management in accordance with articles 171 to 175; and

(ii) financial arrangements in accordance with Annex III, article 13 and article 17, paragraph 1(c);

(z) establish appropriate mechanisms for directing and supervising a staff of inspectors who shall inspect activities in the Area to determine whether this Part, the rules, regulations and procedures of the Authority, and the terms and conditions of any contract with the Authority are being complied with.

Article 163. *Organs of the Council*

1. There are hereby established the following organs of the Council:
   (a) an Economic Planning Commission;
   (b) a Legal and Technical Commission.

2. Each Commission shall be composed of 15 members, elected by the Council from among the candidates nominated by the States Parties. However, if necessary, the Council may decide to increase the size of either Commission having due regard to economy and efficiency.

3. Members of a Commission shall have appropriate qualifications in the area of competence of that Commission. States Parties shall nominate candidates of the highest standards of competence and integrity with qualifications in relevant fields so as to ensure the effective exercise of the functions of the Commissions.

4. In the election of members of the Commissions, due account shall be taken of the need for equitable geographical distribution and the representation of special interests.

5. No State Party may nominate more than one candidate for the same Commission. No person shall be elected to serve on more than one Commission.

6. Members of the Commissions shall hold office for a term of five years. They shall be eligible for re-election for a further term. . . .

8. Members of Commissions shall have no financial interest in any activity relating to exploration and exploitation in the Area. Subject to their responsibilities to the Commissions upon which they serve, they shall not disclose, even after the termination of their functions, any industrial secret, proprietary data which are transferred to the Authority in accordance with Annex III, article 14, or any other confidential information coming to their knowledge by reason of their duties for the Authority.

9. Each Commission shall exercise its functions in accordance with such guidelines and directives as the Council may adopt.

10. Each Commission shall formulate and submit to the Council for approval such rules and regulations as may be necessary for the efficient conduct of the Commission's functions.

11. The decision-making procedures of the Commissions shall be established by the rules, regulations and procedures of the Authority. Recommendations to the Council shall, where necessary, be accompanied by a summary on the divergencies of opinion in the Commission.

12. Each Commission shall normally function at the seat of the Authority and shall meet as often as is required for the efficient exercise of its functions. . . .

Article 164. *The Economic Planning Commission*

1. Members of the Economic Planning Commission shall have appropriate qualifications such as those relevant to mining, management of mineral resource activities, international trade or international economics. The Council shall endeavour to ensure that the membership of the Commission reflects all appropriate qualifications. The Commission shall include at least two members from developing States whose exports of the categories of minerals to be derived from the Area have a substantial bearing upon their economies.

2. The Commission shall:

(a) propose, upon the request of the Council, measures to implement decisions relating to activities in the Area taken in accordance with this Convention;

(b) review the trends of and the factors affecting supply, demand and prices of materials which may be derived from the Area, bearing in mind the interests of both importing and exporting countries, and in particular of the developing States among them;

(c) examine any situation likely to lead to the adverse effects referred to in article 150, subparagraph (h), brought to its attention by the State Party or States Parties concerned, and make appropriate recommendations to the Council;

(d) propose to the Council for submission to the Assembly, as provided in article 151, paragraph 10, a system of compensation or other measures of economic adjustment assistance for developing States which suffer adverse effects caused by activities in the Area. The Commission shall make the recommendations to the Council that are necessary for the application of the system or other measures adopted by the Assembly in specific cases.

Article 165. The Legal and Technical Commission

1. Members of the Legal and Technical Commission shall have appropriate qualifications such as those relevant to exploration for and exploitation and processing of mineral resources, oceanology, protection of the marine environment, or economic or legal matters relating to ocean mining and related fields of expertise. The Council shall endeavour to ensure that the membership of the Commission reflects all appropriate qualifications.

2. The Commission shall:

(a) make recommendations with regard to the exercise of the Authority's functions upon the request of the Council;

(b) review formal written plans of work for activities in the Area in accordance with article 153, paragraph 3, and submit appropriate recommendations to the Council. The Commission shall base its recommendations solely on the grounds stated in Annex III and shall report fully thereon to the Council;

(c) supervise, upon the request of the Council, activities in the Area, where appropriate, in consultation and collaboration with any entity carrying out such activities or State or States concerned and report to the Council;

(d) prepare assessments of the environmental implications of activities in the Area;

(e) make recommendations to the Council on the protection of the marine environment, taking into account the views of recognized experts in that field;

(f) formulate and submit to the Council the rules, regulations and procedures referred to in article 162, paragraph 2(o), taking into account all relevant factors including assessments of the environmental implications of activities in the Area;

(g) keep such rules, regulations and procedures under review and recommend to the Council from time to time such amendments thereto as it may deem necessary or desirable;

(h) make recommendations to the Council regarding the establishment of a monitoring programme to observe, measure, evaluate and analyse, by recognized scientific methods, on a regular basis, the risks or effects of pollution of the marine environment resulting from activities in the Area, ensure that existing regulations are adequate and are complied with and co-ordinate the implementation of the monitoring programme approved by the Council;

(i) recommend to the Council that proceedings be instituted on behalf of the Authority before the Sea-Bed Disputes Chamber, in accordance with this Part and the relevant Annexes taking into account particularly article 187;

(j) make recommendations to the Council with respect to measures to be taken, upon a decision by the Sea-Bed Disputes Chamber in proceedings instituted in accordance with subparagraph (i);

(k) make recommendations to the Council to issue emergency orders, which may include orders for the suspension or adjustment of operations, to prevent serious harm to the marine environment arising out of activities in the Area. Such recommendations shall be taken up by the Council on a priority basis;

(l) make recommendations to the Council to disapprove areas for exploitation by contractors or the Enterprise in cases where substantial evidence indicates the risk of serious harm to the marine environment;

(m) make recommendations to the Council regarding the direction and supervision of a staff of inspectors who shall inspect activities in the Area to determine whether the provisions of this Part, the rules, regulations and procedures of the Authority, and the terms and conditions of any contract with the Authority are being complied with;

(n) calculate the production ceiling and issue production authorizations on behalf of the Authority pursuant to article 151, paragraphs 2 to 7, following any necessary selection among applicants for production authorizations by the Council in accordance with Annex III, article 7. . . .

SUBSECTION D. THE SECRETARIAT

Article 166. The Secretariat

1. The Secretariat of the Authority shall comprise a Secretary-General and such staff as the Authority may require.

2. The Secretary-General shall be elected for four years by the Assembly from among the candidates proposed by the Council and may be re-elected.

3. The Secretary-General shall be the chief administrative officer of the Authority, and shall act in that capacity in all meetings of the Assembly, of the Council and of any subsidiary organ, and shall perform such other administrative functions as are entrusted to the Secretary-General by these organs.

4. The Secretary-General shall make an annual report to the Assembly on the work of the Authority.

Article 167. The Staff of the Authority

1. The staff of the Authority shall consist of such qualified scientific and technical and other personnel as may be required to fulfil the administrative functions of the Authority.

2. The paramount consideration in the recruitment and employment of the staff and in the determination of their conditions of service shall be the necessity of securing the highest standards of efficiency, competence and integrity. Subject to this consideration, due regard shall be paid to the importance of recruiting the staff on as wide a geographical basis as possible.

3. The staff shall be appointed by the Secretary-General. The terms and conditions on which they shall be appointed, remunerated and dismissed shall be in accordance with the rules, regulations and procedures of the Authority.

Article 168. International Character of the Secretariat

1. In the performance of their duties the Secretary-General and the staff shall not seek or receive instructions from any government or from any other source external to the Authority. They shall refrain from any action which might reflect on their position as international officials responsible only to the Authority. Each State Party undertakes to respect the exclusively international character of the responsibilities of the Secretary-General and the staff and not to seek to influence them in the discharge of their responsibilities. Any violation of responsibilities by a staff member shall be submitted to the appropriate administrative tribunal as provided in the rules, regulations and procedures of the Authority.

2. The Secretary-General and the staff shall have no financial interest in any activity relating to exploration and exploitation in the Area. Subject to their responsibilities to the Authority, they shall not disclose, even after the termination of their functions, any industrial secret, proprietary data which are transferred to the Authority in accordance with Annex III, article 14, or any other confidential information coming to their knowledge by reason of their employment with the Authority. . . .

Article 169. Consultation and Co-operation with International and Non-governmental Organizations

1. The Secretary-General shall, on matters within the competence of the Authority, make suitable arrangements, with the approval of the Council, for consultation and co-operation with international and non-governmental organizations recognized by the Economic and Social Council of the United Nations. . . .

SUBSECTION E. THE ENTERPRISE

Article 170. The Enterprise

1. The Enterprise shall be the organ of the Authority which shall carry out activities in the Area directly, pursuant to article 153, paragraph 2(a), as well as the transporting, processing and marketing of minerals recovered from the Area.

2. The Enterprise shall, within the framework of the International legal personality of the Authority, have such legal capacity as is provided for in the Statute set forth in Annex IV. The Enterprise shall act in accordance with this Convention and the rules, regulations and procedures of the Authority, as well as the general policies established by the Assembly, and shall be subject to the directives and control of the Council.

3. The Enterprise shall have its principal place of business at the seat of the Authority.

4. The Enterprise shall, in accordance with article 173, paragraph 2, and Annex IV, article 11, be provided with such funds as it may require to carry out its functions, and shall receive technology as provided in article 144 and other relevant provisions of this Convention.

SUBSECTION F. FINANCIAL ARRANGEMENTS OF THE AUTHORITY

Article 171. Funds of the Authority

The funds of the Authority shall include:

(a) assessed contributions made by members of the Authority in accordance with article 160, paragraph 2(e);

(b) funds received by the Authority pursuant to Annex III, article 13, in connection with activities in the Area;

(c) funds transferred from the Enterprise in accordance with Annex IV, article 10;

(d) funds borrowed pursuant to article 174;

(e) voluntary contributions made by members or other entities; and

(f) payments to a compensation fund, in accordance with article 151, paragraph 10, whose sources are to be recommended by the Economic Planning Commission.

Article 172. Annual Budget of the Authority

The Secretary-General shall draft the proposed annual budget of the Authority and submit it to the Council. The Council shall consider the proposed annual budget and submit it to the Assembly, together with any recommendations thereon. The Assembly shall consider and approve the proposed annual budget in accordance with article 160, paragraph 2(h).

Article 173. Expenses of the Authority

1. The contributions referred to in article 171, subparagraph (a), shall be paid into a special account to meet the administrative expenses of the Authority until the Authority has sufficient funds from other sources to meet those expenses.

2. The administrative expenses of the Authority shall be a first call upon the funds of the Authority. Except for the assessed contributions referred to in article 171, subparagraph (a), the funds which remain after payment of administrative expenses may, *inter alia:*

(a) be shared in accordance with article 140 and article 160, paragraph 2(g);

(b) be used to provide the Enterprise with funds in accordance with article 170, paragraph 4;

(c) be used to compensate developing States in accordance with article 151, paragraph 10, and article 160, paragraph 2(1).

Article 174. Borrowing Power of the Authority

1. The Authority shall have the power to borrow funds.

2. The Assembly shall prescribe the limits on the borrowing power of the Authority in the financial regulations adopted pursuant to article 160, paragraph 2(f).

3. The Council shall exercise the borrowing power of the Authority.

4. States Parties shall not be liable for the debts of the Authority.

Article 175. Annual Audit . . .

SUBSECTION G. LEGAL STATUS, PRIVILEGES AND IMMUNITIES

Article 176. Legal Status

The Authority shall have international legal personality and such legal capacity as may be necessary for the exercise of its functions and the fulfilment of its purposes.

Article 177. Privileges and Immunities

To enable the Authority to exercise its functions, it shall enjoy in the territory of each State Party the privileges and immunities set forth in this subsection. The privileges and immunities relating to the Enterprise shall be those set forth in Annex IV, article 13.

Article 178. Immunity from Legal Process

The Authority, its property and assets, shall enjoy immunity from legal process except to the extent that the Authority expressly waives this immunity in a particular case.

Article 179. Immunity from Search and Any Form of Seizure

The property and assets of the Authority, wherever located and by whomsoever held, shall be immune from search, requisition, confiscation, expropriation or any other form of seizure by executive or legislative action.

Article 180. Exemption from Restrictions, Regulations, Controls and Moratoria

The property and assets of the Authority shall be exempt from restrictions, regulations, controls and moratoria of any nature.

Article 181. Archives and Official Communications of the Authority

1. The archives of the Authority, wherever located, shall be inviolable.
2. Proprietary data, industrial secrets or similar information and personnel records shall not be placed in archives which are open to public inspection.
3. With regard to its official communications, the Authority shall be accorded by each State Party treatment no less favourable than that accorded by that State to other international organizations.

Article 182. Privileges and Immunities of Certain Persons Connected with the Authority

Representatives of States Parties attending meetings of the Assembly, the Council or organs of the Assembly or the Council, and the Secretary-General and staff of the Authority, shall enjoy in the territory of each State Party:

(a) immunity from legal process with respect to acts performed by them in the exercise of their functions, except to the extent that the State which they represent or the Authority, as appropriate, expressly waives this immunity in a particular case;

(b) if they are not nationals of that State Party, the same exemptions from immigration restrictions, alien registration requirements and national service obligations, the same facilities as regards exchange restrictions and the same treatment in respect of travelling facilities as are accorded by that State to the representatives, officials and employees of comparable rank of other States Parties.

Article 183. Exemption from Taxes and Customs Duties

1. Within the scope of its official activities, the Authority, its assets and property, its income, and its operations and transactions, authorized by this Convention, shall be exempt from all direct taxation and goods imported or exported for its official use shall be exempt from all customs duties. The Authority shall not claim exemption from taxes which are no more than charges for services rendered. . . .

SUBSECTION H. SUSPENSION OF THE EXERCISE OF RIGHTS AND PRIVILEGES OF MEMBERS

Article 184. Suspension of the Exercise of Voting Rights

A State Party which is in arrears in the payment of its financial contributions to the Authority shall have no vote if the amount of its arrears equals or exceeds the amount of the contributions due from it for the preceding two full years. The Assembly may, nevertheless, permit such a member to vote if it is satisfied that the failure to pay is due to conditions beyond the control of the member.

Article 185. Suspension of Exercise of Rights and Privileges of Membership

1. A State Party which has grossly and persistently violated the provisions of this Part may be suspended from the exercise of the rights and privileges of membership by the Assembly upon the recommendation of the Council.

2. No action may be taken under paragraph 1 until the Sea-Bed Disputes Chamber has found that a State Party has grossly and persistently violated the provisions of this Part.

SECTION 5. SETTLEMENT OF DISPUTES AND ADVISORY OPINIONS

Article 186. Sea-Bed Disputes Chamber of the International Tribunal for the Law of the Sea

The establishment of the Sea-Bed Disputes Chamber and the manner in which it shall exercise its jurisdiction shall be governed by the provisions of this section, of Part XV and of Annex VI.

Article 187. Jurisdiction of the Sea-Bed Disputes Chamber

The Sea-Bed Disputes Chamber shall have jurisdiction under this Part and the Annexes relating thereto in disputes with respect to activities in the Area falling within the following categories:

(a) disputes between States Parties concerning the interpretation or application of this Part and the Annexes relating thereto;

(b) disputes between a State Party and the Authority concerning:

(i) acts or omissions of the Authority or of a State Party alleged to be in violation of this Part or the Annexes relating thereto or of rules, regulations and procedures of the Authority adopted in accordance therewith; or

(ii) acts of the Authority alleged to be in excess of jurisdiction or a misuse of power;

(c) disputes between parties to a contract, being States Parties, the Authority or the Enterprise, state enterprises and natural or juridical persons referred to in article 153, paragraph 2(b), concerning:

(i) the interpretation or application of a relevant contract or a plan of work; or

(ii) acts or omissions of a party to the contract relating to activities in the Area and directed to the other party or directly affecting its legitimate interests;

(d) disputes between the Authority and a prospective contractor who has been sponsored by a State as provided in article 153, paragraph 2 (b), and has duly fulfilled the conditions referred to in Annex III, article 4, paragraph 6, and article 13, paragraph 2, concerning the refusal of a contract or a legal issue arising in the negotiation of the contract;

(e) disputes between the Authority and a State Party, a state enterprise or a natural or juridical person sponsored by a State Party as provided for in article 153, paragraph 2(b), where it is alleged that the Authority has incurred liability as provided in Annex III, article 22;

(f) any other disputes for which the jurisdiction of the Chamber is specifically provided in this Convention.

Article 188. Submission of Disputes to a Special Chamber of the International Tribunal for the Law of the Sea or an Ad Hoc Chamber of the Sea-Bed Disputes Chamber or to Binding Commercial Arbitration

1. Disputes between States Parties referred to in article 187, subparagraph (a), may be submitted:

(a) at the request of the parties to the dispute, to a special chamber of the International Tribunal for the Law of the Sea to be formed in accordance with Annex VI, articles 15 and 17; or

(b) at the request of any party to the dispute, to an *ad hoc* chamber of the Sea-Bed Disputes Chamber to be formed in accordance with Annex VI, article 36.

2. (a) Disputes concerning the interpretation or application of a contract referred to in article 187, subparagraph (c) (i), shall be submitted, at the request of any party to the dispute, to binding commercial arbitration, unless the parties otherwise agree. A commercial arbitral tribunal

to which the dispute is submitted shall have no jurisdiction to decide any question of interpretation of this Convention. When the dispute also involves a question of the interpretation of Part XI and the Annexes relating thereto, with respect to activities in the Area, that question shall be referred to the Sea-Bed Disputes Chamber for a ruling.

(b) If, at the commencement of or in the course of such arbitration, the arbitral tribunal determines, either at the request of any party to the dispute or *proprio motu,* that its decision depends upon a ruling of the Sea-Bed Disputes Chamber, the arbitral tribunal shall refer such question to the Sea-Bed Disputes Chamber for such ruling. The arbitral tribunal shall then proceed to render its award in conformity with the ruling of the Sea-Bed Disputes Chamber.

(c) In the absence of a provision in the contract on the arbitration procedure to be applied in the dispute, the arbitration shall be conducted in accordance with the UNCITRAL Arbitration Rules or such other arbitration rules as may be prescribed in the rules, regulations and procedures of the Authority, unless the parties to the dispute otherwise agree.

Article 189. Limitation on Jurisdiction with Regard to Decisions of the Authority

The Sea-Bed Disputes Chamber shall have no jurisdiction with regard to the exercise by the Authority of its discretionary powers in accordance with this Part; in no case shall it substitute its discretion for that of the Authority. Without prejudice to article 191, in exercising its jurisdiction pursuant to article 187, the Sea-Bed Disputes Chamber shall not pronounce itself on the question of whether any rules, regulations and procedures of the Authority are in conformity with this Convention, nor declare invalid any such rules, regulations and procedures. Its jurisdiction in this regard shall be confined to deciding claims that the application of any rules, regulations and procedures of the Authority in individual cases would be in conflict with the contractual obligations of the parties to the dispute or their obligations under this Convention, claims concerning excess of jurisdiction or misuse of power, and to claims for damages to be paid or other remedy to be given to the party concerned for the failure of the other party to comply with its contractual obligations or its obligations under this Convention.

Article 190. Participation and Appearance of Sponsoring States Parties in Proceedings

1. If a natural or juridical person is a party to a dispute referred to in article 187, the sponsoring State shall be given notice thereof and shall have the right to participate in the proceedings by submitting written or oral statements.

2. If an action is brought against a State Party by a natural or juridical person sponsored by another State Party in a dispute referred to in article 187, subparagraph (c), the respondent State may request the State sponsoring that person to appear in the proceedings on behalf of that person. Failing such appearance, the respondent State may arrange to be represented by a juridical person of its nationality.

Article 191. Advisory Opinions

The Sea-Bed Disputes Chamber shall give advisory opinions at the request of the Assembly or the Council on legal questions arising within the scope of their activities. Such opinions shall be given as a matter of urgency.

Part XII. Protection and Preservation of the Marine Environment

Section 1. General Provisions

Article 192. General Obligation

States have the obligation to protect and preserve the marine environment.

Article 193. Sovereign Right of States to Exploit Their Natural Resources

States have the sovereign right to exploit their natural resources pursuant to their environmental policies and in accordance with their duty to protect and preserve the marine environment.

Article 194. Measures to Prevent, Reduce and Control Pollution of the Marine Environment

1. States shall take, individually or jointly as appropriate, all measures consistent with this Convention that are necessary to prevent, reduce and control pollution of the marine environment from any source, using for this purpose the best practicable means at their disposal and in accordance with their capabilities, and they shall endeavour to harmonize their policies in this connection.

2. States shall take all measures necessary to ensure that activities under their jurisdiction or control are so conducted as not to cause damage by pollution to other States and their environment, and that pollution arising from incidents or activities under their jurisdiction or control does not spread beyond the areas where they exercise sovereign rights in accordance with this Convention.

3. The measures taken pursuant to this Part shall deal with all sources of pollution of the marine environment. These measures shall include, *inter alia*, those designed to minimize to the fullest possible extent:

(a) the release of toxic, harmful or noxious substances, especially those which are persistent, from land-based sources, from or through the atmosphere or by dumping;

(b) pollution from vessels, in particular measures for preventing accidents and dealing with emergencies, ensuring the safety of operations at sea, preventing intentional and unintentional discharges, and regulating the design, construction, equipment, operation and manning of vessels;

(c) pollution from installations and devices used in exploration or exploitation of the natural resources of the sea-bed and subsoil, in particular measures for preventing accidents and dealing with emergencies, ensuring the safety of operations at sea, and regulating the design, construction, equipment, operation and manning of such installations or devices;

(d) pollution from other installations and devices operating in the marine environment, in particular measures for preventing accidents and dealing with emergencies, ensuring the safety of operations at sea, and regulating the design, construction, equipment, operation and manning of such installations or devices.

4. In taking measures to prevent, reduce or control pollution of the marine environment, States shall refrain from unjustifiable interference with activities carried out by other States in the exercise of their rights and in pursuance of their duties in conformity with this Convention.

5. The measures taken in accordance with this Part shall include those necessary to protect and preserve rare or fragile ecosystems as well as the habitat of depleted, threatened or endangered species and other forms of marine life.

Article 195. Duty Not to Transfer Damage or Hazards or Transform One Type of Pollution into Another

In taking measures to prevent, reduce and control pollution of the marine environment, States shall act so as not to transfer, directly or indirectly, damage or hazards from one area to another or transform one type of pollution into another.

Article 196. Use of Technologies or Introduction of Alien or New Species

1. States shall take all measures necessary to prevent, reduce and control pollution of the marine environment resulting from the use of technologies under their jurisdiction or control, or the intentional or accidental introduction of species, alien or new, to a particular part of the marine environment, which may cause significant and harmful changes thereto.

2. This article does not affect the application of this Convention regarding the prevention, reduction and control of pollution of the marine environment.

SECTION 2. GLOBAL AND REGIONAL CO-OPERATION

Article 197. Co-operation on a Global or Regional Basis

States shall co-operate on a global basis and, as appropriate, on a regional basis, directly or through competent international organizations, in formulating and elaborating international rules, standards and recommended practices and procedures consistent with this Convention, for the protection and preservation of the marine environment, taking into account characteristic regional features.

Article 198. *Notification of Imminent or Actual Damage*

When a State becomes aware of cases in which the marine environment is in imminent danger of being damaged or has been damaged by pollution, it shall immediately notify other States it deems likely to be affected by such damage, as well as the competent international organizations.

Article 199. *Contingency Plans Against Pollution*

In the cases referred to in article 198, States in the area affected, in accordance with their capabilities, and the competent international organizations shall co-operate, to the extent possible, in eliminating the effects of pollution and preventing or minimizing the damage. To this end, States shall jointly develop and promote contingency plans for responding to pollution incidents in the marine environment.

Article 200. *Studies, Research Programmes and Exchange of Information and Data*

States shall co-operate, directly or through competent international organizations, for the purpose of promoting studies, undertaking programmes of scientific research and encouraging the exchange of information and data acquired about pollution of the marine environment. . . .

SECTION 3. TECHNICAL ASSISTANCE

Article 202. *Scientific and Technical Assistance to Developing States*

States shall, directly or through competent international organizations:
 (a) promote programmes of scientific, educational, technical and other assistance to developing States for the protection and preservation of the marine environment and the prevention, reduction and control of marine pollution. . . .
 (b) provide appropriate assistance, especially to developing States, for the minimization of the effects of major incidents which may cause serious pollution of the marine environment;
 (c) provide appropriate assistance, especially to developing States, concerning the preparation of environmental assessments.

Article 203. *Preferential Treatment for Developing States*

Developing States shall, for the purposes of prevention, reduction and control of pollution of the marine environment or minimization of its effects, be granted preference by international organizations in:
 (a) the allocation of appropriate funds and technical assistance; and
 (b) the utilization of their specialized services.

Section 4. Monitoring and Environmental Assessment

Article 204. Monitoring of the Risks or Effects of Pollution

1. States shall, consistent with the rights of other States, endeavour, as far as practicable, directly or through the competent international organizations, to observe, measure, evaluate and analyse, by recognized scientific methods, the risks or effects of pollution of the marine environment.

2. In particular, States shall keep under surveillance the effects of any activities which they permit or in which they engage in order to determine whether these activities are likely to pollute the marine environment.

Article 205. Publication of Reports

States shall publish reports of the results obtained pursuant to article 204 or provide such reports at appropriate intervals to the competent international organizations, which should make them available to all States.

Article 206. Assessment of Potential Effects of Activities

When States have reasonable grounds for believing that planned activities under their jurisdiction or control may cause substantial pollution of or significant and harmful changes to the marine environment, they shall, as far as practicable, assess the potential effects of such activities on the marine environment and shall communicate reports of the results of such assessments in the manner provided in article 205.

Section 5. International Rules and National Legislation to Prevent, Reduce and Control Pollution of the Marine Environment

Article 207. Pollution from Land-based Sources

1. States shall adopt laws and regulations to prevent, reduce and control pollution of the marine environment from land-based sources, including rivers, estuaries, pipelines and outfall structures, taking into account internationally agreed rules, standards and recommended practices and procedures.

2. States shall take other measures as may be necessary to prevent, reduce and control such pollution.

3. States shall endeavour to harmonize their policies in this connection at the appropriate regional level.

4. States, acting especially through competent international organizations or diplomatic conference, shall endeavour to establish global and regional rules, standards and recommended practices and procedures to prevent, reduce and control pollution of the marine environment from land-based sources, taking into account characteristic regional features, the economic capacity of developing States and their need for economic devel-

opment. Such rules, standards and recommended practices and procedures shall be re-examined from time to time as necessary.

5. Laws, regulations, measures, rules, standards and recommended practices and procedures referred to in paragraphs 1, 2 and 4 shall include those designed to minimize, to the fullest extent possible, the release of toxic, harmful or noxious substances, especially those which are persistent, into the marine environment.

Article 208. Pollution from Sea-bed Activities Subject to National Jurisdiction

1. Coastal States shall adopt laws and regulations to prevent, reduce and control pollution of the marine environment arising from or in connection with sea-bed activities subject to their jurisdiction and from artificial islands, installations and structures under their jurisdiction, pursuant to articles 60 and 80.

2. States shall take other measures as may be necessary to prevent, reduce and control such pollution.

3. Such laws, regulations and measures shall be no less effective than international rules, standards and recommended practices and procedures.

4. States shall endeavour to harmonize their policies in this connection at the appropriate regional level.

5. States, acting especially through competent international organizations or diplomatic conference, shall establish global and regional rules, standards and recommended practices and procedures to prevent, reduce and control pollution of the marine environment referred to in paragraph 1. Such rules, standards and recommended practices and procedures shall be re-examined from time to time as necessary.

Article 209. Pollution from Activities in the Area

1. International rules, regulations and procedures shall be established in accordance with Part XI to prevent, reduce and control pollution of the marine environment from activities in the Area. Such rules, regulations and procedures shall be re-examined from time to time as necessary.

2. Subject to the relevant provisions of this section, States shall adopt laws and regulations to prevent, reduce and control pollution of the marine environment from activities in the Area undertaken by vessels, installations, structures and other devices flying their flag or of their registry or operating under their authority, as the case may be. The requirements of such laws and regulations shall be no less effective than the international rules, regulations and procedures referred to in paragraph 1.

Article 210. Pollution by Dumping

1. States shall adopt laws and regulations to prevent, reduce and control pollution of the marine environment by dumping.

2. States shall take other measures as may be necessary to prevent, reduce and control such pollution.

3. Such laws, regulations and measures shall ensure that dumping is not

carried out without the permission of the competent authorities of States.

4. States, acting especially through competent international organizations or diplomatic conference, shall endeavour to establish global and regional rules, standards and recommended practices and procedures to prevent, reduce and control such pollution. Such rules, standards and recommended practices and procedures shall be re-examined from time to time as necessary.

5. Dumping within the territorial sea and the exclusive economic zone or onto the continental shelf shall not be carried out without the express prior approval of the coastal State, which has the right to permit, regulate and control such dumping after due consideration of the matter with other States which by reason of their geographical situation may be adversely affected thereby.

6. National laws, regulations and measures shall be no less effective in preventing, reducing and controlling such pollution than the global rules and standards.

Article 211. Pollution from Vessels

1. States, acting through the competent international organization or general diplomatic conference, shall establish international rules and standards to prevent, reduce and control pollution of the marine environment from vessels and promote the adoption, in the same manner, wherever appropriate, of routeing systems designed to minimize the threat of accidents which might cause pollution of the marine environment, including the coastline, and pollution damage to the related interests of coastal States. Such rules and standards shall, in the same manner, be re-examined from time to time as necessary.

2. States shall adopt laws and regulations for the prevention, reduction and control of pollution of the marine environment from vessels flying their flag or of their registry. Such laws and regulations shall at least have the same effect as that of generally accepted international rules and standards established through the competent international organization or general diplomatic conference.

3. States which establish particular requirements for the prevention, reduction and control of pollution of the marine environment as a condition for the entry of foreign vessels into their ports or internal waters or for a call at their off-shore terminals shall give due publicity to such requirements and shall communicate them to the competent international organization.
... Every State shall require the master of a vessel flying its flag or of its registry, when navigating within the territorial sea of a State participating in such co-operative arrangements, to furnish, upon the request of that State, information as to whether it is proceeding to a State of the same region participating in such co-operative arrangements and, if so, to indicate whether it complies with the port entry requirements of that State. This article is without prejudice to the continued exercise by a vessel of its right of innocent passage or to the application of article 25, paragraph 2.

4. Coastal States may, in the exercise of their sovereignty within their territorial sea, adopt laws and regulations for the prevention, reduction and

control of marine pollution from foreign vessels, including vessels exercising the right of innocent passage. Such laws and regulations shall, in accordance with Part II, section 3, not hamper innocent passage of foreign vessels.

5. Coastal States, for the purpose of enforcement as provided for in section 6, may in respect of their exclusive economic zones adopt laws and regulations for the prevention, reduction and control of pollution from vessels conforming to and giving effect to generally accepted international rules and standards established through the competent international organization or general diplomatic conference.

6. (a) Where the international rules and standards referred to in paragraph 1 are inadequate to meet special circumstances and coastal States have reasonable grounds for believing that a particular, clearly defined area of their respective exclusive economic zones is an area where the adoption of special mandatory measures for the prevention of pollution from vessels is required for recognized technical reasons in relation to its oceanographical and ecological conditions, as well as its utilization or the protection of its resources and the particular character of its traffic, the coastal States, after appropriate consultations through the competent international organization with any other States concerned, may, for that area, direct a communication to that organization, submitting scientific and technical evidence in support and information on necessary reception facilities. Within 12 months after receiving such a communication, the organization shall determine whether the conditions in that area correspond to the requirements set out above. If the organization so determines, the coastal States may, for that area, adopt laws and regulations for the prevention, reduction and control of pollution from vessels implementing such international rules and standards or navigational practices as are made applicable, through the organization, for special areas. These laws and regulations shall not become applicable to foreign vessels until 15 months after the submission of the communication to the organization. . . .

7. The international rules and standards referred to in this article should include *inter alia* those relating to prompt notification to coastal States, whose coastline or related interests may be affected by incidents, including maritime casualties, which involve discharges or probability of discharges.

Article 212. *Pollution From or Through the Atmosphere*

1. States shall adopt laws and regulations to prevent, reduce and control pollution of the marine environment from or through the atmosphere, applicable to the air space under their sovereignty and to vessels flying their flag or vessels or aircraft of their registry, taking into account internationally agreed rules, standards and recommended practices and procedures and the safety of air navigation.

2. States shall take other measures as may be necessary to prevent, reduce and control such pollution.

3. States, acting especially through competent international organizations or diplomatic conference, shall endeavour to establish global and

regional rules, standards and recommended practices and procedures to prevent, reduce and control such pollution.

SECTION 6. ENFORCEMENT

Article 213. Enforcement with Respect to Pollution from Land-based Sources

States shall enforce their laws and regulations adopted in accordance with article 207 and shall adopt laws and regulations and take other measures necessary to implement applicable international rules and standards established through competent international organizations or diplomatic conference to prevent, reduce and control pollution of the marine environment from land-based sources.

Article 214. Enforcement with Respect to Pollution from Sea-bed Activities

States shall enforce their laws and regulations adopted in accordance with article 208 and shall adopt laws and regulations and take other measures necessary to implement applicable international rules and standards established through competent international organizations or diplomatic conference to prevent, reduce and control pollution of the marine environment arising from or in connection with sea-bed activities subject to their jurisdiction and from artificial islands, installations and structures under their jurisdiction, pursuant to articles 60 and 80.

Article 215. Enforcement with Respect to Pollution from Activities in the Area

Enforcement of international rules, regulations and procedures established in accordance with Part XI to prevent, reduce and control pollution of the marine environment from activities in the Area shall be governed by that Part.

Article 216. Enforcement with Respect to Pollution by Dumping

1. Laws and regulations adopted in accordance with this Convention and applicable international rules and standards established through competent international organizations or diplomatic conference for the prevention, reduction and control of pollution of the marine environment by dumping shall be enforced:

(a) by the coastal State with regard to dumping within its territorial sea or its exclusive economic zone or onto its continental shelf;

(b) by the flag State with regard to vessels flying its flag or vessels or aircraft of its registry;

(c) by any State with regard to acts of loading of wastes or other matter occurring within its territory or at its off-shore terminals.

2. No State shall be obliged by virtue of this article to institute proceedings when another State has already instituted proceedings in accordance with this article.

Article 217. Enforcement by Flag States

1. States shall ensure compliance by vessels flying their flag or of their registry with applicable international rules and standards, established through the competent international organization or general diplomatic conference, and with their laws and regulations adopted in accordance with this Convention for the prevention, reduction and control of pollution of the marine environment from vessels and shall accordingly adopt laws and regulations and take other measures necessary for their implementation. Flag States shall provide for the effective enforcement of such rules, standards, laws and regulations, irrespective of where a violation occurs.

2. States shall, in particular, take appropriate measures in order to ensure that vessels flying their flag or of their registry are prohibited from sailing, until they can proceed to sea in compliance with the requirements of the international rules and standards referred to in paragraph 1, including requirements in respect of design, construction, equipment and manning of vessels.

3. States shall ensure that vessels flying their flag or of their registry carry on board certificates required by and issued pursuant to international rules and standards referred to in paragraph 1. States shall ensure that vessels flying their flag are periodically inspected in order to verify that such certificates are in conformity with the actual condition of the vessels. These certificates shall be accepted by other States as evidence of the condition of the vessels and shall be regarded as having the same force as certificates issued by them, unless there are clear grounds for believing that the condition of the vessel does not correspond substantially with the particulars of the certificates.

4. If a vessel commits a violation of rules and standards established through the competent international organization or general diplomatic conference, the flag State, without prejudice to articles 218, 220 and 228, shall provide for immediate investigation and where appropriate institute proceedings in respect of the alleged violation irrespective of where the violation occurred or where the pollution caused by such violation has occurred or has been spotted.

5. Flag States conducting an investigation of the violation may request the assistance of any other State whose co-operation could be useful in clarifying the circumstances of the case. States shall endeavour to meet appropriate requests of flag States.

6. States shall, at the written request of any State, investigate any violation alleged to have been committed by vessels flying their flag. If satisfied that sufficient evidence is available to enable proceedings to be brought in respect of the alleged violation, flag States shall without delay institute such proceedings in accordance with their laws.

7. Flag States shall promptly inform the requesting State and the competent international organization of the action taken and its outcome. Such information shall be available to all States.

8. Penalties provided for by the laws and regulations of States for vessels flying their flag shall be adequate in severity to discourage violations wherever they occur.

Article 218. Enforcement by Port States

1. When a vessel is voluntarily within a port or at an off-shore terminal of a State, that State may undertake investigations and, where the evidence so warrants, institute proceedings in respect of any discharge from that vessel outside the internal waters, territorial sea or exclusive economic zone of that State in violation of applicable international rules and standards established through the competent international organization or general diplomatic conference.

2. No proceedings pursuant to paragraph 1 shall be instituted in respect of a discharge violation in the internal waters, territorial sea or exclusive economic zone of another State unless requested by that State, the flag State, or a State damaged or threatened by the discharge violation, or unless the violation has caused or is likely to cause pollution in the internal waters, territorial sea or exclusive economic zone of the State instituting the proceedings.

3. When a vessel is voluntarily within a port or at an off-shore terminal of a State, that State shall, as far as practicable, comply with requests from any State for investigation of a discharge violation referred to in paragraph 1, believed to have occurred in, caused, or threatened damage to the internal waters, territorial sea or exclusive economic zone of the requesting State. It shall likewise, as far as practicable, comply with requests from the flag State for investigation of such a violation, irrespective of where the violation occurred.

4. The records of the investigation carried out by a port State pursuant to this article shall be transmitted upon request to the flag State or to the coastal State. Any proceedings instituted by the port State on the basis of such an investigation may, subject to section 7, be suspended at the request of the coastal State when the violation has occurred within its internal waters, territorial sea or exclusive economic zone. The evidence and records of the case, together with any bond or other financial security posted with the authorities of the port State, shall in that event be transmitted to the coastal State. Such transmittal shall preclude the continuation of proceedings in the port State.

Article 219. Measures Relating to Seaworthiness of Vessels to Avoid Pollution

Subject to section 7, States which, upon request or on their own initiative, have ascertained that a vessel within one of their ports or at one of their off-shore terminals is in violation of applicable international rules and standards relating to seaworthiness of vessels and thereby threatens damage to the marine environment shall, as far as practicable, take administrative measures to prevent the vessel from sailing. Such States may permit the vessel to proceed only to the nearest appropriate repair yard and, upon removal of the causes of the violation, shall permit the vessel to continue immediately.

Article 220. Enforcement by Coastal States

1. When a vessel is voluntarily within a port or at an off-shore terminal of a State, that State may, subject to section 7, institute proceedings in respect of any violation of its laws and regulations adopted in accordance with this Convention or applicable international rules and standards for the prevention, reduction and control of pollution from vessels when the violation has occurred within the territorial sea or the exclusive economic zone of that State.

2. Where there are clear grounds for believing that a vessel navigating in the territorial sea of a State has, during its passage therein, violated laws and regulations of that State adopted in accordance with this Convention or applicable international rules and standards for the prevention, reduction and control of pollution from vessels, that State, without prejudice to the application of the relevant provisions of Part II, section 3, may undertake physical inspection of the vessel relating to the violation and may, where the evidence so warrants, institute proceedings, including detention of the vessel, in accordance with its laws, subject to the provisions of section 7.

3. Where there are clear grounds for believing that a vessel navigating in the exclusive economic zone or the territorial sea of a State has, in the exclusive economic zone, committed a violation of applicable international rules and standards for the prevention, reduction and control of pollution from vessels or laws and regulations of that State conforming and giving effect to such rules and standards, that State may require the vessel to give information regarding its identity and port of registry, its last and its next port of call and other relevant information required to establish whether a violation has occurred.

4. States shall adopt laws and regulations and take other measures so that vessels flying their flag comply with requests for information pursuant to paragraph 3.

5. Where there are clear grounds for believing that a vessel navigating in the exclusive economic zone or the territorial sea of a State has, in the exclusive economic zone, committed a violation referred to in paragraph 3 resulting in a substantial discharge causing or threatening significant pollution of the marine environment, that State may undertake physical inspection of the vessel for matters relating to the violation if the vessel has refused to give information or if the information supplied by the vessel is manifestly at variance with the evident factual situation and if the circumstances of the case justify such inspection.

6. Where there is clear objective evidence that a vessel navigating in the exclusive economic zone or the territorial sea of a State has, in the exclusive economic zone, committed a violation referred to in paragraph 3 resulting in a discharge causing major damage or threat of major damage to the coastline or related interests of the coastal State, or to any resources of its territorial sea or exclusive economic zone, that State may, subject to section 7, provided that the evidence so warrants, institute proceedings, including detention of the vessel, in accordance with its laws.

7. Notwithstanding the provisions of paragraph 6, whenever appropriate procedures have been established, either through the competent inter-

national organization or as otherwise agreed, whereby compliance with requirements for bonding or other appropriate financial security has been assured, the coastal State if bound by such procedures shall allow the vessel to proceed.

8. The provisions of paragraphs 3, 4, 5, 6 and 7 also apply in respect of national laws and regulations adopted pursuant to article 211, paragraph 6.

Article 221. Measures to Avoid Pollution Arising from Maritime Casualties

1. Nothing in this Part shall prejudice the right of States, pursuant to international law, both customary and conventional, to take and enforce measures beyond the territorial sea proportionate to the actual or threatened damage to protect their coastline or related interests, including fishing, from pollution or threat of pollution following upon a maritime casualty or acts relating to such a casualty, which may reasonably be expected to result in major harmful consequences.

2. For the purposes of this article, "maritime casualty" means a collision of vessels, stranding or other incident of navigation, or other occurrence on board a vessel or external to it resulting in material damage or imminent threat of material damage to a vessel or cargo.

Article 222. Enforcement with Respect to Pollution From or Through the Atmosphere

States shall enforce, within the air space under their sovereignty or with regard to vessels flying their flag or vessels or aircraft of their registry, their laws and regulations adopted in accordance with article 212, paragraph 1, and with other provisions of this Convention and shall adopt laws and regulations and take other measures necessary to implement applicable international rules and standards established through competent international organizations or diplomatic conference to prevent, reduce and control pollution of the marine environment from or through the atmosphere, in conformity with all relevant international rules and standards concerning the safety of air navigation.

Section 7. Safeguards

Article 223. Measures to Facilitate Proceedings

In proceedings instituted pursuant to this Part, States shall take measures to facilitate the hearing of witnesses and the admission of evidence submitted by authorities of another State, or by the competent international organization, and shall facilitate the attendance at such proceedings of official representatives of the competent international organization, the flag State and any State affected by pollution arising out of any violation. The official representatives attending such proceedings shall have such rights and duties as may be provided under national laws and regulations or international law.

Article 224. Exercise of Powers of Enforcement

1. The powers of enforcement against foreign vessels under this Part may only be exercised by officials or by warships, military aircraft, or other ships or aircraft clearly marked and identifiable as being on government service and authorized to that effect. . . .

Article 226. Investigation of Foreign Vessels

1. (a) States shall not delay a foreign vessel longer than is essential for purposes of the investigations provided for in articles 216, 218 and 220. Any physical inspection of a foreign vessel shall be limited to an examination of such certificates, records or other documents as the vessel is required to carry by generally accepted international rules and standards or of any similar documents which it is carrying; further physical inspection of the vessel may be undertaken only after such an examination and only when:

(i) there are clear grounds for believing that the condition of the vessel or its equipment does not correspond substantially with the particulars of those documents;

(ii) the contents of such documents are not sufficient to confirm or verify a suspected violation; or

(iii) the vessel is not carrying valid certificates and records.

(b) If the investigation indicates a violation of applicable laws and regulations or international rules and standards for the protection and preservation of the marine environment, release shall be made promptly subject to reasonable procedures such as bonding or other appropriate financial security.

(c) Without prejudice to applicable international rules and standards relating to the seaworthiness of vessels, the release of a vessel may, whenever it would present an unreasonable threat of damage to the marine environment, be refused or made conditional upon proceeding to the nearest appropriate repair yard. Where release has been refused or made conditional, the flag State of the vessel must be promptly notified, and may seek release of the vessel in accordance with Part XV.

2. States shall co-operate to develop procedures for the avoidance of unnecessary physical inspection of vessels at sea.

Article 227. Non-discrimination with Respect to Foreign Vessels

In exercising their rights and performing their duties under this Part, States shall not discriminate in form or in fact against vessels of any other State.

Article 228. Suspension and Restrictions on Institution of Proceedings

1. Proceedings to impose penalties in respect of any violation of applicable laws and regulations or international rules and standards relating to the prevention, reduction and control of pollution from vessels committed by a foreign vessel beyond the territorial sea of the State instituting proceedings shall be suspended upon the taking of proceedings to impose penalties in respect of corresponding charges by the flag State within six months of

the date on which proceedings were first instituted, unless those proceedings relate to a case of major damage to the coastal State or the flag State in question has repeatedly disregarded its obligation to enforce effectively the applicable international rules and standards in respect of violations committed by its vessels. The flag State shall in due course make available to the State previously instituting proceedings a full dossier of the case and the records of the proceedings, whenever the flag State has requested the suspension of proceedings in accordance with this article. When proceedings instituted by the flag State have been brought to a conclusion, the suspended proceedings shall be terminated. . . .

2. Proceedings to impose penalties on foreign vessels shall not be instituted after the expiry of three years from the date on which the violation was committed, and shall not be taken by any State in the event of proceedings having been instituted by another State subject to the provisions set out in paragraph 1. . . .

Article 229. Institution of Civil Proceedings

Nothing in this Convention affects the institution of civil proceedings in respect of any claim for loss or damage resulting from pollution of the marine environment.

Article 230. Monetary Penalties and the Observance of Recognized Rights of the Accused

1. Monetary penalties only may be imposed with respect to violations of national laws and regulations or applicable international rules and standards for the prevention, reduction and control of pollution of the marine environment, committed by foreign vessels beyond the territorial sea.

2. Monetary penalties only may be imposed with respect to violations of national laws and regulations or applicable international rules and standards for the prevention, reduction and control of pollution of the marine environment, committed by foreign vessels in the territorial sea, except in the case of a wilful and serious act of pollution in the territorial sea. . . .

Article 231. Notification to the Flag State and Other States Concerned

States shall promptly notify the flag State and any other State concerned of any measures taken pursuant to section 6 against foreign vessels, and shall submit to the flag State all official reports concerning such measures. However, with respect to violations committed in the territorial sea, the foregoing obligations of the coastal State apply only to such measures as are taken in proceedings.

Article 232. Liability of States Arising from Enforcement Measures

States shall be liable for damage or loss attributable to them arising from measures taken pursuant to section 6 when such measures are unlawful or exceed those reasonably required in the light of available information. States shall provide for recourse in their courts for actions in respect of such damage or loss.

Article 233. Safeguards with Respect to Straits Used for International Navigation

Nothing in sections 5, 6 and 7 affects the legal régime of straits used for international navigation. However, if a foreign ship other than those referred to in section 10 has committed a violation of the laws and regulations referred to in article 42, paragraph 1(a) and (b), causing or threatening major damage to the marine environment of the straits, the States bordering the straits may take appropriate enforcement measures and if so shall respect *mutatis mutandis* the provisions of this section.

Section 8. Ice-covered Areas

Article 234. Ice-covered Areas

Coastal States have the right to adopt and enforce non-discriminatory laws and regulations for the prevention, reduction and control of marine pollution from vessels in ice-covered areas within the limits of the exclusive economic zone, . . .

Section 9. Responsibility and Liability

Article 235. Responsibility and Liability

1. States are responsible for the fulfilment of their international obligations concerning the protection and preservation of the marine environment. They shall be liable in accordance with international law.
2. States shall ensure that recourse is available in accordance with their legal systems for prompt and adequate compensation or other relief in respect of damage caused by pollution of the marine environment by natural or juridical persons under their jurisdiction.
3. With the objective of assuring prompt and adequate compensation in respect of all damage caused by pollution of the marine environment, States shall co-operate in the implementation of existing international law and the further development of international law relating to responsibility and liability for the assessment of and compensation for damage and the settlement of related disputes, as well as, where appropriate, development of criteria and procedures for payment of adequate compensation, such as compulsory insurance or compensation funds.

Section 10. Sovereign Immunity

Article 236. Sovereign Immunity

The provisions of this Convention regarding the protection and preservation of the marine environment do not apply to any warship, naval auxiliary, other vessels or aircraft owned or operated by a State and used, for the time being, only on government non-commercial service. However, each State shall ensure, by the adoption of appropriate measures not impairing operations or operational capabilities of such vessels or aircraft owned or operated by it, that such vessels or aircraft act in a manner consistent, so far as is reasonable and practicable, with this Convention.

SECTION 11. OBLIGATIONS UNDER OTHER CONVENTIONS ON THE PROTECTION AND PRESERVATION OF THE MARINE ENVIRONMENT

Article 237. Obligations Under Other Conventions on the Protection and Preservation of the Marine Environment

1. The provisions of this Part are without prejudice to the specific obligations assumed by States under special conventions and agreements concluded previously which relate to the protection and preservation of the marine environment and to agreements which may be concluded in furtherance of the general principles set forth in this Convention. . . .

Part XIII. Marine Scientific Research

SECTION 1. GENERAL PROVISIONS

Article 238. Right to Conduct Marine Scientific Research

All States, irrespective of their geographical location, and competent international organizations have the right to conduct marine scientific research subject to the rights and duties of other States as provided for in this Convention.

Article 239. Promotion of Marine Scientific Research

States and competent international organizations shall promote and facilitate the development and conduct of marine scientific research in accordance with this Convention.

Article 240. General Principles for the Conduct of Marine Scientific Research

In the conduct of marine scientific research the following principles shall apply:
   (a) marine scientific research shall be conducted exclusively for peaceful purposes;
   (b) marine scientific research shall be conducted with appropriate scientific methods and means compatible with this Convention;
   (c) marine scientific research shall not unjustifiably interfere with other legitimate uses of the sea compatible with this Convention and shall be duly respected in the course of such uses;
   (d) marine scientific research shall be conducted in compliance with all relevant regulations adopted in conformity with this Convention including those for the protection and preservation of the marine environment.

Article 241. Non-recognition of Marine Scientific Research Activities as the Legal Basis for Claims

Marine scientific research activities shall not constitute the legal basis for any claim to any part of the marine environment or its resources.

Section 2. International Co-operation

Article 242. Promotion of International Co-operation

1. States and competent international organizations shall, in accordance with the principle of respect for sovereignty and jurisdiction and on the basis of mutual benefit, promote international co-operation in marine scientific research for peaceful purposes.

2. In this context, without prejudice to the rights and duties of States under this Convention, a State, in the application of this Part, shall provide, as appropriate, other States with a reasonable opportunity to obtain from it, or with its co-operation, information necessary to prevent and control damage to the health and safety of persons and to the marine environment. . . .

Article 244. Publication and Dissemination of Information and Knowledge

1. States and competent international organizations shall, in accordance with this Convention, make available by publication and dissemination through appropriate channels information on proposed major programmes and their objectives as well as knowledge resulting from marine scientific research. . . .

Section 3. Conduct and Promotion of Marine Scientific Research

Article 245. Marine Scientific Research in the Territorial Sea

Coastal States, in the exercise of their sovereignty, have the exclusive right to regulate, authorize and conduct marine scientific research in their territorial sea. Marine scientific research therein shall be conducted only with the express consent of and under the conditions set forth by the coastal State.

Article 246. Marine Scientific Research in the Exclusive Economic Zone and on the Continental Shelf

1. Coastal States, in the exercise of their jurisdiction, have the right to regulate, authorize and conduct marine scientific research in their exclusive economic zone and on their continental shelf in accordance with the relevant provisions of this Convention.

2. Marine scientific research in the exclusive economic zone and on the continental shelf shall be conducted with the consent of the coastal State.

3. Coastal States shall, in normal circumstances, grant their consent for

marine scientific research projects by other States or competent international organizations in their exclusive economic zone or on their continental shelf to be carried out in accordance with this Convention exclusively for peaceful purposes and in order to increase scientific knowledge of the marine environment for the benefit of all mankind. To this end, coastal States shall establish rules and procedures ensuring that such consent will not be delayed or denied unreasonably.

4. For the purposes of applying paragraph 3, normal circumstances may exist in spite of the absence of diplomatic relations between the coastal State and the researching State.

5. Coastal States may however in their discretion withhold their consent to the conduct of a marine scientific research project of another State or competent international organization in the exclusive economic zone or on the continental shelf of the coastal State if that project:

(a) is of direct significance for the exploration and exploitation of natural resources, whether living or non-living;

(b) involves drilling into the continental shelf, the use of explosives or the introduction of harmful substances into the marine environment;

(c) involves the construction, operation or use of artificial islands, installations and structures referred to in articles 60 and 80;

(d) contains information communicated pursuant to article 248 regarding the nature and objectives of the project which is inaccurate or if the researching State or competent international organization has outstanding obligations to the coastal State from a prior research project.

6. Notwithstanding the provisions of paragraph 5, coastal States may not exercise their discretion to withhold consent under subparagraph (a) of that paragraph in respect of marine scientific research projects to be undertaken in accordance with the provisions of this Part on the continental shelf, beyond 200 nautical miles from the baselines from which the breadth of the territorial sea is measured, outside those specific areas which coastal States may at any time publicly designate as areas in which exploitation or detailed exploratory operations focused on those areas are occurring or will occur within a reasonable period of time. . . .

7. The provisions of paragraph 6 are without prejudice to the rights of coastal States over the continental shelf as established in article 77. . . .

Article 248. Duty to Provide Information to the Coastal State

States and competent international organizations which intend to undertake marine scientific research in the exclusive economic zone or on the continental shelf of a coastal State shall, not less than six months in advance of the expected starting date of the marine scientific research project, provide that State with a full description of:

(a) the nature and objectives of the project;

(b) the method and means to be used, including name, tonnage, type and class of vessels and a description of scientific equipment;

(c) the precise geographical areas in which the project is to be conducted;

(d) the expected date of first appearance and final departure of the research vessels, or deployment of the equipment and its removal, as appropriate;

(e) the name of the sponsoring institution, its director, and the person in charge of the project; and

(f) the extent to which it is considered that the coastal State should be able to participate or to be represented in the project.

Article 249. *Duty to Comply with Certain Conditions*

1. States and competent international organizations when undertaking marine scientific research in the exclusive economic zone or on the continental shelf of a coastal State shall comply with the following conditions:

(a) ensure the right of the coastal State, if it so desires, to participate or be represented in the marine scientific research project, especially on board research vessels and other craft or scientific research installations, when practicable, without payment of any remuneration to the scientists of the coastal State and without obligation to contribute towards the costs of the project;

(b) provide the coastal State, at its request, with preliminary reports, as soon as practicable, and with the final results and conclusions after the completion of the research;

(c) undertake to provide access for the coastal State, at its request, to all data and samples derived from the marine scientific research project and likewise to furnish it with data which may be copied and samples which may be divided without detriment to their scientific value;

(d) if requested, provide the coastal State with an assessment of such data, samples and research results or provide assistance in their assessment or interpretation;

(e) ensure, subject to paragraph 2, that the research results are made internationally available through appropriate national or international channels, as soon as practicable;

(f) inform the coastal State immediately of any major change in the research programme;

(g) unless otherwise agreed, remove the scientific research installations or equipment once the research is completed.

2. This article is without prejudice to the conditions established by the laws and regulations of the coastal State for the exercise of its discretion to grant or withhold consent pursuant to article 246, paragraph 5, including requiring prior agreement for making internationally available the research results of a project of direct significance for the exploration and exploitation of natural resources. . . .

Article 253. *Suspension or Cessation of Marine Scientific Research Activities*

1. A coastal State shall have the right to require the suspension of any marine scientific research activities in progress within its exclusive economic zone or on its continental shelf if:

(a) the research activities are not being conducted in accordance with the information communicated as provided under article 248 upon which the consent of the coastal State was based; or

(b) the State or competent international organization conducting the research activities fails to comply with the provisions of article 249 concerning the rights of the coastal State with respect to the marine scientific research project.

2. A coastal State shall have the right to require the cessation of any marine scientific research activities in case of any non-compliance with the provisions of article 248 which amounts to a major change in the research project or the research activities.

3. A coastal State may also require cessation of marine scientific research activities if any of the situations contemplated in paragraph 1 are not rectified within a reasonable period of time.

4. Following notification by the coastal State of its decision to order suspension or cessation, States or competent international organizations authorized to conduct marine scientific research activities shall terminate the research activities that are the subject of such a notification. . . .

Article 256. *Marine Scientific Research in the Area*

All States, irrespective of their geographical location, and competent international organizations have the right, in conformity with the provisions of Part XI, to conduct marine scientific research in the Area.

Article 257. *Marine Scientific Research in the Water Column Beyond the Exclusive Economic Zone*

All States, irrespective of their geographical location, and competent international organizations have the right, in conformity with this Convention, to conduct marine scientific research in the water column beyond the limits of the exclusive economic zone. . . .

SECTION 5. RESPONSIBILITY AND LIABILITY

Article 263. *Responsibility and Liability*

1. States and competent international organizations shall be responsible for ensuring that marine scientific research, whether undertaken by them or on their behalf, is conducted in accordance with this Convention.

2. States and competent international organizations shall be responsible and liable for the measures they take in contravention of this Convention in respect of marine scientific research conducted by other States, their natural or juridical persons or by competent international organizations, and shall provide compensation for damage resulting from such measures.

3. States and competent international organizations shall be responsible and liable pursuant to article 235 for damage caused by pollution of the marine environment arising out of marine scientific research undertaken by them or on their behalf.

Section 6. Settlement of Disputes and Interim Measures

Article 264. Settlement of Disputes

Disputes concerning the interpretation or application of the provisions of this Convention with regard to marine scientific research shall be settled in accordance with Part XV, sections 2 and 3. . . .

Part XIV. Development and Transfer of Marine Technology

Section 1. General Provisions

Article 266. Promotion of the Development and Transfer of Marine Technology

1. States, directly or through competent international organizations, shall co-operate in accordance with their capabilities to promote actively the development and transfer of marine science and marine technology on fair and reasonable terms and conditions.
2. States shall promote the development of the marine scientific and technological capacity of States which may need and request technical assistance in this field, particularly developing States, including land-locked and geographically disadvantaged States, with regard to the exploration, exploitation, conservation and management of marine resources, the protection and preservation of the marine environment, marine scientific research and other activities in the marine environment compatible with this Convention, with a view to accelerating the social and economic development of the developing States.
3. States shall endeavour to foster favourable economic and legal conditions for the transfer of marine technology for the benefit of all parties concerned on an equitable basis.

Article 267. Protection of Legitimate Interests

States, in promoting co-operation pursuant to article 266, shall have due regard for all legitimate interests including, *inter alia,* the rights and duties of holders, suppliers and recipients of marine technology.

Article 268. Basic Objectives

States, directly or through competent international organizations, shall promote:
    (a) the acquisition, evaluation and dissemination of marine technological knowledge and facilitate access to such information and data;
    (b) the development of appropriate marine technology;
    (c) the development of the necessary technological infrastructure to facilitate the transfer of marine technology;
    (d) the development of human resources through training and educa-

tion of nationals of developing States and countries and especially the nationals of the least developed among them;

(e) international co-operation at all levels, particularly at the regional, subregional and bilateral levels.

Article 269. Measures to Achieve the Basic Objectives

In order to achieve the objectives referred to in article 268, States, directly or through competent international organizations, shall endeavour, *inter alia*, to:

(a) establish programmes of technical co-operation for the effective transfer of all kinds of marine technology to States which may need and request technical assistance in this field, particularly the developing landlocked and geographically disadvantaged States, as well as other developing States which have not been able either to establish or develop their own technological capacity in marine science and in the exploration and exploitation of marine resources or to develop the infrastructure of such technology;

(b) promote favourable conditions for the conclusion of agreements, contracts and other similar arrangements, under equitable and reasonable conditions;

(c) hold conferences, seminars and symposia on scientific and technological subjects, in particular on policies and methods for the transfer of marine technology;

(d) promote the exchange of scientists and of technological and other experts;

(e) undertake projects and promote joint ventures and other forms of bilateral and multilateral co-operation.

SECTION 2. INTERNATIONAL CO-OPERATION . . .

Article 273. Co-operation with International Organizations and the Authority

States shall co-operate actively with competent international organizations and the Authority to encourage and facilitate the transfer to developing States, their nationals and the Enterprise of skills and marine technology with regard to activities in the Area.

Article 274. Objectives of the Authority

Subject to all legitimate interests including, *inter alia*, the rights and duties of holders, suppliers and recipients of technology, the Authority, with regard to activities in the Area, shall ensure that:

(a) on the basis of the principle of equitable geographical distribution, nationals of developing States, whether coastal, land-locked or geographically disadvantaged, shall be taken on for the purposes of training as members of the managerial, research and technical staff constituted for its undertakings;

(b) the technical documentation on the relevant equipment, machinery, devices and processes is made available to all States, in particular developing States which may need and request technical assistance in this field;

(c) adequate provision is made by the Authority to facilitate the acquisition of technical assistance in the field of marine technology by States which may need and request it, in particular developing States, and the acquisition by their nationals of the necessary skills and know-how, including professional training;

(d) States which may need and request technical assistance in this field, in particular developing States, are assisted in the acquisition of necessary equipment, processes, plant and other technical know-how through any financial arrangements provided for in this Convention.

SECTION 3. NATIONAL AND REGIONAL MARINE SCIENTIFIC AND TECHNOLOGICAL CENTRES . . .

Part XV. Settlement of Disputes

SECTION 1. GENERAL PROVISIONS

Article 279. Obligation to Settle Disputes by Peaceful Means

States Parties shall settle any dispute between them concerning the interpretation or application of this Convention by peaceful means in accordance with Article 2, paragraph 3, of the Charter of the United Nations and, to this end, shall seek a solution by the means indicated in Article 33, paragraph 1, of the Charter.

Article 280. Settlement of Disputes by Any Peaceful Means Chosen by the Parties

Nothing in this Part impairs the right of any States Parties to agree at any time to settle a dispute between them concerning the interpretation or application of this Convention by any peaceful means of their own choice.

Article 281. Procedure Where No Settlement Has Been Reached by the Parties

1. If the States Parties which are parties to a dispute concerning the interpretation or application of this Convention have agreed to seek settlement of the dispute by a peaceful means of their own choice, the procedures provided for in this Part apply only where no settlement has been reached by recourse to such means and the agreement between the parties does not exclude any further procedure.

2. If the parties have also agreed on a time-limit, paragraph 1 applies only upon the expiration of that time-limit.

Article 282. Obligations Under General, Regional or Bilateral Agreements

If the States Parties which are parties to a dispute concerning the interpretation or application of this Convention have agreed, through a general, regional or bilateral agreement or otherwise, that such dispute shall, at the request of any party to the dispute, be submitted to a procedure that entails a binding decision, that procedure shall apply in lieu of the procedures provided for in this Part, unless the parties to the dispute otherwise agree.

Article 283. Obligation to Exchange Views

1. When a dispute arises between States Parties concerning the interpretation or application of this Convention, the parties to the dispute shall proceed expeditiously to an exchange of views regarding its settlement by negotiation or other peaceful means.
2. The parties shall also proceed expeditiously to an exchange of views where a procedure for the settlement of such a dispute has been terminated without a settlement or where a settlement has been reached and the circumstances require consultation regarding the manner of implementing the settlement.

Article 284. Conciliation

1. A State Party which is a party to a dispute concerning the interpretation or application of this Convention may invite the other party or parties to submit the dispute to conciliation in accordance with the procedure under Annex V, section 1, or another conciliation procedure.
2. If the invitation is accepted and if the parties agree upon the conciliation procedure to be applied, any party may submit the dispute to that procedure.
3. If the invitation is not accepted or the parties do not agree upon the procedure, the conciliation proceedings shall be deemed to be terminated.
4. Unless the parties otherwise agree, when a dispute has been submitted to conciliation, the proceedings may be terminated only in accordance with the agreed conciliation procedure.

Article 285. Application of This Section to Disputes Submitted Pursuant to Part XI

This section applies to any dispute which pursuant to Part XI, section 5, is to be settled in accordance with procedures provided for in this Part. If an entity other than a State Party is a party to such a dispute, this section applies *mutatis mutandis.*

SECTION 2. COMPULSORY PROCEDURES ENTAILING BINDING DECISIONS

Article 286. Application of Procedures Under This Section

Subject to section 3, any dispute concerning the interpretation or application of this Convention shall, where no settlement has been reached by recourse to section 1, be submitted at the request of any party to the dispute to the court or tribunal having jurisdiction under this section.

Article 287. Choice of Procedure

1. When signing, ratifying or acceding to this Convention or at any time thereafter, a State shall be free to choose, by means of a written declaration, one or more of the following means for the settlement of disputes concerning the interpretation or application of this Convention:

(a) the International Tribunal for the Law of the Sea established in accordance with Annex VI;

(b) the International Court of Justice;

(c) an arbitral tribunal constituted in accordance with Annex VII;

(d) a special arbitral tribunal constituted in accordance with Annex VIII for one or more of the categories of disputes specified therein.

2. A declaration made under paragraph 1 shall not affect or be affected by the obligation of a State Party to accept the jurisdiction of the Sea-Bed Disputes Chamber of the International Tribunal for the Law of the Sea to the extent and in the manner provided for in Part XI, section 5.

3. A State Party, which is a party to a dispute not covered by a declaration in force, shall be deemed to have accepted arbitration in accordance with Annex VII.

4. If the parties to a dispute have accepted the same procedure for the settlement of the dispute, it may be submitted only to that procedure, unless the parties otherwise agree.

5. If the parties to a dispute have not accepted the same procedure for the settlement of the dispute, it may be submitted only to arbitration in accordance with Annex VII, unless the parties otherwise agree.

6. A declaration made under paragraph 1 shall remain in force until three months after notice of revocation has been deposited with the Secretary-General of the United Nations.

7. A new declaration, a notice of revocation or the expiry of a declaration does not in any way affect proceedings pending before a court or tribunal having jurisdiction under this article, unless the parties otherwise agree. . . .

Article 288. Jurisdiction

1. A court or tribunal referred to in article 287 shall have jurisdiction over any dispute concerning the interpretation or application of this Convention which is submitted to it in accordance with this Part.

2. A court or tribunal referred to in article 287 shall also have jurisdiction over any dispute concerning the interpretation or application of an international agreement related to the purposes of this Convention, which is submitted to it in accordance with the agreement.

3. The Sea-Bed Disputes Chamber of the International Tribunal for the Law of the Sea established in accordance with Annex VI, and any other chamber or arbitral tribunal referred to in Part XI, section 5, shall have jurisdiction in any matter which is submitted to it in accordance therewith.

4. In the event of a dispute as to whether a court or tribunal has jurisdiction, the matter shall be settled by decision of that court or tribunal.

Article 289. *Experts*

In any dispute involving scientific or technical matters, a court or tribunal exercising jurisdiction under this section may, at the request of a party or *proprio motu,* select in consultation with the parties no fewer than two scientific or technical experts chosen preferably from the relevant list prepared in accordance with Annex VIII, article 2, to sit with the court or tribunal but without the right to vote.

Article 290. *Provisional Measures*

1. If a dispute has been duly submitted to a court or tribunal which considers that *prima facie* it has jurisdiction under this Part or Part XI, section 5, the court or tribunal may prescribe any provisional measures which it considers appropriate under the circumstances to preserve the respective rights of the parties to the dispute or to prevent serious harm to the marine environment, pending the final decision.

2. Provisional measures may be modified or revoked as soon as the circumstances justifying them have changed or ceased to exist.

3. Provisional measures may be prescribed, modified or revoked under this article only at the request of a party to the dispute and after the parties have been given an opportunity to be heard.

4. The court or tribunal shall forthwith give notice to the parties to the dispute, and to such other States Parties as it considers appropriate, of the prescription, modification or revocation of provisional measures.

5. Pending the constitution of an arbitral tribunal to which a dispute is being submitted under this section, any court or tribunal agreed upon by the parties or, failing such agreement within two weeks from the date of the request for provisional measures, the International Tribunal for the Law of the Sea or, with respect to activities in the Area, the Sea-Bed Disputes Chamber, may prescribe, modify or revoke provisional measures in accordance with this article if it considers that *prima facie* the tribunal which is to be constituted would have jurisdiction and that the urgency of the situation so requires. Once constituted, the tribunal to which the dispute has been submitted may modify, revoke or affirm those provisional measures, acting in conformity with paragraphs 1 to 4.

6. The parties to the dispute shall comply promptly with any provisional measures prescribed under this article.

Article 291. *Access*

1. All the dispute settlement procedures specified in this Part shall be open to States Parties.

2. The dispute settlement procedures specified in this Part shall be open to entities other than States Parties only as specifically provided for in this Convention.

Article 292. *Prompt Release of Vessels and Crews*

1. Where the authorities of a State Party have detained a vessel flying the flag of another State Party and it is alleged that the detaining State has not complied with the provisions of this Convention for the prompt release of the vessel or its crew upon the posting of a reasonable bond or other financial security, the question of release from detention may be submitted to any court or tribunal agreed upon by the parties or, failing such agreement within 10 days from the time of detention, to a court or tribunal accepted by the detaining State under article 287 or to the International Tribunal for the Law of the Sea, unless the parties otherwise agree.

2. The application for release may be made only by or on behalf of the flag State of the vessel.

3. The court or tribunal shall deal without delay with the application for release and shall deal only with the question of release, without prejudice to the merits of any case before the appropriate domestic forum against the vessel, its owner or its crew. The authorities of the detaining State remain competent to release the vessel or its crew at any time.

4. Upon the posting of the bond or other financial security determined by the court or tribunal, the authorities of the detaining State shall comply promptly with the decision of the court or tribunal concerning the release of the vessel or its crew.

Article 293. *Applicable Law*

1. A court or tribunal having jurisdiction under this section shall apply this Convention and other rules of international law not incompatible with this Convention.

2. Paragraph 1 does not prejudice the power of the court or tribunal having jurisdiction under this section to decide a case *ex aequo et bono*, if the parties so agree.

Article 294. *Preliminary Proceedings*

1. A court or tribunal provided for in article 287 to which an application is made in respect of a dispute referred to in article 297 shall determine at the request of a party, or may determine *proprio motu*, whether the claim constitutes an abuse of legal process or whether *prima facie* it is well founded. If the court or tribunal determines that the claim constitutes an abuse of legal process or is *prima facie* unfounded, it shall take no further action in the case.

2. Upon receipt of the application, the court or tribunal shall immediately notify the other party or parties of the application, and shall fix a reasonable time-limit within which they may request it to make a determination in accordance with paragraph 1.

3. Nothing in this article affects the right of any party to a dispute to make preliminary objections in accordance with the applicable rules of procedure.

Article 295. *Exhaustion of Local Remedies*

Any dispute between States Parties concerning the interpretation or application of this Convention may be submitted to the procedures provided for in this section only after local remedies have been exhausted where this is required by international law.

Article 296. *Finality and Binding Force of Decisions*

1. Any decision rendered by a court or tribunal having jurisdiction under this section shall be final and shall be complied with by all the parties to the dispute.

2. Any such decision shall have no binding force except between the parties and in respect of that particular dispute.

SECTION 3. LIMITATIONS AND EXCEPTIONS TO APPLICABILITY OF SECTION 2

Article 297. *Limitations on Applicability of Section 2*

1. Disputes concerning the interpretation or application of this Convention with regard to the exercise by a coastal State of its sovereign rights or jurisdiction provided for in this Convention shall be subject to the procedures provided for in section 2 in the following cases:

(a) when it is alleged that a coastal State has acted in contravention of the provisions of this Convention in regard to the freedoms and rights of navigation, overflight or the laying of submarine cables and pipelines, or in regard to other internationally lawful uses of the sea specified in article 58;

(b) when it is alleged that a State in exercising the aforementioned freedoms, rights or uses has acted in contravention of this Convention or of laws or regulations adopted by the coastal State in conformity with this Convention and other rules of international law not incompatible with this Convention; or

(c) when it is alleged that a coastal State has acted in contravention of specified international rules and standards for the protection and preservation of the marine environment which are applicable to the coastal State and which have been established by this Convention or through a competent international organization or diplomatic conference in accordance with this Convention.

2. (a) Disputes concerning the interpretation or application of the provisions of this Convention with regard to marine scientific research shall be settled in accordance with section 2, except that the coastal State shall not be obliged to accept the submission to such settlement of any dispute arising out of:

(i) the exercise by the coastal State of a right or discretion in accordance with article 246; or

(ii) a decision by the coastal State to order suspension or cessation of a research project in accordance with article 253.

(b) A dispute arising from an allegation by the researching State that with respect to a specific project the coastal State is not exercising its rights under articles 246 and 253 in a manner compatible with this Convention shall be submitted, at the request of either party, to conciliation under Annex V, section 2, provided that the conciliation commission shall not call in question the exercise by the coastal State of its discretion to designate specific areas as referred to in article 246, paragraph 6, or of its discretion to withhold consent in accordance with article 246, paragraph 5.

3. (a) Disputes concerning the interpretation or application of the provisions of this Convention with regard to fisheries shall be settled in accordance with section 2, except that the coastal State shall not be obliged to accept the submission to such settlement of any dispute relating to its sovereign rights with respect to the living resources in the exclusive economic zone or their exercise, including its discretionary powers for determining the allowable catch, its harvesting capacity, the allocation of surpluses to other States and the terms and conditions established in its conservation and management laws and regulations.

(b) Where no settlement has been reached by recourse to section 1 of this Part, a dispute shall be submitted to conciliation under Annex V, section 2, at the request of any party to the dispute, when it is alleged that:

(i) a coastal State has manifestly failed to comply with its obligations to ensure through proper conservation and management measures that the maintenance of the living resources in the exclusive economic zone is not seriously endangered;

(ii) a coastal State has arbitrarily refused to determine, at the request of another State, the allowable catch and its capacity to harvest living resources with respect to stocks which that other State is interested in fishing; or

(iii) a coastal State has arbitrarily refused to allocate to any State, under articles 62, 69 and 70 and under the terms and conditions established by the coastal State consistent with this Convention, the whole or part of the surplus it has declared to exist.

(c) In no case shall the conciliation commission substitute its discretion for that of the coastal State.

(d) The report of the conciliation commission shall be communicated to the appropriate international organizations.

(e) In negotiating agreements pursuant to articles 69 and 70, States Parties, unless they otherwise agree, shall include a clause on measures which they shall take in order to minimize the possibility of a disagreement concerning the interpretation or application of the agreement, and on how they should proceed if a disagreement nevertheless arises.

Article 298. *Optional Exceptions to Applicability of Section 2*

1. When signing, ratifying or acceding to this Convention or at any time thereafter, a State may, without prejudice to the obligations arising under section 1, declare in writing that it does not accept any one or more of the procedures provided for in section 2 with respect to one or more of the following categories of disputes:

(a) (i) disputes concerning the interpretation or application of articles 15, 74 and 83 relating to sea boundary delimitations, or those involving historic bays or titles, provided that a State having made such a declaration shall, when such a dispute arises subsequent to the entry into force of this Convention and where no agreement within a reasonable period of time is reached in negotiations between the parties, at the request of any party to the dispute, accept submission of the matter to conciliation under Annex V, section 2; and provided further that any dispute that necessarily involves the concurrent consideration of any unsettled dispute concerning sovereignty or other rights over continental or insular land territory shall be excluded from such submission;

(ii) after the conciliation commission has presented its report, which shall state the reasons on which it is based, the parties shall negotiate an agreement on the basis of that report; if these negotiations do not result in an agreement, the parties shall, by mutual consent, submit the question to one of the procedures provided for in section 2, unless the parties otherwise agree;

(iii) this subparagraph does not apply to any sea boundary dispute finally settled by an arrangement between the parties, or to any such dispute which is to be settled in accordance with a bilateral or multilateral agreement binding upon those parties;

(b) disputes concerning military activities, including military activities by government vessels and aircraft engaged in non-commercial service, and disputes concerning law enforcement activities in regard to the exercise of sovereign rights or jurisdiction excluded from the jurisdiction of a court or tribunal under article 297, paragraph 2 or 3;

(c) disputes in respect of which the Security Council of the United Nations is exercising the functions assigned to it by the Charter of the United Nations, unless the Security Council decides to remove the matter from its agenda or calls upon the parties to settle it by the means provided for in this Convention.

2. A State Party which has made a declaration under paragraph 1 may at any time withdraw it, or agree to submit a dispute excluded by such declaration to any procedure specified in this Convention.

3. A State Party which has made a declaration under paragraph 1 shall not be entitled to submit any dispute falling within the excepted category of disputes to any procedure in this Convention as against another State Party, without the consent of that party.

4. If one of the States Parties has made a declaration under paragraph 1(a), any other State Party may submit any dispute falling within an excepted category against the declarant party to the procedure specified in such declaration.

5. A new declaration, or the withdrawal of a declaration, does not in any way affect proceedings pending before a court or tribunal in accordance with this article, unless the parties otherwise agree. . . .

Article 299. *Right of the Parties to Agree upon a Procedure*

1. A dispute excluded under article 297 or excepted by a declaration made under article 298 from the dispute settlement procedures provided for in section 2 may be submitted to such procedures only by agreement of the parties to the dispute.

2. Nothing in this section impairs the right of the parties to the dispute to agree to some other procedure for the settlement of such dispute or to reach an amicable settlement.

Part XVI. General Provisions

Article 300. Good Faith and Abuse of Rights

States Parties shall fulfil in good faith the obligations assumed under this Convention and shall exercise the rights, jurisdiction and freedoms recognized in this Convention in a manner which would not constitute an abuse of right.

Article 301. Peaceful Uses of the Seas

In exercising their rights and performing their duties under this Convention, States Parties shall refrain from any threat or use of force against the territorial integrity or political independence of any State, or in any other manner inconsistent with the principles of international law embodied in the Charter of the United Nations.

Article 302. Disclosure of Information

Without prejudice to the right of a State Party to resort to the procedures for the settlement of disputes provided for in this Convention, nothing in this Convention shall be deemed to require a State Party, in the fulfilment of its obligations under this Convention, to supply information the disclosure of which is contrary to the essential interests of its security.

Article 303. Archaeological and Historical Objects Found at Sea

1. States have the duty to protect objects of an archaeological and historical nature found at sea and shall co-operate for this purpose.
2. In order to control traffic in such objects, the coastal State may, in applying article 33, presume that their removal from the sea-bed in the zone referred to in that article without its approval would result in an infringement within its territory or territorial sea of the laws and regulations referred to in that article.
3. Nothing in this article affects the rights of identifiable owners, the law of salvage or other rules of admiralty, or laws and practices with respect to cultural exchanges.
4. This article is without prejudice to other international agreements and rules of international law regarding the protection of objects of an archaelogical and historical nature.

Article 304. Responsibility and Liability for Damage

The provisions of this Convention regarding responsibility and liability for damage are without prejudice to the application of existing rules and the development of further rules regarding responsibility and liability under international law.

Part XVII. Final Provisions

Article 305. Signature

1. This Convention shall be open for signature by:
    (a) all States;
    (b) Namibia, represented by the United Nations Council for Namibia;
    (c) all self-governing associated States which have chosen that status in an act of self-determination supervised and approved by the United Nations in accordance with General Assembly resolution 1514 (XV) and which have competence over the matters governed by this Convention, including the competence to enter into treaties in respect of those matters;
    (d) all self-governing associated States which, in accordance with their respective instruments of association, have competence over the matters governed by this Convention, including the competence to enter into treaties in respect of those matters;
    (e) all territories which enjoy full internal self-government, recognized as such by the United Nations, but have not attained full independence in accordance with General Assembly resolution 1514 (XV) and which have competence over the matters governed by this Convention, including the competence to enter into treaties in respect of those matters;
    (f) international organizations, in accordance with Annex IX. . . .

Article 308. Entry into Force

1. This Convention shall enter into force 12 months after the date of deposit of the sixtieth instrument of ratification or accession.

2. For each State ratifying or acceding to this Convention after the deposit of the sixieth instrument of ratification or accession, the Convention shall enter into force on the thirtieth day following the deposit of its instrument of ratification or accession, subject to paragraph 1.

3. The Assembly of the Authority shall meet on the date of entry into force of this Convention and shall elect the Council of the Authority. The first Council shall be constituted in a manner consistent with the purpose of article 161 if the provisions of that article cannot be strictly applied.

4. The rules, regulations and procedures drafted by the Preparatory Commission shall apply provisionally pending their formal adoption by the Authority in accordance with Part XI.

5. The Authority and its organs shall act in accordance with resolution II of the Third United Nations Conference on the Law of the Sea relating to preparatory investment and with decisions of the Preparatory Commission taken pursuant to that resolution.

Article 309. Reservations and Exceptions

No reservations or exceptions may be made to this Convention unless expressly permitted by other articles of this Convention.

Article 310. Declarations and Statements

Article 309 does not preclude a State, when signing, ratifying or acceding to this Convention, from making declarations or statements, however phrased or named, with a view, *inter alia,* to the harmonization of its laws and regulations with the provisions of this Convention, provided that such declarations or statements do not purport to exclude or to modify the legal effect of the provisions of this Convention in their application to that State.

Article 311.   Relation to Other Conventions and International Agreements

1. This Convention shall prevail, as between States Parties, over the Geneva Conventions on the Law of the Sea of 29 April 1958.

2. This Convention shall not alter the rights and obligations of States Parties which arise from other agreements compatible with this Convention and which do not affect the enjoyment by other States Parties of their rights or the performance of their obligations under this Convention.

3. Two or more States Parties may conclude agreements modifying or suspending the operation of provisions of this Convention, applicable solely to the relations between them, provided that such agreements do not relate to a provision derogation from which is incompatible with the effective execution of the object and purpose of this Convention, and provided further that such agreements shall not affect the application of the basic principles embodied herein, and that the provisions of such agreements do not affect the enjoyment by other States Parties of their rights or the performance of their obligations under this Convention.

4. States Parties intending to conclude an agreement referred to in paragraph 3 shall notify the other States Parties through the depositary of this Convention of their intention to conclude the agreement and of the modification or suspension for which it provides.

5. This article does not affect international agreements expressly permitted or preserved by other articles of this Convention.

6. States Parties agree that there shall be no amendments to the basic principle relating to the common heritage of mankind set forth in article 136 and that they shall not be party to any agreement in derogation thereof.

Article 312.   Amendment

1. After the expiry of a period of 10 years from the date of entry into force of this Convention, a State Party may, by written communication addressed to the Secretary-General of the United Nations, propose specific amendments to this Convention, other than those relating to activities in the Area, and request the convening of a conference to consider such proposed amendments. The Secretary-General shall circulate such communication to all States Parties. If, within 12 months from the date of the circulation of the communication, not less than one half of the States Parties reply favourably to the request, the Secretary-General shall convene the conference.

2. The decision-making procedure applicable at the amendment conference shall be the same as that applicable at the Third United Nations Conference on the Law of the Sea unless otherwise decided by the conference. The conference should make every effort to reach agreement on any amendments by way of consensus and there should be no voting on them until all efforts at consensus have been exhausted.

Article 313. Amendment by Simplified Procedure

1. A State Party may, by written communication addressed to the Secretary-General of the United Nations, propose an amendment to this Convention, other than an amendment relating to activities in the Area, to be adopted by the simplified procedure set forth in this article without convening a conference. The Secretary-General shall circulate the communication to all States Parties.

2. If, within a period of 12 months from the date of the circulation of the communication, a State Party objects to the proposed amendment or to the proposal for its adoption by the simplified procedure, the amendment shall be considered rejected. The Secretary-General shall immediately notify all States Parties accordingly.

3. If, 12 months from the date of the circulation of the communication, no State Party has objected to the proposed amendment or to the proposal for its adoption by the simplified procedure, the proposed amendment shall be considered adopted. The Secretary-General shall notify all States Parties that the proposed amendment has been adopted.

Article 314. Amendments to the Provisions of this Convention Relating Exclusively to Activities in the Area

1. A State Party may, by written communication addressed to the Secretary-General of the Authority, propose an amendment to the provisions of this Convention relating exclusively to activities in the Area, including Annex VI, section 4. The Secretary-General shall circulate such communication to all States Parties. The proposed amendment shall be subject to approval by the Assembly following its approval by the Council. Representatives of States Parties in those organs shall have full powers to consider and approve the proposed amendment. The proposed amendment as approved by the Council and the Assembly shall be considered adopted.

2. Before approving any amendment under paragraph 1, the Council and the Assembly shall ensure that it does not prejudice the system of exploration for and exploitation of the resources of the Area, pending the Review Conference in accordance with article 155.

Article 315. Signature, Ratification of, Accession to and Authentic Texts of Amendments

1. Once adopted, amendments to this Convention shall be open for signature by States Parties for 12 months from the date of adoption, at United Nations Headquarters in New York, unless otherwise provided in the amendment itself. . . .

Article 316. Entry into Force of Amendments

1. Amendments to this Convention, other than those referred to in paragraph 5, shall enter into force for the States Parties ratifying or acceding to them on the thirtieth day following the deposit of instruments of ratification or accession by two thirds of the States Parties or by 60 States Parties, whichever is greater. Such amendments shall not affect the enjoyment by

other States Parties of their rights or the performance of their obligations under this Convention.

2. An amendment may provide that a larger number of ratifications or accessions shall be required for its entry into force than are required by this article.

3. For each State Party ratifying or acceding to an amendment referred to in paragraph 1 after the deposit of the required number of instruments of ratification or accession, the amendment shall enter into force on the thirtieth day following the deposit of its instrument of ratification or accession.

4. A State which becomes a Party to this Convention after the entry into force of an amendment in accordance with paragraph 1 shall, failing an expression of a different intention by that State:

(a) be considered as a Party to this Convention as so amended; and

(b) be considered as a Party to the unamended Convention in relation to any State Party not bound by the amendment.

5. Any amendment relating exclusively to activities in the Area and any amendment to Annex VI shall enter into force for all States Parties one year following the deposit of instruments of ratification or accession by three fourths of the States Parties.

6. A State which becomes a Party to this Convention after the entry into force of amendments in accordance with paragraph 5 shall be considered as a Party to this Convention as so amended. . . .

Annex I. Highly Migratory Species

1. Albacore tuna: *Thunnus alalunga.*
2. Bluefin tuna: *Thunnus thynnus.*
3. Bigeye tuna: *Thunnus obesus.*
4. Skipjack tuna: *Katsuwonus pelamis.*
5. Yellowfin tuna: *Thunnus albacares.*
6. Blackfin tuna: *Thunnus atlanticus.*
7. Little tuna: *Euthynnus alletteratus; Euthynnus affinis.*
8. Southern bluefin tuna: *Thunnus maccoyii.*
9. Frigate mackerel: *Auxis thazard; Auxis rochei.*
10. Pomfrets: Family *Bramidae.*
11. Marlins: *Tetrapturus angustirostris; Tetrapturus belone; Tetrapturus pfluegeri; Tetrapturus albidus; Tetrapturus audax; Tetrapturus georgei; Makaira mazara; Makaira indica; Makaira nigricans.*
12. Sail-fishes: *Istiophorus platypterus; Istiophorus albicans.*
13. Swordfish: *Xiphias gladius.*
14. Sauries: *Scomberesox saurus; Cololabis saira; Cololabis adocetus; Scomberesox saurus scombroides.*
15. Dolphin: *Coryphaena hippurus; Coryphaena equiselis.*
16. Oceanic sharks: *Hexanchus griseus; Cetorhinus maximus;* Family *Alopiidae; Rhincodon typus;* Family *Carcharhinidae;* Family *Sphyrnidae;* Family *Isurida.*

17. Cetaceans: Family *Physeteridae;* Family *Balaenopteridae;* Family *Balaenidae;* Family *Eschrichtiidae;* Family *Monodontidae;* Family *Ziphiidae;* Family *Delphinidae.*

Annex II. Commission on the Limits of the Continental Shelf

Article 1

In accordance with the provisions of article 76, a Commission on the Limits of the Continental Shelf beyond 200 nautical miles shall be established in conformity with the following articles.

Article 2

1. The Commission shall consist of 21 members who shall be experts in the field of geology, geophysics or hydrography, elected by States Parties to this Convention from among their nationals, having due regard to the need to ensure equitable geographical representation, who shall serve in their personal capacities.

2. The initial election shall be held as soon as possible but in any case within 18 months after the date of entry into force of this Convention. At least three months before the date of each election, the Secretary-General of the United Nations shall address a letter to the States Parties, inviting the submission of nominations, after appropriate regional consultations, within three months. The Secretary-General shall prepare a list in alphabetical order of all persons thus nominated and shall submit it to all the States Parties.

3. Elections of the members of the Commission shall be held at a meeting of States Parties convened by the Secretary-General at United Nations Headquarters. At that meeting, for which two thirds of the States Parties shall constitute a quorum, the persons elected to the Commission shall be those nominees who obtain a two-thirds majority of the votes of the representatives of States Parties present and voting. Not less than three members shall be elected from each geographical region.

4. The members of the Commission shall be elected for a term of five years. They shall be eligible for re-election.

5. The State Party which submitted the nomination of a member of the Commission shall defray the expenses of that member while in performance of Commission duties. The coastal State concerned shall defray the expenses incurred in respect of the advice referred to in article 3, paragraph 1(b), of this Annex. The secretariat of the Commission shall be provided by the Secretary-General of the United Nations.

Article 3

1. The functions of the Commission shall be:
 (a) to consider the data and other material submitted by coastal States concerning the outer limits of the continental shelf in areas where those

limits extend beyond 200 nautical miles, and to make recommendations in accordance with article 76 and the Statement of Understanding adopted on 29 August 1980 by the Third United Nations Conference on the Law of the Sea;

(b) to provide scientific and technical advice, if requested by the coastal State concerned during the preparation of the data referred to in subparagraph (a).

2. The Commission may co-operate, to the extent considered necessary and useful, with the Intergovernmental Oceanographic Commission of UNESCO, the International Hydrographic Organization and other competent international organizations with a view to exchanging scientific and technical information which might be of assistance in discharging the Commission's responsibilities.

Article 4

Where a coastal State intends to establish, in accordance with article 76, the outer limits of its continental shelf beyond 200 nautical miles, it shall submit particulars of such limits to the Commission along with supporting scientific and technical data as soon as possible but in any case within 10 years of the entry into force of this Convention for that State. The coastal State shall at the same time give the names of any Commission members who have provided it with scientific and technical advice.

Article 5

Unless the Commission decides otherwise, the Commission shall function by way of sub-commissions composed of seven members, appointed in a balanced manner taking into account the specific elements of each submission by a coastal State. Nationals of the coastal State making the submission who are members of the Commission and any Commission member who has assisted a coastal State by providing scientific and technical advice with respect to the delineation shall not be a member of the sub-commission dealing with that submission but has the right to participate as a member in the proceedings of the Commission concerning the said submission. The coastal State which has made a submission to the Commission may send its representatives to participate in the relevant proceedings without the right to vote.

Article 6

1. The sub-commission shall submit its recommendations to the Commission.

2. Approval by the Commission of the recommendations of the sub-commission shall be by a majority of two thirds of Commission members present and voting.

3. The recommendations of the Commission shall be submitted in writing to the coastal State which made the submission and to the Secretary-General of the United Nations.

Article 7

Coastal States shall establish the outer limits of the continental shelf in conformity with the provisions of article 76, paragraph 8, and in accordance with the appropriate national procedures.

Article 8

In the case of disagreement by the coastal State with the recommendations of the Commission, the coastal State shall, within a reasonable time, make a revised or new submission to the Commission.

Article 9

The actions of the Commission shall not prejudice matters relating to delimitation of boundaries between States with opposite or adjacent coasts.

Annex III. Basic Conditions of Prospecting, Exploration and Exploitation

Article 1. Title to Minerals

Title to minerals shall pass upon recovery in accordance with this Convention.

Article 2. Prospecting

1. (a) The Authority shall encourage prospecting in the Area.

(b) Prospecting shall be conducted only after the Authority has received a satisfactory written undertaking that the proposed prospector will comply with this Convention and the relevant rules, regulations and procedures of the Authority concerning co-operation in the training programmes referred to in articles 143 and 144 and the protection of the marine environment, and will accept verification by the Authority of compliance therewith. The proposed prospector shall, at the same time, notify the Authority of the approximate area or areas in which prospecting is to be conducted.

(c) Prospecting may be conducted simultaneously by more than one prospector in the same area or areas.

2. Prospecting shall not confer on the prospector any rights with respect to resources. A prospector may, however, recover a reasonable quantity of minerals to be used for testing.

Article 3. Exploration and Exploitation

1. The Enterprise, States Parties, and the other entities referred to in article 153, paragraph 2(b), may apply to the Authority for approval of plans of work for activities in the Area.

2. The Enterprise may apply with respect to any part of the Area, but applications by others with respect to reserved areas are subject to the additional requirements of article 9 of this Annex.

3. Exploration and exploitation shall be carried out only in areas specified in plans of work referred to in article 153, paragraph 3, and approved by the Authority in accordance with this Convention and the relevant rules, regulations and procedures of the Authority.

4. Every approved plan of work shall:

(a) be in conformity with this Convention and the rules, regulations and procedures of the Authority;

(b) provide for control by the Authority of activities in the Area in accordance with article 153, paragraph 4;

(c) confer on the operator, in accordance with the rules, regulations and procedures of the Authority, the exclusive right to explore for and exploit the specified categories of resources in the area covered by the plan of work. If, however, the applicant presents for approval a plan of work covering only the stage of exploration or the stage of exploitation, the approved plan of work shall confer such exclusive right with respect to that stage only.

5. Upon its approval by the Authority, every plan of work, except those presented by the Enterprise, shall be in the form of a contract concluded between the Authority and the applicant or applicants.

Article 4. Qualifications of Applicants

1. Applicants, other than the Enterprise, shall be qualified if they have the nationality or control and sponsorship required by article 153, paragraph 2(b), and if they follow the procedures and meet the qualification standards set forth in the rules, regulations and procedures of the Authority.

2. Except as provided in paragraph 6, such qualification standards shall relate to the financial and technical capabilities of the applicant and his performance under any previous contracts with the Authority.

3. Each applicant shall be sponsored by the State Party of which it is a national unless the applicant has more than one nationality, as in the case of a partnership or consortium of entities from several States, in which event all States Parties involved shall sponsor the application, or unless the applicant is effectively controlled by another State Party or its nationals, in which event both States Parties shall sponsor the application. The criteria and procedures for implementation of the sponsorship requirements shall be set forth in the rules, regulations and procedures of the Authority.

4. The sponsoring State or States shall, pursuant to article 139, have the responsibility to ensure, within their legal systems, that a contractor so sponsored shall carry out activities in the Area in conformity with the terms of its contract and its obligations under this Convention. A sponsoring State shall not, however, be liable for damage caused by any failure of a contractor sponsored by it to comply with its obligations if that State Party has adopted laws and regulations and taken administrative measures which are, within the framework of its legal system, reasonably appropriate for securing compliance by persons under its jurisdiction.

5. The procedures for assessing the qualifications of States Parties which are applicants shall take into account their character as States.

6. The qualification standards shall require that every applicant, without exception, shall as part of his application undertake:

(a) to accept as enforceable and comply with the applicable obligations created by the provisions of Part XI, the rules, regulations and procedures of the Authority, the decisions of the organs of the Authority and terms of his contracts with the Authority;

(b) to accept control by the Authority of activities in the Area, as authorized by this Convention;

(c) to provide the Authority with a written assurance that his obligations under the contract will be fulfilled in good faith;

(d) to comply with the provisions on the transfer of technology set forth in article 5 of this Annex.

Article 5. Transfer of Technology

1. When submitting a plan of work, every applicant shall make available to the Authority a general description of the equipment and methods to be used in carrying out activities in the Area, and other relevant non-proprietary information about the characteristics of such technology and information as to where such technology is available.

2. Every operator shall inform the Authority of revisions in the description and information made available pursuant to paragraph 1 whenever a substantial technological change or innovation is introduced.

3. Every contract for carrying out activities in the Area shall contain the following undertakings by the contractor:

(a) to make available to the Enterprise on fair and reasonable commercial terms and conditions, whenever the Authority so requests, the technology which he uses in carrying out activities in the Area under the contract, which the contractor is legally entitled to transfer. This shall be done by means of licenses or other appropriate arrangements which the contractor shall negotiate with the Enterprise and which shall be set forth in a specific agreement supplementary to the contract. This undertaking may be invoked only if the Enterprise finds that it is unable to obtain the same or equally efficient and useful technology on the open market on fair and reasonable commercial terms and conditions;

(b) to obtain a written assurance from the owner of any technology used in carrying out activities in the Area under the contract, which is not generally available on the open market and which is not covered by subparagraph (a), that the owner will, whenever the Authority so requests, make that technology available to the Enterprise under licence or other appropriate arrangements and on fair and reasonable commercial terms and conditions, to the same extent as made available to the contractor. If this assurance is not obtained, the technology in question shall not be used by the contractor in carrying out activities in the Area;

(c) to acquire from the owner by means of an enforceable contract, upon the request of the Enterprise and if it is possible to do so without substantial cost to the contractor, the legal right to transfer to the Enterprise any technology used by the contractor, in carrying out activities in the Area under the contract, which the contractor is otherwise not legally entitled to transfer and which is not generally available on the open market. In cases where there is a substantial corporate relationship between the contractor and the owner of the technology, the closeness of this relationship and the degree of control or influence shall be relevant to the determination whether all feasible measures have been taken to acquire such a right. In cases where the contractor exercises effective control over the owner, failure to acquire from the owner the legal right shall be considered relevant to the contractor's qualification for any subsequent application for approval of a plan of work;

(d) to facilitate, upon the request of the Enterprise, the acquisition by the Enterprise of any technology covered by subparagraph (b), under licence or other appropriate arrangements and on fair and reasonable commercial terms and conditions, if the Enterprise decides to negotiate directly with the owner of the technology;

(e) to take the same measures as are prescribed in subparagraphs (a), (b), (c) and (d) for the benefit of a developing State or group of developing States which has applied for a contract under article 9 of this Annex, provided that these measures shall be limited to the exploitation of the part of the area proposed by the contractor which has been reserved pursuant to article 8 of this Annex and provided that activities under the contract sought by the developing State or group of developing States would not involve transfer of technology to a third State or the nationals of a third State. The obligation under this provision shall only apply with respect to any given contractor where technology has not been requested by the Enterprise or transferred by that contractor to the Enterprise.

4. Disputes concerning undertakings required by paragraph 3, like other provisions of the contracts, shall be subject to compulsory settlement in accordance with Part XI and, in cases of violation of these undertakings, suspension or termination of the contract or monetary penalties may be ordered in accordance with article 18 of this Annex. Disputes as to whether offers made by the contractor are within the range of fair and reasonable commercial terms and conditions may be submitted by either party to binding commercial arbitration in accordance with the UNCITRAL Arbitration Rules or such other arbitration rules as may be prescribed in the rules, regulations and procedures of the Authority. If the finding is that the offer made by the contractor is not within the range of fair and reasonable commercial terms and conditions, the contractor shall be given 45 days to revise his offer to bring it within that range before the Authority takes any action in accordance with article 18 of this Annex.

5. If the Enterprise is unable to obtain on fair and reasonable commercial terms and conditions appropriate technology to enable it to commence in a timely manner the recovery and processing of minerals from the Area, either the Council or the Assembly may convene a group of States Parties composed of those which are engaged in activities in the Area, those which have sponsored entities which are engaged in activities in the Area and other States Parties having access to such technology. This group shall consult together and shall take effective measures to ensure that such technology is made available to the Enterprise on fair and reasonable commercial terms and conditions. Each such State Party shall take all feasible measures to this end within its own legal system.

6. In the case of joint ventures with the Enterprise, transfer of technology will be in accordance with the terms of the joint venture agreement.

7. The undertakings required by paragraph 3 shall be included in each contract for the carrying out of activities in the Area until 10 years after the commencement of commercial production by the Enterprise, and may be invoked during that period.

8. For the purposes of this article, "technology" means the specialized equipment and technical know-how, including manuals, designs, operating instructions, training and technical advice and assistance, necessary to assemble, maintain and operate a viable system and the legal right to use these items for that purpose on a non-exclusive basis.

Article 6. Approval of Plans of Work

1. Six months after the entry into force of this Convention, and thereafter each fourth month, the Authority shall take up for consideration proposed plans of work.

2. When considering an application for approval of a plan of work in the form of a contract, the Authority shall first ascertain whether:

(a) the applicant has complied with the procedures established for applications in accordance with article 4 of this Annex and has given the Authority the undertakings and assurances required by that article. In cases of non-compliance with these procedures or in the absence of any of these undertakings and assurances, the applicant shall be given 45 days to remedy these defects;

(b) the applicant possesses the requisite qualifications provided for in article 4 of this Annex.

3. All proposed plans of work shall be taken up in the order in which they are received. The proposed plans of work shall comply with and be governed by the relevant provisions of this Convention and the rules, regulations and procedures of the Authority, including those on operational requirements, financial contributions and the undertakings concerning the transfer of technology. If the proposed plans of work conform to these requirements, the Authority shall approve them provided that they are in accordance with the uniform and non-discriminatory requirements set forth in the rules, regulations and procedures of the Authority, unless:

(a) part or all of the area covered by the proposed plan of work is included in an approved plan of work or a previously submitted proposed plan of work which has not yet been finally acted on by the Authority;

(b) part or all of the area covered by the proposed plan of work is disapproved by the Authority pursuant to article 162, paragraph 2 (x); or

(c) the proposed plan of work has been submitted or sponsored by a State Party which already holds:

(i) plans of work for exploration and exploitation of polymetallic nodules in non-reserved areas that, together with either part of the area covered by the application for a plan of work, exceed in size 30 per cent of a circular area of 400,000 square kilometres surrounding the centre of either part of the area covered by the proposed plan of work;

(ii) plans of work for the exploration and exploitation of polymetallic nodules in non-reserved areas which, taken together, constitute 2 per cent of the total sea-bed area which is not reserved or disapproved for exploitation pursuant to article 162, paragraph (2) (x).

4. For the purpose of the standard set forth in paragraph 3(c), a plan of work submitted by a partnership or consortium shall be counted on a *pro rata* basis among the sponsoring States Parties involved in accordance with article 4, paragraph 3, of this Annex. The Authority may approve plans of work covered by paragraph 3(c) if it determines that such approval would not permit a State Party or entities sponsored by it to monopolize the conduct of activities in the Area or to preclude other States Parties from activities in the Area.

5. Notwithstanding paragraph 3(a), after the end of the interim period specified in article 151, paragraph 3, the Authority may adopt by means of rules, regulations and procedures other procedures and criteria consistent with this Convention for deciding which applicants shall have plans of work approved in cases of selection among applicants for a proposed area. These procedures and criteria shall ensure approval of plans of work on an equitable and non-discriminatory basis.

Article 7. Selection Among Applicants for Production Authorizations

1. Six months after the entry into force of this Convention, and thereafter each fourth month, the Authority shall take up for consideration applications for production authorizations submitted during the immediately preceding period. The Authority shall issue the authorizations applied for if all such applications can be approved without exceeding the production limitation or contravening the obligations of the Authority under a commodity agreement or arrangement to which it has become a party, as provided in article 151.

2. When a selection must be made among applicants for production authorizations because of the production limitation set forth in article 151, paragraphs 2 to 7, or because of the obligations of the Authority under a commodity agreement or arrangement to which it has become a party, as provided for in article 151, paragraph 1, the Authority shall make the selection on the basis of objective and non-discriminatory standards set forth in its rules, regulations and procedures.

3. In the application of paragraph 2, the Authority shall give priority to those applicants which:

(a) give better assurance of performance, taking into account their financial and technical qualifications and their performance, if any, under previously approved plans of work;

(b) provide earlier prospective financial benefits to the Authority, taking into account when commercial production is scheduled to begin;

(c) have already invested the most resources and effort in prospecting or exploration.

4. Applicants which are not selected in any period shall have priority in subsequent periods until they receive a production authorization.

5. Selection shall be made taking into account the need to enhance opportunities for all States Parties, irrespective of their social and economic systems or geographical locations so as to avoid discrimination against any

State or system, to participate in activities in the Area and to prevent monopolization of those activities.

6. Whenever fewer reserved areas than non-reserved areas are under exploitation, applications for production authorizations with respect to reserved areas shall have priority.

7. The decisions referred to in this article shall be taken as soon as possible after the close of each period.

Article 8. Reservation of Areas

Each application, other than those submitted by the Enterprise or by any other entities for reserved areas, shall cover a total area, which need not be a single continuous area, sufficiently large and of sufficient estimated commercial value to allow two mining operations. The applicant shall indicate the co-ordinates dividing the area into two parts of equal estimated commercial value and submit all the data obtained by him with respect to both parts. Without prejudice to the powers of the Authority pursuant to article 17 of this Annex, the data to be submitted concerning polymetallic nodules shall relate to mapping, sampling, the abundance of nodules, and their metal content. Within 45 days of receiving such data, the Authority shall designate which part is to be reserved solely for the conduct of activities by the Authority through the Enterprise or in association with developing States. This designation may be deferred for a further period of 45 days if the Authority requests an independent expert to assess whether all data required by this article has been submitted. The area designated shall become a reserved area as soon as the plan of work for the non-reserved area is approved and the contract is signed.

Article 9. Activities in Reserved Areas

1. The Enterprise shall be given an opportunity to decide whether it intends to carry out activities in each reserved area. This decision may be taken at any time, unless a notification pursuant to paragraph 4 is received by the Authority, in which event the Enterprise shall take its decision within a reasonable time. The Enterprise may decide to exploit such areas in joint ventures with the interested State or entity.

2. The Enterprise may conclude contracts for the execution of part of its activities in accordance with Annex IV, article 12. It may also enter into joint ventures for the conduct of such activities with any entities which are eligible to carry out activities in the Area pursuant to article 153, paragraph 2(b). When considering such joint ventures, the Enterprise shall offer to States Parties which are developing States and their nationals the opportunity of effective participation.

3. The Authority may prescribe, in its rules, regulations and procedures substantive and procedural requirements and conditions with respect to such contracts and joint ventures.

4. Any State Party which is a developing State or any natural or juridical person sponsored by it and effectively controlled by it or by other developing State which is a qualified applicant, or any group of the foregoing, may notify the Authority that it wishes to submit a plan of work pursuant to

article 6 of this Annex with respect to a reserved area. The plan of work shall be considered if the Enterprise decides, pursuant to paragraph 1, that it does not intend to carry out activities in that area.

Article 10. *Preference and Priority Among Applicants*

An operator who has an approved plan of work for exploration only, as provided in article 3, paragraph 4(c), of this Annex shall have a preference and a priority among applicants for a plan of work covering exploitation of the same area and resources. However, such preference or priority may be withdrawn if the operator's performance has not been satisfactory.

Article 11. *Joint Arrangements*

1. Contracts may provide for joint arrangements between the contractor and the Authority through the Enterprise, in the form of joint ventures or production sharing, as well as any other form of joint arrangement, which shall have the same protection against revision, suspension or termination as contracts with the Authority. . . .

Article 12. *Activities Carried Out by the Enterprise*

1. Activities in the Area carried out by the Enterprise pursuant to article 153, paragraph 2(a), shall be governed by Part XI, the rules, regulations and procedures of the Authority and its relevant decisions.

2. Any plan of work submitted by the Enterprise shall be accompanied by evidence supporting its financial and technical capabilities.

Article 13. *Financial Terms of Contracts*

1. In adopting rules, regulations and procedures concerning the financial terms of a contract between the Authority and the entities referred to in article 153, paragraph 2(b), and in negotiating those financial terms in accordance with Part XI and those rules, regulations and procedures, the Authority shall be guided by the following objectives:

(a) to ensure optimum revenues for the Authority from the proceeds of commercial production;

(b) to attract investments and technology to the exploration and exploitation of the Area;

(c) to ensure equality of financial treatment and comparable financial obligations for contractors;

(d) to provide incentives on a uniform and non-discriminatory basis for contractors to undertake joint arrangements with the Enterprise and developing States or their nationals, to stimulate the transfer of technology thereto, and to train the personnel of the Authority and of developing States;

(e) to enable the Enterprise to engage in sea-bed mining effectively at the same time as the entities referred to in article 153, paragraph 2(b); and

(f) to ensure that, as a result of the financial incentives provided to contractors under paragraph 14, under the terms of contracts reviewed in accordance with article 19 of this Annex or under the provisions of article 11 of this Annex with respect to joint ventures, contractors are not subsidized so as to be given an artificial competitive advantage with respect to land-based miners.

2. A fee shall be levied for the administrative cost of processing an application for approval of a plan of work in the form of a contract and shall be fixed at an amount of $US 500,000 per application. The amount of the fee shall be reviewed from time to time by the Council in order to ensure that it covers the administrative cost incurred. If such administrative cost incurred by the Authority in processing an application is less than the fixed amount, the Authority shall refund the difference to the applicant.

3. A contractor shall pay an annual fixed fee of $US 1 million from the date of entry into force of the contract. If the approved date of commencement of commercial production is postponed because of a delay in issuing the production authorization, in accordance with article 151, the annual fixed fee shall be waived for the period of postponement. From the date of commencement of commercial production, the contractor shall pay either the production charge or the annual fixed fee, whichever is greater.

4. Within a year of the date of commencement of commercial production, in conformity with paragraph 3, a contractor shall choose to make his financial contribution to the Authority by either:

(a) paying a production charge only; or

(b) paying a combination of a production charge and a share of net proceeds.

5. (a) If a contractor chooses to make his financial contribution to the Authority by paying a production charge only, it shall be fixed at a percentage of the market value of the processed metals produced from the polymetallic nodules recovered from the area covered by the contract. This percentage shall be fixed as follows:

(i) years 1–10 of commercial production 5 per cent
(ii) years 11 to the end of commercial production 12 per cent

(b) . . .

6. If a contractor chooses to make his financial contribution to the Authority by paying a combination of a production charge and a share of net proceeds, such payments shall be determined as follows:

(a) The production charge shall be fixed at a percentage of the market value, determined in accordance with subparagraph (b), of the processed metals produced from the polymetallic nodules recovered from the area covered by the contract. This percentage shall be fixed as follows:

(i) first period of commercial production 2 per cent
(ii) second period of commercial production 4 per cent

If, in the second period of commercial production, as defined in subparagraph (d), the return on investment in any accounting year as defined in subparagraph (m) falls below 15 per cent as a result of the payment of the production charge at 4 per cent, the production charge shall be 2 per cent instead of 4 per cent in that accounting year.

(b) The said market value shall be the product of the quantity of the processed metals produced from the polymetallic nodules recovered from the area covered by the contract and the average price for those metals during the relevant accounting year as defined in paragraphs 7 and 8.

(c) (i) The Authority's share of net proceeds shall be taken out of that portion of the contractor's net proceeds which is attributable to the mining of the resources of the area covered by the contract, referred to hereinafter as attributable net proceeds.

(ii) The Authority's share of attributable net proceeds shall be determined in accordance with the following incremental schedule:

Portion of attributable net proceeds	Share of the Authority	
	First period of commercial production	*Second period of commercial production*
That portion representing a return on investment which is greater than 0 per cent, but less than 10 per cent	35 per cent	40 per cent
That portion representing a return on investment which is 10 per cent or greater, but less than 20 per cent	42.5 per cent	50 per cent
That portion representing a return on investment which is 20 per cent or greater . . .	50 per cent	70 per cent

10. The contractor shall make available to the accountants, in accordance with the financial rules, regulations and procedures of the Authority, such financial data as are required to determine compliance with this article.

11. All costs, expenditures, proceeds and revenues, and all prices and values referred to in this article, shall be determined in accordance with generally recognized accounting principles and the financial rules, regulations and procedures of the Authority. . . .

15. In the event of a dispute between the Authority and a contractor over the interpretation or application of the financial terms of a contract, either party may submit the dispute to binding commercial arbitration, unless both parties agree to settle the dispute by other means, in accordance with article 188, paragraph 2.

Article 14. *Transfer of Data*

1. The operator shall transfer to the Authority, in accordance with its rules, regulations and procedures and the terms and conditions of the plan of work, at time intervals determined by the Authority all data which are both necessary for and relevant to the effective exercise of the powers and functions of the principal organs of the Authority in respect of the area covered by the plan of work.

2. Transferred data in respect of the area covered by the plan of work, deemed proprietary, may only be used for the purposes set forth in this article. Data necessary for the formulation by the Authority of rules, regulations and procedures concerning protection of the marine environment and safety, other than equipment design data, shall not be deemed proprietary.

3. Data transferred to the Authority by prospectors, applicants for contracts or contractors, deemed proprietary, shall not be disclosed by the Authority to the Enterprise or to anyone external to the Authority, but data on the reserved areas may be disclosed to the Enterprise. Such data transferred by such persons to the Enterprise shall not be disclosed by the Enterprise to the Authority or to anyone external to the Authority. . . .

Article 16. *Exclusive Right to Explore and Exploit*

The Authority shall, pursuant to Part XI and its rules, regulations and procedures, accord the operator the exclusive right to explore and exploit the area covered by the plan of work in respect of a specified category of resources and shall ensure that no other entity operates in the same area for a different category of resources in a manner which might interfere with the operations of the operator. The operator shall have security of tenure in accordance with article 153, paragraph 6.

Article 17. *Rules, Regulations and Procedures of the Authority*

1. The Authority shall adopt and uniformly apply rules, regulations and procedures in accordance with article 160, paragraph 2(f)(ii), and article 162, paragraph 2 (o)(ii), for the exercise of its functions as set forth in Part XI on, *inter alia,* the following matters:

(a) administrative procedures relating to prospecting, exploration and exploitation in the Area;

(b) operations:

(i) size of area;

(ii) duration of operations;

(iii) performance requirements including assurances pursuant to article 4, paragraph 6(c), of this Annex;

(iv) categories of resources;

(v) renunciation of areas;

(vi) progress reports;

(vii) submission of data;

(viii) inspection and supervision of operations;

(ix) prevention of interference with other activities in the marine environment;

(x) transfer of rights and obligations by a contractor;

(xi) procedures for transfer of technology to developing States in accordance with article 144 and for their direct participation;

(xii) mining standards and practices, including those relating to operational safety, conservation of the resources and the protection of the marine environment;

(xiii) definition of commercial production;

(xiv) qualification standards for applicants;

(c) financial matters:

(i) establishment of uniform and non-discriminatory costing and accounting rules and the method of selection of auditors;

(ii) apportionment of proceeds of operations;

(iii) the incentives referred to in article 13 of this Annex;

(d) implementation of decisions taken pursuant to article 151, paragraph 10, and article 164, paragraph 2(d).

2. Rules, regulations and procedures on the following items shall fully reflect the objective criteria set out below:

(a) Size of areas:

The Authority shall determine the appropriate size of areas for exploration which may be up to twice as large as those for exploitation in order to permit intensive exploration operations. The size of area shall be calculated to satisfy the requirements of article 8 of this Annex on reservation of areas as well as stated production requirements consistent with article 151 in accordance with the terms of the contract taking into account the state of the art of technology then available for sea-bed mining and the relevant physical characteristics of the areas. Areas shall be neither smaller nor larger than are necessary to satisfy this objective.

(b) Duration of operations:

(i) Prospecting shall be without time-limit;

(ii) Exploration should be of sufficient duration to permit a thorough survey of the specific area, the design and construction of mining equipment for the area and the design and construction of small and medium-size processing plants for the purpose of testing mining and processing systems;

(iii) The duration of exploitation should be related to the economic life of the mining project, taking into consideration such factors as the depletion of the ore, the useful life of mining equipment and processing facilities and commercial viability. Exploitation should be of sufficient duration to permit commercial extraction of minerals of the area and should include a reasonable time period for construction of commercial-scale mining and processing systems, during which period commercial production should not be required. The total duration of exploitation, however, should also be short enough to give the Authority an opportunity to amend the terms and conditions of the plan of work at the time it considers renewal in accordance with rules, regulations and procedures which it has adopted subsequent to approving the plan of work.

(c) Performance requirements:

The Authority shall require that during the exploration stage periodic expenditures be made by the operator which are reasonably related to the size of the area covered by the plan of work and the expenditures which would be expected of a *bona fide* operator who intended to bring the area into commercial production within the time-limits established by the Authority. The required expenditures should not be established at a level which would discourage prospective operators with less costly technology than is prevalently in use. The Authority shall establish a maximum time interval, after the exploration stage is completed and the exploitation stage begins, to achieve commercial production. To determine this interval, the Authority should take into consideration that construction of large-scale mining and processing systems cannot be initiated until after the termination of the exploration stage and the commencement of the exploitation stage. Accordingly, the interval to bring an area into commercial production should take into account the time necessary for this construction after the completion of the exploration stage and reasonable allowance should be made for unavoidable delays in the construction schedule. Once commercial production is achieved, the Authority shall within reasonable limits and taking into consideration all relevant factors require the operator to maintain commercial production throughout the period of the plan of work. . . .

(e) Renunciation of areas:

The operator shall have the right at any time to renounce without penalty the whole or part of his rights in the area covered by a plan of work.

(f) Protection of the marine environment:

Rules, regulations and procedures shall be drawn up in order to secure effective protection of the marine environment from harmful effects directly resulting from activities in the Area or from shipboard processing immediately above a mine site of minerals derived from that mine site, taking into account the extent to which such harmful effects may directly result from drilling, dredging, coring and excavation and from disposal, dumping and discharge into the marine environment of sediment, wastes or other effluents.

(g) Commercial production:

Commercial production shall be deemed to have begun if an operator engages in sustained large-scale recovery operations which yield a quantity of materials sufficient to indicate clearly that the principal purpose is large-scale production rather than production intended for information gathering, analysis or the testing of equipment or plant.

Article 18. Penalties

1. A contractor's rights under the contract may be suspended or terminated only in the following cases:

(a) if, in spite of warnings by the Authority, the contractor has conducted his activities in such a way as to result in serious, persistent and wilful violations of the fundamental terms of the contract, Part XI and the rules, regulations and procedures of the Authority; or

(b) if the contractor has failed to comply with a final binding decision of the dispute settlement body applicable to him.

2. In the case of any violation of the contract not covered by paragraph 1(a), or in lieu of suspension or termination under paragraph 1(a), the Authority may impose upon the contractor monetary penalties proportionate to the seriousness of the violation.

3. Except for emergency orders under article 162, paragraph 2(w), the Authority may not execute a decision involving monetary penalties, suspension or termination until the contractor has been accorded a reasonable opportunity to exhaust the judicial remedies available to him pursuant to Part XI, section 5.

Article 19. Revision of Contract

1. When circumstances have arisen or are likely to arise which, in the opinion of either party, would render the contract inequitable or make it impracticable or impossible to achieve the objectives set out in the contract or in Part XI, the parties shall enter into negotiations to revise it accordingly.

2. Any contract entered into in accordance with article 153, paragraph 3, may be revised only with the consent of the parties. . . .

Article 21. Applicable Law

1. The contract shall be governed by the terms of the contract, the rules, regulations and procedures of the Authority, Part XI and other rules of international law not incompatible with this Convention.

2. Any final decision rendered by a court or tribunal having jurisdiction under this Convention relating to the rights and obligations of the Authority and of the contractor shall be enforceable in the territory of each State Party. . . .

Article 22. Responsibility

The contractor shall have responsibility or liability for any damage arising out of wrongful acts in the conduct of its operations, account being taken of contributory acts or omissions by the Authority. Similarly, the Authority shall have responsibility or liability for any damage arising out of wrongful acts in the exercise of its powers and functions, including violations under article 168, paragraph 2, account being taken of contributory acts or omissions by the contractor. Liability in every case shall be for the actual amount of damage.

Annex IV. Statute of the Enterprise

Article 1. Purposes

1. The Enterprise is the organ of the Authority which shall carry out activities in the Area directly, pursuant to article 153, paragraph 2 (a), as well as the transporting, processing and marketing of minerals recovered from the Area.

2. In carrying out its purposes and in the exercise of its functions, the Enterprise shall act in accordance with this Convention and the rules, regulations and procedures of the Authority.

3. In developing the resources of the Area pursuant to paragraph 1, the Enterprise shall, subject to this Convention, operate in accordance with sound commercial principles.

Article 2. Relationship to the Authority

1. Pursuant to article 170, the Enterprise shall act in accordance with the general policies of the Assembly and the directives of the Council.

2. Subject to paragraph 1, the Enterprise shall enjoy autonomy in the conduct of its operations.

3. Nothing in this Convention shall make the Enterprise liable for the acts or obligations of the Authority, or make the Authority liable for the acts or obligations of the Enterprise.

Article 3. Limitation of Liability

Without prejudice to article 11, paragraph 3, of this Annex, no member of the Authority shall be liable by reason only of its membership for the acts or obligations of the Enterprise.

Article 4. Structure

The Enterprise shall have a Governing Board, a Director-General and the staff necessary for the exercise of its functions.

Article 5. Governing Board

1. The Governing Board shall be composed of 15 members elected by the Assembly in accordance with article 160, paragraph 2(c). In the election of the members of the Board, due regard shall be paid to the principle of equitable geographical distribution. In submitting nominations of candidates for election to the Board, members of the Authority shall bear in mind the need to nominate candidates of the highest standard of competence, with qualifications in relevant fields, so as to ensure the viability and success of the Enterprise.

2. Members of the Board shall be elected for four years and may be re-elected; and due regard shall be paid to the principle of rotation of membership.

3. Members of the Board shall continue in office until their successors are elected. If the office of a member of the Board becomes vacant, the Assembly shall, in accordance with article 160, paragraph 2(c), elect a new member for the remainder of his predecessor's term.

4. Members of the Board shall act in their personal capacity. In the performance of their duties they shall not seek or receive instructions from any government or from any other source. Each member of the Authority shall respect the independent character of the members of the Board and shall refrain from all attempts to influence any of them in the discharge of their duties.

5. Each member of the Board shall receive remuneration to be paid out of the funds of the Enterprise. The amount of remuneration shall be fixed by the Assembly, upon the recommendation of the Council.

6. The Board shall normally function at the principal office of the Enterprise and shall meet as often as the business of the Enterprise may require.

7. Two thirds of the members of the Board shall constitute a quorum.

8. Each member of the Board shall have one vote. All matters before the Board shall be decided by a majority of its members. If a member has a conflict of interest on a matter before the Board he shall refrain from voting on that matter.

9. Any member of the Authority may ask the Board for information in respect of its operations which particularly affect that member. The Board shall endeavour to provide such information.

Article 6. Powers and Functions of the Governing Board

The Governing Board shall direct the operations of the Enterprise. Subject to this Convention, the Governing Board shall exercise the powers necessary to fulfil the purposes of the Enterprise, including powers:

(a) to elect a Chairman from among its members;

(b) to adopt its rules of procedure;

(c) to draw up and submit formal written plans of work to the Council in accordance with article 153, paragraph 3, and article 162, paragraph 2(j);

(d) to develop plans of work and programmes for carrying out the activities specified in article 170;

(e) to prepare and submit to the Council applications for production authorizations in accordance with article 151, paragraphs 2 to 7;

(f) to authorize negotiations concerning the acquisition of technology, including those provided for in Annex III, article 5, paragraph 3 (a), (c) and (d), and to approve the results of those negotiations;

(g) to establish terms and conditions, and to authorize negotiations, concerning joint ventures and other forms of joint arrangements referred to in Annex III, articles 9 and 11, and to approve the results of such negotiations;

(h) to recommend to the Assembly what portion of the net income of the Enterprise should be retained as its reserves in accordance with article 160, paragraph 2(f), and article 10 of this Annex;

(i) to approve the annual budget of the Enterprise;

(j) to authorize the procurement of goods and services in accordance with article 12, paragraph 3, of this Annex;

(k) to submit an annual report to the Council in accordance with article 9 of this Annex;

(l) to submit to the Council for the approval of the Assembly draft rules in respect of the organization, management, appointment and dismissal of the staff of the Enterprise and to adopt regulations to give effect to such rules;

(m) to borrow funds and to furnish such collateral or other security as it may determine in accordance with article 11, paragraph 2, of this Annex;

(n) to enter into any legal proceedings, agreements and transactions and to take any other actions in accordance with article 13 of this Annex;

(o) to delegate, subject to the approval of the Council, any non-discretionary powers to the Director-General and to its committees.

Article 7. Director-General and Staff of the Enterprise

1. The Assembly shall, upon the recommendation of the Council and the nomination of the Governing Board, elect the Director-General of the Enterprise who shall not be a member of the Board. The Director-General shall hold office for a fixed term, not exceeding five years, and may be re-elected for further terms.

2. The Director-General shall be the legal representative and chief executive of the Enterprise and shall be directly responsible to the Board

for the conduct of the operations of the Enterprise. He shall be responsible for the organization, management, appointment and dismissal of the staff of the Enterprise in accordance with the rules and regulations referred to in article 6, subparagraph (1), of this Annex. He shall participate, without the right to vote, in the meetings of the Board and may participate, without the right to vote, in the meetings of the Assembly and the Council when these organs are dealing with matters concerning the Enterprise.

3. The paramount consideration in the recruitment and employment of the staff and in the determination of their conditions of service shall be the necessity of securing the highest standards of efficiency and of technical competence. Subject to this consideration, due regard shall be paid to the importance of recruiting the staff on an equitable geographical basis.

4. In the performance of their duties the Director-General and the staff shall not seek or receive instructions from any government or from any other source external to the Enterprise. They shall refrain from any action which might reflect on their position as international officials of the Enterprise responsible only to the Enterprise. Each State Party undertakes to respect the exclusively international character of the responsibilities of the Director-General and the staff and not to seek to influence them in the discharge of their responsibilities.

5. The responsibilities set forth in article 168, paragraph 2, are equally applicable to the staff of the Enterprise.

Article 8. Location

The Enterprise shall have its principal office at the seat of the Authority. The Enterprise may establish other offices and facilities in the territory of any State Party with the consent of that State Party.

Article 9. Reports and Financial Statements

1. The Enterprise shall, not later than three months after the end of each financial year, submit to the Council for its consideration an annual report containing an audited statement of its accounts and shall transmit to the Council at appropriate intervals a summary statement of its financial position and a profit and loss statement showing the results of its operations. . . .

Article 10. Allocation of Net Income

1. Subject to paragraph 3, the Enterprise shall make payments to the Authority under Annex III, article 13, or their equivalent.

2. The Assembly shall, upon the recommendation of the Governing Board, determine what portion of the net income of the Enterprise shall be retained as reserves of the Enterprise. The remainder shall be transferred to the Authority.

3. During an initial period required for the Enterprise to become self-supporting, which shall not exceed 10 years from the commencement of commercial production by it, the Assembly shall exempt the Enterprise from the payments referred to in paragraph 1, and shall leave all of the net income of the Enterprise in its reserves.

Article 11. Finances

1. The funds of the Enterprise shall include:

(a) amounts received from the Authority in accordance with article 173, paragraph 2(b);

(b) voluntary contributions made by States Parties for the purpose of financing activities of the Enterprise;

(c) amounts borrowed by the Enterprise in accordance with paragraphs 2 and 3;

(d) income of the Enterprise from its operations;

(e) other funds made available to the Enterprise to enable it to commence operations as soon as possible and to carry out its functions.

2. (a) The Enterprise shall have the power to borrow funds and to furnish such collateral or other security as it may determine. . . .

3. (a) The Enterprise shall be provided with the funds necessary to explore and exploit one mine site, and to transport, process and market the minerals recovered therefrom and the nickel, copper, cobalt and manganese obtained, and to meet its initial administrative expenses. The amount of the said funds, and the criteria and factors for its adjustment, shall be included by the Preparatory Commission in the draft rules, regulations and procedures of the Authority.

(b) All States Parties shall make available to the Enterprise an amount equivalent to one half of the funds referred to in subparagraph (a) by way of long-term interest-free loans in accordance with the scale of assessments for the United Nations regular budget in force at the time when the assessments are made, adjusted to take into account the States which are not members of the United Nations. Debts incurred by the Enterprise in raising the other half of the funds shall be guaranteed by all States Parties in accordance with the same scale.

(c) If the sum of the financial contributions of States Parties is less than the funds to be provided to the Enterprise under subparagraph (a), the Assembly shall, at its first session, consider the extent of the shortfall and adopt by consensus measures for dealing with this shortfall, taking into account the obligation of States Parties under subparagraphs (a) and (b) and any recommendations of the Preparatory Commission. . . .

4. The funds, assets and expenses of the Enterprise shall be kept separate from those of the Authority. This article shall not prevent the Enterprise from making arrangements with the Authority regarding facilities, personnel and services and arrangements for reimbursement of administrative expenses paid by either on behalf of the other. . . .

5. The records, books and accounts of the Enterprise, including its annual financial statements, shall be audited annually by an independent auditor appointed by the Council.

Article 12. Operations

1. The Enterprise shall propose to the Council projects for carrying out activities in accordance with article 170. Such proposals shall include a formal written plan of work for activities in the Area in accordance with article 153, paragraph 3, and all such other information and data as may be

required from time to time for its appraisal by the Legal and Technical Commission and approval by the Council.

2. Upon approval by the Council, the Enterprise shall execute the project on the basis of the formal written plan of work referred to in paragraph 1.

3. (a) If the Enterprise does not possess the goods and services required for its operations it may procure them. For that purpose, it shall issue invitations to tender and award contracts to bidders offering the best combination of quality, price and delivery time.

　(b) If there is more than one bid offering such a combination, the contract shall be awarded in accordance with:

　　(i) the principle of non-discrimination on the basis of political or other considerations not relevant to the carrying out of operations with due diligence and efficiency; and

　　(ii) guidelines approved by the Council with regard to the preferences to be accorded to goods and services originating in developing States, including the land-locked and geographically disadvantaged among them.

　(c) The Governing Board may adopt rules determining the special circumstances in which the requirement of invitations to bid may, in the best interests of the Enterprise, be dispensed with.

4. The Enterprise shall have title to all minerals and processed substances produced by it.

5. The Enterprise shall sell its products on a non-discriminatory basis. It shall not give non-commercial discounts. . . .

7. The Enterprise shall not interfere in the political affairs of any State Party; nor shall it be influenced in its decisions by the political character of the State Party concerned. Only commercial considerations shall be relevant to its decisions, and these considerations shall be weighed impartially in order to carry out the purposes specified in article 1 of this Annex.

Article 13. Legal Status, Privileges and Immunities

1. To enable the Enterprise to exercise its functions, the status, privileges and immunities set forth in this article shall be accorded to the Enterprise in the territories of States Parties. . . .

2. The Enterprise shall have such legal capacity as is necessary for the exercise of its functions and the fulfilment of its purposes and, in particular, the capacity:

　(a) to enter into contracts, joint arrangements or other arrangements, including agreements with States and international organizations;

　(b) to acquire, lease, hold and dispose of immovable and movable property;

　(c) to be a party to legal proceedings.

3. . . .

　(b) The property and assets of the Enterprise, wherever located and by whomsoever held, shall be immune from all forms of seizure, attachment or execution before the delivery of final judgment against the Enterprise.

4. (a) The property and assets of the Enterprise, wherever located and by whomsoever held, shall be immune from requisition, confiscation, expropriation or any other form of seizure by executive or legislative action. . . .

(d) States Parties shall ensure that the Enterprise enjoys all rights, privileges and immunities accorded by them to entities conducting commercial activities in their territories. . . . If special privileges are provided by States Parties for developing States or their commercial entities, the Enterprise shall enjoy those privileges on a similarly preferential basis.

(e) States Parties may provide special incentives, rights, privileges and immunities to the Enterprise without the obligation to provide such incentives, rights, privileges and immunities to other commercial entities.

Annex V. Conciliation

Section 1. Conciliation Procedure Pursuant to Section 1 of Part XV

Article 1. Institution of Proceedings

If the parties to a dispute have agreed, in accordance with article 284, to submit it to conciliation under this section, any such party may institute the proceedings by written notification addressed to the other party or parties to the dispute.

Article 2. List of Conciliators

A list of conciliators shall be drawn up and maintained by the Secretary-General of the United Nations. Every State Party shall be entitled to nominate four conciliators, each of whom shall be a person enjoying the highest reputation for fairness, competence and integrity. The names of the persons so nominated shall constitute the list. . . .

Article 3. Constitution of Conciliation Commission

The conciliation commission shall, unless the parties otherwise agree, be constituted as follows:

(a) Subject to subparagraph (g), the conciliation commission shall consist of five members.

(b) The party instituting the proceedings shall appoint two conciliators to be chosen preferably from the list referred to in article 2 of this Annex, one of whom may be its national, unless the parties otherwise agree. Such appointments shall be included in the notification referred to in article 1 of this Annex.

(c) The other party to the dispute shall appoint two conciliators in the manner set forth in subparagraph (b) within 21 days of receipt of the notification referred to in article 1 of this Annex. If the appointments are not made within that period, the party instituting the proceedings may, within one week of the expiration of that period, either terminate the proceedings by notification addressed to the other party or request the Secretary-General of the United Nations to make the appointments in accordance with subparagraph (e).

(d) Within 30 days after all four conciliators have been appointed, they shall appoint a fifth conciliator chosen from the list referred to in article 2 of this Annex, who shall be chairman. If the appointment is not made within that period, either party may, within one week of the expiration of that period, request the Secretary-General of the United Nations to make the appointment in accordance with subparagraph (e).

(e) Within 30 days of the receipt of a request under subparagraph (c) or (d), the Secretary-General of the United Nations shall make the necessary appointments from the list referred to in article 2 of this Annex in consultation with the parties to the dispute.

(f) Any vacancy shall be filled in the manner prescribed for the initial appointment.

(g) Two or more parties which determine by agreement that they are in the same interest shall appoint two conciliators jointly. Where two or more parties have separate interests or there is a disagreement as to whether they are of the same interest, they shall appoint conciliators separately.

(h) In disputes involving more than two parties having separate interests, or where there is disagreement as to whether they are of the same interest, the parties shall apply subparagraphs (a) to (f) in so far as possible.

Article 4. Procedure

The conciliation commission shall, unless the parties otherwise agree, determine its own procedure. The commission may, with the consent of the parties to the dispute, invite any State Party to submit to it its views orally or in writing. Decisions of the commission regarding procedural matters, the report and recommendations shall be made by a majority vote of its members.

Article 5. Amicable Settlement

The commission may draw the attention of the parties to any measures which might facilitate an amicable settlement of the dispute.

Article 6. Functions of the Commission

The commission shall hear the parties, examine their claims and objections, and make proposals to the parties with a view to reaching an amicable settlement.

Article 7. Report

1. The commission shall report within 12 months of its constitution. Its report shall record any agreements reached and, failing agreement, its conclusions on all questions of fact or law relevant to the matter in dispute and such recommendations as the commission may deem appropriate for an

amicable settlement. The report shall be deposited with the Secretary-General of the United Nations and shall immediately be transmitted by him to the parties to the dispute.

2. The report of the commission, including its conclusions or recommendations, shall not be binding upon the parties.

Article 8. Termination

The conciliation proceedings are terminated when a settlement has been reached, when the parties have accepted or one party has rejected the recommendations of the report by written notification addressed to the Secretary-General of the United Nations, or when a period of three months has expired from the date of transmission of the report to the parties.

Article 9. Fees and Expenses

The fees and expenses of the commission shall be borne by the parties to the dispute.

Article 10. Right of Parties to Modify Procedure

The parties to the dispute may by agreement applicable solely to that dispute modify any provision of this Annex.

Section 2. Compulsory Submission to Conciliation Procedure Pursuant to Section 3 of Part XV

Article 11. Institution of Proceedings

1. Any party to a dispute which, in accordance with Part XV, section 3, may be submitted to conciliation under this section, may institute the proceedings by written notification addressed to the other party or parties to the dispute.

2. Any party to the dispute, notified under paragraph 1, shall be obliged to submit to such proceedings.

Article 12. Failure to Reply or to Submit to Conciliation

The failure of a party or parties to the dispute to reply to notification of institution of proceedings or to submit to such proceedings shall not constitute a bar to the proceedings.

Article 13. Competence

A disagreement as to whether a conciliation commission acting under this section has competence shall be decided by the commission.

Article 14. Application of Section 1

Articles 2 to 10 of section 1 of this Annex apply subject to this section.

Annex VI. Statute of the International Tribunal for the Law of the Sea

Article 1. General Provisions

1. The International Tribunal for the Law of the Sea is constituted and shall function in accordance with the provisions of this Convention and this Statute.

2. The seat of the Tribunal shall be in the Free and Hanseatic City of Hamburg in the Federal Republic of Germany.

3. The Tribunal may sit and exercise its functions elsewhere whenever it considers this desirable.

4. A reference of a dispute to the Tribunal shall be governed by the provisions of Parts XI and XV.

SECTION 1. ORGANIZATION OF THE TRIBUNAL

Article 2. Composition

1. The Tribunal shall be composed of a body of 21 independent members, elected from among persons enjoying the highest reputation for fairness and integrity and of recognized competence in the field of the law of the sea.

2. In the Tribunal as a whole the representation of the principal legal systems of the world and equitable geographical distribution shall be assured.

Article 3. Membership

1. No two members of the Tribunal may be nationals of the same State. A person who for the purposes of membership in the Tribunal could be regarded as a national of more than one State shall be deemed to be a national of the one in which he ordinarily exercises civil and political rights.

2. There shall be no fewer than three members from each geographical group as established by the General Assembly of the United Nations.

Article 4. Nominations and Elections

1. Each State Party may nominate not more than two persons having the qualifications prescribed in article 2 of this Annex. The members of the Tribunal shall be elected from the list of persons thus nominated.

2. At least three months before the date of the election, the Secretary-General of the United Nations in the case of the first election and the Registrar of the Tribunal in the case of subsequent elections shall address a written invitation to the States Parties to submit their nominations for members of the Tribunal within two months. He shall prepare a list in alphabetical order of all the persons thus nominated, with an indication of the States Parties which have nominated them, and shall submit it to the

States Parties before the seventh day of the last month before the date of each election.

3. The first election shall be held within six months of the date of entry into force of this Convention.

4. The members of the Tribunal shall be elected by secret ballot. Elections shall be held at a meeting of the States Parties convened by the Secretary-General of the United Nations in the case of the first election and by a procedure agreed to by the States Parties in the case of subsequent elections. Two thirds of the States Parties shall constitute a quorum at that meeting. The persons elected to the Tribunal shall be those nominees who obtain the largest number of votes and a two-thirds majority of the States Parties present and voting, provided that such majority includes a majority of the States Parties.

Article 5. Term of Office

1. The members of the Tribunal shall be elected for nine years and may be re-elected; provided, however, that of the members elected at the first election, the terms of seven members shall expire at the end of three years and the terms of seven more members shall expire at the end of six years.

2. The members of the Tribunal whose terms are to expire at the end of the above-mentioned initial periods of three and six years shall be chosen by lot to be drawn by the Secretary-General of the United Nations immediately after the first election.

3. The members of the Tribunal shall continue to discharge their duties until their places have been filled. Though replaced, they shall finish any proceedings which they may have begun before the date of their replacement. . . .

Article 6. Vacancies

1. Vacancies shall be filled by the same method as that laid down for the first election, subject to the following provision: the Registrar shall, within one month of the occurrence of the vacancy, proceed to issue the invitations provided for in article 4 of this Annex, and the date of the election shall be fixed by the President of the Tribunal after consultation with the States Parties. . . .

Article 7. Incompatible Activities

1. No member of the Tribunal may exercise any political or administrative function, or associate actively with or be financially interested in any of the operations of any enterprise concerned with the exploration for or exploitation of the resources of the sea or the sea-bed or other commercial use of the sea or the sea-bed.

2. No member of the Tribunal may act as agent, counsel or advocate in any case.

3. Any doubt on these points shall be resolved by decision of the majority of the other members of the Tribunal present.

Article 8. Conditions Relating to Participation of Members in a Particular Case

1. No member of the Tribunal may participate in the decision of any case in which he has previously taken part as agent, counsel or advocate for one of the parties, or as a member of a national or international court or tribunal, or in any other capacity.

2. If, for some special reason, a member of the Tribunal considers that he should not take part in the decision of a particular case, he shall so inform the President of the Tribunal.

3. If the President considers that for some special reason one of the members of the Tribunal should not sit in a particular case, he shall give him notice accordingly.

4. Any doubt on these points shall be resolved by decision of the majority of the other members of the Tribunal present.

Article 9. Consequence of Ceasing to Fulfil Required Conditions

If, in the unanimous opinion of the other members of the Tribunal, a member has ceased to fulfil the required conditions, the President of the Tribunal shall declare the seat vacant.

Article 10. Privileges and Immunities

The members of the Tribunal, when engaged on the business of the Tribunal, shall enjoy diplomatic privileges and immunities.

Article 11. Solemn Declaration by Members

Every member of the Tribunal shall, before taking up his duties, make a solemn declaration in open session that he will exercise his powers impartially and conscientiously.

Article 12. President, Vice-President and Registrar

1. The Tribunal shall elect its President and Vice-President for three years; they may be re-elected. . . .

Article 13. Quorum

1. All available members of the Tribunal shall sit; a quorum of 11 elected members shall be required to constitute the Tribunal.

2. Subject to article 17 of this Annex, the Tribunal shall determine which members are available to constitute the Tribunal for the consideration of a particular dispute, having regard to the effective functioning of the chambers as provided for in articles 14 and 15 of this Annex.

3. All disputes and applications submitted to the Tribunal shall be heard and determined by the Tribunal, unless article 14 of this Annex applies, or the parties request that it shall be dealt with in accordance with article 15 of this Annex.

Article 14. *Sea-Bed Disputes Chamber*

A Sea-Bed Disputes Chamber shall be established in accordance with the provisions of section 4 of this Annex. Its jurisdiction, powers and functions shall be as provided for in Part XI, section 5.

Article 15. *Special Chambers*

1. The Tribunal may form such chambers, composed of three or more of its elected members, as it considers necessary for dealing with particular categories of disputes.

2. The Tribunal shall form a chamber for dealing with a particular dispute submitted to it if the parties so request. The composition of such a chamber shall be determined by the Tribunal with the approval of the parties.

3. With a view to the speedy dispatch of business, the Tribunal shall form annually a chamber composed of five of its elected members which may hear and determine disputes by summary procedure. Two alternative members shall be selected for the purpose of replacing members who are unable to participate in a particular proceeding.

4. Disputes shall be heard and determined by the chambers provided for in this article if the parties so request.

5. A judgment given by any of the chambers provided for in this article and in article 14 of this Annex shall be considered as rendered by the Tribunal.

Article 16. *Rules of the Tribunal*

The Tribunal shall frame rules for carrying out its functions. In particular it shall lay down rules of procedure.

Article 17. *Nationality of Members*

1. Members of the Tribunal of the nationality of any of the parties to a dispute shall retain their right to participate as members of the Tribunal.

2. If the Tribunal, when hearing a dispute, includes upon the bench a member of the nationality of one of the parties, any other party may choose a person to participate as a member of the Tribunal.

3. If the Tribunal, when hearing a dispute, does not include upon the bench a member of the nationality of the parties, each of those parties may choose a person to participate as a member of the Tribunal.

4. This article applies to the chambers referred to in articles 14 and 15 of this Annex. In such cases, the President, in consultation with the parties, shall request specified members of the Tribunal forming the chamber, as many as necessary, to give place to the members of the Tribunal of the nationality of the parties concerned, and, failing such, or if they are unable to be present, to the members specially chosen by the parties.

5. Should there be several parties in the same interest, they shall, for the purpose of the preceding provisions, be considered as one party only. Any doubt on this point shall be settled by the decision of the Tribunal.

6. Members chosen in accordance with paragraphs 2, 3 and 4 shall fulfil

the conditions required by articles 2, 8 and 11 of this Annex. They shall participate in the decision on terms of complete equality with their colleagues.

Article 18. Remuneration of Members

1. Each elected member of the Tribunal shall receive an annual allowance and, for each day on which he exercises his functions, a special allowance, provided that in any year the total sum payable to any member as special allowance shall not exceed the amount of the annual allowance.

2. The President shall receive a special annual allowance. . . .

8. The salaries, allowances, and compensation shall be free of all taxation.

Article 19. Expenses of the Tribunal

1. The expenses of the Tribunal shall be borne by the States Parties and by the Authority on such terms and in such a manner as shall be decided at meetings of the States Parties.

2. When an entity other than a State Party or the Authority is a party to a case submitted to it, the Tribunal shall fix the amount which that party is to contribute towards the expenses of the Tribunal.

SECTION 2. COMPETENCE

Article 20. Access to the Tribunal

1. The Tribunal shall be open to States Parties.

2. The Tribunal shall be open to entities other than States Parties in any case expressly provided for in Part XI or in any case submitted pursuant to any other agreement conferring jurisdiction on the Tribunal which is accepted by all the parties to that case.

Article 21. Jurisdiction

The jurisdiction of the Tribunal comprises all disputes and all applications submitted to it in accordance with this Convention and all matters specifically provided for in any other agreement which confers jurisdiction on the Tribunal.

Article 22. Reference of Disputes Subject to Other Agreements

If all the parties to a treaty or convention already in force and concerning the subject-matter covered by this Convention so agree, any disputes concerning the interpretation or application of such treaty or convention may, in accordance with such agreement, be submitted to the Tribunal.

Article 23. Applicable Law

The Tribunal shall decide all disputes and applications in accordance with article 293.

Section 3. Procedure

Article 24. Institution of Proceedings

1. Disputes are submitted to the Tribunal, as the case may be, either by notification of a special agreement or by written application, addressed to the Registrar. In either case, the subject of the dispute and the parties shall be indicated.

2. The Registrar shall forthwith notify the special agreement or the application to all concerned.

3. The Registrar shall also notify all States Parties.

Article 25. Provisional Measures

1. In accordance with article 290, the Tribunal and its Sea-Bed Disputes Chamber shall have the power to prescribe provisional measures.

2. If the Tribunal is not in session or a sufficient number of members is not available to constitute a quorum, the provisional measures shall be prescribed by the chamber of summary procedure formed under article 15, paragraph 3, of this Annex. Notwithstanding article 15, paragraph 4, of this Annex, such provisional measures may be adopted at the request of any party to the dispute. They shall be subject to review and revision by the Tribunal.

Article 26. Hearing

1. The hearing shall be under the control of the President or, if he is unable to preside, of the Vice-President. If neither is able to preside, the senior judge present of the Tribunal shall preside.

2. The hearing shall be public, unless the Tribunal decides otherwise or unless the parties demand that the public be not admitted.

Article 27. Conduct of Case

The Tribunal shall make orders for the conduct of the case, decide the form and time in which each party must conclude its arguments, and make all arrangements connected with the taking of evidence.

Article 28. Default

When one of the parties does not appear before the Tribunal or fails to defend its case, the other party may request the Tribunal to continue the proceedings and make its decision. Absence of a party or failure of a party to defend its case shall not constitute a bar to the proceedings. Before making its decision, the Tribunal must satisfy itself not only that it has jurisdiction over the dispute, but also that the claim is well founded in fact and law.

Article 29. Majority for Decision

1. All questions shall be decided by a majority of the members of the Tribunal who are present.

2. In the event of an equality of votes, the President or the member of the Tribunal who acts in his place shall have a casting vote.

Article 30. Judgment

1. The judgment shall state the reasons on which it is based.

2. It shall contain the names of the members of the Tribunal who have taken part in the decision.

3. If the judgment does not represent in whole or in part the unanimous opinion of the members of the Tribunal, any member shall be entitled to deliver a separate opinion.

4. The judgment shall be signed by the President and by the Registrar. It shall be read in open court, due notice having been given to the parties to the dispute.

Article 31. Request to Intervene

1. Should a State Party consider that it has an interest of a legal nature which may be affected by the decision in any dispute, it may submit a request to the Tribunal to be permitted to intervene.

2. It shall be for the Tribunal to decide upon this request.

3. If a request to intervene is granted, the decision of the Tribunal in respect of the dispute shall be binding upon the intervening State Party in so far as it relates to matters in respect of which that State Party intervened.

Article 32. Right to Intervene in Cases of Interpretation or Application

1. Whenever the interpretation or application of this Convention is in question, the Registrar shall notify all States Parties forthwith.

2. Whenever pursuant to article 21 or 22 of this Annex the interpretation or application of an international agreement is in question, the Registrar shall notify all the parties to the agreement.

3. Every party referred to in paragraphs 1 and 2 has the right to intervene in the proceedings; if it uses this right, the interpretation given by the judgment will be equally binding upon it.

Article 33. Finality and Binding Force of Decisions

1. The decision of the Tribunal is final and shall be complied with by all the parties to the dispute.

2. The decision shall have no binding force except between the parties in respect of that particular dispute.

3. In the event of dispute as to the meaning or scope of the decision, the Tribunal shall construe it upon the request of any party.

Article 34. Costs

Unless otherwise decided by the Tribunal, each party shall bear its own costs.

Section 4. Sea-Bed Disputes Chamber

Article 35. Composition

1. The Sea-Bed Disputes Chamber referred to in article 14 of this Annex shall be composed of 11 members, selected by a majority of the elected members of the Tribunal from among them.

2. In the selection of the members of the Chamber, the representation of the principal legal systems of the world and equitable geographical distribution shall be assured. The Assembly of the Authority may adopt recommendations of a general nature relating to such representation and distribution.

3. The members of the Chamber shall be selected every three years and may be selected for a second term.

4. The Chamber shall elect its President from among its members, who shall serve for the term for which the Chamber has been selected.

5. If any proceedings are still pending at the end of any three-year period for which the Chamber has been selected, the Chamber shall complete the proceedings in its original composition.

6. If a vacancy occurs in the Chamber, the Tribunal shall select a successor from among its elected members, who shall hold office for the remainder of his predecessor's term.

7. A quorum of seven of the members selected by the Tribunal shall be required to constitute the Chamber.

Article 36. Ad Hoc Chambers

1. The Sea-Bed Disputes Chamber shall form an *ad hoc* chamber, composed of three of its members, for dealing with a particular dispute submitted to it in accordance with article 188, paragraph 1(b). The composition of such a chamber shall be determined by the Sea-Bed Disputes Chamber with the approval of the parties.

2. If the parties do not agree on the composition of an *ad hoc* chamber, each party to the dispute shall appoint one member, and the third member shall be appointed by them in agreement. If they disagree, or if any party fails to make an appointment, the President of the Sea-Bed Disputes Chamber shall promptly make the appointment or appointments from among its members, after consultation with the parties.

3. Members of the *ad hoc* chamber must not be in the service of, or nationals of, any of the parties to the dispute.

Article 37. Access

The Chamber shall be open to the States Parties, the Authority and the other entities referred to in Part XI, section 5.

Article 38. Applicable Law

In addition to the provisions of article 293, the Chamber shall apply:
 (a) the rules, regulations and procedures of the Authority adopted in accordance with this Convention; and

(b) the terms of contracts concerning activities in the Area in matters relating to those contracts.

Article 39. Enforcement of Decisions of the Chamber

The decisions of the Chamber shall be enforceable in the territories of the States Parties in the same manner as judgments or orders of the highest court of the State Party in whose territory the enforcement is sought.

Article 40. Applicability of Other Sections of This Annex

1. The other sections of this Annex which are not incompatible with this section apply to the Chamber.

2. In the exercise of its functions relating to advisory opinions, the Chamber shall be guided by the provisions of this Annex relating to procedure before the Tribunal to the extent to which it recognizes them to be applicable.

SECTION 5. AMENDMENTS

Article 41. Amendments

1. Amendments to this Annex, other than amendments to section 4, may be adopted only in accordance with article 313 or by consensus at a conference convened in accordance with this Convention.

2. Amendments to section 4 may be adopted only in accordance with article 314.

3. The Tribunal may propose such amendments to this Statute as it may consider necessary, by written communications to the States Parties for their consideration in conformity with paragraphs 1 and 2.

Annex VII. Arbitration

Article 1. Institution of Proceedings

Subject to the provisions of Part XV, any party to a dispute may submit the dispute to the arbitral procedure provided for in this Annex by written notification addressed to the other party or parties to the dispute. The notification shall be accompanied by a statement of the claim and the grounds on which it is based.

Article 2. List of Arbitrators

1. A list of arbitrators shall be drawn up and maintained by the Secretary-General of the United Nations. Every State Party shall be entitled to nominate four arbitrators, each of whom shall be a person experienced in maritime affairs and enjoying the highest reputation for fairness, competence and integrity. The names of the persons so nominated shall constitute the list.

2. If at any time the arbitrators nominated by a State Party in the list

so constituted shall be fewer than four, that State Party shall be entitled to make further nominations as necessary. . . .

Article 3. Constitution of Arbitral Tribunal

For the purpose of proceedings under this Annex, the arbitral tribunal shall, unless the parties otherwise agree, be constituted as follows:

(a) Subject to subparagraph (g), the arbitral tribunal shall consist of five members.

(b) The party instituting the proceedings shall appoint one member to be chosen preferably from the list referred to in article 2 of this Annex, who may be its national. The appointment shall be included in the notification referred to in article 1 of this Annex.

(c) The other party to the dispute shall, within 30 days of receipt of the notification referred to in article 1 of this Annex, appoint one member to be chosen preferably from the list, who may be its national. If the appointment is not made within that period, the party instituting the proceedings may, within two weeks of the expiration of that period, request that the appointment be made in accordance with subparagraph (e).

(d) The other three members shall be appointed by agreement between the parties. They shall be chosen preferably from the list and shall be nationals of third States unless the parties otherwise agree. The parties to the dispute shall appoint the President of the arbitral tribunal from among those three members. If, within 60 days of receipt of the notification referred to in article 1 of this Annex, the parties are unable to reach agreement on the appointment of one or more of the members of the tribunal to be appointed by agreement, or on the appointment of the President, the remaining appointment or appointments shall be made in accordance with subparagraph (e), at the request of a party to the dispute. Such request shall be made within two weeks of the expiration of the aforementioned 60-day period.

(e) Unless the parties agree that any appointment under subparagraphs (c) and (d) be made by a person or a third State chosen by the parties, the President of the International Tribunal for the Law of the Sea shall make the necessary appointments. If the President is unable to act under this subparagraph or is a national of one of the parties to the dispute, the appointment shall be made by the next senior member of the International Tribunal for the Law of the Sea who is available and is not a national of one of the parties. The appointments referred to in this subparagraph shall be made from the list referred to in article 2 of this Annex within a period of 30 days of the receipt of the request and in consultation with the parties. The members so appointed shall be of different nationalities and may not be in the service of, ordinarily resident in the territory of, or nationals of, any of the parties to the dispute.

(f) Any vacancy shall be filled in the manner prescribed for the initial appointment.

(g) Parties in the same interest shall appoint one member of the tribunal jointly by agreement. Where there are several parties having separate interests or where there is disagreement as to whether they are of the same interest, each of them shall appoint one member of the tribunal. The number of members of the tribunal appointed separately by the parties shall always be smaller by one than the number of members of the tribunal to be appointed jointly by the parties.

(h) In disputes involving more than two parties, the provisions of subparagraphs (a) to (f) shall apply to the maximum extent possible.

Article 4. Functions of Arbitral Tribunal

An arbitral tribunal constituted under article 3 of this Annex shall function in accordance with this Annex and the other provisions of this Convention.

Article 5. Procedure

Unless the parties to the dispute otherwise agree, the arbitral tribunal shall determine its own procedure, assuring to each party a full opportunity to be heard and to present its case.

Article 6. Duties of Parties to a Dispute

The parties to the dispute shall facilitate the work of the arbitral tribunal and, in particular, in accordance with their law and using all means at their disposal, shall:

(a) provide it with all relevant documents, facilities and information; and

(b) enable it when necessary to call witnesses or experts and receive their evidence and to visit the localities to which the case relates.

Article 7. Expenses

Unless the arbitral tribunal decides otherwise because of the particular circumstances of the case, the expenses of the tribunal, including the remuneration of its members, shall be borne by the parties to the dispute in equal shares.

Article 8. Required Majority for Decisions

Decisions of the arbitral tribunal shall be taken by a majority vote of its members. The absence or abstention of less than half of the members shall not constitute a bar to the tribunal reaching a decision. In the event of an equality of votes, the President shall have a casting vote.

Article 9. Default of Appearance

If one of the parties to the dispute does not appear before the arbitral tribunal or fails to defend its case, the other party may request the tribunal to continue the proceedings and to make its award. Absence of a party or failure of a party to defend its case shall not constitute a bar to the proceedings. Before making its award, the arbitral tribunal must satisfy itself not only that it has jurisdiction over the dispute but also that the claim is well founded in fact and law.

Article 10. Award

The award of the arbitral tribunal shall be confined to the subject-matter of the dispute and state the reasons on which it is based. It shall contain the names of the members who have participated and the date of the award. Any member of the tribunal may attach a separate or dissenting opinion to the award.

Article 11. Finality of Award

The award shall be final and without appeal, unless the parties to the dispute have agreed in advance to an appellate procedure. It shall be complied with by the parties to the dispute.

Article 12. Interpretation or Implementation of Award

1. Any controversy which may arise between the parties to the dispute as regards the interpretation or manner of implementation of the award may be submitted by either party for decision to the arbitral tribunal which made the award. For this purpose, any vacancy in the tribunal shall be filled in the manner provided for in the original appointments of the members of the tribunal.

2. Any such controversy may be submitted to another court or tribunal under article 287 by agreement of all the parties to the dispute.

Article 13. Application to Entities Other Than States Parties

The provisions of this Annex shall apply *mutatis mutandis* to any dispute involving entities other than States Parties.

Annex VIII. Special Arbitration

Article 1. Institution of Proceedings

Subject to Part XV, any party to a dispute concerning the interpretation or application of the articles of this Convention relating to (1) fisheries, (2) protection and preservation of the marine environment, (3) marine scientific research, or (4) navigation, including pollution from vessels and by dumping, may submit the dispute to the special arbitral procedure provided for in this Annex by written notification addressed to the other party or parties to the dispute. The notification shall be accompanied by a statement of the claim and the grounds on which it is based.

Article 2. Lists of Experts

1. A list of experts shall be established and maintained in respect of each of the fields of (1) fisheries, (2) protection and preservation of the marine environment, (3) marine scientific research, and (4) navigation, including pollution from vessels and by dumping.

2. The lists of experts shall be drawn up and maintained, in the field

of fisheries by the Food and Agriculture Organization of the United Nations, in the field of protection and preservation of the marine environment by the United Nations Environment Programme, in the field of marine scientific research by the Inter-Governmental Oceanographic Commission, in the field of navigation, including pollution from vessels and by dumping, by the International Maritime Organization, or in each case by the appropriate subsidiary body concerned to which such organization, programme or commission has delegated this function.

3. Every State Party shall be entitled to nominate two experts in each field whose competence in the legal, scientific or technical aspects of such field is established and generally recognized and who enjoy the highest reputation for fairness and integrity. The names of the persons so nominated in each field shall constitute the appropriate list.

4. If at any time the experts nominated by a State Party in the list so constituted shall be fewer than two, that State Party shall be entitled to make further nominations as necessary. . . .

Article 3. *Constitution of Special Arbitral Tribunal*

For the purpose of proceedings under this Annex, the special arbitral tribunal shall, unless the parties otherwise agree, be constituted as follows:

(a) Subject to subparagraph (g), the special arbitral tribunal shall consist of five members.

(b) The party instituting the proceedings shall appoint two members to be chosen preferably from the appropriate list or lists referred to in article 2 of this Annex relating to the matters in dispute, one of whom may be its national. The appointments shall be included in the notification referred to in article 1 of this Annex.

(c) The other party to the dispute shall, within 30 days of receipt of the notification referred to in article 1 of this Annex, appoint two members to be chosen preferably from the appropriate list or lists relating to the matters in dispute, one of whom may be its national. If the appointments are not made within that period, the party instituting the proceedings may, within two weeks of the expiration of that period, request that the appointments be made in accordance with subparagraph (e).

(d) The parties to the dispute shall by agreement appoint the President of the special arbitral tribunal, chosen preferably from the appropriate list, who shall be a national of a third State, unless the parties otherwise agree. If, within 30 days of receipt of the notification referred to in article 1 of this Annex, the parties are unable to reach agreement on the appointment of the President, the appointment shall be made in accordance with subparagraph (e), at the request of a party to the dispute. Such request shall be made within two weeks of the expiration of the aforementioned 30-day period.

(e) Unless the parties agree that the appointment be made by a person or a third State chosen by the parties, the Secretary-General of the United Nations shall make the necessary appointments within 30 days of receipt of a request under subparagraphs (c) and (d). The appointments referred to in this subparagraph shall be made from the appropriate list or lists of experts referred to in article 2 of this Annex and in consultation with the parties to the dispute and the appropriate international organization. The members so appointed shall be of different nationalities and may not be in the service of, ordinarily resident in the territory of, or nationals of, any of the parties to the dispute.

(f) Any vacancy shall be filled in the manner prescribed for the initial appointment.

(g) Parties in the same interest shall appoint two members of the tribunal jointly by agreement. Where there are several parties having separate interests or where there is disagreement as to whether they are of the same interest, each of them shall appoint one member of the tribunal.

(h) In disputes involving more than two parties, the provisions of subparagraphs (a) to (f) shall apply to the maximum extent possible.

Article 4. General Provisions

Annex VII, articles 4 to 13, apply *mutatis mutandis* to the special arbitration proceedings in accordance with this Annex.

Article 5. Fact Finding

1. The parties to a dispute concerning the interpretation or application of the provisions of this Convention relating to (1) fisheries, (2) protection and preservation of the marine environment, (3) marine scientific research, or (4) navigation, including pollution from vessels and by dumping, may at any time agree to request a special arbitral tribunal constituted in accordance with article 3 of this Annex to carry out an inquiry and establish the facts giving rise to the dispute.

2. Unless the parties otherwise agree, the findings of fact of the special arbitral tribunal acting in accordance with paragraph 1, shall be considered as conclusive as between the parties.

3. If all the parties to the dispute so request, the special arbitral tribunal may formulate recommendations which, without having the force of a decision, shall only constitute the basis for a review by the parties of the questions giving rise to the dispute.

4. Subject to paragraph 2, the special arbitral tribunal shall act in accordance with the provisions of this Annex, unless the parties otherwise agree.

Annex IX. Participation by International Organizations

Article 1. Use of Terms

For the purposes of article 305 and of this Annex, "international organization" means an intergovernmental organization constituted by States to which its member States have transferred competence over matters governed by this Convention, including the competence to enter into treaties in respect of those matters.

Article 2. Signature

An international organization may sign this Convention if a majority of its member States are signatories of this Convention. At the time of signature an international organization shall make a declaration specifying the matters governed by this Convention in respect of which competence has been transferred to that organization by its member States which are signatories, and the nature and extent of that competence. . . .

Article 4. Extent of Participation and Rights and Obligations

1. The instrument of formal confirmation or of accession of an international organization shall contain an undertaking to accept the rights and obligations of States under this Convention in respect of matters relating to which competence has been transferred to it by its member States which are Parties to this Convention.

2. An international organization shall be a Party to this Convention to the extent that it has competence in accordance with the declarations, communications of information or notifications referred to in article 5 of this Annex.

3. Such an international organization shall exercise the rights and perform the obligations which its member States which are Parties would otherwise have under this Convention, on matters relating to which competence has been transferred to it by those member States. The member States of that international organization shall not exercise competence which they have transferred to it.

4. Participation of such an international organization shall in no case entail an increase of the representation to which its member States which are States Parties would otherwise be entitled, including rights in decision-making. . . .

6. In the event of a conflict between the obligations of an international organization under this Convention and its obligations under the agreement establishing the organization or any acts relating to it, the obligations under this Convention shall prevail.

Article 5. Declarations, Notifications and Communications

1. The instrument of formal confirmation or of accession of an international organization shall contain a declaration specifying the matters governed by this Convention in respect of which competence has been transferred to the organization by its member States which are Parties to this Convention.

2. A member State of an international organization shall, at the time it ratifies or accedes to this Convention or at the time when the organization deposits its instrument of formal confirmation or of accession, whichever is later, make a declaration specifying the matters governed by this Convention in respect of which it has transferred competence to the organization. . . .

ANTARCTIC TREATY

December 1, 1959, 12 U.S.T. 794, T.I.A.S. No. 4780, 402 U.N.T.S. 71*

The governments . . .
Have agreed as follows:

Article I

1. Antarctica shall be used for peaceful purposes only. There shall be prohibited, *inter alia,* any measures of a military nature, such as the establishment of military bases and fortifications, the carrying out of military maneuvers, as well as the testing of any type of weapons.

2. The present Treaty shall not prevent the use of military personnel or equipment for scientific research or for any other peaceful purpose.

Article II

Freedom of scientific investigation in Antarctica and cooperation toward that end, as applied during the International Geophysical Year, shall continue, subject to the provisions of the present Treaty.

Article III

1. In order to promote international cooperation in scientific investigation in Antarctica, as provided for in Article II of the present Treaty, the Contracting Parties agree that, to the greatest extent feasible and practicable:

   (a) information regarding plans for scientific programs in Antarctica shall be exchanged to permit maximum economy and efficiency of operations;

   (b) scientific personnel shall be exchanged in Antarctica between expeditions and stations;

   (c) scientific observations and results from Antarctica shall be exchanged and made freely available.

2. In implementing this Article, every encouragement shall be given to

---

*Signed at Washington, D.C., on December 1, 1959. Entered into force on June 23, 1961.
The 39 parties to the treaty are: Argentina, Australia, Austria, Belgium, Brazil, Bulgaria, Canada, Chile, China, Cuba, Czechoslovakia, Denmark, Ecuador, Finland, France, the Federal Republic of Germany, Greece, Hungary, India, Italy, Japan, the Democratic People's Republic of Korea, the Republic of Korea, Netherlands, New Zealand, Norway, Papua New Guinea, Peru, Poland, Romania, South Africa, Spain, Sweden, Switzerland, Union of Soviet Socialist Republics, United Kingdom, United States, and Uruguay. The 26 Consultative Members under article IX of the treaty are: Argentina, Australia, Belgium, Brazil, Chile, China, Ecuador, Finland, France, the Federal Republic of Germany, India, Italy, Japan, Republic of Korea, Netherlands, New Zealand, Norway, Peru, Poland, South Africa, Spain, Sweden, U.S.S.R., United Kingdom, United States, and Uruguay.

the establishment of cooperative working relations with those Specialized Agencies of the United Nations and other international organizations having a scientific or technical interest in Antarctica.

Article IV

1. Nothing contained in the present Treaty shall be interpreted as:

(a) a renunciation by any Contracting Party of previously asserted rights of or claims to territorial sovereignty in Antarctica;

(b) a renunciation or diminution by any Contracting Party of any basis of claim to territorial sovereignty in Antarctica which it may have whether as a result of its activities or those of its nationals in Antarctica, or otherwise;

(c) prejudicing the position of any Contracting Party as regards its recognition or non-recognition of any other State's right of or claim or basis of claim to territorial sovereignty in Antarctica.

2. No acts or activities taking place while the present Treaty is in force shall constitute a basis for asserting, supporting or denying a claim to territorial sovereignty in Antarctica or create any rights of sovereignty in Antarctica. No new claim, or enlargement of an existing claim, to territorial sovereignty in Antarctica shall be asserted while the present Treaty is in force.

Article V

1. Any nuclear explosions in Antarctica and the disposal there of radioactive waste material shall be prohibited.

2. In the event of the conclusion of international agreements concerning the use of nuclear energy, including nuclear explosions and the disposal of radioactive waste material, to which all of the Contracting Parties whose representatives are entitled to participate in the meetings provided for under Article IX are parties, the rules established under such agreements shall apply in Antarctica.

Article VI

The provisions of the present Treaty shall apply to the area south of 60° South Latitude, including all ice shelves, but nothing in the present Treaty shall prejudice or in any way affect the rights, or the exercise of the rights, of any State under international law with regard to the high seas within that area.

Article VII

1. In order to promote the objectives and ensure the observance of the provisions of the present Treaty, each Contracting Party whose representatives are entitled to participate in the meetings referred to in Article IX of the Treaty shall have the right to designate observers to carry out any inspection provided for by the present Article. Observers shall be nationals of the Contracting Parties which designate them. The names of observers shall be communicated to every other Contracting Party having the right to

designate observers, and like notice shall be given of the termination of their appointment.

2. Each observer designated in accordance with the provisions of paragraph 1 of this Article shall have complete freedom of access at any time to any or all areas of Antarctica.

3. All areas of Antarctica, including all stations, installations and equipment within those areas, and all ships and aircraft at points of discharging or embarking cargoes or personnel in Antarctica, shall be open at all times to inspection by any observers designated in accordance with paragraph 1 of this Article.

4. Aerial observation may be carried out at any time over any or all areas of Antarctica by any of the Contracting Parties having the right to designate observers.

5. Each Contracting Party shall, at the time when the present Treaty enters into force for it, inform the other Contracting Parties, and thereafter shall give them notice in advance, of

(a) all expeditions to and within Antarctica, on the part of its ships or nationals, and all expeditions to Antarctica organized in or proceeding from its territory;

(b) all stations in Antarctica occupied by its nationals; and

(c) any military personnel or equipment intended to be introduced by it into Antarctica subject to the conditions prescribed in paragraph 2 of Article I of the present Treaty.

Article VIII

1. In order to facilitate the exercise of their functions under the present Treaty, and without prejudice to the respective positions of the Contracting Parties relating to jurisdiction over all other persons in Antarctica, observers designated under paragraph 1 of Article VII and scientific personnel exchanged under subparagraph 1(b) of Article III of the Treaty, and members of the staffs accompanying any such persons, shall be subject only to the jurisdiction of the Contracting Party of which they are nationals in respect of all acts or omissions occurring while they are in Antarctica for the purpose of exercising their functions.

2. Without prejudice to the provisions of paragraph 1 of this Article, and pending the adoption of measures in pursuance of subparagraph 1(e) of Article IX, the Contracting Parties concerned in any case of dispute with regard to the exercise of jurisdiction in Antarctica shall immediately consult together with a view to reaching a mutually acceptable solution.

Article IX

1. Representatives of the Contracting Parties named in the preamble to the present Treaty shall meet at the City of Canberra within two months after the date of entry into force of the Treaty, and thereafter at suitable intervals and places, for the purpose of exchanging information, consulting together on matters of common interest pertaining to Antarctica, and formulating and considering, and recommending to their Governments, mea-

sures in furtherance of the principles and objectives of the Treaty, including measures regarding:

(a) use of Antarctica for peaceful purposes only;
(b) facilitation of scientific research in Antarctica;
(c) facilitation of international scientific cooperation in Antarctica;
(d) facilitation of the exercise of the rights of inspection provided for in Article VII of the Treaty;
(e) questions relating to the exercise of jurisdiction in Antarctica;
(f) preservation and conservation of living resources in Antarctica.

2. Each Contracting Party which has become a party to the present Treaty by accession under Article XIII shall be entitled to appoint representatives to participate in the meetings referred to in paragraph 1 of the present Article, during such time as that Contracting Party demonstrates its interest in Antarctica by conducting substantial scientific research activity there, such as the establishment of a scientific station or the despatch of a scientific expedition.

3. Reports from the observers referred to in Article VII of the present Treaty shall be transmitted to the representatives of the Contracting Parties participating in the meetings referred to in paragraph 1 of the present Article.

4. The measures referred to in paragraph 1 of this Article shall become effective when approved by all the Contracting Parties whose representatives were entitled to participate in the meetings held to consider those measures.

5. Any or all of the rights established in the present Treaty may be exercised as from the date of entry into force of the Treaty whether or not any measures facilitating the exercise of such rights have been proposed, considered or approved as provided in this Article.

Article X

Each of the Contracting Parties undertakes to exert appropriate efforts, consistent with the Charter of the United Nations, to the end that no one engages in any activity in Antarctica contrary to the principles or purposes of the present Treaty.

Article XI

1. If any dispute arises between two or more of the Contracting Parties concerning the interpretation or application of the present Treaty, those Contracting Parties shall consult among themselves with a view to having the dispute resolved by negotiation, inquiry, mediation, conciliation, arbitration, judicial settlement or other peaceful means of their own choice.

2. Any dispute of this character not so resolved shall, with the consent, in each case, of all parties to the dispute, be referred to the International Court of Justice for settlement; but failure to reach agreement on reference to the International Court shall not absolve parties to the dispute from the responsibility of continuing to seek to resolve it by any of the various peaceful means referred to in paragraph 1 of this Article.

Article XII

1. (a) The present Treaty may be modified or amended at any time by unanimous agreement of the Contracting Parties whose representatives are entitled to participate in the meetings provided for under Article IX. Any such modification or amendment shall enter into force when the depositary Government has received notice from all such Contracting Parties that they have ratified it.

(b) Such modification or amendment shall thereafter enter into force as to any other Contracting Party when notice of ratification by it has been received by the depositary Government. Any such Contracting Party from which no notice of ratification is received within a period of two years from the date of entry into force of the modification or amendment in accordance with the provisions of subparagraph 1(a) of this Article shall be deemed to have withdrawn from the present Treaty on the date of the expiration of such period. . . .

10

The Law Governing Airspace, Aviation, and Outer Space

CONVENTION ON INTERNATIONAL CIVIL AVIATION (CHICAGO CONVENTION)

December 7, 1944 (as amended)*

PREAMBLE

WHEREAS the future development of international civil aviation can greatly help to create and preserve friendship and understanding among the

---

*Done at Chicago on December 7, 1944. Entered into force on April 4, 1947. 61 Stat. 1180, T.I.A.S. No. 1591, 15 U.N.T.S. 295. Amended several times since. The most recent amendments that are in force are from 1974 and came into force in February 1980. 1175 U.N.T.S. 297. The excerpts here reflect all amendments that are in force. Other amending protocols are awaiting a sufficient number of states to accept them before they come into force.

The 162 parties to the convention are: Afghanistan, Algeria, Angola, Antigua & Barbuda, Argentina, Australia, Austria, The Bahamas, Bahrain, Bangladesh, Barbados, Belgium, Benin, Bhutan, Bolivia, Botswana, Brazil, Burnei, Bulgaria, Burkina Faso, Burma, Burundi, Cambodia, Cameroon, Canada, Cape Verde, Central African Republic, Chad, Chile, China, Colombia, Comoros, Congo, Cook Is., Costa Rica, Cote d'Ivoire, Cuba, Cyprus, Czechoslovakia, Denmark, Djibouti, Dominican Republic, Ecuador, Egypt, El Salvador, Equatorial Guinea, Ethiopia, Fiji, Finland, France, Gabon, Gambia, Germany (Federal Republic), Ghana, Greece, Grenada, Guatemala, Guinea, Guinea-Bissau, Guyana, Haiti, Honduras, Hungary, Iceland, India, Indonesia, Iran, Iraq, Ireland, Israel, Italy, Jamaica, Japan, Jordan, Kenya, Kiribati, Korea (Democratic People's Republic), Korea (Republic of), Kuwait, Laos, Lebanon, Lesotho, Liberia, Libya, Luxembourg, Madagascar, Malawi, Malaysia, Maldives, Mali, Malta, Marshall Islands, Mauritania, Mauritius, Mexico, Micronesia, Monaco, Morocco, Mozambique, Nauru, Nepal, Netherlands, New Zealand, Nicaragua, Niger, Nigeria, Norway, Oman, Pakistan, Panama, Papua New Guinea, Paraguay, Peru, Philippines, Poland, Portugal, Qatar, Romania, Rwanda, Saint Lucia, Saint Vincent & the Grenadines, San Marino, Sao Tome & Principe, Saudi Arabia, Senegal, Seychelles, Sierra Leone, Singapore, Solomon Island, Somalia, South Africa, Spain, Sri Lanka, Sudan, Suriname, Swaziland, Sweden, Switzerland, Syrian Arab Republic, Tanzania, Thailand, Togo, Tonga, Trinidad & Tobago, Tunisia, Turkey, Uganda, Union of Soviet Socialist Republics, United Arab Emirates, United Kingdom, United States, Uruguay, Vanuatu, Venezuela, Vietnam (Socialist Republic), Yemen (Aden), Yemen (Sanaa), Yugoslavia, Zaire, Zambia, and Zimbabwe.

nations and peoples of the world, yet its abuse can become a threat to the general security; and

WHEREAS it is desirable to avoid friction and to promote that cooperation between nations and peoples upon which the peace of the world depends;

THEREFORE, the undersigned governments having agreed on certain principles and arrangements in order that international civil aviation may be developed in a safe and orderly manner and that international air transport services may be established on the basis of equality of opportunity and operated soundly and economically;

Have accordingly concluded this Convention to that end.

Part I. Air Navigation

Chapter I. General Principles and Application of the Convention

Article 1. Sovereignty

The contracting States recognize that every State has complete and exclusive sovereignty over the airspace above its territory.

Article 2. Territory

For the purposes of this Convention the territory of a State shall be deemed to be the land areas and territorial waters adjacent thereto under the sovereignty, suzerainty, protection or mandate of such State.

Article 3. Civil and State Aircraft

(a) This Convention shall be applicable only to civil aircraft, and shall not be applicable to state aircraft.

(b) Aircraft used in military, customs and police services shall be deemed to be state aircraft.

(c) No state aircraft of a contracting State shall fly over the territory of another State or land thereon without authorization by special agreement or otherwise, and in accordance with the terms thereof.

(d) The contracting States undertake, when issuing regulations for their state aircraft, that they will have due regard for the safety of navigation of civil aircraft.

Article 4. Misuse of Civil Aviation

Each contracting State agrees not to use civil aviation for any purpose inconsistent with the aims of this Convention.

Chapter II. Flight over Territory of Contracting States

Article 5. Right of Non-scheduled Flight

Each contracting State agrees that all aircraft of the other contracting States, being aircraft not engaged in scheduled international air services shall have the right, subject to the observance of the terms of this Convention, to make flights into or in transit non-stop across its territory and to make stops for non-traffic purposes without the necessity of obtaining prior permission, and subject to the right of the State flown over to require landing. Each contracting State nevertheless reserves the right, for reasons of safety of flight, to require aircraft desiring to proceed over regions which are inaccessible or without adequate air navigation facilities to follow prescribed routes, or to obtain special permission for such flights.

Such aircraft, if engaged in the carriage of passengers, cargo, or mail for remuneration or hire on other than scheduled international air se. vices, shall also, subject to the provisions of Article 7, have the privilege of taking on or discharging passengers, cargo, or mail, subject to the right of any State where such embarkation or discharge takes place to impose such regulations, conditions or limitations as it may consider desirable.

Article 6. Scheduled Air Services

No scheduled international air service may be operated over or into the territory of a contracting State, except with the special permission or other authorization of that State, and in accordance with the terms of such permission or authorization.

Article 7. Cabotage

Each contracting State shall have the right to refuse permission to the aircraft of other contracting States to take on in its territory passengers, mail and cargo carried for remuneration or hire and destined for another point within its territory. Each contracting State undertakes not to enter into any arrangements which specifically grant any such privilege on an exclusive basis to any other State or an airline of any other State, and not to obtain any such exclusive privilege from any other State.

Article 8. Pilotless Aircraft

No aircraft capable of being flown without a pilot shall be flown without a pilot over the territory of a contracting State without special authorization by that State and in accordance with the terms of such authorization. Each contracting State undertakes to insure that the flight of such aircraft without a pilot in regions open to civil aircraft shall be so controlled as to obviate danger to civil aircraft.

Article 9. Prohibited Areas

(a) Each contracting State may, for reasons of military necessity or public safety, restrict or prohibit uniformly the aircraft of other States from flying over certain areas of its territory, provided that no distinction in this respect is made between the aircraft of the State whose territory is involved, engaged in international scheduled airline services, and the aircraft of the other contracting States likewise engaged. Such prohibited areas shall be of reasonable extent and location so as not to interfere unnecessarily with air navigation. Descriptions of such prohibited areas in the territory of a contracting State, as well as any subsequent alterations therein, shall be communicated as soon as possible to the other contracting States and to the International Civil Aviation Organization.

(b) Each contracting State reserves also the right, in exceptional circumstances or during a period of emergency, or in the interest of public safety, and with immediate effect, temporarily to restrict or prohibit flying over the whole or any part of its territory, on condition that such restriction or prohibition shall be applicable without distinction of nationality to aircraft of all other States.

(c) Each contracting State, under such regulations as it may prescribe, may require any aircraft entering the areas contemplated in subparagraphs (a) or (b) above to effect a landing as soon as practicable thereafter at some designated airport within its territory.

Article 10. Landing at Customs Airport

Except in a case where, under the terms of this Convention or a special authorization, aircraft are permitted to cross the territory of a contracting State without landing, every aircraft which enters the territory of a contracting State shall, if the regulations of that State so require, land at an airport designated by that State for the purpose of customs and other examination. On departure from the territory of a contracting State, such aircraft shall depart from a similarly designated customs airport. Particulars of all designated customs airports shall be published by the State and transmitted to the International Civil Aviation Organization established under Part II of this Convention for communication to all other contracting States.

Article 11. Applicability of Air Regulations

Subject to the provisions of this Convention, the laws and regulations of a contracting State relating to the admission to or departure from its territory of aircraft engaged in international air navigation, or to the operation and navigation of such aircraft while within its territory, shall be applied to the aircraft of all contracting States without distinction as to nationality, and shall be complied with by such aircraft upon entering or departing from or while within the territory of that State.

Article 12. Rules of the Air

Each contracting State undertakes to adopt measures to insure that every aircraft flying over or maneuvering within its territory and that every aircraft carrying its nationality mark, wherever such aircraft may be, shall comply with the rules and regulations relating to the flight and maneuver of aircraft there in force. Each contracting State undertakes to keep its own regulations in these respects uniform, to the greatest possible extent, with those established from time to time under this Convention. Over the high seas, the rules in force shall be those established under this Convention. Each contracting State undertakes to insure the prosecution of all persons violating the regulations applicable.

Article 13. Entry and Clearance Regulations

The laws and regulations of a contracting State as to the admission to or departure from its territory of passengers, crew or cargo of aircraft, such as regulations relating to entry, clearance, immigration, passports, customs, and quarantine shall be complied with by or on behalf of such passengers, crew or cargo upon entrance into or departure from, or while within the territory of that State.

Article 14. Prevention of Spread of Disease

Each contracting State agrees to take effective measures to prevent the spread by means of air navigation of cholera, typhus (epidemic), smallpox, yellow fever, plague, and such other communicable diseases as the contracting States shall from time to time decide to designate, and to that end contracting States will keep in close consultation with the agencies concerned with international regulations relating to sanitary measures applicable to aircraft. Such consultation shall be without prejudice to the application of any existing international convention on this subject to which the contracting States may be parties.

Article 15. Airport and Similar Charges

Every airport in a contracting State which is open to public use by its national aircraft shall likewise, subject to the provisions of Article 68, be open under uniform conditions to the aircraft of all the other contracting States. The like uniform conditions shall apply to the use, by aircraft of every contracting State, of all air navigation facilities, including radio and meteorological services, which may be provided for public use for the safety and expedition of air navigation.

Any charges that may be imposed or permitted to be imposed by a contracting State for the use of such airports and air navigation facilities by the aircraft of any other contracting State shall not be higher,

(a) As to aircraft not engaged in scheduled international air services, than those that would be paid by its national aircraft of the same class engaged in similar operations, and

(b) As to aircraft engaged in scheduled international air services, than those that would be paid by its national aircraft engaged in similar international air services.

All such charges shall be published and communicated to the International Civil Aviation Organization: provided that, upon representation by an interested contracting State, the charges imposed for the use of airports and other facilities shall be subject to review by the Council, which shall report and make recommendations thereon for the consideration of the State or

States concerned. No fees, dues or other charges shall be imposed by any contracting State in respect solely of the right of transit over or entry into or exit from its territory of any aircraft of a contracting State or persons or property thereon.

Article 16. Search of Aircraft

The appropriate authorities of each of the contracting States shall have the right, without unreasonable delay, to search aircraft of the other contracting States on landing or departure, and to inspect the certificates and other documents prescribed by this Convention.

CHAPTER III. NATIONALITY OF AIRCRAFT

Article 17. Nationality of Aircraft

Aircraft have the nationality of the State in which they are registered.

Article 18. Dual Registration

An aircraft cannot be validly registered in more than one State, but its registration may be changed from one State to another.

Article 19. National Laws Governing Registration

The registration or transfer of registration of aircraft in any contracting State shall be made in accordance with its laws and regulations.

Article 20. Display of Marks

Every aircraft engaged in international air navigation shall bear its appropriate nationality and registration marks.

Article 21. Report of Registrations

Each contracting State undertakes to supply to any other contracting State or to the International Civil Aviation Organization, on demand, information concerning the registration and ownership of any particular aircraft registered in that State. In addition, each contracting State shall furnish reports to the International Civil Aviation Organization, under such regulations as the latter may prescribe, giving such pertinent data as can be made available concerning the ownership and control of aircraft registered in that State and habitually engaged in international air navigation. The data thus obtained by the International Civil Aviation Organization shall be made available by it on request to the other contracting States.

CHAPTER IV. MEASURES TO FACILITATE AIR NAVIGATION

Article 22. Facilitation of Formalities

Each contracting State agrees to adopt all practicable measures, through the issuance of special regulations or otherwise, to facilitate and expedite navigation by aircraft between the territories of contracting States, and to prevent unnecessary delays to aircraft, crews, passengers and cargo, especially in the administration of the laws relating to immigration, quarantine, customs and clearance.

Article 23. Customs and Immigration Procedures

Each contracting State undertakes, so far as it may find practicable, to establish customs and immigration procedures affecting international air navigation in accordance with the practices which may be established or recommended from time to time, pursuant to this Convention. Nothing in this Convention shall be construed as preventing the establishment of customs-free airports.

Article 24. Customs Duty

(a) Aircraft on a flight to, from, or across the territory of another contracting State shall be admitted temporarily free of duty, subject to the customs regulations of the State. Fuel, lubricating oils, spare parts, regular equipment and aircraft stores on board an aircraft of a contracting State, on arrival in the territory of another contracting State and retained on board on leaving the territory of that State shall be exempt from customs duty, inspection fees or similar national or local duties and charges. This exemption shall not apply to any quantities or articles unloaded, except in accordance with the customs regulations of the State, which may require that they shall be kept under customs supervision.

(b) Spare parts and equipment imported into the territory of a contracting State for incorporation in or use on an aircraft of another contracting State engaged in international air navigation shall be admitted free of customs duty, subject to compliance with the regulations of the State concerned, which may provide that the articles shall be kept under customs supervision and control.

Article 25. Aircraft in Distress

Each contracting State undertakes to provide such measures of assistance to aircraft in distress in its territory as it may find practicable, and to permit, subject to control by its own authorities, the owners of the aircraft or authorities of the State in which the aircraft is registered to provide such measures of assistance as may be necessitated by the circumstances. Each contracting State, when undertaking search for missing aircraft, will collaborate in coordinated measures which may be recommended from time to time pursuant to this Convention.

Article 26. Investigation of Accidents

In the event of an accident to an aircraft of a contracting State occurring in the territory of another contracting State, and involving death or serious injury, or indicating serious technical defect in the aircraft or navigation facilities, the State in which the accident occurs will institute an inquiry into the circumstances of the accident, in accordance, so far as its laws permit, with the procedure which may be recommended by the International Civil

Aviation Organization. The State in which the aircraft is registered shall be given the opportunity to appoint observers to be present at the inquiry and the State holding the inquiry shall communicate the report and findings in the matter to that State. . . .

Article 28. Air Navigation Facilities and Standard Systems

Each contracting State undertakes, so far as it may find practicable, to:

(a) Provide, in its territory, airports, radio services, meteorological services and other air navigation facilities to facilitate international air navigation, in accordance with the standards and practices recommended or established from time to time, pursuant to this Convention;

(b) Adopt and put into operation the appropriate standard systems of communications procedure, codes, markings, signals, lighting and other operational practices and rules which may be recommended or established from time to time, pursuant to this Convention;

(c) Collaborate in international measures to secure the publication of aeronautical maps and charts in accordance with standards which may be recommended or established from time to time, pursuant to this Convention.

CHAPTER V. CONDITIONS TO BE FULFILLED WITH RESPECT TO AIRCRAFT

Article 29. Documents Carried in Aircraft

Every aircraft of a contracting State, engaged in international navigation, shall carry the following documents in conformity with the conditions prescribed in this Convention:

(a) Its certificate of registration;
(b) Its certificate of airworthiness;
(c) The appropriate licenses for each member of the crew;
(d) Its journey log book;
(e) If it is equipped with radio apparatus, the aircraft radio station license;
(f) If it carries passengers, a list of their names and places of embarkation and destination;
(g) If it carries cargo, a manifest and detailed declarations of the cargo.

Article 30. Aircraft Radio Equipment

(a) Aircraft of each contracting State may, in or over the territory of other contracting States, carry radio transmitting apparatus only if a license to install and operate such apparatus has been issued by the appropriate authorities of the State in which the aircraft is registered. The use of radio transmitting apparatus in the territory of the contracting State whose territory is flown over shall be in accordance with the regulations prescribed by that State.

(b) Radio transmitting apparatus may be used only by members of the flight crew who are provided with a special license for the purpose, issued by the appropriate authorities of the State in which the aircraft is registered.

Article 31. Certificates of Airworthiness

Every aircraft engaged in international navigation shall be provided with a certificate of airworthiness issued or rendered valid by the State in which it is registered.

Article 32. Licenses of Personnel

(a) The pilot of every aircraft and the other members of the operating crew of every aircraft engaged in international navigation shall be provided with certificates of competency and licenses issued or rendered valid by the State in which the aircraft is registered.

(b) Each contracting State reserves the right to refuse to recognize, for the purpose of flight above its own territory, certificates of competency and licenses granted to any of its nationals by another contracting State.

Article 33. Recognition of Certificates and Licenses

Certificates of airworthiness and certificates of competency and licenses issued or rendered valid by the contracting State in which the aircraft is registered, shall be recognized as valid by the other contracting States, provided that the requirements under which such certificates or licenses were issued or rendered valid are equal to or above the minimum standards which may be established from time to time pursuant to this Convention.

Article 34. Journey Log Books

There shall be maintained in respect of every aircraft engaged in international navigation a journey log book in which shall be entered particulars of the aircraft, its crew and of each journey, in such form as may be prescribed from time to time pursuant to this Convention.

Article 35. Cargo Restrictions

(a) No munitions of war or implements of war may be carried in or above the territory of a State in aircraft engaged in international navigation, except by permission of such State. Each State shall determine by regulations what constitutes munitions of war or implements of war for the purposes of this Article, giving due consideration, for the purposes of uniformity, to such recommendations as the International Civil Aviation Organization may from time to time make.

(b) Each contracting State reserves the right, for reasons of public order and safety, to regulate or prohibit the carriage in or above its territory of articles other than those enumerated in paragraph (a): provided that no distinction is made in this respect between its national aircraft engaged in international navigation and the aircraft of the other States so engaged; and provided further that no restriction shall be imposed which may interfere with the carriage and use on aircraft of apparatus necessary for the operation or navigation of the aircraft or the safety of the personnel or passengers.

Article 36. *Photographic Apparatus*

Each contracting State may prohibit or regulate the use of photographic apparatus in aircraft over its territory.

CHAPTER VI. INTERNATIONAL STANDARDS AND RECOMMENDED PRACTICES

Article 37. *Adoption of International Standards and Procedures*

Each contracting State undertakes to collaborate in securing the highest practicable degree of uniformity in regulations, standards, procedures, and organization in relation to aircraft, personnel, airways and auxiliary services in all matters in which such uniformity will facilitate and improve air navigation.

To this end the International Civil Aviation Organization shall adopt and amend from time to time, as may be necessary, international standards and recommended practices and procedures dealing with:

(a) Communications systems and air navigation aids, including ground marking;
(b) Characteristics of airports and landing areas;
(c) Rules of the air and air traffic control practices;
(d) Licensing of operating and mechanical personnel;
(e) Airworthiness of aircraft;
(f) Registration and identification of aircraft;
(g) Collection and exchange of meteorological information;
(h) Log books;
(i) Aeronautical maps and charts;
(j) Customs and immigration procedures;
(k) Aircraft in distress and investigation of accidents;

and such other matters concerned with the safety, regularity, and efficiency of air navigation as may from time to time appear appropriate.

Article 38. *Departures from International Standards and Procedures*

Any State which finds it impracticable to comply in all respects with any such international standards or procedure, or to bring its own regulations or practices into full accord with any international standard or procedure after amendment of the latter, or which deems it necessary to adopt regulations or practices differing in any particular respect from those established by an international standard, shall give immediate notification to the International Civil Aviation Organization of the differences between its own practice and that established by the international standard. In the case of amendments to international standards, any State which does not make the appropriate amendments to its own regulations or practices shall give notice to the Council within sixty days of the adoption of the amendment to the international standard, or indicate the action which it proposes to take. In any such case, the Council shall make immediate notification to all other States of the difference which exists between one or more features of an international standard and the corresponding national practice of that State. . . .

Part II. The International Civil Aviation Organization

CHAPTER VII. THE ORGANIZATION

Article 43. Name and Composition

An organization to be named the International Civil Aviation Organization is formed by the Convention. It is made up of an Assembly, a Council, and such other bodies as may be necessary.

Article 44. Objectives

The aims and objectives of the Organization are to develop the principles and techniques of international air navigation and to foster the planning and development of international air transport so as to:

(a) Insure the safe and orderly growth of international civil aviation throughout the world;
(b) Encourage the arts of aircraft design and operation for peaceful purposes;
(c) Encourage the development of airways, airports, and air navigation facilities for international civil aviation;
(d) Meet the needs of the peoples of the world for safe, regular, efficient and economical air transport;
(e) Prevent economic waste caused by unreasonable competition;
(f) Insure that the rights of contracting States are fully respected and that every contracting State has a fair opportunity to operate international airlines;
(g) Avoid discrimination between contracting States;
(h) Promote safety of flight in international air navigation;
(i) Promote generally the development of all aspects of international civil aeronautics.

Article 45. Permanent Seat

The permanent seat of the Organization shall be at such place as shall be determined at the final meeting of the Interim Assembly of the Provisional International Civil Aviation Organization set up by the Interim Agreement on International Civil Aviation signed at Chicago on December 7, 1944. The seat may be temporarily transferred elsewhere by decision of the Council. . . .

Article 47. *Legal Capacity*

The Organization shall enjoy in the territory of each contracting State such legal capacity as may be necessary for the performance of its functions. Full juridical personality shall be granted wherever compatible with the constitution and laws of the State concerned.

CHAPTER VIII. THE ASSEMBLY

Article 48. *Meetings of Assembly and Voting*

(a) The Assembly shall meet not less than once in three years and shall be convened by the Council at a suitable time and place. An extraordinary meeting of the Assembly may be held at any time upon the call of the Council or at the request of not less than one-fifth of the total number of contracting States addressed to the Secretary General.

(b) All contracting States shall have an equal right to be represented at the meetings of the Assembly and each contracting State shall be entitled to one vote. Delegates representing contracting States may be assisted by technical advisers who may participate in the meetings but shall have no vote.

(c) A majority of the contracting States is required to constitute a quorum for the meetings of the Assembly. Unless otherwise provided in this Convention, decisions of the Assembly shall be taken by a majority of the votes cast.

Article 49. *Powers and Duties of Assembly*

The powers and duties of the Assembly shall be to:

(a) Elect at each meeting its President and other officers;
(b) Elect the contracting States to be represented on the Council, in accordance with the provisions of Chapter IX;
(c) Examine and take appropriate action on the reports of the Council and decide on any matter referred to it by the Council;
(d) Determine its own rules of procedure and establish such subsidiary commissions as it may consider to be necessary or desirable;
(e) Vote annual budgets and determine the financial arrangements of the Organization, in accordance with the provisions of Chapter XII;
(f) Review expenditures and approve the accounts of the Organization;
(g) Refer, at its discretion, to the Council, to subsidiary commissions, or to any other body any matter within its sphere of action;
(h) Delegate to the Council the powers and authority necessary or desirable for the discharge of the duties of the Organization and revoke or modify the delegations of authority at any time;
(i) Carry out the appropriate provisions of Chapter XIII;
(j) Consider proposals for the modification or amendment of the provisions of this Convention and, if it approves of the proposals, recommend them to the contracting States in accordance with the provisions of Chapter XXI;

(k) Deal with any matter within the sphere of action of the Organization not specifically assigned to the Council.

Chapter IX. The Council

Article 50. Composition and Election of Council

(a) The Council shall be a permanent body responsible to the Assembly. It shall be composed of thirty-three contracting States elected by the Assembly. An election shall be held at the first meeting of the Assembly and thereafter every three years, and the members of the Council so elected shall hold office until the next following election.

(b) In electing the members of the Council, the Assembly shall give adequate representation to

1) the States of chief importance in air transport;

2) the States not otherwise included which make the largest contribution to the provision of facilities for international civil air navigation; and

3) the States not otherwise included whose designation will insure that all major geographic areas of the world are represented on the Council. Any vacancy on the Council shall be filled by the Assembly as soon as possible; any contracting State so elected to the Council shall hold office for the unexpired portion of its predecessor's term of office.

(c) No representative of a contracting State on the Council shall be actively associated with the operation of an international air service or financially interested in such a service.

Article 51. President of Council

The Council shall elect its President for a term of three years. He may be reelected. He shall have no vote. The Council shall elect from among its members one or more Vice Presidents who shall retain their right to vote when serving as acting President. The President need not be selected from among the representatives of the members of the Council but, if a representative is elected, his seat shall be deemed vacant and it shall be filled by the State which he represented. The duties of the President shall be to:

(a) Convene meetings of the Council, the Air Transport Committee, and the Air Navigation Commission;
(b) Serve as representative of the Council; and
(c) Carry out on behalf of the Council the functions which the Council assigns to him.

Article 52. Voting in Council

Decisions by the Council shall require approval by a majority of its members. The Council may delegate authority with respect to any particular matter to a committee of its members. Decisions of any committee of the Council may be appealed to the Council by any interested contracting State.

Article 53. Participation without a Vote

Any contracting State may participate, without a vote, in the consideration by the Council and by its committees and commissions on any question which especially affects its interests. No member of the Council shall vote in the consideration by the Council of a dispute to which it is a party.

Article 54. *Mandatory Functions of Council*

The Council shall:

(a) Submit annual reports to the Assembly;
(b) Carry out the directions of the Assembly and discharge the duties and obligations which are laid on it by this Convention;
(c) Determine its organization and rules of procedure;
(d) Appoint and define the duties of an Air Transport Committee, which shall be chosen from among the representatives of the members of the Council, and which shall be responsible to it;
(e) Establish an Air Navigation Commission, in accordance with the provisions of Chapter X;
(f) Administer the finances of the Organization in accordance with the provisions of Chapters XII and XV;
(g) Determine the emoluments of the President of the Council;
(h) Appoint a chief executive officer who shall be called the Secretary General, and make provision for the appointment of such other personnel as may be necessary, in accordance with the provisions of Chapter XI;
(i) Request, collect, examine and publish information relating to the advancement of air navigation and the operation of international air services, including information about the costs of operation and particulars of subsidies paid to airlines from public funds;
(j) Report to contracting States any infraction of this Convention, as well as any failure to carry out recommendations or determinations of the Council;
(k) Report to the Assembly any infraction of this Convention where a contracting State has failed to take appropriate action within a reasonable time after notice of the infraction;
(l) Adopt, in accordance with the provisions of Chapter VI of this Convention, international standards and recommended practices; for convenience, designate them as Annexes to this Convention; and notify all contracting States of the action taken;
(m) Consider recommendations of the Air Navigation Commission for amendment of the Annexes and take action in accordance with the provisions of Chapter XX;
(n) Consider any matter relating to the Convention which any contracting State refers to it.

Article 55. *Permissive Functions of Council*

The Council may:

(a) Where appropriate and as experience may show to be desirable, create subordinate air transport commissions on a regional or other basis and define groups of states or airlines with or through

which it may deal to facilitate the carrying out of the aims of this Convention;
(b) Delegate to the Air Navigation Commission duties additional to those set forth in the Convention and revoke or modify such delegations of authority at any time;
(c) Conduct research into all aspects of air transport and air navigation which are of international importance, communicate the results of its research to the contracting States, and facilitate the exchange of information between contracting States on air transport and air navigation matters;
(d) Study and matters affecting the organization and operation of international air transport, including the international ownership and operation of international air services on trunk routes, and submit to the Assembly plans in relation thereto;
(e) Investigate, at the request of any contracting State, any situation which may appear to present avoidable obstacles to the development of international air navigation; and, after such investigation, issue such reports as may appear to it desirable. . . .

Part III. International Air Transport

CHAPTER XIV. INFORMATION AND REPORTS

Article 67. File Reports with Council

Each contracting State undertakes that its international airlines shall, in accordance with requirements laid down by the Council, file with the Council traffic reports, cost statistics and financial statements showing among other things all receipts and the sources thereof.

CHAPTER XV. AIRPORTS AND OTHER AIR NAVIGATION FACILITIES

Article 68. Designation of Routes and Airports

Each contracting State may, subject to the provisions of this Convention, designate the route to be followed within its territory by any international air service and the airports which any such service may use. . . .

CHAPTER XVIII. DISPUTES AND DEFAULT

Article 84. Settlement of Disputes

If any disagreement between two or more contracting States relating to the interpretation or application of this Convention and its Annexes cannot be settled by negotiation, it shall, on the application of any State concerned in the disagreement, be decided by the Council. No member of the Council shall vote in the consideration by the Council of any dispute to which it is a party. Any contracting State may, subject to Article 85, appeal from the decision of the Council to an *ad hoc* arbitral tribunal agreed upon with the other parties to the dispute or to the Permanent Court of International Justice. Any such appeal shall be notified to the Council within sixty days of receipt of notification of the decision of the Council.

Article 85. Arbitration Procedure

If any contracting State party to a dispute in which the decision of the Council is under appeal has not accepted the Statute of the Permanent Court of International Justice and the contracting States parties to the dispute cannot agree on the choice of the arbitral tribunal, each of the contracting States parties to the dispute shall name a single arbitrator who shall name an umpire. If either contracting State party to the dispute fails to name an arbitrator within a period of three months from the date of the appeal, an arbitrator shall be named on behalf of that State by the President of the Council from a list of qualified and available persons maintained by the Council. If, within thirty days, the arbitrators cannot agree on an umpire, the President of the Council shall designate an umpire from the list previously referred to. The arbitrators and the umpire shall then jointly constitute an arbitral tribunal. Any arbitral tribunal established under this or the preceding Article shall settle its own procedure and give its decisions by majority vote, provided that the Council may determine procedural questions in the event of any delay which in the opinion of the Council is excessive.

Article 86. Appeals

Unless the Council decides otherwise, any decision by the Council on whether an international airline is operating in conformity with the provisions of this Convention shall remain in effect unless reversed on appeal. On any other matter, decisions of the Council shall, if appealed from, be suspended until the appeal is decided. The decisions of the Permanent Court of International Justice and of an arbitral tribunal shall be final and binding.

Article 87. Penalty for Non-conformity of Airline

Each contracting State undertakes not to allow the operation of an airline of a contracting State through the airspace above its territory if the Council has decided that the airline concerned is not conforming to a final decision rendered in accordance with the previous Article.

Article 88. Penalty for Non-conformity by State

The Assembly shall suspend the voting power in the Assembly and in the Council of any contracting State that is found in default under the provisions of this Chapter.

CHAPTER XIX. WAR

Article 89. War and Emergency Conditions

In case of war, the provisions of this Convention shall not affect the freedom of action of any of the contracting States affected, whether as belligerents or as neutrals. The same principle shall apply in the case of any contracting State which declares a state of national emergency and notifies the fact to the Council.

CHAPTER XX. ANNEXES

Article 90. *Adoption and Amendment of Annexes*

(a) The adoption by the Council of the Annexes described in Article 54, subparagraph (l), shall require the vote of two-thirds of the Council at a meeting called for that purpose and shall then be submitted by the Council to each contracting State. Any such Annex or any amendment of an Annex shall become effective within three months after its submission to the contracting States or at the end of such longer period of time as the Council may prescribe, unless in the meantime a majority of the contracting States register their disapproval with the Council.

(b) The Council shall immediately notify all contracting States of the coming into force of any Annex or amendment thereto. . . .

CHAPTER XXII. DEFINITIONS

Article 96

For the purpose of this Convention the expression:

(a) "Air service" means any scheduled air service performed by aircraft for the public transport of passengers, mail or cargo.

(b) "International air service" means an air service which passes through the airspace over the territory of more than one State.

(c) "Airline" means any air transport enterprise offering or operating an international air service.

(d) "Stop for non-traffic purposes" means a landing for any purpose other than taking on or discharging passengers, cargo or mail. . . .

OUTER SPACE TREATY

January 27, 1967, 18 U.S.T. 2410, T.I.A.S. No. 6347, 610 U.N.T.S. 205*

The States Parties to this Treaty,
Inspired by the great prospects opening up before mankind as a result of man's entry into outer space,
Recognizing the common interest of all mankind in the progress of the exploration and use of outer space for peaceful purposes,
Believing that the exploration and use of outer space should be carried on for the benefit of all peoples irrespective of the degree of their economic or scientific development,
Desiring to contribute to broad international co-operation in the scientific as well as the legal aspects of the exploration and use of outer space for peaceful purposes,
Believing that such co-operation will contribute to the development of mutual understanding and to the strengthening of friendly relations between States and peoples,
Recalling resolution 1962 (XVIII), entitled "Declaration of Legal Principles Governing the Activities of States in the Exploration and Use of Outer Space", which was adopted unanimously by the United Nations General Assembly on 13 December 1963,
Recalling resolution 1884 (XVIII), calling upon States to refrain from placing in orbit around the earth any objects carrying nuclear weapons or any other kinds of weapons of mass destruction or from installing such weapons on celestial bodies, which was adopted unanimously by the United Nations General Assembly on 17 October 1963,
Taking account of United Nations General Assembly resolution 110 (II) of 3 November 1947, which condemned propaganda designed or likely to provoke or encourage any threat to the peace, breach of the peace or act

---

*Officially entitled the Treaty on Principles Governing the Activities of States in the Exploration and Use of Outer Space Including the Moon and Other Celestial Bodies. Done at Washington, London, and Moscow on January 27, 1967. Entered into force on October 10, 1967.

The 98 parties to the treaty are: Afghanistan, Antigua & Barbuda, Argentina, Australia, Austria, The Bahamas, Bangladesh, Barbados, Belgium, Benin, Brazil, Brunei, Bulgaria, Burkina Faso, Burma, Byelorussian SSR, Canada, Chile, China, Cuba, Cyprus, Czechoslovakia, Denmark, Dominica, Dominican Republic, Ecuador, Egypt, El Salvador, Fiji, Finland, France, German Democratic Republic, Germany (Federal Republic), Greece, Grenada, Guinea-Bissau, Hungary, Iceland, India, Iraq, Ireland, Israel, Italy, Jamaica, Japan, Kenya, Korea, Kuwait, Laos, Lebanon, Libya, Madagascar, Mali, Mauritius, Mexico, Mongolia, Morocco, Nepal, Netherlands, New Zealand, Niger, Nigeria, Norway, Pakistan, Papua New Guinea, Peru, Poland, Romania, Saint Kitts & Nevis, Saint Lucia, San Marino, Saudi Arabia, Seychelles, Sierra Leone, Singapore, Solomon Islands, South Africa, Spain, Sri Lanka, Swaziland, Sweden, Switzerland, Syrian Arab Republic, Thailand, Tonga, Tunisia, Turkey, Uganda, Ukrainian SSR, Union of Soviet Socialist Republics, United Kingdom, United States, Uruguay, Venezuela, Vietnam (Socialist Republic), Yemen (Aden), and Zambia.

of aggression, and considering that the aforementioned resolution is applicable to outer space,

Convinced that a Treaty on Principles Governing the Activities of States in the Exploration and Use of Outer Space, including the Moon and Other Celestial Bodies, will further the Purposes and Principles of the Charter of the United Nations,

Have agreed on the following:

Article I

The exploration and use of outer space, including the moon and other celestial bodies, shall be carried out for the benefit and in the interests of all countries, irrespective of their degree of economic or scientific development, and shall be the province of all mankind.

Outer space, including the moon and other celestial bodies, shall be free for exploration and use by all States without discrimination of any kind, on a basis of equality and in accordance with international law, and there shall be free access to all areas of celestial bodies.

There shall be freedom of scientific investigation in outer space, including the moon and other celestial bodies, and States shall facilitate and encourage international co-operation in such investigation.

Article II

Outer space, including the moon and other celestial bodies, is not subject to national appropriation by claim of sovereignty, by means of use or occupation, or by any other means.

Article III

States Parties to the Treaty shall carry on activities in the exploration and use of outer space, including the moon and other celestial bodies, in accordance with international law, including the Charter of the United Nations, in the interest of maintaining international peace and security and promoting international co-operation and understanding.

Article IV

States Parties to the Treaty undertake not to place in orbit around the earth any objects carrying nuclear weapons or any other kinds of weapons of mass destruction, instal such weapons on celestial bodies, or station such weapons in outer space in any other manner.

The moon and other celestial bodies shall be used by all States Parties to the Treaty exclusively for peaceful purposes. The establishment of military bases, installations and fortifications, the testing of any type of weapons and the conduct of military manœuvres on celestial bodies shall be forbidden. The use of military personnel for scientific research or for any other peaceful purposes shall not be prohibited. The use of any equipment or facility necessary for peaceful exploration of the moon and other celestial bodies shall also not be prohibited.

Article V

States Parties to the Treaty shall regard astronauts as envoys of mankind in outer space and shall render to them all possible assistance in the event of accident, distress, or emergency landing on the territory of another State Party or on the high seas. When astronauts make such a landing, they shall be safely and promptly returned to the State of registry of their space vehicle.

In carrying on activities in outer space and on celestial bodies, the astronauts of one State Party shall render all possible assistance to the astronauts of other States Parties.

States Parties to the Treaty shall immediately inform the other States Parties to the Treaty or the Secretary-General of the United Nations of any phenomena they discover in outer space, including the moon and other celestial bodies, which could constitute a danger to the life or health of astronauts.

Article VI

States Parties to the Treaty shall bear international responsibility for national activities in outer space, including the moon and other celestial bodies, whether such activities are carried on by governmental agencies or by non-governmental entities, and for assuring that national activities are carried out in conformity with the provisions set forth in the present Treaty. The activities of non-governmental entities in outer space, including the moon and other celestial bodies, shall require authorization and continuing supervision by the appropriate State Party to the Treaty. When activities are carried on in outer space, including the moon and other celestial bodies, by an international organization, responsibility for compliance with this Treaty shall be borne both by the international organization and by the States Parties to the Treaty participating in such organization.

Article VII

Each State Party to the Treaty that launches or procures the launching of an object into outer space, including the moon and other celestial bodies, and each State Party from whose territory or facility an object is launched, is internationally liable for damage to another State Party to the Treaty or to its natural or juridical persons by such object or its component parts on the Earth, in air space or in outer space, including the moon and other celestial bodies.

Article VIII

A State Party to the Treaty on whose registry an object launched into outer space is carried shall retain jurisdiction and control over such object, and over any personnel thereof, while in outer space or on a celestial body. Ownership of objects launched into outer space, including objects landed or constructed on a celestial body, and of their component parts, is not affected by their presence in outer space or on a celestial body or by their return to the Earth. Such objects or component parts found beyond the limits of the State Party to the Treaty on whose registry they are carried shall be returned to that State Party, which shall, upon request, furnish identifying data prior to their return.

Article IX

In the exploration and use of outer space, including the moon and other celestial bodies, States Parties to the Treaty shall be guided by the principle of co-operation and mutual assistance and shall conduct all their activities in outer space, including the moon and other celestial bodies, with due regard to the corresponding interests of all other States Parties to the Treaty. States Parties to the Treaty shall pursue studies of outer space, including the moon and other celestial bodies, and conduct exploration of them so as to avoid their harmful contamination and also adverse changes in the environment of the Earth resulting from the introduction of extraterrestrial matter and, where necessary, shall adopt appropriate measures for this purpose. If a State Party to the Treaty has reason to believe that an activity or experiment planned by it or its nationals in outer space, including the moon and other celestial bodies, would cause potentially harmful interference with activities of other States Parties in the peaceful exploration and use of outer space, including the moon and other celestial bodies, it shall undertake appropriate international consultations before proceeding with any such activity or experiment. A State Party to the Treaty which has reason to believe that an activity or experiment planned by another State Party in outer space, including the moon and other celestial bodies, would cause potentially harmful interference with activities in the peaceful exploration and use of outer space, including the moon and other celestial bodies, may request consultation concerning the activity or experiment.

Article X

In order to promote international co-operation in the exploration and use of outer space, including the moon and other celestial bodies, in conformity with the purposes of this Treaty, the States Parties to the Treaty shall consider on a basis of equality any requests by other States Parties to the Treaty to be afforded an opportunity to observe the flight of space objects launched by those States.

The nature of such an opportunity for observation and the conditions under which it could be afforded shall be determined by agreement between the States concerned.

Article XI

In order to promote international co-operation in the peaceful exploration and use of outer space, States Parties to the Treaty conducting activities in outer space, including the moon and other celestial bodies, agree to inform the Secretary-General of the United Nations as well as the public and the international scientific community, to the greatest extent feasible and practicable, of the nature, conduct, locations and results of such activities. On receiving the said information, the Secretary-General of the United Nations should be prepared to disseminate it immediately and effectively.

Article XII

All stations, installations, equipment and space vehicles on the moon and other celestial bodies shall be open to representatives of other States Parties to the Treaty on a basis of reciprocity. Such representatives shall give reasonable advance notice of a projected visit, in order that appropriate consultations may be held and that maximum precautions may be taken to assure safety and to avoid interference with normal operations in the facility to be visited.

Article XIII

The provisions of this Treaty shall apply to the activities of States Parties to the Treaty in the exploration and use of outer space, including the moon and other celestial bodies, whether such activities are carried on by a single State Party to the Treaty or jointly with other States, including cases where they are carried on within the framework of international inter-governmental organizations.

Any practical questions arising in connexion with activities carried on by international inter-governmental organizations in the exploration and use of outer space, including the moon and other celestial bodies, shall be resolved by the States Parties to the Treaty either with the appropriate international organization or with one or more States members of that international organization, which are Parties to this Treaty. . . .

11

International Environmental Law

STOCKHOLM DECLARATION, OR THE DECLARATION OF THE UNITED NATIONS CONFERENCE ON THE HUMAN ENVIRONMENT

June 16, 1972, U.N. Doc. A/CONF. 48/14, 11 I.L.M. 1416 (1972)[*]

The United Nations Conference on the Human Environment,
Having met at Stockholm from 5 to 16 June 1972,
Having considered the need for a common outlook and for common principles to inspire and guide the peoples of the world in the preservation and enhancement of the human environment, . . .

II. Principles

States the common conviction that:

Principle 1

Man has the fundamental right to freedom, equality and adequate conditions of life, in an environment of a quality that permits a life of dignity and well-being, and he bears a solemn responsibility to protect and improve the environment for present and future generations. In this respect, policies promoting or perpetuating *apartheid,* racial segregation, discrimination, colonial and other forms of oppression and foreign domination stand condemned and must be eliminated.

---

[*]More formally known as the Report of the U.N. Conference on the Human Environment, from the U.N. Conference in Stockholm, Sweden, June 5-16, 1972.

Principle 2

The natural resources of the earth including the air, water, land, flora and fauna and especially representative samples of natural ecosystems must be safeguarded for the benefit of present and future generations through careful planning or management, as appropriate.

Principle 3

The capacity of the earth to produce vital renewable resources must be maintained and, wherever practicable, restored or improved.

Principle 4

Man has a special responsibility to safeguard and wisely manage the heritage of wildlife and its habitat which are now gravely imperilled by a combination of adverse factors. Nature conservation including wildlife must therefore receive importance in planning for economic development.

Principle 5

The non-renewable resources of the earth must be employed in such a way as to guard against the danger of their future exhaustion and to ensure that benefits from such employment are shared by all mankind.

Principle 6

The discharge of toxic substances or of other substances and the release of heat, in such quantities or concentrations as to exceed the capacity of the environment to render them harmless, must be halted in order to ensure that serious or irreversible damage is not inflicted upon ecosystems. The just struggle of the peoples of all countries against pollution should be supported.

Principle 7

States shall take all possible steps to prevent pollution of the seas by substances that are liable to create hazards to human health, to harm living resources and marine life, to damage amenities or to interfere with other legitimate uses of the sea.

Principle 8

Economic and social development is essential for ensuring a favourable living and working environment for man and for creating conditions on earth that are necessary for the improvement of the quality of life.

Principle 9

Environmental deficiencies generated by the conditions of underdevelopment and natural disasters pose grave problems and can best be remedied by accelerated development through the transfer of substantial quantities of financial and technological assistance as a supplement to the domestic effort of the developing countries and such timely assistance as may be required.

Principle 10

For the developing countries, stability of prices and adequate earnings for primary commodities and raw material are essential to environmental management since economic factors as well as ecological processes must be taken into account.

Principle 11

The environmental policies of all States should enhance and not adversely affect the present or future development potential of developing countries, nor should they hamper the attainment of better living conditions for all, and appropriate steps should be taken by States and international organizations with a view to reaching agreement on meeting the possible national and international economic consequences resulting from the application of environmental measures.

Principle 12

Resources should be made available to preserve and improve the environment, taking into account the circumstances and particular requirements of developing countries and any costs which may emanate from their incorporating environmental safeguards into their development planning and the need for making available to them, upon their request, additional international technical and financial assistance for this purpose.

Principle 13

In order to achieve a more rational management of resources and thus to improve the environment, States should adopt an integrated and coordinated approach to their development planning so as to ensure that development is compatible with the need to protect and improve the human environment for the benefit of their population.

Principle 14

Rational planning constitutes an essential tool for reconciling any conflict between the needs of development and the need to protect and improve the environment.

Principle 15

Planning must be applied to human settlements and urbanization with a view to avoiding adverse effects on the environment and obtaining maximum social, economic and environmental benefits for all. In this respect projects which are designed for colonialist and racist domination must be abandoned.

Principle 16

Demographic policies, which are without prejudice to basic human rights and which are deemed appropriate by Governments concerned, should be applied in those regions where the rate of population growth or excessive population concentrations are likely to have adverse effects on the environment or development, or where low population density may prevent improvement of the human environment and impede development.

Principle 17

Appropriate national institutions must be entrusted with the task of planning, managing or controlling the environmental resources of States with the view to enhancing environmental quality.

Principle 18

Science and technology, as part of their contribution to economic and social development, must be applied to the identification, avoidance and control of environmental risks and the solution of environmental problems and for the common good of mankind.

Principle 19

Education in environmental matters, for the younger generation as well as adults, giving due consideration to the underprivileged, is essential in order to broaden the basis for an enlightened opinion and responsible conduct by individuals, enterprises and communities in protecting and improving the environment in its full human dimension. It is also essential that mass media of communications avoid contributing to the deterioration of the environment, but, on the contrary, disseminate information of an educational nature, on the need to protect and improve the environment in order to enable man to develop in every respect.

Principle 20

Scientific research and development in the context of environmental problems, both national and multinational, must be promoted in all countries, especially the developing countries. In this connexion, the free flow of up-to-date scientific information and transfer of experience must be supported and assisted, to facilitate the solution of environmental problems; environmental technologies should be made available to developing countries on terms which would encourage their wide dissemination without constituting an economic burden on the developing countries.

Principle 21

States have, in accordance with the Charter of the United Nations and the principle of international law, the sovereign right to exploit their own resources pursuant to their own environmental policies, and the responsibility to ensure that activities within their jurisdiction or control do not cause damage to the environment of other States or of areas beyond the limits of national jurisdiction.

Principle 22

States shall co-operate to develop further the international law regarding liability and compensation for the victims of pollution and other environmental damage caused by activities within the jurisdiction or control of such States to areas beyond their jurisdiction.

Principle 23

Without prejudice to such criteria as may be agreed upon by the international community, or to standards which will have to be determined nationally, it will be essential in all cases to consider the systems of values prevailing in each country and the extent of the applicability of standards which are valid for the most advanced countries but which may be inappropriate and of unwarranted social cost for the developing countries.

Principle 24

International matters concerning the protection and improvement of the environment should be handled in a co-operative spirit by all countries, big or small, on an equal footing. Co-operation through multilateral or bilateral arrangements or other appropriate means is essential to effectively control, prevent, reduce and eliminate adverse environmental effects resulting from activities conducted in all spheres, in such a way that due account is taken of the sovereignty and interests of all States.

Principle 25

States shall ensure that international organizations play a co-ordinated, efficient and dynamic role for the protection and improvement of the environment.

Principle 26

Man and his environment must be spared the effects of nuclear weapons and all other means of mass destruction. States must strive to reach prompt agreement, in the relevant international organs, on the elimination and complete destruction of such weapons. . . .

VIENNA CONVENTION FOR THE PROTECTION OF THE OZONE LAYER

March 22, 1985, — U.S.T. — , T.I.A.S. No. — , 26 I.L.M. 1516 (1987)*

Preamble

The Parties to this Convention,

Aware of the potentially harmful impact on human health and the environment through modification of the ozone layer,

Recalling the pertinent provisions of the Declaration of the United Nations Conference on the Human Environment, and in particular principle 21, which provides that "States have, in accordance with the Charter of the United Nations and the principles of international law, the sovereign right to exploit their own resources pursuant to their own environmental policies, and the responsibility to ensure that activities within their jurisdiction or control do not cause damage to the environment of other States or of areas beyond the limits of national jurisdiction",

Taking into account the circumstances and particular requirements of developing countries,

Mindful of the work and studies proceeding within both international and national organizations and, in particular, of the World Plan of Action on the Ozone Layer of the United Nations Environment Programme,

Mindful also of the precautionary measures for the protection of the ozone layer which have already been taken at the national and international levels,

Aware that measures to protect the ozone layer from modifications due to human activities require international co-operation and action, and should be based on relevant scientific and technical considerations,

Aware also of the need for further research and systematic observations to further develop scientific knowledge of the ozone layer and possible adverse effects resulting from its modification,

---

*Done at Vienna on March 22, 1985. Entered into force on September 22, 1988. The United States ratified the convention on August 27, 1986.

The 60 parties to the convention are: Australia, Austria, Belgium, Burkina Faso, Byelorussian S.S.R., Cameroon, Canada, Chad, China, Denmark, Egypt, Equatorial Guinea, European Economic Community, Fiji, Finland, France, German Democratic Republic, Germany (Federal Republic), Ghana, Greece, Guatemala, Hungary, Iceland, Ireland, Italy, Jordan, Japan, Kenya, Liechtenstein, Luxembourg, Malaysia, Maldives, Malta, Mexico, Netherlands, New Zealand, Nigeria, Norway, Panama, Peru, Portugal, Singapore, South Africa, Spain, Sri Lanka, Sweden, Switzerland, Syria, Thailand, Trinidad & Tobago, Tunisia, Uganda, Ukrainian S.S.R., Union of Soviet Socialist Republics, United Arab Emirates, United Kingdom, United States, Uruguay, Venezuela, and Zambia.

Determined to protect human health and the environment against adverse effects resulting from modifications of the ozone layer,
HAVE AGREED AS FOLLOWS:

Article 1. Definitions

For the purposes of this Convention:

1. "The ozone layer" means the layer of atmospheric ozone above the planetary boundary layer.

2. "Adverse effects" means changes in the physical environment or biota, including changes in climate, which have significant deleterious effects on human health or on the composition, resilience and productivity of natural and managed ecosystems, or on materials useful to mankind.

3. "Alternative technologies or equipment" means technologies or equipment the use of which makes it possible to reduce or effectively eliminate emissions of substances which have or are likely to have adverse effects on the ozone layer.

4. "Alternative substances" means substances which reduce, eliminate or avoid adverse effects on the ozone layer.

5. "Parties" means, unless the text otherwise indicates, Parties to this Convention.

6. "Regional economic integration organization" means an organization constituted by sovereign States of a given region which has competence in respect of matters governed by this Convention or its protocols and has been duly authorized, in accordance with its internal procedures, to sign, ratify, accept, approve or accede to the instruments concerned.

7. "Protocols" means protocols to this Convention.

Article 2. General Obligations

1. The Parties shall take appropriate measures in accordance with the provisions of this Convention and of those protocols in force to which they are party to protect human health and the environment against adverse effects resulting or likely to result from human activities which modify or are likely to modify the ozone layer.

2. To this end the Parties shall, in accordance with the means at their disposal and their capabilities:

(a) Co-operate by means of systematic observations, research and information exchange in order to better understand and assess the effects of human activities on the ozone layer and the effects on human health and the environment from modification of the ozone layer;

(b) Adopt appropriate legislative or administrative measures and co-operate in harmonizing appropriate policies to control, limit, reduce or prevent human activities under their jurisdiction or control should it be found that these activities have or are likely to have adverse effects resulting from modification or likely modification of the ozone layer;

(c) Co-operate in the formulation of agreed measures, procedures and standards for the implementation of this Convention, with a view to the adoption of protocols and annexes;

(d) Co-operate with competent international bodies to implement effectively this Convention and protocols to which they are party.

3. The provisions of this Convention shall in no way affect the right of Parties to adopt, in accordance with international law, domestic measures additional to those referred to in paragraphs 1 and 2 above, nor shall they affect additional domestic measures already taken by a Party, provided that these measures are not incompatible with their obligations under this Convention.

4. The application of this article shall be based on relevant scientific and technical considerations.

Article 3. Research and Systematic Observations

1. The Parties undertake, as appropriate, to initiate and co-operate in, directly or through competent international bodies, the conduct of research and scientific assessments on:

(a) The physical and chemical processes that may affect the ozone layer;

(b) The human health and other biological effects deriving from any modifications of the ozone layer, particularly those resulting from changes in ultra-violet solar radiation having biological effects (UV-B);

(c) Climatic effects deriving from any modifications of the ozone layer;

(d) Effects deriving from any modifications of the ozone layer and any consequent change in UV-B radiation on natural and synthetic materials useful to mankind;

(e) Substances, practices, processes and activities that may affect the ozone layer, and their cumulative effects;

(f) Alternative substances and technologies;

(g) Related socio-economic matters;

and as further elaborated in annexes I and II.

2. The Parties undertake to promote or establish, as appropriate, directly or through competent international bodies and taking fully into account national legislation and relevant ongoing activities at both the national and international levels, joint or complementary programmes for systematic observation of the state of the ozone layer and other relevant parameters, as elaborated in annex I.

3. The Parties undertake to co-operate, directly or through competent international bodies, in ensuring the collection, validation and transmission of research and observational data through appropriate world data centres in a regular and timely fashion.

Article 4. Co-operation in the Legal, Scientific and Technical Fields

1. The Parties shall facilitate and encourage the exchange of scientific, technical, socio-economic, commercial and legal information relevant to this Convention as further elaborated in annex II. Such information shall be supplied to bodies agreed upon by the Parties. Any such body receiving information regarded as confidential by the supplying Party shall ensure that such information is not disclosed and shall aggregate it to protect its confidentiality before it is made available to all Parties.

2. The Parties shall co-operate, consistent with their national laws,

regulations and practices and taking into account in particular the needs of the developing countries, in promoting, directly or through competent international bodies, the development and transfer of technology and knowledge. Such co-operation shall be carried out particularly through:

(a) Facilitation of the acquisition of alternative technologies by other Parties;

(b) Provision of information on alternative technologies and equipment, and supply of special manuals or guides to them;

(c) The supply of necessary equipment and facilities for research and systematic observations;

(d) Appropriate training of scientific and technical personnel.

Article 5. Transmission of Information

The Parties shall transmit, through the secretariat, to the Conference of the Parties established under article 6 information on the measures adopted by them in implementation of this Convention and of protocols to which they are party in such form and at such intervals as the meetings of the parties to the relevant instruments may determine.

Article 6. Conference of the Parties

1. A Conference of the Parties is hereby established. The first meeting of the Conference of the Parties shall be convened by the secretariat designated on an interim basis under article 7 not later than one year after entry into force of this Convention. Thereafter, ordinary meetings of the Conference of the Parties shall be held at regular intervals to be determined by the Conference at its first meeting.

2. Extraordinary meetings of the Conference of the Parties shall be held at such other times as may be deemed necessary by the Conference, or at the written request of any Party, provided that, within six months of the request being communicated to them by the secretariat, it is supported by at least one third of the Parties.

3. The Conference of the Parties shall by consensus agree upon and adopt rules of procedure and financial rules for itself and for any subsidiary bodies it may establish, as well as financial provisions governing the functioning of the secretariat.

4. The Conference of the Parties shall keep under continuous review the implementation of this Convention, and, in addition, shall:

(a) Establish the form and the intervals for transmitting the information to be submitted in accordance with article 5 and consider such information as well as reports submitted by any subsidiary body;

(b) Review the scientific information on the ozone layer, on its possible modification and on possible effects of any such modification;

(c) Promote, in accordance with article 2, the harmonization of appropriate policies, strategies and measures for minimizing the release of substances causing or likely to cause modification of the ozone layer, and make recommendations on any other measures relating to this Convention;

(d) Adopt, in accordance with articles 3 and 4, programmes for research, systematic observations, scientific and technological co-operation, the exchange of information and the transfer of technology and knowledge;

(e) Consider and adopt, as required, in accordance with articles 9 and 10, amendments to this Convention and its annexes;

(f) Consider amendments to any protocol, as well as to any annexes thereto, and, if so decided, recommend their adoption to the parties to the protocol concerned;

(g) Consider and adopt, as required, in accordance with article 10, additional annexes to this Convention;

(h) Consider and adopt, as required, protocols in accordance with article 8;

(i) Establish such subsidiary bodies as are deemed necessary for the implementation of this Convention;

(j) Seek, where appropriate, the services of competent international bodies and scientific committees, in particular the World Meteorological Organization and the World Health Organization, as well as the Co-ordinating Committee on the Ozone Layer, in scientific research, systematic observations and other activities pertinent to the objectives of this Convention, and make use as appropriate of information from these bodies and committees;

(k) Consider and undertake any additional action that may be required for the achievement of the purposes of this Convention.

5. The United Nations, its specialized agencies and the International Atomic Energy Agency, as well as any State not party to this Convention, may be represented at meetings of the Conference of the Parties by observers. Any body or agency, whether national or international, governmental or non-governmental, qualified in fields relating to the protection of the ozone layer which has informed the secretariat of its wish to be represented at a meeting of the Conference of the Parties as an observer may be admitted unless at least one-third of the Parties present object. The admission and participation of observers shall be subject to the rules of procedure adopted by the Conference of the Parties.

Article 7. *Secretariat*

1. The functions of the secretariat shall be:

(a) To arrange for and service meetings provided for in articles 6, 8, 9 and 10;

(b) To prepare and transmit reports based upon information received in accordance with articles 4 and 5, as well as upon information derived from meetings of subsidiary bodies established under article 6;

(c) To perform the functions assigned to it by any protocol;

(d) To prepare reports on its activities carried out in implementation of its functions under this Convention and present them to the Conference of the Parties;

(e) To ensure the necessary co-ordination with other relevant international bodies, and in particular to enter into such administrative and contractual arrangements as may be required for the effective discharge of its functions;

(f) To perform such other functions as may be determined by the Conference of the Parties.

2. The secretariat functions will be carried out on an interim basis by the United Nations Environment Programme until the completion of the first ordinary meeting of the Conference of the Parties held pursuant to article 6. At its first ordinary meeting, the Conference of the Parties shall designate the secretariat from amongst those existing competent international organizations which have signified their willingness to carry out the secretariat functions under this Convention.

Article 8. Adoption of Protocols

1. The Conference of the Parties may at a meeting adopt protocols pursuant to article 2.

2. The text of any proposed protocol shall be communicated to the Parties by the secretariat at least six months before such a meeting.

Article 9. Amendment of the Convention or Protocols

1. Any Party may propose amendments to this Convention or to any protocol. Such amendments shall take due account, *inter alia,* of relevant scientific and technical considerations.

2. Amendments to this Convention shall be adopted at a meeting of the Conference of the Parties. Amendments to any protocol shall be adopted at a meeting of the Parties to the protocol in question. The text of any proposed amendment to this Convention or to any protocol, except as may otherwise be provided in such protocol, shall be communicated to the Parties by the secretariat at least six months before the meeting at which it is proposed for adoption. The secretariat shall also communicate proposed amendments to the signatories to this Convention for information.

3. The Parties shall make every effort to reach agreement on any proposed amendment to this Convention by consensus. If all efforts at consensus have been exhausted, and no agreement reached, the amendment shall as a last resort be adopted by a three-fourths majority vote of the Parties present and voting at the meeting, and shall be submitted by the Depositary to all Parties for ratification, approval or acceptance.

4. The procedure mentioned in paragraph 3 above shall apply to amendments to any protocol, except that a two-thirds majority of the parties to that protocol present and voting at the meeting shall suffice for their adoption.

5. Ratification, approval or acceptance of amendments shall be notified to the Depositary in writing. Amendments adopted in accordance with paragraphs 3 or 4 above shall enter into force between parties having accepted them on the ninetieth day after the receipt by the Depositary of notification of their ratification, approval or acceptance by at least three-fourths of the Parties to this Convention or by at least two-thirds of the parties to the protocol concerned, except as may otherwise be provided in such protocol. Thereafter the amendments shall enter into force for any other Party on the ninetieth day after that Party deposits its instrument of ratification, approval or acceptance of the amendments.

6. For the purposes of this article, "Parties present and voting" means Parties present and casting an affirmative or negative vote.

Article 10. Adoption and Amendment of Annexes

1. The annexes to this Convention or to any protocol shall form an integral part of this Convention or of such protocol, as the case may be, and, unless expressly provided otherwise, a reference to this Convention or its protocols constitutes at the same time a reference to any annexes thereto. Such annexes shall be restricted to scientific, technical and administrative matters.

2. Except as may be otherwise provided in any protocol with respect to its annexes, the following procedure shall apply to the proposal, adoption and entry into force of additional annexes to this Convention or of annexes to a protocol:

(a) Annexes to this Convention shall be proposed and adopted according to the procedure laid down in article 9, paragraphs 2 and 3, while annexes to any protocol shall be proposed and adopted according to the procedure laid down in article 9, paragraphs 2 and 4;

(b) Any party that is unable to approve an additional annex to this Convention or an annex to any protocol to which it is party shall so notify the Depositary, in writing, within six months from the date of the communication of the adoption by the Depositary. The Depositary shall without delay notify all Parties of any such notification received. A Party may at any time substitute an acceptance for a previous declaration of objection and the annexes shall thereupon enter into force for that Party;

(c) On the expiry of six months from the date of the circulation of the communication by the Depositary, the annex shall become effective for all Parties to this Convention or to any protocol concerned which have not submitted a notification in accordance with the provision of subparagraph (b) above.

3. The proposal, adoption and entry into force of amendments to annexes to this Convention or to any protocol shall be subject to the same procedure as for the proposal, adoption and entry into force of annexes to the Convention or annexes to a protocol. Annexes and amendments thereto shall take due account, *inter alia,* of relevant scientific and technical considerations.

4. If an additional annex or an amendment to an annex involves an amendment to this Convention or to any protocol, the additional annex or amended annex shall not enter into force until such time as the amendment to this Convention or to the protocol concerned enters into force.

Article 11. Settlement of Disputes

1. In the event of a dispute between Parties concerning the interpretation or application of this Convention, the parties concerned shall seek solution by negotiation.

2. If the parties concerned cannot reach agreement by negotiation, they may jointly seek the good offices of, or request mediation by, a third party.

3. When ratifying, accepting, approving or acceding to this Convention, or at any time thereafter, a State or regional economic integration organization may declare in writing to the Depositary that for a dispute not resolved in accordance with paragraph 1 or paragraph 2 above, it accepts one or both of the following means of dispute settlement as compulsory:

(a) Arbitration in accordance with procedures to be adopted by the Conference of the Parties at its first ordinary meeting;

(b) Submission of the dispute to the International Court of Justice.

4. If the parties have not, in accordance with paragraph 3 above, accepted the same or any procedure, the dispute shall be submitted to conciliation in accordance with paragraph 5 below unless the parties otherwise agree.

5. A conciliation commission shall be created upon the request of one of the parties to the dispute. The commission shall be composed of an equal number of members appointed by each party concerned and a chairman chosen jointly by the members appointed by each party. The commission shall render a final and recommendatory award, which the parties shall consider in good faith.

6. The provisions of this article shall apply with respect to any protocol except as otherwise provided in the protocol concerned. . . .

Article 15. Right to Vote

1. Each Party to this Convention or to any protocol shall have one vote.

2. Except as provided for in paragraph 1 above, regional economic intergration organizations, in matters within their competence, shall exercise their right to vote with a number of votes equal to the number of their member States which are Parties to the Convention or the relevant protocol. Such organizations shall not exercise their right to vote if their member States exercise theirs, and vice versa. . . .

Article 18. Reservations

No reservations may be made to this Convention. . . .

Annex I. Research and Systematic Observations

1. The Parties to the Convention recognize that the major scientific issues are:

(a) Modification of the ozone layer which would result in a change in the amount of solar ultra-violet radiation having biological effects (UV-B) that reaches the Earth's surface and the potential consequences for human health, for organisms, ecosystems and materials useful to mankind;

(b) Modification of the vertical distribution of ozone, which could change the temperature structure of the atmosphere and the potential consequences for weather and climate.

2. The Parties to the Convention, in accordance with article 3, shall co-operate in conducting research and systematic observations and in formulating recommendations for future research and observation in such areas as:

(a) *Research into the physics and chemistry of the atmosphere* . . .
(b) *Research into health, biological and photodegradation effects* . . .
(c) *Research on effects on climate* . . .
(d) *Systematic observations on:*

(i) The status of the ozone layer (i.e. the spatial and temporal variability of the total column content and vertical distribution) by making the

Global Ozone Observing System, based on the integration of satellite and ground-based systems, fully operational; . . .

4. The following chemical substances of natural and anthropogenic origin, not listed in order of priority, are thought to have the potential to modify the chemical and physical properties of the ozone layer.

(a) Carbon substances

(i) *Carbon monoxide (CO)*

Carbon monoxide has significant natural and anthropogenic sources, and is thought to play a major direct role in tropospheric photochemistry, and an indirect role in stratospheric photochemistry.

(ii) *Carbon dioxide (CO_2)*

Carbon dioxide has significant natural and anthropogenic sources, and affects stratospheric ozone by influencing the thermal structure of the atmosphere.

(iii) *Methane (CH_4)*

Methane has both natural and anthropogenic sources, and affects both tropospheric and stratospheric ozone.

(iv) *Non-methane hydrocarbon species* . . .

(b) Nitrogen substances

(i) *Nitrous oxide (N_2O)*

The dominant sources of N_2O are natural, but anthropogenic contributions are becoming increasingly important. Nitrous oxide is the primary source of stratospheric NO_x, which play a vital role in controlling the abundance of stratospheric ozone.

(ii) *Nitrogen oxides (NO_x)*

Ground-level sources of NO_x play a major direct role only in tropospheric photochemical processes and an indirect role in stratosphere photochemistry, whereas injection of NO_x close to the tropopause may lead directly to a change in upper tropospheric and stratospheric ozone.

(c) Chlorine substances . . .

(d) Bromine substances . . .

(e) Hydrogen substances . . .

Annex II. Information Exchange

1. The Parties to the Convention recognize that the collection and sharing of information is an important means of implementing the objectives of this Convention and of assuring that any actions that may be taken are appropriate and equitable. Therefore, Parties shall exchange scientific, technical, socio-economic, business, commercial and legal information.

2. The Parties to the Convention, in deciding what information is to be collected and exchanged, should take into account the usefulness of the information and the costs of obtaining it. The Parties further recognize that co-operation under this annex has to be consistent with national laws, regulations and practices regarding patents, trade secrets, and protection of confidential and proprietary information. . . .

MONTREAL PROTOCOL ON SUBSTANCES THAT DEPLETE THE OZONE LAYER (1987)

September 16, 1987, 26 I.L.M. 1541 (1987), 52 Fed. Reg. 47,489, 47,515-47,519*

The Parties to this Protocol, . . .
[See with the 1990 changes at p. 731.]
Have agreed as follows:

Article 1. Definitions

For the purposes of this Protocol:
1. "Convention" means the Vienna Convention for the Protection of the Ozone Layer, adopted on 22 March 1985.
2. "Parties" means, unless the text otherwise indicates, Parties to this Protocol.
3. "Secretariat" means the secretariat of the Convention.
4. "Controlled substance" means a substance listed in Annex A to this Protocol, whether existing alone or in a mixture. It excludes, however, any such substance or mixture which is in a manufactured product other than a container used for the transportation or storage of the substance listed.
5. "Production" means the amount of controlled substances produced minus the amount destroyed by technologies to be approved by the Parties.
6. "Consumption" means production plus imports minus exports of controlled substances.
7. "Calculated levels" of production, imports, exports and consumption means levels determined in accordance with Article 3.
8. "Industrial rationalization" means the transfer of all or a portion of the calculated level of production of one Party to another, for the purpose of achieving economic efficiencies or responding to anticipated shortfalls in supply as a result of plant closures.

---

*Concluded at Montreal on September 16, 1987. Entered into force on January 1, 1989. The United States ratified the protocol on April 21, 1988.

The 57 parties to the protocol are: Australia, Austria, Belgium, Brazil, Burkina Faso, Byelorussian SSR, Cameroon, Canada, Chile, Denmark, Egypt, European Economic Community, Fiji, Finland, France, German Democratic Republic, Germany (Federal Republic), Ghana, Greece, Guatemala, Hungary, Iceland, Ireland, Italy, Japan, Jordan, Kenya, Liechtenstein, Luxembourg, Malaysia, Maldives, Malta, Mexico, Netherlands, New Zealand, Nigeria, Norway, Panama, Portugal, Singapore, South Africa, Spain, Sri Lanka, Sweden, Switzerland, Syria, Thailand, Trinidad & Tobago, Tunisia, Uganda, Ukrainian SSR, Union of Soviet Socialist Republics, United Arab Emirates, United Kingdom, United States, Venezuela, and Zambia.

Article 2. Control Measures

1. Each Party shall ensure that for the twelve-month period commencing on the first day of the seventh month following the date of the entry into force of this Protocol, and in each twelve-month period thereafter, its calculated level of consumption of the controlled substances in Group I of Annex A does not exceed its calculated level of consumption in 1986. By the end of the same period, each Party producing one or more of these substances shall ensure that its calculated level of production of the substances does not exceed its calculated level of production in 1986, except that such level may have increased by no more than ten per cent based on the 1986 level. Such increase shall be permitted only so as to satisfy the basic domestic needs of the Parties operating under Article 5 and for the purposes of industrial rationalization between Parties.

2. Each Party shall ensure that for the twelve-month period commencing on the first day of the thirty-seventh month following the date of the entry into force of this Protocol, and in each twelve month period thereafter, its calculated level of consumption of the controlled substances listed in Group II of Annex A does not exceed its calculated level of consumption in 1986. Each Party producing one or more of these substances shall ensure that its calculated level of production of the substances does not exceed its calculated level of production in 1986, except that such level may have increased by no more than ten per cent based on the 1986 level. Such increase shall be permitted only so as to satisfy the basic domestic needs of the Parties operating under Article 5 and for the purposes of industrial rationalization between Parties. The mechanisms for implementing these measures shall be decided by the Parties at their first meeting following the first scientific review.

3. Each Party shall ensure that for the period 1 July 1993 to 30 June 1994 and in each twelve-month period thereafter, its calculated level of consumption of the controlled substances in Group I of Annex A does not exceed, annually, eighty per cent of its calculated level of consumption in 1986. Each Party producing one or more of these substances shall, for the same periods, ensure that its calculated level of production of the substances does not exceed, annually, eighty per cent of its calculated level of production in 1986. However, in order to satisfy the basic domestic needs of the Parties operating under Article 5 and for the purposes of industrial rationalization between Parties, its calculated level of production may exceed that limit by up to ten per cent of its calculated level of production in 1986.

4. Each Party shall ensure that for the period 1 July 1998 to 30 June 1999, and in each twelve-month period thereafter, its calculated level of consumption of the controlled substances in Group I of Annex A does not exceed, annually, fifty per cent of its calculated level of consumption in 1986. Each Party producing one or more of these substances shall, for the same periods, ensure that its calculated level of production of the substances does not exceed, annually, fifty per cent of its calculated level of production in 1986. However, in order to satisfy the basic domestic needs of the Parties operating under Article 5 and for the purposes of industrial rationalization

between Parties, its calculated level of production may exceed that limit by up to fifteen per cent of its calculated level of production in 1986. This paragraph will apply unless the Parties decide otherwise at a meeting by a two-thirds majority of Parties present and voting, representing at least two-thirds of the total calculated level of consumption of these substances of the Parties. This decision shall be considered and made in the light of the assessments referred to in Article 6.

5. Any Party whose calculated level of production in 1986 of the controlled substances in Group I of Annex A was less than twenty-five kilotonnes may, for the purposes of industrial rationalization, transfer to or receive from any other Party, production in excess of the limits set out in paragraphs 1, 3 and 4 provided that the total combined calculated levels of production of the Parties concerned does not exceed the production limits set out in this Article. Any transfer of such production shall be notified to the secretariat, no later than the time of the transfer.

6. Any Party not operating under Article 5, that has facilities for the production of controlled substances under construction, or contracted for, prior to 16 September 1987, and provided for in national legislation prior to 1 January 1987, may add the production from such facilities to its 1986 production of such substances for the purposes of determining its calculated level of production for 1986, provided that such facilities are completed by 31 December 1990 and that such production does not raise that Party's annual calculated level of consumption of the controlled substances above 0.5 kilograms per capita.

7. Any transfer of production pursuant to paragraph 5 or any addition of production pursuant to paragraph 6 shall be notified to the secretariat, no later than the time of the transfer or addition.

8. (a) Any Parties which are Member States of a regional economic integration organization as defined in Article 1(6) of the Convention may agree that they shall jointly fulfil their obligations respecting consumption under this Article provided that their total combined calculated level of consumption does not exceed the levels required by this Article.

(b) The Parties to any such agreement shall inform the secretariat of the terms of the agreement before the date of the reduction in consumption with which the agreement is concerned.

(c) Such agreement will become operative only if all Member States of the regional economic integration organization and the organization concerned are Parties to the Protocol and have notified the secretariat of their manner of implementation.

9. (a) Based on the assessments made pursuant to Article 6, the Parties may decide whether:

(i) adjustments to the ozone depleting potentials specified in Annex A should be made and, if so, what the adjustments should be; and

(ii) further adjustments and reductions of production or consumption of the controlled substances from 1986 levels should be undertaken and, if so, what the scope, amount and timing of any such adjustments and reductions should be.

(b) Proposals for such adjustments shall be communicated to the Parties by the secretariat at least six months before the meeting of the Parties at which they are proposed for adoption.

(c) In taking such decisions, the Parties shall make every effort to reach agreement by consensus. If all efforts at consensus have been exhausted, and no agreement reached, such decisions shall, as a last resort, be adopted by a two-thirds majority vote of the Parties present and voting representing at least fifty per cent of the total consumption of the controlled substances of the Parties.

(d) The decisions, which shall be binding on all Parties, shall forthwith be communicated to the Parties by the Depositary. Unless otherwise provided in the decisions, they shall enter into force on the expiry of six months from the date of the circulation of the communication by the Depositary.

10. (a) Based on the assessments made pursuant to Article 6 of this Protocol and in accordance with the procedure set out in Article 9 of the Convention, the Parties may decide:

(i) whether any substances, and if so which, should be added to or removed from any annex to this Protocol; and

(ii) the mechanism, scope and timing of the control measures that should apply to those substances;

(b) Any such decision shall become effective, provided that it has been accepted by a two-thirds majority vote of the Parties present and voting.

11. Notwithstanding the provisions contained in this Article, Parties may take more stringent measures than those required by this Article.

Article 3. *Calculation of Control Levels*

For the purposes of Articles 2 and 5, each Party shall, for each Group of substances in Annex A, determine its calculated levels of:

(a) production by:

(i) multiplying its annual production of each controlled substance by the ozone depleting potential specified in respect of it in Annex A; and

(ii) adding together, for each such Group, the resulting figures;

(b) imports and exports, respectively, by following, *mutatis mutandis,* the procedure set out in subparagraph (a); and

(c) consumption by adding together its calculated levels of production and imports and subtracting its calculated level of exports as determined in accordance with subparagraphs (a) and (b). However, beginning on 1 January 1993, any export of controlled substances to non-Parties shall not be subtracted in calculating the consumption level of the exporting Party.

Article 4. *Control of Trade with Non-Parties*

1. Within one year of the entry into force of this Protocol, each Party shall ban the import of controlled substances from any State not party to this Protocol.

2. Beginning on 1 January 1993, no Party operating under paragraph

1 of Article 5 may export any controlled substance to any State not party to this Protocol.

3. Within three years of the date of the entry into force of this Protocol, the Parties shall, following the procedures in Article 10 of the Convention, elaborate in an annex a list of products containing controlled substances. Parties that have not objected to the annex in accordance with those procedures shall ban, within one year of the annex having become effective, the import of those products from any State not party to this Protocol.

4. Within five years of the entry into force of this Protocol, the Parties shall determine the feasibility of banning or restricting, from States not party to this Protocol, the import of products produced with, but not containing, controlled substances. If determined feasible, the Parties shall, following the procedures in Article 10 of the Convention, elaborate in an annex a list of such products. Parties that have not objected to it in accordance with those procedures shall ban or restrict, within one year of the annex having become effective, the import of those products from any State not party to this Protocol.

5. Each Party shall discourage the export, to any State not party to this Protocol, of technology for producing and for utilizing controlled substances.

6. Each Party shall refrain from providing new subsidies, aid, credits, guarantees or insurance programmes for the export to States not party to this Protocol of products, equipment, plants or technology that would facilitate the production of controlled substances.

7. Paragraphs 5 and 6 shall not apply to products, equipment, plants or technology that improve the containment, recovery, recycling or destruction of controlled substances, promote the development of alternative substances, or otherwise contribute to the reduction of emissions of controlled substances.

8. Notwithstanding the provisions of this Article, imports referred to in paragraphs 1, 3 and 4 may be permitted from any State not party to this Protocol if that State is determined, by a meeting of the Parties, to be in full compliance with Article 2 and this Article, and has submitted data to that effect as specified in Article 7.

Article 5. *Special Situation of Developing Countries*

1. Any Party that is a developing country and whose annual calculated level of consumption of the controlled substances is less than 0.3 kilograms per capita on the date of the entry into force of the Protocol for it, or any time thereafter within ten years of the date of entry into force of the Protocol shall, in order to meet its basic domestic needs, be entitled to delay its compliance with the control measures set out in paragraphs 1 to 4 of Article 2 by ten years after that specified in those paragraphs. However, such Party shall not exceed an annual calculated level of consumption of 0.3 kilograms per capita. Any such Party shall be entitled to use either the average of its annual calculated level of consumption for the period 1995 to 1997 inclusive or a calculated level of consumption of 0.3 kilograms per capita, whichever is the lower, as the basis for its compliance with the control measures.

2. The Parties undertake to facilitate access to environmentally safe alternative substances and technology for Parties that are developing countries and assist them to make expeditious use of such alternatives.

3. The Parties undertake to facilitate bilaterally or multilaterally the provision of subsidies, aid, credits, guarantees or insurance programmes to Parties that are developing countries for the use of alternative technology and for substitute products.

Article 6. Assessment and Review of Control Measures

Beginning in 1990, and at least every four years thereafter, the Parties shall assess the control measures provided for in Article 2 on the basis of available scientific, environmental, technical and economic information. At least one year before each assessment, the Parties shall convene appropriate panels of experts qualified in the fields mentioned and determine the composition and terms of reference of any such panels. Within one year of being convened, the panels will report their conclusions, through the secretariat, to the Parties.

Article 7. Reporting of Data

1. Each Party shall provide to the secretariat, within three months of becoming a Party, statistical data on its production, imports and exports of each of the controlled substances for the year 1986, or the best possible estimates of such data where actual data are not available.

2. Each Party shall provide statistical data to the secretariat on its annual production (with separate data on amounts destroyed by technologies to be approved by the Parties), imports, and exports to Parties and non-Parties, respectively, of such substances for the year during which it becomes a Party and for each year thereafter. It shall forward the data no later than nine months after the end of the year to which the data relate.

Article 8. Non-Compliance

The Parties, at their first meeting, shall consider and approve procedures and institutional mechanisms for determining non-compliance with the provisions of this Protocol and for treatment of Parties found to be in non-compliance.

Article 9. Research, Development, Public Awareness and Exchange of Information

1. The Parties shall co-operate, consistent with their national laws, regulations and practices and taking into account in particular the needs of developing countries, in promoting, directly or through competent international bodies, research, development and exchange of information on:

    (a) best technologies for improving the containment, recovery, recycling or destruction of controlled substances or otherwise reducing their emissions;

    (b) possible alternatives to controlled substances, to products containing such substances, and to products manufactured with them; and (c) costs and benefits of relevant control strategies.

2. The Parties, individually, jointly or through competent international bodies, shall co-operate in promoting public awareness of the environmental effects of the emissions of controlled substances and other substances that deplete the ozone layer.

3. Within two years of the entry into force of this Protocol and every two years thereafter, each Party shall submit to the secretariat a summary of the activities it has conducted pursuant to this Article.

Article 10. Technical Assistance

1. The Parties shall, in the context of the provisions of Article 4 of the Convention, and taking into account in particular the needs of developing countries, co-operate in promoting technical assistance to facilitate participation in and implementation of this Protocol.

2. Any Party or Signatory to this Protocol may submit a request to the secretariat for technical assistance for the purposes of implementing or participating in the Protocol.

3. The Parties, at their first meeting, shall begin deliberations on the means of fulfilling the obligations set out in Article 9, and paragraphs 1 and 2 of this Article, including the preparation of workplans. Such workplans shall pay special attention to the needs and circumstances of the developing countries. States and regional economic integration organizations not party to the Protocol should be encouraged to participate in activities specified in such workplans.

Article 11. Meetings of the Parties . . .

[See with the one change made in the 1990 document.]

Article 12. Secretariat . . .

[See the 1990 document. The article is not changed.]

Article 13. Financial Provisions . . .

[See the 1990 document. The article is not changed.]

Article 14. Relationship of This Protocol to the Convention

Except as otherwise provided in this Protocol, the provisions of the Convention relating to its protocols shall apply to this Protocol. . . .

Annex A

CONTROLLED SUBSTANCES . . .

[See the 1990 document. Annex A is not changed.]

HELSINKI DECLARATION ON THE PROTECTION OF THE OZONE LAYER

May 2, 1989, 28 I.L.M. 1335 (1989)*

The Governments and the European Communities Represented at the First Meetings of the Parties to the Vienna Convention and the Montreal Protocol

Aware of the wide agreement among scientists that depletion of the ozone layer will threaten present and future generations unless more stringent control measures are adopted

Mindful that some ozone depleting substances are powerful greenhouse gases leading to global warming

Aware also of the extensive and rapid technological development of environmentally acceptable substitutes for the substances that deplete the ozone layer and the urgent need to facilitate the transfer of technologies of such substitutes especially to developing countries

ENCOURAGE all states that have not done so to join the Vienna Convention for the Protection of the Ozone Layer and its Montreal Protocol

AGREE to phase out the production and the consumption of CFC's controlled by the Montreal Protocol as soon as possible but not later than the year 2000 and for that purpose to tighten the timetable agreed upon in the Montreal Protocol taking due account of the special situation of developing countries

AGREE to both phase out halons and control and reduce other ozone-depleting substances which contribute significantly to ozone depletion as soon as feasible

AGREE to commit themselves, in proportion to their means and resources, to accelerate the development of environmentally acceptable substituting chemicals, products and technologies

AGREE to facilitate the access of developing countries to relevant scientific information, research results and training and to seek to develop appropriate funding mechanisms to facilitate the transfer of technology and replacement of equipment at minimum cost to developing countries.

*Done at Helsinki, Finland, on May 2, 1989. The declaration was adopted by a consensus at a meeting of the states participating in the Vienna Convention, at p. 714, and the Montreal Protocol, at p. 723. The declaration expresses the intent of the parties. A 1990 meeting was scheduled to discuss amendments. These amendments are provided next.

MONTREAL PROTOCOL ON SUBSTANCES THAT DEPLETE THE OZONE LAYER
(as amended and adjusted)

June 1990 [New or amended language is in bold print.]*

The Parties to this Protocol,

Being Parties to the Vienna Convention for the Protection of the Ozone Layer,

Mindful of their obligation under that Convention to take appropriate measures to protect human health and the environment against adverse effects resulting or likely to result from human activities which modify or are likely to modify the ozone layer,

Recognizing that world-wide emissions of certain substances can significantly deplete and otherwise modify the ozone layer in a manner that is likely to result in adverse effects on human health and the environment,

Conscious of the potential climatic effect of emissions of these substances,

Aware that measures taken to protect the ozone layer from depletion should be based on relevant scientific knowledge, taking into account technical and economic considerations,

Determined to protect the ozone layer by taking precautionary measures to control equitably total global emissions of substances that deplete it, with the ultimate objective of their elimination on the basis of developments in scientific knowledge, taking into account technical and economic considerations **and bearing in mind the developmental needs of developing countries,**

Acknowledging that special provision is required to meet the needs of developing countries, **including the provision of additional financial resources and access to relevant technologies, bearing in mind that the magnitude of funds necessary is predictable, and the funds can be expected to make a substantial difference in the world's ability to address the scientifically established problem of ozone depletion and its harmful effects,**

Noting the precautionary measures for controlling emissions of certain

---

*This document is a result of the second meeting of the parties to the Montreal Protocol (excerpted earlier), which took place in London on June 27-29, 1990. The meeting adopted an amendment to the Montreal Protocol in accordance with paragraph 4 of Article 9 of the Vienna Convention for the Protection of the Ozone Layer (excerpted earlier). In accordance with paragraphs 4 and 9 of Article 2 of the Montreal Protocol, the meeting also adopted the adjustments and reductions of production and consumption of the controlled substances listed in Annex A to the Protocol.

The source for this document is the U.N. Environment Programme's (UNEP) Report of the Second Meeting of the Parties to the Montreal Protocol . . . , UNEP/OzL.Pro.2/3 (29 June 1990).

chlorofluorocarbons that have already been taken at national and regional levels,

Considering the importance of promoting international cooperation in the research, development **and transfer of alternative technologies** relating to the control and reduction of emissions of substances that deplete the ozone layer, bearing in mind in particular the needs of developing countries,

HAVE AGREED AS FOLLOWS:

Article 1. Definitions

For the purposes of this Protocol:

1. "Convention" means the Vienna Convention for the Protection of the Ozone Layer, adopted on 22 March 1985.

2. "Parties" means, unless the text otherwise indicates, Parties to this Protocol.

3. "Secretariat" means the secretariat of the Convention.

4. "Controlled substance" means a substance listed in Annex A **or in** Annex B to this Protocol, whether existing alone or in a mixture. It **includes the isomers of any such substance, except as specified in the relevant Annex, but** excludes any **controlled** substance or mixture which is in a manufactured product other than a container used for the transportation or storage of **that** substance.

5. "Production" means the amount of controlled substances produced minus the amount destroyed by technologies to be approved by the Parties **and minus the amount entirely used as feedstock in the manufacture of other chemicals. The amount recycled and reused is not to be considered as "production".**

6. "Consumption" means production plus imports minus exports of controlled substances.

7. "Calculated levels" of production, imports, exports and consumption means levels determined in accordance with Article 3.

8. "Industrial rationalization" means the transfer of all or a portion of the calculated level of production of one Party to another, for the purpose of achieving economic efficiencies or responding to anticipated shortfalls in supply as a result of plant closures.

9. **"Transitional substance" means a substance in Annex C to this Protocol, whether existing alone or in a mixture. It includes the isomers of any such substance, except as may be specified in Annex C, but excludes any transitional substance or mixture which is in a manufactured product other than a container used for the transportation or storage of that substance.**

Article 2. Control Measures

5. Any Party may, for any one or more control periods, transfer to another Party any portion of its calculated level of production set out in Articles 2A to 2E, provided that the total combined calculated levels of production of the Parties concerned for any group of controlled substances do not exceed the production limits set out in those Articles for that group. Such transfer of production shall be notified to the Secretar-

iat by each of the Parties concerned, stating the terms of such transfer and the period for which it is to apply.

6. Any Party not operating under Article 5, that has facilities for the production of **Annex A or Annex B** controlled substances under construction, or contracted for, prior to 16 September 1987, and provided for in national legislation prior to 1 January 1987, may add the production from such facilities to its 1986 production of such substances for the purposes of determining its calculated level of production for 1986, provided that such facilities are completed by 31 December 1990 and that such production does not raise that Party's annual calculated level of consumption of the controlled substances above 0.5 kilograms per capita.

7. Any transfer of production pursuant to paragraph 5 or any addition to production pursuant to paragraph 6 shall be notified to the secretariat, no later than the time of the transfer or addition.

8. (a) Any Parties which are Members States of a regional economic integration organization as defined in Article 1(6) of the Convention may agree that they shall jointly fulfill their obligations respecting consumption under this Article **and Articles 2A to 2E** provided that their total combined calculated level of consumption does not exceed the levels required by this Article **and Articles 2A to 2E**.

(b) The Parties to any such agreement shall inform the secretariat of the terms of the agreement before the date of the reduction in consumption with which the agreement is concerned.

(c) Such agreement will become operative only if all Member States of the regional economic integration organization and the organization concerned are Parties to the Protocol and have notified the secretariat of their manner of implementation.

9. (a) Based on the assessments made pursuant to Article 6, the Parties may decide whether:

(i) Adjustments to the ozone depleting potentials specified in Annex A **and/or Annex B** should be made, and, if so, what the adjustments should be; and

(ii) Further adjustments and reductions of production or consumption of the controlled substances should be undertaken and, if so, what the scope, amount and timing of any such adjustments and reductions should be;

(b) Proposals for such adjustments shall be communicated to the Parties by the secretariat at least six months before the meeting of the Parties at which they are proposed for adoption;

(c) In taking such decisions, the Parties shall make every effort to reach agreement by consensus. If all efforts at consensus have been exhausted, and no agreement reached, such decisions shall, as a last resort, be adopted by a two-thirds majority vote of the Parties present and voting representing **a majority of the Parties operating under paragraph 1 of Article 5 present and voting and a majority of Parties not so operating present and voting.**

(d) The decisions, which shall be binding on all Parties, shall forthwith be communicated to the Parties by the Depositary. Unless otherwise provided in the decisions, they shall enter into force on the expiry of six months from the date of the circulation of the communication by the Depositary.

10. Based on the assessments made pursuant to Article 6 of this Protocol and in accordance with the procedure set out in Article 9 of the Convention, the Parties may decide:

(i) whether any substances, and if so which, should be added to or removed from any annex to this Protocol; and

(ii) the mechanism, scope and timing of the control measures that should apply to those substances.

11. Notwithstanding the provisions contained in this Article **and Articles 2A to 2E,** Parties may take more stringent measures than those required by this Article **and Articles 2A to 2E.**

Article 2A. CFCS

1. Each Party shall ensure that for the twelve-month period commencing on the first day of the seventh month following the date of the entry into force of this Protocol, and in each twelve-month period thereafter, its calculated level of consumption of the controlled substances in Group I of Annex A does not exceed its calculated level of consumption in 1986. By the end of the same period, each Party producing one or more of these substances shall ensure that its calculated level of production of the substances does not exceed its calculated level of production in 1986, except that such level may have increased by no more than ten per cent based on the 1986 level. Such increase shall be permitted only so as to satisfy the basic domestic needs of the Parties operating under Article 5 and for the purposes of industrial rationalization between Parties.

2. Each Party shall ensure that for the period from 1 July 1991 to 31 December 1992 its calculated levels of consumption and production of the controlled substances in Group I of Annex A do not exceed 150 per cent of its calculated levels of production and consumption of those substances in 1986; with effect from 1 January 1993, the twelve-month control period for these controlled substances shall run from 1 January to 31 December each year.

3. Each Party shall ensure that for the twelve-month period commencing on 1 January 1995, and in each twelve-month period thereafter, its calculated level of consumption of the controlled substances in Group I of Annex A does not exceed, annually, fifty per cent of its calculated level of consumption in 1986. Each Party producing one or more of these substances shall, for the same periods, ensure that its calculated level of production of the substances does not exceed, annually, fifty per cent of its calculated level of production in 1986. However, in order to satisfy the basic domestic needs of the Parties operating under paragraph 1 of Article 5, its calculated level of production may exceed that limit by up to ten per cent of its calculated level of production in 1986.

4. Each Party shall ensure that for the twelve-month period commencing on 1 January 1997, and in each twelve-month period thereafter, its calculated level of consumption of the controlled substances in Group I of Annex A does not exceed, annually, fifteen per cent of its calculated level of consumption in 1986. Each Party producing one or more of these substances shall, for the same periods, ensure that its calculated level of production of the substances does not exceed, annually, fifteen per cent

of its calculated level of production in 1986. However, in order to satisfy the basic domestic needs of the Parties operating under paragraph 1 of Article 5, its calculated level of production may exceed that limit by up to 10 per cent of its calculated level of production in 1986.

5. Each Party shall ensure that for the twelve-month period commencing on 1 January 2000, and in each twelve-month period thereafter, its calculated level of consumption of the controlled substances in Group I of Annex A does not exceed zero. Each Party producing one or more of these substances shall, for the same periods, ensure that its calculated level of production of the substances does not exceed zero. However, in order to satisfy the basic domestic needs of the Parties operating under paragraph 1 of Article 5, its calculated level of production may exceed that limit by up to fifteen percent of its calculated level of production in 1986.

6. In 1992, the Parties will review the situation with the objective of accelerating the reduction schedule.

Article 2B. Halons

1. Each Party shall ensure that for the twelve-month period commencing on 1 January 1992, and in each twelve-month period thereafter, its calculated level of consumption of the controlled substances in Group II of Annex A does not exceed, annually, its calculated level of consumption in 1986. Each Party producing one or more of these substances shall, for the same periods, ensure that its calculated level of production of the substances does not exceed, annually, its calculated level of production in 1986. However, in order to satisfy the basic domestic needs of the Parties operating under paragraph 1 of Article 5, its calculated level of production may exceed that limit by up to ten per cent of its calculated level of production in 1986.

2. Each Party shall ensure that for the twelve-month period commencing on 1 January 1995, and in each twelve-month period thereafter, its calculated level of consumption of the controlled substances in Group II of Annex A does not exceed, annually, fifty per cent of its calculated level of consumption in 1986. Each Party producing one or more of these substances shall, for the same periods, ensure that its calculated level of production of the substances does not exceed, annually, fifty per cent of its calculated level of production in 1986. However, in order to satisfy the basic domestic needs of the Parties operating under paragraph 1 of Article 5, its calculated level of production may exceed that limit by up to ten per cent of its calculated level of production in 1986. This paragraph will apply save to the extent that the Parties decide to permit the level of production or consumption that is necessary to satisfy essential uses for which no adequate alternatives are available.

3. Each Party shall ensure that for the twelve-month period commencing on 1 January 2000, and in each twelve-month period thereafter, its calculated level of consumption of the controlled substances in Group II of Annex A does not exceed zero. Each Party producing one or more of these substances shall, for the same periods, ensure that its calculated level of production of the substances does not exceed zero. However, in

order to satisfy the basic domestic needs of the Parties operating under paragraph 1 of Article 5, its calculated level of production may exceed that limit by up to fifteen per cent of its calculated level of production in 1986. This paragraph will apply save to the extent that the Parties decide to permit the level of production or consumption that is necessary to satisfy essential uses for which no adequate alternatives are available.

4. By 1 January 1993, the Parties shall adopt a decision identifying essential uses, if any, for the purposes of paragraphs 2 and 3 of this Article. Such decision shall be reviewed by the Parties at their subsequent meetings.

Article 2C. Other Fully Halogenated CFCS

1. Each Party shall ensure that for the twelve-month period commencing on 1 January 1993, and in each twelve-month period thereafter, its calculated level of consumption of the controlled substances in Group I of Annex B does not exceed, annually, eighty per cent of its calculated level of consumption in 1989. Each Party producing one or more of these substances shall, for the same periods, ensure that its calculated level of production of the substances does not exceed, annually, eighty per cent of its calculated level of production in 1989. However, in order to satisfy the basic domestic needs of the Parties operating under paragraph 1 of Article 5, its calculated level of production may exceed that limit by up to ten per cent of its calculated level of production in 1989.

2. Each Party shall ensure that for the twelve-month period commencing on 1 January 1997, and in each twelve-month period thereafter, its calculated level of consumption of the controlled substances in Group I of Annex B does not exceed, annually, fifteen percent of its calculated level of consumption in 1989. Each Party producing one or more of these substances shall, for the same periods, ensure that its calculated level of production of the substances does not exceed, annually, fifteen per cent of its calculated level of production in 1989. However, in order to satisfy the basic domestic needs of the Parties operating under paragraph 1 of Article 5, its calculated level of production may exceed that limit by up to ten per cent of its calculated level of production in 1989.

3. Each Party shall ensure that for the twelve-month period commencing on 1 January 2000, and in each twelve-month period thereafter, its calculated level of consumption of the controlled substances in Group I of Annex B does not exceed zero. Each Party producing one or more of these substances shall, for the same periods, ensure that its calculated level of production of the substances does not exceed zero. However, in order to satisfy the basic domestic needs of the Parties operating under paragraph 1 of Article 5, its calculated level of production may exceed that limit by up to fifteen per cent of its calculated level of production in 1989.

Article 2D. Carbon Tetrachloride

1. Each Party shall ensure that for the twelve-month period commencing on 1 January 1995, and in each twelve-month period thereafter, its calculated level of consumption of the controlled substance in Group

II of Annex B does not exceed, annually, fifteen per cent of its calculated level of consumption in 1989. Each Party producing the substance shall, for the same period, ensure that its calculated level of production of the substance does not exceed, annually, fifteen per cent of its calculated level of production in 1989. However, in order to satisfy the basic domestic needs of the Parties operating under paragraph 1 of Article 5, its calculated level of production may exceed that limit by up to ten per cent of its calculated level of production in 1989.

2. Each Party shall ensure that for the twelve-month period commencing on 1 January 2000, and in each twelve-month period thereafter, its calculated level of consumption of the controlled substance in Group II of Annex B does not exceed zero. Each Party producing the substance shall, for the same periods, ensure that its calculated level of production of the substance does not exceed zero. However, in order to satisfy the basic domestic needs of the Parties operating under paragraph 1 of Article 5, its calculated level of production may exceed that limit by up to fifteen per cent of its calculated level of production in 1989.

Article 2E. 1,1,1-Trichloroethane (Methyl Chloroform)

1. Each Party shall ensure that for the twelve-month period commencing on 1 January 1993, and in each twelve-month period thereafter, its calculated level of consumption of the controlled substance in Group III of Annex B does not exceed, annually, its calculated level of consumption in 1989. Each Party producing the substance shall, for the same periods, ensure that its calculated level of production of the substance does not exceed, annually, its calculated level of production in 1989. However, in order to satisfy the basic domestic needs of the Parties operating under paragraph 1 of Article 5, its calculated level of production may exceed that limit by up to ten per cent of its calculated level of production in 1989.

2. Each Party shall ensure that for the twelve-month period commencing on 1 January 1995, and in each twelve-month period thereafter, its calculated level of consumption of the controlled substance in Group III of Annex B does not exceed, annually, seventy per cent of its calculated level of consumption in 1989. Each Party producing the substance shall, for the same periods, ensure that its calculated level of production of the substance does not exceed, annually, seventy per cent of its calculated level of consumption in 1989. However, in order to satisfy the basic domestic needs of the Parties operating under paragraph 1 of Article 5, its calculated level of production may exceed that limit by up to ten per cent of its calculated level of production in 1989.

3. Each Party shall ensure that for the twelve-month period commencing on 1 January 2000, and in each twelve-month period thereafter, its calculated level of consumption of the controlled substance in Group III of Annex B does not exceed, annually, thirty per cent of its calculated level of consumption in 1989. Each Party producing the substance shall, for the same periods, ensure that its calculated level of production of the substance does not exceed, annually, thirty per cent of its calculated level of production in 1989. However, in order to satisfy the basic domestic

needs of Parties operating under paragraph 1 of Article 5, its calculated level of production may exceed that limit by up to ten per cent of its calculated level of production in 1989.

4. Each Party shall ensure that for the twelve-month period commencing on 1 January 2005, and in each twelve-month period thereafter, its calculated level of consumption of the controlled substance in Group III of Annex B does not exceed zero. Each Party producing the substance shall, for the same periods, ensure that its calculated level of production of the substance does not exceed zero. However, in order to satisfy the basic domestic needs of the Parties operating under paragraph 1 of Article 5, its calculated level of production may exceed that limit by up to fifteen percent of its calculated level of production in 1989.

5. The Parties shall review in 1992 the feasibility of a more rapid schedule of reductions than that set out in this Article.

Article 3. Calculation of Control Levels

For the purposes of Articles 2, **2A to 2E,** and 5, each Party shall, for each group of substances in Annex A **or Annex B,** determine its calculated level of:

(a) Production by:

(i) Multiplying its annual production of each controlled substance by the ozone depleting potential specified in respect of it in Annex A **or Annex B;** and

(ii) Adding together, for each such Group, the resulting figures;

(b) Imports and exports, respectively, by following, *mutatis mutandis,* the procedure set out in subparagraph (a); and

(c) Consumption by adding together its calculated levels of production and imports and subtracting its calculated level of exports as determined in accordance with subparagraphs (a) and (b). However, beginning on 1 January 1993, any export of controlled substances to non-Parties shall not be subtracted in calculating the consumption level of the exporting Party.

Article 4. Control of Trade with Non-Parties

1. **As of 1 January 1990, each Party shall ban the import of the controlled substances in Annex A from any State not party to this Protocol.**

1 *bis.* Within one year of the date of the entry into force of this **paragraph,** each Party shall ban the import of **the** controlled substances **in Annex B** from any State not party to this Protocol.

2. **As of 1 January 1993, each Party shall ban the export of any controlled substances in Annex A to any State not party to this Protocol.**

2 *bis.* **Commencing one year after the date of entry into force of this paragraph, each Party shall ban the export of any controlled substances in Annex B to any State not party to this Protocol.**

3. **By 1 January 1992, the Parties shall, following the procedures in Article 10 of the Convention, elaborate in an annex a list of products containing controlled substances in Annex A. Parties that have not objected to the annex in accordance with those procedures shall ban, within

one year of the annex having become effective, the import of those products from any State not party to this Protocol.

3 *bis*. **Within three years of the date of the entry into force of this paragraph,** the Parties shall, following the procedures in Article 10 of the Convention, elaborate in an annex a list of products containing controlled substances in Annex B. Parties that have not objected to the annex in accordance with those procedures shall ban, within one year of the annex having become effective, the import of those products from any State not party to this Protocol.

4. **By 1 January 1994, the Parties shall determine the feasibility of banning or restricting, from States not party to this Protocol, the import of products produced with, but not containing, controlled substances in Annex A.** If determined feasible, the Parties shall, following the procedures in Article 10 of the Convention, elaborate in an annex a list of such products. Parties that have not objected to the annex in accordance with those procedures shall ban, within one year of the annex having become effective, the import of those products from any State not party to this Protocol.

4 *bis*. Within five years of the **date of the** entry into force of this paragraph, the Parties shall determine the feasibility of banning or restricting, from States not party to this Protocol, the import of products produced with, but not containing, controlled substances **in Annex B.** If determined feasible, the Parties shall, following the procedures in Article 10 of the Convention, elaborate in an annex a list of such products. Parties that have not objected to **the annex** in accordance with those procedures shall ban or restrict, within one year of the annex having become effective, the import of those products from any State not party to this Protocol.

5. Each Party **undertakes to the fullest practicable extent to** discourage the export to any State not party to this Protocol of technology for producing and for utilizing controlled substances.

6. Each Party shall refrain from providing new subsidies, aid, credits, guarantees or insurance programmes for the export to States not party to this Protocol of products, equipment, plants or technology that would facilitate the production of controlled substances.

7. Paragraphs 5 and 6 shall not apply to products, equipment, plants or technology that improve the containment, recovery, recycling, or destruction of controlled substances, promote the development of alternative substances, or otherwise contribute to the reduction of emissions of controlled substances.

8. Notwithstanding the provisions of this Article, imports referred to in paragraphs 1, **1** *bis*, 3, **3** *bis*, 4 and **4** *bis*, **and exports referred to in paragraphs 2 and 2** *bis*, may be permitted from, **or to,** any State not party to this Protocol, if that State is determined by a meeting of the Parties to be in full compliance with Article 2, **Articles 2A to 2E,** and this Article and have submitted data to that effect as specified in Article 7.

9. **For the purposes of this Article, the term "State not party to this Protocol" shall include, with respect to a particular controlled substance, a State or regional economic integration organization that has not agreed to be bound by the control measures in effect for that substance.**

Article 5. Special Situation of Developing Countries

1. Any Party that is a developing country and whose annual calculated level of consumption of the controlled substances **in Annex A** is less than 0.3 kilograms per capita on the date of the entry into force of the Protocol for it, or any time thereafter **until 1 January 1999,** shall, in order to meet its basic domestic needs, be entitled to delay for ten years its compliance with the control measures set out in **Articles 2A to 2E.**

2. However, any Party operating under paragraph 1 of this Article shall exceed neither an annual calculated level of consumption of the controlled substances in Annex A of 0.3 kilograms per capita nor an annual calculated level of consumption of the controlled substances of Annex B of 0.2 kilograms per capita.

3. When implementing the control measures set out in Articles 2A to 2E, any Party operating under paragraph 1 of this Article shall be entitled to use:

(a) for controlled substances under Annex A, either the average of its annual calculated level of consumption for the period 1995 to 1997 inclusive or a calculated level of consumption of 0.3 kilograms per capita, whichever is the lower, as the basis for determining its compliance with the control measures;

(b) for controlled substances under Annex B, the average of its calculated level of consumption for the period 1998 to 2000 inclusive or a calculated level of consumption of 0.2 kilograms per capita, whichever is the lower, as the basis for determining its compliance with the control measures.

4. If a Party operating under paragraph 1 of this Article, at any time before the control measures obligations in Articles 2A to 2E become applicable to it, finds itself unable to obtain an adequate supply of controlled substances, it may notify this to the Secretariat. The Secretariat shall forthwith transmit a copy of such notification to the Parties, which shall consider the matter at their next Meeting, and decide upon appropriate action to be taken.

5. Developing the capacity to fulfil the obligations of the Parties operating under paragraph 1 of this Article to comply with the control measures set out in Article 2A to 2E and their implementation by those same Parties will depend upon the effective implementation of the financial co-operation as provided by Article 10 and transfer of technology as provided by Article 10A.

6. Any Party operating under paragraph 1 of this Article may, at any time, notify the Secretariat in writing that, having taken all practicable steps, it is unable to implement any or all of the obligations laid down in Articles 2A to 2E due to the inadequate implementation of Articles 10 and 10A. The Secretariat shall forthwith transmit a copy of the notification to the Parties, which shall consider the matter at their next Meeting, giving due recognition to paragraph 5 of this Article, and shall decide upon appropriate action to be taken.

7. During the period between notification and the Meeting of the Parties at which the appropriate action referred to in paragraph 6 above is to be decided, or for a further period if the Meeting of Parties so

decides, the non-compliance procedures referred to in Article 8 shall not be invoked against the notifying Party.

8. A Meeting of the Parties shall review, not later than 1995, the situation of the Parties operating under paragraph 1 of this Article, including the effective implementation of financial co-operation and transfer of technology to them, and adopt such revisions that may be deemed necessary regarding the schedule of control measures applicable to those Parties.

9. Decisions of the Parties referred to in paragraphs 4, 6 and 7 of this Article shall be taken according to the same procedure applied to decision-making under Article 10.

Article 6. *Assessment and Review of Control Measures*

Beginning in 1990, and at least every four years thereafter, the Parties shall assess the control measures provided for in Article 2, **Articles 2A to 2E, and the situation regarding production, imports and exports of the transitional substances in Group I of Annex C,** on the basis of available scientific, environmental, technical and economic information. At least one year before each assessment, the Parties shall convene appropriate panels of experts qualified in the fields mentioned and determine the composition and terms of reference of any such panels. Within one year of being convened, the panels will report their conclusions, through the secretariat, to the Parties.

Article 7. *Reporting of Data*

1. Each Party shall provide to the Secretariat, within three months of becoming a Party, statistical data on its production, imports and exports of each of the controlled substances **in Annex A** for the year 1986, or the best possible estimates of such data where actual data are not available.

2. **Each Party shall provide to the Secretariat statistical data on its production, imports and exports of each of the controlled substances in Annex B and each of the transitional substances in Group I of Annex C, for the year 1989, or the best possible estimates of such data where actual data are not available, not later than three months after the date when the provisions set out in the Protocol with regard to the substances in Annex B enter into force for that Party.**

3. Each Party shall provide statistical data to the Secretariat on its annual production (as defined in paragraph 5 of Article 1), and, separately,

—amounts used for feedstocks,
—amounts destroyed by technologies approved by the Parties,
—imports and exports to Parties and non-Parties, respectively,

of each of the controlled substances listed in Annexes A and B as well as of the transitional substances in Group I of Annex C, for the year during which provisions concerning the substances in Annex B entered into force for that Party and for each year thereafter. Data shall be forwarded not later than nine months after the end of the year to which the data relate.

4. For Parties operating under the provisions of paragraph 8(a) of Article 2, the requirements in paragraphs 1, 2 and 3 of this Article in respect of statistical data on imports and exports shall be satisfied if the regional economic integration organization concerned provides data on imports and exports between the organization and States that are not members of that organization.

Article 8. Non-Compliance

The Parties, at their first meeting, shall consider and approve procedures and institutional mechanisms for determining non-compliance with the provisions of this Protocol and for treatment of Parties found to be in non-compliance.

Article 9. Research, Development, Public Awareness and Exchange of Information

1. The Parties shall cooperate, consistent with their national laws, regulations and practices and taking into account in particular the needs of developing countries, in promoting, directly or through competent international bodies, research, development and exchange of information on:

(a) Best technologies for improving the containment, recovery, recycling or destruction of controlled **and transitional** substances or otherwise reducing their emissions;

(b) Possible alternatives to controlled substances, to products containing such substances, and to products manufactured with them; and

(c) Costs and benefits of relevant control strategies.

2. The Parties, individually, jointly or through competent international bodies, shall cooperate in promoting public awareness of the environmental effects of the emissions of controlled substances and other substances that deplete the ozone layer.

3. Within two years of the entry into force of this Protocol and every two years thereafter, each Party shall submit to the secretariat a summary of the activities it has conducted pursuant to this Article.

Article 10. Financial Mechanism

1. The Parties shall establish a mechanism for the purposes of providing financial and technical co-operation, including the transfer of technologies, to Parties operating under paragraph 1 of Article 5 of this Protocol to enable their compliance with the control measures set out in Articles 2A to 2E of the Protocol. The mechanism, contributions to which shall be additional to other financial transfers to Parties operating under that paragraph, shall meet all agreed incremental costs of such Parties in order to enable their compliance with the control measures of the Protocol. An indicative list of the categories of incremental costs shall be decided by the meeting of the Parties.

2. The mechanism established under paragraph 1 shall include a

Multilateral Fund. It may also include other means of multilateral, regional and bilateral co-operation.

3. The Multilateral Fund shall:

(a) Meet, on a grant or concessional basis as appropriate, and according to criteria to be decided upon by the Parties, the agreed incremental costs;

(b) Finance clearing-house functions to:

(i) Assist Parties operating under paragraph 1 of Article 5, through country specific studies and other technical co-operation, to identify their needs for co-operation;

(ii) Facilitate technical co-operation to meet these identified needs;

(iii) Distribute, as provided for in Article 9, information and relevant materials, and hold workshops, training sessions, and other related activities, for the benefit of Parties that are developing countries; and

(iv) Facilitate and monitor other multilateral, regional and bilateral co-operation available to Parties that are developing countries.

(c) Finance the secretarial services of the Multilateral Fund and related support costs.

4. The Multilateral Fund shall operate under the authority of the Parties who shall decide on its overall policies.

5. The Parties shall establish an Executive Committee to develop and monitor the implementation of specific operational policies, guidelines and administrative arrangements, including the disbursement of resources, for the purpose of achieving the objectives of the Multilateral Fund. The Executive Committee shall discharge its tasks and responsibilities, specified in its terms of reference as agreed by the Parties, with the co-operation and assistance of the International Bank for Reconstruction and Development (World Bank), the United Nations Environment Programme, the United Nations Development Programme or other appropriate agencies depending on their respective areas of expertise. The members of the Executive Committee, which shall be selected on the basis of balanced representation of the Parties operating under paragraph 1 of Article 5 and of the Parties not so operating, shall be endorsed by the Parties.

6. The Multilateral Fund shall be financed by contributions from Parties not operating under paragraph 1 of Article 5 in convertible currency or, in certain circumstances, in kind and/or in national currency, on the basis of the United Nations scale of assessments. Contributions by other Parties shall be encouraged. Bilateral and, in particular cases agreed by a decision of the Parties, regional co-operation may, up to a percentage and consistent with any criteria to be specified by decision of the Parties, be considered as a contribution to the Multilateral Fund, provided that such co-operation, as a minimum:

(a) Strictly relates to compliance with the provisions of this Protocol;

(b) Provides additional resources; and

(c) Meets agreed incremental costs.

7. The Parties shall decide upon the programme budget of the Multi-

lateral Fund for each fiscal period and upon the percentage of contributions of the individual Parties thereto.

8. Resources under the Multilateral Fund shall be disbursed with the concurrence of the beneficiary Party.

9. Decisions by the Parties under this Article shall be taken by consensus whenever possible. If all efforts at consensus have been exhausted and no agreement reached, decisions shall be adopted by a two-thirds majority of the Parties present and voting, representing a majority of the Parties operating under paragraph 1 of Article 5 present and voting and a majority of the Parties not so operating present and voting.

10. The financial mechanism set out in this Article is without prejudice to any future arrangements that may be developed with respect to other environmental issues.

Article 10A. *Transfer of Technology*

Each Party shall take every practicable step, consistent with the programmes supported by the financial mechanism, to ensure:

(a) that the best available, environmentally safe substitutes and related technologies are expeditiously transferred to Parties operating under paragraph 1 of Article 5, and

(b) that the transfers referred to in subparagraph (a) occur under fair and most favourable conditions.

Article 11. *Meeting of the Parties*

1. The Parties shall hold meetings at regular intervals. The secretariat shall convene the first meeting of the Parties not later than one year after the date of the entry into force of this Protocol and in conjunction with a meeting of the Conference of the Parties to the Convention, if a meeting of the latter is scheduled within that period.

2. Subsequent ordinary meetings of the parties shall be held, unless the Parties otherwise decide, in conjunction with meetings of the Conference of the Parties to the Convention. Extraordinary meetings of the Parties shall be held at such other times as may be deemed necessary by a meeting of the Parties, or at the written request of any Party, provided that, within six months of such a request being communicated to them by the secretariat, it is supported by at least one third of the Parties.

3. The Parties, at their first meeting, shall:

(a) Adopt by consensus rules of procedure for their meetings;

(b) Adopt by consensus the financial rules referred to in paragraph 2 of Article 13;

(c) Establish the panels and determine the terms of reference referred to in Article 6;

(d) Consider and approve the procedures and institutional mechanisms specified in Article 8; and

(e) Begin preparation of workplans pursuant to paragraph 3 of Article 10.

4. The functions of the meetings of the Parties shall be to:

(a) Review the implementation of this Protocol;

(b) Decide on any adjustments or reductions referred to in paragraph 9 of Article 2;

(c) Decide on any addition to, insertion in or removal from any annex of substances and on related control measures in accordance with paragraph 10 of Article 2;

(d) Establish, where necessary, guidelines or procedures for reporting of information as provided for in Article 7 and paragraph 3 of Article 9;

(e) Review requests for technical assistance submitted pursuant to sub-paragraph (c) of Article 12;

(f) Review reports prepared by the secretariat pursuant to subparagraph (c) of Article 12;

(g) Assess, in accordance with Article 6, the control measures and the situation regarding transitional substances;

(h) Consider and adopt, as required, proposals for amendment of this Protocol or any annex and for any new annex;

(i) Consider and adopt the budget for implementing this Protocol; and

(j) Consider and undertake any additional action that may be required for the achievement of the purposes of this Protocol.

5. The United Nations, its specialized agencies and the International Atomic Energy Agency, as well as any State not party to this Protocol, may be represented at meetings of the Parties as observers. Any body or agency, whether national or international, governmental or non-governmental, qualified in fields relating to the protection of the ozone layer which has informed the secretariat of its wish to be represented at a meeting of the Parties as an observer may be admitted unless at least one third of the Parties present object. The admission and participation of observers shall be subject to the rules of procedure adopted by the Parties.

Article 12. *Secretariat*

For the purposes of this Protocol, the secretariat shall:

(a) Arrange for and service meetings of the Parties as provided for in Article 11;

(b) Receive and make available, upon request by a Party, data provided pursuant to Article 7;

(c) Prepare and distribute regularly to the Parties reports based on information received pursuant to Articles 7 and 9;

(d) Notify the Parties of any request for technical assistance received pursuant to Article 10 so as to facilitate the provision of this Protocol;

(e) Encourage non-Parties to attend the meetings of the Parties as observers and to act in accordance with the provisions of this Protocol;

(f) Provide, as appropriate, the information and requests referred to in subparagraphs (c) and (d) to such non-party observers; and

(g) Perform such other functions for the achievement of the purposes of this Protocol as may be assigned to it by the Parties.

Article 13. *Financial Provisions*

1. The Funds required for the operation of this Protocol, including those for the functioning of the secretariat related to this Protocol, shall be charged exclusively against contributions from the Parties.

2. The Parties, at their first meeting, shall adopt by consensus financial rules for the operation of this Protocol.

Article 14. Relationship of This Protocol to the Convention

Except as otherwise provided in this Protocol, the provisions of the Convention relating to its protocols shall apply to this Protocol.

Article 15. Signature . . .

Article 16. Entry into Force

1. This Protocol shall enter into force on 1 January 1989, provided that at least eleven instruments of ratification, acceptance, approval of the Protocol or accession thereto have been deposited by States or regional economic integration organizations representing at least two-thirds of 1986 estimated global consumption of the controlled substances, and the provisions of paragraph 1 of Article 17 of the Convention have been fulfilled. In the event that these conditions have not been fulfilled by that date, the Protocol shall enter into force on the ninetieth day following the date on which the conditions have been fulfilled.

2. For the purposes of paragraph 1, any such instrument deposited by a regional economic integration organization shall not be counted as additional to those deposited by member States of such organization.

3. After the entry into force of this Protocol, any State or regional economic integration organization shall become a Party to it on the ninetieth day following the date of deposit of its instrument of ratification, acceptance, approval or accession.

Article 17. Parties Joining After Entry into Force

Subject to Article 5, any State or regional economic integration organization which becomes a Party to this Protocol after the date of its entry into force, shall fulfill forthwith the sum of the obligations under Article 2, as well as under **Articles 2A to 2E, and** Article 4, that apply at that date to the States and regional economic integration organizations that became Parties on the date the Protocol entered into force.

Article 18. Reservations

No reservations may be made to this Protocol.

Article 19. Withdrawal

Any Party may withdraw from this Protocol by giving written notification to the Depositary at any time after four years of assuming the obligations specified in **paragraph 1 of Article 2A.** Any such withdrawal shall take effect upon expiry of one year after the date of its receipt by the Depositary, or on such later date as may be specified in the notification of the withdrawal. . . .

ANNEX A
Controlled Substances

Group	Substance		Ozone Depleting Potential*
Group I			
	$CFCl_3$	(CFC-11)	1.0
	CF_2Cl_2	(CFC-12)	1.0
	$C_2F_3Cl_3$	(CFC-113)	0.8
	$C_2F_4Cl_2$	(CFC-114)	1.0
	C_2F_5Cl	(CFC-115)	0.6
Group II			
	CF_2BrCl	(halon-1211)	3.0
	CF_3Br	(halon-1301)	10.0
	$C_2F_4Br_2$	(halon-2402)	(to be determined)

*These ozone depleting potentials are estimates based on existing knowledge and will be reviewed and revised periodically.

ANNEX B
Controlled Substances

Group	Substance		Ozone-Depleting Potential
Group I			
	CF_3Cl	(CFC-13)	1.0
	C_2FCl_5	(CFC-111)	1.0
	$C_2F_2Cl_4$	(CFC-112)	1.0
	C_3FCl_7	(CFC-211)	1.0
	$C_3F_2Cl_6$	(CFC-212)	1.0
	$C_3F_3Cl_5$	(CFC-213)	1.0
	$C_3F_4Cl_4$	(CFC-214)	1.0
	$C_3F_5Cl_3$	(CFC-215)	1.0
	$C_3F_6Cl_2$	(CFC-216)	1.0
	C_3F_7Cl	(CFC-217)	1.0
Group II			
	CCl_4	carbon tetrachloride	1.1
Group III			
	$C_2H_3Cl_3$*	1,1,1-trichloroethane (methyl chloroform)	0.1

*This formula does not refer to 1,1,2-trichloroethane.

ANNEX C
Transitional Substances

Group	Substance	Ozone-Depleting Potential
Group I		
$CHFCl_2$	(HCFC-21)	
CHF_2Cl	(HCFC-22)	
CH_2FCl	(HCFC-31)	
C_2HFCl_4	(HCFC-121)	
$C_2HF_2Cl_3$	(HCFC-122)	
$C_2HF_3Cl_2$	(HCFC-123)	
C_2HF_4Cl	(HCFC-124)	
$C_2H_2FCl_3$	(HCFC-131)	
$C_2H_2F_2Cl_2$	(HCFC-132)	
$C_2H_2F_3Cl$	(HCFC-133)	
$C_2H_3FCl_2$	(HCFC-141)	
$C_2H_3F_2Cl$	(HCFC-142)	
C_3HFCL_6	(HCFC-221)	
$C_3HF_2Cl_5$	(HCFC-222)	
$C_3HF_3Cl_4$	(HCFC-223)	
$C_3HF_4Cl_3$	(HCFC-224)	
$C_3HF_5Cl_2$	(HCFC-225)	
C_3HF_6Cl	(HCFC-226)	
$C_3H_2FCl_5$	(HCFC-231)	
$C_3H_2F_2Cl_4$	(HCFC-232)	
$C_3H_2F_3Cl_3$	(HCFC-233)	
$C_3H_2F_4Cl_2$	(HCFC-234)	
$C_3H_2F_5Cl$	(HCFC-235)	
$C_3H_3FCl_4$	(HCFC-241)	
$C_3H_3F_2Cl_3$	(HCFC-242)	
$C_3H_3F_3Cl_2$	(HCFC-243)	
$C_3H_3F_4Cl$	(HCFC-244)	
$C_3H_4FCl_3$	(HCFC-251)	
$C_3H_4F_2Cl_2$	(HCFC-252)	
$C_5H_4F_3Cl$	(HCFC-253)	
$C_3H_5FCl_2$	(HCFC-261)	
$C_3H_5F_2Cl$	(HCFC-262)	
C_3H_6FCl	(HCFC-271)	

12

Use of Force and Arms Control

U.N. "UNITING FOR PEACE" RESOLUTION
U.N. G.A. Res. 337A (V 1950)*

A

The General Assembly,
Recognizing that the first two stated Purposes of the United Nations are:

To maintain international peace and security, and to that end: to take effective collective measures for the prevention and removal of threats to the peace, and for the suppression of acts of aggression or other breaches of the peace, and to bring about by peaceful means, and in conformity with the principles of justice and international law, adjustment or settlement of international disputes or situations which might lead to a breach of the peace, and

To develop friendly relations among nations based on respect for the principle of equal rights and self-determination of peoples, and to take other appropriate measures to strengthen universal peace,

Reaffirming that it remains the primary duty of all Members of the United Nations, when involved in an international dispute, to seek settlement of such a dispute by peaceful means through the procedures laid down in Chapter VI of the Charter, and recalling the successful achievements of the United Nations in this regard on a number of previous occasions,

Finding that international tension exists on a dangerous scale,

Recalling its resolution 290 (IV) entitled "Essentials of peace", which states that disregard of the Principles of the Charter of the United Nations

---

*Adopted by the U.N. General Assembly on November 3, 1950. The vote was 52 states for, 5 against (Byelorussian S.S.R., Czechoslovakia, Poland, Ukrainian S.S.R., and the U.S.S.R.), and 2 abstaining (Argentina and India).

is primarily responsible for the continuance of international tension, and desiring to contribute further to the objectives of that resolution,

Reaffirming the importance of the exercise by the Security Council of its primary responsibility for the maintenance of international peace and security, and the duty of the permanent members to seek unanimity and to exercise restraint in the use of the veto,

Reaffirming that the initiative in negotiating the agreements for armed forces provided for in Article 43 of the Charter belongs to the Security Council, and desiring to ensure that, pending the conclusion of such agreements, the United Nations has at its disposal means for maintaining international peace and security,

Conscious that failure of the Security Council to discharge its responsibilities on behalf of all the Member States, particularly those responsibilities referred to in the two preceding paragraphs, does not relieve Member States of their obligations or the United Nations of its responsibility under the Charter to maintain international peace and security,

Recognizing in particular that such failure does not deprive the General Assembly of its rights or relieve it of its responsibilities under the Charter in regard to the maintenance of international peace and security,

Recognizing that discharge by the General Assembly of its responsibilities in these respects calls for possibilities of observation which would ascertain the facts and expose aggressors; for the existence of armed forces which could be used collectively; and for the possibility of timely recommendation by the General Assembly to Members of the United Nations for collective action which, to be effective, should be prompt,

A

1. *Resolves* that if the Security Council, because of lack of unanimity of the permanent members, fails to exercise its primary responsibility for the maintenance of international peace and security in any case where there appears to be a threat to the peace, breach of the peace, or act of aggression, the General Assembly shall consider the matter immediately with a view to making appropriate recommendations to Members for collective measures, including in the case of a breach of the peace or act of aggression the use of armed force when necessary, to maintain or restore international peace and security. If not in session at the time, the General Assembly may meet in emergency special session within twenty-four hours of the request therefor. Such emergency special session shall be called if requested by the Security Council on the vote of any seven members, or by a majority of the Members of the United Nations;

2. *Adopts* for this purpose the amendments to its rules of procedure set forth in the annex to the present resolution;

B

3. *Establishes* a Peace Observation Commission which, for the calendar years 1951 and 1952, shall be composed of fourteen Members, namely: China, Colombia, Czechoslovakia, France, India, Iraq, Israel, New Zealand, Pakistan, Sweden, the Union of Soviet Socialist Republics, the United King-

dom of Great Britain and Northern Ireland, the United States of America and Uruguay, and which could observe and report on the situation in any area where there exists international tension the continuance of which is likely to endanger the maintenance of international peace and security. Upon the invitation or with the consent of the State into whose territory the Commission would go, the General Assembly, or the Interim Committee when the Assembly is not in session, may utilize the Commission if the Security Council is not exercising the functions assigned to it by the Charter with respect to the matter in question. Decisions to utilize the Commission shall be made on the affirmative vote of two-thirds of the members present and voting. The Security Council may also utilize the Commission in accordance with its authority under the Charter;

4. *Decides* that the Commission shall have authority in its discretion to appoint sub-commissions and to utilize the services of observers to assist it in the performance of its functions;

5. *Recommends* to all governments and authorities that they co-operate with the Commission and assist it in the performance of its functions;

6. *Requests* the Secretary-General to provide the necessary staff and facilities, . . .

C

7. *Invites* each Member of the United Nations to survey its resources in order to determine the nature and scope of the assistance it may be in a position to render in support of any recommendations of the Security Council or of the General Assembly for the restoration of international peace and security;

8. *Recommends* to the States Members of the United Nations that each Member maintain within its national armed forces elements so trained, organized and equipped that they could promptly be made available, in accordance with its constitutional processes, for service as a United Nations unit or units, upon recommendation by the Security Council or the General Assembly, without prejudice to the use of such elements in exercise of the right of individual or collective self-defence recognized in Article 51 of the Charter;

9. *Invites* the Members of the United Nations to inform the Collective Measures Committee provided for in paragraph 11 as soon as possible of the measures taken in implementation of the preceding paragraph;

10. *Requests* the Secretary-General to appoint, with the approval of the Committee provided for in paragraph 11, a panel of military experts who could be made available, on request, to Member States wishing to obtain technical advice regarding the organization, training, and equipment for prompt service as United Nations units of the elements referred to in paragraph 8;

D

11. *Establishes* a Collective Measures Committee consisting of fourteen Members, namely: Australia, Belgium, Brazil, Burma, Canada, Egypt,

France, Mexico, Philippines, Turkey, the United Kingdom of Great Britain and Northern Ireland, the United States of America, Venezuela and Yugoslavia, and directs the Committee, in consultation with the Secretary-General and with such Member States as the Committee finds appropriate, to study and make a report to the Security Council and the General Assembly, not later than 1 September 1951, on methods, including those in section C of the present resolution, which might be used to maintain and strengthen international peace and security in accordance with the Purposes and Principles of the Charter, taking account of collective self-defence and regional arrangements (Articles 51 and 52 of the Charter);

12. *Recommends* to all Member States that they cooperate with the Committee and assist it in the performance of its functions;

13. *Requests* the Secretary-General to furnish the staff and facilities necessary for the effective accomplishment of the purposes set forth in sections C and D of the present resolution;

E

14. *Is fully conscious* that, in adopting the proposals set forth above, enduring peace will not be secured solely by collective security arrangements against breaches of international peace and acts of aggression, but that a genuine and lasting peace depends also upon the observance of all the Principles and Purposes established in the Charter of the United Nations, upon the implementation of the resolutions of the Security Council, the General Assembly and other principal organs of the United Nations intended to achieve the maintenance of international peace and security, and especially upon respect for and observance of human rights and fundamental freedoms for all and on the establishment and maintenance of conditions of economic and social well-being in all countries; and accordingly

15. *Urges* Member States to respect fully, and to intensify, joint action, in co-operation with the United Nations, to develop and stimulate universal respect for and observance of human rights and fundamental freedoms, and to intensify individual and collective efforts to achieve conditions of economic stability and social progress, particularly through the development of under-developed countries and areas.

Annex

The rules of procedure of the General Assembly are amended in the following respects:

1. The present text of rule 8 shall become paragraph *(a)* of that rule, and a new paragraph *(b)* shall be added to read as follows:

"Emergency special sessions pursuant to resolution 377A (V) shall be convened within twenty-four hours of the receipt by the Secretary-General of a request for such a session from the Security Council, on the vote of any seven members thereof, or of a request from a majority of the Members of the United Nations expressed by vote in the Interim Committee or otherwise, or of the concurrence of a majority of Members as provided in rule 9."

2. The present text of rule 9 shall become paragraph *(a)* of that rule and a new paragraph *(b)* shall be added to read as follows:

"This rule shall apply also to a request by any Member for an emergency special session pursuant to resolution 377 A (V). In such a case the Secretary-General shall communicate with other Members by the most expeditious means of communication available."

3. Rule 10 is amended by adding at the end thereof the following:

". . . In the case of an emergency special session convened pursuant to rule 8(b), the Secretary-General shall notify the Members of the United Nations at least twelve hours in advance of the opening of the session."

4. Rule 16 is amended by adding at the end thereof the following:

". . . The provisional agenda of an emergency special session shall be communicated to the Members of the United Nations simultaneously with the communication summoning the session."

5. Rule 19 is amended by adding at the end thereof the following:

". . . During an emergency special session additional items concerning the matters dealt with in resolution 377 A (V) may be added to the agenda by a two-thirds majority of the Members present and voting."

6. There is added a new rule to precede rule 65 to read as follows:

"Notwithstanding the provisions of any other rule and unless the General Assembly decides otherwise, the Assembly, in case of an emergency special session, shall convene in plenary session only and proceed directly to consider the item proposed for consideration in the request for the holding of the session, without previous reference to the General Committee or to any other Committee; the President and Vice-Presidents for such emergency special sessions shall be, respectively, the Chairman of those delegations from which were elected the President and Vice-Presidents of the previous session."

B

For the purpose of maintaining international peace and security, in accordance with the Charter of the United Nations, and, in particular, with Chapters V, VI and VII of the Charter,

The General Assembly

Recommends to the Security Council:

That it should take the necessary steps to ensure that the action provided for under the Charter is taken with respect to threats to the peace, breaches of the peace or acts of aggression and with respect to the peaceful settlement of disputes or situations likely to endanger the maintenance of international peace and security;

That it should devise measures for the earliest application of Articles 43, 45, 46 and 47 of the Charter of the United Nations regarding the placing of armed forces at the disposal of the Security Council by the States Members of the United Nations and the effective functioning of the Military Staff Committee;

The above dispositions should in no manner prevent the General Assembly from fulfilling its functions under resolution 377 A (V).

C

The General Assembly,

Recognizing that the primary function of the United Nations Organization is to maintain and promote peace, security and justice among all nations, . . .

Recognizing that the Charter charges the Security Council with the primary responsibility for maintaining international peace and security,

Reaffirming the importance of unanimity among the permanent members of the Security Council on all problems which are likely to threaten world peace,

Recalling General Assembly resolution 190 (III) entitled "Appeal to the Great Powers to renew their efforts to compose their differences and establish a lasting peace",

Recommends to the permanent members of the Security Council that:

(a) They meet and discuss, collectively or otherwise, and, if necessary, with other States concerned, all problems which are likely to threaten international peace and hamper the activities of the United Nations, with a view to their resolving fundamental differences and reaching agreement in accordance with the spirit and letter of the Charter;

(b) They advise the General Assembly and, when it is not in session, the Members of the United Nations, as soon as appropriate, of the results of their consultations.

U.N. PARTICIPATION ACT
22 U.S.C. §287c-d (1982)

§287c. Economic and Communication Sanctions Pursuant to United Nations Security Council Resolution

(a) *Enforcement Measures; Importation of Rhodesian Chromium*

Notwithstanding the provisions of any other law, whenever the United States is called upon by the Security Council to apply measures which said Council has decided, pursuant to article 41 of said Charter, are to be employed to give effect to its decisions under said Charter, the President may, to the extent necessary to apply such measures, through any agency which he may designate, and under such orders, rules, and regulations as may be prescribed by him, investigate, regulate, or prohibit, in whole or in part, economic relations or rail, sea, air, postal, telegraphic, radio, and other means of communication between any foreign country or any national thereof or any person therein and the United States or any person subject to the jurisdiction thereof, or involving any property subject to the jurisdiction of the United States. Any Executive order which is issued under this subsection and which applies measures against Southern Rhodesia pursuant to any United Nations Security Council Resolution may be enforced, notwithstanding the provisions of any other law. The President may exempt from such Executive order any shipment of chromium in any form which is in transit to the United States on March 18, 1977.

(b) *Penalties*

Any person who willfully violates or evades or attempts to violate or evade any order, rule, or regulation issued by the President pursuant to subsection (a) of this section shall, upon conviction, be find not more than $10,000 or, if a natural person, be imprisoned for not more than ten years, or both; and the officer, director, or agent of any corporation who knowingly participates in such violation or evasion shall be punished by a like fine, imprisonment, or both, and any property, funds, securities, papers, or other articles or documents, or any vessel, together with her tackle, apparel, furniture, and equipment, or vehicle, or aircraft, concerned in such violation shall be forfeited to the United States. . . .

(Dec. 20, 1945, c.583, §5, 59 Stat. 620; Oct. 10, 1949, c.660, §3, 63 Stat. 735; Mar. 18, 1977, Pub. L. 95-12, §1, 91 Stat. 22.)

§287d. Use of Armed Forces; Limitations

The President is authorized to negotiate a special agreement or agreements with the Security Council which shall be subject to the approval of the Congress by appropriate Act or joint resolution, providing for the numbers and types of armed forces, their degree of readiness and general location, and the nature of facilities and assistance, including rights of passage, to be made available to the Security Council on its call for the purpose of maintaining international peace and security in accordance with article 43 of said Charter. The President shall not be deemed to require the authorization of the Congress to make available to the Security Council on its call in order to take action under article 42 of said Charter and pursuant to such special agreement or agreements the armed forces, facilities, or assistance provided for therein: *Provided,* That, except as authorized in section 287d-1 of this title, nothing herein contained shall be construed as an authorization to the President by the Congress to make available to the Security Council for such purpose armed forces, facilities, or assistance in addition to the forces, facilities, and assistance provided for in such special agreement or agreements.

(Dec. 20, 1945, c.583, §6, 59 Stat. 621; Oct. 10, 1949, c.660, §4, 63 Stat. 735.)

§287d-1. Noncombatant Assistance to United Nations

(a) *Armed Forces Details; Supplies and Equipment; Obligation of Funds; Procurement and Replacement of Requested Items*

Notwithstanding the provisions of any other law, the President, upon the request by the United Nations for cooperative action, and to the extent that he finds that it is consistent with the national interest to comply with such request, may authorize, in support of such activities of the United Nations as are specifically directed to the peaceful settlement of disputes and not involving the employment of armed forces contemplated by chapter VII of the United Nations Charter—

(1) the detail to the United Nations, under such terms and conditions as the President shall determine, of personnel of the armed forces of the United States to serve as observers, guards, or in any non-combatant capacity, but in no event shall more than a total of one thousand of such personnel be so detailed at any one time: *Provided,* That while so detailed, such personnel shall be considered for all purposes as acting in the line of duty including the receipt of pay and allowances as personnel of the armed forces of the United States, credit for longevity and retirement, and all other perquisites appertaining to such duty: *Provided further,* That upon authorization or approval by the President, such personnel may accept directly from the United Nations (a) any or all of the allowances or perquisites to which they are entitled under the first proviso hereof, and (b) extraordinary expenses and perquisites incident to such detail;

(2) the furnishing of facilities, services, or other assistance and the loan

of the agreed fair share of the United States of any supplies and equipment to the United Nations by the Department of Defense, under such terms and conditions as the President shall determine;

(3) the obligation, insofar as necessary to carry out the purposes of clauses (1) and (2) of this subsection, of any funds appropriated to the Department of Defense or any department therein, the procurement of such personnel, supplies, equipment, facilities, services, or other assistance as may be made available in accordance with the request of the United Nations, and the replacement of such items, when necessary, where they are furnished from stocks.

(b) *Reimbursement from United Nations; Waiver of Reimbursement*

Whenever personnel or assistance is made available pursuant to the authority contained in subsection (a)(1) and (2) of this section, the President shall require reimbursement from the United Nations for the expense thereby incurred by the United States: *Provided,* That in exceptional circumstances, or when the President finds it to be in the national interest, he may waive, in whole or in part, the requirement of such reimbursement: *Provided further,* That when any such reimbursement is made, it shall be credited, at the option of the appropriate department of the Department of Defense, either to the appropriation, fund, or account utilized in incurring the obligation, or to an appropriate appropriation, fund, or account currently available for the purposes for which expenditures were made.

(c) *Additional Appropriation Authorizations*

In addition to the authorization of appropriations to the Department of State contained in section 287e of this title, there is hereby authorized to be appropriated to the Department of Defense, or any department therein, such sums as may be necessary to reimburse such departments in the event that reimbursement from the United Nations is waived in whole or in part pursuant to authority contained in subsection (b) of this section. . . .

(Dec. 20, 1945, c.583, §7, as added Oct. 10, 1949, c.660, §5, 63 Stat. 735, and amended Aug. 10, 1949, c.412, §12(a), 63 Stat. 591.)

PROPOSED INTELLIGENCE AUTHORIZATION ACT FOR FISCAL YEAR 1991

S. 2834, 101st Cong., 2d Sess.*

TITLE VI — OVERSIGHT OF INTELLIGENCE ACTIVITIES

REPEAL OF HUGHES-RYAN AMENDMENT

Sec. 601. Section 662 of the Foreign Assistance Act of 1961 (22 U.S.C. 2422) is repealed.

OVERSIGHT OF INTELLIGENCE ACTIVITIES

Sec. 602. Title V of the National Security Act of 1947 is amended by striking out section 501 (50 U.S.C. 413) and inserting in lieu thereof the following new sections:

GENERAL PROVISIONS

Sec. 501. (a)(1) The President shall ensure that the Select Committee on Intelligence of the Senate and the Permanent Select Committee on Intelligence of the House of Representatives (hereinafter in this title referred to as the 'intelligence committees') are kept fully and currently informed of the intelligence activities of the United States, including any significant anticipated intelligence activities, as required by this title.

(2) Nothing contained in this title shall be construed as requiring the approval of the intelligence committees as a condition precedent to the initiation of such activities.

(b) The President shall ensure that any illegal intelligence activity is reported promptly to the intelligence committees, as well as any corrective action that has been taken or is planned in connection with such illegal activity.

(c) The President and the intelligence committees shall establish such procedures as may be necessary to carry out the provisions of this title.

(d) The House of Representatives and the Senate, in consultation with the Director of Central Intelligence, shall each establish, by rule or resolution of such House, procedures to protect from unauthorized dis-

---

*President Bush refused to sign this bill within ten working days after it reached his desk, thus "pocket-vetoing" it. See Casebook at p.1354.

closure all classified information and all information relating to intelligence sources and methods furnished to the intelligence committees or to Members of Congress under this title. In accordance with such procedures, each of the intelligence committees shall promptly call to the attention of its respective House, or to any appropriate committee or committees of its respective House, any matter relating to intelligence activities requiring the attention of such House or such committee or committees.

(e) Nothing in this Act shall be construed as authority to withhold information from the intelligence committees on the grounds that providing the information to the intelligence committees would constitute the unauthorized disclosure of classified information or information relating to intelligence sources and methods.

(f) As used in this section, the term 'intelligence activities' includes, but is not limited to, covert actions as defined in section 503(e).

REPORTING INTELLIGENCE ACTIVITIES OTHER THAN COVERT ACTION

Sec. 502. To the extent consistent with due regard for the protection from unauthorized disclosure of classified information relating to sensitive intelligence sources and methods or other exceptionally sensitive matters, the Director of Central Intelligence and the heads of all departments, agencies, and other entities of the United States Government involved in intelligence activities shall —

(1) keep the intelligence committees fully and currently informed of all intelligence activities, other than a covert action as defined in section 503(e), which are the responsibility of, are engaged in by, or are carried out for or on behalf of, any department, agency, or entity of the United States Government, including any significant anticipated intelligence activity and any significant intelligence failure; . . .

PRESIDENTIAL APPROVAL AND REPORTING OF COVERT ACTIONS

Sec. 503(a). The President may not authorize the conduct of a covert action by departments, agencies, or entities of the United States Government unless the President determines such an action is necessary to support identifiable foreign policy objectives of the United States and is important to the national security of the United States, which determination shall be set forth in a finding that shall meet each of the following conditions:

(1) Each finding shall be in writing, unless immediate action by the United States is required and time does not permit the preparation of a written finding, in which case a written record of the President's decision shall be contemporaneously made and shall be reduced to a written finding as soon as possible but in no event more than forty-eight hours after the decision is made.

(2) Except as permitted by paragraph (1), a finding may not authorize or sanction covert actions, or any aspect of such actions, which have already occurred.

(3) Each finding shall specify each and every department, agency, or entity of the United States Government authorized to fund or otherwise participate in any significant way in such actions. . . .

(4) Each finding shall specify whether it is contemplated that any third party which is not an element of, or a contractor or contract agent of, the United States Government, or is not otherwise subject to United States Government policies and regulations, will be used to fund or otherwise participate in any significant way in the covert action concerned, or be used to undertake the covert action concerned on behalf of the United States.

(5) A finding may not authorize any action that would violate the Constitution or any statute of the United States.

(b) To the extent consistent with due regard for the protection from unauthorized disclosure of classified information relating to sensitive intelligence sources and methods or other exceptionally sensitive matters, the Director of Central Intelligence and the heads of all departments, agencies, and entities of the United States Government involved in a covert action —

(1) shall keep the intelligence committees fully and currently informed of all covert actions which are the responsibility of, are engaged in by, or are carried out for or on behalf of, any department, agency, or entity of the United States Government, including significant failures; and

(2) shall furnish to the intelligence committees any information or material concerning covert actions which is in the possession, custody, or control of any department, agency, or entity of the United States Government and which is requested by either of the intelligence committees in order to carry out its authorized responsibilities.

(c)(1) The President shall ensure that any finding approved pursuant to subsection (a) shall be reported to the intelligence committees as soon as possible after such approval and prior to the initiation of the covert actions authorized by the finding, except as otherwise provided in paragraph (2) and paragraph (3).

(2) If the President determines it is essential to limit access to the finding to meet extraordinary circumstances affecting vital interests of the United States, such finding may be reported to the Chairmen and Ranking Minority Members of the intelligence committees, the Speaker and Minority Leader of the House of Representatives, the Majority and Minority Leaders of the Senate, and such other Member or members of the joint congressional leadership as may be included by the President.

(3) On rare occasions, the President may direct that covert actions be initiated before reporting such actions to the intelligence committees. On such occasions, the President shall fully inform the intelligence committees in a timely fashion and shall provide a statement of the reasons for not giving prior notice.

(4) In a case under paragraph (1), (2) or (3), a copy of the finding, signed by the President, shall be provided to the chairman of each intelligence committee. Where access to a finding is limited to the Members of Congress specified in paragraph (2), a statement of the reasons for limiting such access shall also be provided.

(d) The President shall ensure that the intelligence committees, or, if applicable, the Members of Congress specified in subsection (c)(2), are notified of any significant change in a previously approved covert action, or any significant undertaking pursuant to a previously approved finding, in the same manner as findings are reported pursuant to subsection (c).

(e) As used in this title, the term 'covert action' means an activity or activities conducted by an element of the United States Government to influence political, economic, or military conditions abroad so that the role of the United States Government is not intended to be apparent or acknowledged publicly, but does not include —

(1) activities the primary purpose of which is to acquire intelligence, traditional counterintelligence activities, traditional activities to improve or maintain the operational security of United States Government programs, or administrative activities;

(2) traditional diplomatic or military activities or routine support to such activities;

(3) traditional law enforcement activities conducted by United States Government law enforcement agencies or routine support to such activities; or

(4) activities to provide routine support to the covert activities (other than activities described in paragraph (1), (2), or (3)) of other United States Government agencies abroad.

A request by any department, agency, or entity of the United States to a foreign government or a private citizen to conduct a covert action on behalf of the United States shall be deemed to be a covert action.

(f) No covert action may be conducted which is intended to influence United States political processes, public opinion, policies, or media.

LIMITATIONS ON USE OF FUNDS

Sec. 603. Section 502 of the National Security Act of 1947 (50 U.S.C. 414) —

(1) is redesignated as section 504;

(2) is amended in subsection (a)(2) by striking out "501" and inserting in lieu thereof "503"; and

(3) is amended by adding at the end the following:

(d) No funds appropriated for, or otherwise available to, any department, agency, or entity of the United States Government, may be expended, or may be directed to be expended, for any covert action, as defined in section 503(e), unless and until a Presidential finding required by subsection (a) of section 503 has been signed or otherwise issued in accordance with that subsection.

(e) Except as provided in section 204(b) (appearing under the heading 'GENERAL PROVISIONS — DEPARTMENT OF JUSTICE') of the Department of Justice Appropriations Act, 1988 (contained in Public Law 100-202) and in section 423 of title 10, United States Code, funds available to an intelligence agency which are not appropriated funds may be obligated or expended for an intelligence or intelligence related activity only if they are used for activities reported to the appropriate congressional committees pursuant to procedures jointly agreed upon by such committees and, as appropriate, the Director of Central Intelligence or the Secretary of Defense, which identify types of activities for which nonappropriated funds may be expended and under what circumstances an activity must be reported as a significant anticipated intelligence activity before such funds can be expended. . . .

WAR POWERS RESOLUTION

November 7, 1973, Pub. L. No. 93-148, 87 Stat. 555, 50 U.S.C. §§1541-1548 (as amended)

§1541. Purpose and Policy

(a) Congressional Declaration

It is the purpose of this chapter to fulfill the intent of the framers of the Constitution of the United States and insure that the collective judgment of both the Congress and the President will apply to the introduction of United States Armed Forces into hostilities, or into situations where imminent involvement in hostilities is clearly indicated by the circumstances, and to the continued use of such forces in hostilities or in such situations.

(b) Congressional Legislative Power Under Necessary and Proper Clause

Under article I, section 8, of the Constitution, it is specifically provided that the Congress shall have the power to make all laws necessary and proper for carrying into execution, not only its own powers but also all other powers vested by the Constitution in the Government of the United States, or in any department or officer hereof.

(c) Presidential Executive Power as Commander-in-Chief; Limitation

The constitutional powers of the President as Commander-in-Chief to introduce United States Armed Forces into hostilities, or into situations where imminent involvement in hostilities is clearly indicated by the circumstances, are exercised only pursuant to (1) a declaration of war, (2) specific statutory authorization, or (3) a national emergency created by attack upon the United States, its territories or possessions, or its armed forces.

(Pub. L. 93-148, §2)

§1542. Consultation; Initial and Regular Consultations

The President in every possible instance shall consult with Congress before introducing United States Armed Forces into hostilities or into situations where imminent involvement in hostilities is clearly indicated by the circumstances, and after every such introduction shall consult regularly with the

Congress until United States Armed Forces are no longer engaged in hostilities or have been removed from such situations.

(Pub. L. 93-148, §3.)

§1543. Reporting Requirement

(a) Written Report; Time of Submission; Circumstances Necessitating Submission; Information Reported

In the absence of a declaration of war, in any case in which United States Armed Forces are introduced —

(1) into hostilities or into situations where imminent involvement in hostilities is clearly indicated by the circumstances;

(2) into the territory, airspace or waters of a foreign nation, while equipped for combat, except for deployments which relate solely to supply, replacement, repair, or training of such forces; or

(3) in numbers which substantially enlarge United States Armed Forces equipped for combat already located in a foreign nation;

the President shall submit within 48 hours to the Speaker of the House of Representatives and to the President pro tempore of the Senate a report, in writing, setting forth —

(A) the circumstances necessitating the introduction of United States Armed Forces;

(B) the constitutional and legislative authority under which such introduction took place; and

(C) the estimated scope and duration of the hostilities or involvement.

(b) Other Information Reported

The President shall provide such other information as the Congress may request in the fulfillment of its constitutional responsibilities with respect to committing the Nation to war and to the use of United States Armed Forces abroad.

(c) Periodic Reports; Semiannual Requirement

Whenever United States Armed Forces are introduced into hostilities or into any situation described in subsection (a) of this section, the President shall, so long as such armed forces continue to be engaged in such hostilities or situation, report to the Congress periodically on the status of such hostilities or situation as well as on the scope and duration of such hostilities or situation, but in no event shall he report to the Congress less often than once every six months.

(Pub. L. 93-148, §4.)

§1544. Congressional Action

(a) Transmittal of Report and Referral to Congressional Committees; Joint Request for Convening Congress

Each report submitted pursuant to section 1543(a)(1) of this title shall be transmitted to the Speaker of the House of Representatives and to the President pro tempore of the Senate on the same calendar day. Each report so transmitted shall be referred to the Committee on Foreign Affairs of the House of Representatives and to the Committee on Foreign Relations of the Senate for appropriate action. If, when the report is transmitted, the Congress has adjourned sine die or has adjourned for any period in excess of three calendar days, the Speaker of the House of Representatives and the President pro tempore of the Senate, if they deem it advisable (or if petitioned by at least 30 percent of the membership of their respective Houses) shall jointly request the President to convene Congress in order that it may consider the report and take appropriate action pursuant to this section.

(b) Termination of Use of United States Armed Forces; Exceptions; Extension Period

Within sixty calendar days after a report is submitted or is required to be submitted pursuant to section 1543(a)(1) of this title, whichever is earlier, the President shall terminate any use of United States Armed Forces with respect to which such report was submitted (or required to be submitted), unless the Congress (1) has declared war or has enacted a specific authorization for such use of United States Armed Forces, (2) has extended by law such sixty-day period, or (3) is physically unable to meet as a result of an armed attack upon the United States. Such sixty-day period shall be extended for not more than an additional thirty days if the President determines and certifies to the Congress in writing that unavoidable military necessity respecting the safety of United States Armed Forces requires the continued use of such armed forces in the course of bringing about a prompt removal of such forces.

(c) Concurrent Resolution for Removal by President of United States Armed Forces

Notwithstanding subsection (b) of this section, at any time that United States Armed Forces are engaged in hostilities outside the territory of the United States, its possessions and territories without a declaration of war or specific statutory authorization, such forces shall be removed by the President if the Congress so directs by concurrent resolution.

(Pub. L. 93-148, §5.)

§1545. Congressional Priority Procedures for Joint Resolution or Bill

(a) Time Requirement; Referral to Congressional Committee; Single Report

Any joint resolution or bill introduced pursuant to section 1544(b) of this title at least thirty calendar days before the expiration of the sixty-day period specified in such section shall be referred to the Committee on Foreign Affairs of the House of Representatives or the Committee on Foreign Relations of the Senate, as the case may be, and such committee shall report one such joint resolution or bill, together with its recommendations, not later than twenty-four calendar days before the expiration of the sixty-day period specified in such section, unless such House shall otherwise determine by the years and nays.

(b) Pending Business; Vote

Any joint resolution or bill so reported shall become the pending business of the House in question (in the case of the Senate the time for debate shall be equally divided between the proponents and the opponents), and shall be voted on within three calendar days thereafter, unless such House shall otherwise determine by yeas and nays.

(c) Referral to Other House Committee

Such a joint resolution or bill passed by one House shall be referred to the committee of the other House named in subsection (a) of this section and shall be reported out not later than fourteen calendar days before the expiration of the sixty-day period specified in section 1544(b) of this title. The joint resolution or bill so reported shall become the pending business of the House in question and shall be voted on within three calendar days after it has been reported, unless such House shall otherwise determine by yeas and nays.

(d) Disagreement Between Houses

In the case of any disagreement between the two Houses of Congress with respect to a joint resolution or bill passed by both Houses, conferees shall be promptly appointed and the committee of conference shall make and file a report with respect to such resolution or bill not later than four calendar days before the expiration of the sixty-day period specified in section 1544(b) of this title. In the event the conferees are unable to agree within 48 hours, they shall report back to their respective Houses in disagreement. Notwithstanding any rule in either House concerning the printing of conference reports in the Record or concerning any delay in the consideration of such reports, such report shall be acted on by both Houses not later than the expiration of such sixty-day period.

(Pub. L. 93-148, §6.)

§1546. Congressional Priority Procedures for Concurrent Resolution

(a) Referral to Congressional Committee; Single Report

Any concurrent resolution introduced pursuant to section 1544(c) of this title shall be referred to the Committee on Foreign Affairs of the House of Representatives or the Committee on Foreign Relations of the Senate, as the case may be, and one such concurrent resolution shall be reported out by such committee together with its recommendations within fifteen calendar days, unless such House shall otherwise determine by the yeas and nays.

(b) Pending Business; Vote

Any concurrent resolution so reported shall become the pending business of the House in question (in the case of the Senate the time for debate shall be equally divided between the proponents and the opponents) and shall be voted on within three calendar days thereafter, unless such House shall otherwise determine by yeas and nays.

(c) Referral to Other House Committee

Such a concurrent resolution passed by one House shall be referred to the committee of the other House named in subsection (a) of this section and shall be reported out by such committee together with its recommendations within fifteen calendar days and shall thereupon become the pending business of such House and shall be voted upon within three calendar days, unless such House shall otherwise determine by yeas and nays.

(d) Disagreement Between Houses

In the case of any disagreement between the two Houses of Congress with respect to a concurrent resolution passed by both Houses, conferees shall be promptly appointed and the committee of conference shall make and file a report with respect to such concurrent resolution within six calendar days after the legislation is referred to the committee of conference. Notwithstanding any rule in either House concerning the printing of conference reports in the Record or concerning any delay in the consideration of such reports, such report shall be acted on by both Houses not later than six calendar days after the conference report is filed. In the event the conferees are unable to agree within 48 hours, they shall report back to their respective Houses in disagreement.

(Pub. L. 93-148, §7.)

§1546a. Expedited Procedures for Certain Joint Resolutions and Bills

Any joint resolution or bill introduced in either House which requires the removal of United States Armed Forces engaged in hostilities outside the territory of the United States, its possessions and territories, without a declaration of war or specific statutory authorization shall be considered in accordance with the procedures of section 601(b) of the International Security Assistance and Arms Export Control Act of 1976, except that any such resolution or bill shall be amendable. If such a joint resolution or bill should be vetoed by the President, the time for debate in consideration of the veto message on such measure shall be limited to twenty hours in the Senate and in the House shall be determined in accordance with the Rules of the House.

(Pub. L. 98-164, title X, §1013, Nov. 22, 1983, 97 Stat. 1062.)

§1547. Interpretation of Joint Resolution

(a) *Inferences from Any Law or Treaty*

Authority to introduce United States Armed Forces into hostilities or into situations wherein involvement in hostilities is clearly indicated by the circumstances shall not be inferred —

(1) from any provision of law (whether or not in effect before November 7, 1973), including any provision contained in any appropriation Act, unless such provision specifically authorizes the introduction of United States Armed Forces into hostilities or into such situations and states that it is intended to constitute specific statutory authorization within the meaning of this chapter; or

(2) from any treaty heretofore or hereafter ratified unless such treaty is implemented by legislation specifically authorizing the introduction of United States Armed Forces into hostilities or into such situations and stating that it is intended to constitute specific statutory authorization within the meaning of this chapter.

(b) *Joint Headquarters Operations of High-level Military Commands*

Nothing in this chapter shall be construed to require any further specific statutory authorization to permit members of United States Armed Forces to participate jointly with members of the armed forces of one or more foreign countries in the headquarters operations of high-level military commands which were established prior to November 7, 1973, and pursuant to the United Nations Charter or any treaty ratified by the United States prior to such date.

(c) *Introduction of United States Armed Forces*

For purposes of this chapter, the term "introduction of United States Armed Forces" includes the assignment of members of such armed forces to command, coordinate, participate in the movement of, or accompany the regular or irregular military forces of any foreign country or government when such military forces are engaged, or there exists an imminent threat that such forces will become engaged, in hostilities.

(d) Constitutional Authorities or Existing Treaties Unaffected; Construction Against Grant of Presidential Authority Respecting Use of United States Armed Forces

Nothing in this chapter —

(1) is intended to alter the constitutional authority of the Congress or of the President, or the provisions of existing treaties; or

(2) shall be construed as granting any authority to the President with respect to the introduction of United States Armed Forces into hostilities or into situations wherein involvement in hostilities is clearly indicated by the circumstances which authority he would not have had in the absence of this chapter.

(Pub. L. 93-148, §8.)

§1548. Separability of Provisions

If any provision of this chapter or the application thereof to any person or circumstance is held invalid, the remainder of the chapter and the application of such provision to any other person or circumstance shall not be affected thereby.

(Pub. L. 93-148, §9.)

U.N. SECURITY COUNCIL RESOLUTIONS RE: IRAQI INVASION AND OCCUPATION (1990)

RESOLUTION 660
August 2, 1990*

The Security Council,
Alarmed by the invasion of Kuwait on 2 August 1990 by the military forces of Iraq,
Determining that there exists a breach of international peace and security as regards the Iraqi invasion of Kuwait,
Acting under Articles 39 and 40 of the Charter of the United Nations,
1. *Condemns* the Iraqi invasion of Kuwait;
2. *Demands* that Iraq withdraw immediately and unconditionally all its forces to the positions in which they were located on 1 August 1990;
3. *Calls upon* Iraq and Kuwait to begin immediately intensive negotiations for the resolution of their differences and supports all efforts in this regard, and especially those of the League of Arab States;
4. *Decides* to meet again as necessary to consider further steps to ensure compliance with the present resolution.

RESOLUTION 661
August 6, 1990†

The Security Council,
Reaffirming its resolution 660 (1990) of 2 August 1990,
Deeply concerned that that resolution has not been implemented and that the invasion by Iraq of Kuwait continues with further loss of human life and material destruction,
Determined to bring the invasion and occupation of Kuwait by Iraq to an end and to restore the sovereignty, independence and territorial integrity of Kuwait,
Noting that the legitimate Government of Kuwait has expressed its readiness to comply with resolution 660 (1990),
Mindful of its responsibilities under the Charter of the United Nations for the maintenance of international peace and security,
Affirming the inherent right of individual or collective self-defence, in

---

*S.C. Res. 660. Adopted by a vote of 14-0, with Yemen abstaining.
†Adopted by a vote of 13-0, with Cuba and Yemen abstaining.

response to the armed attack by Iraq against Kuwait, in accordance with Article 51 of the Charter,

Acting under Chapter VII of the Charter of the United Nations,

1. *Determines* that Iraq so far has failed to comply with paragraph 2 of resolution 660 (1990) and has usurped the authority of the legitimate Government of Kuwait;

2. *Decides,* as a consequence, to take the following measures to secure compliance of Iraq with paragraph 2 of resolution 660 (1990) and to restore the authority of the legitimate Government of Kuwait;

3. *Decides* that all States shall prevent:

(a) The import into their territories of all commodities and products originating in Iraq or Kuwait exported therefrom after the date of the present resolution;

(b) Any activities by their nationals or in their territories which would promote or are calculated to promote the export or trans-shipment of any commodities or products from Iraq or Kuwait; and any dealings by their nationals or their flag vessels or in their territories in any commodities or products originating in Iraq or Kuwait and exported therefrom after the date of the present resolution, including in particular any transfer of funds to Iraq or Kuwait for the purposes of such activities or dealings;

(c) The sale or supply by their nationals or from their territories or using their flag vessels of any commodities or products, including weapons or any other military equipment, whether or not originating in their territories but not including supplies intended strictly for medical purposes, and, in humanitarian circumstances, foodstuffs, to any person or body in Iraq or Kuwait or to any person or body for the purposes of any business carried on in or operated from Iraq or Kuwait, and any activities by their nationals or in their territories which promote or are calculated to promote such sale or supply of such commodities or products;

4. *Decides* that all States shall not make available to the Government of Iraq or to any commercial, industrial or public utility undertaking in Iraq or Kuwait, any funds or any other financial or economic resources and shall prevent their nationals and any persons within their territories from removing from their territories or otherwise making available to that Government or to any such undertaking any such funds or resources and from remitting any other funds to persons or bodies within Iraq or Kuwait, except payments exclusively for strictly medical or humanitarian purposes and, in humanitarian circumstances, foodstuffs;

5. *Calls upon* all States, including States non-members of the United Nations, to act strictly in accordance with the provisions of the present resolution notwithstanding any contract entered into or licence granted before the date of the present resolution;

6. *Decides* to establish, in accordance with rule 28 of the provisional rules of procedure of the Security Council, a Committee of the Security Council consisting of all the members of the Council, to undertake the following tasks and to report on its work to the Council with its observations and recommendations:

(a) To examine the reports on the progress of the implementation of the present resolution which will be submitted by the Secretary-General;

(b) To seek from all States further information regarding the action taken by them concerning the effective implementation of the provisions laid down in the present resolution;

7. *Calls upon* all States to co-operate fully with the Committee in the fulfilment of its task, including supplying such information as may be sought by the Committee in pursuance of the present resolution;

8. *Requests* the Secretary-General to provide all necessary assistance to the Committee and to make the necessary arrangements in the Secretariat for the purpose;

9. *Decides* that, notwithstanding paragraphs 4 through 8 above, nothing in the present resolution shall prohibit assistance to the legitimate Government of Kuwait, and *calls upon* all States:

(a) To take appropriate measures to protect assets of the legitimate Government of Kuwait and its agencies;

(b) Not to recognize any régime set up by the occupying Power;

10. *Requests* the Secretary-General to report to the Council on the progress of the implementation of the present resolution, the first report to be submitted within thirty days;

11. *Decides* to keep this item on its agenda and to continue its efforts to put an early end to the invasion by Iraq.

RESOLUTION 662

August 9, 1990*

The Security Council, . . .

Gravely alarmed by the declaration by Iraq of a "comprehensive and eternal merger" with Kuwait,

Demanding, once again, that Iraq withdraw immediately and unconditionally all its forces to the positions in which they were located on 1 August 1990,

Determined to bring the occupation of Kuwait by Iraq to an end and to restore the sovereignty, independence and territorial integrity of Kuwait,

Determined also to restore the authority of the legitimate Government of Kuwait,

1. *Decides* that annexation of Kuwait by Iraq under any form and whatever pretext has no legal validity, and is considered null and void;

2. *Calls upon* all States, international organizations and specialized agencies not to recognize that annexation, and to refrain from any action or dealing that might be interpreted as an indirect recognition of the annexation;

3. *Further demands* that Iraq rescind its actions purporting to annex Kuwait; . . .

*Adopted by a vote of 15-0.

RESOLUTION 664

August 18, 1990*

The Security Council, . . .

Deeply concerned for the safety and well being of third state nationals in Iraq and Kuwait,

Recalling the obligations of Iraq in this regard under international law, . . .

Acting under Chapter VII of the United Nations Charter:

1. *Demands* that Iraq permit and facilitate the immediate departure from Kuwait and Iraq of the nationals of third countries and grant immediate and continuing access of consular officials to such nationals;

2. *Further demands* that Iraq take no action to jeopardize the safety, security or health of such nationals;

3. *Reaffirms* its decision in resolution 662 (1990) that annexation of Kuwait by Iraq is null and void, and therefore demands that the government of Iraq rescind its orders for the closure of diplomatic and consular missions in Kuwait and the withdrawal of the immunity of their personnel, and refrain from any such actions in the future; . . .

RESOLUTION 665

August 25, 1990†

The Security Council, . . .

Having decided in resolution 661 (1990) to impose economic sanctions under Chapter VII of the Charter of the United Nations,

Determined to bring an end to the occupation of Kuwait by Iraq which imperils the existence of a Member State and to restore the legitimate authority, and the sovereignty, independence and territorial integrity of Kuwait which requires the speedy implementation of the above resolutions, . . .

Gravely alarmed that Iraq continues to refuse to comply with resolutions 660 (1990), 661 (1990), 662 (1990) and 664 (1990) and in particular at the conduct of the Government of Iraq in using Iraqi flag vessels to export oil,

1. *Calls upon* those Member States co-operating with the Government of Kuwait which are deploying maritime forces to the area to use such measures commensurate to the specific circumstances as may be necessary under the authority of the Security Council to halt all inward and outward maritime shipping in order to inspect and verify their cargoes and destinations and to ensure strict implementation of the provisions related to such shipping laid down in resolution 661 (1990);

2. *Invites* Member States accordingly to co-operate as may be necessary to ensure compliance with the provisions of resolution 661 (1990) with

---

*Adopted by a vote of 15-0.
†Adopted by a vote of 13-0, with Cuba and Yemen abstaining.

maximum use of political and diplomatic measures, in accordance with paragraph 1 above;

3. *Requests* all States to provide in accordance with the Charter such assistance as may be required by the States referred to in paragraph 1 of this resolution;

4. *Further requests* the States concerned to co-ordinate their actions in pursuit of the above paragraphs of this resolution using as appropriate mechanisms of the Military Staff Committee and after consultation with the Secretary-General to submit reports to the Security Council and its Committee established under resolution 661 (1990) to facilitate the monitoring of the implementation of this resolution; . . .

RESOLUTION 666
September 13, 1990*

The Security Council,

Recalling its resolution 661 (1990), paragraphs 3 (c) and 4 of which apply, except in humanitarian circumstances, to foodstuffs,

Recognizing that circumstances may arise in which it will be necessary for foodstuffs to be supplied to the civilian population in Iraq or Kuwait in order to relieve human suffering,

Noting that in this respect the Committee established under paragraph 6 of that resolution has received communications from several Member States,

Emphasizing that it is for the Security Council, alone or acting through the Committee, to determine whether humanitarian circumstances have arisen,

Deeply concerned that Iraq has failed to comply with its obligations under Security Council resolution 664 (1990) in respect of the safety and well-being of third State nationals, and reaffirming that Iraq retains full responsibility in this regard under international humanitarian law including, where applicable, the Fourth Geneva Convention,

Acting under Chapter VII of the Charter of the United Nations,

1. *Decides* that in order to make the necessary determination whether or not for the purposes of paragraph 3 (c) and paragraph 4 of resolution 661 (1990) humanitarian circumstances have arisen, the Committee shall keep the situation regarding foodstuffs in Iraq and Kuwait under constant review;

2. *Expects* Iraq to comply with its obligations under Security Council resolution 664 (1990) in respect of third State nationals and reaffirms that Iraq remains fully responsible for their safety and well-being in accordance with international humanitarian law including, where applicable, the Fourth Geneva Convention;

3. *Requests,* for the purposes of paragraphs 1 and 2 of this resolution, that the Secretary-General seek urgently, and on a continuing basis, information from relevant United Nations and other appropriate humanitarian

*Adopted by a vote of 13-2, with Cuba and Yemen dissenting.

agencies and all other sources on the availability of food in Iraq and Kuwait, such information to be communicated by the Secretary-General to the Committee regularly;

4. *Requests further* that in seeking and supplying such information particular attention will be paid to such categories of persons who might suffer specially, such as children under 15 years of age, expectant mothers, maternity cases, the sick and the elderly;

5. *Decides* that if the Committee, after receiving the reports from the Secretary-General, determines that circumstances have arisen in which there is an urgent humanitarian need to supply foodstuffs to Iraq or Kuwait in order to relieve human suffering, it will report promptly to the Council its decision as to how such need should be met;

6. *Directs* the Committee that in formulating its decisions it should bear in mind that foodstuffs should be provided through the United Nations in co-operation with the International Committee of the Red Cross or other appropriate humanitarian agencies and distributed by them or under their supervision in order to ensure that they reach the intended beneficiaries;

7. *Requests* the Secretary-General to use his good offices to facilitate the delivery and distribution of foodstuffs to Kuwait and Iraq in accordance with the provisions of this and other relevant resolutions;

8. *Recalls* that resolution 661 (1990) does not apply to supplies intended strictly for medical purposes, but in this connection recommends that medical supplies should be exported under the strict supervision of the Government of the exporting State or by appropriate humanitarian agencies.

RESOLUTION 667

September 16, 1990*

The Security Council, . . .

Recalling the Vienna Conventions of 18 April 1961 on diplomatic relations and of 24 April 1963 on consular relations, to both of which Iraq is a party,

Considering that the decision of Iraq to order the closure of diplomatic and consular missions in Kuwait and to withdraw the immunity and privileges of these missions and their personnel is contrary to the decisions of the Security Council, the international Conventions mentioned above and international law,

Deeply concerned that Iraq, notwithstanding the decisions of the Security Council and the provisions of the Conventions mentioned above, has committed acts of violence against diplomatic missions and their personnel in Kuwait,

Outraged at recent violations by Iraq of diplomatic premises in Kuwait and at the abduction of personnel enjoying diplomatic immunity and foreign nationals who were present in these premises,

Considering that the above actions by Iraq constitute aggressive acts and

*Adopted by a vote of 15-0.

a flagrant violation of its international obligations which strike at the root of the conduct of international relations in accordance with the Charter of the United Nations,

Recalling that Iraq is fully responsible for any use of violence against foreign nationals or against any diplomatic or consular mission in Kuwait or its personnel,

Determined to ensure respect for its decisions and for Article 25 of the Charter of the United Nations,

Further considering that the grave nature of Iraq's actions, which constitute a new escalation of its violations of international law, obliges the Council not only to express its immediate reaction but also to consult urgently to take further concrete measures to ensure Iraq's compliance with the Council's resolutions,

Acting under Chapter VII of the Charter of the United Nations,

1. *Strongly condemns* aggressive acts perpetrated by Iraq against diplomatic premises and personnel in Kuwait, including the abduction of foreign nationals who were present in those premises;

2. *Demands* the immediate release of those foreign nationals as well as all nationals mentioned in resolution 664 (1990);

3. *Further demands* that Iraq immediately and fully comply with its international obligations under resolutions 660 (1990), 662 (1990) and 664 (1990) of the Security Council, the Vienna Conventions on diplomatic and consular relations and international law;

4. *Further demands* that Iraq immediately protect the safety and well-being of diplomatic and consular personnel and premises in Kuwait and in Iraq and take no action to hinder the diplomatic and consular missions in the performance of their functions, including access to their nationals and the protection of their person and interests;

5. *Reminds* all States that they are obliged to observe strictly resolutions 661 (1990), 662 (1990), 664 (1990), 665 (1990) and 666 (1990);

6. *Decides* to consult urgently to take further concrete measures as soon as possible, under Chapter VII of the Charter, in response to Iraq's continued violation of the Charter, of resolutions of the Council and of international law.

RESOLUTION 669

September 24, 1990*

The Security Council,

Recalling its resolution 661 (1990) of 6 August 1990,

Recalling also Article 50 of the Charter of the United Nations,

Conscious of the fact that an increasing number of requests for assistance have been received under the provisions of Article 50 of the Charter of the United Nations,

Entrusts the Committee established under resolution 661 (1990) concerning the situation between Iraq and Kuwait with the task of examining

*Adopted by a vote of 15-0.

requests for assistance under the provisions of Article 50 of the Charter of the United Nations and making recommendations to the President of the Security Council for appropriate action.

RESOLUTION 670
September 25, 1990*

The Security Council, ...

Condemning Iraq's continued occupation of Kuwait, its failure to rescind its actions and end its purported annexation and its holding of third State nationals against their will, in flagrant violation of resolutions 660 (1990), 662 (1990), 664 (1990) and 667 (1990) and of international humanitarian law,

Condemning further the treatment by Iraqi forces of Kuwaiti nationals, including measures to force them to leave their own country and mistreatment of persons and property in Kuwait in violation of international law,

Noting with grave concern the persistent attempts to evade the measures laid down in resolution 661 (1990), ...

Determined to ensure by all necessary means the strict and complete application of the measures laid down in resolution 661 (1990),

Determined to ensure respect for its decisions and the provisions of Articles 25 and 48 of the Charter of the United Nations,

Affirming that any acts of the Government of Iraq which are contrary to the above-mentioned resolutions or to Articles 25 or 48 of the Charter of the United Nations, such as Decree No. 377 of the Revolution Command Council of Iraq of 16 September 1990, are null and void,

Reaffirming its determination to ensure compliance with Security Council resolutions by maximum use of political and diplomatic means, ...

Underlining to the Government of Iraq that its continued failure to comply with the terms of resolutions 660 (1990), 661 (1990), 662 (1990), 664 (1990), 666 (1990) and 667 (1990) could lead to further serious action by the Council under the Charter of the United Nations, including under Chapter VII,

Recalling the provisions of Article 103 of the Charter of the United Nations,

Acting under Chapter VII of the Charter of the United Nations,

1. *Calls upon* all States to carry out their obligations to ensure strict and complete compliance with resolution 661 (1990) and in particular paragraphs 3, 4 and 5 thereof;

2. *Confirms* that resolution 661 (1990) applies to all means of transport, including aircraft;

3. *Decides* that all States, notwithstanding the existence of any rights or obligations conferred or imposed by any international agreement or any contract entered into or any licence or permit granted before the date of the present resolution, shall deny permission to any aircraft to take off from their territory if the aircraft would carry any cargo to or from Iraq or Kuwait

---

*Adopted by a vote of 14-1, with Cuba opposed.

other than food in humanitarian circumstances, subject to authorization by the Council or the Committee established by resolution 661 (1990) and in accordance with resolution 666 (1990), or supplies intended strictly for medical purposes or solely for UNIIMOG;

4. *Decides further* that all States shall deny permission to any aircraft destined to land in Iraq or Kuwait, whatever its State of registration, to overfly its territory unless:

(a) The aircraft lands at an airfield designated by that State outside Iraq or Kuwait in order to permit its inspection to ensure that there is no cargo on board in violation of resolution 661 (1990) or the present resolution, and for this purpose the aircraft may be detained for as long as necessary; or

(b) The particular flight has been approved by the Committee established by resolution 661 (1990); or

(c) The flight is certified by the United Nations as solely for the purposes of UNIIMOG;

5. *Decides* that each State shall take all necessary measures to ensure that any aircraft registered in its territory or operated by an operator who has his principal place of business or permanent residence in its territory complies with the provisions of resolution 661 (1990) and the present resolution;

6. *Decides further* that all States shall notify in a timely fashion the Committee established by resolution 661 (1990) of any flight between its territory and Iraq or Kuwait to which the requirement to land in paragraph 4 above does not apply, and the purpose for such a flight;

7. *Calls upon* all States to co-operate in taking such measures as may be necessary, consistent with international law, including the Chicago Convention, to ensure the effective implementation of the provisions of resolution 661 (1990) or the present resolution;

8. *Calls upon* all States to detain any ships of Iraqi registry which enter their ports and which are being or have been used in violation of resolution 661 (1990), or to deny such ships entrance to their ports except in circumstances recognized under international law as necessary to safeguard human life;

9. *Reminds* all States of their obligations under resolution 661 (1990) with regard to the freezing of Iraqi assets, and the protection of the assets of the legitimate Government of Kuwait and its agencies, located within their territory and to report to the Committee established under resolution 661 (1990) regarding those assets;

10. *Calls upon* all States to provide to the Committee established by resolution 661 (1990) information regarding the action taken by them to implement the provisions laid down in the present resolution; . . .

12. *Decides* to consider, in the event of evasion of the provisions of resolution 661 (1990) or of the present resolution by a State or its nationals or through its territory, measures directed at the State in question to prevent such evasion;

13. *Reaffirms* that the Fourth Geneva Convention applies to Kuwait and that as a High Contracting Party to the Convention Iraq is bound to comply fully with all its terms and in particular is liable under the Convention in respect of the grave breaches committed by it, as are individuals who commit or order the commission of grave breaches.

RESOLUTION 674
October 29, 1990*

The Security Council, . . .

Stressing the urgent need for the immediate and unconditional withdrawal of all Iraqi forces from Kuwait, for the restoration of Kuwait's sovereignty, independence and territorial integrity and of the authority of its legitimate Government,

Condemning the actions by the Iraqi authorities and occupying forces to take third-state nationals hostage and to mistreat and oppress Kuwait and third-state nationals, and the other actions reported to the Council such as the destruction of Kuwaiti demographic records, forced departure of Kuwaitis and relocation of population in Kuwait and the unlawful destruction and seizure of public and private property in Kuwait including hospital supplies and equipment, in violation of the decisions of this Council, the Charter of the United Nations, the Fourth Geneva Convention, the Vienna Conventions on Diplomatic and Consular Relations and international law,

Expressing grave alarm over the situation of nationals of third states in Kuwait and Iraq, including the personnel of the diplomatic and consular missions of such states,

Reaffirming that the Fourth Geneva Convention applies to Kuwait and that as a high contracting party to the convention, Iraq is bound to comply fully with all its terms and in particular is liable under the convention in respect of the grave breaches committed by it, as are individuals who commit or order the commission of grave breaches, . . .

Deeply concerned at the economic cost, and at the loss and suffering caused to individuals in Kuwait and Iraq as a result of the invasion and occupation of Kuwait by Iraq,

Acting under Charter VII of the United Nations Charter, . . .

Reaffirming its determination to insure compliance by Iraq with the Security Council resolutions by maximum use of political and diplomatic means,

1. *Demands* that the Iraqi authorities and occupying forces immediately cease and desist from taking third-state nationals hostage, and mistreating and oppressing Kuwait and third-state nationals, and from any other actions such as those reported to the Council and described above, violating the decisions of this Council, the Charter of the United Nations, the Fourth Geneva Convention, the Vienna Conventions on Diplomatic and Consular Relations and international law;

2. *Invites* states to collate substantiated information in their possession or submitted to them on the grave breaches by Iraq as per paragraph 1 above and to make this information available to the Council;

3. *Reaffirms* its demand that Iraq immediately fulfill its obligations to third-state nationals in Kuwait and Iraq, including the personnel of diplomatic and consular missions, under the Charter, the Fourth Geneva Convention, the Vienna Conventions on Diplomatic and Consular Relations, general principles of international law and the relevant resolutions of the Council;

*Adopted by a vote of 13-0, with Cuba and Yemen abstaining.

4. *Reaffirms further* its demand that Iraq permit and facilitate the immediate departure from Kuwait and Iraq of those third-state nationals, including diplomatic and consular personnel who wish to leave;

5. *Demands* that Iraq insure the immediate access to food, water and basic services necessary to the protection and well-being of Kuwaiti nationals and of nationals of third states in Kuwait and Iraq, including the personnel of diplomatic and consular missions in Kuwait;

6. *Reaffirms* its demand that Iraq immediately protect the safety and well-being of diplomatic and consular personnel and premises in Kuwait and in Iraq, take no action to hinder these diplomatic and consular missions in the performance of their functions, including access to their nationals and the protection of their person and interests and rescind its orders for the closure of diplomatic and consular missions in Kuwait and the withdrawal of the immunity of their personnel;

7. *Requests* the Secretary General, in the context of the continued exercise of his good offices concerning the safety and well-being of third-state nationals in Iraq and Kuwait, to seek to achieve the objectives of paragraphs 4, 5 and 6 and in particular the provision of food, water and basic services to Kuwaiti nationals and to the diplomatic and consular missions in Kuwait and the evacuation of third-state nationals;

8. *Reminds* Iraq that under international law it is liable for any loss, damage or injury arising in regard to Kuwait and third states, and their nationals and corporations, as a result of the invasion and illegal occupation of Kuwait by Iraq;

9. *Invites* states to collect relevant information regarding their claims, and those of their nationals and corporations, for restitution or financial compensation by Iraq with a view to such arrangements as may be established in accordance with international law;

10. *Requires* that Iraq comply with the provisions of the present resolution and its previous resolutions, failing which the Council will need to take further measures under the Charter;

11. *Decides to* remain actively and permanently seized of the matter until Kuwait has regained its independence and peace has been restored in conformity with the relevant resolutions of the Security Council. . . .

RESOLUTION 677
November 28, 1990*

The Security Council,

Recalling resolutions 660 (1990) of 2 August 1990, 662 (1990) of 6 August 1990 and 674 (1990) of 29 October 1990,

Reiterating its concern for the suffering caused to individuals in Kuwait as a result of the invasion and occupation of Kuwait by Iraq,

Gravely concerned at the ongoing attempt by Iraq to alter the demographic composition of the population of Kuwait and to destroy the civil records maintained by the legitimate Government of Kuwait,

*S.C. Res. 677. Adopted by a unanimous vote of 15-0.

Acting under Chapter VII of the Charter of the United Nations,

1. *Condemns* the attempts by Iraq to alter the demographic composition of the population of Kuwait and to destroy the civil records maintained by the legitimate Government of Kuwait;

2. *Mandates* the Secretary-General to take custody of a copy of the population register of Kuwait the authenticity of which has been certified by the legitimate Government of Kuwait which covers the population registration up to 1 August 1990;

3. *Requests* the Secretary-General to establish, in co-operation with the legitimate Government of Kuwait, an Order of Rules and Regulations governing access and use of the said copy of the population register.

RESOLUTION 678
November 29, 1990*

The Security Council,

Recalling and reaffirming its Resolutions 660 (1990), 661 (1990), 662 (1990), 664 (1990), 665 (1990), 666 (1990), 667 (1990), 669 (1990), 670 (1990), 674 (1990) and 677 (1990),

Noting that, despite all efforts by the United Nations, Iraq refuses to comply with its obligation to implement Resolution 660 (1990) and subsequent resolutions, in flagrant contempt of the Council,

Mindful of its duties and responsibilities under the Charter of the United Nations for the maintenance and preservation of international peace and security,

Determined to secure full compliance with its decisions,

Acting under Chapter VII of the Charter of the United Nations,

1. *Demands* that Iraq comply fully with Resolution 660 (1990) and all subsequent relevant resolutions and decides, while maintaining all its decisions, to allow Iraq one final opportunity, as a pause of good will, to do so;

2. *Authorizes* member states cooperating with the Government of Kuwait, unless Iraq on or before Jan. 15, 1991, fully implements, as set forth in paragraph 1 above, the foregoing resolutions, to use all necessary means to uphold and implement the Security Council Resolution 660 and all subsequent relevant resolutions and to restore international peace and security in the area;

3. *Requests* all states to provide appropriate support for the actions undertaken in pursuance of paragraph 2 of this resolution; and

4. *Requests* the states concerned to keep the Council regularly informed on the progress of actions undertaken pursuant to paragraphs 2 and 3 of this resolution;

5. *Decides* to remain seized of the matter.

*S.C. Res. 678. Adopted by a vote of 12-2, with Cuba and Yemen opposed and China abstaining.

AUTHORIZATION FOR USE OF MILITARY FORCE AGAINST IRAQ RESOLUTION

H.J. Res. 77, 102d Cong., 1st Sess. (January 12, 1991)*

To authorize the use of United States Armed Forces pursuant to United Nations Security Council Resolution 678.

Whereas the Government of Iraq without provocation invaded and occupied the territory of Kuwait on August 2, 1990; and

Whereas both the House of Representatives (in H.J. Res. 658 of the 101st Congress) and the Senate (in S. Con. Res. 147 of the 101st Congress) have condemned Iraq's invasion of Kuwait and declared their support for international action to reverse Iraq's aggression; and

Whereas Iraq's conventional, chemical, biological, and nuclear weapons and ballistic missile programs and its demonstrated willingness to use weapons of mass destruction pose a grave threat to world peace; and

Whereas the international community has demanded that Iraq withdraw unconditionally and immediately from Kuwait and that Kuwait's independence and legitimate government be restored; and

Whereas the U.N. Security Council repeatedly affirmed the inherent right of individual or collective self-defense in response to the armed attack by Iraq against Kuwait in accordance with Article 51 of the U.N. Charter; and

Whereas, in the absence of full compliance by Iraq with its resolutions, the U.N. Security Council in Resolution 678 has authorized member states of the United Nations to use all necessary means, after January 15, 1991, to uphold and implement all relevant Security Council resolutions and to restore international peace and security in the area; and

Whereas Iraq has persisted in its illegal occupation of, and brutal aggression against Kuwait: Now, therefore, be it

Resolved by the Senate and House of Representatives of the United States of America in Congress assembled,

Section 1. Short Title.

This joint resolution may be cited as the "Authorization for Use of Military Force Against Iraq Resolution."

*This joint resolution was passed by Congress on January 12, 1991. The Senate vote was 52-47, and the vote in the House of Representatives was 250-183.

Section 2. Authorization for Use of United States Armed Forces.

(a) AUTHORIZATION.—The President is authorized, subject to subsection (b), to use United States Armed Forces pursuant to United Nations Security Council Resolution 678 (1990) in order to achieve implementation of Security Council Resolutions 660, 661, 662, 664, 665, 666, 667, 669, 670, 674, and 677.

(b) REQUIREMENT FOR DETERMINATION THAT USE OF MILITARY FORCE IS NECESSARY.—Before exercising the authority granted in subsection (a), the President shall make available to the Speaker of the House of Representatives and the President pro tempore of the Senate his determination that—

(1) the United States has used all appropriate diplomatic and other peaceful means to obtain compliance by Iraq with the United Nations Security Council resolutions cited in subsection (a); and (2) that those efforts have not been and would not be successful in obtaining such compliance.

(c) WAR POWERS RESOLUTION REQUIREMENTS.—

(1) SPECIFIC STATUTORY AUTHORIZATION.—Consistent with section 8(a)(1) of the War Powers Resolution, the Congress declares that this section is intended to constitute specific statutory authorization within the meaning of section 5(b) of the War Powers Resolution.

(2) APPLICABILITY OF OTHER REQUIREMENTS.—Nothing in this resolution supersedes any requirement of the War Powers Resolution.

Section 3. Reports to Congress.

At least once every 60 days, the President shall submit to the Congress a summary on the status of efforts to obtain compliance by Iraq with the resolutions adopted by the United Nations Security Council in response to Iraq's aggression.

PRESIDENT BUSH'S LETTER TO CONGRESS RE: ATTACK ON IRAQ

January 16, 1991*

Dear Mr. Speaker:
[Dear Mr. President:]

Pursuant to section 2(b) of the Authorization for Use of Military Force Against Iraq Resolution (H.J. Res. 77, Public Law 102-1), I have concluded that:

    1. the United States has used all appropriate diplomatic and other peaceful means to obtain compliance by Iraq with U.N. Security Council Resolutions 660, 661, 662, 664, 665, 666, 667, 669, 670, 674, 677, and 678; and
    2. that those efforts have not been and would not be successful in obtaining such compliance.

Enclosed is a report that supports my decision.

Sincerely,

George Bush

Report for Use in Connection with Section 2(b) of the Joint Congressional Resolution Authorizing the Use of Military Force Against Iraq

    The report that follows is a summary of diplomatic and other peaceful means used in an attempt to obtain compliance by Iraq with the twelve U.N. Security Council resolutions relating to its invasion and occupation of Kuwait. It is not a definitive rendition of these means, because the Administration cannot, of necessity, include at this time all the factual data that would support a complete historical record. This report, therefore, should be considered in light of formal and informal information already provided to the Congress and that which will be provided in the future.

---

*President Bush sent this letter and report to House Speaker Thomas S. Foley (D.-Wash.) and Senate President Pro Tem Robert C. Byrd (D-W.Va.) at the opening of hostilities against Iraq on Wednesday, January 16, 1991.

1. BACKGROUND

For over five and a half months, the international community has sought with unprecedented unity to reverse Iraq's brutal and unprovoked aggression against Kuwait. The United States and the vast majority of governments of the world, working together through the United Nations, have been united both in their determination to compel Iraq's withdrawal from Kuwait and in their strong preference for doing so through peaceful means. Since August 2, we have sought to build maximum diplomatic and economic pressure against Iraq. Regrettably, Iraq has given no sign whatever that it intends to comply with the will of the international community; nor is there any indication that diplomatic and economic means alone would ever compel Iraq to do so. Instead, Iraq has continued to reject the relevant U.N. Security Council resolutions and refuses to recognize them.

From the beginning of the Gulf crisis, the United States has consistently pursued four basic objectives: (1) the immediate, complete, and unconditional Iraqi withdrawal from Kuwait; (2) the restoration of the legitimate Government of Kuwait; (3) the protection of U.S. citizens abroad; and (4) the security and stability of a region vital to U.S. national security. In pursuit of these objectives, we have sought and obtained action by the UN Security Council, resulting in twelve separate resolutions that have been fully consistent with U.S. objectives.

The last of these twelve resolutions, UN Security Council Resolution 678 of 29 November 1990, authorizes UN Member States to use "all necessary means" to implement Resolution 660 and all subsequent relevant resolutions of the Security Council, and to restore international peace and security in the area, unless Iraq fully implements those resolutions on or before January 15, 1991.

The nearly seven week "pause of goodwill" established in UN Security Council Resolution 678 has now passed. Iraq has taken no steps whatever to fulfill these requirements. Iraq has forcefully stated that it considers the Security Council's resolutions invalid and has no intention of complying with them at any time. Iraqi forces remain in occupation of Kuwait, and have been substantially reinforced in recent weeks rather than withdrawn. Iraq has strongly and repeatedly reiterated its annexation of Kuwait and stated its determination that Kuwait will remain permanently a part of Iraq. The Iraqi closure of diplomatic and consular missions in Kuwait has in no way been rescinded.

In short, the Government of Iraq remains completely intransigent in rejecting the UN Security Council's demands—despite the exhaustive use by the United States and the United Nations of all appropriate diplomatic, political and economic measures to persuade or compel Iraq to comply.

This has been a truly international effort. More than two dozen other countries have sent their own military forces to the Gulf region, including more than 250,000 troops. They have given or pledged substantial funds and other assistance to us for our operations, including over $8 billion in calendar year 1990 alone. They have taken on the responsibility for assisting those nations that have suffered the most from the effects of international sanctions against Iraq and higher energy prices. As additional costs are incurred during 1991, we will look to our allies to shoulder their fair share of our military expenses and exceptional economic assistance efforts.

2. Diplomatic and Political Actions

The extensive diplomatic and political efforts undertaken by the United States, other countries, regional organizations including the Arab League and the European Community and the United Nations to persuade or compel Iraq to withdraw from Kuwait have not succeeded. The UN Security Council and General Assembly have overwhelmingly and repeatedly condemned the Iraqi invasion and demanded Iraq's immediate and unconditional withdrawal from Kuwait. The Security Council has invoked its extraordinary authority under Chapter VII of the UN Charter, not only to order comprehensive economic sanctions, but to authorize the use of all other means necessary, including the use of force. The Security Council has directed other UN organizations (e.g., the International Atomic Energy Agency) to take appropriate actions toward the same end within their areas of competence, and they have done so where relevant.

The President, the Secretary of State and other U.S. officials have engaged in an exhaustive process of consultation with other governments and international organizations. . . .

Most recently, on January 9, the Secretary of State met at length in Geneva with the Iraqi Foreign Minister, who in six and one-half hours of talks demonstrated no readiness whatever to implement the U.N. Security Council resolutions. The Iraqi Foreign Minister even refused to receive a diplomatic communication from the President intended for Saddam Hussein. On January 13, the U.N. Secretary-General was rebuffed by Iraq for a second time, in this case in a direct attempt to persuade Saddam Hussein to withdraw from Kuwait peacefully. Many other heads of state, foreign ministers and private persons have made similar attempts. In short, the international community has in an unprecedented way directed the full scope and vigor of its political and diplomatic means to produce an Iraqi withdrawal.

These exhaustive efforts have produced not the slightest indication of any intention by Saddam Hussein to meet the demands of the international community for immediate and unconditional withdrawal from Kuwait. For our part, the Administration made clear that there could be no reward for aggression lest we undermine prospects for an expanded constructive role for the UN Security Council and for a new, more peaceful world order. Attempts to link resolution of Iraq's aggression against Kuwait with other issues were rejected on the grounds that these issues were unrelated to Iraq's aggression and that such efforts would only serve to divert attention from the immediate challenge posed by Iraq.

3. Economic Sanctions

Since August 2 (in the case of the United States) and August 9 (in the case of the Security Council and the other UN Member States), comprehensive economic sanctions have been imposed on Iraq, prohibiting all trade and financial transactions with Iraq, with the exception of goods for a very limited category of essential humanitarian purposes. These sanctions have since August 25 been backed by an extensive maritime interception effort involving warships of many states, and since September 25 by rigorous controls on air traffic to and from Iraq. The United States and other countries have engaged in tireless efforts during this period to uncover and defeat attempted evasions of these sanctions around the world, whether by direct attempts to pass through the allied interception cordon or by the use of financial and trade intermediaries.

Our efforts have resulted in a very substantial reduction of the volume of trade to and from Iraq, and significant shortages in Iraq's financial resources. The most serious impact on Iraq thus far has been on the financial sector, where hard currency shortages have led Baghdad to take a variety of unusual steps to conserve or obtain foreign exchange. The sanctions have shut off 97% of Iraq's exports and more than 90% of its imports, and have prevented Baghdad from reaping the proceeds of higher oil prices or its seizure of Kuwaiti oil fields. The departure of foreign workers and the cutoff of imported industrial inputs has caused problems for a variety of industries.

Notwithstanding the substantial economic impact of sanctions to date, and even if sanctions were to continue to be enforced for an additional six to twelve months, economic hardship alone is highly unlikely to compel Saddam to retreat from Kuwait or cause regime-threatening popular discontent in Iraq. Due to a reduction of domestic consumption, cannibalization of Kuwaiti facilities, smuggling, and use of existing stockpiles, the most vital Iraqi industries do not appear to be threatened. The price of foodstuffs for the Iraqi population has sharply increased and rations have been reduced, but there is still access to sufficient staple foods, and new supplies are being injected from the fall harvest and smuggling.

While we might succeed in substantially reducing the overall Iraqi supply of food and other essential consumer commodities, Saddam Hussein has made clear his willingness to divert such supplies to his military forces, even at the cost of severe deprivation of his civilian population. Even if the international community were prepared to deprive the Iraqi civilian population of food, there is no reason to believe that this would change Saddam Hussein's policies.

The ability of Iraqi armed forces to defend Kuwait and southern Iraq is unlikely to be eroded substantially over the next six to twelve months even if effective sanctions could be maintained. Iraq's infantry and artillery forces probably would not suffer significantly, since Iraq could maintain the relatively simple Soviet-style weaponry of these forces. Low-technology defensive preparations could also be expanded. Iraq's armored and mechanized forces would be degraded somewhat, but Iraq has large stocks of spare parts and other supplies that would ameliorate this effect. Iraqi air forces and air defenses would likely be hit far more severely by continued effective sanctions, but in any case, Iraqi air defense and air forces would play a limited role—in relation to the ground forces—with respect to Iraq's ability to hold Kuwait.

In short, while sanctions might degrade to some extent the operational readiness of some portion of the Iraqi armed forces, it is clear that Iraq would still retain very large and powerful land and air forces, as well as substantial capability to replace ammunition and other essential replacement items. Delay would also have important military consequences that might make any eventual military action more costly and increase U.S. and coalition casualties. Iraq has already exploited its five-month occupation of Kuwait to increase significantly its ability to resist coalition efforts to restore that country's sovereignty and to increase further its already formidable military capability. Iraq has increased the size of its forces in the Kuwait Theater of Operations by 450,000 personnel and has increased the overall size of its armed forces by mobilizing many thousands of combat veterans and reservists. Additional time has already permitted the Iraqis to extend and reinforce their fortifications along the Saudi border; more time would only make these defenses more formidable. Delay also would give the Iraqis more time to further develop, produce and weaponize weapons of mass destruction, thus making any eventual conflict more destructive and strengthening Iraq's ability to coerce other nations with the threat of mass destruction. Delay may also degrade the readiness of coalition forces.

In short, international sanctions have not caused Iraq to comply with the January 15, 1991 deadline in UN Security Council Resolution 678, or to retreat from its insistence that its annexation of Kuwait is permanent. Even if the world community were able to maintain the current high level of success in sanctions enforcement, these economic results would not produce such compliance.

Further, the longer the sanctions continue, the more likely it is that leaks in the sanctions enforcement system will develop, that intermediaries will devise ways to circumvent sanctions, and that Iraq will find means of using its own resources to fill critical shortfalls. Even more important, if the coalition fails now to carry through on the UN Security Council's demands for immediate Iraqi withdrawal from Kuwait, there will be strong pressures and temptations on various countries to ease their enforcement of sanctions and to compromise on demands that Iraq meet existing objectives fully and unconditionally.

In summary, diplomatic and economic pressures have not diminished Iraq's intransigence despite five and one-half months of unparalleled international effort, and continued reliance upon them alone could risk achieving the basic objective of bringing about Iraq's complete and unconditional withdrawal from Kuwait.